The Middle East and the Peace Process

The Middle East and the Peace Process

The Impact of the Oslo Accords

Edited by Robert O. Freedman

University Press of Florida

Gainesville Tallahassee Tampa Boca Raton
Pensacola Orlando Miami Jacksonville

2

03 02 01 00 99 98   6 5 4 3 2 1

Library of Congress Cataloging-in-Publication Data

The Middle East and the peace process: the impact of the Oslo Accords
/ edited by Robert O. Freedman.
Papers presented at a conference held on November 5, 1995, at
Baltimore Hebrew University.
Includes bibliographical references (p.) and index.
ISBN 0-8130-1554-5 (alk. paper)
1. Geopolitics—Middle East—Congresses. 2. Middle East—Politics and
government—1979—Congresses. I. Freedman, Robert Owen.
DS63.1.M4847 1998 97-20336
956.05—dc21

The University Press of Florida is the scholarly publishing agency for
the State University System of Florida, comprised of Florida A&M
University, Florida Atlantic University, Florida International University,
Florida State University, University of Central Florida, University of
Florida, University of North Florida, University of South Florida, and
University of West Florida.

University Press of Florida
15 Northwest 15th Street
Gainesville, FL 32611

To Harold Baron,

loving husband, father, and grandfather

and dedicated friend of Baltimore Hebrew University

Contents

Publication of the Center for the Study of Israel and the Contemporary Middle East, Baltimore Hebrew University

Preface

The Middle East has long been one of the most volatile regions on the globe. Wars, coups d'état, rapid shifts in alliances and alignments, numerous intra-Arab, intrastate, and regional conflicts, and constant intervention by the superpowers have wracked the region since the first Arab-Israeli war in 1948. In an effort to increase public understanding of this complex region, the Center for the Study of Israel and the Contemporary Middle East was founded at Baltimore Hebrew University in 1977. It has held a series of conferences bringing together Middle Eastern specialists from various perspectives to analyze and discuss the region.

The first conference, held in 1978, examined the impact of the Arab-Israeli conflict on the Middle East, and the papers were later published as *World Politics and the Arab-Israeli Conflict*, edited by Robert O. Freedman (New York: Pergamon, 1979). The second conference, held in 1979 (two years into the administration of Israeli Prime Minister Menachem Begin), made a preliminary analysis of the dynamics of the Begin regime. Following the Israeli election of 1981, the papers were updated and published as *Israel in the Begin Era*, edited by Robert O. Freedman (New York: Praeger, 1982). The third conference, which took place in 1982, dealt with Middle Eastern developments in the period between the Camp David agreements of 1978 and the Israeli invasion of Lebanon in 1982. These papers were published as *The Middle East since Camp David*, edited by Robert O. Freedman (Boulder, Colo.: Westview Press, 1984).

Just as the Camp David agreements marked a major turning point in the Middle East, so too did the Israeli invasion of Lebanon. For that reason, a fourth conference at Baltimore Hebrew University met three years after the invasion in order to analyze its impact on the Middle East. The papers were published as *The Middle East after the Israeli Invasion of Lebanon*, edited by Robert O. Freedman (Syracuse: Syracuse University Press, 1986). The Iran-Contra affair was yet another key event in Middle East politics that had major ramifications throughout the region, and a fifth conference was held at Baltimore Hebrew University in 1988 to assess the impact of the affair on the course of Middle East history. The conference papers were published as *The Middle East from the Iran-Contra Affair to the Intifada,* edited by Robert O. Freedman (Syracuse: Syracuse University Press, 1991).

In December 1989, as the intifada (Palestinian uprising) entered its third year, a conference was held to analyze its impact. The papers presented at that conference were published as *The Intifada: Its Impact on Israel, the Arab World, and the Superpowers,* edited by Robert O. Freedman (Gainesville: University Press of Florida, 1991). The Iraqi invasion of Kuwait in August 1990 was another seminal event in Middle Eastern affairs. Fifteen months after the invasion, in November 1991, with the Madrid Arab-Israeli peace talks having just begun, a conference was held at Baltimore Hebrew University to assess the impact of the Iraqi invasion and the subsequent Gulf War. The conference papers were published as *The Middle East after Iraq's Invasion of Kuwait,* edited by Robert O. Freedman (Gainesville: University Press of Florida, 1993).

The return of the Labor Party to power in Israel as a result of the June 1992 election was another major turning point in Middle Eastern politics. Unlike the Likud-led government of Yitzhak Shamir, which preceded it, the Labor-led government of Yitzhak Rabin was genuinely interested in an Arab-Israeli peace settlement. A conference was held at Baltimore Hebrew University in November 1993, two months after the signing of the Oslo I agreement, to evaluate the domestic and foreign policy changes in Israel precipitated by the 1992 Israeli elections. The conference papers were published as *Israel under Rabin,* edited by Robert O. Freedman (Boulder, Colo.: Westview Press, 1995).

The Oslo I agreement of September 1993 was another major turning point in Middle East politics. It was followed by a peace treaty between Israel and Jordan in October 1994, and by the Oslo II Palestinian-Israeli agreement in September 1995. The Arab-Israeli peace process, spurred by these events, was jeopardized by the tragic assassination of Israeli Prime Minister Yitzhak Rabin by an Israeli religious fanatic on November 4, 1995.

Ironically, less than twelve hours after that event, on November 5, 1995, a conference was held at Baltimore Hebrew University to evaluate the progress of the Arab-Israeli peace process and the thrust of Middle Eastern political developments since the Oslo I agreement. This book, the ninth in our series on the Middle East, is the outgrowth of that conference.

Many individuals and institutions are to be thanked for their help in making possible both the conference and the book that emerged from it. First and foremost, generous grants from the Jack Pearlstone Institute for

Living Judaism and Baltimore Hebrew University provided the bulk of the financial support for the conference. Second, I want to thank the chairman of the Board of Trustees of Baltimore Hebrew University, George Hess, for his strong support for the Center for the Study of Israel and the Contemporary Middle East. Third, the director of Baltimore Hebrew University's library, Dr. Steven Fine, assistant director Barbara Salit Michel, and staff assistant Jeanette Katkoff provided special assistance in expediting publication of the book, as did Liya Slobodsky, who has helped to maintain the center's research files on the Middle East.

Fourth, I want to thank the administrative assistant to the president of Baltimore Hebrew University, Jean Bernstein, for her constant and able support during my period of service as acting president of Baltimore Hebrew University, as I sought to combine my scholarly pursuits with the requirements of managing a university. Finally, I owe special thanks to my long-time secretary, Elise Baron, who handled the physical arrangements for the conference and prepared the manuscript for publication while at the same time maintaining the Graduate Office of Baltimore Hebrew University in an exemplary manner. Sadly, as the manuscript was in the last stages of production, her husband of fifty years, Harold Baron, passed away, and it is to his memory that this book is dedicated.

Robert O. Freedman

Introduction

The signing of the Oslo I agreement by Israeli Prime Minister Yitzhak Rabin and PLO leader Yasser Arafat on September 13, 1993, was a major turning point in the Middle East. The Israeli-PLO agreement led, in October 1994, to a peace treaty between Israel and Jordan and, almost one year after that, to Oslo II, a second major agreement between Israel and the PLO. Following the Oslo II agreement, however, came the assassination of Rabin by an Israeli Jew opposed to the peace process. Rabin's successor, Shimon Peres, sought to expedite the peace process by accelerating the withdrawal of Israeli troops from major Palestinian cities on the West Bank (except Hebron)—a development that enabled the Palestinians to hold an election for their legislative council on January 20, 1996—and by beginning intensive peace talks with Syria. The peace process, however, received a major blow in late February and early March when a series of terrorist attacks by Palestinian Islamic militants undermined the Israeli-PLO dialogue and also put an end to the peace talks between Israel and Syria, which, in any case, had made little progress. The terrorist attacks were also the primary reason behind the election of a right-wing coalition government headed by Likud leader Benyamin Netanyahu on May 29, 1996, and Netanyahu quickly made it clear that—despite his campaign pledges of peace with security—he was far less interested in the Middle East peace process than his predecessor had been.

Against the background of these events, both regional and extraregional powers sought to shape their policies in the Middle East. In this book a group of scholars, in addition to analyzing U.S. and Russian policy toward the Middle East since the Oslo agreements, also examine the positions of twenty Middle Eastern countries and the Palestinians toward the Arab-Israeli peace process, as well as the central issues in the domestic and foreign policies of these countries. In some Middle Eastern states like Israel, Jordan, and Syria, the Arab-Israeli peace process has been the central factor in their foreign policy and often in their domestic politics as well. In other countries, such as Turkey, Iran, and Iraq, the Arab-Israeli issue has been a less salient political factor. Nonetheless, the signing of the Oslo agreement of September 13, 1993, was a major turning point for all of the Middle East, and the authors in this book use it as a focal point in their analyses, which, as in previous books in this series, examine events in the Middle East from domestic, regional, and external perspectives.

Myron J. Aronoff and Yael S. Aronoff begin with an analysis of the evolution of Israeli policy toward the Palestinians from the election of the Labor government in June 1992 until the assassination of Yitzhak Rabin in November 1995. They argue that the dovish composition of the Labor cabinet, and the influence of both Yossi Beilin and Shimon Peres, helped persuade Rabin to move toward peace with the Palestinians, despite strong opposition from militant members of Israel's right wing. They note that the process of moving toward peace with the Palestinians dramatically improved Israel's position in the world and made possible the Israeli peace treaty with Jordan but the authors presciently warned that Rabin's successor as prime minister, Shimon Peres, had to use the "bully pulpit" of his office to educate the Israeli public about the importance of the peace process to their long-term security and welfare. Peres's failure to do this adequately, coupled with a series of Hamas and Islamic Jihad terrorist attacks against Israelis in February and March 1996, led to his loss in the election in May 1996 to Likud leader Benyamin Netanyahu.

The impact of the election on the Middle East peace process is dealt with by Mark Rosenblum. He notes that during the election campaign, Netanyahu ran more against Arafat than against Peres, and, exploiting the terrorist attacks, condemned Peres for "subcontracting" Israeli security to the PLO and the Palestinian authority. At the same time, he sought to win over the doves in the Israeli electorate by calling for a "secure peace," pledging to honor previous agreements and to continue the peace process, even if at a slower pace and with an eye on "security first." Yet on taking office, Netanyahu appeared to be intent more on reversing than continuing the peace process. Despite a fractious coalition that included some ministers more hawkishly and others more dovishly inclined than Netanyahu, he embarked on a program of enlarging Jewish settlements on the West Bank, humiliating Arafat, and stalling on the promised redeployment from Hebron. Furthermore, in a move that precipitated major battles between the Israeli army and armed Palestinian police, Israel's erstwhile allies against Palestinian terrorism, he secretly arranged for opening a tunnel in Jerusalem running beside the Temple Mount, where the al-Aksa and Dome of the Rock mosques are located. Whether Netanyahu will be able to recover from this event and restore the momentum of the peace process, remains to be seen.

The Palestinians, the central partners of Israel in the peace process, function intellectually in the larger Arab world, and the interplay of Palestinian and other Arab perspectives on the peace process is the central theme of Muhamhad Muslih's analysis of Arab thinking toward Israel. Muslih argues that Palestinians, like other Arabs, are strongly divided on the need to make peace with Israel, with some, like Edward Said, arguing that the Oslo agreement was nothing more than another Versailles, imposed by U.S. and Israeli power. Others, on Arab national or religious grounds, continue to oppose a sovereign Jewish state in the Middle East. However, another viewpoint argues that, on both religious and security grounds, an honorable peace (a Palestinian state on the West Bank and Gaza and Israeli withdrawal from Lebanon and the Golan Heights) is possible and that Arab and Islamic civilization is strong enough to resist the perceived threat of Israeli economic, political, and cultural domination during the process of normalization between Israel and her Arab neighbors.

If differing attitudes toward Israel pervaded Palestinian ranks, the same could be said for Jordan, with one major difference. Unlike Arafat, who was challenged both by Islamic radical groups such as Hamas and Islamic Jihad and by secularists calling for increased democratization in Palestinian-controlled areas, King Hussein remained firmly in control of his country and sought to introduce limited political pluralism even as he sought to build support within Jordan for the peace treaty with Israel that he signed in October 1994. Adam Garfinkle discusses Jordan's path to peace after Oslo and the impact of the agreement on Jordan's foreign policy and domestic politics. Garfinkle notes that the Oslo agreement enabled Jordan to make its own deal with Israel, and the resulting peace treaty, which even led to military cooperation between the two countries, quickly created a far warmer relationship between Israel and Jordan than between Israel and Egypt even though the Israeli-Egyptian treaty had been signed fifteen years earlier. Garfinkle also points up the areas of friction between the king and Yasser Arafat and raises questions about a possible future Jordanian-Palestinian confederation that has the potential of unleashing Palestinian irredentism against Jordan. Finally, he also discusses the reversal of Jordan's alignment with Iraq, and the kingdom's return, after a period of estrangement during the Gulf war, to a close relationship with the United States.

If Jordan, Israel's neighbor to the east, has moved to improve relations with Israel, Syria, Israel's northern neighbor, and Syria's Lebanese protectorate, have not. Nonetheless, Raymond A. Hinnebusch argues that Syrian

President Hafiz Assad is indeed interested in peace with Israel, if only because his regime needs a growing economy to appease the Syrian bourgeoisie—which he is increasingly coopting into his regime—and to absorb the rapidly increasing number of job seekers fueled by Syria's high population growth. However Assad has clear demands in return for a peace treaty with Israel: full Israeli withdrawal to the 1967 prewar lines (there remains some dispute over whether this includes, in addition to Israel's withdrawal from the Golan Heights, Syrian access to the Sea of Galilee) and an independent Palestinian state. However, Hinnebusch hints that Assad may accept less than this as Syria undergoes a change in its national identity away from Arabism and toward a Syrian identity. In any case, the Syrian leader, in the ups and downs of negotiations with Rabin, Peres, and Netanyahu, has proved willing to use Hizbollah attacks on Israeli forces in southern Lebanon as a prod to get Israel to recognize Syria's critical role in the peace process, although he has also been badly discomfited by the independent moves toward peace with Israel by PLO leader Yasser Arafat and King Hussein of Jordan.

While Syria has been a critical factor in determining whether there would be an overall Arab-Israeli peace settlement, Egypt has often sought to facilitate such a settlement. Yet in recent years, as Louis J. Cantori has noted, economic stagnation, administrative incapacity, widespread corruption, and political repression have weakened Egypt internally and reduced its influence in Middle Eastern affairs, even though it continues to receive more than $2 billion annually in economic aid from the United States. The regime's main internal opponent is the Gamaa Islamiyya, which garners support, Cantori notes, because of increasing poverty and maldistribution of income accompanied by government ineptitude and lack of political imagination. Cantori concludes by noting that with the increasing integration of the Arab state system into the larger Middle East regional system, the role of Egypt may be in decline, and this is one reason why Egypt has had to assert itself so vigorously against Israel on issues such as Israel's presumed nuclear capacity.

While Syria, Jordan, Egypt, Israel, and the Palestinians have all been intensively involved in the Middle East peace process in recent years, particularly after the Oslo I agreement of September 1993, Turkey has also become a factor in the Arab-Israeli relationship. As George E. Gruen points out, Turkey has become active in establishing closer economic, diplomatic, and even military ties with Israel while at the same time elevating its diplomatic relations with the Palestinians and offering the nascent Palestinian entity economic aid, even though Turkey's own economy is beset by serious difficulties, including runaway inflation. At the same time, despite its escalating clash with Syria over the water of the Euphrates River, Turkey has offered to sell its excess water to water-poor countries of the Middle East like Israel, Jordan, and the Palestinian entity, hoping thereby to lubricate the Middle East peace process. The advent of the coalition government headed by Islamist leader Necmettin Erbakan in July 1996 threatened to reverse the rapidly warming relationship between Turkey and Israel—leading Turkey to tilt toward the Arabs and away from Israel—had Erbakan managed to stay in power and consolidate his position, something he proved unable to do.

While Turkey, despite Erbakan, remains an ally of the United States, Iraq, under Saddam Hussein, remains the main American enemy in the Middle East. Phoebe Marr analyzes the question of why, in the face of international sanctions, Saddam Hussein has been able to remain in power despite his defeat in the Gulf war in 1991. Marr notes that while Saddam's power has clearly eroded since 1991, accompanied by a precipitous decline in the standard of living of the Iraqi population, Saddam has managed to remain in power because of a relatively weak and divided opposition on the one hand and his own brutality on the other. She asserts, though, that Saddam has become increasingly dependent on the Iraqi tribes and that, for this reason, the highly centralized administration of the Ba'athist regime may be undercut. In addition, she contends that if Saddam's regime falls apart and if a successor regime fails either to accommodate Iraq's various communities or to meet appropriate demands from the international community, Iraq could slide toward instability and collapse.

While Iraq under Saddam Hussein has been subject to the "dual containment" policy of the United States, so too has Iran under Hashemi Rafsanjani. In his analysis of Iran since the end of its war with Iraq, Shaul Bakhash traces the problems Iran has encountered since the Gulf war because of its divided leadership and the resulting conflict of domestic and foreign policies. Rafsanjani sought to privatize and liberalize the Iranian economy and integrate Iran into the international community by trying to rein in Iran's revolutionary organizations, but his efforts were checked: by Ayatollah Ali Khamenei, who followed Ayatollah Khomeini as Iran's supreme guide and who sought to shore up his questionable Islamic credentials by taking a hard line on domestic social policy and foreign policy issues, and by others in the Iranian religious establishment. One of these others was the speaker of Iran's Parliament, the Ayatollah Ali Akbar Nateq-Nuri, who opposed Rafsanjani's technocratic approach and his efforts to improve ties with Western Europe, if not with the United States. This was evident in parliamentary opposition to Rafsanjani's efforts to back off from Khomeini's *fatwa* calling for the death of writer Salman Rushdie and in the wave of attacks on Iranian dissidents living in Europe—attacks that severely damaged Rafsanjani's attempts to improve ties with countries like France and Germany.

While both Iran and Iraq have been beset by serious economic and political problems, their Gulf neighbors to the south and southwest, the Gulf Cooperation Council (GCC) states, have also run into their share of difficulties, though not as severe. In his analysis of the GCC states and Yemen, F. Gregory Gause III notes that shrinking financial revenues have begun to cause political problems in these states and that if they prove unable to provide jobs, goods, and services to their people as they have done in the past, their populations may become restive and demand a greater political role. Gause suggests that economic problems may have been a major cause of the serious unrest in Bahrein, although there have also been problems, caused primarily by radical Islamic forces, in Oman and Saudi Arabia. As far as foreign policy is concerned, all the GCC states have become militarily dependent on the United States, but they differ among themselves as to their relations with the United States and with the two U.S. enemies in the Gulf, Iraq and Iran. In addition, while all have supported the Arab-Israeli peace process begun at Madrid, they have done so to different degrees, with Oman, Qatar, and Bahrein taking the lead, albeit cautiously, in developing ties with Israel.

North Africa, while farther removed from the Arab-Israeli relationship than either the core Arab-Israeli area or the Gulf, nonetheless has moved cautiously, as Mary Jane Deeb notes, to participate in the peace process with Israel. While Morocco has taken the lead and Tunisia has made several important gestures toward Israel, Algeria, beset by a civil war with Islamic militants, has been more cautious. Libya, also beset by an Islamic opposition that opposes the peace process with Israel, has made a few small moves toward improving ties with Israel. Deeb also notes that, economically and politically, Morocco and Tunisia have made important strides in the 1990s, while in Algeria the civil war has been the major impediment to economic growth, and Libya's economic development has been hampered by international sanctions. Deeb believes that the key to the region's development may be a closer economic and political relationship with the European Union.

While the other North African states are challenged to a greater or lesser degree by Islamic opposition groups, in Sudan an Islamic party, the National Islamic Front, is in power. Nonetheless, as Anne Mosely Lesch points out, Sudan is isolated internationally, wracked by civil war, and impoverished economically. She also notes that the foreign and domestic policies adopted by the Islamic regime have enhanced its isolation: its harboring of terrorist leaders and groups and its efforts to spearhead the spread of Islamist movements into East and North Africa have alienated most of its neighbors, especially Egypt, Uganda, Eritrea, Ethiopia, Algeria, and Tunisia. Sudan can consider only one country—Islamist Iran—an ally from whom assistance in the form of Pasdaran soldiers and other forms of military aid has been flowing, although Sudan also cooperates with Iraq and Yemen as well as China, from which it receives military assistance, often paid for by Iran. As far as the Arab-Israeli peace process is concerned, the leading Islamist in the Sudanese regime, Hassan Tarabi, whom many see as the real power in Sudan, openly denounced the Oslo accords as "a peace and capitulation plan which conflicts with the Palestinian, Arab and Islamic principle rejecting Israel." Tarabi did try, however, to bridge the gap between Arafat and Hamas, which has activists in Khartoum.

When it comes to promoting the Arab-Israeli peace process, no country is more important than the United States. Don Peretz underlines the important role of the United States in Arab-Israeli peacemaking, noting that despite the U.S.-mediated Israeli-Egyptian peace treaty of 1979, it was not until the first Oslo agreement, in 1993, that the United States scored a major regional success in its peacemaking efforts, as that agreement was followed by a peace treaty between Israel and Jordan and the beginning of peace talks between Israel and Syria. Peretz sees U.S. policy toward the Gulf as less successful and raises important questions about the "dual containment" policy the United States is pursuing against Iran and Iraq, although he acknowledges America's growing dependence on oil from the Middle East, particularly from Saudi Arabia.

If the United States has had a clear policy toward the Middle East since the Gulf war, with many of the policy makers of the Bush administration, such as Dennis Ross, being retained by President Bill Clinton, the same cannot be said about Russian foreign policy. Although it emerged as the primary successor state after the collapse of the Soviet Union in December 1991, as Robert O. Freedman points out, Russian policy toward the region was often confused, the subject of rival foreign policy fiefdoms, and increasingly subject to the vagaries of Russia's domestic politics, which tended to affect Russian policy toward Iraq and Israel. Only in the case of Russian policy toward Iran was there real continuity from the latter part of the Gorbachev era, and, Freedman argues, this was due in large part to the restrained policies Iran was following in the newly independent states of

Central Asia and the Transcaucasus, through which Russian policy makers were increasingly viewing the Middle East.

In sum, these authors present a variety of perspectives on developments in the Middle East since the Oslo I agreement of September 1993, with particular attention to the impact of the Arab-Israeli peace process and the rise of Islamic opposition movements in the region. The depth and breadth of the views presented, which offer domestic, regional, and external frameworks of analysis of the key events in the region, present the reader with tools for understanding the political dynamics of the contemporary Middle East.

PART I

The Arab-Israeli Core Area

1: Domestic Determinants of Israeli Foreign Policy

The Peace Process from the Declaration of Principles
to the Oslo II Interim Agreement

Myron J. Aronoff and Yael S. Aronoff

The major shift in the balance of international power that came with the disintegration of the Soviet Union significantly altered the regional balance of power in the Middle East. The aftermath of the Gulf war, which further consolidated U.S. hegemony and eroded the political and economic viability of the PLO, coupled with the growing challenge of militant Islamic movements, constituted the "necessary" conditions that made possible the historic shift in Israeli foreign policy. However, the political composition of the government formed as a result of the 1992 election, in the context of a changing political culture, constituted the "sufficient" condition for rapprochement between Israel and the PLO. That, in turn, facilitated the peace with Jordan and the increasing normalization of relations with much of the Arab world.[1] As Theodore Friedgut, a professor at the Hebrew University of Jerusalem, has noted, "the signing of the Declaration of Principles for peace negotiations between the Palestine Liberation Organization and the government of Israel in September 1993 was one of those rare moments in world politics when all the necessary and sufficient conditions fell into place and a historic turning point was reached."[2]

Four Key Events in the Policy Breakthrough

Four key events in the past dozen years set the scene for the evolution of current Israeli policy. The first was Israel's war against the PLO in Lebanon (1982–85), euphemistically named (with overtones of Orwell's *1984*) "Peace for Galilee." The war broke the military back of the PLO, drove it farther into exile, and diminished its control over day-to-day affairs in the occupied territories. This contributed to the eventual outbreak of the intifada. Shimon Peres argues that it also created the impression that the war was between equals. He claims, thereby, "the seeds of the Intifada and of Israeli recognition of the need for bilateral talks were planted."[3]

A second key event was the failure of the 1987 London accord. Rejection of this framework for negotiation between Israel and a joint Jordanian-Palestinian delegation, worked out between Foreign Minister Peres and King Hussein, aborted a process that might have prevented the intifada. Peres argues, "We could have avoided the need to negotiate with a Palestinian-only delegation controlled by PLO headquarters if only Likud leaders had not been blindsighted by pipe dreams and an impossible political ideal in whose name they were prepared to wreak havoc with the most significant breakthrough since Sadat's visit to Jerusalem."[4] However, Prime Minister Shamir was not the only key actor who had reservations about this framework. It is unclear whether Yasser Arafat would have given his blessings to talks without direct PLO representation at the time.[5] Without his sanction it is doubtful that credible Palestinian leaders from the West Bank and Gaza would have participated in the talks.

The third, and most decisive, factor was the intifada, the Palestinian popular uprising that began in December 1988 and continued, at varying rates of intensity, through the initial stages of the peace process.[6] Among other things, it convinced most Israelis that the status quo of occupation was untenable. It also further polarized the Israeli public regarding which policy initiatives needed to be made.[7] As I observed well before the Madrid conference, "Ironically, the Intifada, which began without PLO initiative or direction, has proven that Israel cannot achieve a political resolution of the conflict without negotiating with the PLO and meeting the legitimate demands of the Palestinians."[8]

"The Intifada set off a chain of events that eventually led to the breakup of the National Unity government in March 1990 and the historic preliminary peace conference in Madrid during late October and early November 1991."[9] Paradoxically, the intifada "brought to the Palestinians the feeling that they were capable of forging their own fate and future."[10] Yet five years of struggle led only to intensified Israeli military presence and Israeli settlement in the territories. The growth of Hamas, which turned the intifada into an armed struggle and challenged PLO dominance, further contributed to perception that the Palestinian rejection of autonomy under the Camp David agreements had been a missed opportunity, and another missed opportunity could be fatal to the Palestinian national moment. "As much as any other factor, this growing sentiment among Palestinians convinced Israelis that the Palestinian public was now ripe for substantive discussions toward a modus vivendi."[11]

The political stalemate that led to the breakup of the government formed after the 1988 election was the fourth set of events that set the scene for the return of Labor to power and the dramatic advance in the peace talks. Among other factors, pressure from the United States led to the Madrid conference, where the Likud government entered into indirect negotiations with the PLO. However, Shamir intended to stonewall the talks indefinitely while his government created more settlements in the territories.[12] The deterioration of U.S.-Israel relations was one of several issues that aided Labor in the 1992 elections.

Moshe Arens (Likud), foreign minister during this period, argues that relations between the two formerly close allies plummeted to "an unprecedented low, with the Bush Administration interfering in the Israeli domestic political arena in an undisguised attempt to bring down the democratically elected government of Israel."[13] He blames the United States for causing a number of government crises in Israel that contributed to the downfall of the Shamir government. While Arens's partisan analysis is exaggerated and oversimplified, it is not entirely without merit.[14] There has also been considerable speculation and controversy over the indirect role the PLO played in the election.[15]

The Pivotal Role of the Labor Party

We first examine the pivotal position of the Labor party. Without an understanding of the dynamics of internal power relations within Labor and of its movement towards a more dovish position on the Palestinian issue, there can be no adequate explanation of the breakthrough in the peace talks. We argue that progress with the Palestinians was a prerequisite for the conclusion of a peace treaty with Jordan and for progress on the other fronts.

Over the years scores of Israelis and Palestinians challenged the mutual nonrecognition, demonization, and taboos on contacts with the "enemy" camp. Following is a brief discussion of one outstanding example, a prominent official of the Labor party, which illustrates how the trail was blazed and the price paid for being a pioneer, ahead of one's time.

In 1970 Arie Lova Eliav, who was secretary-general of the Labor party at the time, charged his party with ignoring the political rights of the Palestinians and challenged Israel's continued occupation of territories as an obstacle to peace.[16] In so doing he entered into a collision course with Prime Minister Golda Meir, which led to his resignation from his position and eventually from the party.[17] "Eliav paid a high price for his personal integrity and political conscience."[18] A man who might have become prime minister spent the next thirteen years in the relative obscurity of the political opposition. Eliav, along with many others, made a significant contribution in paving the way for the present peace process.

Eliav first met secretly with Issam Sartawi in Paris in 1975 under the auspices of Pierre Mendes-France. A year later, after Sartawi had renounced terrorism, Eliav told Prime Minister Yitzhak Rabin that there were PLO leaders with whom Israel could negotiate.[19] Rabin, according to Eliav, replied, "I'll meet them on the battlefield."[20] Eliav and Sartawi shared the Kriesky Peace Prize in 1980 for their efforts to establish an Israeli-Arab dialogue. It is most likely that Sartawi was acting as a weather balloon, testing the Palestinian political climate for the possibility of a shift in PLO tactics and policy. The assassination of Sartawi by Abu Nidal in 1984 at a meeting of the Socialist International in Portugal was tragic proof of the high stakes paid by courageous Palestinian pioneers of the peace process.[21]

How did Rabin and Peres, who led the Labor party until Rabin was assassinated by a fanatic Jewish opponent of the peace process on November 4, 1995, move from rejection of the possibility of meeting secretly with moderate elements within the PLO in 1976 to their support for Oslo I and II? In his examination of Labor positions on national security issues, Efraim Inbar's analysis of the movement of Labor to the left in the 1980s is a most instructive point of departure. He cites multiple causes for this movement— in spite of a movement of the Israeli electorate in the opposite direction during the same period. Whereas Inbar tends to conflate causes and effects of the ideological shift, we suggest a clearer causal chain.[22]

Inbar concludes, correctly in our assessment, that the perception of threat is a major determinant of security policy. In fact, we argue that it is one of two major factors shaping ideological polarization in Israeli political culture on this issue.[23] Top party leaders came to perceive a fundamental change in Arab aims concerning Israel. Whereas Inbar does not explain the reasons for this perceptual shift, we suggest that it was the result, first, of the breaking down of stereotypes of mutual demonization by pioneers like Eliav and Sartawi, and second, of their perception of gradual shifts in PLO policy, which we discuss in more detail later.

The perception of the reduction of threat was a fundamental cause of the greater flexibility and willingness of Labor leaders to take risks. The results were Labor's recognition of the Palestinian national movement as a factor in regional arrangements, its willingness to make greater territorial concessions, its greater openness to a Palestinian state, and its greater reluctance to engage in large-scale military operations.

Inbar suggests that a move leftward was also necessary to stress the difference between Labor and the Likud—particularly as their differences narrowed on social, economic, and religious affairs. The exodus of the most hawkish elements from Labor, along with peer group pressure from external groups (the Socialist International) and internal pressures from intellectuals and the media contributed to the leftward shift. Additional factors were the return of the Sinai for a peace treaty, increased awareness of the "demographic problem," fatigue from constant and continuous conflict, the lack of an acceptable alternative to the dovish position in Labor, and sensitivity to outside constraints—particularly the need to maintain cordial relations with the United States.

Finally, Inbar concludes, personnel changes at the elite level led to the advancement of more doves than hawks into the Knesset and into higher levels of leadership within the party and eventually within the government. However, Inbar fails to explain this phenomenon. We suggest that the recruitment of a coterie of influential younger advisers and party activists by Shimon Peres during his tenure as party chairman is the primary explanation. Internal party reforms played an important role as well. The most prominent of the Peres coterie were elected to the Knesset because of the more open and democratic forms of candidate selection adopted by Labor prior to the last two elections, which helped to bring Labor to power in 1992.[24] The democratic reforms facilitated the upward mobility of younger and more dovish leaders.[25]

In the first national primary election held by Labor, on February 21, 1992, Yitzhak Rabin barely managed to top the 40 percent that avoided a run-off against his perennial rival, Peres, for the top spot on Labor's Knesset list. He won because most Laborites, including several prominent Peres supporters, came to the conclusion that Rabin had a better chance of leading Labor to an electoral victory. However, Peres mobilized majority support in several key elections, for example, Eli Dayan as Knesset party faction chairman, Nissim Zvili as secretary general of the party, and Ezer Weizman as the party's nominee for president of Israel.

Peres managed to place his supporters strategically in the cabinet as well. For example, his most trusted protégé, Yossi Beilin, who as his deputy foreign minister initiated and supervised the critical early stages in the Oslo talks, was later promoted to minister of economy and planning. Beilin was replaced in the Foreign Ministry by Eli Dayan.[26] These supporters are even more dovish than Peres, much less than was Rabin. The political coalition that made possible the peace initiatives of the Rabin government combined the strongly dovish Meretz cabinet members and Knesset delegation with the parliamentary support of the even more dovish members of the Arab Democratic Party and the Democratic Movement for Peace and Equality.

Although the rivalry between Rabin and Peres was muted, it did not disappear altogether, especially in the first year.[27] Yet, had these two leaders not managed to find a modus vivendi for cooperation, the significant progress in the peace talks could never have been made. On the other hand, the government continues to face challenges from two groups that, in large part, emerged from within Labor.

Challenges Emerging from Labor

The first group, led by Histadrut secretary-general Chaim Ramon (who ran on an independent list aligned with Shas and the Arab-Jewish List) ended Labor's seventy-five-year control over the powerful Histadrut and thereby greatly diminished the support Labor has traditionally mobilized through this institution and the resources it controls. Ramon also exposed the alleged corruption of several top Labor leaders who used Histadrut funds to finance their primary campaigns. His predecessor as secretary-general and the former treasurer have been charged and will stand trial for alleged illegal misuse of funds. Transportation Minister Yisrael Kesar may face similar charges.[28] This scandal may cost Labor crucial votes in the next election. (This was indeed one of the factors leading to Labor's loss in the May 1996 elections, though certainly not the dominant one.) Ramon (a former minister of health in the Rabin government) was expelled from the party, but the expulsion was later revoked. Ramon announced his unconditional return to the party in the aftermath of Rabin's assassination.[29]

The second group poses an even more immediate parliamentary threat to the survival of the present government and to Labor's chances to form a government after the next election. The Third Way, led by disgruntled Labor Knesset member Avigdor Kahalani and supported by Labor MK Emanuel Zissman, began as a movement protesting withdrawal from the Golan Heights. It has become a political party that will compete in the 1996 Knesset elections.[30] One survey predicted it could receive between five and six mandates.[31] By claiming the center of the political map, the Third Way might possibly attract more Labor supporters than Likud supporters and, like the Democratic Movement for Change in 1967, pave the way for a Likud-led coalition.[32] The movement's leaders indicate they will form a coalition with the party whose candidate is elected premier. (The

Third Way won four seats in the May 1996 elections and joined the Likud-led coalition.)

The deep division of the nation expressed in the narrow margin of parliamentary support and the fragility of the coalition government had a significant impact on the manner in which it could negotiate the peace process. Given these constraints, it is remarkable that it accomplished as much as it did. Had Yitzhak Rabin succeeded in his initial goal of forming a broader coalition including the militantly nationalist Tsomet, such progress would have been impossible.[33]

Labor's Coalition Partners and Parliamentary Allies

The volatile disputes between Meretz leader Shulamit Aloni and Shas leader Aryeh Deri diverted much of Rabin's time and energy in the first year of his government.[34] The exodus of Shas from the coalition, lengthy futile negotiations to get it to return, and the continued uncertainty of parliamentary support from Shas increased government dependence on the votes of the Arab parties. This, in turn, strengthened the opposition charges that fateful decisions relating to the future of the nation were being made without the support of a Jewish-Zionist majority.[35] The legitimacy of such decisions was thereby called into question for the more nationalistic sector of the population. That is why Rabin brought into the coalition two of the three renegades from Tsomet who had split off to form Yi'ud.[36]

This new junior partner did not play any direct role in foreign policy. However, on crucial votes in which confidence in the government was involved, such as the Golan bill, the vote of Yi'ud member Alex Goldfarb created a 59–59 tie, which prevented passage of the law and the defeat of the government.[37] The interim agreement (popularly known as Oslo II) passed the Knesset by a slightly more comfortable margin (61–59) after a tumultuous fifteen-hour debate. It passed in spite of the negative votes of Kahalani and Zissman (Third Way), who officially represented Labor in the Knesset. The junior partners (at different times) and the Arab parties provided the crucial votes to maintain a parliamentary majority.

Labor's main partner, Meretz, was more directly influential in the peace process. Environment Minister Yossi Sarid played a particularly active role in negotiations with Arafat and various other PLO leaders. Arguably the most dovish member of the cabinet, Sarid, a former long-standing Labor Knesset member, became a close confidant of Prime Minister Rabin.[38] Through their close working relationship, he helped persuade Rabin of the necessity of following the path that the government took.

While he was defense minister in the unity government led by Shamir, Rabin became convinced that only a political solution would end the intifada. However, he had to be persuaded by his more dovish colleagues in the cabinet to accept the necessity of negotiating with the PLO.[39] While not the most hawkish member of his government, he was clearly the most hawkish of the three key decision makers who shaped his government's policy during the peace process.[40] Of the three, Yossi Beilin is clearly the most dovish. Shimon Peres is less dovish than Beilin but more so than Rabin was.[41]

Parliamentary and Nonparliamentary Opposition

Given the polarization of Israeli politics—particularly on the Palestinian question—opposition to the Oslo I accord and to the interim agreement has been militant and occasionally extreme to the point of violence. Likud has led the parliamentary opposition.[42] Just as the more militant nationalist parties to the Likud's right have been riven by internal disputes, splintering off into factions that have formed independent Knesset caucuses, so has Likud suffered from internal turmoil. Former Foreign Minister David Levy, titular leader of a segment of Jews of Middle Eastern background, announced in July 1995 that he would establish a new political party tentatively called the New Way and that he would compete for the premiership,[43] but he later formed a coalition with Likud to run in the May 1996 elections.

The most important ramification for the peace process of the disunity and competition among the nationalist and ultranationalist parties has been the encouragement of irresponsible rhetoric and actions in opposition to the process.[44] Even more militant and less responsible nonparliamentary opposition is led by the settlers in the territories and a new group called Zo Artzenu (This Is Our Land). The result has been a concerted effort to delegitimate the government through charges that the absence of a Zionist-Jewish parliamentary majority leaves it with no authority to negotiate on behalf of the nation.[45] The Zo Artzenu leader, Moshe Feiglin, has repeatedly charged that the Labor-led government was "illegitimate."[46]

The more extreme elements charged the government with treason. Posters portraying Prime Minister Rabin with his head adorned in a kaffiya, looking like Arafat and labeled traitor (boged), were prominent at almost every antigovernment demonstration. Several demonstrators at a rally against the signing of the interim accord carried images of Prime Minister Rabin dressed in a Nazi uniform decorated with swastikas.[47] Verbal and symbolic violence led to physical violence. Dozens of demonstrators threatened Housing Minister Binyamin Ben Eliezer as he left the Knesset. They

attacked his car with stones and clubs, smashing the headlights and punc-
turing the tires. Knesset security guards rescued Ben Eliezer and his driver
from the angry mob. Demonstrators were also forced off the top of Prime
Minister Rabin's car. Objects were thrown at the police.[48]

The security establishment, despite its concern about the attacks on
government ministers, the inflammatory rhetoric expressed in antigovernment demonstrations, and the threats to the life of the prime minister, failed
to prevent the assassination of Rabin.[49] Likud leader Benjamin Netanyahu,
who has been criticized for not doing enough to stop the violence, had
called for a meeting with Rabin before his assassination to lower tensions
among the public.[50] After the assassination of Prime Minister Rabin, the
Jewish extremists who oppose the peace process matched their militant
Palestinian counterparts in terms of violence. The militant Jewish opponents of the peace process, especially those who participated in or supported the assassination of Rabin, are the mirror image of Hamas and Islamic Jihad in their attempts to abort the process. Such actions are an
expression of the political weakness and desperation of the groups engaging in them.[51]

There are many indications that all but the most militant Jewish and
Palestinian opponents of the peace process have come to recognize the
impossibility of reversing it. Herb Keinon suggests that everyone—especially the settlers—realizes that the reality has changed and that the Palestinians will be determining their own fate.[52] This is precisely the perception of reality that Rabin attempted to create.[53] On October 6, 1995, the day
of the Knesset vote on the interim accords, the nationalistic *Jerusalem Post*'s
editorial stated: "The investment of effort, prestige and international approval, not to mention the difficulty that all politicians have in admitting
error, makes retreat from such pacts virtually impossible."[54] Similarly the
Hamas representative in Beirut was reported by Reuters to have credited
Arafat with victory by stating that "the Middle East peace process is irre-
versible."[55] Support for Hamas on the West Bank and even in Gaza has
declined.[56]

Key Policy Designers and the Role of Cognitive Change

Beilin, in his former capacity as deputy foreign minister, played a vanguard role for the Israeli side in initiating the Oslo process. Without the
support of Peres and Rabin the process could not have succeeded. Yet,
without the daring of Beilin the process might never have gotten underway.[57] Jane Corbin reconstructs the "Oslo Channel," emphasizing the human relationships and the personal and political trust that developed among

the participants.[58] "The incrementalism of the process, as well as the skill of the individuals involved in understanding how that could be made attractive to those to whom they answered were keys to success."[59]

Michael Keren, who credits Beilin with supervising the back-channel negotiations in Oslo, identifies Peres as their main architect.[60] Keren criticizes as "outdated" the "belief that conflicts are resolved as a result of cognitive changes, that is, changes in people's sensing and thinking."[61] "The truth, however, is that there was little cognitive change involved in the Oslo Accord; if anything, it was the making of professionals rather than intellectuals. . . . The Oslo Accords were made by a knowledge-power nexus, dominated by Peres and his allies among Israel's professionals, who had little concern for cognitive changes. On the contrary, their main assumption was that no such changes were possible in the Middle East; hence the need to reach an agreement that would allow them to manage the conflict rather than to resolve it."[62]

Keren's thesis requires elucidation and demands a response. First of all, his distinction between professionals and intellectuals is highly problematic. The key negotiators for Israel in the initial stages of the Oslo process were intellectuals. Ya'ir Hirschfeld and Ron Pundak are academics. They were joined by professionals like Uri Savir and Yoel Zinger only after initial progress had been made. Keren writes, "Peres mobilized the professionals. He formed a close circle of academically trained aides, worked closely with government-employed professionals, called scientists in for consultations, founded both ongoing and ad hoc policy-making forums, held endless meetings with heads of universities and media organizations, and established a network of informal contacts between his office and academia".[63]

Such close cooperation demonstrates the futility of trying to separate the contributions of intellectuals and professionals in this context. Indeed, some of them, like Beilin, fit both categories.

Second, while Keren insists that Beilin is a technocrat, Klieman argues that "Beilin was guided at each step of the way by a defined political philosophy."[64] Klieman calls Peres visionary, while Keren insists he is also a technocrat. We suggest that the two views need not be mutually exclusive. Pragmatism can be ideological, particularly when faith in technological solutions becomes visionary, as it clearly does with Peres. Such pragmatism is an ideological position in which even Keren appears to have faith.[65]

Finally, Keren fails to specify either the level or the extent to which cognitive changes need be manifest if the utility of the concept is to be evaluated. Whereas there was no appearance of widespread public changes in perceptions preceding the Oslo process, such changes had taken place among key participants in the process. Furthermore, these changes became even more pronounced as a result of the lengthy negotiations of both Oslo I and Oslo II. Helena Cobban stresses the importance of "citizen diplomacy"—in which close working relationships were built over years of contacts between individual Palestinians, such as Nabil Shaath, and individual Israelis, such as Yossi Beilin, Efraim Sneh, and Yossi Sarid (all ministers in the Rabin government), as well as many others.[66]

Cobban's conclusions about personal relationships of trust built up by the participants in the isolated Norway talks apply also to the success of Israeli-Palestinian negotiations. Under similar conditions, larger numbers of negotiators, roughly one hundred each of Israelis and Palestinians, were virtually locked together for more than two months in the same hotel in Eilat. The result was reported to be significant alterations of mutual suspicion and the development of relationships of trust and even friendships. Most visibly, the leaders of the respective delegations that hammered out the Oslo II interim agreement, Ahmed Korei (Abu Ala'a) and Uri Savir (director-general of the Foreign Ministry), have become close personal friends.[67]

The Role of Cultural Change

We suggest this change in perceptions and relations between some Israeli and Palestinian leaders is part of a much broader process in which the prevailing assumptions of the dominant Zionist discourse have been challenged in recent years by traditionally marginalized groups such as Israeli Arabs and haredim, as well as by members of the establishment such as iconoclastic young Labor leaders (most conspicuously Yossi Beilin, chairman of the Jewish Agency Avraham Burg, and Chaim Ramon) and by intellectuals and artists whom some call "post-Zionist."[68] We have shown that the support of the Arab parties and the haredi Shas kept the government in power during the critical negotiations. Beilin, the leading Labor iconoclast in the government, was shown to have played a pivotal role in the peace process.

The fact that the Arab parties and Labor iconoclasts have challenged dominant assumptions, including the demonization of the Palestinian Other, at a time when traditional Zionism is undergoing a crisis, facilitated the breakthrough in policy. Furthermore, the success of the peace process has helped to erode mutual negative stereotypes among the wider public. "Already many, if not most, Israelis make cognitive (and political) distinctions between 'good' Palestinians (who support the peace process) and 'bad' Palestinians (Hamas terrorists). Palestinians are thus no longer seen as a single, monolithic outgroup—except by those who distrust the peace process and question the sincerity of the 'good' Palestinians."[69]

Palestinians are also making more sophisticated distinctions between Israelis in terms of their support for, or rejection of, the peace process. The fact that many now distinguish between the policies of Labor and the Likud illustrates such newly acquired political sophistication through the erosion of monolithic stereotypes. It is significant in this context that Hamas politically targeted the Rabin government in its efforts to undermine the peace process.[70]

Klieman calls "the revitalization of Israeli foreign and economic relations" the most tangible benefit of the peace process—nothing less than "a far reaching diplomatic revolution."[71] Israel had recovered from the nadir of the 1975 UN resolution equating Zionism with racism, which was revoked in 1991. From its all-time low of having diplomatic relations with only 65 nations, Israel as of March 1995 had formal contacts with 142 nations. These include formal diplomatic relations with the two Arab nations with which Israel shares the longest borders—Egypt and Jordan—and ongoing relations with Morocco, Tunisia, Oman, Qatar, and many other Muslim nations. Israel under the Labor government enjoyed unprecedented close political and economic relations with the United States and the European Union. A dramatic testament to this change was the gathering of world leaders in Jerusalem for Yitzhak Rabin's funeral, including King Hussein, King Hassan, President Hosni Mubarak, and representatives of Gulf states with which Israel does not yet have formal diplomatic relations.

Klieman notes the psychological healing process of Israel's rapprochement with states in the region and elsewhere in the world: "Broad segments of the Israeli public do indicate a non-ideological flexibility and willingness to revise thinking and attitudes toward: a) sharing confidence and trust with foreigners; b) the efficacy of pursuing foreign relations; and c) the larger historical-philosophical Jewish debate from the time of the biblical patriarchs . . . over the proper place of 'Israel among the nations' and in a non-Jewish world."[72]

In the inaugural address in which he presented his new government to the Knesset on July 13, 1992, Prime Minister Rabin boldly declared, "We must overcome the sense of isolation that has held us in thrall for almost half a century. We have to stop thinking the whole world is against us."[73] We argue that Rabin thereby signaled a fundamental ideological shift in cultural perceptions of political reality for his government, away from emphasis on the Holocaust and Israel's isolation in the world, which were the ideological motifs of the Likud governments. Rabin's vision reflects the perception of Israel as a "light unto the nations," the universalistic orientation of humanist Zionism. This perception is in contrast to the vision of Israel as a "people that dwells alone" (the more particularistic worldview of nationalist Zionism) and of "Esau hates Jacob" (the paranoid worldview of ultranationalist Zionism).[74]

This shift in ideological interpretation of the dominant Zionist paradigm provides the cultural explanation for the dramatic shift in Israeli policy toward the Palestinians. Particularly in the wake of the tragic death of Rabin, Prime Minister Peres needed to use the "bully pulpit" of his office to educate the public about the importance of the process to their long-term security and welfare. (The fact that he did not do so effectively was one of the reasons why Peres lost the May 1996 elections. The lack of attention to communicating with and educating the Israeli and Palestinian publics effectively is one of the greatest threats to the continued success of the peace process.)

Success of the peace process primarily depends upon the success of the Palestinian Authority in preventing terrorism, establishing law and order, and developing a democratic Palestinian state. As Beilin has observed, "If terrorism decreased, it is a whole new ball game. The view of the people and everything else will change."[75] There is a direct causal relationship between Israelis' perceptions of personal and collective security and their support for the peace process. The greater the sense of security, the stronger the support for the process. Success will generate even broader support, just as failure will undermine the process.

Peace with Jordan

The contrast between public reactions to and parliamentary support of the "painful" peace agreements with the Palestinians and the relatively "easy" peace treaty with Jordan is instructive. The Jordan-Israel declaration was approved by the Knesset 91–3 on August 10, 1994. Only the three Moledet MKs voted against, while two Likud MKs abstained.[76] The Knesset vote on October 26, 1994, readily affirmed the peace treaty with Jordan: 105 in favor, 3 opposed, 6 abstaining, and 6 not present. The support was even larger than for the peace treaty with Egypt.[77] The vote approving the Oslo accord, on September 23, 1993, was 61 to 50 with 9 abstentions and absences, whereas the vote on the interim agreement on October 6, 1995, was 61–59. Tzachi Hanegbi, one of the most hawkish members of the Likud, admitted that peace with Jordan meant the end of the "Jordan is Palestine" line. "This line is no longer a political principle . . . and we have to accept it."[78]

The decades of "secret" contacts between Israeli and Jordanian leaders, including Yitzhak Shamir and King Hussein—most of the meetings known eventually to the Israeli public—helped create greater receptivity for the treaty with Jordan.[79] Labor leaders since Golda Meir had met with King Abdullah and his successor, King Hussein. As discussed earlier, an accord was reached between King Hussein and Shimon Peres in 1987. Hussein and Rabin developed particularly close rapport, as dramatically revealed in Hussein's moving eulogy at Rabin's funeral. Based on perceived intentions rather than on objective military capabilities, Jordan is perceived by most Israelis, including members of the Knesset, to pose a lesser threat to Israeli security than do the Palestinians.

Rabin called the peace treaty with Jordan "the greatest achievement of my career."[80] With major agreements on transportation and tourism concluded within the first year of peace, Israel's relations with Jordan are "warmer" than they are with Egypt, with whom Israel has been at peace since 1979. For example, the Egyptian newspaper *Al-Shaab* complained that whereas Egypt would be proposing 75 investment projects at the Amman economic summit on October 29–31, 1995, Jordan had made a list of 250 projects, mostly for bilateral cooperation with *"the Zionist entity."*[81] At the economic summit Egyptian Foreign Minister Amr Moussa criticized Jordan for "chasing" after peace and "rushing" to normalize relations with Israel. King Hussein replied, with an edge in his voice, with reference to the seventeen years that Egypt had been at peace with Israel, "If we take into account the necessity to make up for lost time on behalf of the Palestinians, Jordanians, the Egyptians, the Syrians, and the Lebanese, we must not only hurry up, but really run."[82] Egyptian President Mubarak's first visit to Jerusalem and Israel to attend Rabin's funeral drew strong criticism in Egypt.

However, lasting peace with Jordan depends ultimately on final settlement with the Palestinians. Jordanian ambassador to Israel, Marwan Muasher, has made clear that without final status agreements between Israel and the Palestinians, the peace with Jordan will not be "durable."[83] This position confirms our thesis that the breakthrough in relations with the PLO made possible the rapid conclusion of the treaty with Jordan.

Israeli-Jordanian-Palestinian Confederation

The top Israeli decision makers favor a confederation of Israel, Jordan, and a Palestinian "entity." Rabin was most reluctant to discuss plans for the final settlement during the negotiations over the interim accords. Although he made statements favoring confederation, he also repeatedly talked about separation between Israel and the Palestinian entity, a seeming contradiction. He even rebuked Beilin for discussing confederation with Arafat when they met in Tunis in October 1993. Peres, on the other hand, has written and spoken extensively on the subject.[84]

The Israeli foreign minister held discussions with both King Hussein and Yasser Arafat on the subject in Washington, when they attended the ceremonial signing of the interim agreement. Peres said, "I have spoken with Hussein and he said this was a possibility that he has always considered. Both Hussein and Arafat understand this is the preferred option. They still need to find the magic formula to live together."[85] Arafat said decisions had already been taken in PLO institutions on the issue of confederation. He noted that the Jordanians and Palestinians are related peoples, to which Hussein agrees.

At the economic conference in Amman, most of the Israeli government's regional development projects were designed to serve as the basis for the foundation of an Israeli-Jordanian-Palestinian economic bloc. They included the construction of new bridges over the Jordan River, the development of tourism around the Dead Sea and the Mediterranean coast, the creation of special commercial regions, and a program to link the electrical systems of Israel, Egypt, Jordan, and the Palestinian Authority.[86] The European Union pledged $6 billion to fund regional development projects such as the development of the Dead Sea region, the creation of a tourist region north of the Red Sea, and the construction of a promenade between El-Arish and Ashkelon.[87]

Syria: What's the Hurry?

The rapid conclusion of a treaty with Jordan contrasts sharply with the glacial pace of on-again, off-again talks with the Syrians. Before Rabin's assassination, the motto for both sides in these talks appeared to be "What's the hurry?" There is significant disagreement among Israeli experts regarding Syrian intentions. Uri Saguy, former head of military intelligence (Aman), strongly believes Syria is ready for peace with Israel and has expressed his views to Israeli policy makers. Ya'acov Ami-Dror, head of the research division that produces the annual national intelligence assessment, equally strongly disagrees with his ex-boss.[88]

Academic experts like Mark Heller and Eyal Zisser, both of Tel Aviv University, are skeptical about the chances for peace with Syria in the near future. Heller, emphasizing Assad's rigidity, argues that for both Israel and Syria the status quo is not intolerable, and the political risks of change could be costly to both.[89] Zisser (protégé of the former Israeli ambassador to the United States, Itamar Rabinovich, who was chief negotiator with Syria) is convinced that Assad, unlike Peres, does not want a new Middle East. "Unlike other Israeli experts, Zisser is not certain that once the Syrian president agrees to a deal, he can be trusted to keep it."[90] Ann Mosely Lesch has observed, "Syria's Levant Security Doctrine was not only undermined but also potentially challenged by an alternative system embracing Israel, the Palestinians, Jordan, and Egypt."[91]

Among Israeli policy makers, even Yossi Beilin expressed his doubts that Assad has made a genuine commitment to peace with Israel. Former Israeli ambassador to the United States, Itamar Rabinovich, has called Syria stubborn and hostile in its positions. Whereas at an earlier stage it appeared that Prime Minister Rabin might have preferred a peace treaty with Syria prior to the conclusion of a treaty with the Palestinians, at the time of his death he had apparently decided, for domestic political reasons and in response to Syrian intransigence, not to push hard for the resumption of talks. His successor, Shimon Peres, through concerted efforts and with help from the Clinton administration, revived talks with Syria at the end of 1995.

When Rabin was taking a hard line, Foreign Minister Peres told the Labor Knesset faction, "I do not want to reach a situation where Israel could be accused of not being interested in reaching a peace settlement [with Syria]. We will try not to be the ones who turn off the light."[92] Because in his vision Syria is the key to a comprehensive peace in the Middle East, Peres, when he succeeded Rabin, pushed more assiduously to reopen a dialogue with Assad. Perhaps the assassination of Rabin helped convince Assad of the seriousness of the opposition to peace in Israel. Given the more flexible conditions for negotiation to which Peres's government agreed, renewed talks between Israel and Syria got underway in the new year of 1996. In this instance not only the political composition of the government but also the ideological vision of its leader played a key role in overcoming a serious impasse in negotiations.

Conclusions

We have maintained that the formation of a dovish government as the outcome of the 1992 election was the essential or "sufficient" condition for the radical departure from long-standing Israeli foreign policy that had precluded political negotiations with the Palestine Liberation Organization. This change took place in the context of far-reaching changes in Israeli political culture that have called into question certain assumptions, including the taboo against negotiations with the PLO. We further contend that the breakthrough that opened the dialogue between Israel and the PLO made possible the peace with Jordan, the improvement of Israeli relations with other Arab and Muslim states, and closer political and economic ties with the European Union and the United States. The dramatically improved position of Israel in the world has given many Israelis greater self-confidence and a sense of security, which in turn generate support for continuation of the peace process.

We suggest that the dovish composition of the cabinet was critical in persuading Prime Minister Rabin, who was already committed to the peace process, to agree reluctantly in the end to negotiate with the PLO. We credit Yossi Beilin, the most prominent member of the younger generation of Labor leaders in the cabinet and an iconoclast in the vanguard of challenges to old sacred cows, with having had the courage to respond positively to the Norwegian initiative. That initiative brought together, first of all, "surrogates" and eventually official representatives of the Israeli government and of the PLO. Shimon Peres provided Beilin with political backing and contributed significantly to the vision that led to the Oslo accords and eventually to the interim agreement. Neither could have been accomplished without the full support of Prime Minister Rabin at each step in the process.

Prime Minister Shamir admitted that he planned to stall the Madrid talks indefinitely while intensifying Jewish settlement in order to prevent the return of territories occupied by Israel in 1967. The unequivocal condemnation of the Labor government's agreements with the PLO by Shamir's successor as head of the Likud, Benyamin Netanyahu, makes it abundantly clear that had he been able to form the government in 1992, no shift in Israeli policy would have taken place.

We therefore conclude that the changes in domestic politics—the shift in participation of political parties in the government coalition—are an essential variable in any explanation of the dramatic shift in Israeli foreign policy. The structural changes in the international system and their ramifications in the region provided the necessary conditions for the change in Israeli policy. However, the sufficient conditions were a government coalition with the ideological commitment to make such changes as well as leaders with the courage, vision, and commitment to make the changes in spite of their fragile parliamentary majority and militant opposition in a highly polarized polity.

In the wake of sympathy and remorse immediately after the assassination of Prime Minister Rabin, three-fourths of Israelis polled expressed support for the government's handling of the peace process. While such high support is obviously influenced by a volatile emotional reaction to the traumatic loss of their leader, the long-range impact of this surge of support may well be significant.[93] Widespread shock at the consequences of the escalation of verbal and symbolic violence to physical violence and political assassination, may also lead to more civil political discourse. Agreement on this issue between Prime Minister Peres and Likud leader Benjamin Netanyahu is an important first step in that direction.

Notes

1. Norwegian Foreign Minister Johan Holst, in a speech at the National Press Club on October 4, 1993, cited the return of Labor to power as the critical turning point for the Oslo process. Cited in Zeva Flamhaft, "Israel and the Arab-Israeli Peace Process," 63.

2. Theodore H. Friedgut, "Israel's Turn toward Peace," 71–89.

3. Shimon Peres, *The New Middle East*, 16, 55–57.

4. Ibid., 57.

5. Hanan Ashrawi seriously doubts that Arafat at that time would have sanctioned negotiations with Israel by any delegation not officially tied to the PLO. Response to a question posed by one of the authors at a lecture by Ashrawi at Columbia University, October 13, 1995.

6. There have been several studies of the intifada. For a good analysis of its impact on Israel, the Arab world, and the superpowers, see Freedman, *The Intifada*.

7. See, for example, Asher Arian, "Israeli Public Opinion and the Intifada," 269–92; Myron J. Aronoff, "The Labor Party and the Intifada, 325–42; Aronoff, *Israeli Visions and Divisions*, 145–60; Mordecai Bar-On, "Israeli Reactions to the Palestinian Uprising," 42; Ephraim Yuchtman-Yaar, "The Israeli Public and the Intifada: Attitude Change or Entrenchment?" 235–51.

8. Aronoff, "The Labor Party and the Intifada," 338; reprinted in Aronoff, *Power and Ritual in the Israel Labor Party*, 216.

9. Aronoff, *Power and Ritual in the Israel Labor Party*, xii.

10. Friedgut, "Israel's Turn Toward Peace," 80.

11. Ibid., 81.

12. In an interview in *Ma'ariv* three days after his electoral defeat in 1992, Shamir admitted that his secret agenda for the peace talks had been to stall forever while continuing to build Jewish settlements. "I would have carried on autonomy talks for ten years," he said, "and meanwhile we would have reached half a million people in Judea and Samaria." Cited in Avi Shlaim, "Prelude to the Accord: Likud, Labor, and the Palestinians," 10.

13. Moshe Arens, *Broken Covenant: American Foreign Policy and the Crisis between the U.S. and Israel*, 9.

14. See Barry Rubin, "U.S.-Israel Relations and Israel's 1992 Election," 193–203, for a more balanced appraisal.

15. Much of the controversy was sparked in Israel by the publication by Mahmud

Abbas (also known as Abu Mazen, of *Through Secret Channels* [Reading: Gamet, 1995]) of his account of the Oslo negotiations. Abbas, head of the PLO's Israeli desk, led the Palestinian delegation in Oslo. He claimed that Labor's Ephraim Sneh (minister of health in the previous Labor Government) conspired with Said Kanaan (PLO) to help Labor win the 1992 election. See Yossi Olmert, "Gossip and Fairy Tales," *Jerusalem Post International Edition*, April 22, 1995, 16, for a highly critical review of such assertions and of the book by a scholar not normally sympathetic to Labor. For a scholarly analysis of the PLO role in the 1992 election, see Hillel Frisch, "The PLO and the 1992 Elections—A Skillful Participant?" 177–91. Helena Cobban, in "Israel and the Palestinians," 91–110, notes the Palestinian preference for Labor. She suggests that Arafat attempted to keep the situation in the occupied territories calm preceding the Israeli elections of June 23.

16. Arie Lova Eliav published a number of articles and interviews in the Israeli press and a particularly controversial article in *Time*. His most comprehensive manifesto was a book published in Hebrew by Am Oved in 1972, two years later in English: *Land of the Hart: Israelis, Arabs, The Territories, and a Vision of the Future*.

17. Eliav returned to the party fold and was elected to the Knesset on the Labor ticket in 1988. He received the second largest number of votes on the central list in the internal party primary even though he did not participate in any of the pre-election deals. See Aronoff, *Power and Ritual in the Israel Labor Party*, 193.

18. Ibid., 135.

19. Sartawi had masterminded an attack on a Lufthansa jet in which Israeli actress Hanna Marron lost a leg.

20. Netty C. Gross, "Alone in the Desert," *Jerusalem Post International Edition*, May 20, 1995, 14–15.

21. Eliav says, "Sartawi paid with his life. . . . I paid with my career. . . . Sartawi was the bravest of the brave, an extraordinary man. It pains me that the PLO today hasn't done much to rehabilitate his memory" (ibid., 15). Unfortunately Sartawi was neither the first nor the last Palestinian leader assassinated for daring to talk with Israelis in the pursuit of peace.

22. Efraim Inbar, *War and Peace in Israeli Politics*, especially chap. 7, 149–57. The uses of *left* and *right, dove,* and *hawk* are imprecise metaphors that tend to oversimplify complex phenomena. Inbar gives the latter two greater precision than most scholars using them. The restricted sense in which we use the term *dovishness* constitutes a sliding scale similar to that used by Inbar. A *dove* recognizes the legitimacy of national Palestinian rights, is willing to make territorial concessions, willing to negotiate with the PLO, and willing to accept an independent Palestinian state.

23. Aronoff, *Israeli Visions and Divisions*, chap. 6, esp. 135–37.

24. See Aronoff, *Power and Ritual in the Israel Labor Party*, esp. chaps. 10 and 12.

25. There is an analogy with the reforms in the U.S. Democratic Party that resulted in greater representation of liberal delegates to the national party conventions.

26. Beilin became minister without portfolio in the office of the prime minister with special responsibilities for the peace process in the reconstituted government led by Prime Minister Peres.

27. Myron J. Aronoff, "Labor in the Second Rabin Era: The First Year of Leadership," in Freedman, ed., *Israel under Rabin*, 129–42.

28. *Ha'aretz* reported in *Israel Line*, October 24, 1995.

29. Ramon, after rejoining Labor, became minister of the interior in the reconstituted government. He aspires to become prime minister. If Peres does not run in a future election, Ramon's likely opponents in Labor will be Yossi Beilin and Ehud Barak. (In a Labor Party vote in 1997, Barak was chosen as successor to Peres.)

30. Rabin received considerable criticism for his handling of Kahalani and his cohorts. It is widely believed among party insiders that had Rabin courted rather than rebuffed them, he could have prevented their defection. The two thousand members of the movement's council met at Kibbutz Shafaim and declared the formation of a political party. Kahalani was elected as party chairman.

31. Michal Yudelman, "Peace, the Third Way's Way," *Jerusalem Post International Edition*, September 2, 1995, 8.

32. The DMC won fifteen Knesset seats, at least ten of them from former Labor supporters.

33. We note the significance of the unplanned consequences of actions. Rabin made a serious effort to form a broader coalition. His failure to do this made possible his success in the peace talks. Aronoff, "Labor in the Second Rabin Era," in Freedman, ed. *Israel under Rabin*, esp. 130. See also Gregory S. Mahler, "Domestic Politics, Israeli Security, and the New Order in the Middle East," a paper presented at the annual meeting of the American Political Science Association, Chicago, 1995, for a general discussion of coalition building in Israeli politics as well as a discussion of the formation of the twenty-fifth government in 1992.

34. Ibid.

35. Ironically, in light of such charges, the nationalistic opposition parties joined the Arab parties in a vote of no-confidence in the government, a vote called by the Arab parties to oppose the expropriation of land in Jerusalem. Rehavam Ze'evi, the leader of the ultranationalist Moledet, said, "The end justifies the means, even if it means wearing very dirty clothes": Liat Collins, "Arafat attempts to stifle a Knesset no-confidence motion," *Jerusalem Post International Edition*, May 27, 1995, 32. This was the first time that Israeli Arab political parties nearly toppled a government— in this case one that they generally supported. However, their strong opposition to the government's attempt to expropriate more land in Jerusalem led them to take this forceful measure. When the opposition parties opportunistically announced they would vote with the Arab parties against the government (in spite of the fact that they supported the annexation), the government was forced to back down.

36. The split in Tsomet followed a similar split in Moledet, the most extreme of the ultranationalist parties represented in the Knesset. Tsomet's split came in the wake of allegations by the maverick Knesset members of financial irregularities

and other improprieties that contradicted Raphael (Raful) Eitan's squeaky-clean image, which accounted for the party's surprisingly successful showing in the 1992 election. Eitan, the party leader and former chief of staff, was accused of dishonesty and of being a dictator (among other allegations). Three of the renegade MKs formed the new Yi'ud Knesset faction. Yi'ud was further divided when Esther Salmovitz refused to join her two colleagues in the Labor-led coalition government. Faction leader Gonen Segev became minister of energy and his colleague, Alex Goldfarb, became deputy housing minister. Shortly thereafter, Hemi Doron, secretary-general of the new party, resigned in a huff.

37. The bill would have required a special majority of seventy Knesset members, or 50 percent of eligible voters in a national referendum, before any concessions could be made to the Syrians on the Golan.

38. Sarid was a protégé of the late Pinchas Sapir, who, as treasury minister and secretary-general of the Labor party, was a powerful patron. Sarid left Labor and joined Meretz during the Eleventh Knesset in 1984 in protest against the unity government of Labor and Likud. See Aronoff, *Power and Ritual in the Israel Labor Party.*

39. Aronoff, "Labor in the Second Rabin Era," 132–34.

40. For example, Religious Affairs Minister Shimon Shitreet (Labor) and Energy and Infrastructure Minister Gonen Segev (Yi'ud) did not vote in favor of the interim agreement in the cabinet as reported in *Israel Line,* September 27, 1995.

41. Klieman, "New Directions in Israel's Foreign Policy," correctly credits Beilin as one of the three shapers of policy along with the prime minister and the foreign minister.

42. Ilan Peleg, "The Likud under Rabin II: Between Ideological Purity and Pragmatic Readjustment."

43. Shas leader Aryeh Deri indicated that his party would endorse the prime ministerial candidacy of Levy. Had he drawn sufficient support, Levy could have forced a runoff between Labor's candidate (Peres) and the Likud's candidate (Benyamin Natanyahu). Deri did not indicate which of the two candidates he would urge his supporters to back. Shas joined the Likud government led by Netanyahu.

44. Peleg, "The Likud Under Rabin II," 159, quotes Doron Rosenblum, from *Ha'aretz,* May 7, 1993: "The radicalization of Likud looks like political suicide, taking into account that it achieved the height of its popularity particularly in the short periods in which it masqueraded as a pragmatic centrist party which seeks compromise and peace."

45. The latter used unconventional tactics such as having motorists halt traffic in major cities. The authorities have dealt quickly and severely with the leaders of this group, and its popular support appears to be limited. In the period before the assassination of Rabin, the attempt to block the Tel Aviv–Jerusalem highway in protest against the interim agreement was unsuccessful.

46. See, for example, his letter to the editor of the *Jerusalem Post International Edition,* October 21, 1995, 11.

47. *Yediot Aharonot* reported in *Israel Line,* October 10, 1995.

48. *Davar* reported in *Israel Line*, October 10, 1995.

49. Repeated disruptions by loudspeaker, such as that by Likud MK Tzachi Hanegbi during Rabin's speech at the ceremony concluding the Jerusalem parade, are another tactic used by the opposition. Rabin was also prevented from speaking to a meeting of Israelis from English-speaking countries. In reaction the party mobilized volunteers from the Histadrut, the Labor Young Guard, and the United Kibbutz Movement to accompany and protect government ministers at public appearances. Michal Yudelman, "Labor forms unit to fight 'right-wing violence,'" *Jerusalem Post International Edition*, October 28, 1995, 4.

50. *Ha'aretz* reported in *Israel Line*, October 13, 1995.

51. Gabriel Sheffer, "A weapon of the weak," *Jerusalem Post International Edition*, October 7, 1995, 12. Sheffer is a professor of political science at The Hebrew University of Jerusalem.

52. Herb Keinon, "A new state of affairs," *Jerusalem Post International Edition*, October 7, 1995, 3.

53. David Makovsky, "Past the point of no return," *Jerusalem Post International Edition*, September 30, 1995, 7, 14.

54. "Now it is in force," editorial, *Jerusalem Post*, October 6, 1995, republished in the *Jerusalem Post International Edition*, October 14, 1995, 10.

55. "Arafat has triumphed—Hamas official," *Jerusalem Post International Edition*, October 7, 1995, 5.

56. Immediately after the signing of the interim accords, Yasir Arafat entered into negotiations with Hamas. In return for a suspension of attacks on Israel from territories controlled by the Palestinian Authority, Hamas was given greater leeway in forming parties and publishing newspapers. A struggle is taking place within Hamas between those who favor accommodation and working through the political process and the militants who reject compromise. David Afek, head of the Foreign Ministry's Center for Political Research, *Davar* reported, claims that progress in the peace process has cost Hamas significant political support among the Palestinians. He also suggested that a political agreement between the PLO and Hamas may bring about the separation of the military wing from Hamas (*Israel Line*, October 20, 1995). A survey conducted October 7, 1995, by the Jerusalem Media and Communication Center indicated that support for Hamas declined from 18 percent to 11 percent after their June poll. "Hamas-PA deal reported," *Jerusalem Post International Edition*, October 28, 1995, 6. Hamas decided not to participate officially in the elections but allowed candidates identified with the movement to compete under the banner of the National Salvation Party (*Ha'aretz*, reported in *Israel Line*, December 20, 1995).

57. Most scholars fail to credit Beilin for the initiative and instrumental role he has played. Peres even fails to mention Beilin in his book *The New Middle East* and does not give him his due credit in *Battling for Peace: A Memoir*. Aharon Klieman is one of the few scholars who has given Beilin the full credit he deserves. Although less risky than Lova Eliav's earlier initiatives, had Beilin's gamble not paid off, it could have damaged his most promising political future.

58. Jane Corbin, *Gaza First: The Secret Norway Channel to Peace Between Israel and the PLO.*

59. Charles Tripp, "Timing Is Everything: The Making of the Israel-PLO Deal," 167.

60. Michael Keren, "Israeli Professionals and the Peace Process."

61. Ibid, 149.

62. Ibid., 150.

63. Ibid., 153.

64. Klieman, 107. He cites Beilin's book *Israel—Forty Plus* (Tel Aviv: Yediot Aharonot Publishing House, 1993).

65. "Such a technocratic approach may not satisfy the quest for 'peace' propounded by most intellectuals; but there would seem to be no viable alternative to pragmatism, which promises at least some hope in great despair" (Keren, 162).

66. Helena Cobban, "Israel and the Palestinians," 94–101.

67. Serge Schmemann, "Negotiators, Arab and Israeli, Built Friendship from Mistrust," *New York Times,* September 28, 1995, 1, A10. For an even more dramatic example, see Basam Abu-Sharif and Uzi Mahnaimi, *Best of Enemies* (New York: Little Brown, 1995). Abu-Sharif is a former militant in the Popular Front for the Liberation of Palestine (wounded by a letter bomb reputedly sent by Israeli intelligence); Mahnaimi is a former Israeli intelligence officer who was involved in espionage.

68. Myron J. Aronoff and Pierre M. Atlas, "The Peace Process and Competing Challenges to the Dominant Zionist Discourse."

69. Ibid., 23; Ilan Peleg, "Otherness and Israel's Arab Dilemma," in Laurence J. Silberstein and Robert L. Cohen, eds., *The Other in Jewish Thought and History: Constructions of Jewish Culture and Identity* (New York: New York University Press, 1994), 264.

70. See, for example, Serge Schmemann, "Bus Bombing Kills Five in Jerusalem: 100 Are Wounded," *New York Times,* August 22, 1995, A1, A6.

71. Klieman, "New Directions in Israel's Foreign Policy," 96.

72. Ibid., 102.

73. Aronoff, "Labor in the Second Rabin Era," 130.

74. Aronoff, *Power and Ritual in the Israel Labor Party,* 132–37.

75. David Makovsky and Steve Rodan, "Beilin talks about his talks," *Jerusalem Post International Edition,* October 30, 1993, 12.

76. David Makovsky, "Israel, Jordan move towards peace," *Jerusalem Post International Edition,* August 13, 1995, 4.

77. Clyde Haberman, "Ceremony Will Be Hot, Windy, and Made for TV," *New York Times,* October 26, 1994.

78. Ibid.

79. Shamir met secretly with King Hussein in London on January 5, 1991, at Hussein's invitation. Shamir promised not to violate Jordanian airspace in return for Hussein's promise to bar Iraq from using Jordanian bases against Israel and to bar Iraqi planes from using Jordanian airspace to attack Israel. This agreement was a significant factor in Shamir's decision not to retaliate against Iraqi attacks with

Scud missiles. Moshe Zak, "Gulf War revelations," *Jerusalem Post International Edition*, September 20, 1995, 15.

80. Liat Collins, "Rabin family plays tourist in Petra," *Jerusalem Post International Edition*, May 13, 1995, 24.

81. Thomas L. Friedman, "Almost Egypt," *New York Times*, October 25, 1995, A21 (emphasis added).

82. Serge Schmemann, "Mideast Leaders Talk, This Time of Business," *New York Times*, October 30, 1995, A9. Tension between Jordan and Egypt over the location of the headquarters of the new Middle East Development Bank was resolved in a compromise. It will have headquarters in Cairo, and a permanent secretariat for economic cooperation will be located in Amman. Economics and Planning Minister Yossi Beilin called the compromise a major achievement for the Steering Committee (of which he was a member). *Ha'aretz*, reported in *Israel Line*, October 30, 1995.

83. David Makovsky, "Peace with Jordan depends on final settlement with Palestinians," *Jerusalem Post International Edition*, September 23, 1995, 6.

84. Shimon Peres, The New Middle East, chap. 13, 163–79.

85. *Ma'ariv* report in *Israel Line*, September 29, 1995.

86. Schmemann, "Mideast Leaders Talk, This Time of Business"; also Schmemann, *Israel Line*, October 26, 1995.

87. *Ha'aretz*, reported in *Israel Line*, October 30, 1995.

88. Steve Rodan, "Of Two Minds at the Top," *Jerusalem Post International Edition*, October 29, 1994, 11.

89. Mark Heller, "Assad's rigidity," *Jerusalem Post International Edition*, August 12, 1995, 12.

90. Steve Rodan, "The sphinx and the skeptic," *Jerusalem Post International Edition*, October 21, 1995, 20–21.

91. Ann Mosely Lesch, "Israeli Negotiations with Syria, Lebanon, and Jordan: The Security Dimension," 117.

92. *Ha'aretz*, reported in *Israel Line*, October 24, 1995.

93. Three and a half weeks after the assassination of Prime Minister Rabin, support for the Oslo agreements remained steady at 58 percent, after rising 11 percentage points in the wake of the murder. General support for the peace process, which rose 20 points, to 73.1 percent, in the wake of the assassination, declined to 65.7 percent. *Ha'aretz*, reported in *Israel Line*, December 20, 1995.

2: Netanyahu and Peace

From Sound Bites to Sound Policies?

Mark Rosenblum

The Oslo journey for Arab-Israeli peacemaking was destined to be a long uphill road, even if Shimon Peres had won his fourth and final bid for the prime ministership. Sufyan Abu Zaidah, head of the Israel desk at the Palestinian Planning Ministry, acknowledged as much in his response to the political upheaval in Israel. "We expected difficult negotiations in any case with Labor and Peres. We didn't think a state was in the pocket. We had different opinions on all the final status issues—borders, refugees, Jerusalem and the settlements. But the problem now for the Palestinians is not the final settlement. It's the implementation of the interim agreement."[1] Benjamin Netanyahu's cliff-hanger victory has turned this uphill climb into an up-mountain marathon.

Israel and Peace: Two Slogans, One Policy

The June 1992 election of the Rabin-led Labor government was a decisive factor in making the Oslo quest for peace plausible. For the first time in the history of the Israeli-Palestinian conflict, two pragmatic national leaderships were in power at the same time. This overlapping rule, of the Labor-led government in Israel and the Fatah-dominated Palestine Liberation Organization, facilitated negotiations toward and implementation of the only peace possible: a historic swap, withdrawal for security.

Thus, in 1992, Israelis elected, if ever so narrowly, a new government that dismissed two discredited slogans and embraced the only viable policy. The first slogan discarded was Likud's offer to the Arab world of "peace for peace." Without any territorial compromise—without any Israeli withdrawal—this call for "Greater Israel" had absolutely no prospect of producing partners in the Arab world. Worse, it was a prescription for what Abba Eban characterized as "suicide through annexation."[2] Extending Israel's geography to include the West Bank and Gaza would create a crisis in demography and polity. The specter of a binational state wracked by violence and civil war has discredited this Likud option.

The second slogan that has been dismissed is the supposed Labor party alternative of "land for peace." This simplistic formula omits the single most important variable—security. Without security arrangements that help offset and compensate Israel for the military advantages associated with specific territory and topography, no Israeli government would engage in an exchange that included withdrawal.

Beyond this strategic, existential security imperative, the Oslo process and the suicidal terrorist attacks have highlighted a second dimension of security: personal, individual security. There was little anticipation of the kind of suicidal terrorism that has ravaged Israel following the Oslo accords. During the August 30, 1993, cabinet meeting in which Prime Minister Rabin submitted the agreement for approval, two kinds of criticism emerged—but neither addressed the issue of personal security.

First, Elyakim Rubinstein, chief negotiator with the Palestinians, complained that the Oslo I accord compromised Israel's goal of entering final status negotiations with all options open, including the option of asserting Israeli sovereignty over the territories.[3] The other criticism was articulated by Chief of Staff Ehud Barak, who focused on security concerns. While not unmindful of the political advantages of the agreement, Barak was deeply worried about undermining Israeli Defense Forces (IDF) combat readiness and assigning the Israeli army a thankless task: protecting some 100,000 settlers scattered throughout the 130 settlements of the West Bank and Gaza while Israel simultaneously relinquished jurisdiction to the Palestinians. Thus security fears were voiced from the outset of the Oslo process. Barak's attention was riveted on the problems of IDF readiness and the vulnerability of Jewish settlers who were living and traveling throughout the West Bank and Gaza.[4] Militant Palestinians and settlers bristling with arms and buttressed by animosities, often living cheek to jowl, were the security nightmare Barak most feared. Suicide terrorist attacks against Israelis within the green line were not yet the preoccupation of Israeli politicians or generals. They soon haunted the governments of Peres and Rabin and Israeli generals. Yet in spite of this new security challenge, there is only one formula for combating Israel's security dangers and ending its hundred years' war with Arab neighbors: "security and peace for land."

This exchange has been the backbone of Arab-Israeli peacemaking. The old zero-sum politics of the Arab-Israeli conflict has been slowly but surely redirected toward the possibility of win-win policies. Many presumed that sustaining these policies would require the electoral legitimization of the pragmatic national leaderships on both sides of the divide. The specter of messianic nationalists of either "Greater Israel" or "Greater Palestine" hurtling Arabs and Israelis to a still less secure, more territorially irredentist future remains a haunting possibility.

Ballots over Bullets: The Legitimization of the Palestinian Authority

On November 4, 1995, an Israeli political assassin had just such a future in mind when he killed Prime Minister Rabin. However, Yigal Amir failed to halt the Israeli withdrawal and transfer of power in six cities in the West Bank. The Peres-led government remained committed to completing its redeployment in Hebron, albeit only with continuing evidence of the Palestinian Authority's crackdown on terrorism and only after the Palestinian National Council rescinded those parts of the Palestinian Charter that were in violation of the Oslo agreements. Having fulfilled these two Israeli demands, Arafat was nevertheless compelled to accept a further delay in redeployment, as Peres for obvious domestic political reasons wanted to avoid a struggle around the volcanic Hebron issue until the Israeli elections had taken place. In the meantime, the Israeli Labor party tried to mollify Arafat by doing some of its own rescinding. It excised from its platform the clause opposing the creation of a Palestinian state. Hence, redeployment from Hebron, complicated because of the residence of 450 militant messianic Jewish settlers in the midst of 120,000 Palestinians, remains an agreement waiting to be implemented. As of late summer 1996, Prime Minister Netanyahu was still "studying" the "complicated" situation.[5]

By honoring its Oslo obligations (except for Hebron) to evacuate the population centers of the West Bank and yield power to Palestinian authority there, the Peres government facilitated the first-ever national elections in the West Bank and Gaza. Thus, in January 1996 ballots prevailed over bullets. Israeli enlightened self-interest and Palestinian self-determination were both winners. Israeli soldiers were liberated from the fearful burden of chasing Palestinians through the casbahs of the West Bank, and the Palestinian legislators freely elected by their fellow citizens prepared to govern an emerging nation.

This represented the high point in the uphill struggle for peace. Transferring Gaza and a notch of the West Bank—Jericho—to the Palestinians and converting Israel's de facto peace with Jordan into an official, public relationship barely took us into the foothills of the negotiations. With the successful implementation of this phase of the interim agreement, the peace-makers entered the really rugged political terrain that many skeptics thought was beyond reach.

Political pundits took turns explaining either why the Israelis would never redeploy from the cities of the West Bank, or why Arafat would never hold elections. Prime Minister Peres suggested that "there were various hints during the Oslo process that the elections might be deferred or might not be held at all." He acknowledged, "I did not see [elections] as a neces-sary condition [for making peace]." Nor did he believe "democracy can be imposed artificially on another society."[6] Yossi Beilin, one of the architects of Oslo, also remained doubtful that elections would ever take place, given Arafat's antidemocratic instincts.[7]

The comments of Naseer Aruri, a Palestinian activist and scholar, were illustrative of Palestinians' skepticism about the Israeli's will to redeploy. He argued that "the Gaza-Jericho first formula is the bait. . . . Ironically, for Israel, it opened the gateway to the Arab world, but it simultaneously closed to the Palestinians the doors to the West Bank."[8] For Aruri, "The demo-graphic and geographic character of the 140 Jewish settlements in the West Bank would make it nearly impossible for any Israeli government to ex-tend limited self-rule from Gaza to the West Bank."[9] Article 13 of Oslo's Declaration of Principles, which had linked the holding of Palestinian elec-tions to Israel's redeploying "outside populated areas," was presumed by Aruri to be an exercise in political alchemy.[10] Instead of there being neither redeployment nor elections as Aruri expected, Israelis and Palestinians experienced both. Confounding the critics, this would be the last accom-plishment of the Peres-Arafat partnership.

Bombs and Ballots: Peres's Struggle for Political Survival

Within six weeks of the historic Palestinian national elections in the West Bank and Gaza, military units of Hamas and Islamic Jihad launched a new cycle of suicide bombings in Jerusalem, Ashkelon, and Tel Aviv. The nego-tiations and the election of Peres were in grave jeopardy.

Crackdown on Arafat

For the first time, the Peres government specifically linked additional Is-raeli withdrawal to a series of reciprocal security-related moves on the Palestinian side. Peres demanded that Arafat and the Palestinian Author-ity wage a comprehensive war against Palestinian terrorism. Arafat's poli-tics of co-opting Hamas would have to be supplemented with coercive military policies. The thirteen most wanted military leaders of Hamas and

Islamic Jihad would have to be captured, arrested, tried, and punished with the full force of the law. All militias had to be declared illegal and disarmed. During this period of crackdown, Peres's contact with Arafat was largely limited to television interviews or government press releases. Amnon Shahak, Israel's army chief of staff, personally delivered Peres's demand that the Palestinian Authority arrest the thirteen members of Hamas's military arm.[11] As one Palestinian minister suggested,"Israeli generals are telling our police what they expect them to do."[12]

The Israeli government was also pressuring the Palestinian Authority to mobilize the public and nongovernmental organizations in a campaign against violence. Arafat initiated a crackdown on Palestinian institutions from mosques to universities. The Palestinian Authority helped mobilize demonstrations in several cities in the West Bank and Gaza under the banner of "yes to peace, no to closure."[13] In addition, they insisted that the Palestinian National Council officially revoke those parts of its covenant that contradicted agreements signed by the PLO and the Palestinian Authority with the Israeli government. A date certain for completing this revocation process was included for the first time in the September 1995 interim agreement. The Israelis were adamant that the May 7 deadline be met. If the Palestinians did not honor this commitment, the Israelis would continue to defer the redeployment in Hebron (originally scheduled for March 28) as well as postpone final status negotiations set for May 4. Hanan Ashrawi, former spokesperson for the Palestinian negotiating team in Madrid and member of the Palestinian Council, captured the sentiment of Palestinians and perhaps objective reality as well: "The entire peace process is now subordinated to the electoral issue of the Israelis' personal security."[14]

"Total Closure"

In addition to these demands on Arafat, the Peres government imposed a "total closure" on the West Bank and Gaza as part of its antiterrorism measures. This total closure stopped all movement of people and goods into Israel from the Palestinian self-governing areas. Even those Palestinians who had been granted permits to work in Israel during periods of "normal closure" were prevented from leaving the self-governing areas.[15] Palestinian access to Jordan and Egypt from the West Bank and Gaza was also radically curtailed.[16] While the Israeli defense establishment was overwhelmingly opposed to the closures, fearing an increase in both economic privation and violence in the West Bank and Gaza, Rabin and Peres found it a domestic political asset.[17] In the words of one former Likud minister,

"The public just doesn't want to be knifed. It cares less about where the border is than the fact that it exists and Arabs are on the other side."[18] The politics of separation and the reestablishment of the border have been a powerful motivating force behind the Labor Party's closure policy.

As part of its crackdown on terrorism, the Peres government imposed an unprecedented security measure, an "internal closure." This effectively cantonized the West Bank's 1.3 million Palestinians into their 465 villages and towns, preventing all movement from one place to another. The internal closure applied both to zone C, the 70 percent of the West Bank still under exclusive Israeli authority, and to areas under the jurisdiction of the recently elected Palestinian Authority. The Peres government not only hinted that it reserved the right to fight Palestinian terrorists "everywhere." It also used its security coordination mechanisms with Palestinians to request Palestinian police "to step aside" in order to allow Israeli forces to conduct selective security sweeps in Palestinian villages during the March security crisis.[19] The Israeli government also reactivated its policy of punishing the families of terrorists by demolishing several of their houses. In addition Peres announced that the final status agreement with the Palestinians would be submitted to a plebiscite separate from and after the national elections of May 29, 1996.

In short, Shimon Peres's response to the February-March terrorist assaults was swift, dramatic, and in some respects draconian. Security was becoming the third rail of the triangular exchange of "security and peace for land." Without a response to the crisis in Israeli personal security, peace and the upcoming elections would be lost. Hence, three months before the election of Netanyahu, Prime Minister Peres effectively froze the peace negotiations with the Palestinians, making further progress contingent on the Palestinian Authority's honoring its commitments, particularly in the security field.

Lebanon: A Bloody Return to the Status Quo Ante

This crisis on the Israeli-Palestinian track was preceded by a protracted stalemate on the Syrian front—one that dated back to the end of 1995. Unable to get a firm commitment for a summit with Assad and disappointed by Assad's inflexibility on security arrangements, normalization questions, and border demarcations, Peres decided to go for early elections without a negotiating breakthrough with Syria. Assad in turn apparently felt betrayed and slighted by Peres—betrayed by the latter's decision to submit any deal on the Golan to an Israeli plebiscite. The specter of the Israeli public deciding what to do with Syrian territory in a

national referendum was a violation of Assad's understanding of the negotiating rules. It was, from his perspective, also an act of national humiliation or, more to the point, regime humiliation. Neither Sadat nor King
Hussein had to endure a special Israeli plebiscite. Assad also felt slighted
by Peres's decision to run his electoral campaign on the basis of progress
with the Palestinians and Jordan only. Assad does not like being left out.
He fancies himself as the deal maker or deal breaker.[20] Feeling little incentive to rein in Hizbollah and sensing no military threat from Israel, Syria
allowed the war of attrition in southern Lebanon to heat up. With Israel's
"security zone" being bled, the Galilee under Katyusha assault, and Lebanese civilians killed in Peres's "Grapes of Wrath" military campaign, Assad
held court in Damascus as the would-be peacemaker.

Meanwhile, Peres tried to sell a return to the status quo ante as a victory. There were few buyers. Most of the world would remember only the
carnage at the Lebanese town of Qana caused by an Israeli artillery response to Hizbollah shelling, and Israeli voters did not reward Peres for
looking tough in Lebanon. The very Israeli politician who had helped extract Israel from Likud's 1982 folly was stuck in the Lebanese briar patch.

Peres's get-tough policy with the Palestinian Authority was not convincing to either Israeli voters or the Palestinians. Many Israelis, like Binnie
Zerah, who reject the politics of "Greater Israel," were deeply troubled by
the timing of Peres's crackdown on Arafat and terrorism. "Now Peres thinks
that Arafat can and will do more to fight the butchers of Hamas. Where
were our demands and pressures earlier, before March 4? What planet was
Peres visiting during the earlier bombings in Tel Aviv and Jerusalem? Part
of me feels that what Peres has done is a case of 'better late then never.' But
most of me thinks he is just unforgivably late. Maybe we should have held
early-early elections. Like last year. Then Peres might have read the riot act
to Arafat, and we might have had less terrorism. The man got it right only
on the eve of elections, only when his political life is on the line. I think he
is too late."[21]

The Closure: Security Boon or Boomerang?

While Peres's crackdown on Arafat came too late and raised too many un-
flattering questions among some Israelis about his electoral opportunism,
Palestinians have experienced the closures too often, and with consequences
that do not bode well for either the Palestinian Authority or Israeli security.

According to the UN Office of the Special Coordinator in the Occupied
Territories, the Israeli closure policy, including Peres's "total closure" after

the February-March bombings, cost the Palestinians in the West Bank and Gaza about $800 million in 1996. About $300 million of this was lost wages, and $500 million was lost gross domestic product. This $800 million in lost income is approximately equal to what the international donors pledged to the Palestinian Authority for all of 1996. Unfortunately, only about 10 percent of the money pledged has actually been disbursed.[22]

Palestinian income flow from Israel in the form of jobs, trade, and taxes is simply irreplaceable. About 60 percent of Palestinian Authority revenues come from Israel.[23] Given these lost revenues, it is not surprising that the World Bank is anticipating a 20 percent decline in economic output in the West Bank and Gaza in 1996.[24]

On the eve of the Israeli elections, only some 20,000 Palestinians were permitted to work in Israel.[25] Prior to the first closure in March 1993, the number of Palestinians from the territories working in Israel had exceeded 120,000.[26] The most recent closure, following the February-March suicide terrorism, cost 50,000 Palestinian jobs in the West Bank and Gaza, approximately one-third of the estimated 150,000-member labor force.[27] Of the 50,000 jobs lost by Palestinians, 20,000 were in Israel and the rest in Gaza.[28] Of the jobs lost in Gaza, the majority, about 23,000, were in the construction sector, which has been plagued by shortages of material—shortages also attributable to the closure.[29]

Prior to the last closure, the Palestinian deficit for 1996 was projected at $75 million.[30] This figure was based on assumptions that at least 35,000 Palestinian workers would have access to Israeli labor markets and that the Palestinian domestic product would grow by 7.5 percent.[31] As a result of the closure, the deficit is likely to be at least double.[32] This could create a devastating budget deficit crisis given that donors pledged to cover the deficit as it was projected before the last closure.

It is a tragic paradox that Shimon Peres, who had spoken so often and so elegantly of Israel's self-interest in helping to create a vibrant Palestinian economy, has passed on such an impoverished inheritance to Netanyahu. With a sharp decline in both Palestinian living standards and the Palestinian Authority's revenues, a severe social and liquidity crisis could combine in strengthening Hamas and Islamic Jihad.

Israeli Security vs. Palestinian Economy

The military wing of Hamas and Islamic Jihad have discovered the exposed Achilles heel of the Oslo agreement. Israeli security has been pitted against Palestinian economy. Through a handful of young men armed with plastique and messianic faith, Hamas and Islamic Jihad have violated Israeli personal security and challenged the elected Palestinian Authority. Their suicidal terrorist attacks against Israeli civilians in their nation's urban heartland have triggered an Israeli security retaliation that has had devastating consequences for the West Bank and Gaza economy. Hoping to foster popular disillusionment about peace on both Israeli and Palestinian streets, they have succeeded in sowing fear in Ramat Gan and increasing poverty in Jubalya. While Islamic Jihad and the military wing of Hamas would surely like to foster conflict and enmity between the common citizens of Tel Aviv and Gaza, they are also determined to disrupt the partnership that has emerged between the pragmatic national elites in both communities. From the perspective of Hamas's military underground, Shimon Peres and his government were the most dangerous kind of enemies. They are would-be partners in compromise—a compromise that might attract Hamas's own Palestinian constituents and challenge its ideological maximalism.[33]

Having mistakenly boycotted the January Palestinian elections, Hamas was decidedly less shy about using its lethal influence on the May 29 Israeli elections. It bombed Prime Minister Peres and the Labor party into electoral oblivion. The four suicidal bombings in February and March frightened away a key swing constituency, the nonideological "hawks of fear."[34]

Peres was hoping that a series of positive developments in the security sphere would win them back. He helped mobilize support for the Sharm el-Sheik peace and antiterrorism conference. A new security agreement with the United States provided Israel with antimissile and antiterrorism technology. Finally, the Palestinian Authority intensified its fight against terrorism. Yet this embryonic partnership against terrorism and a ten-week respite from suicide attacks inside Israel could not break the spell-like "terrorist watch" that haunted the Israelis, daily reminding them of their vulnerability. Nor could it offset the orthodox bloc voting for Netanyahu or the small but important backlash among Israeli Arabs whose blank ballots were yet another indication of the bitter harvest reaped by Peres's "Operation Grapes of Wrath" in Lebanon.

Netanyahu: Running against Arafat, Defeating Peres

By casting their terrorist vote for Likud and the forces of "Greater Israel," Hamas and Islamic Jihad created an opening for Binyamin Netanyahu. Exploiting their suicidal terrorism, Netanyahu ran against Yasser Arafat and defeated Shimon Peres.

Netanyahu was relentless in attacking the Labor-led government for supposedly "subcontracting" Israelis' security to the PLO and the Palestinian Authority. "Yasser Arafat will not protect us; he is not capable of protecting us; he doesn't want to protect us." If elected, Netanyahu promised, "We will change this. Security will be put in the hands of the IDF, security will be in the hands of the Shin Bet."[35]

During their only TV debate, shortly before the election, Netanyahu achieved perfection of the sound bite in lecturing Peres. "You have created asylum cities [in the West Bank] while our front line is under bombardment."[36] Peres, in contrast, seemed arrogantly aloof in yielding his only direct opportunity to challenge his opponent with a concluding question.

Netanyahu's one-liners seemingly resonated with Israel's swing constituency of "security hawks." Peres's trademark aphorisms, on the other hand, were often perceived as naively futuristic and out of sync with the immediate politics of fear. Netanyahu replayed the nightmare images of exploding bombs and charred buses. Peres fast-forwarded to dreamy visions of "tomatoes bigger than Toyotas."[37] With the Israeli public understandably obsessing over the next terrorist bombing, Peres suggested that "in the future the only generals in the Middle East will be General Motors and General Electric."[38]

While Netanyahu will not be able to ignore the generals or even the captains of industry and finance, he campaigned with a laser-like focus on terrorism, projecting himself as Mr. Security. He promised all the dividends of peace with none of its liabilities. Never a general, he will nevertheless be judged as prime minister by whether he honors his commitment to fight against terrorism and for peace. Netanyahu ran his electoral campaign to the center and pledged to make a "secure peace." Can he run a government to the center and deliver either security or peace, much less the two together, without a willingness to negotiate significant territorial withdrawal? His mastery of electronic politics and sound bites is not in question. What remains to be answered is his capacity to lead a nation in pursuit of sound policies.

Tripartite Coalition, Dual Tendencies, One Boss

Before exploring the implications of Netanyahu's victory on the embryonic Arab-Israeli peace, it is worth briefly discussing the nature of his mandate and his capacity to act given his unwieldy coalition of competing interests and parties.

Israel's fourteenth national elections were not a mandate either for "Greater Israel" or against Oslo. To be sure there were, and will continue to be, public and substantive differences between Netanyahu and Peres, and Labor and Likud, both on specific issues such as a Palestinian state, settlements, and negotiations with Syria, and on general willingness to compromise, much less negotiate, key final-status issues such as Jerusalem and refugees. Yet in spite of these central differences, Netanyahu felt compelled to campaign to the middle. He pledged to honor previous agreements and continue the current peace process, even if at a slower pace and with an eye on "security first." Netanyahu ran to the center because running to the right on a rollback or annexationist platform would have made him unelectable.

The composition of the Knesset and of the new governing coalition suggests similar conclusions. This is no triumph for "Greater Israel." The new Knesset is divided roughly among four blocs, the largest bloc being composed of hard-core doves. Four parties—Labor (34), Meretz, (9) Hadash (5), and the United Arab List (4)—represent 52 seats in this dovish bloc. They lost 9 seats in the election, thereby depriving them of the all-important strategic advantage that they had held in the previous Knesset: a blocking majority. Having lost both their blocking majority and the prime ministership, these 52 MKs represent the initial basis for a parliamentary opposition.

The remaining three blocs combined have a total of 66 members—the new tripartite coalition, led by the first prime minister to have been directly elected, independent of his party. Although the 2 members of the Knesset representing Moledet are not included in the government because their policy of favoring the "transfer" of Palestinians is too radical for Netanyahu, they are likely to support the government from the outside. In other words, Netanyahu can depend on a majority of 68 at the outset of his term.

The second largest bloc in the new Knesset is composed of the hardcore hawks of "Greater Israel." There are three parties in this bloc: Likud, including Tsomet and Gesher (32); the National Religious Party, or NPR (9); and Moledet (2). Holding 43 seats in the Knesset, they have collectively lost 6 seats since the last election. Not all of the Knesset members in these parties are advocates of territorial status quo. There are Knesset members in Likud, in David Levy's Gesher faction, and even in the NRP who are more moderate and less ideological than their parties' platforms might indicate.[39]

The third largest bloc in the new Knesset is made up of the ultraorthodox parties Shas (10) and United Torah Judaism (4). On peace and security issues, they are more political opportunists than true believers. They represent a core agnostic constituency on questions of Arab-Israeli negotiations. Both of these parties are moved primarily by theological questions of Sabbath observance, religious conversion, and Kashrut (Jewish dietary laws). These religious priorities are increasingly intertwined with the worldly servicing of their ethnic and religious constituencies. This latter interest requires cash, housing allotments, and, of course, ministry appointments and Knesset seats, which in turn ensure all the bounties associated with political power.

Shas has not been averse to joining Labor governments in the past. It was a coalition partner in Rabin's government until a cloud of scandal and an official corruption investigation forced Aryeh Deri, the party's leader, to leave the government.[40] While Shas became increasingly critical of subsequent agreements with the Palestinians, Rabbi Ovadia Yosef, the renowned spiritual leader of the party, has consistently issued Halachic (Jewish legal) rulings in favor of peace and territorial withdrawal. The positions of United Torah Judaism are more hawkish. The revered, aging rabbinical leader of one of its two factions, Rabbi Eliezer Schach, is strongly averse to the culture and leadership of the secular dovish parties. In spite of this personal and cultural animus, even this party is not necessarily a lock for Likud and the secular core of the annexationist camp.

The last, smallest, and newest of the four blocs in the Knesset is composed of two centrist parties, Natan Sharansky's Yisrael Ba'aliya Russian immigrant party (7) and the Third Way (4), a breakaway faction from the Labor party that has focused on maintaining Israeli sovereignty in those parts of the Golan Heights where there are Jewish settlements, water resources, and "vital lines of defense."[41] While both of these parties identify certain red lines in their platforms on both the Palestinian and Syrian fronts, they are open to territorial compromise. Their red lines are drawn for largely pragmatic security reasons, not out of absolute ideological commitments. Positive developments with Arab and Palestinian neighbors of Israel and improvement in Israel's security situation could convert them to two new centrist parties, from "security hawks" to "security doves."[42]

Netanyahu's governing coalition is riven with conflicts and competing interests on religious social domestic issues and on peace and security questions. These coalitional differences are significant and likely to tax his conflict resolution skills. First, his skills will be tested in trying to reconcile the ultraorthodox demands with the positions of the secular forces of Tzomet, Yisrael Ba'aliya, the Third Way, and many Likudniks. Second, they will be tested in mediating the policy differences between Netanyahu's right flank (the Likud-Tzomet secular hawks and the NRP-Yesha messianic nationalists) and the more territorially centrist wing of his coalition (Yisrael Ba'aliya, the Third Way, Shas, Gesher, and key Likud MKs).

It is not unimaginable that Netanyahu could face rebellions from both annexationists and centrists. Yet at the end of the day, those new parties that have come from nowhere, Yisrael Ba'aliya and the Third Way, as well as those who won stunning increases in the election, the NRP and Shas, have compelling reasons not to bring Netanyahu down. They would be committing political suicide. The new election law makes it very difficult to bring about new prime ministerial elections without dissolving the Knesset at the same time. Scenarios for Knesset gridlock and crisis abound. However, prospects for the dissolution of the Knesset or a special election for a new prime minister seem dim. Whatever the pain or gain of "Bibi-land," we are likely to experience the whole term.[43]

Disquieting Appointments: Bulldozers and "Hebrew Only"

It is premature to speak with any certainty about how Prime Minister Netanyahu intends to pursue his election mandate of providing security and peace for Israel. However, there are hints of a direction, based on his appointments of ministers and other executive positions, the *Guidelines of the Government of Israel*, initial discussions with U.S. officials and Arab interlocutors, and his government's initial behavior in the field.

His appointments have generally been met with relief by those who had been fearful that hawks like Ariel Sharon and Raful Eytan would be given strategic ministries from which they could send the IDF back into Gaza City, Ramallah, and perhaps even Beirut. Both men have been shut out of the ministries they most coveted. Eytan is head of Agriculture and Environment, and Sharon, after haggling over a customized portfolio, has landed the powerful National Infrastructure Ministry, tailored to suit his sizable ambitions in the West Bank, Gaza, and the Golan Heights. Sharon has won wide-ranging authority over national energy, road construction, and state lands. This dynamic duo, which orchestrated Israel's 1982 debacle in Lebanon, could still end up playing havoc with the Oslo agreements. While these two ambitious former warriors no longer command the tanks, they may yet control the bulldozers. Their commitment to taking and holding land makes them, even out of uniform, key allies for settlement activists of YESHA (the Council of Jewish Settlements in Judea, Samaria, and the Gaza Strip).

Following the Oslo breakthrough, Sharon was active with Amana, the settlement arm of YESHA, in creating a blueprint for a massive new settlement drive in the West Bank. The plan included a $4 billion construction effort that would triple the settler population in the territories by the beginning of the next millennium.[44] This settlement boom would be carried out under the rubric of "expanding" and "thickening" the larger preexisting settlements—particularly those that were de facto suburbs of Jerusalem with easy access to the extensive series of bypass roads paved in the wake of the Oslo agreement. There were twelve new settlements in the plan, settlements that were actually approved while Shamir was prime minister.[45] Yet even these new settlements were targeted for areas outside the territorial jurisdiction of the Palestinian Authority.[46] By focusing a massive settlement drive on either state lands or within the master plan boundaries of existing settlements, Sharon and Amana were hoping to blunt foreign criticism. The financing of this settlement campaign was also planned with an eye toward minimizing dissent. Rather than depend on large-scale governmental assistance, Amana and Sharon were counting on mobilizing private-sector financing.[47]

The operative word here is *natural:* as in "natural" growth of preexisting settlements, as in private financing from the marketplace, as in consistency with Oslo accords. After all, the $600 million bypass road system that these settlements would use had been built by the Labor Party and accepted by the Palestinian Authority. The land where these settlements would be built will be outside the self-governing areas and within Israeli state lands. The PA, in the interim agreement of September 1995, recognized Israel's "legal right" over state lands.[48]

It seems reasonable to presume that Sharon and Eytan will, at the minimum, use this ambitious blueprint of settlement expansion so as to contain any further territorial expansion of the PA and to preclude the emergence of a Palestinian state.[49] While Sharon and Eytan have gotten all the attention, two other cabinet appointments may also complicate negotiating and implementing the Oslo accords. Benni Begin, who has been an inveterate ideological enemy of Oslo since its inception, has been appointed minister of science. Initially refusing the appointment, he accepted after the influential inner cabinet was expanded to include him. His presence in the inner sanctum of this new government will strengthen its most ideological and unyielding tendencies. For Begin, Oslo was a horrific pact that has been nullified, wiped out by the violence of the "terrorists of the Palestinian Authority." He claims the new government has inherited no negotiating obligations vis-à-vis the Palestinians.[50] Its only obligation is to begin defending Israeli citizens against "Arafat the terrorist" and "his murderous army."[51]

It is hardly surprising that Begin has led the campaign within the Netanyahu government against meetings with representatives of the Palestinian Authority. Although Netanyahu delayed meeting Arafat until August 1996, he then gradually expanded contacts with him. When Netanyahu's foreign policy adviser, Dore Gold, met with Arafat at the end of June, Begin denounced the meeting in an exchange with Netanyahu at their June 28 cabinet session.[52] Begin proved unable to stop these "dialogues" with Arafat, which moved from Dore Gold to David Levy to Yitzhak Mordechai and eventually to Prime Minister Netanyahu. Yet by advocating the most extreme positions within the cabinet, Begin may both make Netanyahu look moderate by comparison and help forge Israeli policies that stymie Oslo.

A second appointment that has been largely ignored is that of Eli Suissa, to the Ministry of Interior. While Suissa is not a member of the Knesset, he is a relative of Rabbi Ovadia Yosef, who has made his mark as a Shas functionary, working most recently as the Interior Ministry's Jerusalem District head and as chair of the Regional Planning Board of Jerusalem. In these capacities, he recently refused to accept a letter written in Arabic from Arab residents of Um Tuba and Beit Sahur.[53] They were objecting to a controversial building project in southern Jerusalem. The project they were opposing was the building of a Jewish neighborhood on land confiscated from them at Har Homa. The Arab residents of the two villages of Um Tuba and Beit Sahur, which border Har Homa, were given sixty days by law to submit their objections to the Regional Planning Board of Jerusalem. The Palestinian plaintiffs and their lawyer Daniel Seideman received a letter from Suissa declaring their objections unacceptable because they had been written in Arabic. They were given three days to provide a letter in Hebrew. If they failed to meet this deadline, they would be denied the right to present their objections to the commission. Ir Shalem, a Jerusalem-based educational and legal project, broke the story to the Israeli press, and Suissa subsequently reversed his patently illegal "Hebrew only" policy. Under the scrutiny of the media, the Jerusalem municipality translated the letter.[54]

As minister of interior, Suissa will have much broader powers over the daily lives of Jerusalem's 170,000 Palestinian residents. From family reunification to land expropriation, the response of his ministry appears to be a variation of "Hebrew only." In one of his first acts as minister of interior, Suissa reversed a decision of the former Labor Party minister, by instructing the Jerusalem Planning Board to expedite the plan for building a new Jewish settler enclave in Ras el-Amud.[55] This settlement project had been halted by the outgoing minister because the Planning Board (chaired by Suissa) had abused its powers in an earlier attempt to allow the construction of the enclave.[56] Gross inequalities disqualified this project in its earlier incarnation. Suissa's interaction with Palestinians of East Jerusalem is not a good omen for the fragile peace process.

Several other appointments have been reassuring in projecting moderation. Dan Meridor's assignment as finance minister has won near-unanimous praise. A man of high integrity, he has been critical of the violence and intolerance associated with the Israeli militants. When in power as minister of justice under Shamir, he earned a reputation as an honest and fair advocate of justice. Even in the face of vilification and threats by Israeli extremists, he honored his professional responsibilities. These included defending and protecting the rights of Palestinian nationalists like Faisal Husseini who were subjected to a campaign of death threats and intimidation. (Meridor was to resign in 1997 as a protest to Netanyahu's policies.)

The appointment of David Levy has also suggested a relatively pragmatic tendency in defense and foreign policy. Before the government was a week old, Levy was apparently contradicting his government's *Guidelines* by suggesting that territorial withdrawal in the Golan Heights was possible.[57] The foreign minister also staked out a conciliatory position within the new government when he was pressed to clarify what he meant, reiterating that Israel would negotiate with the Palestinian Council. Did he mean Arafat? He answered, "Can one recognize an authority without a leader?"[58]

The Sword and the Shekel

There were two other early signs of potential pragmatism in the Netanyahu government. He initially attempted to create an institutional presence for security experts and professional economists in his government. First, he suggested the creation of a National Security Council under the guidance of David Ivri, a former close adviser of Rabin. If it came into being, the council might help insulate defense and security policy formulation from hawkish ideologues and religious fundamentalists. Ivri, a former head of the Israeli Air Force, is a nonpartisan defense technocrat who has been director general of the Defense Ministry, responsible for managing Israel's extensive military relationship with the United States. His responsibilities include oversight of key national projects like the Amos satellite and the Arrow antimissile missile.[59] Second, the creation of a new Council of Economic Advisors under the professional stewardship of Jacob Frenkel, governor of the Bank of Israel, might highlight Israel's economic motivation for peacemaking. In a June 10, 1996, speech to the Institute of International Bankers in New York, Frenkel suggested that "the more you have the business sector involved, the larger is the base of individuals who have a stake in the continuation of the [peace] process."[60]

These two new governmental agencies represent the two most important domestic constituencies for peace in Israel. It has been the nation's professional security experts and generals, along with its business leaders, who have been the most credible in making the Machiavellian, self-interested case for peace.[61] A disproportionate number of Israel's elites, who help manage their nation's sword and shekel, are supporters of Oslo for reasons of security and finance.[62] Could their influence be greater in the new policy bodies than it was during the last electoral contest? We may never know.

These two new agencies, which might have built some restraint into the Netanyahu defense and security policies, seem likely to be stillborn. Netanyahu is having second thoughts. This seems to suit Frenkel, who prefers to run Netanyahu's economic policy from the Bank of Israel, and Dore Gold, who continues to assemble his own foreign policy staff. Meanwhile, Ivri waits to see if his prime minister intends to create a serious National Security Council that would include operational responsibilities and not just coordinating activities.[63] If these two new councils are created in the end, U.S. interests and opinions may be given additional institutional weight by the men who head them. They are keenly aware of the inextricable link between Israel's security and economy and the United States. While Netanyahu prides himself on his savvy in managing the relationship with Washington, his new councillors might help him avoid the kind of economic and security decisions that a previous Likud leader made in poisoning relations with the United States.

Guidelines to the Past

While the *Guidelines* are only that, they do suggest a policy direction if not an exact final destination. That direction is not necessarily forward, in terms of the peace process.

Syria and Israel: Preconditions of a Crisis

There are two primary reasons for concern. First, the *Guidelines* seem to foreclose the possibility of reengaging Syria in any substantive negotiations. There are a half dozen relevant articles in the *Guidelines* that seemingly lead to a dead end. The one article that would be hopeful if it was the only guideline for negotiations with Syria, is article 3, section 1. It calls for "negotiations with Syria without pre-conditions."[64] Nearly all of the remaining articles in the *Guidelines* that relate to Syria establish Israeli preconditions for negotiating. For example, article 9, section 1, presents the Israeli terms for an agreement without any ambiguity: "The Government views the Golan Heights as essential to the security of the State and its water resources. Retaining Israeli sovereignty over the Golan will be the basis for an arrangement with Syria."[65] Zeev Schiff, the military analyst for *Ha'aretz*, noted that the Hebrew version of the document did not translate as "over the Golan" but was "b'Golan," meaning "on" or "in."[66] This linguistic nuance suggests an even more firmly grounded Israeli possession of the Golan.

Israel's terms for negotiating the status of the settlements in the Golan are also asserted with finality in article 8, section 1: "In any political arrangement, Israel shall insist on ensuring the existence and security of Jewish settlements and their affinity with the state of Israel."[67] The *Guidelines* reiterate the government's commitment to the settlements on the Golan Heights in article 1, section 6, ("Settlement").

Given these positions, it is difficult to imagine how the Netanyahu government will be able to pursue two other goals that are linked to negotiations with Syria, as spelled out in the *Guidelines*: "to bring home the prisoners of war and missing in action, . . . and remove the threat to the northern border."[68]

Recent diplomatic efforts indicated that the final chapter on the tragic story of Israeli armed forces missing in action (MiAs) would only be written when there is a negotiating breakthrough with the Syrians. The Israeli MiAs, alive or not, seemed hostage to Syrian-Israeli relations that are growing very acrimonious. The battlefield in Lebanon appeared closer than the negotiating table in Washington. Yet in less than two months the Netanyahu government succeeded at what had eluded Labor governments for the previous three and one-half years: getting the remains of Israeli MiAs in an exchange with Hizbollah. This exchange of bodies and prisoners between Israel and Hizbollah fueled rumors of additional exchanges involving the four remaining missing soldiers, including the only potential survivor, Israeli navigator Ron Arad. This July 21, 1996, prisoner and body exchange has also been followed by a flurry of diplomatic activity attempting to create a breakthrough on the Israeli-Lebanese front.

Bibi Begin?

Menachem Begin is a revered model for those hoping that Netanyahu's *Guidelines* become blueprints for an unexpected leap into the future. It is worth remembering that Begin's leap was in part a response to an initiative by Sadat. He also had the benefit of two imaginatively pragmatic former military heroes, Foreign Minister Moshe Dayan and Defense Minister Ezer Weizman. Drawn by Sadat's opening and pushed by Dayan and Weizman,

Begin withdrew from the Sinai, every inch of it, taking every settlement and soldier with him. Israel received, in exchange, sweeping security arrangements and peace. The peace has never been more than tepid. However, the security arrangements and the peace have withstood the political assassination of Sadat, several wars—in Lebanon and the Gulf—and the intifada. Begin did not make this historic swap to establish himself or his agreement with Egypt as a model to be emulated. Quite the contrary. Begin saw this as a withdrawal to end all withdrawals. In particular he was trying to protect and make permanent Israel's hold on the West Bank and Gaza.[69]

Netanyahu can appreciate Begin's feat. He successfully consolidated Israeli control in the West Bank, creating settlement facts while he was making a separate peace with half of the Arab world—Egypt. The question is: On which front, with which Arab regime can Netanyahu make such a bold exchange? With Egypt and Jordan already at peace with Israel, there is but one candidate: Lebanon. There is an offer Netanyahu can make—the one Rabin articulated and for which Peres expressed sympathy. Unfortunately, Peres's sympathy was seemingly never translated into a policy priority. Perhaps it awaited his next term. However, Lebanon did not wait. It captured his attention, late and tragically in his tenure as prime minister. Does Netanyahu have an exit from the Land of Cedars? One that, Begin-like, would spare him the pain of withdrawing from zone C of the West Bank?

The basis for a Beginesque deal in Lebanon, the one that Peres missed and Netanyahu covets, entails repackaging Rabin's earlier offer of withdrawal. Rather than hold out for a formal security agreement that includes a six-month trial period prior to the withdrawal of the IDF, as the Labor party demanded, Netanyahu might accept a more modest "understanding" that could be implemented much more rapidly. The IDF would engage in a phased withdrawal over a four-month period. A special multinational force drawn from key moderate Arab states (Morocco, Egypt, Jordan, the Gulf Cooperation Council states, and perhaps Syria) along with European units would replace the Israelis during this initial transfer of security responsibilities.[70] Israel's client militia, the South Lebanon Army (SLA), would be dissolved and its former fighters integrated into a local police force. The entire area south of the Zahrani River, some 45 kilometers from the Israeli border, would be "militia free," thus implicitly banning Hizbollah and other guerilla units from an area larger than Israel's present "security zone." At a later stage, the Lebanese Army would assume control of this area. This could all be packaged as part of an interim agreement, with Syrian consent and participation, leading to the rejuvenation of Israeli-Syrian negotiations.[71]

However tempting this deal might be to the Lebanese government, Assad is unlikely to agree to any such interim understanding that does not include negotiations over the Golan. What could the Netanyahu government offer Assad on the Golan? The most moderate position, associated with Foreign Minister Levy, suggests meeting Syria "in the middle." Once again it is hard to imagine Assad negotiating on these terms. He got Peres, in effect, to recognize Syrian sovereignty over the Golan and to begin talking about an Israeli retreat to the international border. Even these terms did not satisfy Assad, who continued to play brinkmanship right through the Israeli election. According to MK Ori Orr, former deputy defense minister and commander of Israel's northern front, "Assad made up his mind for peace—but *his* peace—a peace that required us to accept the June 4 borders. Assad, with proper security concessions, might have gotten to the international borders but not the Sea of Galilee."[72] Unless the prime minister translates "meeting Syria halfway" into something very similar to what the Labor Party was prepared to negotiate, it is difficult to see how he can stop the war of attrition in Lebanon, much less achieve a secure withdrawal from that country.

Unwilling to persuade the Syrians to bite on his proposal, Netanyahu has yet another option. He can implement a muscular variation of unilateral withdrawal. Israel would satisfy UN Resolution 425, which calls for the complete and unconditional withdrawal of Israeli forces. However, the withdrawal would be accompanied by a dire warning that cross-border attacks against Israel would be met with overwhelming force. Although a unilateral withdrawal cannot be ruled out, it seems unlikely, given escalating IDF casualties in Lebanon and the growing morale problems of the SLA. Netanyahu would encounter opposition not only from the Labor party and Meretz but, more important, from the IDF.[73]

Denied a negotiated exit from Lebanon and not being bold or foolish enough (depending on one's point of view) to withdraw unilaterally, Netanyahu may yet derive political benefit from this failed negotiating gambit. A recalcitrant Syrian regime that has become a main target in his campaign against regional and international terrorism will be blamed.

All the speculation around Netanyahu's Lebanon initiative may yet end up having less to do with negotiating peace in the Middle East than with political positioning within the Beltway of Washington, D.C.: Netanyahu, democracy, and security vs. Assad, dictatorship, and terrorism. Netanyahu is likely to devote his considerable telegenic talents as well as those of his highly ideological Director of Policy Planning and Communications David Bar-Ilan to winning this battle in Washington.[74]

Netanyahu and Arafat: Security and Peace without Partnership?

The *Guidelines* of the new government and the political orientations of a hard-core group of messianic nationalists and secular annexationists within the government also make progress on the Palestinian negotiating front problematic.

The *Guidelines* state that "the Government will negotiate with the Palestinian Authority, with the intent of reaching a permanent arrangement, on the condition that the Palestinians fulfill all their commitments fully."[75] It is certainly reasonable for the Netanyahu government to insist that the Palestinians honor their obligations under the Oslo agreements if the Israelis honor theirs. This was the formula Prime Minister Peres adopted after the February-March round of suicide terrorist attacks. Linkage and reciprocity are a fundamental component of the Oslo agreements. Peres did not reconvene the Palestinian negotiations until May 4, after the Palestinian Authority had intensified its antiterrorism efforts and after the PNC had voted to rescind the covenant that called for the destruction of Israel.

However, Netanyahu's approach to the problem of Palestinian violations does not necessarily suggest a policy of linkage and reciprocity. Rather the *Guidelines* and Netanyahu's statements indicate a policy of one-sided preconditioning. The Palestinian Authority must honor "all" of their commitments "fully," regardless of the Israeli performance.

The simple truth is that the Israeli government has also violated a number of its commitments in the Oslo agreements. It remains in violation of its agreements with the Palestinians for not having freed female prisoners, for closing the Netzarim Junction, for not having opened the "safe passage" between Gaza and Jericho, and for placing roadblocks in forbidden places.[76]

If the new government's *Guidelines* are any indication, Netanyahu intends to add to this list of violations. According to the *Guidelines*, the government "will oppose the right of return of the Arab populations to any part of the land of Israel west of the Jordan River."[77] The Oslo agreement provides for the return of displaced persons and refugees from the 1967 Six Day War to the PA's territories. This was to be done, obviously, with the consent of the Israelis.[78]

Arafat and Peres (and before him, Rabin) kept long lists of each other's violations of the agreements. As Chemi Shalev, correspondent for *Ma'ariv,* suggests, "Until now there was a tacit agreement between the two sides not to turn the issue of the infringements into a main bone of contention. Some of the violations were corrected at quiet negotiations between the two sides, some turned out to be unimportant, some remained a matter for future discussions."[79] Some violations were side-stepped because correcting them would have generated a backlash on either the Israeli or Palestinian street. For example, the PA could not extradite Palestinian terrorists without losing the trust of many Palestinians who were already being besieged with Hamas's claims that Arafat had become an Israeli stooge. In turn, the Israeli government could not free Palestinian female prisoners who were involved in murder cases without creating a major backlash on the Israeli street.[80] Hence, the PA implemented "fast trials" to avoid the embarrassment of extraditing Palestinian prisoners to Israel and to assuage Israeli concern that terrorists are not going unpunished.[81] The Palestinians then deferred to a later time the Israeli pledge to free female prisoners. Two national leaderships, both with significant domestic opposition, were trying to preserve an embryonic peace that could be delivered only if their fragile partnership survived.

The rhetoric and policy guidelines of the Netanyahu government might tempt it to discard this partnership and pursue a violations campaign against the PA. The battle over violations will not be one-sided. There is ammunition enough on both sides. As Chemi Shalev suggests, "for every Palestinian infraction there is an Israeli infringement."[82] This does not mean that major grievances and problems are subject to endless trade-offs or ignored. There are moments of profound crisis when business as usual is impossible. February and March of 1996 represented just such a crisis. Terrorism had become and remains a strategic threat to the fragile peace, not just to the electoral chances of one of the partners. Adjustments were made. New pressure on Arafat and the PA yielded results. Yet the results of the partnership on the security front were infrequently if ever acknowledged by the Israeli opposition and Netanyahu, its leader. The Israeli public experienced and emotionally recorded images of buses and bombs. They have no access to the Israeli intelligence and security files that document all the acts of terrorism that have been preempted and prevented by cooperative work of the security agencies of the PA and their Israeli counterparts. According to the head of the Shin Bet Security Service, the effective cooperation with Palestinian security bodies prevented at least fourteen suicide terrorist attacks in the months prior to the Israeli elections.[83]

As members of the new government gain access to these files and hear Defense official briefings, they may discover that their policy of "security first" leads back to partnership with the Palestinians. The politics of uni-lateralism, preconditions, and exclusivity runs through the government's *Guidelines* and political philosophy. One-sided preconditions that require the PA to come "fully in compliance" with "all" their obligations, and ex-clusivist Israeli policies that preclude the possibility of a Palestinian state or any Palestinian political or national presence in Jerusalem and call "for strengthening, broadening, and developing settlement in Israel,"[84] all point in one direction. It is not forward.

Bibi Shamir?

Prime Minster Netanyahu is unlikely to become a second Begin. He also seems too ambitious and too sensitive to his U.S. allies' interests to become a second Shamir. To be sure, it might be seductive for Prime Minister Netan-yahu to orchestrate a "stallmate," à la Shamir,[85] this time without being blamed. Yet it is arguable that Prime Minister Netanyahu is exhibiting a certain tactical flexibility on the Palestinian front that casts doubt on the "Bibi Shamir" stallmate-breakdown scenario. Such a stallmate would be in defiance of the strategic interests of the United States. It would be in disregard of the moderate Arabs with whom Israel has already negotiated peace agreements (Egypt, Jordan, and the PA). Such a stallmate would be-tray the prime minister's mandate to forge a secure peace, let alone protect the economic peace dividends that have accrued to the benefit of Israel. Hirsh Goodman has suggested that these considerations are the very con-straining forces that will bend Netanyahu's hard line in a more concilia-tory direction.[86]

The Muddle-Through: Oslo II

Netanyahu seems to have acknowledged these constraining forces, and he is likely to try to defer and disguise as much as possible those policies that would precipitate a showdown with the United States or endanger the peace with either Egypt or Jordan. His first visit as prime minister to an Arab country, Egypt, was a transparent attempt to reassure Mubarak that he is not a younger version of Shamir. This may be more than a public relations ploy. Netanyahu may even have a policy that he hopes will medi-ate the conflict between serving the ideology he was weaned on, "Greater Israel," and confronting the reality he has inherited, the post-Oslo struc-ture of peace. His compromise with reality may entail rejecting the break-down/stallmate policies of Shamir in favor of a Netanyahu strategy of breakthrough (with Lebanon) and muddle-through (with the PA).

Whatever comes of Netanyahu's attempted exit from Lebanon and political domination in Washington, his true face as either a hard-line ideologue or flexible statesman, as well as his political fate, is likely to be revealed on the Palestinian front. Given his ideological rejection of a Palestinian state and his refusal to negotiate on Jerusalem, there is virtually no chance of a negotiating breakthrough. Having removed any incentives for the Palestinians to negotiate the final status issues, radical settlers and their parliamentary supporters could trigger a breakdown in implementing the interim agreement. Without any prospect of a breakthrough and a good chance of a breakdown, Netanyahu will have to summon all of his tactical flexibility to muddle through the next few years.

In his muddle-through strategy, Netanyahu may exploit the exceedingly low expectations many have for his government's peace policies. He will not have to display much moderation in order to evoke sighs of relief that he is not as extreme as many feared. Netanyahu exploited this sentiment during his mid-July visit to Cairo, when he revealed elements of a muddle-through strategy with the Palestinians.

1. The primacy of economics.—Netanyahu is apparently determined to try to succeed where Rabin and Peres failed, in giving the Palestinians an economic peace dividend. His government is fond of distinguishing its preference for open borders and coexistence in contrast to Labor's fixation on separation and disengagement. This is consistent with Likud's ideological antipathy toward territorial compromise and its reticence to recognize a border that would divide Eretz Yisrael. However, in Cairo Netanyahu was not debating revisionist ideology but revealing a new flexibility. He announced the easing of the closure, permitting an additional ten thousand Palestinians to work in Israel.[87] On July 26, 1996, several days after that closure was relaxed, the Netanyahu government was rocked by its first act of terrorism, as three Israelis were killed in a drive-by shooting within the green line. The total closure was immediately reimposed.[88] Arafat responded with the speedy arrest of a group of Palestinians associated with the Popular Front, a PLO faction that has militantly opposed the Oslo agreements. The next day the blockade was lifted. This raised questions about whether the Netanyahu government was really prepared to break out of the terrorism-retaliation cycle and about a devastating contradiction between Israeli security and Palestinian economy. Was Likud going to fall into the same trap Palestinian terrorists set for the Labor party?[89] Some voices in Likud and the Netanyahu government were offering a bold new direction. Likud MK Gideon Ezra, a former deputy director of Shin Bet, dismissed the premise that closing the borders represented an effective security measure. "No Palestinian with a work permit has been connected with the recent terror attacks. We should aim to improve the economic lot of Palestinians."[90]

Yet the prime minister has not been this candid about how effective the closure is in preventing terrorism. While he is committed to relieving what Terje Larsen, the UN's coordinator in the territories, calls a "living conditions crisis," he still insists on having his closure policy "fluctuate according to the condition of security."[91] In Amman the prime minister was determined to bring good news. With King Hussein at his side on August 5, he announced further relaxation of the closure, permitting an additional five thousand Palestinian workers to work in Israel.[92] The prime minister had succeeded in pleasing the king but not in freeing his closure policy from being held hostage to terrorism.

While the prime minister zigs and zags on the closure/security dilemma, his government is moving to replace a foreign labor force that has grown dramatically since 1993. Recent government figures indicate that there are nearly 200,000 foreign workers in Israel, recruited mostly from Eastern Europe and Southeast Asia.[93] The prime minister has an opportunity to exploit the desire of Shas to deport illegal foreign workers who have been brought to Israel to replace Palestinian labor.[94] Apparently Shas's clerical leadership is worried by reports of Jewish women entering into relationships with foreign workers.[95]

Other official explanations for reducing the number of foreign workers in Israel are more directly motivated by the desire to reemploy Palestinians from the West Bank and Gaza. Shlomo Dror, Israel's coordinator of activities in the territories, suggested that whereas the foreign workers were present only under temporary permits, "the Palestinians are people we have some responsibility for. We have complaints from many Israelis who do not have enough workers for their factories and farms."[96] Hence Netanyahu's government intends to reduce dramatically the number of foreign workers in Israel and to boost the number of Palestinian employees in Israel to eighty thousand. This is still some forty thousand fewer than there were before Rabin implemented the first closure at the end of March 1993.[97]

No matter how successful Netanyahu is in realizing the original Oslo Accord, which envisioned open borders and free movement of goods and people between Israel and the "self-governing areas," he is likely to find it difficult to get by on the Palestinian front with bread alone. In fact, the political decision to emphasize the economic dimension of Oslo is dependent on restraint from resealing the West Bank and Gaza with every act of Palestinian terrorism.

2. *Continuity in security policies.* This muddle-through strategy presumes

that Netanyahu will not send the IDF back into the casbahs of Nablus and Gaza in the name of Israeli security. Instead, this scenario presumes a security policy under Netanyahu that more or less represents continuity with the Labor party's approach following the February-March 1996 cycle of suicide bombings. This approach included a demand for reciprocity from the PA in the implementation of agreements. Yet, ultimately, muddling through relies on joint patrols, cooperative intelligence, and further institutionalization of common security interests. This will require reconvening the Israeli-Palestinian coordination committee, ending the hiatus that followed the wave of suicide bombings in February and March of 1996.

To be sure, Netanyahu has continued to issue stern warnings to the Palestinians that Israel "will collect a very heavy price"[98] if there is an upsurge in terrorism. On the other hand, the prime minister has also praised the Israeli and Palestinian security agencies for working together "in the full sense of the word."[99] Brigadier General Yaakov Amidror, head of the research department of military intelligence, praised Arafat for his resolve and tenacity in battling against Hamas's terrorist infrastructure.[100]

Without a partnership in security, terrorism is likely to intensify, triggering more closures and further impoverishment of the West Bank-Gaza, as well as a collapse of the peace process. Netanyahu would be stripped of his credentials as a pragmatist and would risk facing an electorate as one who had violated his mandate to win both security and peace. One can expect Prime Minister Netanyahu to try to avoid such a calamity, in part by ending his personal boycott of Arafat, as he did at the end of August 1996.

If Prime Minister Netanyahu's quest for Israeli security is dependent upon maintaining the nascent partnership with the security agencies of the PA, it is also incumbent upon his government to address the political, national, and territorial dimensions of the Oslo agreements. While Arafat and the Palestinian Council are unquestionably the weak party in this negotiating battle, they are not without their negotiating resources.[101] As a partner in the struggle against terrorism, the PA, along with external support, particularly from the United States may be able to encourage the prime minister's pragmatic tendencies, helping him avoid getting bogged down in the muddle so that he can get through—at least in implementing Oslo II.

3. *Hebron, a muscular redeployment.*—Netanyahu's pre-election position on Hebron was clear and public: "I don't see any reason to evacuate Hebron."[102] His reasoning as prime minister has become less clear. Haggai Segal, writing in *Yediot Ahranot*, sees a new de facto policy emerging that he characterizes as a "momentum of delay."[103] While Netanyahu might

have difficulty officially blocking the redeployment, he might try to postpone it indefinitely. Netanyahu's indefinite postponement might be couched in terms of a security rationale that he used in mid-August. "Hebron is not only Israel's problem. If we act hastily there and lose control and there is an act of terror and perhaps bloodshed on both sides, that will blow up the whole peace process."[104]

While the decision not to redeploy from Hebron may have a security rationale, it will also be driven by political calculations. Will the settlers in Hebron and their hard-core ideologues of Yesha be perceived as too volatile and be granted an anticipatory veto over Israel's redeployment commitments? Will Arafat engage in only theatrical protest and then, as Haggai Segal suggests, resign himself to the latest disappointment because "three years after the Oslo agreement he has no way back? To admit the Oslo process's failure would undermine his public standing and lead to his ousting."[105]

This may be a very dangerous calculation. Arafat may not be in a position to absorb many more negotiating deferrals and disappointments. In early August Arafat was struggling to contain a mini-intifada in Nablus and Tulkarem against the PA for human rights abuses, including the torture of Palestinian prisoners. The crushing burdens of the enclosure and massive unemployment had not yet been relieved in spite of Likud's promises. The Israeli government was slowly but surely expanding settlement activity. Finally, Netanyahu had declared that Jerusalem was nonnegotiable. In these circumstances it is not surprising to hear dissident Palestinian voices like that of Sheik Na'ef Rajoub on the Palestinian street—voices that are not harbingers of Palestinian submission.

Sheik Na'ef Rajoub, imam of Dura (a town on the outskirts of Hebron) and brother of Jibril Rajoub, head of the Palestinian preventive security organization, suggested that Oslo was turning Arafat into Antoine Lahad (head of the SLA), something which "the Palestinian people will not tolerate."[106]

Unless Netanyahu finds a talmudic formulation for honoring Israel's redeployment in Hebron, the city may become a religious battleground, with Hamas displacing the Palestinian Authority. Such a formula might include a redeployment accompanied by additional security arrangements within Hebron and between Hebron and Kiryat Arba, along with tough talk about how these Jewish communities will remain an eternal part of Eretz Yisrael. (An agreement on Hebron was finally reached in January 1997 after tortuous negotiations mediated by the United States.)

4. Reciprocal implementation of Oslo II.—Netanyahu is likely to continue the Labor Party's post–February-March crackdown on the PA and pressure Arafat to honor his commitments, particularly in the security realm and in Jerusalem. While there will be periodic tension and threats to close down Orient House or PA offices doing official business in the city, these are not likely to be deal breakers. Other Jerusalem hot spots that will be discussed here are likely to threaten the muddle-through scenario. Similarly, while Netanyahu may demand further evidence that the PNC did in fact honor its commitment to rescind its covenant in April 1996, he is likely, no matter how reluctantly, to accept Arafat's clarifications, which will be recertified by Washington.

This constant background noise, of higgling and haggling over two competing sets of violations, need not stop cautious, plodding implementation of Oslo 2. The highly symbolic release of the Palestinian female prisoners and of Sheikh Ahmad Yassin, the ailing quadriplegic founder of Hamas, coupled with the belated opening of the Gaza-Jericho safe passage, may not create what Peres has characterized as "thoroughbred" peacemaking.[107] Yet combined with other agreements, including three separate redeployments scheduled at six-month intervals from unspecified zones in area C, some forward movement is possible. Tortoise-like as it may be, this movement could take us to the abyss of final status talks in 1998.

What stands in the way of even this modest forward movement are the issues of settlements and Jerusalem. Although they are both the subjects of final status negotiations, they symbolically and substantively represent the core of the conflict and any political resolution of it.

5. *Settlement expansion: more than Rabin and Peres, less than Begin and Shamir.*—Netanyahu is likely to try to find that middle ground of tolerable dissatisfaction for both his government's pro-settlement constituency and his nation's most valuable partners, the United States, Egypt, and Jordan. Both sides will be disappointed by his policies. The militants of Yesha will never get the 500,000 settlers they want by the end of the century, and the U.S. government will not get a freeze on settlement activity. Yet unless Washington draws credible red lines, Netanyahu is bound to engage in political cost/benefit tradeoffs that redound to the advantage of those Israelis living beyond the green line.

Prime Minister Netanyahu tried to strike a compromise between his pro-settlement politics and his desire not to offend President Clinton during his first trip to Washington in July 1996. After claiming that the settler population had increased by fifty percent under the previous government, he quipped, "I assume nobody here expects us to do less than the Labor government." His percentages were dubious.[108] His intentions were clear:

Labor had continued to build bypass roads and housing for settlers, and the Oslo process was not endangered. What was good for Labor was good for him.

In late July, Minister of National Infrastructures Ariel Sharon began to draw attention not to the continuity of the new government's settlements policy but to the unmistakable change that Likud was introducing. His announcement of a $65 million construction plan to build three highways in the West Bank was headline news, signaling a "hard line on land."[109] Sharon also reportedly intends to have these roads "flanked by new Jewish buildings."[110] While Sharon's plan was technically a revival of earlier plans that Labor had shelved, it revived memories of "madness repeating itself."[111]

The creeping clarification of the government's settlement policy took another step forward in early August. The Israeli cabinet decided to end the previous government's declared freeze on settlements. Netanyahu characterized this move as an end of "the discrimination against Jewish settlements in Judea, Samaria and the Gaza Strip." [112] Although declaring a new policy, Netanyahu did not specifically commit the government to any new projects. Rather, he was keeping his options open, including the one of building new settlements. However, his emphasis was on natural growth within existing communities.

Netanyahu resisted calls by Agriculture Minister Raful Eytan to establish a ministerial committee on settlement expansion.[113] Netanyahu's refusal was apparently meant to limit Sharon's involvement and to assuage the concerns of both Washington and the Arab world.[114] It seemed to work. The U.S. and Jordanian governments put on brave faces. The U.S. State Department spokesman said that America considered the Israeli decision a "quite complex statement" to be discussed further with Prime Minister Netanyahu.[115] King Hussein's response was much more supportive. With Netanyahu standing next to him at a news conference in Amman, the king said, "I believe that there is too much speculation, and there is too much of an attempt to blow things out of proportion at times and create areas of misunderstanding. . . . I hope and I trust that the Israeli government will act very prudently and will make sure that it does not create obstacles but instead create incentives and opportunities for progress towards achieving peace in the time ahead."[116]

The king was engaging in more than the legendary Hashemite hospitality. He was pursuing Jordan's vital economic and political interests. King Hussein increasingly sees his lifeline tied to Israel, specifically to the Netanyahu government. Long gone are the days when Likud claimed Jordan was Palestine. Now the king apparently views Netanyahu as a more reliable ally than the Labor party in the joint enterprise of restraining Palestinian national ambition.[117]

The "hope and trust" the king so graciously referred to are growing shorter in supply. On August 8, 1996, settlement mania had even reached Gaza. Hundreds of Gazans demonstrated against Israeli plans to seize Arabowned land in order to build a new access road to a Jewish settlement.[118] In a speech to the legislative council Arafat characterized the decision to expand Jewish settlements "an outrageous violation of all the peace agreements."[119] He called for a comprehensive plan "to resist this conspiracy against peace."[120]

On August 11 Minister of Defense Yitzhak Mordechai announced he had eased procedures for obtaining building permits in the West Bank and Gaza and had approved a request by settlers to set up three hundred mobile homes in settlements.[121] The same day Minister of Interior Eli Suissa pledged $5 million dollars of immediate aid to help compensate for past financial burdens the settlers had to bear "as a result of the Israeli-Palestinian agreements."[122] The next day Israeli officials confirmed that Uri Ariel, a key settlement leader, would be named as a government coordinator for settlement construction in the West Bank and Gaza Strip.[123]

Twenty-four hours later Michael Eitan, head of the ruling Likud party faction in the Knesset, claimed that this Israeli government would be creating "new neighborhoods [in the West Bank and Gaza], and many Jews will come and live there."[124] The same day Ma'ariv reported that settlers had put forward approximately two hundred plans for building thousands of new houses.[125] By mid-August the Palestinian Council had sent Arafat a request "to study the possibility of suspending the negotiations should the Israelis continue with settlement activity."[126]

The Netanyahu government has already shattered the status quo on the issue of Jewish settlements. It is not a question of three hundred new trailers or three new highways. It is Netanyahu's commitment to expand settlements as part of a broader hard-line ideological policy—a policy that rejects the principle of territorial compromise, a Palestinian state, and negotiations over Jerusalem. The settlements policy is likely to be seen increasingly as a fundamental break from the Labor Party's policies. The Labor Party also agreed that settlements would not be uprooted. By annexing 10 percent of the West Bank, 70 percent of the settlers would be incorporated into a slightly larger Jewish state. The rest of the settlers were to remain in Palestine. The Labor Party was clearly moving toward endorsing a Palestinian state. Its party platform in the spring of 1996 had excised a clause that excluded the possibility. Yossi Beilin and Mahmoud Abbas (Abu Mazen) had supervised "a document of understanding" in which, according to Yair Hirschfeld, the Israelis "agreed with the Palestinians on the establishment of [a demilitarized] independent state."[127] Likud, in contrast, is using its settlement policy as an instrument of denial of another nation. The difference between the Labor Party's negotiated affirmation of Palestine and Netanyahu's categorical rejection is likely to create a breakdown in the peace process and a potential crisis within Israel between the Netanyahu government and its critical allies.

6. *Jerusalem flashpoints and the breakdown of Oslo II.*—If the muddle-through strategy will be sorely tested on the question of settlements, it faces its final exam on the issue of Jerusalem. The "J word," as the State Department nervously refers to Jerusalem, is littered with time bombs that will have to be defused—not only in order to facilitate negotiating final status arrangements, which do not seem imminent, but to maintain the fragile status quo of the city.

By excluding Jerusalem as a negotiable final status issue and declaring that no compromise is imaginable, Prime Minister Netanyahu is likely to increase popular anti-Israeli sentiment and poison relationships between Israel and its Arab negotiating partners. The absence of a political negotiating vehicle and the discrediting of the peace process on the Palestinian street is likely to increase political violence.

Second, there are already early indications that the Netanyahu victory has rejuvenated the activities of militant Jewish settlers whose provocative incursions into Arab neighborhoods of East Jerusalem had been curtailed by the Labor government in 1992.[128] According to Ir Shalem and attorney Daniel Seideman, there are plans to expand this campaign to take over Palestinian properties in Silwan (the City of David), the Moslem Quarter of the Old City, Sheikh Jarakh, and Ras el-Amud.[129]

Third, Netanyahu is likely to reverse the policy that Prime Minister Yitzhak Rabin announced in May 1995, that no new expropriations would be carried out in East Jerusalem without the Palestinians' approval. This followed Rabin's near-disastrous attempt to expropriate two parcels of land in East Jerusalem the previous month. Domestic and international dissent led him to reconsider.

Chastened by this experience, Rabin and Peres were hesitant to break ground in yet another expropriation project in East Jerusalem, Har Homa—a project that began in the fall of 1994.[130] Israeli extraparliamentary peace groups had been effectively preventing groundbreaking in Har Homa by a combination of legal interventions and private meetings with ministers of the previous government.[131]

The building of Har Homa could be the detonating act that blows up the interim agreement, but it is the combination of the new government's policies and cumulative tensions that make the status of Jerusalem such a combustible issue. The lack of sensitivity of new ministers like Eli Suissa toward Palestinians is likely to add to this explosive mixture. Palestinian Jerusalemites who have been residing abroad may find it increasingly difficult to renew their identity cards and return as residents to their city.[132] In addition there is a festering problem of government efforts to collect back property taxes from East Jerusalemites who own land that remains "unplanned" and is consequently taxed.[133]

Ir Shalem and other Israeli human rights organizations that succeeded in getting the Labor government's Ministry of Finance to intervene when tax authorities attempted to auction Palestinian lands to collect back taxes may find less friendly governmental offices.[134] Daniel Seideman, the principal attorney for Ir Shalem, anticipates more land auctions under the Netanyahu government. In addition there is the possibility of an upsurge in administrative demolition orders (a draconian power depriving residents of due process) issued to Palestinian Jerusalemites and a continued paucity of building permits granted to them.[135]

While the headline stories in the early summer of 1996 continued to focus on Orient House and PA offices in the city, they were dwarfed by a new conflict in Jerusalem that attracted regional and international attention—the opening of the Hasmonean tunnel.

Tunnel at the End of the Light

On September 25, 1996, a crisis was triggered by the Netanyahu government's opening of a second entrance to a Hasmonean tunnel running along the side of the Temple Mount. Some sixty-five Palestinians and fifteen Israelis were killed as violence engulfed the West Bank and Gaza. Beyond the tragic loss of life, the three days of violence struck at the heart of the Oslo accords. The joint patrols and cooperation between Palestinian policemen and Israeli soldiers gave way to deadly gun battles, thus calling into question the security partnership that was one of the pillars of the fragile peace. The Israelis had evidence that some two hundred Palestinian police had been caught on camera opening fire on Israeli soldiers. The Palestinians claimed that the Israeli soldiers had started the lethal gun battles by firing into crowds of Palestinian protesters. The Israeli newspaper *Ha'aretz* cited an Israeli commander in Gaza who indicated that, at least in the sector near the Jewish settlement of Kfar Dorom, settlers and Israeli soldiers engaged in "indiscriminate shooting [which] was what caused this whole situation."[136]

The pitched battles between some of the Palestinian police and Israeli soldiers opened a fundamental breach in the Oslo agreements. While the primary question was whether the Israeli and Palestinian security agencies could rebuild their shattered trust and reestablish their effective cooperation in the field, there were two other troubled relationships that were exposed in the "tunnel war." Both of them represent severe challenges to Netanyahu: one on the domestic front with his own military and the other with his friendliest neighbor, Jordan.

Netanyahu's relationship with his nation's military and security branches has gone from bad to worse. In early August 1996, he bluntly summarized a discussion he had held with his generals: "I told them I don't want them in the peace process."[137] They would offer him their intelligence assessments, but they were to be excluded from playing any policy role, as he suggested they had during the previous Labor government. True to his word, the heads of Israel's military and intelligence agencies have been banned from policy making and their intelligence recommendations ignored, with devastating consequences for both Israeli security and the peace negotiations. Both the General Security Service (the Shin Bet, Israel's domestic intelligence agency) and the military intelligence branch of the Israel Defense Force had been warning the prime minister of the possibility of a massive outbreak of violence and a collapse of security.[138] They feared that it would only take a spark to ignite a rebellion and violence. In August Major General Oren Shahor, the coordinator of activities in the territories, warned the prime minister in writing of Arafat's and the Palestinian Authority's vulnerable status.[139] On August 13 Chief of Staff Amnon Lipkin-Shahak met with key commanders to prepare operational plans in the event that the Palestinian Authority collapsed. Written summaries of their meeting, including a specific warning of the possibility of "overall chaos in the entire territory" were sent to both the defense minister and the prime minister.[140] Thus Netanyahu had been warned repeatedly and dramatically about the highly volatile situation in the territories and the fragility of the Palestinian Authority. Dismissing his military commanders' general security concerns, the prime minister also rejected the specific counsel of the head of the Shin Bet. Ami Ayalon, director of the Shin Bet, had recommended opening the second entrance to the tunnel in the

Islamic Quarter of the Old City, but *only* as part of a "package deal."[141] Israel would get the opening of the tunnel and would give the Palestinians Solomon's Stables (a prayer site underneath the Temple Mount, which the Palestinians had been renovating based on an understanding worked out with the previous Labor government) and the redeployment from Hebron.[142] Netanyahu not only rejected the advice of Ayalon, he also excluded the entire defense and security establishment from his ill-fated decision: the defense minister, his chief of staff, his deputy, the head of army intelligence, the commanding general of the Central region (which includes the West Bank), the coordinator of activities in the territories, and, of course, scores of others who had to bear the brunt of the consequences in the field.[143]

The growing schism between Prime Minister Netanyahu and his military and intelligence heads was highlighted in a prime-time televised press conference that the prime minister called on September 27, 1996. At the press conference, both Ayalon and Military Intelligence Chief Bugi Ya'alon rejected Netanyahu's claim that Arafat had personally ordered the Palestinian police to fire their weapons on Israeli soldiers.[144] Though both men held Arafat responsible for inciting civil disturbances in response to what he perceived as a new Israeli provocation in the battle over the future of East Jerusalem, both characterized the situation as one that had "spun out of control."[145]

Netanyahu's relationship with the Israeli military had gotten so out of control that in mid-October 1996 the Shin Bet ordered Israeli troops to appear without their rifles when the prime minister visited their army base.[146] Some of the soldiers complained to opposition Labor Party MK Hagai Merom. Merom argued that the order "showed distrust of the defense forces, their soldiers and their officers."[147] Zeev Maoz, the head of Tel Aviv University's Jaffee Center for Strategic Studies, feared that the military had become so upset at being excluded from crucial security decisions that "we have moved a step on the slippery slope" to a coup. This is a four-letter word that is virtually never uttered in Israel, particularly by a serious analyst from an established academic institute.

The second relationship that turned very stormy with the "tunnel war" is the rapport with King Hussein. The king was unsettled by Israel's unilateral decision to open the entrance to the tunnel, which in his eyes deprived Jordan of its special status as guardian of Islamic holy sites in Jerusalem, a status specifically granted under the terms of the 1994 accord. He was doubly disturbed when Netanyahu's foreign policy adviser, Dore Gold, failed to inform him of Israel's plans during a visit to Amman only days before the entrance to the tunnel was opened. The king was sufficiently angry to remind Netanyahu of those perilous days during the Gulf War when the words he spoke on behalf of a previous Israeli government had been filtered through a gas mask.

King Hussein's potential influence in altering Israel's policies in Jerusalem should not be dismissed. He may yet help to defuse a city packed with detonating issues.

King Hussein: Damage Control in Jerusalem

Perhaps no one can play as decisive a role in attempting damage control in Jerusalem as King Hussein. One little-known historical precedent suggests his potential capacity for positive intervention in the city. In April 1995 the Rabin government became embroiled in an ill-advised attempt to confiscate 131 acres of land in two Arab neighborhoods, Beit Hanina and Beit Safafa. Most of the land in question was being expropriated from Arabs in order to build seven thousand apartments for Jews. The popular retelling of this story is that Rabin's sudden rescinding of the expropriation order was nothing more than regime survival. The five Arab parliamentarians who had ensured Rabin his 61-vote majority in the Knesset were supposedly poised to vote against the Rabin government because they were enraged by its expropriation order. The Likud opposition, though fervently pro-annexationist, was prepared to join the motion of no confidence in order to unseat Labor and save Greater Israel. Facing sure defeat, so the story goes, Prime Minister Rabin abandoned the annexation. This is, however, only half the truth at best. The more interesting side of the story—which is omitted—concerns Arafat's behavior, and the king's position and its decisive impact.

Arafat did not remain on the sidelines. He was active in trying to ensure that Rabin's misstep did not bring down his peace partner. Arafat lobbied Abdel Wahab Darawshe, head of the Arab Democratic Party, not to file his no-confidence motion, which could topple the government.[148] Arafat had his eyes set on the next step of the Oslo agreement—Israeli redeployment from the cities of the West Bank. He was hoping for a July agreement, and 131 acres in Jerusalem was not going to stop him from gaining control of 30 percent of the West Bank. Darawshe responded to Arafat's lobbying by suggesting that any decision he made would be based solely on Israeli interests.[149] Although the leaders of the ADP and Hadash could defiantly proclaim that "they were not captives of this government and the support of it was never unconditional,"[150] it was clear that they were far from committed to voting Rabin out of power. An interview with Darawshe suggests he was proudly independent but politically shrewd enough not to bring down the "most pragmatic government we are likely to get."[151]

Politics for Israel does not stop at its shore or its borders. Rabin's calculations were strongly influenced by King Hussein's intervention. The initial Jordanian expression of "profound concerns about the Jerusalem expropriation fiasco" was communicated to Yossi Beilin and Uri Savir.[152] Neither of them seemed to treat the Jordanian concerns with urgency. Shimon Peres was approached without any satisfaction. Domestic criticism against the Israeli expropriation grew within the kingdom. There were hints that the Jordanian parliament might reconvene in order to freeze the peace agreement with Israel.[153] The king grew more agitated and sent a personal message to Rabin, a warm but urgent note. The king and Rabin had a strong personal connection. According to Marwan Muasher, the talented young Jordanian minister of information who had been the Jordanian government's spokesman at the peace talks, the king's note indicated that the expropriations were too much for the still fragile peace to bear and that they complicated the king's ability to rule. Graciously, but decisively, King Hussein drew a red line. The next day Rabin rescinded the expropriation order. The prime minister had accepted the limits of a partner.

Rabin had much more difficulty in embracing Arafat and Palestinians as partners and in accepting their limits. Yet his government and that of his successor Shimon Peres did produce a red line for themselves in negotiating with the Palestinians. It was most clearly expressed by Uri Savir, the director general of the Israeli Foreign Ministry and chief negotiator with the Palestinians. "Our greatest negotiating challenge is not to win too much. We are the stronger party, but our interests will not be served if we take all that we can."[154] This red line was not always honored. That it was articulated at all is a sign of how far Arabs and Israelis had come in settling their hundred years' war.

How far peace has been set back by the election of Binyamin Netanyahu is likely to be measured by whether or not a partnership of red lines can be established—not just between Prime Minister Netanyahu and King Hussein. Arafat and the Palestinians must be integrated as full partners in a triangular relationship of Israelis, Palestinians, and Jordanians. This challenge will take us into the next millennium and the electoral judgment on whether Prime Minister Netanyahu has honored his mandate to achieve security and peace.

Notes

1. Quoted by Isabel Kershner, "Facts on the Ground," *Jerusalem Report*, June 27, 1996, 28.

2. Abba Eban's characterization of Likud's policies during a memorial lecture following the assassination of Prime Minister Rabin, New York City, November 8, 1996.

3. David Makovsky, *Making Peace with the PLO: The Rabin Government's Road to the Oslo Accord*, 76.

4. Ibid.

5. The redeployment negotiated under Oslo II provided for the Israelis to hand over 80 percent of Hebron to the Palestinian Authority, which would deploy some four hundred uniformed policemen. The remaining 20 percent of the city, the eastern side that included the small isolated enclaves of Jewish settlers and their holy places (Beit Hadassah, Tel Romeidah, Beit Romano, Cave of the Makhpela, and Avraham Avinu), was to remain under Israeli control, as were the roads linking the city to the adjacent Jewish community of six thousand in Kiryat Arba. The settler leadership opposes the redeployment and is lobbying for expanding the Jewish presence in Hebron. Their plan calls for building homes for some six hundred families by the year 2000. Nearly half of the new homes would be built on the city's wholesale market, which has been closed since Baruch Goldstein's massacre of twenty-nine Arab worshipers on February 25, 1994. Peter Hirschberg, "The Trouble with Hebron," *Jerusalem Report*, July 25, 1996, 18–22. An agreement was finally reached in January 1997.

6. Makovsky, 57.

7. Ibid.

8. Naseer Aruri, *The Obstruction of Peace: The United States, Israel, and the Palestinians* (Monroe, Maine: Common Courage Press, 1995), 347.

9. Ibid., 348.

10. Ibid., 349.

11. "Israel and Palestine: A Matter of Confidence," *Economist*, April 6, 1996, 46.

12. Ibid.

13. "West Bank and Gaza Closed Down," *Economist*, March 23, 1996, 39.

14. "Israel and Palestine: A Matter of Confidence," 44.

15. For a brief but lucid description of "total closure," "normal closure," and "internal closure" and their debilitating impact on the Palestinian economy, see "West Bank and Gaza, Closed Down," 39. For a more academic approach to the closures, see Geri Ovensen, "The Border Closure and Its Effects on the Labor Market and the Palestinian Household Economy," in *The Economy of Peace in the Middle East* (Paris: Maisonneuve et Larose, 1995). For an interesting overview of the economic crisis of the PA that focuses largely on nonclosure issues, see Barbara Balaj, Ishac Diwan, and Bernard Philippe, "External Assistance to the Palestinians: What Went Wrong?" forthcoming in *Politique Etrangère*. Perhaps the most authoritative

general study relevant to the economic status of Gaza is Sara Roy, *The Gaza Strip: The Political Economy of De-development*, (Washington: Institute for Palestine Studies, 1995).

16. "West Bank and Gaza Closed Down," 44.

17. Makovsky, 89.

18. Quoted in Makovsky, 89.

19. "West Bank and Gaza Closed Down," 39.

20. The Syrians' assertion of their centrality to the peace process was driven home in my meetings with Syrian government officials and cabinet ministers following the Oslo agreement in 1993 and again in November of 1994. Rislan Allush, the deputy foreign minister, repeated the theme that "without Syria there can be no real peace. We are the missing variable." Rislan made this comment at a meeting at the Syrian Foreign Ministry, November 8, 1994.

21. Interview with Binnie Zerah, Ashdod, Israel, May 3, 1996.

22. Interview with Rick Hooper, the outgoing deputy director of the UN Office of the Special Coordinator in the Occupied Territories, Gaza City, May 4, 1996.

23. UN Office of Special Coordinator, "Local Aid Coordination Committee Meets in Gaza with Palestinian Authority President Yasser Arafat," June 7, 1996, 1.

24. Stanley Reed, "Squeezing the Palestinians Could Set Off Another Intifada," *Business Week*, June 24, 1996, 62.

25. UN Office of the Special Coordinator, "Emerging Humanitarian Plan," paper presented to the Ad Hoc Liaison Committee, Brussels, April 12, 1996, 1.

26. Estimates of the number of Palestinians from the West Bank and Gaza working in Israel prior to the Oslo agreement and the closure policy vary from 100,000 to 180,000. The latter number reflects an estimate including illegal Palestinian laborers who used to work in Israel. For a typical example of how the elite Western media has presented these estimates, see Ilene Prusha, "Israel Eases the Blockade, but Not the Pain," *Financial Times*, July 24, 1996, 5.

27. UN Office of the Special Coordinator, "Emerging Humanitarian Plan," 1.

28. Ibid.

29. Ibid.

30. UN Office of the Special Coordinator, "Local Aid Coordination Committee Meets President Arafat," 2.

31. Ibid.

32. Ibid.

33. In an interview in Gaza City, January 23, 1996, Ghazi Hamid, a leading activist and intellectual associated with Hamas in Gaza, told me, "Jews are our enemies who we are destined to combat to the end. Yet we are seeing that our people want peace—and soon." The conflict between the absolute ideology he articulates and Hamas's desire to lead a popular cause—one that reflects the desires of the people—has triggered tensions within the movement. The Labor Party's relatively moderate peace policies challenged the pristine ideological moorings of Hamas.

34. Israeli post-election analysis focused on this swing constituency and the "bomb in the air" pre-election environment that moved these nonideological hawks

to vote for Netanyahu. See Hirsh Goodman, "For His Next Success: Peace," *Jerusalem Report*, June 27, 1996, 56, and Ehud Ya'ari, "Bibi's Middle East," ibid., 29.

35. Quoted in *Mideast Mirror*, March 20, 1996, 2.

36. David Gardner, "Peace Hangs in the Balance," *Financial Times*, May 31, 1996, 17.

37. Ehud Ya'ari, 29.

38. David Gardner, "Poll serves as referendum on Labour leader's vision of peace," *Financial Times*, May 29, 1996, 6.

39. Even the NRP ran a more moderate electoral campaign. Rather than repeating its militant campaign for "Greater Israel" as it did in the last election, the party emphasized Jewish values and courted secular voters. It is estimated that one of its nine seats, up from six in the last Knesset, is a result of this more pragmatic electoral face. See Peter Hirschberg, "With God on Their Side," *The Jerusalem Report*, June 27, 1996, 23.

40. Deri is on trial, charged with accepting bribes and arranging for the transfer of millions of dollars to Shas when he was interior minister within the Rabin government.

41. The Third Way Platform, April 1996. The Third Way may also have sharp differences with Netanyahu on the settlements issue. The leader of the Third Way, Internal Security Minister Avigdor Kahalani, has reportedly protested any settlement plans that go beyond the expansion of *existing* "settlement blocs." David Makovsky and Evelyn Gordon, "Cabinet Unfreezes Settlements," *Jerusalem Post International Edition*, August 10, 1996, 2.

42. Interview with MK Maria Solotkin, Jerusalem, July 4, 1996. Solotkin, a centrist member of Yisrael B'Aliyah (Immigrants) party is illustrative of this moderate tendency. She argued that the Russians are not ideologically hawkish or necessarily against territorial compromise. She suggested that two-thirds of the Russian immigrant vote for Netanyahu in the 1996 elections was based on perceptions that the Labor party "humiliated" them by actions like appointing an Israeli ambassador to Russia who could not speak Russian, when many linguistically and diplomatically skilled people were available for the ambassadorship.

43. There is a caveat in presuming a full term for Netanyahu. It revolves around David Levy, who threatened to resign three times in the first two months. His party's defection would still leave Netanyahu in power if Moledet supported the coalition from the outside. However, if Shas ministers are forced to resign as scandals grow, it is not inconceivable that Netanyahu's presumed mathematical lock on the prime ministership could prove illusory.

44. "Settlers Propose Massive Settlement Program after Elections," Foundation for Middle East Peace, *Report on Israeli Settlement in the Occupied Territories*, May 1996, 3.

45. Ibid.

46. Ibid.

47. Yehiel Leiter, head of the foreign desk of the Council of Jewish Communities in Judea, Samaria, and Gaza, shares this expectation that any settlement expansion

will be fueled by private construction. Leiter believes that the Netanyahu government has too many budget constraints to engage in massive spending in the West Bank or Gaza. Leiter is counting on the forces of the marketplace and the political sympathies of the new Israeli government to create a new building and buying boom in the territories. Given the infrastructure of the new bypass road built by Labor and the prohibitive cost of housing in pre-1967 Israel's urban centers, Leiter presumes young families will be pulled toward the quality-of-life settlements that are now within a short, safe drive to Tel Aviv and Jerusalem. Larry Derfner, "Bypass Surgery," *Jerusalem Post International Edition,* August 10, 1996, p. 28.

48. "Settlers Propose Massive Settlement Program after Elections," 3.

49. Yehiel Leiter speaks openly of "the [Yesha] council's strategic goal of preventing a Palestinian state. The only way to prevent such a state is to ensure that there is no territorial contiguity between major Palestinian population centers" in area C, which constitutes over 70 percent of the West Bank. Quoted in Dan Leon, "Settlements or Peace," *Jerusalem Post International Edition,* August 10, 1996, 13.

50. Quotation from a meeting with Benni Begin, Jerusalem, July 4, 1996.

51. Ibid.

52. "Israeli Aide Meets Arafat," *International Herald Tribune,* June 29–30, 1996, 5. (Begin was later to resign from the government.)

53. "Ministry official tries to block building objections in Arabic," *Jerusalem Post,* January 23, 1996, 3.

54. Ibid.

55. Interview with Daniel Seideman, Jerusalem, July 2, 1996.

56. Ibid.

57. *Mideast Mirror, Israel Section,* June 24, 1996, 2.

58. Department of Communications and Public Affairs, Consulate General of Israel in New York, *Israel Line,* June 26, 1996, 2.

59. Hirsh Goodman, "Professional Defense," *Jerusalem Report,* July 11, 1996, 60.

60. Stanley Reed, "Squeezing the Palestinians," *Business Week,* June 24, 1996, 62.

61. While the annexationist side of the Israeli political map has its generals and security experts, a disproportionate number of Israel's leading military officers and security experts have identified with a policy of territorial withdrawal coupled with security arrangements. Peace Now, Israel's largest and oldest parliamentary peace movement, emerged in March of 1978 with the now-famous Officer's Letter of 348 reserve officers and combat soldiers. The dovish Council for Israeli Peace and Security has recruited a notable group of former generals, high-ranking officers, and security experts. The perception that Israel's military elite is disproportionately dovish is apparently also shared by some leaders in Likud. In August 1996 Likud MK and chair of the prestigious Knesset Foreign Affairs and Defense Committee Uzi Landau went so far as to accuse IDF staff command officers and senior members of the defense establishment of having a political bias in favor of the Oslo accords and the Labor Party's security and defense policies. Defense Minister Yitzhak Mordechai published a fierce rejection of these charges, and Netanyahu

also disassociated himself from Landau's remarks. Yet it is noteworthy that Netanyahu has excluded the military from formulating policies, as in the case of Hebron, that entail very specific security arrangements to be enforced by the IDF. In an interview with Channel 2 television on August 2, 1996, the prime minister summarized his discussions with the various Israeli security branches: "I told them I don't want them in the peace process." Under his watch, the various security branches would offer their intelligence assessments. However, they would not have any policy role, as he suggested they did during the Labor government. *Mideast Mirror, Israel Section,* August 8, 1996, 4.

62. The Israeli business elite has been bullish on the Oslo peace process. During the election campaign, twenty leading executives placed full-page pro-Peres ads in Israeli dailies. Their message was that the peace process was vital to Israel's future prosperity. Benjamin Gaon, CEO of Koor Industries, a profitable $4 billion industrial group, suggested that Netanyahu "needs the economy to grow rapidly, and that depends entirely on the peace process." Aharon Fogel, chairman of Enhro, a Tel Aviv–based private power company and one of the architects of Israel's recent economic liberalization, argues that "no Israeli government has an option other than peace." John Rossant and Neal Sandler, "Bibi Has Business Biting Its Nails," *Business Week,* June 17, 1996, 52, 54.

63. David Makovsky, "Netanyahu's dreams of new advisory councils fading away," *Jerusalem Post International Edition,* August 10, 1996, 4.

64. Embassy of Israel, Office of Public Affairs, *Guidelines of the Government of Israel,* June 17, 1996, 2.

65. Ibid.

66. Quoted in *Mideast Mirror, Israel Section,* June 28, 1996, 3.

67. *Guidelines of the Government,* 2.

68. Ibid., 5.

69. Mark Tessler, *A History of the Israeli-Palestinian Conflict,* 516.

70. *Mideast Mirror, Arab/Islamic World Section,* July 30, 1996, 2. The details of this "Lebanon First" scheme were developed in considerable detail in a front-page story in *Al-Hayat* of July 30, 1996, written by the newspaper's political editor, Khairallah Khairallah. On August 9, 1996, Prime Minister Netanyahu did reveal aspects of his "Lebanon first" proposal, saying that Israel was prepared to withdraw from Lebanon if three conditions were met: disarming Hizbollah, deployment of the Lebanese Army to the international border with Israel, and protection of the IDF's client South Lebanon Army (SLA). *Mideast Mirror, Israel Section,* August 9, 1996, 2.

71. Ibid.

72. Meeting with Ori Orr, Jerusalem, July 3, 1996.

73. David Makovsky, "Leaving Lebanon," *Jerusalem Post International Edition,* August 10, 1996, 7. In an interview with the author, Jerusalem, July 3, 1996, MK Ori Orr indicated that "security doves" like him would be firmly opposed to a unilateral withdrawal without a *negotiated* security arrangement that guarantees Israel's northern border. Without such negotiated security arrangements, Israel could not

prevent Hizbollah or other militias from retaking positions along Israel's border and resuming attacks against northern Israel: "There is only one way out of Lebanon, an agreement with Syria."

74. David Bar-Ilan projected just such a scenario in the meeting with a delegation of American Jews, Jerusalem, July 4, 1996.

75. *Guidelines of the Government*, 1.

76. *Mideast Mirror, Israel Section*, June 19, 1996, 13–14.

77. *Guidelines of the Government*, 2.

78. *Mideast Mirror, Israel Section*, June 19, 1996, 14.

79. Ibid.

80. Ibid.

81. Ibid.

82. Ibid.

83. Hirsh Goodman documents additional evidence of the PA's cooperation with Israeli security agencies in his article "For His Next Success: Peace," *Jerusalem Report*, June 27, 1996, 56.

84. *Guidelines of the Government*, 1.

85. In an interview with the Israeli newspaper *Ma'ariv* on June 28, 1992, Yitzhak Shamir was quoted as saying, "If I had been reelected, I would have continued negotiations on Palestinian autonomy for ten years, and in that time half a million Israelis would have settled on the West Bank." Shamir's office subsequently suggested that the prime minister was misunderstood. He meant only to suggest that final status negotiations could last ten years. *Mideast Mirror*, June 30, 1992, 8; *Le Figaro*, May 26, 1993, 5.

86. Hirsh Goodman, "For His Next Success: Peace," 56.

87. "West Bank and Gaza, the Banging Door," *Economist*, August 3, 1996, 39.

88. Ibid.

89. Between the signing of the Oslo agreement in September 1993 and the end of its term in June, the Labor-led government imposed approximately two hundred days of total closure and one hundred days of partial closure in the West Bank and Gaza. Ibid.

90. Ibid.

91. *Mideast Mirror, Israel Section*, August 5, 1996, 4.

92. Ibid.

93. "West Bank and Gaza: the Banging Door."

94. "Likud to ease closure?" *Palestine Report*, Jerusalem Media and Communication Centre, July 12, 1996, 1–3.

95. Ibid.

96. Ilene Prusher, "Israel eases the blockade, but not the pain, "*Financial Times*, July 24, 1996, 5.

97. "Likud to ease closure?" 1.

98. *Mideast Mirror, Arab/Islamic World Section*, July 31, 1996, 8.

99. *Mideast Mirror, Israel Section*, August 2, 1996, 2.

100. Ibid., 9.

101. Danni Rubinstein, one of Israel's premier analysts of the Palestinian issue, argues that Arafat is a master of brinkmanship. Although he cannot order an intifada (it starts from below), he can order his 35,000-strong "small light army. . . . Bibi does not want to draw Fatah back onto the battlefield, and area B is a field full of potential tension points. Arafat can pick his battle points. Here a road block, there a demonstration. He does not need to declare a war or even a strike to exploit Israel's fear about having to become occupiers again and face a revived domestic opposition and new international pressure." Quoted in an interview with Danni Rubinstein, Jerusalem, July 5, 1996.

102. *Mideast Mirror, Israel Section,* August 13, 1996, 3.

103. Ibid.

104. Ibid.

105. Ibid., 4.

106. Ada Ushpiz, "Alas, the Authority Has Finished Us," *Ha'aretz,* August 9, 1996, B2.

107. Meeting with Shimon Peres, Jerusalem, July 6, 1995.

108. Peace Now argued that under the Labor government the number of settlers increased 39 percent, not 50 percent as alleged by Prime Minister Netanyahu. More importantly, the report attributes this growth predominantly to Labor's willingness to complete the ten thousand housing units on which construction began under Shamir's Likud government. The Labor government froze government funding for construction of *new* settlements in the West Bank and Gaza Strip. The report states: "With the exception of the housing units already in progress and selective expansion around Jerusalem, the Labor government permitted very little new construction in the settlements, because continued expansion of the settlements would have impeded implementation of the peace process." *Peace Now Settlement Watch Report* no. 8, July 1996.

Yesha spokesman Yehiel Leiter presented data suggesting that the increase in the number of settlers under Labor was significantly less than Peace Now reported. Leiter claimed that the increase was only about 20 percent—from 127,000 settlers to 150,000. (Yesha's figures on the total number of settlers are about 10 percent below those of Israel's Central Bureau of Statistics.) Larry Derfner, "Boom Town in the West Bank?" *Jewish Week,* July 19, 1996.

109. The first four-lane highway will be six miles long and will enter Jerusalem from the north, extending travel from Israel's coastal plain by slicing through the West Bank. The second road will run east from an area north of Tel Aviv through the West Bank for about twelve miles, where it will intersect with an existing road near Ariel. The third construction plan entails widening and repairing sections of a north-south highway that runs the entire length of the West Bank along the Jordan Valley. Minister Sharon has also instructed the Department of Public Works, an agency under his control, to replace with wider spans two narrow bridges over the Jordan River in order to accommodate "the growing population of the Golan." Joel

Greenberg, "Israel Maps Roads across West Bank: Plan for 2 Golan Bridges Signals Hard Line on Land," *New York Times,* July 30, 1996, 1, 5.

110. David Landau, "New Settlements Likely to Surge, but Impact on Peace Is Uncertain," *JTA*, August 7, 1996, 3.

111. Joel Greenberg, "Israel Maps Roads."

112. David Makovsky and Evelyn Gordon, "Cabinet Unfreezes Settlements," *Jerusalem Post International Edition,* August 10, 1996, 1.

113. Ibid.

114. Ibid.

115. *Mideast Mirror, Israel Section,* August 5, 1996, 3.

116. Ibid., 3–4.

117. For an interesting assessment of the conflicts between Jordan and the PA, as well as the promise and peril this affords Israel, see Ehud Ya'ari, "The Waiting Game," *Ma'ariv,* August 9, 1996, Supplement 9. See also the chapter by Adam Garfinkle in this volume.

118. *Mideast Mirror, Israel Section,* August 8, 1996, 5.

119. Ibid.

120. Ibid.

121. Ibid., August 13, 1996, 1.

122. Ibid.

123. Ibid., August 14, 1996, 3.

124. Ibid.

125. Ibid.

126. Cited in ibid.

127. This "understanding" that Yossi Beilin and Abu Mazen helped shepherd through twenty secret meetings culminated in a broad agreement on permanent borders and an approach to resolving the Jerusalem problem. This exercise in final status thinking ended successfully after two years on November 1, 1995, only days before the assassination of Rabin. Yossi Beilin argued that these talks demonstrated that a final agreement could be reached within the Israeli national consensus. First, there would be a demilitarized Palestinian state, not "a Palestinian state with an army." Second, the problem of Palestinian refugees would be resolved *outside* Israel's borders. Israel would agree to family reunification within Palestinian territory. Third, Jerusalem would not be redivided. According to the understanding, a Palestinian capital—"Al-Quds"—would be established in Abu-Dis, outside Jerusalem municipal jurisdiction. Palestinians would have free access to the Temple Mount (Haram Ash-Shareef) and would have the right to fly a Palestinian flag there. The Old City would be "without sovereignty" but in practice would remain under Israeli jurisdiction and the control of the Jerusalem municipality. There was also an understanding that the issue of sovereignty in East Jerusalem would be deferred for later discussion. Teddy Kollek's "quarters" plan, modeled on the Greater London boroughs system, was to be introduced into Arab neighborhoods in East Jerusalem. When presented with these understandings, neither Arafat nor Peres was fully con-

vinced that they were an adequate basis for negotiations. Ze'ev Schiff, *Ha'aretz*, February 22, 1996. For the full text of the Hirschfeld interview and Prime Minister Peres's and President Arafat's objections to the understanding, see *Mideast Mirror, Israel Section*, July 31, 1996, 1–5.

128. Daniel Sternoff, "Netanyahu's Win a Boost for West Bank Settlers," *Washington Times*, June 8, 1996, 1. The expropriations in Silwan (the City of David) came to a head in 1991. After discovering irregularities in the purchasing of these properties, the Rabin government halted the acquisitions. An intergovernmental committee, named after Director General of the Justice Department Chaim Klugman, completed its investigation in September 1992. It found the takeovers were riddled with irregularities and evidence of corruption. Houses were purchased without a legal tender. In addition, public monies that were listed as loans for first- time home buyers were channeled to settlers. Ibid., 10.

129. Interview with Daniel Seideman, Jerusalem, July 4, 1996.

130. Meeting with Yossi Beilin, Israeli minister without portfolio, who is deeply involved in monitoring the Har Homa issue, Jerusalem, January 15, 1996.

131. Interview with Mossi Raz, director of Ir Shalem, Jerusalem, January 16, 1996.

132. A number of Palestinian and Israeli human rights organizations and research institutions in Jerusalem have been reporting this as an increasing problem. Interview with Maha Abu Dayyeh Shames, director of Women's Centre for Legal Aid and Counseling, New York City, August 8, 1996.

133. Interview with Daniel Seideman, Jerusalem, July 2, 1996.

134. Ibid., July 7, 1996.

135. According to Palestinian attorney and member of the Palestinian Council Ziad abu Zayyad, some thirty new demolition orders were issued to residents of Issawiya in early July 1996.

136. Colleen Siegel, "Settlers, Soldiers Blamed in Clash," *Washington Times*, October 1, 1996, A10.

137. *Mideast Mirror (Israel Section)*, August 8, 1996, 4.

138. Ze'ev Schiff, "Who Failed?," *Ha'aretz*, October 4, 1996, B1.

139. Ibid.

140. Ibid.

141. Ibid.

142. Ibid.

143. Lawrence Cohler and Larry Derfner, "Bibi Rapped on Two Key Fronts," *Jewish Week*, October 11, 1996, 35.

144. Ibid.

145. Ibid.

146. Martin Sieff, "Israeli troops disarmed for Netanyahu's visit," *Washington Times*, October 17, 1996, 14.

147. Ibid.

148. *Mideast Mirror*, May 22, 1995, 2.

149. Ibid.

150. Ibid.

151. Interview with Abdel Wahab Darawshe, Jerusalem, July 1, 1995.

152. Meeting with Marwan Muasher, Amman, July 7, 1996.

153. Ibid.

154. Uri Savir at the Conference of Presidents of Major American Organizations, New York City, October 6, 1995.

3: Palestinian and Other Arab Perspectives on the Peace Process

Muhammad Muslih

In this essay I will attempt to listen to Arab society's dialogue with itself in the aftermath of two major events, Israel's "Operation Grapes of Wrath" against Lebanon in April 1996 and Likud's victory in the Israeli elections of May 1996. This dialogue offers a revealing picture of how Arabs viewed themselves in the changing world of the early and mid-1990s, taking into account the traumatizing effects of the second Gulf War; internal Arab divisions; the quality of Arab leadership; the peace process; the intrusion of outside powers; and above all the balance of power, which has worked in favor of non-Arab actors, primarily Israel and to a lesser degree Turkey.

Two major events provide the context for the Arab dialogue: the Gulf War of 1991 and the Middle East peace process that followed the war. Arab political writings in the first half of the 1990s were primarily focused on these events. The interpretations offered in these writings tend to fall into two categories: those stressing the consolidation of U.S. and Israeli hegemony throughout the region and those emphasizing the need to establish a U.S.-led regional security system that would serve as a bulwark against any post-Saddam defiant Iraqi regime. In the first category is the view eloquently expressed by the Syrian poet Nizar Qabbani, that the Arabs live in a state of *sharshaha* (shameful weakness).[1] According to this view, the state of sharshaha manifests itself in almost all facets of Arab life. Arab society suffers from fragmentation and alienation, lament the advocates of this view; Arab governments have succumbed to the combined power of the United States and Israel; Arab oil resources are under the tight control of the U.S. government.

Arab cultural life is falling behind in reaction to the harsh impact of authoritarian governments; the socioeconomic status quo favors the oil-rich dynasties; and the potential Arab deterrence of Israel has been wiped out through the destruction of Iraq.[2]

This state of affairs is poignantly illustrated by one Palestinian intellectual's commentary on the Gulf crisis. "The crisis," wrote Naseer Aruri, "simply highlights a dependency which has been for some time the Arab world's most serious problem: its inability and/or unwillingness to utilize its potential to become independent in real economic, political, military and cultural terms."[3] The dependency takes on another dimension as the oil-rich Gulf dynasties opt for a protective U.S. security umbrella and allow a massive buildup of American troops on the Arabian peninsula. Aruri considers that the buildup completes a process of recolonization that has been going on for many years. In short, the Arabs have been "voluntarily recolonized."[4]

Abd al-Rahman Munif,[5] the distinguished Saudi novelist who was stripped of his Saudi citizenship for political reasons, expressed the view that the U.S. motive for using such overwhelming force against Iraq was more than just the liberation of Kuwait, or even the destruction of Iraq. The larger U.S. goal was to intimidate others and create a new order under the exclusive domination of the United States. "Iraq was hit with this degree of mercilessness," Munif commented, "in order to make it an example to others, including friends, and to demonstrate the extent of the power of the United States at the present time and under conditions called the new world order. Therefore all people must be aware of the dangers that await them in the future, and must understand that the white sheep [Arab countries of the Gulf] was eaten in the same day during which the black sheep [Iraq] was eaten."[6] This feeling, accompanied by a widespread belief that the United States wreaked so much destruction upon Iraq in order to consolidate Israel's regional hegemony, significantly compounded the Arab sense of alienation from the West and from Arab governments regarded as subservient to foreign powers.

The views discussed here reflect not only the sentiments of leftist Arab circles but also those of centrist Arab circles. The main complaint of both is that Saddam Hussein's invasion of Kuwait merely provided the United States the formal excuse to destroy the technological and military capacity of Iraq, thus causing Arabs to feel a greater measure of weakness or fear vis-à-vis Israel and the West.[7]

In the second category of views on the Gulf crisis, by contrast, the point of departure is the security of the Gulf dynasties. The Iraqi invasion of Kuwait demonstrates that neither individually nor through their subregional organization, the Gulf Cooperation Council (GCC), were the Gulf states able to establish an effective self-defense plan. Saudi Arabia, the strongest partner of the small member-states that constitute the GCC, sought U.S. military assistance and permitted the stationing of foreign troops on its soil in the wake of the Iraqi invasion of Kuwait. Prince Bandar bin Sultan, Saudi Arabia's ambassador to the United States, is reported to have told representative Stephen J. Solarz, Democrat of Brooklyn, New York, that the reason Iraq did not invade the kingdom was the presence by October 1990 of more than 200,000 American troops and more than 1,000 American airplanes.[8]

These reactions of vulnerability, particularly the feeling that a protective U.S. military umbrella was an absolute necessity, may be noted in other Gulf countries. When the GCC opened its eleventh annual summit meeting in Doha, Qatar, on December 22, 1990, the emir of Qatar at the time, Sheikh Khalifa bin Hamad al-Thani, implicitly recognized this problem by stressing that the Gulf states "must establish a more effective security system."[9] In the eyes of the Gulf rulers, there was no substitute for continued U.S. military presence. And, unlike their attitude in the past, they were not coy about such a presence. As one observer has put it, the Gulf governments believed that "the more overt, permanent, and substantial it [the U.S. presence] is on the land, in the sea, and in the air, the greater its deterrent value."[10]

This position found clear expression in the Gulf governments' attacks against those Arabs who supported Iraq or abstained from participation in the U.S.-led anti-Iraq coalition. An open letter that the Saudi ambassador to the United States addressed to King Hussein of Jordan in 1990 captures the new boldness of the Gulf governments. King Hussein had suggested in a speech to the American people on CNN during the third week of September 1990 that the forces of foreign powers must leave Saudi Arabia and that the Iraqi-Kuwaiti border had been created by the colonial British. The Saudi prince responded: "Your Majesty, you should be the last one to say that. Not only all your borders, but your whole country was created by the same colonial British. And do you remember when the British troops were invited by you into your country in 1958? We did not object or question your motives and judgement over that."[11]

In their quest for a security umbrella, the Gulf governments wanted the role played by foreign powers to be confined to the West, principally the United States. Thus these governments were not favorably disposed toward allowing their two non-Gulf Arab allies, Syria and Egypt, to play the security role envisioned for them in the Damascus Declaration of March 1991. At the core of this Gulf position was the deep-seated suspicion that their poorer Arab partners would interfere in domestic Gulf politics.

Three other reasons precluded a security role for Egypt and Syria. First, an isolationist trend, or a desire to act outside the framework of the Arab consensus on the Arab-Israeli conflict, was increasingly on the rise in some Gulf countries. Second, the cost of even a token Arab force at a time of economic decline in the Gulf states provided another barrier against an Egyptian or Syrian security role. The initial $15 billion pledge of peninsular Arabs to their non-Gulf Arab partners was quickly scaled down to a substantially reduced sum, mainly in the form of a conditional loan.[12] Third, the Egyptians and Syrians were not capable of meeting Gulf security needs in terms of either skilled soldiers or sophisticated military hardware.

It was against the background of this state of Arab trauma that the Middle East peace process was launched in October 1991. Israeli Prime Minister Yitzhak Shamir was dragged to the peace process. Among all parties, he was the least inclined to participate in a peace conference that was based on a land-for-peace formula, a formula that was inconsistent with his ideological beliefs. The Arabs, by contrast, showed the flexibility needed to facilitate the implementation of the Madrid formula for achieving peace with Israel. The formula provided a multifaceted process based on the following points:

· The peace process would aim at a settlement based on Security Council Resolutions 242 and 338.
· The peace settlement would be reached through direct, two-track negotiations to be conducted in phases following the opening meeting in Madrid.
· The bilateral negotiations would be the centerpiece of the process, but multilateral negotiations also would be launched, involving, in addition to the parties participating in the bilaterals, governments that had interests in the region related to security, water, and other issues.
· The conference would have no decision-making powers and no mechanism for handling differences of opinion or for achieving simultaneous progress on all tracks.
· The United Nations would play only the role of an observer.

Within the framework of the Madrid formula, the Palestinians were allowed to participate in the peace process, though under procedural constraints imposed by the Likud government. Emerging from the Gulf crisis weak and isolated, the Palestine Liberation Organization (PLO) accepted Israel's conditions for Palestinian participation: any Palestinian delegation must be formed by non-PLO Palestinians from the West Bank and Gaza; members of the delegation would not have any direct connection with East Jerusalem; and members should not have formal links with the PLO. Having made painful concessions on procedure, the Palestinians hoped for a better deal on interim self-government arrangements and final status issues, particularly the questions of sovereignty, Jerusalem, and refugees.

Arab participation in the Middle East peace conference gave rise to an Arab debate that revolved around three questions: participation in the peace process, the Israel-PLO Declaration of Principles (DOP), and normalization of relations with Israel. There were two views as to whether or not Arab states should take part in the peace process. The first tended to explain Arab participation in terms of a realpolitik policy aimed at *inqadh ma yumkin inqadhuhu* ("salvaging whatever could be salvaged")—in other words, the recovery through negotiations of the Arab territories conquered by Israel in June 1967 and the settlement of the Palestinian question on the basis of pragmatic justice. In other words, some kind of Palestinian entity would be established in the West Bank and Gaza. Those who subscribe to this view argued that the balance of power favored Israel in a decisive way that made the status quo a sweet deal for the Jewish state.

On the other hand, the status quo did not augur well for the Arabs, being a source of regional tensions and domestic instability. Moreover, the dissolution of the Soviet Union, together with the immense U.S. investments in the Gulf in the form of oil interests and direct military presence, were bound to diminish the significance of Israel in U.S. strategic calculations. This, in turn, held the promise of convincing the United States to bring its prestige, power, and leverage to bear in the cause of Middle East peace. In short, Arab supporters of the peace process believed that the Gulf War and its aftermath in the region opened a window of opportunity for paving the way to Arab-Israeli peace.[13]

The Palestinian component of this view was represented by what might be called a proactive trend. The proactive view did not oppose Palestinian participation in the peace conference, but insisted that the PLO (1) be given guarantees from the United States that the peace conference would produce a comprehensive and equitable settlement; (2) play a role in selecting the Palestinian delegation to the peace talks; and (3) democratize the PLO policy-making process, which was dominated by Yasir Arafat.[14]

The view of those who were not prepared to accept Arab participation in the peace process rested mainly on two grounds: realpolitik and ideological considerations. The realpolitik argument was that the superiority of Israel's power position vis-à-vis the Arabs had significant implications for the negotiating process. Advocates of this view asked the following questions: Would Israeli leaders make the concessions necessary for peace (that is, adhere to the so-called land for peace formula), or would they press for a still more favorable position for their country? And how, in any event, might the Arabs secure an honorable settlement when inter-Arab disputes were legion and when the Arab world was traumatized by the horrendous effects of the Gulf War? The negative answers to these questions were summed up by a Syrian academician: "The role and influence of the Arab homeland and the world around have diminished. The Arab ability to influence the world order has declined perceptibly. The Arabs are becoming increasingly dependent on the industrial capitalist world (technology, trade, capital, skilled labor, etc.); they are also more dependent than before in terms of their food needs (more than 50 percent of the Arab markets import their loaves of bread); the Arab economic performance is in a state of deterioration (our international debts are increasing, our arms purchases are consuming our growth potential); Arab internal disputes still persist."[15]

These and similar considerations have driven wide sectors of the Arab intelligentsia and Arab public opinion to conclude not only that the Arabs were at a dangerous disadvantage in the peace process, but also that the United States aimed at exploiting the Arab weakness to achieve certain long-term regional objectives for itself as well as for Israel. According to Arab analyses, these included the tightening of U.S. control over the Gulf; the intimidation of the Arabs; and the integration of Israel into the region not as an equal partner but as a hegemonic actor in the political, economic, and military fields.[16]

In an ideological context, those who opposed Arab participation in the peace process were of two views, one based on Islam and one on secular Arab nationalism. The first view holds that Palestine is Islamic *waqf* (religious endowment), that no Muslim can cede even a tiny portion of its territory to a non-Muslim and that mobilizing all Muslim resources was the only way of restoring Muslim Arab rights.[17] The more radical adherents of this view categorically reject the interpretation supported by Muslim jurists who endorsed the peace process—that it is permissible for a Muslim to conclude peace with the Jews on the condition that Muslim rights be restored.[18] In rejecting this interpretation, advocates of the radical view rely on a strict interpretation of the Quranic sura that says, "But if the enemy incline towards peace, do thou [also] incline towards peace, and trust in God."[19] Radical Islamists point to the fact that the verse says, "If the enemy incline towards peace," and not "If the Muslims incline."[20] The implication is that the Jews are not predisposed toward peace, but toward imposing their will upon the world of Arabdom and Islam.

Secular Arab nationalists' ideas about reconciliation with Israel derived mainly from Ba'athism and Nasserism. Many still believed that Arab unity was bound to happen and that what had been created by the colonial powers could be unmade and remade with a revitalized and united Arab nation. Writing in 1994, the Iraqi politician Sa'dun Hamadi expressed this sentiment as follows: "Modern Arab nationalism is a movement of progress and reform. It is a historical and inevitable fact for which there is no substitute. The difficulties that lie ahead do not mean the acceptance of the present situation. The position of incumbent regimes is no basis for discussing the question of unity. Unity is the business of the *umma* [nation], and not the business of the governments."[21]

These and related Arab unity themes coalesce in the publications of the Beirut-based Center for Arab Unity Studies (*markaz dirasat al-wahda al-Arabiyya*), which are highly regarded by Arab intellectuals and publicists. The books and articles published by the center and written from a Pan-Arab perspective use a language far more subdued than that of the pre-1967 era. The language is deferential to the Arab heritage, but it differs from the publications of the 1950s and 1960s by being less threatening to the prerogatives of incumbent political elites in the Arab world. Their style reflects the change in the balance of power that favors local nationalism (*al-tawajjuh al-iqlimi*) in the parlance of Pan-Arabists.

The Pan-Arab perspective on the peace process is that reconciliation with a state that has "usurped" an integral part of the Arab homeland is too big a concession and that the Arabs should spend their energies on the question of unity. The notion that Arab unity was inevitable did not go unchallenged. A large segment of the Arab intelligentsia questioned this thesis not because they were against pan-Arabism but because they believed that unity was not the real issue. From their perspective the fundamental political and cultural questions related to what they call the Arab mind (*al-'aql al-Arabi*). According to this view, it was not merely foreign domination or the nature and occupation of the regimes in power that stood between the Arabs and unity. Even more important was the structure of the Arab mind and the tools of analysis that Arabs use to understand their society and politics. "The Arab mind," wrote the Moroccan thinker Muhammad 'Abid al-Jabiri, "deals more with words than with concepts; its point of departure is a principle (*asl*) that guides and leads to conclusions, a principle that is supported by the authority of the ancestors *(salaf)* and expressed either in the form of words or in the form of ideas; the Arab mind uses analogy (or rhetorical analogy, *al-qiyas al-bayani*) and comparative analogy (or cognitive analogy, *al-qiyas al-`irfani*) as tools with which to acquire rather than produce knowledge. In doing all this the Arab mind relies on godly sanction *(tajwiz)* as an axiom and a general rule upon which it establishes its methodology and its view of the world."[22]

Such a statement may be dismissed as Orientalist thinking by certain Arab intellectuals,[23] but, contends al-Jabiri, it closely reflects the prevailing mode of Arab thinking. This, asserts al-Jabiri, not only produces what he calls a body of alienated thought *(sahat fikr mughtarib)*,[24] but it also precludes the possibility of Arab revival and Arab unity because it reinforces tribalism and dogmatism and hampers the prospects for rational economic development. Al-Jabiri carefully shows how "the Arab mind" is at odds with the modern world. Thus the first thing that the Arabs should do in order to have a place under the sun, and by implication in order to regain their rights, is to be critical of themselves. "Contemporary Arab thinkers," he writes, "are duty bound to criticize Arab society, the Arab economy, and the Arab mind, both the abstract mind and the political mind. . . . Without objective criticism all kinds of talk about revival, progress, and unity in the Arab homeland will continue to be based on hopes and dreams."[25]

The Declaration of Principles, or the Oslo agreement, signed between Israel and the PLO in September 1993 revealed more than any political development since the Gulf crisis of 1991 the dilemmas that the Arabs confronted. Not many Arabs, including Palestinians, celebrated this agreement. Even its staunchest supporters knew that they had to accept it, both because the balance of power was decisively in favor of Israel and because the Oslo agreement was the only option available for the Palestinians. For many, including Arafat and his inner circle, the Olso agreement did not promise an instant remaking of the painful world in which Palestinians lived, a settling of all the problems between Israel and the Palestinians, a compensation for past injustices inflicted on the Palestinians. What it promised was something that should in the final analysis correspond to the legitimate needs and interests of both sides. This view is expressed by Palestinian intellectual Ahmad Khalidi: "For the Palestinians, Oslo and the DOP may have marked the end of the era of cumulative loss and defeat, but their aspirations had already been largely reduced and dissipated by the imbalance of power and successive tragedies of the post-1948 period. In the end, nothing can make up for this loss, but nothing can be gained in the futile pursuit of the past either. What is needed from Israel is not self-righteousness in peace but rather a genuine appreciation of how—despite everything—the Palestinians are willing to look forward, not back."[26]

This, of course, was not a universal feeling in the Arab world. In a curious way, the DOP registered among wide sectors of mass opinion and of the intelligentsia a degree of concern about larger, more serious Arab questions than the launching of the peace process itself. This reaction was partly a product of political and cultural defensiveness against the advancing tide of Israeli hegemony and partly an affirmation that the Palestinian question remains central and preeminent, though not in all Arab circles. There is in this reaction both a strictly Palestinian attempt to understand the agreement and what it holds for the future of Palestine, as well as a wider Arab concern focused on Palestine despite the setback the Palestinians suffered as a result of their support for Iraq during the Gulf War. Indeed, one finds in the wider Arab speculation about the DOP a proxy debate about the harvest of modern Arab history, about the role of the Arabs and their place in the world.

The backdrop common to all other Arab reactions to the DOP might be seen as having three interrelated themes—nationalistic, governance-related, and cultural-civilizational. The nationalist theme is that most of those who criticized or opposed the DOP did so for the following reasons: (1) the belief that Israel had no intention of ever allowing a Palestinian state to emerge; (2) the absence in the agreement of a provision that commits Israel to stop the settlement process; (3) a belief that the autonomy arrangements of the agreement would lead to the cantonization of the West Bank and Gaza, thus severely compromising their territorial integrity; and (4) a built-in bias in the agreement that allows Israel to focus on the West Bank and Gaza and ignore the rights of about 3 million diaspora-based Palestinians.[27] Although this reaction was articulated mainly by Palestinians, it was also evident in the comments of wide sectors of Arab intellectuals and publicists.[28]

The governance theme, which is difficult to separate from the nationalist theme, revolves around Arafat's leadership and his ability to govern. Although misgivings about Arafat's leadership existed in a suppressed form long before Oslo, the signing of the agreement brought them to the surface. Arafat negotiated the DOP agreement secretly, without consultation, and outside the framework of the PLO policy-making process. As Arafat extended his authority over the self-rule areas that came under his partial control after the Olso agreement, many Palestinians were alarmed at the prospect that his shadowy government was developing into an autocratic regime led by a more or less absolute leader. Human rights organizations drew a disturbing picture of human rights violations against Gaza and West Bank Palestinians at the hands of Arafat's security apparatuses, most notably the Palestinian Preventive Security Service.[29] The impact of these violations was significantly compounded by the blockade and other harsh Israeli security measures instituted after the Hamas and Islamic Jihad terrorist attacks of February and March 1996, which shattered an already weak Palestinian economy.

Equally painful was the impact of the closure in the social and psychological domains. The closure measures undertaken by Israel disconnected Palestinian cities and regions in the West Bank from one another and isolated the West Bank and Gaza from the outside world. In many instances married Palestinian couples and Palestinians who hailed from the same family were barred from being with each other or seeing each other. Thus in addition to the economic strangulation that the Israeli-imposed siege visited upon the Palestinian territory, it also caused the Palestinians deep psychological pain, compounding their sense of alienation from Israel and from the Palestine National Authority.

Palestinian advocates of human rights were not coy about criticizing Arafat in the international media. "People are intimidated," charged Iyyad al-Sarraj, a Palestinian psychiatrist and human rights advocate, in an interview with Anthony Lewis of the *New York Times*. "There is an overwhelming sense of fear. The regime is corrupt, dictatorial, oppressive."[30] Palestinians believe that Israel has encouraged Arafat's oppressive policies to crack down on internal dissent, especially after the suicide attacks of Islamic extremists in February and March of 1996. "Why does anyone believe that peace and security can be won through political persecution and economic impoverishment?" asked a Palestinian lawyer. "These policies will only deepen misery and despair in Gaza and the West Bank—perfect conditions for political and religious extremism."[31]

In his own remarkable language, Edward Said makes similar assertions. After arguing that the DOP was a "Palestinian Versailles"[32] and that it was a patchwork of "incomplete procedural suggestions, deliberate ambiguities and obfuscations,"[33] he stated that, given the Arabs' subserviency to U.S. policy that is fixated on Israel's interests, the "looming danger is that Arafat's rule, if perpetuated, will produce assassinations, chaos and civil war."[34] The way out, according to Said, is to speak out and to organize courageously in resistance to both Israel and Arafat's rule.[35]

The cultural-civilizational theme conveyed a nostalgia for purity that survives in every civilization that is on the defensive. After the defeat of 1967, the Palestinian revolution that Arafat has led promised a defeated

Arab world a settling of the great score with Israel and a remaking of the painful realities created in 1948 and 1967. This was at least the view of those who wanted the liberation of all of Palestine. To these people, the Oslo agreement represented a retreat that was politically and culturally unacceptable. They saw in it both a betrayal of the revolution and a sell-out of Palestine. An Arab intellectual's reaction to pictures in the pan-Arab media depicting the bed in which Arafat may sleep in Jericho illustrates this point:

> The picture published on the front page of Arab newspapers show-ing two young Palestinian women preparing the bed in which Pales-tinian president Yasir Arafat may sleep in case he visits Jericho sliced me into two halves, and caused me dizziness and nausea. . . . Who will sleep in this regal and bridal bed that befits two newly wed hon-eymooners? Is the Palestinian cause ready for a honeymoon with a bedroom having a Louis XVI bed, a toilette table and furniture up-holstered with chiffon? Have you ever heard of a revolution that has taken off its boots . . . put its pistol on a coat hanger . . . and slept on a pillow made of birds' feathers? . . . The issue is not a picture distrib-uted by news agencies. . . . It is rather the issue of the Palestinian homeland which we depicted to ourselves and to our children as a sword. . . . But lo and behold, some stupid media people have pre-sented it as a bed.[36]

One finds in this passage a nostalgia for the 1967–73 interlude during which the Palestinian revolution promised to redraw the Arab political map that emerged after 1948 and after 1967—in other words, to liberate Palestine through armed struggle. To be sure, Qabbani, the writer of this passage, understood that this was a far-fetched goal, but at least he and many oth-ers expected the Palestinian revolution to restore Arab dignity. Comment-ing on her return to Gaza in April 1996, Layla Khalid, a Palestinian woman with a radical revolutionary past, had this to say, "I dreamt of a different kind of return. I dreamt of returning with all our people. But I returned alone. . . . My family cannot return yet. . . . It would have been great had we returned and exercised sovereignty over our land."[37]

Another aspect of the cultural-civilizational theme is the Arab debate over the question of normalization with Israel. The measures taken by a number of Arab countries to normalize relations with Israel in the after-math of the Oslo agreement touched off heated discussions among Arab intellectuals and political activists. Three opinions emerged. Advocates of the first view objected to normalization in the name of cultural authenticity. They argue that developments in the post-1973 era, particularly the 1982 Israeli invasion of Lebanon, proved to the Israeli government that the cost of imposing its hegemony through military power was unaffordable given Israel's size and population. To offset this disadvantage, Israel, according to this view, has embarked on a new strategy of economic and cultural penetration.

The new strategy is seen as being more dangerous in the long run than military power because it pursues penetration behind a veil of economic and cultural disguises. In other words, Israel's aim behind seeking normalization is not in the main cultural or economic. It is instead hegemonic and it may acquire an imperialistic character if the state of Arab disarray and weakness persists. The role of the Arabs in the political and cultural spheres would be marginalized by a hegemonic Israel. In this context, the power of Israel, of an ascendant political and economic entity supported by the West, forced many Arabs to look for means of resistance: "We should say 'no' to normalization, and 'yes' to a real and effective program of development in the economic, social, political, and cultural spheres. A weak party will be always vulnerable to any invasion and to any attempt aimed at imposing hegemony or domination. If we fail to mobilize our resources and our capabilities which are abundant in all domains in order to develop our societies in every sphere, our future will be uncertain in the face of this serious Israeli challenge which infringes upon our very national existence."[38]

In a poem entitled "al-muharwilun" (Those who rush to normalization), which won acclaim throughout the Arab world, Nizar Qabbani did battle with normalization with the weapon of his artistic skills:

> After this secret flirtation in Oslo we emerged barren . . .
> They granted us a homeland smaller than a grain of wheat . . .
> A homeland that we swallow without water like an aspirin
>   tablet . . . After fifty years . . .
> we sit on this wasteland without residence . . .
> like thousands of dogs.
> After fifty years . . .
> we can't find a homeland to dwell in
> . . . Except illusory visions . . .
> It is not peace . . .
> That peace which was plunged into us like a dagger . . .
> It is rather an act of rape!
> What good is rushing to peace [harwala]?

When the conscience of the people is alive like the fuse of a
bomb
. . . All the Oslo signatures are not worth one mustard seed!! [39]

Proponents of the second view stress that the Arabs are bearers of a glori-
ous civilization and that their culture will not be compromised when they
interact with Israel, even though Israel is superior in the military and technological spheres. In an interdependent world, all societies interact. This is
as true of the most sophisticated societies as it is of the least technologi-
cally developed. Moreover, those who subscribe to this view argue that
once a process of political normalization has started between Arabs and
Israelis, cultural normalization will have to follow, and the Arabs need not
fear that process; no one is asking them to disavow their civilizational heritage. As a Palestinian writer has put it: "Life goes on. Different peoples in
different parts of the world are open to each other. We can develop our-
selves by reaching out to others and by learning from their experiences in
all fields of life, including the cultural field. I am absolutely sure that our
mission as intellectuals is to call for cultural openness. Our first priority
should be the fight against introversion. Introversion will not protect our
culture even if the culture of Israel were superior." [40]

The meeting ground, the relationship between a vanquished party and
a victorious party, is the thread running through this debate among Arab
intellectuals. Advocates of the first view are concerned about Israeli domination in all domains of life. "Even Arab oil," wrote Abd al-Karim Ghallab,
"will be influenced by normalization and therefore will become Israeli oil."[41]
Other advocates of this view have also expressed their fear that interaction
with Israel, especially in the cultural and social spheres, may corrupt the
moral fabric of Arab society through the infiltration of ideas and practices
alien to the Arab Muslim social code.[42]

Advocates of the second view begin with a different premise. They are
sure of the strength of their culture, and for this reason they do not feel
apprehensive about contact with Israeli culture. After all, they argue, cultural interaction is a road that the Arabs will have to travel, but with open
eyes.[43]

The third perspective is that of Arab intellectuals and politicians who
object to normalization in the political and cultural fields not because they
have not come to terms with the reality of Israel, nor because they are concerned about Israeli domination, but because they believe that Israel pursues policies that are inconsistent with peace. They cite several problems

that in their view should discourage the Arabs from engaging in normal relations with Israel, including (1) Israel's refusal to recognize the right of the Palestinians to establish their own independent state in the West Bank and Gaza; (2) Israel's insistence on retaining Arab East Jerusalem; (3) Israel's refusal to withdraw from the Golan and South Lebanon; and (4) Israel's refusal to subscribe to the policy of a nuclear-free Middle East. The general feeling among holders of this view is that normalization will become a practical proposition only when all aspects of the Palestinian question, including Jerusalem, are resolved, and when there is a breakthrough on the Syrian and Lebanese fronts. The success of normalization, they also believe, requires more than just agreements between governments. Above all, success requires peace-building activities, most notably concrete Israeli policies that demonstrate no territorial ambitions beyond the lines of June 4, 1967.[44]

This perspective was illuminated by Arab discussions of the participation of Adonis (the pen name of the internationally acclaimed Syrian poet and essayist Ali Ahmad Said) in the UNICEF-sponsored conference in Granada, Spain, in December 1993, attended by Arab and Israeli intellectuals. Two points in particular alarmed Arab intellectuals critical of Adonis. The first was Adonis's suggestion that "Israel geographically belongs to a region of the world whose culture has been based on an interaction and diversity since the days of the Sumarians, the Canaanites, and the Pharaohs."[45] The second point was Adonis's query about whether or not Israel would give Judaism a pluralistic dimension by legitimizing intermarriages and adopting a multicultural approach toward education.[46]

Most Arab critics of Adonis raised the following questions: If Israel still occupies Arab land, and if it still follows hegemonic policies in the region, then why didn't Adonis focus in his Granada speech on those policies instead of raising prematurely questions about cultural diversity and pluralism? If Israel had not accepted international legitimacy with respect to the question of withdrawal from all occupied Arab territories, then why should Adonis support political and cultural normalization with the Jewish state?[47]

These reservations of Arab critics did not amount to an unconditional rejection of normalization, but in the end the depth of Arab frustration with Israel's procrastination, especially in policies toward Lebanon and the Palestinians in the West Bank and Gaza, led to the dismissal of Adonis from the Syrian Union of Arab Writers on January 27, 1995. Yet some of those who voted for his dismissal (90 out of a total of 115 Arab writers) were expressing their opposition to any form of cultural normalization with Israel, irrespective of the outcome of the peace process. "We will reject cultural normalization," stressed Ali Uqla Irsan, president of the Union of Arab Writers, "and we will preserve our cultural citadel, a citadel which has safeguarded throughout history the irrevocable principles and moral values of our nation, and protected our rights and our land."[48]

As Israel stiffened its punitive measures against the Palestinians in the West Bank and Gaza and as it resorted to massive military assaults against Lebanon in April 1996, particularly the Qana massacre of that month, Arab frustration with Israel's policies and U.S. solidarity and empathy with these policies acquired greater depth. The scale and ubiquity of Arab resentment can be gauged from the following lines written by Nizar Qabbani in the aftermath of the massacre of Qana, in which more than one hundred Lebanese civilians were killed by Israel.

Anyone who writes about the history of Qana will call it
Karbala II . . .
Qana took off the mantle
And we saw America
Clad in an old coat of a Jewish rabbi
And leading a massacre . . .
Firing at our children without a cause . . .
At our wives without a cause . . .
At our trees without a cause . . .
At our thoughts without a cause . . .
Is the constitution of the mistress of the world written in Hebrew
In order to humiliate the Arabs?[49]

Such Arab resentment reflected the fear of an unrestrained Israel unleashing its military might to subjugate its Arab neighbors. In the aftermath of Qana, the worst of these fears have been confirmed in the Arab consciousness, particularly in the Arab countries neighboring Israel. And just as the Qana massacre has traumatized the Arab psyche, reinforcing Arab skepticism about Israel's declared interest in peace, the victory of right-wing Likud leader Benjamin Netanyahu in the Israeli elections of May 29, 1996, only served to reinforce the argument of those who saw no potential benefits for the Arabs in the peace process.

The depth of Arab skepticism should not come as a surprise to Western readers, considering the hawkish ideology of the Likud and the intransigent positions expressed by Netanyahu both before and after his election victory. Likud's platform explicitly stated that Israel "will oppose the establishment of an independent Palestinian state," that "united and undivided Jerusalem is the capital of the state of Israel," and that the Likud government will "apply Israeli law, jurisdiction, and administration on the Golan Heights, thus setting Israeli sovereignty over the area."[50] The *Guidelines* of the government of Israel, communicated by Prime Minister–elect Netanyahu's bureau on 17 June 1996, reiterated the Likud platform's principles. The guidelines stressed, inter alia, that Israel "will oppose the establishment of a Palestinian state or any foreign sovereignty west of the Jordan River," reiterated the "status of Jerusalem as the eternal capital of the Jewish people," and emphasized that "retaining Israeli sovereignty over the Golan will be the basis for an arrangement with Syria."[51]

Fear in the Arab world over these developments did not lead to rash acts. Rather, it led to official Arab attempts aimed at salvaging the peace process. It was this desire that led to the Arab summit meeting in Cairo, Egypt, during June 21–23, 1996. Twenty-one Arab countries attended the summit, including fifteen heads of state. Iraq was omitted because the Gulf countries were by no means prepared to help the government of Saddam Hussein return to the Arab fold.

Put within the historical context of Arab summits, the Cairo meeting was unique in underlining the Arab governments' commitment to pursue the course of peace with Israel. In contrast to previous summits, the message of this one was unmistakably clear: to bring about permanent and comprehensive peace as a strategic option. This attitude seemed to rest on the basic reckoning that any deviation by the Likud government from the land-for-peace formula would mean the victory of radical forces in the region and that, if this were to happen, Arab-Israeli relations would slide back into the abyss of violence and confrontation.

Concerning the question of peace, the most significant aspect of the Cairo summit was that it represented the first collective Arab endorsement not only of the peace process but also of the agreements reached between Israel and the Palestinians, and between Israel and a number of Arab governments, including the Israeli-Jordanian peace agreement and the Israeli-Syrian pact of May 1995 on the principles that should govern security arrangements on the Golan.[52]

In conclusion, Arab perspectives on the peace process have been shaped by three central issues: the issue of territory, that is, Israel's withdrawal from the Arab territories it conquered in June, 1967; the question of self-determination by the Palestinian people in whatever is left of their ancestral homeland (the West Bank and Gaza); and the geopolitical role of the Arabs in the shadow of a dominant and U.S-supported Israel. There is in these perspectives a recognition of Arab weakness and disarray, yet there is also in some of them a call to the Arabs to look for means of improving their position vis-à-vis Israel and other outside powers. Some Arabs reject the peace process in the name of ideological purity, and in the name of protecting Arab culture and values. At the same time many Arabs, most notably the political elites in power, have expressed their commitment to pursue peace with Israel as a strategic option. They believe that peace based on pragmatic justice and a balance of interest can serve as a corrective, an antidote to cynicism, and a check against the forces of radicalism.

Notes

1. Nizar Qabbani, "Layla tulaqi al-dhi'b" (Layla meets the wolf), *al-Hayat*, June 7, 1996, 20.

2. See, for example, Muhammad Sa'id Talib, *al-nidham al-'alami al-jadid wal-qadaya al-arabiyya al-rahina* (The New World Order and contemporary Arab questions) (Damascus: Dar al-Ahali, 1994), 239–42.

3. Naseer Aruri, "Recolonizing the Arabs," *Middle East International* no. 385 (October 12, 1990): 18.

4. Ibid., 20.

5. Author of *Cities of Salt, sharq al-mutawassit* (East of the Mediterranean), and other novels.

6. See Rina Sharbil's interview with Abd al-Rahman Munif in *al-Adab* 42, nos. 8–9 (August/September 1994), 33.

7. See the papers presented at the panel discussion organized in Cairo by the Beirut-based Center of Arab Unity Studies on April 21–22, 1991, in *azamat al-khalij wa-tada'iyatuha ala al-watan al-Arabi* (The Gulf crisis and its devastating impact on the Arab homeland) (Beirut: Markaz Dirasat al-Wahda al-Arabiyya, 1991); for a concise analysis of this point, see Walid Khalidi, *The Middle East Postwar Environment* (Washington: Institute for Palestine Studies, 1991), 9–11.

8. Judith Miller, "Saudis Tell of Iraq Hot-Line Drama," *New York Times*, October 4, 1990.

9. Judith Miller, "Six Gulf Nations Meet on Preventing Invasions," *New York Times*, December 23, 1990.

10. Khalidi, *The Middle East Postwar Environment*, 16.

11. Bandar bin Sultan Al-Saud, "An Open Letter to King Hussein," *Washington Post*, September 26, 1990.

12. *Mideast Mirror*, May 11, 1992, 19–20; Muhammad Faour, *The Arab World after Desert Storm*, 86–90.

13. For articles on this point see *Qira'at Siyasiyya* (Political review), an Arabic quarterly sponsored and published by World and Islam Studies Enterprise, vol. 1, nos. 2 and 3; interview with Nabil Shaath, *Journal of Palestine Studies* 23, no. 1 (Autumn 1993): 5–14; and the opinion pages of *al-Hayat*, November-December 1992.

14. For a detailed analysis of this question, see Muhammad Muslih, "The Shift in Palestinian Thinking," *Current History* 91, no. 561 (January 1992): 24–27.

15. Khayriyya Qasimiyya, *al-watan al-Arabi wal-nidham al-'alami, awda ila al-madi wa-waqfa 'inda al-hadir* (The Arab homeland and the world order, a retrospect and a look at the present) (Damascus: al-Dawudi Press, 1994), 128–129. For a similar analysis presented from a Palestinian point of view, see "mashru' wathiqa lil-hiwar" (Draft proposal for negotiations), prepared by Hani al-Hasan, senior member of Fatah's Central Committee, in *Qira'at Siyasiyya* 3, no. 1 (Winter 1993): 203–32. Similar views were expressed by a large number of Arab intellectuals. See in particular Shafiq al-Masri, *al-nidham al-'alami al-jadid, malamih wa-makhatir* (The New World Order, characteristics and dangers) (Beirut: Dar al-Ilm Lil-malayin, 1992), 125–131.

16. See, for example, Hisham al-Dajani, *al-idarat al-amrikiyya wa-Israel* (The American administrations and Israel) (Damascus: Manshurat Wizarat al-Thaqafa), 1994, 167–68.

17. See Ziyad Abu Ghanima, "Filastin al-Islamiyya hiya Filastin al-muharrara" (Islamic Palestine is liberated Palestine), *Liwa' al-Islam* 10 (January 9, 1989), 25ff., and the Charter of the Islamic Resistance Movement (Hamas), August 18, 1988.

18. For discussions of this view, see Muhammad Muslih, "Palestinian Civil Society," *Middle East Journal* 47, no. 2 (Spring 1993): 268–70; Ziad Abu Amr, *Islamic Fundamentalism in the West Bank and Gaza* (Bloomington: Indiana University Press, 1994), 23–53; Hasan Hanafi, *al-usuliyya al-Islamiyya* (Islamic fundamentalism) (Cairo: Maktabat Madbuli, 1989).

19. *Quran*, Sura 8, al-Anfa, verse 61; quotation here is from the translation by Abdullah Yusuf Ali.

20. See Umar 'Abd al-Rhaman, *kalimat haq* (A word of truth) (Cairo: Dar al-I'tisam, n.d.), 127–29.

21. Sa'dun Hamadi, "munaqaqwa li-dawr afil-nahda al-Arabiyya" (A discourse on the role of thought in the Arab renaissance), in *qadaya ishkaliyya fil-fikr al-Arabi al-mu'asir* (Ambiguous questions in contemporary Arabic thought) (Beirut: Markaz Dirasat al-Wahda al-Arabiyya, 1995), 26.

22. Muhammad Abid al-Jabiri, *bunyat al-aql al-arabu, dirasa tahliliyya naqdiyya li-nudhum al-ma'rifa fil-thaqafa al-Arabiyya* (The structure of the Arab mind: An analytic and critical study of the systems of knowledge in Arab culture) (Beirut: al-Markaz al-Thaqafi al-Arabi, 1993), 564.

23. See, for example, Hisham Ghasib, *hal hunaka aql Arabi? qira' naqdiyya li-mashru' Muhammad 'Abid al-Jabiri* (Is there an Arab mind? A critical analysis of the project of Muhammad Abid al-Jabiri) (Beirut: al-Mu'assassa al-Arabiyya lil-Dirasat wal-Nashr, 1993). The term *project* refers to al-Jabiri's analytical framework, which incorporates suggestions for bringing about a real Arab renaissance.

24. Al-Jabiri, *bunyat al-aql*, 572.

25. Muhammad Abid al-Jabiri, *al-aql al-siyasi al-Arabi, muhaddidatuhu wa-ajaliyyatuhu* (The Arab political mind, its determinants and its manifestations) (Beirut: al-Markaz al-Thaqafi al-Arabi, 1991), 374.

26. Ahmad S. Khalidi, "Current Dilemmas, Future Challenges," *Journal of Palestine Studies* 24, no. 94 (Winter 1995): 13.

27. See survey of Palestinian opinion on the DOP in the Jerusalem Arabic daily *al-Quds*, September 1, 1993, 4; interview with Haydar 'Abd al-Shafi, *Journal of Palestine Studies* 23, no. 89 (Autumn 1993): 14–19.

28. For articles and interviews that reflect a position of criticism towards the Oslo agreement, see issues of *Journal for Palestine Studies* (Winter 1994–Summer 1996).

29. See, for example, *Neither Law Nor Justice: Extra-Judicial Punishment, Abduction, Unlawful Arrest, and Torture of Palestinian Residents of the West Bank by the Palestinian Preventive Security Service*, a report published by B'TSELEM, Israeli Information Center for Human Rights in the Occupied Territories, Jerusalem, August 1995; *The Gaza Strip and Jericho: Human Rights under Palestinian Partial Self-Rule*, report published by Human Rights Watch (Middle East), New York City, February 1995.

30. See Anthony Lewis's column in *New York Times*, May 6, 1996.

31. Ghassan Abu Sitta and Abdullah Mufawi, "Arafat's Oppression, Israel's Demands," *New York Times*, July 2, 1996, A1.

32. Edward Said, "Palestinian Versailles," *The Progressive*, December 1993, 22.

33. Edward Said, "For Palestinian Independence," *The Nation*, February 14, 1994, 190.

34. Edward Said, "The Palestinian Case against Arafat," *Washington Post*, December 25, 1994, C4.

35. *Ibid*.

36. Nizar Qabbani, *sariru al-ra'is* (The president's bed), *al-Hayat*, September 4, 1993, 16.

37. Interview with Layla Khalid, *al-Quds*, April 27, 1996, 11.

38. Quoted from the paper delivered by Muhammad Kishli (Lebanon) at the Constituent Assembly of the National Conference against Normalization, Beirut, January 28, 1995, in *al-Manabir*, 9, no. 77 (April/May 1995): 129. For similar views see articles in *al-Adab* (Beirut) 41, no. 11 (1993); *al-Muwajaha* (Cairo), no. 3 (June 1992); and *al-Yasar* (Cairo) no. 30 (August 1992), and no. 31 (September 1992).

39. Nizar Qabbani, "al-Muharwilun" (Those who rush to peace), *al-Hayat*, September 28, 1995.

40. Safi Safi, "al-tatbi' al-thaqafi" (Cultural normalization), *al-Katib* (Jerusalem) 15, no. 159 (December 31, 1994), 6. For similar views, see the comments of 'Abd al-Qadir Salih and Ahmad Barqawi in *al-Adab* 41, no. 11 (1993), as well as articles in *al-Arabi* (Kuwait), March 1995.

41. Quoted in *al-Arabi* no. 449 (April 1996), 12.

42. See Hamid 'Ammar, "lil-ikhtiraq hudud lil-sahyana hudud" (Penetration has its limits, Zionization has its limits too!!), *al-Ahali* (Cairo), May 6, 1992; see also the view of the Jordanian writer Wahib al-Sha'ir as outlined by 'Abd al-Qadir Salih, "al-masar al-thaqafi li-ittifaq Ghazza-Ariha wa-subul al-muwajaha" (The cultural course of the Gaza-Jericho agreement and the methods for confronting it), *al-Adab* (Beirut) 41 (November 1993), 47. This view is expressed in detail in the literature of radical Islamists, particularly in Egypt.

43. A brief but telling exposition of this view can be found in the essay written by Muhammad al-Rumayhi, editor of the Kuwaiti monthly magazine *al-Arabi*, under the title "halat al-laharb wal-lasilim . . . thaqafiyyan" (The cultural dimension of the state of war and no peace), *al-Arabi* no. 449 (April 1996).

44. For arguments expressing this view, see editorial of the Egyptian publication *al-Muwajaha* no. 3 (June 1992): 2; see also the statement of al-Sayyid Yasin, Egyptian intellectual and secretary general of the Arab Thought Forum (mumtada al-fikr al-Arabi) in *al-Ahali* (Cairo), no. 551 (April 29, 1992).

45. Quoted in *al-Adab* (Beirut) 42, nos. 8 and 9 (August/September 1994), 14.

46. See *al-Adab* (Beirut) 43, nos. 3 and 4 (March/April 1995), 21.

47. For this point see "thalathat rudud ala-Adonis" (Three perspectives of Adonis), ibid., 15–42; see also *al-Safir* (Beirut), January 5, 1994; *al-Nahar* (Beirut), April 19, 1994; and the nine issues of *al-Adab* from September/October 1993 through October 1994.

48. *al-Hayat*, January 29, 1995, 1, 4.

49. Nizar Qabbani, "Rachel wa-akhawatuha" (Rachel and her sisters), *al-Hayat*, May 10, 1996, 20.

50. Likud Party, *Peace and Security, Platform for the Elections to the 14th Knesset* (Washington: Embassy of Israel, Office of Public Affairs, May 1996).

51. *Guidelines of the Government of Israel* (Jerusalem: Prime Minister-Elect Netanyahu's Bureau, June 17, 1996).

52. See *al-bayan al-khitami li-mu'tamar al-qimma al-Arabi, al-Qahira, 21–23 Yuniu 1996* (Final communiqué of the Arab Summit Conference, Cairo, June 21–23, 1996) (New York: Egypt Mission to the United Nations, June 23, 1996).

4: The Transformation of Jordan, 1991–1995

Adam Garfinkle

To say that the four-year period from the Madrid summit of October 1991 to the Amman summit of October 1995 was dramatic for the Hashemite Kingdom of Jordan comes close to undermining the very meaning of the word through understatement. Particularly since the famous handshake on the White House lawn between Yitzhak Rabin and Yasir Arafat on September 13, 1993, Jordan's national life has undergone a form of accelerated experience that is massively reshaping the basic architecture of its foreign relations and domestic circumstances, both mainly for the better.

Jordan has been formally at peace with Israel since October 1994 and, among other results, it is better able to sort out its relations with the Palestinians and Palestinian nationalism—a historical challenge of the first order. The kingdom has also improved its standing in Washington, an adjustment that promises greater and less complicated political, economic, and strategic benefits than ever before. Jordan, in turn, moved to rebalance its inter-Arab relationships and by the summer of 1996 had made good progress in this necessary, if never-ending and often frustrating, effort.

Meanwhile, Jordan's domestic economy escaped the acute crises of the 1989–92 period—posting 5–6 percent growth for 1995 and 1996[1]—and its current trajectory is arguably upward bound. While many have hoped for more progress since peace with Israel became a reality, there is little doubt that Jordan's current situation would have been much worse if the many things that have gone basically right for Jordan in the years 1991–95 had instead gone basically wrong. As important, perhaps, is that Jordan's careful experiment in political pluralism, begun in earnest in 1989, has survived the pressure of recent events and emerged the stronger for it. This is notwithstanding the regime's determination to "amend" the pace of this experiment from time to time in the interest of overall social stability.[2]

But all change, even when it is for the better, can be disconcerting. Jordan finds itself today in early contemplation of the consequences of its successes. It is often remarked that Israel might have nearly as difficult a time dealing with the normalcy that peace could bring as it has had with the state of war that has lasted for nearly fifty years. That observation also applies, in its own way, to Jordan. After all, Jordan's history, political psychology, and public agenda have been shaped by the Arab-Israeli conflict no less substantially than have Israel's.

With any luck at all—if the peace process eventually brings peace—both Israel and Jordan will encounter the anticlimax of normalcy. The passing of a difficult but in many ways heroic era will require a new public agenda. Domestic cleavages heretofore submerged in the demands of national security will seem to grow, even if in truth they are only emerging from the shadow of weightier problems since solved. Even if the Arab-Israeli conflict ends, neither history nor politics will end with it, and so we should not be surprised if Goethe in Arabic translation should become popular in Amman, for it was Goethe who warned, "Beware of what you wish for in youth, for you may get it in middle age."

Human beings seem born to complain, to take the shorter rather than the longer view of things; if their objective circumstances are improved, they obey no obligation to humility or gratitude as a result. This is why even successful governments and statesmen sometimes get the wrong kind of respite when they least expect it—like Winston Churchill, cast forth from Number Ten Downing Street by the British electorate at the very apex of achievement in 1945. Mass publics have short memories of great challenges overcome and little patience for delay in solving the lesser problems of the moment. If over the next few years the erstwhile Hussein ibn Talal of Jordan escapes Churchill's plight, it may be only because the office of king of Jordan is not elective.

Perhaps the best way to take the measure of Jordan's present circumstances and its likely future is to look backward to see how it has arrived at the current station. As always in the case of Jordan, telling its tale involves a mélange of relationships: with Israel; with the Palestinians without and within the kingdom; with the regional Arab and Muslim environment; with the United States and, to a lesser degree, the other states of the "first world"; and with how all these relationships impinge on Jordan's domestic political and economic circumstances. Two other constants also bear on the story: Jordan's relative weakness next to nearly all its neighbors is such that its government's reactions to others, more than its own decisions, drive regional dynamics; and both Jordan's demography and geography are such that foreign and domestic issues are never as distinct from one another as they are in most other states. Having said that, let us begin.[3]

Madrid and Beyond

There has never been much doubt among careful observers of the Israeli-Jordanian relationship over the years that Jordan would make peace with Israel if it could do so at an acceptable risk with respect to both its inter-Arab and its internal relationships. It is not the will that has been lacking since King Abdallah came within a few clauses and a few signatures of a peace treaty with Israel in 1951, but the way. Hashemite Jordan's relationship with Israel over the years has been one of mixed amity and enmity, "a state of war with a wink," as Shimon Peres once called it. King Hussein and several generations of Israeli leaders have dealt directly with each other, developed a mutual respect and, especially after 1967, carefully calibrated their policies to reflect a range of common interests. But though they came close, in 1971–72, to an agreement that would have led to formal peace, Jordan's multiple weaknesses prevented it from accepting the maximum that Israel could offer. Jordan's longstanding geopolitical requirements for making peace are worth reviewing in brief as a sort of shorthand guide for the possibly perplexed.

These requirements in 1991 were, as ever before, fourfold: an Israeli government prepared to satisfy Jordan's minimal requirements concerning Hashemite legitimacy, security, land, and water; either protection from or weakness in that part of the Arab periphery opposed to peace; a "downloading," so to speak, of the Palestinian issue onto accepted representatives of the Palestinians; and a U.S. administration that could either facilitate the deal diplomatically and economically or at least avoid doing harm to a deal evolving on its own. Given Jordan's inherent weaknesses, all of these conditions had to be in line simultaneously, as well.

Before the end of the Cold War and the Gulf War, Jordan's "planets" had never lined up properly; afterwards, by the spring of 1991, alignment seemed to be in prospect. Though not without a natural trepidation at the sheer magnitude of what was developing, the king saw that he might soon have the chance of a lifetime to grab the brass ring for Jordan and fulfill at least some of his revered grandfather's dream. Both Abdallah and Hussein recognized that the state of war guaranteed a dangerous double bind for Jordan: being enfolded within an implacable Arab opposition to peace exposed Jordan to a stronger Israel, but making a solo deal with Israel exposed Jordan to stronger Arab states and to the wrath of its own majority-Palestinian population. Both knew that peace was the only way that Jordan's external and internal relations could be brought into potential harmony. Already at Madrid it was clear (to some observers, at least) that if Jordan's planets did line up, Hussein would seize the opportunity that such an alignment represented.[4]

The first of Jordan's conditions was fulfilled with the election of a Labor government in Israel in June 1992. The end of the Cold War and of the Soviet Union itself left the Arab rejectionists without their external support, and the temporary Gulf War alignment of Syria with Saudi Arabia—along with the flattening of Iraq—marginalized the rejectionists still further. Together, these developments delivered the second of Jordan's four requirements. The September 1993 "handshake" took care of the third, and the benign, if accidental, juxtaposition of an activist Bush administration and a quietist Clinton administration at just the right times completed the circle. And indeed, when Jordan's planets lined up, King Hussein launched forth peace. The lining up process may be said to have evolved over a three-year period, from October 1991 to October 1994.

In that part of 1991 before the Madrid conference, the potential for change was in the air but not yet much manifest on the ground. The Madrid summit, the product of a single-minded and highly concerted U.S. diplomacy, began to turn potentiality into reality. The invitations to Madrid tendered by the United States had the air of invitations refused only at one's peril, and when the Syrian government agreed to show up, Israel's could not do otherwise. Securing Israel's presence, however, meant circumscribing the nature of Palestinian representation, for the Shamir government of that day, like both its Likud and Labor predecessors, would not sit with the representatives of a Palestine Liberation Organization whose raison d'être was the destruction of the Jewish state. Bush administration principals judged correctly that regional diplomacy would get nowhere if U.S.-Israeli relations deteriorated too far, and despite the difficult personal relationships between the Shamir government and the Bush administration, the Bush-Baker management of the peace process at that stage delivered to Israel every one of its preconditions for an international conference aimed at ameliorating the conflict.

All of this put Jordan in a very peculiar position. To solve the problem of Palestinian representation, Jordan agreed to provide an "umbrella" for the Palestinians by going to Madrid as one delegation with two parts. Inevitably, and to some extent deliberately, ambiguity enveloped this arrangement as interests collided among the principal parties.

From the Israeli perspective, the Jordanian umbrella lowered the Palestinian profile, which was its chief attraction for the Likud government. But by considering the Jordanian and Palestinian tracks together, the Likud was acting more like Labor, which had since 1967 championed various forms of a "Jordanian option" for solving the problem. A Labor government would have been eager to emphasize the connection, for the greater the Jordanian quotient in a contemplated future Israeli withdrawal, the easier it would pass political muster in Israel. It seemed a strange move, however, for Likud, which opposed turning any of the West Bank back to Jordan as much as it opposed withdrawing the IDF in favor of the Palestinians.

For the Palestinians, the joint delegation was a humiliation, but the only way to get to Madrid. Some Palestinians had a long-term reconnection with Jordan in mind anyway, and for them the arrangement was not problematic. But for the majority of Palestinians, it was a condition to be dispensed with as soon as possible, as in fact occurred soon after Madrid when the Palestinian delegation became, in effect, separate. This majority decided to take its chances with Israel rather than risk falling once again under the Hashemite robe.

For Jordan, the provision of such an umbrella had certain advantages: It promised heightened influence over Palestinian decisions; it played well domestically, as the Jordanian monarchy again told its people that, as in 1948 and 1967, it had spared no effort to help Jordan's Palestinian Arab brothers; it maneuvered the Likud into a less overtly anti-Hashemite attitude; and it advanced the peace process generally, in which Jordan had maintained a long and sincere interest. On the other hand, there was no gainsaying that the PLO in Tunis would have a strong, if incomplete, influence over the Palestinian half of the delegation, and Jordan's desire to promote the PLO was, at best, tepid. Such diplomatic engagements over the years, whether with the European Community or the United States, tended to drive the PLO leadership toward tactical if not genuine moderation, a longstanding goal of Hashemite diplomacy. But helping the PLO too much raised the serious longer-term risk that a successful Palestinian nationalism would undermine the security and national cohesion of Jordan itself.

There were other considerations as well. Jordan was an ally of the United States that had seemed to offer sharply diminishing returns during the Gulf War.[5] To be helpful to American diplomacy in the war's aftermath was, whatever other interests were at stake, at least a chance to mend Jordan's most critical extraregional political relationship. Perhaps most important, unlike many of the participants at Madrid, Jordan genuinely wanted and needed peace. While most countries accepted Washington's invitation because they wanted to make peace with the United States, almost universally referred to as "the only superpower," Jordan was in fact eager to make peace with Israel if the circumstances allowed. It was therefore a matter of some frustration to Jordan that, of all the participants in Madrid, it was the most politically encumbered, by the Palestinian issue, and the most dependent on progress in the Palestinian and possibly the Syrian track. There is hardly a better illustration of Jordan's general predicament.

After Madrid produced the Washington venue for simultaneous bilateral negotiations, the prospects for the peace process depended on decisions by the various parties that they wanted to make peace not with Washington but with each other. In the Syrian case, its decision still is not clear, and that has put the Lebanese case into cryogenic stasis. Jordan's intentions were never in doubt, but its progress was limited by what happened on the Palestinian track. For several months, very little that was good happened.

But while Jordan's public diplomacy was limited by a lack of progress in the Israeli-Palestinian attempt to negotiate an accord on interim self-government, private Israeli-Jordanian understandings evolved nonetheless. Before the June 1992 Israeli election, these were limited to be sure—but not entirely absent. In the course of the Kuwait crisis Yitzhak Shamir and King Hussein met twice; the go-between from the Israeli side was cabinet secretary Elyakim Rubinstein. While the density of private Israeli-Jordanian dealings, and the feelings of respect and trust they engendered, were never as pronounced during periods of Likud rule after May 1977, they were never entirely dropped.[6] Moreover, the Gulf War had a sobering effect on Likud ideologues who had long chanted "Jordan is Palestine." Had Jordan *been* Palestine in January 1991 when the Gulf War started, Iraqi forces might well have been just across the Jordan River instead of several hundred kilometers to the east. The experience taught Yitzhak Shamir and others the value of Jordan as a buffer state (even to the point that, in early 1995, some Likud principals, including Likud leader Benyamin Netanyahu, raised the notion of a Jordanian role in the West Bank in opposition to Labor's elevation of the Palestinian claim and the status of the PLO).[7]

But—true enough—Israeli-Jordanian private negotiations really took off only after Yitzhak Rabin and Shimon Peres returned to power in Israel. Along with the king and his closest aides, Rabin and Peres inherited many years of practical, if limited, cooperation with the Jordanians in such matters as water and agriculture, security and intelligence, communications and navigation, and more besides.[8] Led respectively by Elyakim Rubinstein and Fayez al-Tarawneh, the Jordanian ambassador to the United States, Israel and Jordan assembled the pieces of their peace in anticipation of possible forward movement on the Israeli-Palestinian track. Some of these pieces were updates and reaffirmations of past cooperation (as with banking, for example), some grappled with issues that had never been taken up, and still others focused specifically on how Israel and Jordan could help each other protect their respective interests from a novel factor in the regional equation: a future Palestinian entity less than fully sovereign but still very real. By October 1992 Israel and Jordan came secretly to agreement on the text of a Declaration of Principles—and it was duly leaked and detailed in the Israeli press. But it was put in escrow against the day that Israel and the Palestinians would reach the same stage. That day came about ten months later, in Oslo, on the evening of August 20, 1993.

The Handshake

From mid-1992 on, every advance in the Israeli-Palestinian track was followed quickly, as if in lockstep, by a sometimes less dramatic-sounding but usually more substantive advance in the Israeli-Jordanian track. This was the case even when the Oslo channel emerged into the sunlight and took everyone's breath away—including King Hussein's.

At first the revelation of the Oslo deal shocked and worried the king and his court, not because the king did not expect to deal with the PLO at some point but because he wanted to do so only if the PLO entered the picture along with the West Bank-Gaza Palestinian delegation, not instead of it, and under Jordan's wing to the extent possible.[9] That the Israeli Labor Party had decided to bring the PLO into the picture without warning Jordan, whereas for years Hussein had counted on Labor's sense of Israel's self-interest to keep them out, doubtlessly threw into question one of the king's basic assumptions: that for all practical purposes there could be no solution to the problem of the West Bank (and maybe Gaza) without a level of Jordanian input sufficient to provide leverage against dangerous outcomes. The most dangerous outcomes were associated with high PLO profiles, the least with low PLO profiles.

But the situation is not so simple as this, because the lack of peace was understood to be as dangerous to Jordan as making peace the "wrong" way. The Israel-Jordan-Palestinian triangle has always consisted of offsetting valences: Israel and Jordan are objective allies against unrestrained

Palestinian nationalism and irredentism, but Jordan and the Palestinians are objective allies against the Israeli occupation and all of the distempers it causes—the *intifada*, militant Islamization, and the scourge of regional terrorism all being cases in point. Jordan has objected both to the occupation and to the PLO's being the main vehicle of its termination. With the handshake, the dangers of the former declined as those of the latter rose.

King Hussein is not merely a survivor but a skillful, realistic, and principled survivor. He soon adjusted Jordan's diplomacy to make the best—or prevent the worst—of the new reality. The basic strategy was clear: If Jordan had to deal with the PLO as a virtual diplomatic equal, Hussein would use the peace process to assure genuine moderation of Palestinian aims to the extent possible, and he would simultaneously strive to limit Arafat's freedom of action in areas impinging on Jordanian interests: regional economic relations, the problems of refugees and displaced persons, water, security, and Jerusalem. The solution was to strike deals with Israel on these key issues, in which all three actors had a stake, *before* the PLO could do so. In other words, if Arafat had stolen a march on Hussein at Oslo, Hussein intended to steal it back in multiples. And that is what he did.

The very day after the famous September 13 Rabin-Arafat handshake, a less dramatic but no less important Declaration of Principles was signed in the State Department Treaty Room between Fayez al-Tarawneh of Jordan and Elyakim Rubinstein of Israel.[10] The declaration had been waiting for its public debut for nearly a year before the king activated it. He followed up by meeting Rabin secretly on September 26 on a yacht in the Gulf of Elat.

When the full history of Israeli-Jordanian relations is written, with archives open and memoirs completed, it will become clear how important this meeting was. A general understanding appears to have been reached, and Foreign Minister Shimon Peres's nine-hour meeting at Nadwa Palace in Amman on November 2–3 translated that understanding into writing. Jordan committed itself to a formal peace, and Israel committed itself to accepting in principle Jordan's demands with respect to land and water rights. Some have also speculated that even at this early stage Rabin agreed on behalf of Israel to take Jordan into its air defense sphere—which amounted to a strategic partnership.

Details of the agreement gave Jordan important practical influence over Palestinian autonomy. Jordan requested, and Israel agreed, that Israel maintain control over the Jordan River bridges. Much to the PLO's eventual consternation, Israel and Jordan also agreed that Jordanian banks and the

Jordanian dinar would dominate in the West Bank, thus curtailing the Palestinian bid for an independent currency. Meanwhile, rumors surfaced that Jordan would commence aspects of normalization with Israel before the signing of a peace treaty, and on October 4 Crown Prince Hassan went so far as to address a United Jewish Appeal Women's Division meeting in Washington.

All of these developments left Arafat angrier and more anxious about Jordan than he had been for years, reviving latent antagonism from the years after 1970, when Arafat and the king had been mortal enemies. But just as the Israeli-Jordanian negotiating track seemed to gather real speed in the winter of 1993–94, it stalled. Speaking to reporters in Israel after his return from Amman, Peres charged them to "remember November 3" as a great day, a turning point. The Israeli press soon guessed the essence of what had been agreed on and slapped it on the front page, thereby embarrassing the king. The king then temporized, not in reaction to the indiscretion but because the Israeli-PLO negotiations faltered badly. By late February, thanks in large part to the malign effects of the February 25 massacre perpetrated at Hebron's Ibrahimi mosque by Baruch Goldstein, the Jordanians had fully thrown on the brakes.

But Jordan's basic strategy had not changed, as it showed in other ways. For example, UN Security Council resolution 904 was an attempt to get Israel and the PLO back to the negotiating table by deploring and encouraging "all the usual subjects"—as Inspector Louis Renard might have put it. Although the king had no objection to restarting the Israeli-PLO talks, which resumed on March 31, he asserted that the mention of Jerusalem in resolution 904 was a mistake, complaining vigorously that Jordan had not been consulted. Everyone got the point.

Nonetheless, on the larger question, it was not clear in Amman—or anywhere else—that Rabin and Arafat would be able to translate September's Declaration of Principles into a concrete plan of action. If they could not, then Jordan would again have to wait. In the meantime, Rabin, a bit angry that Jordan's stalling had reduced an element of pressure on Arafat, and fighting a series of waves of terror, lobbed an insult at the king after Jordanian TV televised Hamas threats and showed Palestinians gloating after the Afula terror bomb of April 6, 1994. On April 25, it is likely that Hussein and Rabin, along with Warren Christopher, met privately in London to iron out recent problems and report on the result of Crown Prince Hassan's reported quick visit to Washington on April 20.[11] No doubt they also discussed the next phase, for by April 25 Rabin knew that there would *be* a next phase.

To the Washington Declaration

As it turned out, Rabin and Arafat did manage to translate the September 1993 Declaration of Principles into a plan of action. The May 4 Israel-PLO accord that actually launched limited Palestinian autonomy in Gaza and Jericho gave birth to a three-way peace diplomacy.

The first path, between Israel and the PLO, reached a point where the actual performance of the Palestinian side became important. The second, that between Israel and Syria, remained maddeningly slow, although there were episodic portents of significant movement. The third path of diplomacy, between Israel and Jordan, became dramatic when the May 4 accord sharply reduced King Hussein's remaining inhibitions with respect to a public embrace of Israel. Hussein soon moved with lightning speed from a private agreement in principle with Rabin and Peres to a point just short of a final peace treaty in public view. On the whole, Jordan's appearance as a peacemaker, surprising to some, increased the pressure on the PLO to perform and on Syria to move.

Basic Chronology

1993

September 14	Israel-Jordan Declaration of Principles signed
September 26	Rabin-Hussein secret summit in Gulf of Elat
November 2–3	Peres at the king's palace in Amman

1994

May 4	Gaza-Jericho implementation accord signed
May 19	Rabin-Hussein secret summit in London
June 7	Breakthrough announced in Washington trilateral meeting
July 2	Yasir Arafat arrives in Gaza
July 15	Hussein-Rabin Washington summit announced
July 18	Israeli-Jordanian bilateral talks start at Ein Evrona
July 20	Peres and Christopher in Jordan for trilateral meetings
July 25	Rabin-Hussein Washington summit
August 8	Rabin-Hussein summit at Aqaba
August 24	Israel-PLO early empowerment accord signed
October 26	Israel-Jordan peace treaty signed

For sheer drama, nothing that had happened after September 13, 1993, matched the seemingly sudden reemergence of that fabled wonder of Arab-Israeli diplomacy: the Jordanian option. The fact of the May 4 agreement was good news to Jordan, but the agreement itself held some unpleasant surprises. The Israeli-Palestinian economic accord was far more specific and seemingly more serious than Jordan had expected. Preexisting Jordanian-Israeli understandings concerning agriculture, banking, and other issues were thrown into doubt, and the Israeli-Palestinian agreement to create a single economic space confronted Jordan with a major decision: join the free-trade area west of the river and formally junk the Arab boycott, or risk missing what might be the economic opportunity of the century. Jordan's long-term structural economic problems being what they are, essentially a growing mismatch between population and resources, missing that boat was probably tantamount to drowning.

The king's choice was obvious and he moved decisively. On May 19, the very day after Israel's redeployment in Gaza was completed, Hussein and Rabin again met secretly, this time in London.[12] A few days later Crown Prince Hassan talked matters over with Likud head, Benyamin Netanyahu, also in London, to make sure that an Israeli-Jordanian deal would also be supported by the Likud.[13] Thus assured, on the evening of May 23, the king called Ambassador Tarawneh from London to time the Israel-Jordan public breakthrough to coincide with the forthcoming June 6–7 Washington meeting of the trilateral committee.[14] Evidently, word leaked out within Israeli circles; on June 2, Teddy Kollek, the long-time mayor of Jerusalem, publicly—and perhaps prematurely—invited Hussein to worship there.

On June 7, the State Department spokesman issued a statement that "Israel and Jordan, following consultations held on the occasion of the trilateral meeting, reached a number of understandings in the context of bilateral negotiations leading to a Treaty of Peace." It also stated that the two parties had agreed to meet *in the region* starting in mid-July 1994. Astonishingly, every major U.S. newspaper missed the significance of this statement, running only short, unsigned, nondescript articles off the front page the next morning. To anyone who was paying attention, the phrase "reached a number of understandings in the context of bilateral negotiations leading to a Treaty of Peace" meant that peace was in fact at hand. The announcement of the movement of the diplomacy to the region, while everyone else was still bivouacked in the State Department building in Washington, was an unmistakable sign of a major breakthrough. On June 10, the king took a final internal precaution, bringing a broad-based group of parliamentarians into the cabinet to isolate expected Islamist opposition to the announcement of peace with Israel.[15]

On July 2 Yasir Arafat finally made his entry into Gaza. But he was soon upstaged; a week later, Hussein told the Jordanian people on live television that he would meet publicly with Yitzhak Rabin if that would advance Jordan's interests. "I would consider it a duty and an honor," said the king, emphasizing the word *honor*, "We shall never bow except to God, with God's assistance."[16] Six days later came the surprise announcement that the Hussein-Rabin summit would be held in Washington on July 25. In advance of that summit, bilateral Israeli-Jordanian meetings were scheduled, one of them involving the Israeli foreign minister, Jordan's prime minister, and U.S. Secretary of State Warren Christopher, assembled on Jordanian soil. This was the first time that an Israeli cabinet minister had gone to Jordan—in public.

Some kind of document was needed to make the July 25 summit more than just a photo op. The king had been careful not to promise publicly a final peace treaty; he still preferred not to conclude a *de jure* peace with Israel before some degree of Palestinian self-government was institutionalized. The parties therefore decided to end the "state of belligerency," a dubious distinction between war and peace that the Arabs had long held to be meaningful but that has little basis in international law. In ten days of hard work—much of it facilitated by a Mossad principal, Efraim Halevi—what became the Washington Declaration was spiced with warm diplomatic language, a listing of cooperative projects long on the table awaiting the right moment to blossom forth, and lavish praise for President Bill Clinton.

U.S. participation in the drafting of the declaration was deemed unnecessary by both Hussein and Rabin. A very small number of Israelis and Jordanians—five each, including Hussein and Rabin—drafted the Washington Declaration in utter secrecy. Finally, on Sunday afternoon, at the White House's pleading, the two sides agreed to show the text to President Clinton, who incorporated its main points into his address the next day.

Clearly, the decision to move to the summit was Hussein's, whereas the location reflected a desire by both Israel and Jordan to get U.S. support and money into the picture in return for a much-needed boost for Clinton's beleaguered foreign policy. It worked. After a joint Hussein-Rabin appearance before a joint session of Congress on July 26, the United States agreed to forgive the first $220 million chunk of nearly $1 billion in Jordanian debts to the United States.

Thus did the fabled Jordanian option finally materialize, although not in the simpler territorial form of a simpler day. Rabin and Hussein, both old soldiers in the Arab-Israeli conflict, exhibited the warmth and camaraderie so notably lacking between Rabin and Arafat. Immediately thereafter, the formal vestiges of war began to disappear. On August 3, King Hussein piloted a Lockheed Tristar over Tel Aviv and Jerusalem; as he did, he spoke with Rabin on the ground and the whole conversation was broadcast live on radio. Meanwhile, workers razed old border fortifications and detonated land mines as a new border crossing point just north of Aqaba-Elat was created. On August 8 the king received Prime Minister Rabin publicly in Aqaba—in Jordan. The day before, a direct telephone connection was inaugurated when Israeli President Ezer Weizmann invited King Hussein formally to visit Jerusalem. The dizzying pace left some exhilarated, others numb with wonder. Either way it did not reduce its historical importance.

To the Peace Treaty

The most striking part of the Washington Declaration was its prominent mention of Jordan's past, present, and *future* role in Jerusalem: "Israel respects the present special role of the Hashemite Kingdom of Jordan in Muslim Holy Shrines in Jerusalem. When negotiations on the permanent status will take place, Israel will give high priority to the Jordanian historic role in these shrines."

Both this point and an Israeli invitation to the king to pray at the mosques on the Temple Mount were aimed directly at Arafat's aspiration to make East Jerusalem the possession—and the capital—of a sovereign Palestinian state. For months Arafat had been talking up Jerusalem, and the Palestinians had attempted to turn their headquarters at Orient House into a kind of government center. At this the Israelis drew the line. The Rabin government found in King Hussein's own claims to a special role in caring for the Muslim Holy Places (a descendent of the prophet Muhammad, he had recently regilded the golden dome on the Mosque of the Rock at his own expense) the perfect instrument for its purpose. Arafat's stridency over Jerusalem had gained him only a public humiliation.

A furious Arafat retaliated against Jordan. On July 27 he shut down *an-Nahar*, a pro-Jordanian Jerusalem–West Bank newspaper, in turn creating an uproar of protest against the PLO's alleged dictatorial tendencies. But there was not much more that Arafat could do, and as it turned out, the language about Jerusalem to which Arafat objected was repeated in spirit, if not to the letter, in the peace treaty itself.[17] The point that Arafat was meant to grasp was that from then on the PLO would find Hashemite salt on its tail. Jordan could not wholly displace the PLO in deciding the future of the West Bank and Gaza; that possibility had already gone by the boards in the mid-1970s. But, as mentioned, there were several intersecting issues among Israel, Jordan, and the Palestinians, including economic arrangements, security, refugee compensation, water, and Jerusalem, and Jordan meant to use its historical and personal advantages to get the best deals it could. The result was a kind of bidding contest between Jordan and the PLO, with Israel occasionally getting to choose the proposal it liked best.

The pace did not lag either. After the Knesset approved the Washington Declaration on August 3 by a vote of 91–3, Rabin led an Israeli delegation to Aqaba on August 8 to hammer out the details of a treaty with the king. On August 10 the delegations adjourned, reporting progress on issues such as tourism, electrical grids, and other functional matters. On the same day that Hussein paid a courtesy call to Arafat at the Erez crossing, one of Crown Prince Hassan's sons visited the Israeli city of Ashdod. Soon thereafter, not coincidentally, Israel announced that it would import $30 million worth of goods from Jordan in the near future.

While all this was going on, Jordan was also carrying on a negotiation of sorts with the Palestinian Authority. With the PLO fuming over what appeared to it to be Israel's deliberate stalling while talks with Jordan rushed toward conclusion, the king strived to keep Palestinian anxieties from boiling over. On September 27, for example, Jordan severed all *waqf* (Islamic endowment) links to the West Bank, ended the salaries of their employees, and invited the PA to take over the tasks—but there was no severing in Jerusalem. (On January 25, 1995, Arafat visited Hussein in Amman for the first time since the May 4 accord; Arafat was seething with complaint over Jerusalem. The king let him complain.)

Between the month of August and the signing of the Israel-Jordan treaty in October, carefully paced symbolic normalization paralleled progress in the negotiations. On August 29 talks on border and water issues resumed; while decisions in principle had already been made, working out the particulars was not always easy, and ultimately Hussein and Rabin themselves had to intercede to make the last major reciprocal concessions. Another round of talks resumed on September 12 at Beit Gavriel, near Lake Tiberias; at the same time Jordan announced that Israelis who were dual citizens were welcome to visit Jordan on their non-Israeli passports.

On September 29 *Ma'ariv* reported that the sides had finished their discussions about the border, and only final details with respect to water were left. To discuss this and other matters, Rabin met Hussein in Aqaba on September 30. The final substantive negotiations required before the treaty draft was finished took place on October 10 in Elat: four days of talks between the two sides all but wrapped up the effort. Rabin and Peres went to Amman on October 12 and again on October 16, mainly to discuss the nature of the signing ceremony. The next day Rabin and Hussein initialed the treaty and scheduled the signing ceremony in the Arava for October 26.[18] The king then made his first public visit to Israel, an informal one to Beit Gavriel, on November 10, 1994.[19] After an impassioned speech at Yitzhak Rabin's funeral on November 6, 1995,[20] Hussein paid his first official state visit to Israel on January 10, 1996.

Israel and Jordan after the Peace

The larger Arab-Israeli peace process walked from the autumn of 1994 into the winter of 1995 with an angel of peace on one hand and the specter of failure on the other. Even as bells rang out and doves took flight to celebrate the Israeli-Jordan Peace Treaty on October 26, 1994, terror stalked Israeli streets while deepening despair and poverty haunted the Palestinian redoubt in Gaza. The peace treaty opened a new chapter in Israel's history, pointing to a new regional and international stature, whereas the failure to pass the joint test of security for Israel and economic stabilization for the Palestinians threatened the inner core of the peace process itself.

There is no doubt that the Israel-Jordan breakthrough helped Israel broaden rapidly a pattern of normalization with Arab and Muslim states that heretofore would have no public dealings with it. From the Casablanca economic summit at the end of October 1994 to Israel's bilateral engagement with several Arab states, it was clear that a new regional psychology and political dynamic were being created. The Arab states would openly pursue their own interests with no more than rhetorical regard for the Palestinian issue, the crucible of Pan-Arabist pretension since the creation of the Arab League in 1945. Not all the Arab states would rush to make peace with Israel nor would those already at peace necessarily seek a warm relationship. But the fate of the Palestinians was now a matter for Palestinians alone to reckon.

Jordan's role in shaping this new dynamic has been considerable. The Jordanian government has done everything in its power to ensure a warm peace with Israel, and it has emphatically refused to link the ups and downs of the Israeli-Palestinian relationship to the Israeli-Jordanian one. Israeli-Jordanian relations made steady strides forward, whereas Israeli-Palestinian relations remained mired in difficulty for the most part. Despite efforts in Jordan by Palestinian-dominated professional organizations and Islamist groups to retard normalization, ambassadors were exchanged, Israel withdrew on schedule from Jordanian territories as specified in the peace treaty, the two sides began working together to raise money for water and other joint projects, Israel lobbied effectively in the U.S. Congress on behalf of aid to Jordan, and there have even been joint Israeli-Jordanian diplomatic forays—in support of Bosnian refugees, for example.

Also, rumors (probably accurate) emerged about the extent of quiet Israeli-Jordanian military and intelligence cooperation against potential threats to the north and east.[21] Symbols have been unfurled, too, some suggestive of military cooperation still below the line of sight. On October 22, 1995, for example, shortly before the first anniversary of the treaty signing, Israeli F-15s and F-16s flew in formation with Jordanian Mirages and F-5s, along with Jordanian and Israeli helicopters bearing the countries' two flags and a banner proclaiming peace. The air show passed over Tel Aviv, Jerusalem, Tiberias, Acre, Amman, Irbid, and Zarqa.[22] In March 1996, the Jordanian chief of staff, General Abed el-Hafez el-Kabanna, paid a two-day visit to Israel to discuss Israeli-Jordanian military cooperation. Following the December 1995 trip by a large Israeli delegation to Amman to discuss border security and other matters, the Palestine Authority must have wondered just what all this Israeli-Jordanian cooperation was aimed at.

Meanwhile, Jordanian and Israeli businesspeople have been doing business—even if much of it is still sub rosa[23]—and the flow of people and goods both ways across the border has become increasingly smooth and routine despite mighty efforts by those opposed to peace to punish the Jordanian pioneers of normalization in journalism, business, and the arts.[24] Within sixteen months after the signing of the treaty, no fewer than fourteen significant bilateral accords were signed between Israel and Jordan, and the majority have been implemented as well. One of the most important, the transportation agreement allowing bus and private vehicular traffic between Israel and Jordan, was wrapped up in January and implemented in April 1996. Even before the transportation agreement went into effect, tourism in Jordan in 1995 had increased by 25 percent over that in 1994.[25] Both sides expected significant further increases.

Many big commercial deals were also cut; on October 29, 1995, for example, Israeli megabusinessman Shaul Eisenberg left for Amman to sign a $50 million joint investment in Dead Sea–related projects.[26] Other large deals lie just ahead, from water infrastructure projects to Jordan's serving as a terminus for Qatari natural gas destined for both Jordan and Israel. Although many enthusiasts of peace have been impatient for the economic benefits of the peace treaty to flow to ordinary people, in fact the record is not bad.

At Home and Abroad after the Peace

Among developments in Israeli-Jordanian relations since October 1994, the most important are Jordan's relationships with the Palestinian Authority, with the United States, and with the rest of the Arab world.

Hussein and Arafat: Not Together Again

The Israeli-Palestinian agreements and the Israeli-Jordanian Treaty have transformed in important ways the whole gamut of Jordanian-Palestinian relations on both the official level, between the Jordanian government and the Palestinian Authority, and the sociopolitical level within Jordan. The sociopolitical area includes Jordan's democracy experiment and the prospects for long-term social stability after the tenure of the current king.

As to official relations, it is clear that Jordan is reconciled to a PLO-led entity of some sort in the West Bank and Gaza. Since this is an element in regional peace, which Jordan desires, Amman cannot reject such an entity, but the king and his court have never trusted Arafat and his entourage. King Hussein once told a U.S. confidant, a close colleague of an American diplomat with extensive experience in Jordan, that he would rather give the key to al-Aksa mosque to the confidant than to Yasir Arafat. In the gut feeling of many Jordanians who have been through the diplomatic and literal wars with the PLO over the years is a gnawing suspicion that Arafat has not really changed, and that when he finds his ambitions blocked by a strong Israel, he will use his West Bank base to undermine, irritate, and discomfit Jordan. They may be right, too. In any event, until time clears the picture, Jordan is not inclined to see the Palestinian domain grow very far or very fast. Economic relations are one way Jordan hopes to deal with this problem.

Many Palestinians, as well as supporters of the PLO in the United States, argue that if Israel enforces closures against the Palestinians as a whole as an element of a strategy aimed at defeating Islamist terror, then at least Israel should allow the West Bank and Gaza's border to be opened to Jordan and Egypt, respectively. Israel may choose separation, they say, but it should relieve the Palestinian pressure cooker by allowing economic access to and from Jordan and Egypt. What they seem not to recognize—or are not willing to admit—is that neither the Jordanian nor the Egyptian government particularly desires open economic relations with the Palestinians. Most Jordanian exporters (including those who are Palestinian) prefer more vibrant markets than the poor Palestinian one, while Jordanians who produce for the home market are less than enthusiastic about a flood of lower-cost Palestinian vegetables, clothing, ceramics, and tourist items into Jordan. Indeed, some Jordanians even speak—albeit quietly—of Jordanian laborers eventually replacing "unreliable" Palestinians in the Israeli economy.[27]

Jordan signed agreements concerning agriculture and trade with the Palestinians only in late January 1995, several months after the Israel-Jordan treaty.[28] The terms were vague and heavily favored Jordan. Earlier, the PLO had resisted several Jordanian demands, and Amman's response was to apply the squeeze: The Jordanians simply stopped all trade.[29] The PA has sought to revise the January 1995 agreements in the Palestinians' favor, but this has not worked out well.[30] The result is that Jordan, in effect, shares Israel's policy of squeezing the Palestinians, and there is to date more economic cooperation between Jordan and Israel than there is between Jordan and the Palestinians.[31] One Palestinian expressed his ire this way: "The markets in the OPT [occupied Palestinian territories] are full of Arab and non-Arab products that were imported as a result of trade contacts and economic agreements with Israel. This is an attempt to marginalize the Palestinian economy and a violation of the agreement. Why is Israel importing a large quantity of Jordanian olive oil, as was recently announced? It is an intentional attack on the Palestinian economy."[32]

Clearly, Jordan's pervasive wariness toward Palestine is equaled by Palestinians' suspicions of Jordan. To cite one small but telling matter, the Palestinian Authority decided to start Ramadan on January 31, 1995, one day earlier than in Jordan—the Palestinians taking their cue from the Saudis, who saw the crescent moon before the Jordanians did.[33] A somewhat larger matter was Arafat's belief that Jordan was conspiring against him with Hamas, when in fact Jordan's sufferance of some Hamas spokesmen had other, lesser causes.[34]

Most members of the Palestinian elite believe that Jordan wants to hurt them by making sweet deals with Israel at their expense. They find Jordan's claims in Jerusalem to be maddening, and Jordan's reappointment of a mufti in 1994, in parallel to the appointment of one by the PA, to be confrontational. They also suspect that Jordan conspires with Israel to keep them penned up in their truncated lands, and the PA—including Arafat himself, with some vehemence[35]—has also claimed that Jordan is in league with Hamas, the aim being to return Hashemite rule to the West Bank.[36] Some believe as well that the king is trying to parlay his new relationship with Israel and the United States into a megalomaniacal bid for regional Arab leadership.[37] "Talking about his grandfather's assassination here at the hands of a Palestinian in the '50s and drawing parallels between that and the death of Rabin is far from innocent," said a senior Palestinian Authority official just days after Rabin's funeral. "This is not just emotional. The king is vying for a new role in the region with Israel and America's help at our expense."[38] Hassan Asfour, a leading member of the PA and a close colleague of Mahmud Abbas, stated just before Hussein's arrival: "I do not believe there are any implications to [Hussein's] visit. It is only a matter of giving condolences and participating in the funeral of one of the partners in the peace process. We *hope* there will be no political implications of the visit."[39] But soon thereafter Jordan raised the idea of offering West Bank residents passports, which are more easily obtained than Palestinian travel documents—as if to say, life would be easier under Jordanian rule. To drive home the point that Jordanian dominance is not what he has in mind, Arafat ordered in March 1996 that the Jordanian term *West Bank* no longer be used to describe what he ordered to be called the Northern Districts (al-alwiyah al-shamaliyah) of Palestine.[40]

Nevertheless, Palestinian officials, including Arafat himself, speak frequently about confederation between an independent Palestine and Jordan. In late January 1996, shortly after the Palestinian election, Arafat reportedly said: "It is a very important springboard for the establishment of the Palestinian state that will unite us with our Jordanian twin brother in a confederation. This is something of which we are proud. We await a sign from our big twin brother, his majesty the King."[41] Why does Arafat say such things? Is he really sincere about confederation or, when he uses the phrase "twin brother," is he implying equality now but thinking that in the long run Palestinians will overwhelm east bankers and take control on both sides of the river? Does he aim such remarks at Jordan's Palestinian population in an effort to undermine Hashemite rule? Or is he trying only to butter up the king to get him to relent on the economic and diplomatic pressures Jordan applies to the Palestinians? Depending on when and how Arafat speaks, all of these possibilities seem to be at work.

Just as Israelis are often at a loss to figure out why Arafat does what he does and says what he says, so are Jordanians. But they typically think the worst of his intentions—perhaps as much as do most Israelis nowadays. So there will be no go sign from the king anytime soon on confederation. But the Jordanians do not dismiss the notion out of hand; they play the game, too. Following a meeting with Chairman Arafat after the Palestinian elections, for example, Abdul Karim al-Kabariti, who was then Jordanian foreign minister, said that Jordan can support in principle a future federation, but sooner than that Jordan would like to see a council established to discuss "strategic issues" between the two people. It would be impolite and an unnecessarily roiling of public opinion to speak otherwise, but nowadays—as opposed to the case a decade ago—it is Jordan that plays hard to get over confederation. The shift shows that when the king felt the Palestinians still weak enough to be contained, confederation served as a vehicle for containment, but when he came to believe that they were too strong to be contained, confederation would instead serve as a contaminant to Jordan.

The matter of Jordanian-Palestinian confederation is complicated by Israel's attitude. Most of the Israeli Labor Party and much of the Likud nowadays want as large a Jordanian role within the Palestinian domain as possible, for all the old reasons and some new ones.[42] Indeed, Shimon Peres is reported to have rejected a preliminary final status paper prepared by Yossi Beilin in the fall of 1995 in part because it failed to specify a formal link between a future Palestinian entity and Jordan.[43] According to Ma'ariv, Peres himself forced Arafat and Hussein to discuss the matter in his presence in September 1995; after the meeting Peres confessed that while Hussein and Arafat "understand that this is the preferred solution," they "still need to find the magic formula to live together."[44]

None of this means that Jordan wants Palestinians in the West Bank and Gaza to remain isolated and desperately poor, for that makes them politically unreconciled to peace and stability. In the best of all possible worlds, the international community would keep its promises and help the Palestinians get to their feet. There is no bias in Jordan against the Palestinians getting aid, just not money that would otherwise go to the Jordanians. In general, Israeli-Jordanian arrangements on several levels—building bridge crossings that avoid the West Bank, keeping the Jordanian dinar legal tender in the Palestinian areas, reaching water sharing and development agreements separate from the Palestinians, and so forth—facilitate Jordan's economic interests. Yossi Alpher has put the basic dynamic well: "On the one hand, Jordan favors the establishment of a Palestinian entity capable of absorbing Jordan's own surplus Palestinian population, i.e., its refugee population. This implies the emergence of a Palestinian entity with a fairly robust socioeconomic and political profile, one that could maintain stability and prevent the departure of disgruntled Palestinians eastward, to Jordan. This attitude is reflected in the Jordanians' use of the term 'demographic security.' Yet on the other hand, it is important to Jordan that the Palestinian entity not be so strong or dynamic . . . that it poses a threat toward the Hashemite Kingdom: the threat of economic or demographic 'Palestinianization.'"[45]

On the domestic social level, the Palestinianization issue dominates too, albeit in a different way. From 1948 through 1967 Hashemite Jordan tried to Jordanize the Palestinians, indeed to expunge the very notion of Palestinians from the cultural and historical air. It was no coincidence that King Abdallah chose the name West Bank instead of the Transjordanian province of Palestine. In the 1967 war, however, Israel's greatest military victory unleashed its worst political demon—Palestinian nationalism—from the clutches of the Arab states.

After 1967, what had been an aggressive cultural effort at Jordanization became gradually a defensive one. The sharpening of Palestinian identity led in due course to a reciprocal sharpening of east banker identity as well, but in a transtribal form. Economic problems coupled with the migration of much better educated, younger east bankers to the cities has created more antagonism among groups in Jordan, not less as is commonly believed.[46] Whatever the causes, many Palestinians feel they are second-class citizens in Jordan, and that alone is enough to make a Palestinian homeland just to their west seem symbolically attractive. Hence, some counsel Jordan to stop competing with the Palestinian Authority entirely and to rectify inequality within Jordan in order to strengthen the Jordanian identity of the Palestinians there. Jordan is also advised to accept wholeheartedly the establishment of a maximally sovereign Palestinian state because, writes Ali Jarbawi, "that is the only framework that can possibly guarantee the containment of the Palestinians and pose a limit on their aspirations."[47] But nowhere does Jarbawi lay out the logic behind this claim: How does making a Palestinian state maximally sovereign and strong reduce its appeal to Palestinians in Jordan?

But this does not identify Jordan's dilemma: If Jordan represses its Palestinian citizens, it makes Palestinian identity more attractive. But if it doesn't place limits, then Jordan Palestinizes itself by default. It's another kind of Jordanian double bind, and there is no way out of it. At the very least, Jordan will force Palestinians to choose between identities, allowing no form of dual Palestinian-Jordanian citizenship. It enforces choice through devices such as selective rules on eligibility for a Jordanian passport. After the July 31, 1988, Jordanian disengagement from the West Bank, most Palestinians could not get passports, only lesser, two-year "travel documents." In late December 1995, however, in an appeal to the loyalty of certain higher strata of Palestinians in Jordan, Amman again began granting passports, to many but not all Palestinians, saying that "mistakes had been made."

"All Jordanians are equal," proclaimed the king, "and they are a part of this country until they decide of their own will to take a different course."[48] In this way, clearly, Jordan hopes to marginalize the Palestinian refugee population on the east bank—some 300,00 to 350,000 people still residing in refugee camps—in the hope that they will eventually depart for the West Bank; meanwhile, Jordan will integrate other Palestinians. Both dimensions of this approach may well be politically popular in Jordan, not only among east bankers but also among the more socially and economically well-positioned of Jordan's Palestinian population.

But the issue is not easy to deal with by any stretch of the imagination; Jordanians—both Palestinians and east bankers—are sharply divided over how to handle the country's divisions in light of new realities west of the river.[49] While a majority seem in favor of some kind of future confederation between Jordan and a Palestinian entity, some Palestinians want to turn Jordan into a Palestinian base from which to destroy all of Israel. Some ultranationalist east bankers, like the gadfly Ahmed Oweidi Abbadi, a former parliamentary deputy, insist that Palestinians not enjoy Jordanian citizenship and that the government tax 51 percent of all Palestinian earnings in Jordan. Peace process diplomacy has, if anything, sharpened the division of views—but that was an inevitable development if the matter is ever to be brought to real resolution.

Jordan and the Second Anglo-Imperial Epoch

Jordan's relationship with the United States has a new layer as well. Aside from direct financial rewards, which, while appreciated, have been a disappointment to Jordan,[50] Jordan figures prominently in the U.S. strategic views of the region as a whole. There are several reasons for this.

Jordan is a bulwark of moderation in the region, both politically and religiously, and it has the best record of politically containing—without overt violence and repression—a rising Muslim tide.[51] Jordan's king was the first Middle Eastern leader to take the measure of the threat posed by the Iranian revolution in 1978–79. (The king is, after all, a descendent of a prophet.) The United States wants others in the region to follow Jordan's general path, even if Jordan's circumstances cannot be replicated elsewhere.

Moreover, the only region in the world where U.S. military power is growing is the Middle East, particularly in the Persian Gulf. The U.S. Navy has created the Fifth Fleet and has bolstered its military presence and ties throughout the Gulf. Much as British interest in the Levant at the time of World War I was related to the Gulf (due to India), the United States sees as crucial a stable Jordanian buffer between the many distempers of the Gulf and the Eastern Mediterranean. The Jordan leadership sees itself within the framework of the second Anglo-imperial epoch of the century in the Middle East.

Beyond that, Jordan's skilled military has stood as both actual and potential proxy for the United States—and before that, for the British—in the Gulf emirates. While 1980s talk of a Jordanian Rapid Deployment Force for the Gulf was stillborn because of excessive, premature public discussion, the idea is still basically sound. Now that Jordan's relationship with Israel has entered a wholly new phase in defense-related matters, not only is Jordan freed up for duty to its east but Israel also forms a kind of strategic depth for it in this regard.

Against this background, it is hardly surprising that when Iraqi forces made threatening noises immediately after Saddam Hussein's sons-in-law defected to Jordan in August 1995, the United States promised to defend Jordan with Tomahawk cruise missiles if Iraq intervened.[52] The United States also quickly received Israeli permission to overfly Israel to help Jordan in an emergency with U.S. naval forces in the Mediterranean.

In mid-January 1996 the U.S. Defense Department announced that it would give Jordan twelve used F-16A fighters, four F-16B fighters, fifty M60A3 tanks, an AC-130 cargo plane, a helicopter, and other equipment worth about $300 million. The United States also provided about $200 million for hangar construction, training, spare parts, and F-16 upgrades. All this equipment was past its "height of life" usefulness to the United States and had been mothballed. Israel and Jordan announced that they would consider an Israeli bid to provide maintenance for the aircraft, and the United States looked kindly upon the possibility. As Secretary of Defense William Perry put it at the time: "Israeli leaders welcomed my announcement that the U.S. would supply a squadron of F-16 fighters to Jordan. A few years ago Israel and Jordan were in a state of war, and this weapons transfer would have been truly unthinkable. Today, it is another step toward peace."[53]

In a March 1996 move that was perhaps a bit more surprising, though logical, the U.S. Air Force announced that it would dispatch thirty-four fighters to Jordan in a show of power against Iraq. The F-15s and F-16s began in April to fly reconnaissance missions over the "no fly" zone in southern Iraq from bases in eastern Jordan, the first time that the United States and Jordan cooperated in such an endeavor. The announced reason for the program was that the aircraft carrier *Nimitz* was leaving the Gulf (for the general vicinity of the Taiwan Straits) and its replacement, the USS *George Washington*, would not arrive until July.[54] The announcement, however, coincided with the king's annual springtime visit to Washington and clearly indicated a heightened level of integration and coordination among the United States and Jordan and Israel with regard to the Gulf. Indeed, Shimon Peres went so far as to suggest a U.S.-supported regional alliance during his visit with President Clinton on December 14, 1995. The alliance was to include only Israel and Jordan at first (not Egypt), perhaps others later.[55] This prospect seemed far-fetched to many at the time, but on December 27 a large Israeli military delegation traveled to Jordan to discuss issues ranging from joint electronic border to more general matters.[56] In February Israel and Turkey reached a major military agreement, and the shape of a regional partnership in fact began to emerge.

The path of the new U.S.-Jordanian relationship has not always been smooth, the mood of Congress being the cause for most of the bumps. Even achieving forgiveness of Jordan's $375 million debt to the United States was difficult, though it was small change compared with the kind of money the United States fronted for Israel and Egypt at the time of the Camp David accords. Nearly $100 million of the debt was written off in 1994, but further installations were held up for weeks by Congressman Sonny Callahan (R–Ala.), chairman of the House Foreign Operations Subcommittee, who slashed the remaining $275 million to $50 million and who seemed oblivious to the significance of the matter. President Clinton accused him of being an isolationist, which only made him more determined to be obstructionist.[57] (Callahan was at it again in February 1996, when he opposed the arrangement for the United States to provide Jordan with mothballed F-16 aircraft because he was piqued that the administration had failed to consult properly with Congress. This made for much heartburn in the Jordanian Embassy but in the end little more trouble than that.)[58]

Between Iraq and a Hard Place in the Gulf

On the basis of the strengthened foundation of the Jordanian-Israeli peace and improved U.S.-Jordanian cooperation, King Hussein has concentrated much attention since the summer of 1995 on reshuffling his regional hand. In this he has received considerable encouragement and diplomatic support from the United States.[59] What the king has tried to do, the Israeli and American "rear" having been secured, is to move away from Iraq to the maximum extent possible without a total break, in order to restore normal—but not dependent—relations with Saudi Arabia and Kuwait.

The king's movement away from Ba'athist Iraq has involved letting the U.S. Air Force use Jordanian bases to overfly Iraq, cutting Iraq's trade with Jordan (Jordan being its main and only legal outlet to the outside world),[60] shutting down the most flagrant Iraqi business fronts operating from Jordan,[61] reducing the size of the Iraqi "diplomatic" legation in Jordan, hosting Saddam Hussein's defected sons-in-law in August 1995 until their ill-fated return to Iraq in February 1996, hosting a variety of other regime dropouts,[62] intercepting illicit material headed toward Iraq that somehow had gotten through before,[63] and trying to coordinate Iraqi opposition groups into a force capable of replacing Saddam and the Ba'ath.[64]

Taken together, this was strong medicine with which to douse a man like Saddam Hussein. The Iraqi media response was remarkably restrained, and, in what appeared to be a bizarre juxtaposition, Iraq and Jordan managed to extend a special arrangement by which Jordan took Iraqi oil at special prices as debt repayment, and they did so in the very midst of Jordan's anti-Saddam campaign. This would seem to confirm Iraq's dependence on Jordan as its only window to the world, which was the subject of a joke that Crown Prince Hassan told foreign correspondents: "Have you heard the Israeli political joke? The Israeli says to the Jordanian—the usual Israeli complaint—'We're surrounded by enemies.' And the Jordanian says, 'You think you have a problem? We're surrounded by friends!'"[65]

As all of this was going on, no doubt, the Jordanians were looking over their shoulders to see if they could detect smiles on the faces of Saudi and Kuwaiti princes. It took a long time to raise them, and it took a little midcourse correcting as well. At one point, the king had called for a "federal" Iraq, but he backed off when suspicious Saudi minds read into his words an attempt by Hussein to reestablish the Hashemites by hook or by crook in Baghdad.[66] Adjustments made, Jordanian efforts finally, by late 1995, raised the intended smiles—at least to some extent.

The rapprochement began directly after the defection of Saddam's sons-in-law. King Hussein assented to a Saudi request to "interview" the two men; Prince Turki al-Faisal, the Saudi intelligence chief, paid an unannounced visit to Amman in late August 1995 to do so. In October the king met in New York with Prince Sultan bin Abdel-Aziz, the Saudi deputy prime minister.[67] On November 11, a new Saudi ambassador, Abdallah Budairi, arrived in Amman. In January 1996 Saudi Foreign Minister Saud al-Faisal paid a one-day visit to Amman, and not long after that the king made the minor pilgrimage (umra) to Mecca. King Fahd did not yet receive King Hussein, a disappointment that his own ministers had not predicted, but Hussein did see Crown Prince Abdallah.[68] By mid-March 1996, even the Kuwaitis were beginning to show signs of accepting a thaw in relations frozen since August 1990.

Jordan has not had much success at improving its relations with Syria or Egypt. Hafiz al-Asad's vitriolic reaction to Jordan after October 26, 1994, was strong and has been unrelenting. Trade between the neighbors is virtually nil, and Hussein remains exasperated by thuggish Syrian gestures. As Ehud Ya'ari reported, "Hussein gripes that the Syrians often place loudspeakers by the border post at Ramtha and blast propaganda, 'North Korean-style,' into the Hashemite Kingdom."[69]

But loudspeakers represent a distinct improvement over the days when Asad sponsored deadly bombings in Amman. The Jordanians are so confident that Syria is too weak to be a spoiler that in December 1995 they transferred pipes purchased in Turkey across Syrian territory. The pipes will carry the Jordanian water quota from the pumping station at Beit Zera on the Israeli side to feed the Ghor Canal on the Jordanian side. Also, as Ya'ari reported at a mid-December 1995 international arms control workshop at Petra, "participants described the condition of the Syrian army in the bleakest of colors."[70]

As for Egypt, its relations with Jordan have been cool even before Madrid. Egyptian Foreign Minister Amr Musa rebuked Jordan at the October 1995 Amman economic summit for rushing ahead with normalization with Israel at an unseemly speed. In a tart response, the king recalled Egypt's unerring unilateralism in the 1977–79 period when it made peace with Israel against the Arab consensus. "If moving toward peace is rushing," said the king, "it [Egypt] preceded us 17 years ago." This brought an outbreak of applause. "If we have in mind a sincere, serious attempt to compensate for wasted time," the king continued, "we will not only rush, but run to compensate for the time to give our people a free and honorable life."[71]

To some extent, the coolness in Jordanian-Egyptian relations is personal: Hussein and Hosni Mubarak lack a positive interpersonal chemistry. But Egypt has also been stung by several Israeli-Jordanian infrastructure projects that threaten Egyptian economic interests, although not gravely so, including the utility and value of the Suez Canal. Egypt is simply having trouble asserting its big-brother status at the latest phase of the peace process, which ironically has made the Egyptian role as the bridge from Israel to the Arab world less central. Jordan, as a small country that failed to muster beneath Egypt's leadership in August 1990, pays a price for Egypt's injured pride.

In short, Jordan's relations with Syria are bad, with Egypt are cool, with Iraq uncertain, and with the Gulf states are not improving quickly enough. The point, however, is that all of this is easier to live with now that Jordan's stronger neighbor, Israel, is its friend and the Palestinian Authority is very, very weak.

Another Day, Another Dolor

It is hard not to be impressed by Jordan's achievements in the years 1991–95. In the late 1980s and through 1991–92, the country remained fixed in its historic dilemma: a moderate, pragmatic, and civilized country sandwiched tightly between worried Israelis and avaricious Arabs and prone to be a victim of circumstances determined mainly by others—"Hell's firewood," Crown Prince Hassan once called it. Jordan's internal situation was tense: Islamists threatened the country's social comity and, potentially, the crown itself; there was sporadic political violence and before November 1989 long-unmet demands from Jordan's growing middle classes for democratization. The king was sick with cancer and possibly other medical problems. The economy was in deep trouble, with as many as a quarter million mainly Palestinian "returnees" from the Gulf complicating matters. Relations with Egypt and the Gulf states were terrible, the latter contributing much to Jordan's economic woes. Because of the economic crisis and other problems, social tension between the Palestinian and east bank halves of the country worsened, and irreconcilable, contradictory demands plagued the royal house in consequence.

By the summer of 1996, in contrast, Jordan was at peace with Israel and had gained a more solid protector of last resort in Israel than it ever had in the United States.[72] Perhaps as important an improvement, Palestinian nationalism has lost much of its romantic luster as it struggles with actual governance. Thanks to the triangular diplomacy of the Zionist-Hashemite-Palestinian domain, too, Jordan has a leg up on the Palestinian Authority in several important areas—Jerusalem included—and the Palestinians know it. Jordan's broader inter-Arab relations are mending even without its being forced to give up the Iraqi connection entirely.

Internally, the Islamists have been reduced in power through the regime's skillfully managed strategy of political inclusion; there is little overt opposition to the government and virtually no political violence. Democratization is working more or less as planned: slowly and under experimental control. The king appears healthy, as does the economy in general, the Gulf War returnees having been integrated reasonably well. Conflict between Palestinians and east bankers within the kingdom still exists, but it has been displaced to some degree by intra-Palestinian cleavages, between those who oppose normalization with Israel and those determined to get rich from it. Meanwhile, Jordan's tribesmen look forward to the prospect of many of the country's unintegrated refugees leaving for the West Bank.

However, intuition tells us that a small, vulnerable, poor country cannot possibly have such good luck for long. What might go wrong?

If the king should die before long, his talented and well-intended brother might nevertheless be unable to duplicate the king's successes. The population probably will continue to outrun even solid economic growth. The victory of the Gama'a Islamiya in Egypt—however unlikely—might set off a mousetrap effect and revive Islamic fortunes in Jordan. Iraq might collapse into three or more pieces and result in Shiite-Iranian power perched on Jordan's eastern border. Numbing conflict with Israel over refugee compensation and other issues could blunt and even reverse normalization, particularly now—as of May 29, 1996—that a Likud government rules Israel.

Many Likud sympathizers and some others reasoned that King Hussein and his government were secretly pulling for the Likud, and were quietly elated by its victory.[73] The logic behind this: If Palestinian nationalism is the Hashemites' most serious long-term threat, then, after the dizzying historical reversal in recent years, Likud is today a far more reliable objective ally than Labor. There is also some evidence of Hussein's support. After Israel's Operation Grapes of Wrath against Hizbollah forces in Lebanon went bad in April 1996, Hussein told Peres that he would not be welcome in Amman during the Israeli campaign—a gesture thought at the time to be aimed at propitiating an aroused Jordanian opinion and nothing more. Also, Hussein's remarks upon Netanyahu's victory were remarkably placid and restrained, certainly compared to those of other Arab leaders.[74]

Perhaps this is what the king thought, but the matter was neither clear nor simple. Publicly at least, Hussein maintained that he would not be a substitute for Arafat, no matter what Israel's new prime minister supposed, nor would he entertain proposals concerning Jordanian-Palestinian confederation until a Palestinian state had come into being. More important, Hussein had to know that if the Israeli-Palestinian arrangement comes undone thanks to Likud intransigence, it would be impossible to continue and expand Israeli-Jordanian normalization, and the economic benefits that go with it, in the face of mass public arousal. It would also make Jordan too tempting a target not only for Syria and Iraq but also for Saudi Arabia and the Gulf states; the king would likely jettison his patient campaign to reorient and improve Jordan's inter-Arab relations. Then again, on this matter Hussein is fairly far out in front of his people and most of the Arab states, and such miscalculation runs in the family: King Abdallah did something similar in 1950–51 and paid for it with his life.

Jordan's most serious long-term problem, however near-term maneuvers turn out, is that the attention of Jordan's Palestinian population is almost inevitably bound to be drawn westward to some extent—even if most do not actually leave, as is probable. A kind of symbolic irredentism could well hurt deeply Jordan's effort to foster a firm and functional national identity, especially if the country does not prosper materially.[75]

Jordan's troubles are thus not over; indeed there is no last word in the real political life of nations. The pantheon of the country's public symbols has been pulled down. Symbolic debts have shifted. High-minded talk of the burdens of Arabism, of being small and victimized but noble and true, now ring nearly hollow after so many years of sounding true and of playing such an important role. As in Israel, a sense of almost permanent crisis held the country together in some respects, however misanthropic, and made the monarchy into an indispensable corpus colosseum between the two halves of Jordanian society. All this seems less urgent, less pressing, less epochal now.

Normal times brings their own dangers, in Jordan no less than in Israel—or in the United States, for that matter. No less than U.S. statesmen are caught between worlds, with the Cold War over and the next epoch still unnamed, so are Jordanian ones likely to be caught. We wish them luck, and bid them ponder Goethe in Amman.

Notes

1. See the *Financial Times* survey on Jordan, October 25, 1995, 27–30, for a good overview. For the broader view see the World Bank's pamphlet *Peace and the Jordanian Economy* (Washington: IBRD and the World Bank, 1994).

2. Symbolically central here was the regime's arrest of a prominent Islamic politician, Laith Shubayleth, in December 1995. Also of symbolic importance, Shubayleth was reelected in February 1996 by an overwhelming margin as head of his Engineers Union while in prison.

3. It should be noted at the outset that the diplomatic dimension alone of what occurred between Israel and Jordan from 1991 through 1995 could fill a book, and a large one at that. In this space we are limited to a sketch, particularly inasmuch as we are obliged to mention several other topics—Jordan's internal situation and its broader Arab diplomacy among them.

4. It is "common knowledge" that no one predicted Jordan's general policy trajectory after the end of the Cold War and the Gulf War. This is not strictly true. See my 1989 essay "The Importance of Being Hussein: Jordanian Foreign Policy and Peace in the Middle East."

5. See my "Allies of Diminishing Returns: The Hashemite Question."

6. Ali Jarbawi is wrong to assert that they were dropped entirely. See Jarbawi, "The Triangle of Conflict," 97–98.

7. Moshe Katzav said that the Likud plan depended on Jordan; Qol Yisrael, February 5, 1995, in *FBIS-NEA*, February 6, 1995, 39. See Benjamin Netanyahu's comments in this regard "Netanyahu Discusses Likud Political Plan," Qol Yisrael, February 4, 1995, in *FBIS-NEA*, February 6, 1995, 36, and in "Meeting Detailed," *Ha'aretz*, March 12, 1995, 3.

8. Much detail is contained in my *Israel and Jordan in the Shadow of War: Functional Ties and Futile Diplomacy in a Small Place.*

9. This critical point is made in Asher Susser, "Jordan," ed. Ami Ayalon, *Middle East Contemporary Survey* 17 (Boulder: Westview, 1996), 470.

10. It was no coincidence that Rubinstein was the principal on the Israeli side for these negotiations. As mentioned earlier, he had been the key liaison for Israel with Jordan during the Likud government. He knew all the principals and all the issues, and was respected by the Jordanian side.

11. The Christopher-Hussein meeting was public knowledge; Rabin was on his way to a state visit in Russia, but his schedule would have allowed a stopover in London. This is one of several points in the historical narrative of the period that only future archives and memoirs will verify, or not.

12. There are reports that they met yet again in London on June 1, but this too is unconfirmed.

13. Reported in *Ma'ariv,* June 17, 1994, 1.

14. The Trilateral Committee was a U.S.-designed committee set up after September 14, 1993, mainly to facilitate and spotlight U.S. financial support for Israeli-Jordanian economic cooperation.

15. Rabin and Hussein were now communicating frequently by telephone. Details of this telephone diplomacy appeared in *Yediot Aharonot* on July 11, 1994.

16. The king's speech of July 9, 1994, can be found in *FBIS-NEA,* July 11, 1994, 61–65.

17. Syria, in theory, could have done more but limited itself to a stream of verbal bombast against Jordan, beginning on July 28 and not ended as of 1996.

18. The treaty text, with analysis, may be found in the extremely useful pamphlet by Steven A. Cook, "Jordan-Israel Peace, Year One: Laying the Foundation," Washington Institute for Near East Policy, *Policy Focus,* December 1995. For details and historical background of past summits and the agreement on water and land, see my "This Week's Rabin-Hussein Summit Will Cap Decades of Secret Talks," *JTA Daily News Bulletin,* July 25, 1994, and "Israel-Jordanian Water and Border Deals Lean on Much History," *Turkish Times,* November 15, 1994.

19. After an unseemly delay, the first Israeli ambassador to Jordan, Shimon Shamir, finally arrived in Amman on February 16, 1995.

20. Virtually the entire text was reprinted in the *Jordan Times,* November 7, 1995, 1, 7. Soon after the funeral, Crown Prince Hassan traveled to West Jerusalem to pay a call on Leah Rabin. The *Jordan Times,* and, more important, two Arabic dailies, gave the visit first-page coverage, with photo, on November 8, 1995.

21. See *Ha'aretz,* April 7, 1996, A3, for an example.

22. Noted in Cook, 3.

23. For details see Kirk Albrecht, "The Road Less Travelled," *The Middle East,* March 1996, 19; and Amy Dockser Marcus, "Business Ties Expand among Palestinians, Jordanians and Israelis," *Wall Street Journal,* May 8, 1996.

24. Anecdotal evidence can be found in John Lancaster and Barton Gellman,

"For Old Mideast Foes, Public Peace Clouds Personal Enmity," *Washington Post*, February 27, 1996, A1, A14.

25. According to Jordan's Tourism Ministry, quoted in the *Washington Post*, February 26, 1996, A14.

26. "Rabin Addresses Jerusalem Business Conference," Qol Yisrael, October 29, 1995, in *FBIS-NEA*, November 3, 1995, 1.

27. Majid Jibarah, "Labor Minister—No Objections to Exporting Labor to Israel," *Al-Ra'y*, March 13, 1996, 1, 17, in *FBIS-NEA*, March 14, 1996, 57.

28. "Various Jordanian-Palestinian Accords Published," *Al-Ra'y*, January 29, 1995, in *FBIS-NEA*, January 31, 1995, 37–43.

29. See "Uncertain Future for Trade," *Palestine Report*, January 8, 1995, 12.

30. See, for example, "Abd-Rabbuh: Talks with Jordan Suspended," Israeli Television in Arabic, April 19, 1995, in *FBIS-NEA*, April 20, 1995, 7.

31. Note, for example, "Israel Asks Jordan to Permit Passage of Produce to Gulf States," Qol Yisrael, January 23, 1996, in *FBIS-NEA*, January 24, 1996, 27.

32. Muhammed Al-Murabi, "Israel's Tactics," *Al-Quds*, November 1, 1995, translated in *Palestine Report*, November 10, 1995, 13.

33. Noted in the *Jerusalem Report*, February 23, 1995, 11. And the Saudis soon rewarded them by giving $30 million to Faisal Husseini. Ori Nir, "Husseini: Saudis to Give $30 Million to Projects in East Jerusalem," *Ha'aretz*, February 3, 1995.

34. It was easier to monitor Hamas activities in Jordan by allowing them to remain public. Israel acquiesced in this for a time but then insisted on Jordan expelling Musa Abu-Marzuq, which it did in June 1995; Marzuq subsequently tried to enter the United States and was arrested; Israel requested his extradition. Jordan still suffers the presence of Ibrahim Ghowshah, but because he is a Jordanian national and has broken no laws, Jordan lets him be. Meanwhile, Jordanian commentators ask in so many words why Arafat accuses Jordan of helping Hamas but says nothing of the much larger Syrian role. See Tariq Masawirah, "We Do Not Like to Believe," *Al Ra'y*, April 15, 1995, in *FBIS-NEA*, April 19, 1995, 43.

35. Salwa Kanaana, "Arafat Slams Jordan over Hamas," *Palestine Report*, April 19, 1996, 16.

36. See *Al-Ittihad* (Abu Dhabi), April 2, 1996, 26, in *FBIS-NEA*, April 4, 1996, 3.

37. They may not be totally wrong. Princely descendants of the Baghdadi branch of the Hashemite family do exist and, from time to time, speak with the king. What they talk about is not known.

38. Quoted in Youssef M. Ibrahim, "Talks Resume, but Palestinians Worrying about Keeping Self-Rule on Course," *New York Times*, November 8, 1995.

39. Salwa Kanaana, interview with Hassan Asfour in *Palestine Report*, November 10, 1995, 7.

40. "Palestine," *Palestine Report*, March 22, 1996, 8; *FBIS-NEA*, March 18, 1996, 11.

41. Arafat quoted in *Foreign Report*, February 1, 1996, 8.

42. One new reason is the possibility, not often spoken of in public, that should

the PLO collapse, Jordan might join Israel in a temporary administration of the West Bank and Gaza.

43. Ze'ev Schiff, February 22, 1996, *Ha'aretz*; this article is the basic source for this document.

44. *Ma'ariv*, September 29, 1995, 2.

45. Yossi Alpher, "Settlement and Borders," *Final Status Issues: Israel-Palestinians*, no. 3 (Tel Aviv: Jaffee Center for Strategic Studies, 1994), 17–18.

46. I have detailed this in "The Next Generation in Jordan: Implications for Domestic and Regional Political Developments," in *The Next Generation in Four Key Arab Societies*, a study for the Office of Near East–South Asia Affairs, Office of Leadership Analysis, Central Intelligence Agency, July 1989 (unclassified).

47. Jarbawi, 106.

48. The king quoted in *Palestine Report*, December 29, 1995, 13. It is worth noting too that Israel and Jordan had a prior agreement over passports in which Israel undertook to return to Jordan all passports from those Jerusalemites who had applied for Israeli citizenship. *Palestine Report*, December 15, 1995, 12.

49. See Raed Al Abed, "Jordanian-Palestinian Relationship Faces Renewed Challenge," *The Star* (Amman), November 9–15, 1995, 1–2.

50. In July 1995, Prime Minister Zaid bin-Shaker publicly expressed Jordan's dissatisfaction with U.S. largesse. See Peter Feuilherade, "Jordan: Facing the Challenges of Change," *The Middle East*, October 1995, 21. The State Department sought and received expert advice in advance of President Clinton's address to the Jordanian parliament on October 27, 1994. The experts warned against mentioning specific sums of money or raising expectations that would not be met. The White House ignored this warning, the president spoke of money, expectations were raised, and they were frustrated (author's personal knowledge).

51. One discussion of this is Lawrence Tal, "Dealing with Radical Islam: The Case of Jordan," *Survival* 37, no. 3 (Autumn 1995).

52. Bill Geertz and Rowan Scarborough, "Perry Warns Iraq to Back Off," *Washington Times*, August 15, 1995, A1.

53. William Perry, "Inaugural Les Aspin Memorial Lecture on U.S. National Security in the Middle East," as *Policywatch* 185 (February 8, 1996): 1.

54. In fact, contrary to what had been announced in March, the U.S.S. *George Washington* was in place before the operation commenced. See Douglas Jehl, "Jordan Allowing U.S. to Use Its Air Base for Flights over Iraq," *New York Times*, April 9, 1996, A9.

55. Reported in *Ha'aretz*, December 15, 1995, 1.

56. Ibid., December 18, 1995, 1.

57. Details can be had from Sidney Blumenthal, "The Western Front," *The New Yorker*, June 5, 1995, 41.

58. See Thomas W. Lippman, "Jordan Plane Deal Draws GOP Criticism," *Washington Post*, February 14, 1996.

59. In particular, the United States was reported to be urging Saudi Arabi to

supply Jordan with oil so that the king could further distance himself from Iraq. The vehicle for this shift was the repair of the tapline that runs near Zarka in Jordan. See "A New Twist in the Middle East," *Foreign Report*, September 28, 1995, 3–4; and *MEM* (Middle East Memo), October 1995, 13.

60. "Jordanian Trade with Iraq to be Cut in Half," Radio Monte Carlo (Paris), January 22, 1996, in *FBIS-NEA*, January 24, 1996, 29.

61. See *Foreign Report*, December 14, 1995, 3.

62. The asylum request of Iraq's former chief of staff, General Nizar Al-Khazraji, was accepted in March 1996. See *FBIS-NEA*, March 23, 1996, 29.

63. Note "Jordanians Intercept Chemicals Bound for Iraq," *New York Times*, December 28, 1995.

64. See Kamran Karadaghi, "King Hussein in Washington: View from the Iraqi Opposition," *Policywatch* 188 (March 6, 1996); Karen Dabrowska, "King Hussein and the Iraqi Opposition," *Middle East International*, January 19, 1996, 18–19.

65. Quoted in Douglas Jehl, "Jordan Offers Help to Iraq's Foes," *New York Times*, December 7, 1995, A13.

66. See Lamis Andoni, "Two Goals Achieved," *Middle East International*, January 19, 1996, 9.

67. Reported in *Jordan Times*, November 12, 1995, 1.

68. See the coverage in Douglas Jehl, "Jordan Now Succeeding in Mending Gulf Ties Frayed by Iraq," *New York Times*, February 6, 1996, A15.

69. Ehud Ya'ari, "Bittersweet," *Jerusalem Report*, February 8, 1996, 28.

70. Ehud Ya'ari, "The War is On!" *Jerusalem Report*, January 11, 1995, 28.

71. "King Hussein on Palestine Issue," Amman Jordanian Television, October 29, 1995, in *FBIS-NEA*, October 30, 1996, 14. Musa's speech is found on pages 15–16 in the same document.

72. A lesson well learned from the Jordan Crisis of 1970. See my "U.S. Decision-Making in the Jordan Crisis of 1970: Correcting the Record."

73. The *New York Times* articles were almost unanimous; see William Safire, "'Ish' vs. Issues," May 23, 1996, A29; A. L. Rosenthal, "The Warp from Israel,'" June 4, 1996, A15; and Thomas Friedman, "Israel's Arab Fallout," June 5, 1996, A21.

74. Douglas Jehl, "Jordan's King Says Election Won't Derail Peace Effort," *New York Times*, June 2, 1996, A9.

75. It is worth noting here that Jordan is taking responsibility for its own economic future and is not depending on its ties with Israel and international charity alone to solve its problems. It has undertaken significant reform, and reform is working. In the fall of 1995 Jordan passed a new investment law and cut both personal income and selected business taxes while raising the sales tax. See Andrew Album, "Jordan: Privatisation, key to growth," *The Middle East*, February 1996, 28–8; Peter Feuilherade, "Jordan: Implementing Checks and Balances," ibid., January 1996, 19–20; and *MEM*, October 1995, 13.

5: Syria and the Transition to Peace

Raymond A. Hinnebusch

The Challenge of Peace

It once appeared that the Syrian Ba'th regime neither wanted nor could survive a peace with Israel. Syria's authoritarian minority-ruled regime, some pundits insisted, fostered confrontation abroad to justify repressive rule at home and to extract the military and financial largesse for which the conflict made it eligible.[1]

Today such claims seem less credible. For roughly two decades, Syria has claimed it wanted a political settlement under UN resolutions 242 and 338, and it has been engaged in serious peace negotiations with Israel since 1991.

But if the Syrian regime did not invent the conflict with Israel for domestic purposes, it nevertheless used the external threat to justify its rule. The enormous national security apparatus created under President Hafiz al-Asad to carry on the struggle with Israel could lose its raison d'être under peace. As a front-line state, the regime has received plentiful aid from the Arab oil states, which it could not expect to continue at the same levels once the conflict is resolved; the private investment that could potentially replace it will be largely funneled to the private sector, not the state. The regime's main source of legitimacy has been its claim to represent Arab interests in the struggle with Israel, whereas the peace settlement that is shaping up cannot readily be depicted as a nationalist achievement. The peace process does, therefore, represent a serious challenge to the Syrian regime. From the moment he seized power in 1970, Asad designed his state to fight Israel; signs are that he is now incrementally redesigning it.

Regime Consolidation and a Rational Actor Foreign Policy

In Asad's authoritarian state, foreign policy, far from being an irrational product of domestic instability, is largely governed by a raison d'état compatible with the peace process. This is possible because Asad's consolidation of the Ba'th regime gave him relative autonomy in terms of domestic constraints on his foreign policy. Asad achieved this autonomy by concentrating power in a "presidential monarchy" through a policy of balancing social forces. The radical Ba'thists who preceded him (1963–70) had achieved autonomy relative to the dominant classes by breaking their control over the means of production and mobilizing workers and peasants through the Ba'th party. After 1970 Asad used the army to free himself from party ideological constraints; built up his *jama'a*—a core largely of personal followers of the Alawi minority Islamic sect—to enhance his autonomy in terms of both army and party; and fostered a state-dependent new bourgeoisie as a fourth leg of support to minimize dependence on the others.

In this authoritarian national security state, Asad enjoys wide latitude in decision making. Foreign policy making is not subject to bureaucratic politics in which hawkish or dovish factions can shape or veto his decisions. Nor is public opinion a direct constraint: Asad has taken several unpopular foreign policy decisions, notably the 1976 intervention against the PLO in Lebanon and the alignment with Iran in the Iran-Iraq war and against Iraq after its invasion of Kuwait.

The policy process approximates the rational actor model, namely a unified leadership able to make foreign policy decisions on grounds of geopolitics and to adapt strategies freely to the external power balance.[2] Thus, Syrian policy is shaped by two geopolitical constants: residual anti-Israeli irredentism and natural geopolitical rivalry with Israel over spheres of influence in the Levant, and Israeli military superiority and the consequent need both to accept the reality of Israel and to contain its power. To reconcile these somewhat contrary imperatives, Asad tailored Syria's goals to its limited means while upgrading its means to match its goals.

Revisionist aims gave way to limited goals, above all acceptance of peace with Israel in return for its withdrawal from the occupied territories under UN resolution 242. This was the main issue over which Asad overthrew his radical rivals in 1970. Yet Asad, seeing himself as the last Arab nationalist leader, stubbornly refused to follow other Arab leaders who accepted less than full Israeli withdrawal. For a quarter century he has sought, with remarkable consistency and great patience, to roll Israel back behind its 1967 lines.

As a realist convinced that power is what counts in international politics, Asad has consistently sought to build the military capability needed to make his diplomacy credible and to contain Israel. And like a prudent rational actor, he has adapted Syria's strategies to the balance of power. In

1973 he sought to retake the Golan through conventional war, and when this failed he entered the Kissinger-sponsored negotiations with Israel. When Egypt's separate deals with Israel undermined Syria's hand, Asad adopted after 1978 a "tactical rejectionism" that sought to obstruct the peace process until a Syrian military buildup restored a power balance with Israel necessary to a credible Syrian hand. Finally, when the collapse of the USSR and the bipolar world exhausted this strategy and deprived Asad of a military card, he took advantage of the Gulf War to win Western acceptance as a responsible power whose interests should be recognized, and when that seemed to happen, he entered the peace process.

This is not to argue there are no constraints on Asad's foreign policy decisions, only that they are *indirect:* Political wisdom dictates that he take account of their impact on his domestic constituencies and on the wider nationalist legitimacy of the regime. The domestic risks to his rule from involvement in the peace process appear to be declining.

Asad must, presumably, be sensitive to elite opinion. Although he has shown that he is willing to be out in front of it, he tries to govern by intra-elite consensus rather than imposing his views. This was most apparent in the disengagement agreements after the 1973 war, when he took pains to consult Syria's political elite (in contrast to Sadat's unilateral decisions), although as his preeminence has since been consolidated, he has seemed in less need of such consultation.[3] There apparently was dissent among the elite over acceptance of the 1991 US invitation to the Madrid peace conference, which accommodated few of Syria's traditional procedural conditions. Asad's attempt to forge a consensus may have accounted for the time lag in accepting the invitation. Throughout the subsequent negotiations, Vice President Abd al-Halim Khaddam has, by comparison with Asad, been outspokenly anti-Israel, but he has always been Asad's faithful lieutenant, and Khaddam's anti-Israel stand might be a tactic to give the appearance that Asad faces constraints that prevent him making concessions. In reality none of his lieutenants have seriously challenged or constrained Asad's foreign policy.

The Alawi security barons were reputedly unhappy with the prospect of peace negotiations, perhaps for fear they would be the victims of internal political liberalization or a foreign policy realignment toward the West, which might accompany a peace. The army may fear that peace would threaten its dominant societal role and would bring Israeli demands for reductions in the size of Syria's forces. Recently, observers thought senior security chief Ali Duba and several of his subordinates had been fired by Asad to "remove . . . centers of power that could resist the restructuring of the army in the post-peace era."[4] Duba in fact remains in power, but a shakeup among his subordinates reflected Asad's policy of rotation to prevent clientage networks from congealing into fiefdoms beyond his control. As long as Asad keeps a hand on appointments and dismissals, no baron can staff his domain with durable clients enabling him to stand against the president.

It is, moreover, not a foregone conclusion that the Alawi and military elites cannot adapt to postwar conditions. They would retain their dominant positions in the officer corps and security forces, even if these sectors are scaled down. Though officers have been told to expect reductions in their forces after peace, Alawi-dominated elite units such as the presidential guard will be the core of a slimmed-down professional army. The Syrian military was unnerved by the easy defeat of Iraq and is aware that another war in which it could be devastated might be the alternative to the peace process. Asad has portrayed the peace process to the army as an honorable struggle: "Our stance in the battle for peace will not be less courageous than our stances on the battlefield."[5] The Alawis' business connections to the Sunni bourgeoisie should allow them to share in any economic prosperity that accompanies peace, and the capital that they accumulated illicitly might be laundered via investment in legitimate businesses.

The Ba'ath party might be expected to reject a peace settlement that does not measure up to Ba'thist standards and that threatens to take away its nationalist raison d'être. Yet the Ba'th party has been downgraded, deideologized, and turned into a patronage machine with little capacity for independent action. It has not made key decisions, above all in the foreign policy field, in a long time. Asad no longer appears at party functions; party national secretary Abdullah al-Ahmar or vice president Khaddam stands in for him. A party congress is overdue by a decade, perhaps because Asad does not want to make a public defense of his foreign policies, notably the peace process, before they have delivered results. The party central committee was, however, assembled to hear the regime's justification for entering the peace process. The meeting brought together the Regional Command (the assemblage of the highest elite of generals, top party apparatchiki, and senior ministers) and the second-rank elite (party branch secretaries and committees, governors, university presidents, leaders of the popular organizations, junior ministers, army commanders, and chairmen of Peoples' Assembly committees). Party secretaries Suleiman al-Qad-dah and Abdullah al-Ahmar and Prime Minister Mahmoud al-Zubi presided, and Khaddam addressed the assembly. The assembled elites approved the peace process and dispersed to justify it to their constituents.[6]

Although the bourgeoisie is ambivalent or split over the kind of peace shaping up, it will accept whatever Asad decides. Though some Syrian businessmen fear Israeli dumping on the internal market under normalization of relations, most merchants believe that Syrian commercial acumen will allow them to compete. Some fear that Syria will face competition from Israel's superior technology in the Saudi and Gulf markets they want for themselves. Although they hope Asad will obstruct overly rapid normalization in Syria and the Arab world in general, they understand that a stable peace is needed for long-term investment and that Syrian business must learn to compete in the international market.

It is frequently argued that economic constraints have forced Syria into the peace process. There is scant evidence that Asad has ever allowed economic constraints to force foreign policy decisions that would not otherwise have been taken on strategic grounds. Thus, in the 1980s, when Arab aid declined and a resource gap sent the Syrian economy into crisis, Asad remained immovable on policies that antagonized his Gulf paymasters, such as the Iran alliance and the Syrian role in Lebanon. On the other hand, Asad joined the current peace process at a time when a combination of austerity at home and a windfall of aid for Syria's stand in the Gulf war had lifted the economy out of the doldrums. To be sure, there has been a decline in the diversification of Syria's external suppliers of resources—the Eastern Bloc, Europe, Iran, and Gulf Arabs—which formerly eased the constraints that any single donor could have put on Syria's options. But during the period of the peace negotiations, economic constraints have faded into the background, and there is little reason to think that such factors would force Syria to abandon its strategic goals in the Arab-Israeli conflict.

Moreover, the economic consequences of a peace settlement do not uniformly attract or repel the Syrian regime sufficiently to be a decisive factor in its foreign policy calculations. In the short run, the Arab financial aid to which Syria has been entitled as a front-line state has declined and is no longer a motive for avoiding peace, and it will continue to do so as the Arab-Israeli conflict is defused, regardless of Syrian policy. Such aid has at least been channeled through the state, however, while much of the investment the regime could expect after peace is reached would bolster the private bourgeoisie—appeasing but also strengthening a social force that the state cannot wholly trust.

In the long run, both regime and bourgeoisie realize that sustained eco-

nomic prosperity requires a peace settlement. Since the collapse of the socialist bloc, the country needs further incorporation into the world capitalist economy. As statist development strategies reached their limits, the economy has become increasingly dependent on private investment (Arab,
expatriate, or Western); the private sector proportion of overall investment
increased from 29 percent in 1975 to 66 percent in 1992. The shift reflects
both a private sector revival and a decline in Arab transfers funneled into
the public sector.[7] A "no-war-no-peace" situation, isolated from an Arab
world at peace with Israel, is not a favorable investment climate for private capital. The regime needs a growing economy to appease the bourgeoisie and to absorb the burgeoning numbers of job seekers fueled by
high population growth.

Public opinion sets certain indirect bounds on policy toward the Arab-
Israeli conflict. Since independence, Syrians have seen themselves not as a
distinct nationality but as Arabs—indeed the most Arab of the Arabs. Under Asad, the state's foreign policy role was, therefore, to defend the Arab
nation against Israel and to win an honorable peace. Such legitimacy as
the regime enjoyed rested on its claim to represent the national interest
against Israel. No nationalist regime—especially an Alawi-dominated one—
could, without grave risk, accept a dishonorable peace.

Much, however, depends on what the public perceives to be an honorable or realistic settlement. The vast majority of Syrians are tired of years
of conflict and stalemate, and have long wanted a peace settlement, although not at any price: The regime position—full Israeli withdrawal to
the 1967 lines and Palestinian rights, including an independent state—long
reflected the mainstream view fairly accurately.

However, the kind of peace Syria is currently likely to attain will fall
far short of that. An Israeli-dominated Palestinian administration in the
West Bank and Gaza, leaving Diaspora Palestinians in limbo, will be difficult to depict as an achievement of Palestinian rights. A return of the
Golan will bring an unwelcome normalization of relations with Israel.
Such a settlement will be hard to depict as a vindication of Syria's thirty-
year-long struggle.

This is not to say that public opinion is unchanging. After the 1973 war,
the Asad regime accustomed a formerly rejectionist public to accept an eventual peace settlement. Once Syria entered the current peace talks, the Syrian
media began to promote the economic benefits of peace. Asad's commitment to "normal relations" with Israel during the January 1994 Asad-Clinton
meeting was broadcast to Damascus.[8]

Most recently, public opinion seems to be embracing a significant reduction in its conception of an acceptable peace, putting the regime into a better position to sell the less-than-comprehensive settlement that appears in the cards. This sea change in opinion was precipitated by the Oslo accord in which the Palestinians took their own road to peace with Israel. Syria, most Syrians feel, cannot reject a settlement that the Palestinian leadership itself accepts. The regime has successfully argued that the PLO's submission to Israel deprived Syria of the diplomatic leverage to help win the liberation of the West Bank and Gaza. The subsequent Israeli-Jordanian peace treaty convinced Syrians that Syria could not afford to sacrifice opportunities that might achieve its own vital interest in a return of the Golan. In a September 1994 speech to parliament, Asad observed that "for decades Syria waged the Arabs' battle against the Israeli occupation" and carried the principal burden of the confrontation; now, however, the "enormity of the damage that unilateralism [of the Jordanians and Palestinians] has inflicted on the core of the causes for which we have long fought and struggled" had become unambiguously clear.[9] "What can we do since the others have left us and gone forward?," he lamented.[10]

There has even been a sort of backlash against Arab nationalism and Pan-Arab commitments. This development, which has the potential of shrinking the unit of political identity and turning Syrians inward to their own affairs, may seem compatible with the sort of peace shaping up. However, a Syrian identity has not yet become a viable substitute for Arabism and the regime will continue to see its legitimacy linked to a leading role in inter-Arab politics. The regime will not face much overt resistance to normalization of relations with Israel, but forcing such a move on Syria is unlikely to reduce public animosity against Israel, at least in the short run. Whereas their concern for the Palestine cause has declined, Syrians' hostility to Israel has not done so, and many are emotionally resistant to the prospect of relations with Israelis. But the Syrian public now takes a resolution of the conflict for granted, to the extent that people speak of the future in terms of "bad as-salaam"—after the peace.[11]

In conclusion, there appears to be no irresistible pressure on the regime either to reject the sort of deal with Israel that now seems plausible or to make concessions to Israel in pursuit of such a deal.

Syrian Foreign Policy in a Post-Bipolar World

Asad has freely and successfully adapted his policies to the dramatic transformation in the post-bipolar balance of power. With the disappearance of Soviet support, an exposed Syria scrambled to repair and diversify its connections to other powers. Asad entered the anti-Iraq Gulf War coalition in part because he sensed the end of bipolarity and was determined that Syria would not become a victim of whatever "New World Order" replaced it. He effectively took advantage of the Gulf crisis to show the West that Syria was a factor for stability and would eschew terrorism and play by Western rules. Syria reestablished its damaged relations with Western Europe, an alternative source of aid to the USSR.

Asad also deftly came to terms with the remaining superpower, the United States. American acceptance of Syrian interests in Lebanon, the Gulf War, and the peace process put U.S.-Syrian relations on a better footing. But Syria remained suspicious of U.S. motives for various reasons: the 1993 U.S. blocking of Syrian weapons acquisitions, its failure to remove Syria from the terrorism list (combined with the targeting of Libya and the implicit threat that Syria could be next), its role in excluding Syria from Gulf security arrangements, its loan guarantees to Israel, and its failure to broker the peace process in a manner sensitive to Syrian interests. Syria became convinced that the United States would not reward it for its Gulf War role nor acknowledge its "strategic weight."

Despite Syria's inclusion in the Gulf War coalition, Asad perceived the "New World Order" as largely biased against Arab and Syrian interests. The balance of power, he declared, had been upset [by the collapse of bipolarity], and the "main winners have been the Arabs' enemies. Perhaps they expect we shall weaken and collapse but we shall not surrender."[12] A new balance of power would in time be established; unfortunately, while other parts of the world were forming regional blocs, the Arab world was going in the opposite direction: "Some Arabs are absorbed in their own interests or are more at ease with foreigners than brother Arabs and look to them for protection."[13]

Syria has sought to contain the post–Gulf War tendencies toward unipolarity of the global system as it impacted on the Middle East. Syria sought alternative arms sources in China and North Korea. Using their desire for debt repayment as leverage, Syria had some success in reestablishing economic and arms relations with Russia and Eastern Europe and evidently acquired much high-quality equipment at cut-rate prices; Gulf Arab aid serviced some of these connections.[14] Perhaps most important, Russia evidently forgave much of Syria's military debt and resumed some arms and spare parts shipments on a commercial basis, though reputedly deferring to Israeli demands that it restrain advanced weapons deliveries.[15] Syria also preserved its Iranian alliance as a counter to U.S. dominance in the Gulf and as a partner in the development of an arms industry. Nevertheless, the current world order is far less favorable to Syrian interests than the bipolar world, in which it could not only rely on a Soviet patron for arms and protection but also, by exploiting the U.S. desire to contain Soviet influence, could obtain U.S. mediation in the conflict with Israel.

Syria's relative position in the Middle East regional system was marginally improved after the anti-Iraq Gulf War. Syria's incorporation into the Damascus Declaration "6 plus 2" group, including Egypt, Saudi Arabia, and the other GCC states, ended the isolation that Damascus had suffered from in the 1980s. The Gulf War put an end to the Iraqi threat. That war also enabled Syria to smash Maronite resistance to its role in Lebanon and to establish a virtual protectorate over most of the country; this ended much of Israel's ability to intervene through Maronite clients in Lebanese politics. Syria subsequently demonstrated an ability to orchestrate the Lebanese political process to ensure a client regime in Beirut. Syria is determined to maintain military forces in Lebanon, at least until Israel withdraws from its "security zone" in the south.

Damascus is using the "Lebanese card" in the peace negotiations with Israel: Ironically, the security zone has become a Syrian asset in that it enables Damascus, through Hizbollah, to put military pressure on Israel without the risks of directly engaging with superior Israeli power. Syria can either heat up the Lebanese-Israeli border or rein in Hizbollah as a way of demonstrating its indispensability to any resolution of the south Lebanon conflict. Indeed, this became abundantly clear during Israel's ill-fated "Grapes of Wrath" military operation against Hizbollah in April 1996. Syria expects, in return for its services in such a resolution and as part of a general peace settlement, that Lebanon will be acknowledged as its sphere of influence, and there are indications that Israel will accept this.

On the other hand, Syria faces an enhanced threat on its northern border with Turkey. Syrian-Turkish relations have been strained over historic Syrian resentment of Turkish annexation of Iskanderun (Alexandretta) and Turkish accusations of Syrian support for "terrorism" carried out by Kurdish PKK guerrillas against Turkey. Disputes over Syrian rights to a share of the Euphrates water that Turkey controls have been acrimonious; the Turkish-sponsored "peace pipeline," which would have channeled Euphrates water to Israel, was seen as a threat by Syria. Syria might have to fear Turkish-Israeli encirclement: The 1993 attempt by Turkish Foreign Minister Hikmat Cetin to strike an accord with Israel against terrorism, specifically against Syrian support for Bekaa-based groups such as the PKK and Hizbollah, may be a sign of things to come, as was the military agreement signed between Israel and Turkey in February 1996. Iranian-Turkish rivalries mean that Syria and Iran share a perception of threat from Turkey, and this makes the Syrian-Iranian alliance of new value to Damascus. A Syrian-Iranian alliance confronting an Israeli-Turkish one is the classic checkerboard power-balancing typical of "realist" geopolitics.

The Syrian-Israeli Peace Negotiations

Shimon Peres has claimed that "Asad is conducting the peace process just as one conducts a military campaign—slowly, patiently, directed by strategic and tactical considerations."[16] Negotiations with Israel are now the only avenue by which Asad can attain his goals, but given the largely unfavorable balance of power, he must exploit every possible source of leverage.

Asad had long accepted a land-for-peace settlement of the conflict with Israel along the lines of UN resolution 242. Throughout the 1980s, however, believing that the strategic imbalance in Israel's favor precluded an honorable settlement, Asad opposed negotiations until Israel committed itself to full withdrawal, and he sought to obstruct attempts to bypass Syria and broker Israeli deals with Jordan or the Palestinians.

That Asad joined the U.S.-sponsored peace process after the Gulf War was a measure of the radical change in his strategy. The power balance was even more unfavorable than in the 1980s, but Asad's options had narrowed. The first effect of this imbalance was Syria's procedural concessions. As conditions for negotiations, Asad had long insisted on (1) a united Arab delegation so that Israel could not divide the Arabs; (2) UN sponsorship, which would make UN resolutions 242 and 338 the basis of a settlement and would mobilize global pressures on Israel; and (3) prior Israeli commitment to the principle of full withdrawal. Instead, Syria accepted direct unconditional bilateral negotiations with Israel. The best Asad could get was U.S. assurances that the United States considered UN resolution 242 to apply on all fronts and the Israeli annexation of the Golan to be illegitimate.[17]

Asad's adhesion to the peace process protected his investment in joining the anti-Iraq coalition. With no military option left, he could no longer sacrifice diplomatic opportunities that did not meet his full terms for participation. Israel was out to depict Syria as a threat to peace and the next candidate after Iraq for forced disarming; joining the peace process deflected international pressures from Syria.

Asad had traditionally insisted that peace must be comprehensive, and in the negotiations he rebuffed efforts to draw him into a separate agreement, divorced from a settlement of the Palestinian issue. Syrian prospects of achieving a full Israeli withdrawal to the 1967 lines depended on orchestrating a common Arab front and demonstrating that Israel could not have peace without it.

At first, Asad was optimistic about his chances because the Gulf crisis had allowed the formerly isolated Syria to resituate itself at the Arab center and had weakened the PLO and Jordan, making them potentially dependent on Damascus. It was Israel, however, that proved able to take advantage of their weaknesses; Syria's hopes of imposing its strategy in the peace negotiations were dashed as the PLO and Jordan reached separate agreements with Israel and the Gulf Arab states moved toward normalization of relations with Israel in the absence of a comprehensive peace. The result was to undermine Syria's leverage over the other "fronts," thereby confining it, in practical terms, to bilateral negotiations over the Golan. In accepting Israel's procedural terms, Asad was maneuvered into a choice between accepting or rejecting a separate peace settlement over the Golan.

Syrian-Israeli negotiations have therefore focused on the Golan-for-peace equation. Asad's key condition is the full return of the Golan Heights. Israel wants to keep some presence there, not only to avoid uprooting more than twenty Israeli settlements there but also because the Golan contains extensive water resources and is a security buffer. For Asad, however, recovering a mere part of the Golan is hardly attractive since its main values are symbolic (recovering the lost honor of the 1967 defeat) and security-connected (removing the threat to Damascus posed by the Israelis' presence on the plateau). Only a full withdrawal would attain these ends. While Asad is unlikely to accept any compromise of full Syrian sovereignty over the Golan, demilitarized zones and international peacekeeping forces there are acceptable.

Syria originally insisted that under UN resolution 242 all it needed to concede in return for Israeli withdrawal was a treaty ending the war between the two states. However, Israel demanded normalization—diplomatic relations, trade, tourism, and the rest. Asad is loath to concede this because of Syrians' deep mistrust of Israel.

The negotiations have brought the two sides closer together but have not fully bridged the gap. At first Israel insisted that its withdrawal would be only partial and that it would not reveal the extent of withdrawal until Syria detailed its commitment to normalization of relations. Syria refused to commit itself on peace until Israel conceded the principle of full withdrawal. To do so, Asad felt, would undermine Syria's bargaining position.

To break this impasse, Syria proposed that the more land Israel conceded, the more "peace" it could have. Israel responded that the depth of withdrawal would correspond to the scope of peace. The two sides seemed very close in principle. In a January 1994 meeting with President Clinton, Asad publicly committed himself to "normal and full relations" with Israel in return for full withdrawal; Israel, however, fears Asad is including the West Bank in his definition of full withdrawal. Moreover, while Asad will certainly concede formal diplomatic relations, he wants to keep the peace as "cold" as possible, as in the Egyptian precedent, and to phase normalization in over a long time period.

Israel hinted and perhaps conveyed privately its willingness for full withdrawal, but Prime Minister Rabin would not commit himself publicly. Asad remarked: "I've said full peace but Rabin hasn't said full withdrawal."[18]

Even if, as many believe, agreement tacitly existed by 1994 on the core principles of full withdrawal for full peace, a year later the issue of their phasing had not yet been resolved. The Israeli offer on the table in 1995 seemed to be a modest pullback, followed by Syria's implementation of full peace; if Israel was satisfied with this, it would complete the withdrawal. Asad, pointing to Israeli reluctance to fulfill the Oslo Accords, rejected any agreement that would leave the outcome to Israeli discretion. He also wanted full withdrawal achieved within about a year's time.

Another issue was the definition of full withdrawal: Syria argued that this meant a return to the 1967 borders, within which Syria retained some access to Lake Tiberias; Israel insisted on the borders of the Palestine Mandate (1922–48), which would put all lake access in Israel. A settlement in southern Lebanon, presumably exchanging Israeli withdrawal for security guarantees on the Israeli-Lebanese border, would also have to be part of any Israeli-Syrian agreement.

Although it is possible that the two sides have merely leapfrogged over unresolved issues of principle, it was arguably a good sign that they also entered discussions over the practical security considerations on the Golan accompanying a withdrawal. Although such issues seemed more susceptible to compromise than the core issues, these negotiations did not go smoothly.

Israel wanted more than the demilitarization of the Golan that Syria was offering. It demanded a Syrian military pullback virtually to Damascus and a major downsizing of the Syrian army. To Asad, this demand would threaten Syrian security and sovereignty. His counterposition was to call for symmetrical demilitarization on both sides of the border. This was no more than a bargaining position, and subsequently Syria conceded that these zones could be different in size as long as the security position of both sides was balanced. The negotiations stalled and were broken off in mid-1995 over the Israeli demand to exchange early warning stations. Asad, believing that a continued Israeli presence on Mount Hermon would be a political embarrassment and an affront to Syria's sovereignty, insisted that aerial or satellite surveillance was adequate.

Asad refused to make further concessions in the apparent belief that he had some leverage. Asad could orchestrate the Lebanese hizbollah and rejectionist Palestinians to stir up trouble in southern Lebanon if Syrian interests were ignored. Syria probably retained a sufficient military deterrent against Israel to make such a policy less than suicidal.

Also, without Syria's imprimatur no Arab-Israeli peace can be legitimate. Israeli normalization of relations with the Arab world would arguably remain limited without peace on the Syrian front; a Syria opposed to the peace process, in alliance with Iran and possibly with Iraq, could conceivably destabilize the Middle East. The alliance with Iran remained insurance against a conservative Arab attempt to isolate Syria. The United States and Israel appear convinced that no durable regional peace is viable if it excludes Syria, and they have considerable investments in the process. The change of leadership in Israel after the assassination of Rabin, specifically the seeming greater priority put by Prime Minister Peres on reaching a settlement, apparently lured Asad back to the bargaining table in late 1995, but the victory of Likud leader Binyamin Netanyahu in the May 1996 Israeli elections again chilled relations because of Netanyahu's avowed unwillingness to make concessions on the Golan.

Even should a peace agreement be reached, Syria and Israel will remain rivals for influence in the Levant, and Syria's position is threatened by what Damascus sees as Israel's drive to incorporate the Palestinians and Jordan as virtual political and economic satellites. This move could cut Syria off from the fallen-away parts of Greater Syria, leaving only Lebanon in its orbit. As against those promoting a Middle East system in which economic ties bridged national cleavages, thereby integrating Israel into the region, Asad rejoined: "There has been much talk about interests in this historic stage of international development. . . . [But] interests . . . mean . . . not just economic interests, but [national] sentiments and common culture and heritage."[19] Israeli efforts to absorb Jordan and the West Bank into its sphere of influence contradicted natural national ties.

Both Syria and Israel seemingly accept the notion of peace in principle, but they remain ambivalent about it in practice. For Asad, a separate peace and normalization of relations is a high price to pay for the Golan. A Syrian-Israeli settlement that leaves the Palestinian issue unresolved could remain dangerous for the regime if Palestinian-Israeli conflict continued while Israelis walked the streets of Damascus. If this peace also includes the compromises of Syrian sovereignty on the Golan that Israel seems to want, Asad may decide to wait for a favorable shift in the power balance and take the risk that the window of opportunity for a settlement may close.

Domestic Politics and Regime Durability in the Transition to Peace

Would a Syrian-Israeli peace endure? Asad certainly has the power to prevent resistance to such a peace. His sense of honor dictates that he respect his agreements; even his archfoe, Menachem Begin, referred to him as a man "who has always kept his agreements." In fact, the Golan Heights disengagement agreement of 1974 has been scrupulously adhered to.

But is the regime that signs a peace with Israel likely to survive for long the two looming challenges it faces: the end of the era of confrontation and the question of leadership succession? Even an "honorable" peace would require the Syrian regime to adapt, notably to public expectations of political liberalization, and to find a substitute for the Arab nationalist ideology that has helped to cement its support base. But the kind of settlement currently in the cards is unlikely to win the regime much political capital that it could expend in the transition to the era of peace. Its current attempts to prepare itself for the transition give mixed signals as to the likely outcome.

The main threat to regime stability may well be a succession crisis. Indicative of the extent to which Syria's political institutions have been weakened by the personalization of power is the fact that the most credible succession scenario has been dynastic. Asad appeared to be grooming his son Basil for succession until he was killed in an automobile accident. Another son, Bash'shar Asad, has taken over Basil's role as his father's right-hand man, but he lacks Basil's popularity and military experience.

An alternative scenario is collective leadership. The dominant elite has been in power for decades: Vice President Abd al-Halim Khaddam, Chief of Staff Hikmat al-Shihabi, and intelligence boss Ali Duba are probably the most powerful of Asad's lieutenants. Asad has reputedly appointed a committee of the top elites who head the main pillars of power to steer a succession. While the regime institutions themselves have little autonomy, the men who head them are strong and experienced, and they may well stick together in the succession. As long as they do, they have the firepower, demonstrated ruthlessness, and stake in regime survival to turn back any challenge from below. Moreover, there is no viable counter-coalition that could challenge the ruling coalition. In the long run, however, collective leadership appears unsustainable. If a peace settlement is not reached before succession or if the one reached is widely perceived to be illegitimate, it is entirely possible that it could become an issue in a succession power struggle.

Asad appears, however, to be altering his regime to prepare for the era after peace is reached. On the one hand, the core of the regime remains intact. The quadruple pillars of power—army, party, security police, and bureaucracy—have reliable chains of command and appear quite capable of defending the regime. Asad has downgraded the power of the Ba'th party, but its structure still incorporates a Sunni and rural base that Asad needs—if only to balance the Alawi jama'a and the Sunni urban bourgeoisie.

On the other hand, Asad is pursuing a strategy of calculated political decompression as a substitute for substantial political pluralization. This denotes that more elements of the bourgeoisie are more securely incorporated into his regime as a way to balance the Alawis and the Ba'thists. It also means relaxing state control over society, with the aim of releasing private energies able to assume a larger share of the burdens of development. It means adapting political structures to absorb the participation pressures that this may stimulate without loss of regime control or autonomy. The regime may be able to preserve the current political system with merely modest adaptations required to open it to the strongest forces hitherto opposed to it—the bourgeoisie and the Islamists.

Politically, a bourgeois class organized enough and conscious enough to constrain regime autonomy hardly exists. Rather, Asad's co-optation of fractions of it allows him to divide it and to play it off against other classes in the regime's constituency. Asad's strategy of co-optation takes several forms. Members of old families have been brought into government. The Chambers of Commerce and of Industry have growing access to government, and they are not mere transmission belts but semiofficial NGOs; although they are committed to support the regime's economic strategy, within that framework they can press their interests and protect the private sector from arbitrary interference or changes in regulations.

Parliament, previously overwhelmingly dominated by the Ba'th party and its allies, has been expanded to include independents, thus co-opting a broader array of societal forces. Perhaps indicative of the new confidence of the bourgeoisie is the 1994 parliamentary election campaign of Ihsan Sankar, a millionaire Mercedes dealer. He reportedly spent millions of Syrian pounds on his campaign and openly announced his intention to work for reversal of such populist measures as rent control, land reform ceilings, and the progressive tax code and to push for a stock exchange and private education. Riyad Saif, one of Syria's few private industrialists, was also elected.[20] Independents in parliament have not, however, organized as a bloc to contest government policy, and they seek parliamentary seats mostly for prestige, privileges (such as the right to import and sell a car at a big profit), and political access. Parliament advances the regime's strategy of co-optation: The regime nominates influential people in the neighborhoods as candidates and allows members of parliament a bit of patronage and scope to intervene with the bureaucracy on behalf of constituents.

The bourgeoisie seems prepared to defer demands for political power: Rather than leading a democracy movement, it has been satisfied by Asad's distancing himself from the Ba'th, co-opting more of its own into government, and according it greater political access. Since the inegalitarian consequences of capitalism are likely to heighten popular discontent, the bourgeoisie no more wants full democratization than does the regime. But the Sunni bourgeoisie does want a full partnership in the regime, whereas the Alawis want to keep the upper hand.

Regime stability and a stable peace both depend on bourgeois investment replacing wartime "rent" and generating the prosperity needed to make the peace palatable. According to one assessment, investment under the 1991 Law no. 10 to encourage private and foreign capital has exceeded that of the public sector in recent years.[21] Sources of capital formation are diversifying. Gulf money is coming in—some heading to the public sector as the continuing reward for Asad's stand against Iraq in the Gulf War— but an increasing share is taking the form of private investment. Expatriate capital is testing the waters. The village petite bourgeoisie has given rise to a Ba'thi connected business strata and the suq petite bourgeoisie has generated indigenous industrialists such as the Saif brothers. Private investment companies tolerated by the regime recently mobilized tremendous hidden middle-class savings, which government banks had failed to tap. Syria enjoyed growth rates of around 8 percent per year from 1990 through 1993.[22] Some observers are skeptical, however, of the quality and durability of investment. By 1993, around $1.8 billion had been put into 474 Law no. 10 projects, mostly tertiary ones, and some light manufacturing such as food industries.[23] A lot of the new investment was possibly a temporary boom. Sharp operators took immediate advantage of Law no. 10 to set up phony car rental agencies to get around the state monopoly in importing cars. The failure of many speculative private investment companies may cause a liquidity crisis. Constraints on investment are built into the political system, including fear of post-Asad instability and continued bureaucratic obstruction. Corruption is rampant at every level: Business has to make payoffs to get projects, and the best opportunities are reputedly reserved for friends of the regime. Long-awaited further reforms necessary to sustain private investment, notably permitting private banking and a stock market, have not been forthcoming. However, economic liberalization is according the bourgeoisie greater autonomy to reconstruct a business-centered civil society, and the regime, having opted to depend on private capital investment, cannot reverse the current tendency to respond, albeit incrementally, to the bourgeoisie's expectations of greater rule of law and a more favorable investment climate.

The Islamic movement has represented the main opposition to the Ba'th regime. Although the regime crushed its uprising in the early eighties, there remains an antiregime Islamic opposition in exile, which could exploit a peace settlement with Israel. Broadcasting from Iraq, it accuses the Asad family of being ready to trade peace with Israel for money and continued power over Syria.[24] Stability and advances in political liberalization depend on a historic compromise between the Ba'th and political Islam. Asad, well aware of this, has put a high priority on reconciliation with political Islam. Since the collapse of the USSR and socialism, he has been developing the "Islamic card," fostering Islam in the media, portraying himself as pious, and generally trying to add Islam to the formula for legitimizing the regime as Ba'thism erodes.

To this end, Asad has tried to bring the Alawis into the Islamic mainstream, building mosques in the Alawi region of Syria and depicting Alawis as genuine Muslims. Basil Asad's funeral was presided over by a Sunni cleric, and the Alawi sheikhs were shown in Sunni rituals as if there was little difference between the sects. Asad is attempting to co-opt and appease the Islamic mainstream, while marginalizing more radical elements. He has fostered a conservative (al-Azhar-like) Islamic establishment to channel Islamic currents and legitimate the regime. Some Islamists have been co-opted as independents into parliament. To the very considerable extent that the Islamic opposition expressed the reaction of the suq and sections of the bourgeoisie to Ba'thist socialism, economic liberalization could advance a détente with the regime.

A main challenge facing the regime is to preside over economic liberalization without excessively damaging and alienating its original populist (rural petit bourgeois–worker–peasant) constituency. The government-employed middle class has been squeezed between inflation, recently running at 15 percent a year, and the government's refusal to raise salaries. The poor are not yet paying the full costs of liberalization. Although subsidies have been cut, driving up the price of necessities such as *mazout* (heating fuel) and bread at their expense, these commodities are still sold below cost. The urban-rural gap does not appear to be widening. Fertilizer subsidies for peasants have been cut, but producer prices have increased. Agriculture is booming and villages seem prosperous, with much new building of schools and mosques.

The mobilization of opposition to pro-capitalist policies requires a populist ideology, which is currently lacking. Marxism has lost credibility while opposition Islam, which has elsewhere mobilized the victims of economic liberalization, has in Syria so far espoused a free market ideology. But economic discontent, if fused with nationalism and radical Islam, could still generate counterregime activism. Such a scenario cannot be excluded if the regime is perceived to have become a client of the West or to have made a dishonorable peace settlement. Whether a settlement with Israel becomes a potent opposition grievance depends on whether it is perceived as just and rooted in mutual interests. Assuming a settlement returns the Golan to Syria, its legitimization is likely to depend on whether it also satisfies Palestinian rights over the longer term.

If the peace settlement lacks legitimacy, it will always be vulnerable. But if it has some legitimacy, it could generate powerful interests with a stake in preserving it. It would probably produce an influx of private Arab and foreign investment, bolstering bourgeois civil society, tying Syria further into the international political economy, and proliferating transnational ties with the Western world. This could accelerate internal pluralization and ultimately open the foreign policy process itself to the constraining impact of domestic and transnational economic interests.

Conclusion

The view that Asad's regime needs the conflict with Israel and cannot survive peace is very much exaggerated. Asad, far from shaping Syria's policy according to the survival needs of domestic politics, achieved substantial autonomy in foreign policy making. Now, as foreign policy goals are altering, he is making the internal alterations needed to preserve regime autonomy and stability in an era of peace. Although he has preserved the patrimonial core of the regime, he has sought to shift the balance away from reliance on the party, army, and Alawi jama'a toward the bourgeoisie. By diversifying and broadening the regime coalition, he has enhanced his ability to balance above it. Economic alternatives to wartime "rent" from the rich Arab Gulf states are already being fostered by economic liberalization.

If Asad feels forced to settle for less than full Israeli withdrawal on all fronts, he faces little domestic constraint. As Arab nationalism becomes less relevant as a basis of legitimacy, the regime is seeking it in greater economic liberalism and in prosperity and political decompression. The likely peace settlement is probably a legitimacy liability but is rendered less dangerous by a subtle alteration in national identity away from Arabism toward a Syrian identity more compatible with scaled-down foreign policy goals.

In the short term, Asad has resisted any constraint on his foreign policy autonomy, such as substantial political liberalization could well entail. Regime stability appears secure in the absence of a major succession crisis. In the longer term, stability requires a gradual upgrading of institutions to accommodate the inevitable demands for more autonomous political participation, which the revival of civil society under peace will encourage.

Notes

1. Daniel Pipes, *Greater Syria: The History of an Ambition*; Robert Kaplan Lecture, U.S. Institute of Peace, December 7, 1993.

2. This model is adumbrated in Graham Allison, "Conceptual Models and the Cuban Missile Crisis," *American Political Science Review* (September 1969): 689–718. For the definitive study of Asad's foreign policy that depicts him as a masterful chess player in the rational actor mode, see Patrick Seale, *Asad: The Struggle for the Middle East*.

3. Edward Sheehan, "How Kissinger Did It: Step by Step in the Middle East," *Foreign Policy* 22 (Spring 1976).

4. Robert K. Lifton, "Talking with Asad: A Visit to the Middle East in Transition, 10.

5. *BBC Summary of World Broadcasts*, August 3, 1993.

6. Ibid., July 23, 1991.

7. Raymond A. Hinnebusch, "The Political Economy of Economic Liberalization in Syria," *International Journal of Middle East Studies* 27 (1995): 318.

8. *Middle East Mirror*, January 21, 1994.

9. *Middle East Insight* (September/October 1994): 8.

10. *The Middle East*, September 1994, 8.

11. David W. Lesch, *Christian Science Monitor*, December 6, 1995.

12. *Middle East Mirror*, April 1, 1992, 13.

13. *BBC Summary of World Broadcasts*, March 14, 1992.

14. Israel Shahak, "Israel and Syria: Peace through Strategic Parity?" *Middle East International*, December 16, 1994, 18–19.

15. *al-Hiyat* in *Middle East Mirror*, May 5, 1994, 25. See also chapter 14 by Robert O. Freedman in this volume.

16. *BBC Summary of World Broadcasts*, August 3, 1993.

17. *Middle East Mirror,* October 15-16, 1991.

18. Ibid., March 10, 1994.

19. Ibid., March 10, 1994.

20. Volker Perthes, "Syria's Parliamentary Elections: Remodeling Asad's Political Base," *Middle East Report* 174 (January/February 1992), 35; *The Middle East,* October 1994, 18; *Middle East Insight,* September/October, 1994, 5.

21. Sylvia Poelling, "Investment Law No. 10: Which Future for the Private Sector?" in Eberhard Kienle, ed., *Contemporary Syria: Liberalization between Cold War and Cold Peace,* 14.

22. *Syria Country Report,* Economist Intelligence Unit, 2nd Quarter 1994, 3.

23. Ibid., 11.

24. *BBC Summary of World Broadcasts,* February 24, 1994.

6: Egypt at the Crossroads

Domestic, Economic, and Political Stagnation and
Foreign Policy Constraints

Louis J. Cantori

[Egyptians] will never give in to mercenary gangs ruled by an oppressive
[Sudanese] clique that distorts God's religion, works against the people's
interest and devotes its efforts to serving Satan.
   Brothers and Sisters: Regarding the conspiracy that targeted me, all persons are mortals but the homeland is immortal while we are mortals. Regardless of the importance of our roles, we are mere pieces of a noble history that dates back 7,000 years.

Husni Mubarak, speech, Cairo Radio Network, July 23, 1995 (anniversary
of the July 23, 1952, Revolution) (FBIS, July 24, 1995).

Egypt's obsession with conspiracies that are said to originate in the Sudan
and Iran and its fears regarding political Islam in Algeria and Gaza reveal
a nation uncharacteristically on the defensive in foreign policy. This defensiveness is a direct reflection of its domestic vulnerabilities and insufficiencies. The "homeland" may be "immortal" and it may have a seven-
thousand-year "noble history," but it is also at an impasse in domestic
politics and foreign policy. Evidence of the impasse is the Egyptian state's
loss of its characteristic ability to pursue shrewdly its foreign policy interests significantly free from domestic political considerations. This handi-
cap, moreover, is occurring at a time when changes that limit its foreign
policy options are taking place in a Middle Eastern regional environment
that is subordinated to the international environment. The combination of
a bloody repression of armed Islamist attacks largely in the south of the
country and a virtually nonperforming microeconomy in spite of impres-
sive macroeconomic indicators contribute to lethargy and lack of political
performance. Paradoxically, however, all these failings give little expectation of short-term political instability.

There is a theoretical argument to make regarding the interpretation of Egyptian foreign policy. Is this policy to be understood in terms of the pursuit of Egyptian national interests free from domestic determinants, or is it an extension of domestic political factors? Is the pursuit of power and influence the primary motivation, or is legitimacy and regime survival at stake?[1] This chapter analyzes the domestic political impasse in Egypt, the international and regional context of Egyptian foreign policy, the nature of the Egyptian state and the foreign policy process, and Egyptian foreign policy since the conclusion of the second Gulf War in 1991.

The Impasse of the Egyptian Economy and Politics

Domestic policy in Egypt reveals evidence of macroeconomic successes, microeconomic insufficiencies, and political inadequacies. The macroeconomic successes are in fact largely successes in foreign policy.[2] As a reward for its role in forming the Arab alliance in the 1991 Gulf War, Egypt's $40 billion debt was reduced by 1993 to $26 billion. Its foreign currency reserves rose from $2.7 billion in 1990 to $12 billion by 1993. The budget deficit fell from 20 percent of Gross Domestic Product in 1990 to 3 percent in 1993. In the same period, inflation fell from 25 percent to slightly less than 10 percent.[3] Egypt not only collects the rents of foreign economic assistance ($4 billion in 1994) but also has its four "pillars" of hard-currency earnings: worker remittances from oil-rich countries ($6.2 billion, 1994); the rents of oil revenues ($1.5 billion, 1994); Suez Canal receipts ($2 billion, 1994); and tourism receipts ($2.1 billion, 1994).[4] Egypt's small oil reserves figured in its foreign policy in the mid-1970s, when they were recovered from Israeli control in the Sinai II agreement of 1975 between the two countries. Worker remittances, on the other hand, tend to be the way oil wealth is redistributed in the Middle East from the oil-rich countries. One of the sensitivities of this is the way in which millions of Egyptian workers in countries like Libya and Saudi Arabia condition relationships; Egypt's less critical view of Libya can be understood in this way.[5]

If the preceding macroeconomic successes represent foreign policy rewards and sound fiscal management, Egypt's economic performance is another matter. Per capita GDP growth fell from $680 in 1986 to $600 in 1993. Comparing growth of production rates in the two periods 1970–80 and 1980–93, agricultural, industrial, and services rates fell from 40 percent to 80 percent. Unemployment by 1993 reached perhaps as high as 20% The UN Development Program has termed Egypt one of four failed states in the world.[6] Egypt's economy has been stabilized but has not undergone structural reform. More than half the annual GDP still comes from public enterprises and hardly any have been privatized.[7] Food subsidies have been cut, further impoverishing the masses, whereas steps to make the economy productive are not acted upon. The masses are called upon to make sacrifices while the political class, firmly entrenched in the management of public enterprises, continues to benefit.

Just as the economic gaps widen, so do the political ones. Participatory politics is not the hallmark of the corporatist state defined here. During presidential elections, the masses have the opportunity to "support" the single candidate, as in October 1993 when there was 95 percent support, and in parliamentary elections the official National Democratic Party receives similar support.[8] The party system is based on gradations in the opinions of segments of the political class, but they are also prevented from working to achieve grass roots electoral support, especially since 1990. In addition, intellectuals are taken into custody and later released, and newspaper editors are imprisoned for what they have written.[9] Riding roughshod over people is the treatment not only for the masses but also the political class, whose support is necessary for regime stability. Somewhat ominously, the situation resembles incidents in September 1981, when Sadat had very similarly alienated nearly all of his expected supporters by imprisoning them. He was assassinated the following month. Mubarak has thus far survived two attempts on his life.

Foreign policy has not only generated the resources for economic stabilization but has also been providing support for the military, upon which the regime's support depends. It received over half of the annual $2.2 billion a year given Egypt by the United States. This money, plus 19 percent of total government expenditures and unknown receipts from military-owned factories that also produce consumer goods, appears to be what is needed to keep the army out of politics.[10] Foreign policy can be seen as benefiting the regime in terms of foreign rents that stabilize the economy and assure the loyalty of the army. Otherwise, however, the economy is not producing, the masses are deprived, and important segments of the political class are alienated.

From Unipolarity to Multipolarity in the International System

The post–Cold War world has been a unipolar one of continued U.S. dominance. The international political economy strongly suggests that the economic powers of Germany, Japan, China, Taiwan, and the emerging states of Malaysia, Brazil, Indonesia, and others are already playing major international roles in their respective regions. The potential is for regional hegemonies and rivalries to begin to herald the emergence of a new multipolar system. The United States in this anticipated new system would still be dominant, but increasingly it would be "first among more equals."[11] For the present, however, a critical view of the sole superpower role of the United States is that it has in fact yielded to the "imperial temptation" in opting for courses of action that favor military security rather than diplomatic means.[12] This "imperial" impulse is accompanied by a characteristic cultural messianism that sees the American version of European Enlightenment values of democracy, human rights, and a market economy being imposed upon peoples of contrasting communal and collective values.[13]

The evidence of this compulsiveness of U.S. policy can be seen in the Middle East. The result is deep American policy commitment. Critics would argue that the decision to go to war with Iraq before having exhausted diplomatic means illustrates this, as does the continued U.S. military commitment in the Gulf. A policy of dual containment is carried out by military rather than diplomatic means, and the military means is American rather than, possibly, Syrian or Egyptian.[14] Evidence of American cultural messianism can be seen in the rhetoric and sometimes the concreteness of preferred democratization in the form of U.S. foreign economic assistance, as in Morocco, Tunisia, and Egypt. Much more bold is the advocacy of what might be called the American economic culture and its version of capitalism—that is, economic restructuring and privatization of state-owned enterprises. There is, after all, the perhaps more culturally relevant model of state-led capitalism termed "the Asian way."[15]

The foregoing suggests that if the "imperial temptation" of U.S. policy is global, the temptation is perhaps the greatest in the Middle East, where the world's greatest concentration of oil and a sizable domestic political constituency supporting the democratic state of Israel are found in combination with the intersections of strategically important land, air, and sea routes. The internal problems of Russia and a preoccupation with existing and potential successor states from the old Soviet Union continue to reduce Russia's profile in the Middle East.

The implication of the preceding is that American policy in the Middle East seeks maximum influence and control. This is achieved not simply by military and economic imposition but also by specific U.S. foreign policy interests that are often complementary to those of indigenous states, such as Saudi Arabian or Egyptian and American antiterrorism. However, even in the case of two of America's greatest economic and military beneficiaries, Egypt and Israel, the indigenous states can, from time to time, challenge U.S. efforts at control. Instances of U.S.-Egyptian tension will be described later, but the pattern of close U.S.-Egyptian ties since 1991 has been noted previously. (Egypt benefited to a major degree from its role of constructing the Arab alliance in Operation Desert Storm; its U.S. debt of $40 billion was cut in half, and the International Monetary Fund and other lenders followed suit, thus saving Egypt an estimated $1 billion annually in debt servicing.) Egypt's usefulness in the Gulf War as well as its continued service in the Israeli-Palestinian peace process has not only preserved its $2.3 billion annual economic and military assistance in spite of cost cutting by the U.S. Congress, but its short-term future also seems assured.

The Regional Context of Egyptian Foreign Policy

Arab international relations in the aftermath of the 1967 war and Syrian, Egyptian, and Jordanian territorial losses to Israel became enmeshed in the Palestine question. Egypt's foreign and military policies of the 1970s resulted in the bilateral peace treaty with Israel in 1979 and the regaining of occupied Sinai in 1982. The absence of Egypt from the Arab equation facilitated the Israeli invasion of Lebanon in 1982, and the 1989 reentry of Egypt into the Arab state system made it evident that without Egypt's assistance the Arab states could neither recover their own territorial losses nor alleviate the repression of the Palestinians by Israelis seeking to suppress the intifada.[16] Meanwhile, the overthrow of the shah in Iran in 1979 put in motion circumstances leading to the Iraqi invasion of Iran in 1980, which resulted in a second crisis in Middle Eastern international relations. The end of that war in 1988 brought a brief interruption of conflict. The second Gulf crisis, in 1990–91, became a further benchmark event. The Arab state system had already been riven by the 1967, 1980, and 1982 wars. The Gulf War of 1991 fundamentally ended the usefulness of the concept "Arab state system." Even Arab observers now have noted that the concept has been replaced by that of the Middle East (and possibly North African) state system.[17] The non-Arab states of Turkey and Iran are now active international players, and the peace process has now accomplished the same thing for Israel. The Middle East is now a system of conventional international relations.

Egypt's historical foreign policy leadership role has been affected by the preceding developments. The Arabism of Egypt's assumed leadership role in the past has now been transformed from a political ideology into a meaningful cultural identity. As a consequence, Egypt's ability, as recently as perhaps the Arab alliance of 1990–91, to be *the* Arab leader and also to be the interlocutor between the U.S. and Arab states is now significantly ended. Egypt's present and future diplomatic role is likely to be based on its geopolitical position, the size of its population, its military capabilities, its economic strength, and its continued leadership of Arab culture—all of which are conventional factors of international power.

The Egyptian State and Foreign Policy

The Egyptian state is an autonomous corporatist *(takafalliyya)* state, which means that symbolically and institutionally it possesses authority separate from the actual holders of power (for example, "the homeland is immortal"). The state's legitimacy is derived from patriarchical-patrimonial models of authority; that is, the state concentrates authority in the hands of the executive but is understood also to have a custodial role to play in society. Such a state can range from being consultative *(shura)* in its political style (like Saudi Arabia) to being more participatory and democratic (like Egypt). It should be noted, however, that such consultation takes place with the political class and participation is also by segments of the same class. The corporatist state's politics are intrinsically elitist.

As such a state, Egypt is top-down in its politics; the president is surrounded by a ruling class made up of his personal staff and his cabinet. Below these, there is a political class, made up of the 20 percent of the population who receive over 50 percent of the income of the country. This class is the attentive public who can play key consultative roles because they are also the leaders of the functional corporatist groups that carry out support services for the regime system (lawyers' associations, engineering societies, trade unions, and the like). These groups are licensed by the state, based on a "contractual" agreement. This licensing is both informal and formal. In formal terms it is Law 32 of 1964, as administered by the minister of social welfare, that defines the legal relationship and licenses the group. Generally, the "contract" stipulates that in exchange for not engaging in oppositional politics, the organization has a monopoly in that activity (for example, Islamic charity organizations). The corporatist state therefore facilitates elitist foreign policy decision making.[18]

Islam and Egyptian Foreign Policy

The preceding is useful for understanding what otherwise appears a paradox of an Egyptian state that brutally crushes the Gamaa Islamiyya (Islamic Group) while the regime itself, which until the 1980s was secularist, is becoming progressively Islamized. There has been underway since the 1967 war a deep recommitment to religious values by Muslim and Coptic Christian alike. This Islamization process has preceded both from below and from the top. From below, during the 1980s and continuing until now, the government has been licensing Islamic health care centers, Islamic charities, and Islamic elementary schools as alternatives to public agencies and institutions. The result has been that the urban poor population has received free services that the government itself is administratively unable to deliver. These services have generally been politically neutral and in the societal conservative mainstream.[19] However, the health care workers and physicians, social workers, and other professionals have in a general sense been affiliated with this mainstream but also with a previously radical group, the Muslim Brethren *(Ikhwan al-Muslimun)*. Religious groups are by law not allowed to organize as political parties, but beginning in the 1987 parliamentary elections personally popular Muslim Brethren have run as independents in affiliation with established parties and have thereby gained entry into the parliament. From the point of view of the government, those persons who wish to play the political game by democratic rules have in effect violated their nonpolitical "contract," and the results have been widespread arrests, torture, mass trials, and harsh prison sentences.

At the same time, from the top, the formal religious institutions such as the center of Islamic learning, Al-Azhar University, have been allowed to issue increasingly conservative edicts and decrees. Also, what was previously a highly secular French-inspired system of law has begun to adopt similarly conservative religious points of view, such as supporting the involuntary divorce of a couple when the scholar husband has been accused of being an apostate.[20]

But even while the government itself slides to the right, it has been engaging in full-fledged combat with the Gamaa Islamiyya and its campaign of killing police officials and foreign tourists. The Gamaa Islamiyya is probably itself a small organization, but its support and that of the Islamic trend itself is partly a result of deepening poverty and maldistribution of income accompanied by government ineptitude and lack of political imagination. The government response is to search for scapegoats, and hence the Islamic opposition is said to originate abroad with foreign agitators from Iran but perhaps mainly Sudan.

There is a little evidence to support these allegations regarding Sudan, but they have led to harangue and even bloodshed in the case of the disputed southeastern border area of Helaib on the Red Sea.[21] In these instances the generic term "antiterrorism" is employed, a term and policy that Egypt shares with the United States and Israel. In the process, what was once the widely admired and shrewdly pursued Egyptian foreign policy process has become reflective of desperate responses to an internal threat. On other more conventional issues such as the peace process, how-

ever, the essential elitism of the corporatist state's foreign policy process
still serves the Egyptian national interest well.

Egyptian Foreign Policy and the Peace Process

Egypt is unusual among third world states for the amounts it has been
able to collect as foreign economic assistance "rents" and the length of time
it has done so. This sense of "rents" rather than being conventionally termed
assistance in promoting development is the clearest in the case of U.S. economic and military assistance. From its modest inception in 1977 such assistance was an implicit political payment for cooperation in the U.S.-led
effort to gain Egyptian commitment to various U.S. administrations' versions of peace between Israel and its Arab neighbors. Egypt had shown in
the 1973 war that it had a genuine military destructive capability. Beginning with Sadat and the achievement of bilateral peace with Israel in 1979,
such assistance was intended to show the military security and development assistance benefits that peace could bring. The turbulence of the tacit
U.S. approval of the Israeli invasion of Lebanon in 1982 and its aftermath
prevented Egypt during the 1980s from playing a facilitating role in
brokering a peace with the Palestinians, but on the other hand, Egypt did
honor its treaty commitment to the Israelis during this difficult decade. It
was to be both the peace initiatives of the Bush administration and Egypt's
leadership role in the Gulf War alliance that clearly demonstrated the usefulness of the U.S.-Egyptian relationship. Egypt had meanwhile replaced
Iran after 1979 as an important political cornerstone of U.S. policy in the
region.

From 1989 onward, with the return of Egypt to the Arab state system
and the consistent peace efforts by President Bush and Secretary of State
James Baker, Egypt became a full partner in the search for a peace settlement. From the Madrid conference of 1991 onward, the Egyptian involvement increased in spite of the Israeli Likud government's continued ob-
structionism.[22] With the election of a Labor government under Prime Minister
Yitzhak Rabin and his successor Shimon Peres, the working relationships
have improved but at the cost of Egyptian prominence. The Oslo Declaration of Principles of September 1993 was not only prepared in secret by
Rabin and Arafat but was unknown to the United States or the Egyptians
or anyone else for that matter. More recently, therefore, Egypt's role has
receded from important interlocutor to useful facilitator. When there are
frictions, Egypt provides a meeting place and intermediation. At this point
in the peace process, and diplomatically in general, the Israelis have made

their own peace with Jordan and, until the cooling of the peace process after March 1997, had established their own working relationships with Morocco, Qatar, Oman, and even indirectly with Saudi Arabia.[23]

Meanwhile, Egypt had vigilantly worked to create an independence of policy as well, and in the process has reminded Americans and Israelis alike that it cannot be taken for granted. For example, the issue of the U.N. renewal of the Nuclear Non-Proliferation Treaty gave Egypt the opportunity to insist that if it were to sign the treaty, then Israel should as well. The issue involved in the dispute is the generally acknowledged supposition that Israel possesses two hundred or more nuclear bomb devices. Israel denies this, and U.S. policy is one of supporting Israel. In the final analysis the issue was finessed but not before Egypt had made its point.[24] The Nuclear Non-Proliferation Treaty issue was also, however, evidence of Egyptian reservations about Israel's future role in the Middle East after the establishment of an Israeli-Palestinian peace. Egypt's view of Israel and its constant call for normalization was characterized by Egypt's foreign minister as follows: "If Israel's idea about normalization is that we should honor it in every area and not annoy it, we reject this idea. We will not be anybody's puppet. . . . We will implement our own agenda whether it makes Israel happy or miserable."[25] Egypt has voiced anger about a nuclear-armed Israel as a rival to its own hegemony. *Al-Ahram* editorialized on the nuclear issue, "It is not our intention to have peace at the expense of Egypt."[26] From this perspective, chemical weapons of mass destruction by Libya are seen as a counterweight to what is viewed as a connected U.S.-Israel policy of maintaining Israel as the sixth most militarily powerful state in the world and denying Middle Eastern states chemical and intermediate missile counterweights. Even more immediately, Egypt is worried that Israel will not only emerge as a militarily powerful rival but will also dominate in economic terms. The fear is that Palestine as the second largest export market for Israeli goods will be replicated in the region and that Arab cheap labor will also fuel the Israeli economy.[27]

This receding of the Egyptian diplomatic role over time has coincided with the emergence of the conventionalization of the Middle Eastern state relationships and the end of Arabism and Egypt's "Arab" leadership role. Islamism has now emerged as a frequently misunderstood phenomenon most seemingly threatening in terms of its potential for coming to power and creating political instability. Egypt's human rights excesses in putting down its Islamic radicals have thus not met strong objections. Meanwhile its own Islamic rebellion is useful for justifying the continuation of U.S. aid.

Conclusion

Economic stagnation, administrative incapacity, widespread corruption, and political repression have created a condition of Egyptian domestic political and economic stagnation. In the midst of this stagnation, the Islamic revival represents a general clarity of purpose and the means for meeting the social needs of the population.

Islamic political extremism on the other hand, is without mass popular support, but the regime is so disoriented by it and so unable to acknowledge its own failings that it seeks scapegoats abroad in its foreign policy pronouncements.[28] The desperateness of those complaints, however, are not a distraction from the ability of the regime to continue to collect U.S. and other foreign assistance rents. These rents work to stabilize the economy and the political systems. Meanwhile, however, the foreign policy room for maneuver of the regime is declining. As long as the peace process progresses, the Middle Eastern regional international system is becoming conventionalized. The battle of Arab versus Arab in the Gulf War ended the Arabism that Egypt had always sought to lead and use to its own advantage. This trend has been reinforced by the progress thus far in the peace process. Not only has each Arab state begun to see its own possible individual advantage in being on the peace train, but Israel and Turkey see the opportunities as well. The presence of non-Arab states has created fluidity and conventionality in the system of international relations. Syria already nearly equals Egypt in military capability terms and Iraq in its inevitable national recovery will not be far behind.

Egypt's present economic and political weaknesses do not bode well for dealing with the "new" powerful Middle Eastern states of Israel, Iran, and Turkey. To return to the theoretical points raised at the beginning of this chapter, the executive has nearly always been able to externalize its economic difficulties. The scapegoating of its Islamic opposition is further evidence of this externalization. But this externalization has had success in the past because Egypt has been able to manipulate and even dominate its external environment. It has been assisted in this by the Palestinian-Israeli issue. Its role as an important intermediary has declined with the advancement of peace. However, the deterioration of the peace process in 1997 has given it new diplomatic opportunities. This analysis suggests that it has been losing its ability to do so. Egypt can in all likelihood continue for a time in its present mode, but greater economic and military strength will be needed if Egypt is to achieve the greatness it expects of itself.

Notes

1. Four recent papers address these questions in regard to the Middle East, three of them by way of generalizing about the interpretation of Middle Eastern international relations: Michael Barnett, "Identity and Security in the Middle East"; Michael C. Hudson, "'Rogue' Regimes or Security Regimes? The Dialectics of Inclusion and Exclusion in the Middle East"; Shibley Telhami, "Power and Legitimacy in Arab Alliances"; and (from the specific point of view of Egyptian foreign policy) Martin Malin, "International Inclusion and Domestic Exclusion in the Making of Egyptian Foreign Policy." These papers were presented to the Conference Group on the Middle East, American Political Science Association, New York, September 1–4, 1994.

2. This is the argument of Ali Hilal Dessouki, "The Primacy of Economics: The Foreign Policy of Egypt." It is also analyzed in Gregory Aftandilian, *Egypt's Bid for Arab Leadership*, and it is Malin's argument as well, accompanied by detailed analysis of the phenomenon in the Nasser and Sadat eras.

3. These figures are taken from Cassandra, "The Impending Crisis in Egypt," *Middle East Journal* 49, no. 1 (Winter 1995), 11. *Financial Times, Egypt*, May 15, 1995, 1.

4. *Financial Times*, May 15, 1995, 2.

5. There are an estimated 350,000 Egyptian workers in Libya.

6. Cassandra, 13, and *World Development Report 1995*, 164.

7. *Financial Times*, May 15, 1995, 2. With the new government of Kamel el-Ganzouri in January 1996, Egypt once again is *saying* it will privatize more energetically and has received a further $4 billion debt relief from the IMF; *Financial Times*, March 7, 1996.

8. On the referendum for Mubarak to be allowed a third term, see *Financial Times*, October 6, 1993, and on government interference in a landslide victory for the official National Democratic Party, see Mona Makram Ebeid, "Egypt's 1995 Elections: One Step Forward, Two Steps Back."

9. For example, Muhammad Tuham, editor of the well-respected satirical review *Ruz al-Yusuf*, was sentenced to two years' hard labor for criticizing Islamists (*New York Times*, December 31, 1995). This is an example of the Islamization of the Mubarak government even while cracking down on Islamists.

10. *Financial Times*, May 15, 1995, and Cassandra, 23.

11. This argument is expanded upon in Louis J. Cantori, "The Middle East in the New World Order." The recommendation of U.S. global leadership as opposed to multipolarity or neo-isolationism is in Zalmay Khalilzad, ed., *Strategic Appraisal* (Santa Monica: Rand Corporation, 1996), 4.

12. Robert W. Tucker and David C. Hendrickson, *The Imperial Temptation:The New World Order and America's Purpose*.

13. On American messianism, see Mustapha Filali, "La Guerre du Golfe: Prelude à un Nouvel Ordre Regonal Arabe," in Chadly Ayari et al., *La Guerre du Golfe et l'Avenir des Arabes* (Casablanca: EDIFF, 1991), 95.

14. This argument is in Louis J. Cantori, "Regional Solutions to Regional Problems: The Gulf and Somalia," *Middle East Policy* 3, no. 3 (1994), 234–40.

15. Cantori, "Privatization," and Cantori, "The 'Asian Way,' the 'Western Way,' and the 'Islamic Way,' to Economic Growth," *The Diplomat* (London) 2, no. 4 (February 1997), 44–45.

16. Louis J. Cantori, "Egypt Reenters the Arab State System."

17. According to Hicham Djait, the Arab nation in the aftermath of the Gulf War now has only the meaning of a single culture, and politically one now must speak of the Middle East. "Repercussions de la guerre du golfe sur la culture politique Arabe," in Ayari et al., 185–86.

18. This theoretical discussion of corporatism is derived from Hegel, *Grundlinien der Philosophie des Rechts* (The philosophy of right) (Frankfurt: Suhrkamp Verlag, 1986), vol. 7, first published in Berlin in 1821. These ideas are elaborated in Louis J. Cantori and Drew Ziegler, eds., *Comparative Politics in the Post-Behavioral Era*, 75–77, 417–26; Cantori, "Islamic Revivalism: Conservatism and Progress in Contemporary Egypt"; Cantori, "Muhafazawa al-Taqaddam: Misr al-Ahya al-Islamiyya," *Qirat al-Siyasiyya* (Beirut), 3 (1993): 8–26; Cantori, "Privatization."

19. On the general point of the Islamization of a regime bent on repressing both an extreme Islamism and a moderate Islamism, see Fuad Ajami, "The Sorrows of Egypt. On Islamic service organizations, see Denis J. Sullivan, *Private Voluntary Organizations in Egypt: Islamic Development, Private Initiative and State Control.*

20. See Ajami.

21. On the Egyptian preoccupation with Sudan, see the epigraph at the beginning of this chapter. On the Egyptian view in general, see Francis Deng, "Egypt's Dilemma on the Sudan," *Middle East Policy* 4, nos. 1–2 (September 1995): 50–56, including putting into perspective the attack on Mubarak's life in Ethiopia (June 26, 1995) and Egyptian allegations of Sudanese involvement. Sudan's alleged terrorism is a vexed one, including the U.S. policy of labeling Sudan a "terrorist" state. There is little factual evidence to support the Egyptian and American allegations. One U.S. official has said the American concurrence in the label "terrorist" may be a "friendly service," i.e., a U.S. professional intelligence courtesy to a friendly fellow service, Egyptian intelligence. On the Halaib issue, see Economist Intelligence Unit, *Country Report: Egypt,* 14. Since the 1956 independence of Sudan, Egypt has had sovereign rights and Sudan administrative responsibilities. Oil is now thought possible in the area.

22. See Cantori, "Unipolarity and Egyptian Hegemony in the Middle East."

23. Ajami, 86–87.

24. For a detailed discussion of Egypt and the NPT issue in the overall context of U.S. nonproliferation policy, see Paul Power, "Middle East Nuclear Issues in Global Perspective," *Middle East Policy* 4, nos. 1–2 (September 1995): 201–6.

25. FBIS, Middle East News Agency, March 6, 1996.

26. For a critical analysis of Egyptian-Israeli relations, see Fawaz Gerges, "Egyptian-Israeli Relations Turn Sour," 72, for the Foreign Minister Mousa quote.

27. Ibid.

28. Not only does Islamism have a clarity of vision regarding remedies to the domestic policy insufficiencies of the government of Egypt but it has a foreign policy

vision as well. Should the peace process go awry, there is a sizable Islamic literature prepared to argue that the failure would be one of Zionist-U.S. government collusion. The general argument would be that the terms of peace are already so weighted in favor of Israel that a resumption of conflict is inevitable. See Yvonne Yazbeck Haddad, "Islamist Perceptions of U.S. Policy in the Middle East," in David Lesch, ed., *The Middle East and the United States: A Historical and Political Assessment* (Boulder: Westview Press, 1996), 419–37.

PART II

Turkey and the Gulf States

7: Turkey and the Middle East after Oslo I

George E. Gruen

The Turkish government enthusiastically endorsed the mutual recognition by Israel and the Palestine Liberation Organization that was formalized by the signing of the historic Declaration of Principles (the Oslo I agreement) on the White House lawn in September 1993. The unprecedented handshake between Prime Minister Yitzhak Rabin and PLO Chairman Yasir Arafat at the urging of President Clinton symbolized the beginning of the process of Palestinian-Israeli reconciliation that Ankara had long called for. It also highlighted the continuing importance of the American role in the peace process that the United States had initiated at Madrid in October 1991.

From the Turkish perspective, these developments were not only welcome but long overdue. The agreement between Israel and the Palestine Liberation Organization reinforced Ankara's decision to be actively involved in the multilateral working groups of the Middle East peace process. Moreover, the willingness of the PLO and Israel to deal openly with one another, following the start of direct bilateral peace talks between Israel and the individual states of Jordan, Syria, and Lebanon, finally removed from the minds of the Turkish foreign policy establishment the last obstacle to close and public cooperation between Turkey and Israel. Previously Ankara always weighed carefully the negative impact of its ties with Israel on Turkey's efforts to improve its relations with the Arab and Islamic worlds. As a result of Arab economic and political pressures, Ankara had downgraded the formal level of Turkish-Israel relations in 1956, at the time of the Sinai campaign, and in 1980, following the Knesset's adoption of the Jerusalem law. During the mid-1950s, as Turkey was seeking to recruit Arab participation in U.S.-sponsored Middle East defense arrangements, Ankara had decided to minimize public signs of cooperation with Israel. Nevertheless, because of basic Turkish-Israeli mutual interests, both economic and strategic, and because of shared pro-Western secular perspectives, Ankara rejected Arab demands to totally break off all relations with the Jewish state.

The Oslo Agreement Ends Turkish Ambivalence

The various factors influencing Turkish policy in the early years are analyzed in my Columbia University doctoral dissertation, "Turkey, Israel and the Palestine Question, 1948–1960." In view of conflicting pressures and the resultant fluctuations in Turkish policy toward Israel, the work is subtitled "A Study in the Diplomacy of Ambivalence."[1] The September 1993 Palestinian-Israeli agreement ended Ankara's ambivalence because it removed the dilemma and changed the calculus in the Middle East.

Turkey no longer has to choose between supporting either Israel or the Arab states. Ankara now speaks of Israel as a key player in the new strategic alliance being forged in the region. At a joint press conference in Ankara with visiting Israeli Foreign Minister Shimon Peres in April 1994, Turkish Foreign Minister Hikmet Çetin announced that Turkey and Israel had agreed to play "leadership" roles in setting up the Conference on Security and Cooperation in the Middle East (CSCME); it was to be modeled on the Conference [now renamed the Organization] on Security and Cooperation in Europe. Among its objectives would be discussing and defusing threats to peace and stability in the region, including the escalating missile race, as well as fostering economic and technical cooperation. The Turkish and Israeli leaders said they hoped to draw in the moderate Arab states, which increasingly see terrorism from Islamic fundamentalists and other radical groups as a major threat to regional stability.[2]

Thus, on one side of the new equation that has emerged following the Gulf War and the Madrid conference are Turkey and Israel, joined by Jordan, Egypt, the Palestinians, and other Arab states working toward peace (such as Morocco and Tunisia, and the Gulf sheikhdoms of Oman and Qatar). On the opposing side of the equation are the rejectionist elements in the region. These include militantly Islamic Iran, Sudan, and groups among Lebanese Shi'ites (Hizbollah) and Palestinians (Hamas, Islamic Jihad), as well as secular anti-American and anti–peace process radical elements, such as Libya, Iraq, George Habbash's Popular Front for the Liberation of Palestine, and nine other Palestinian rejectionist groups headquartered in Damascus.

One subject of continuing discussion and debate among Ankara, Jerusalem, and Washington has been: Where is Syria to be placed in this equation of supporters and opponents of peace and stability in the Middle East? The oft-expressed Turkish and Israeli hope is that eventually Syria will realize the economic benefits of interdependence and mutual cooperation in peaceful relations with all of its neighbors. From the Turkish perspective, however, Syria continues to be a disruptive element, supporting not only such terrorist groups as the Palestinian rejectionists but also radical groups seeking to destabilize Turkey, most notably the Kurdistan Workers Party (PKK), which has employed terrorism in its decade-long bloody secessionist struggle against Turkey.[3] (Discussions that follow will consider the Turkish-Syrian dispute over the quantity of water to be supplied by Turkey to Syria from the Euphrates—and the recent linkage of the dispute to the Syrian-Israeli negotiations over the Golan Heights and the headwaters of the Jordan River. Also discussed later are the Turkish offers—as part of Ankara's contribution to the peace process—to export water to alleviate the shortages facing the Palestinians, Israelis, and Jordanians.)

Evolution of Ankara's Position on the "Palestine Question"

Before considering the details of Ankara's involvement in the peace process, a brief discussion of the evolution of Turkey's position may be helpful. The PLO-Israel agreement incorporated principles that Ankara had long championed. The Turkish government had consistently argued that a peaceful solution of the Arab-Israel conflict required, first, Israeli withdrawal from territories occupied in the June 1967 war and, second, the Arab states' recognition of Israel's right to live within secure and recognized borders. While these basic principles were included in UN Security Council resolution 242, of November 22, 1967, the resolution was silent about the political future of the Palestinians and spoke only of the necessity of a "just settlement of the refugee problem." Moreover, as pointed out by Ambassador Arthur Goldberg, the U.S. representative to the United Nations and a coauthor of the resolution, the deliberate exclusion of the adjective *Palestinian* or *Arab* before the word *refugees* was meant to indicate that a comprehensive settlement would also have to address the claims of Jews from Arab countries who were expelled or felt pressured to leave their native countries as a result of the Arab-Israel conflict.[4]

Ankara had always been far more explicit in its support of Palestinian national aspirations. In November 1947, when the UN General Assembly debated the future of Palestine, Turkey had joined with the Arab and Muslim states in calling for establishment of a unitary independent Arab state in all of Palestine when the British Mandate ended. Ankara was also part of the minority that opposed the General Assembly resolution that recommended partitioning western Palestine into two independent states, one Jewish and one Arab, with a special UN administration of Jerusalem. However, true to the basic pragmatism of its foreign policy, once Turkey saw that the state of Israel had demonstrated its viability by defeating the Arab attacks in the 1948 war of independence and by establishing ties with the United States and other world powers, Ankara recognized the Jewish state in March 1949 and established diplomatic relations with Israel the following year.

Ankara had remained strictly neutral during the 1948 Arab-Israel conflict. Once the fighting was over, Turkey permitted its Jewish citizens to emigrate freely to Israel. Commercial ties and direct aerial and maritime links also quickly developed between the two countries. Turkey had come to realize the difficulties in resolving the Arab-Israel conflict when it served with the United States and France on the Palestine Conciliation Commission (PCC) set up by the U.N. in December 1948. The commission's purpose was to help the Arab states and Israel negotiate "a final settlement of all questions outstanding between them." The Turkish representative was generally regarded as skillful and fair, but the PCC was unable to bring about Arab recognition of Israel, and it abandoned the effort in the mid-1950s. Ankara downgraded the formal level of relations with Israel in response to Arab political pressure during the 1956 Suez conflict with Egypt, when Israeli forces had occupied the Sinai, and to Arab economic pressures, as well as domestic religious opposition to the Israeli Knesset's 1980 reaffirmation of the annexation of Jerusalem.

Early Clandestine Strategic Cooperation with Israel

Nevertheless, Turkey rejected Arab demands to break all ties with Israel. Commercial links, joint ventures, and quiet cooperation on intelligence and on issues of mutual strategic interest continued between these two pro-Western, non-Arab states. For example, in the aftermath of the Iraqi revolution that overthrew the pro-Western monarchy in July 1958, United States Secretary of State John Foster Dulles encouraged Turkey and Israel to cooperate more closely to combat Soviet-backed subversion of the region. Israeli Prime Minister David Ben-Gurion envisaged this expanded cooperation between Jerusalem and Ankara as part of an informal and unpublicized pro-Western alliance that, as he explained in a memo to President Eisenhower, "would be able to firmly withstand the Soviet expansion via Nasser." This alliance of like-minded countries on the periphery of the Arab world would include "two non-Arab Muslim states (Turkey and Iran), a Christian state (Ethiopia) and the State of Israel."[5] Ben-Gurion secretly flew to Ankara to discuss closer strategic cooperation with Prime Minister Adnan Menderes.[6] (To prevent leaks to the press, Turkish Foreign Ministry staff served as waiters at the official dinner.)[7] Ben-Gurion reportedly was not happy with Turkey's demand that the relationship be secret. He was said to complain, "The Turks have always treated us as one treats a mistress, and not as a partner in an openly avowed marriage." In this earlier period, before the start of Arab-Israeli peace talks, I heard Turkish diplomats and academics make the same analogy in private conversations about Turkey's relations with Israel and the Arab states: "A man may love his mistress more than his wife, and we admire Israel and share common interests, but Muslim Arabs are our family, we must keep up appearances in public." They also noted that the Arab wife brought with her a large dowry—the oil resources upon which Turkey depends.[8]

Ankara's Post-1967 Position on Solving the Arab-Israel Conflict

Following the Six Day War of June 1967, Ankara supported UN peace efforts, and its views were generally consistent with those of the mainstream Arab states and the European Community, as outlined in the Venice Declaration of 1980. This essentially called for Israeli withdrawal from the occupied territories, Arab recognition of Israel, and establishment of a Palestinian state alongside Israel. Turkey had since the 1950s repeatedly called for "a just settlement of the Palestine question in accordance with United Nations resolutions."[9]

Yet it was only in 1979, some fifteen years after the founding of the Palestine Liberation Organization, that Turkey finally allowed the PLO to open an office in Ankara. Turkish-Palestinian relations have at times been strained by hostile actions within Turkey by Palestinian terrorists.[10] Moreover, in June 1982, when the Israeli Defense Forces (IDF) overran PLO bases in southern Lebanon and Beirut, they captured twenty-six Turkish terrorists among the Palestinians. The IDF also provided Ankara with documentary evidence that not only Turkish extremists but also members of ASALA, the Armenian group that had been assassinating Turkish diplomats, were receiving training at PLO bases. Realizing the value of this information, General Kenan Evren, who had become president of Turkey following the military intervention of 1980, quietly authorized closer cooperation between the Turkish and Israeli defense and intelligence establishments. However, on the public diplomatic front Turkish-Israeli relations remained frozen at the low "second-secretary" level as Ankara sought to gain important construction contracts and other economic ventures in the Arab oil-producing countries and Iran.

Open Turkish-Israeli Defense Cooperation after Oslo I

It was only after Oslo I that the defense ministries in Ankara and Tel Aviv entered into formal and public cooperation, including major joint ventures of their defense industries. The most important of these is the $650 million five-year contract the Turkish military negotiated in 1995 with Israel Aircraft Industries to upgrade fifty-four of its U.S.-supplied F-4 Phantom jets.[11] The Israeli company won the contract over U.S. and German competitors, on the strength of Israel's demonstrated ability to lengthen the combat life of its own U.S.-supplied planes by fifteen to twenty years using state-of-the-art sophisticated Israeli radar systems, air-to-air missiles, and advanced avionics. General Çevik Bir, deputy chief of the Turkish General Staff, went to Israel in February 1996 to conclude additional protocols detailing the areas of joint cooperation.[12] According to General Bir, these areas include establishment of a high-level working group to analyze common threats; a mechanism for intelligence gathering and sharing; the supply of Israeli surveillance equipment for Turkey's use in combating terrorist infiltration across its border with Iraq; and joint training and exercises between their respective air forces and navies. David Ivry, director general of Israel's Ministry of Defense, was appointed to head the Israeli side. It is hoped that the Jordanians will soon join in this new regional security effort.[13]

The military training program was inaugurated on April 16, 1996, when eight Israeli F-16 fighter-bombers and their crews arrived at an air base outside Ankara for a week of training. Turkish F-16 pilots were to go to Israel for training later in the year, according to Turkish Defense Ministry spokesman Kemal Baolum.[14] This evidence of Turkish-Israeli defense cooperation was strongly condemned by Arab and Islamic countries and reportedly led to the cancellation of a planned visit to Turkey in mid-April by Egyptian Foreign Minister Amr Moussa. The visit was rescheduled after Onur Oymen, the undersecretary of the Turkish Foreign Ministry, was hastily dispatched to Cairo to reassure the Egyptians that the Turkish-Israeli military training and defense production agreement was "not directed against the interests of any Arab or neighboring country." Rather, he said, it was similar to agreements that Turkey had with sixteen other countries, including Egypt, and was simply a reflection of the normalization of relations between the two countries. He added that technical cooperation was developing in many areas, noting particularly that Turkey would be receiving Israeli expertise on developing water resources. Oymen decried as "baseless" and "completely wrong" allegations that Turkey would use the knowledge it acquired about Israeli air tactics in its war against the PKK separatists. He declared categorically, "The Israeli-Turkish military agreement does not include the establishment of a strategic alliance between the two countries or with any other country."[15] (See later discussion here of the Turkish-Israeli military cooperation agreement and its possible implications for Turkish-Syrian relations and the peace negotiations between Israel and Syria.)

Ankara among First to Recognize PLO-Led "Palestinian State"

While Turkey was improving its relations with Israel, Ankara continued its support of the Palestinian national movement despite the record of collusion in hostile acts against Turkey by some Palestinian militant groups. Thus, when the Palestine National Council, at its November 1988 meeting in Algiers, proclaimed an independent Palestinian state in "the occupied territories," Ankara was one of the first states to recognize the new PLO-led entity. The U.S. State Department opposed the PLO move—as it did any Israeli annexation of the territories—for seeking to achieve a "unilateral determination of the outcome of negotiations," while the British Foreign Office called the Palestinian declaration "premature."[16] In Jerusalem, the Turkish chargé d'affaires, Ekrem Güvendiren, was summoned to the Foreign Ministry and informed of Israel's "disappointment, regret and dissatisfaction in the clearest words possible." At the same time, the Israelis expressed the hope that Turkish-Israeli relations would not be hurt. Güvendiren pointedly reminded the Israelis that Turkey was "the first country in Asia" to recognize Israel. (Significantly, in keeping with the secularist principles of the Turkish Republic, he refrained from repeating what foreign press reports had emphasized at the time—that Turkey was the first Muslim country to recognize Israel.) He characterized the PNC's declaration of independence and its support for an international peace conference as "realistic and constructive" acts.[17]

The Turkish action was also questioned by a delegation of leaders of the American Jewish Committee when they met with Foreign Minister Mesut Yilmaz in Ankara on February 13, 1989. Minister Yilmaz declared that Turkey's policy on the Palestine issue was "consistent and rational" and that Ankara had sought to find a solution without taking sides. He recalled that Arafat had come to Ankara shortly before the PNC meeting in Algiers, and in meetings with Prime Minister Turgut Özal and himself, the PLO leader had asked for Turkey's recommendations. "We told him that he has to recognize Israel's right to exist and to renounce terrorism. In our opinion, the PNC met the preconditions." The foreign minister added that the PLO was now insisting that its representation in Ankara be raised to embassy level; the Turkish prerequisite, however, was that the PLO take "other encouraging steps," such as participation in an international peace conference. Minister Yilmaz indicated that he had similarly told the Israelis that "if Israel takes positive steps with regard to moving to a solution," the level of Turkish-Israeli relations would be upgraded. He also revealed that Turkey had already agreed to intensify its trade and air transport ties with Israel and had approved the renewal of Israeli participation in international fairs held in Turkey.[18]

Rise and Fall of Islamic Petrodollar Influence

Turkish-Israeli relations were indeed being quietly strengthened in the late 1980s as the economic leverage of the Arab and Iranian oil decreased when oil prices sharply declined. Özal's economic liberalization policies, instituted in 1980, enabled Ankara to greatly expand its trade with the industrialized countries of the OECD. For example, in 1982, 47 percent of all Turkish exports went to the Islamic world and 44 percent to Turkey's OECD partners. As will be noted, a decade later exports to the OECD countries had risen to 63 percent while exports to the Islamic world had declined to 20 percent of Turkey's total exports. In the period 1980–84, construction projects by Turkish contractors in Saudi Arabia, Iran, Iraq, Kuwait, and Libya quadrupled to more than $14 billion. Tens of thousands of Turkish workers also benefited from the oil boom of the early 1980s. However, the boom in Turkish-Arab economic relations was to be shortlived. By the late 1980s Turkish exporters and entrepreneurs no longer benefited from the special circumstances that had favored economic ties with the Arab countries and Iran. For example, the year 1988 brought the end of the Iran-Iraq war, from which Turkey had profited by selling to both sides. The failure of Libya to pay its debts to Turkish contractors on time and the economic problems in Iran and Iraq made them less valuable and less reliable customers, even before the UN imposed sanctions on Iraq following its invasion of Kuwait in 1990. The sanctions brought a virtual halt to official trade between Ankara and Baghdad. In an open split in the Arab world, Egypt and Syria supported the American-led allied coalition against Saddam Hussein and the Saudis and Kuwaitis cut off their financial support for the PLO. The split meant that Ankara did not have to worry about retaliation from the oil-rich Arab states if it chose to improve its ties with Israel, especially if it did so in an even-handed fashion.

Turks React to Arab "Ingratitude" and Lack of Reciprocity

The Turks were also upset at what they regarded as the ingratitude of the Arab countries for Turkish political and economic support. Officials in Ankara reportedly had hoped that in exchange for its consistent diplomatic support for the Palestinian cause, which the Arab states had made a "litmus test" of Turkish friendship, the Arab world would join Turkey in supporting the beleaguered Muslim Turkish minority in Cyprus.[19] Yet since the eruption of the crisis in the mid-1960s—especially following the Turkish military intervention in 1974—the Arabs have supported the Greek position. As Alan Makovsky points out, the Arab world persisted in seeing the Cyprus issue not as a matter requiring Muslim solidarity but as yet another example of occupation, recalling the Israeli occupation of Arab land and the past Ottoman domination of the Arab world. The Arabs roundly condemned the Turkish Cypriot declaration of independence in 1983, and the Islamic Conference Organization has never accorded the Turkish Cypriot community more than observer status. (Turkey is the only country officially to recognize the Turkish Republic of Northern Cyprus.)[20]

Yet even in instances when the Turkish position has been in line with that of the international community, Arab ingratitude has rankled the Turks. Thus, for example, Turkish contractors complained that they were not favored and in fact faced great difficulties in obtaining any contracts to help rebuild Kuwait,[21] even though Turkey's compliance with the UN decision to shut down the Iraqi-Turkish oil pipeline and suspend trade with Baghdad has recently been estimated by President Demirel to have cost the Turkish economy more than $20 billion in lost revenues.[22]

The declining importance of the Islamic countries of the Middle East for Ankara was apparent even before the September 1993 Palestinian-Israeli agreement. For example, in September 1992, when I asked Dr. Emre Gönensay, a senior economic adviser to the Turkish prime minister, about Turkish-Arab economic relations, he indicated that he had not even been asked to follow this area. His priorities were Turkey's relations with the European Community and the United States, exploration of the possibilities in Eastern Europe and Central Asia, and privatization of state enterprises. He was supportive of expanding Turkish-Israeli economic cooperation and expressed interest in plans to export Turkish water to Israel.[23]

The growth and increasing sophistication of Turkey's manufacturing and industrial sectors has enabled it to find markets in the developed world. In 1992 more than two-thirds of Turkey's trade was with the industrialized countries of the OECD, mainly with the members of the European Community. OECD countries took 63 percent of Turkey's exports and provided 69 percent of its imports. Only 20 percent of Turkey's exports went to the "Islamic countries," a category that includes Indonesia, Pakistan, and the Turkish Republic of Northern Cyprus, as well as the Arab countries of the Middle East and North Africa and Iran. The Islamic countries supplied 14 percent of Turkey's imports, and 80 percent of the total was oil from Saudi Arabia, the United Arab Emirates, and Libya.[24] As a percentage of Turkey's total exports, trade with Islamic countries has continued to decline. In 1994, exports to Islamic countries accounted for only 17% of total Turkish exports. Some U.S. analysts believe that as a result of Turkey's customs union with the European Union, which went into effect on January 1, 1996, the relative importance of Turkey's trade with the Islamic countries of the Middle East will probably decrease even further.[25] (In terms of absolute numbers, Turkey's economic relations with the Palestinians and some Arab countries may eventually improve if the peace process results in regional economic cooperation as envisaged in the Casablanca and Amman economic summits. The ending of the UN sanctions on Iraq would also clearly benefit Turkish-Iraqi trade.)

Turkey Remains Committed to Ties with West, Rejects Islamist Appeals

The appointment of Gönensay as foreign minister in the center-right Motherland–True Path (Anayol, in Turkish) coalition formed in March 1996 indicated that his pro-Western orientation and priority on ties with the OECD countries would continue under the new government.[26] Turkish and Western foreign policy experts were reportedly pleased at Gönensay's appointment, describing him as "polished" and "creative and very articulate." They note that he has "strong ties with the West and most recently served as Turkey's point man in its successful bid to negotiate the deal for an oil pipeline from Azerbaijan."

The only challenge to this approach has come from the pro-Islamic party named Refah (meaning welfare or prosperity). The Welfare Party's longtime leader, Necmettin Erbakan, has opposed Turkey's close ties with the United States, NATO, and the European Union. He has called instead for creation of a "just order" by abolishing interest rates, getting rid of the Western presence and Western influence on the country, and focusing Turkey's economic and political efforts on strengthening ties with the Islamic countries and the creation of an Islamic Common Market.[27] Although the Welfare Party came in first, by a narrow margin, in the December 24, 1995, parliamentary elections, with 21.3 percent of the total vote and 158 seats in Turkey's 550-member Grand National Assembly, Erbakan initially failed in his efforts to lead a government or even to become a coalition partner. After months of negotiations, with behind-the-scenes prodding from the internationally oriented Turkish business community and the secularist military establishment, the two center-right parties reached agreement for rotation of prime ministers. Mesut Yilmaz, leader of the Motherland Party, assumed the post for the first year.[28]

The new coalition was able to win a vote of confidence in parliament only because of the tacit support of Bulent Ecevit, leader of the Democratic Left Party, who had his seventy-six delegates abstain. The veteran leftist leader and former prime minister indicated that he disagreed with the new government's economic liberalization and privatization programs and some of the other policies of the center-right Anayol coalition, and he promised in the future to "fulfil our responsibilities as an opposition party." He said that he had nevertheless decided not to block the new government because it was preferable to the two other possible outcomes: protracted crisis at a time "when the country is beset by very urgent internal and external problems" or the formation of a government led by the Welfare Party, which he feared would gravely endanger Turkey's secular tradition. He claimed that these fears were shared by the "great majority" of the Turkish people.[29]

While critical of some of the government's economic and foreign policies, Ecevit was fully supportive of its Middle East peace efforts. Ecevit and his wife and political partner, Rahşan Ecevit, paid a five-day visit to Israel in April 1995, at the invitation of Foreign Minister Shimon Peres, and met with all the political leaders, including Prime Minister Rabin, Peres, and PLO leader Arafat. Noting Israel's economic, educational, and technological achievements, Ecevit indicated that he saw great value in strengthening Turkish-Israeli ties in all areas, and he expressed strong support for the peace process. He indicated that despite its own economic difficulties, Turkey would help in the economic rehabilitation of the Palestinian territories. He advocated closer regional cooperation among Turkey, Israel, Jordan, and the Palestinians, and he foresaw "great benefit to Turkey from the successful completion of the peace process."[30]

Thanks to a total of 80 abstentions, the government won a vote of confidence on March 12, 1996, by a comfortable margin of 257 to 207. However, the following month the Turkish parliament dealt a serious blow to the political prospects of former Prime Minister Tansu Çiller, who was scheduled to become prime minister again in 1997. The blow came when 70 deputies from secular parties joined in the populist Islamist Welfare Party's demand for a commission to investigate charges that she and her husband had manipulated government contracts for personal gain. Tansu Çiller, who maintained her innocence, denounced the vote as a plot to bring her down.[31] The fractious center-right coalition fell apart in early June, only three months after taking office.

On June 10, 1996, President Demirel once again asked Welfare Party leader Erbakan to attempt to form a coalition government, as he succeeded in doing in early July. His populist conservative party had gained some additional strength in the June 2 municipal by-elections, and some in the business community welcomed any coalition that would be strong enough to end the ruinous stalemate and begin to tackle the country's worsening problems. However, there was reportedly still strong resistance to a Welfare-led government among the secular establishment, particularly the powerful military, which sees itself as the defender of the modern Turkish state. Like the late President Turgut Özal, Erbakan has espoused an activist Turkish policy toward the Middle East, but unlike Özal and Demirel, Erbakan rejects the idea of a close strategic partnership between Turkey and Israel. On the contrary, Erbakan has repeatedly denounced the leaders of the secular parties for their relations with Israel, especially for the recently concluded air and naval training agreement. During his campaign speeches, Erbakan had called for Turkey to withdraw from its Western alliances and help create "an Islamic United Nations, an Islamic NATO, and an Islamic version of the European Union."[32]

In a campaign speech on May 21, 1996, Erbakan explicitly charged that the secular Turkish coalition government that had concluded the deal with Israel was acting as agents of "the Jews who bombed our Muslim brothers" in Lebanon. He went on to warn that a vote for any party other than Welfare in the June 2 municipal by-elections was giving "a vote to the Jews. Islamic martyrs and saints will strike down such people."[33] This diatribe was issued only three days after an unsuccessful assassination attempt on May 18 against President Suleyman Demirel by a declared Welfare Party supporter, who said he was acting to stop the Turkish-Israeli cooperation. While Erbakan condemned the attempted killing as a "despicable act," he continued his vitriolic rhetoric. Shrugging off the assassination attack, Demirel vowed the following day, after visting the mausoleum of Kemal Ataturk in Ankara, that he would continue to support the secularist principles established by the founder of the modern Turkish Republic.

Özal Initiates Ankara's More Activist Middle East Policy

A more active Turkish policy on the Middle East was initiated by Turgut Özal early in the 1990s, after the fall of the Berlin Wall in November 1989. The freeing of Eastern Europe from Soviet domination and ultimately the breakup of the Soviet Union itself spelled the end of the Cold War and left Ankara in search of a new international role, now that its position as the southeastern anchor of NATO was greatly reduced in significance. The collapse of the Soviet Union opened up new horizons for Turkey in regions from which it had long been cut off.[34] The potential significance of the changes brought about by the collapse of the Soviet Union was summarized by Mustafa Akşin, Turkey's ambassador to the United Nations, in an address at Columbia University in the fall of 1992: "With the collapse of communism we now have the luxury of adding an Eastern European, Balkan, Black Sea, Caucasus, Central Asian and Middle Eastern dimension to our traditional Western Europe oriented diplomacy." Turkey's strategic role had changed "from being a dike holding back Soviet expansion," he said, to becoming "a bridge to a new, emerging world" and the "crossroads where three continents and two seas meet."

For the Turks "by far the most exciting development in this period of profound change" was the coming into being of the Turkic Republics of Azerbaijan, Turkmenistan, Kazakhstan, Uzbekistan, and Kyrgyzstan as independent states. Despite continuing wariness about Russian long-term political ambitions, Turkey has encouraged the democratization and economic liberalization efforts in Russia, and Ankara has been actively pursuing expanded economic links with the states of the former Soviet Union. In November 1992 a Turkish official noted that trade with Russia had increased in the past five years from $400 million to nearly $2 billion, and he estimated that by the end of the decade "our bilateral trade will amount to $10 or $12 billion." In view of the deep economic crisis gripping Russia and the lesser economic difficulties facing Turkey, these figures may prove to be overly optimistic. Nevertheless, as early as 1992 Turkey was providing Russians with goods ranging from textiles and medicine to buses and other industrial equipment. Turkish contractors had obtained building contracts amounting to $1.5 billion, and more than ten thousand Turkish engineers and workers were building hotels, housing, hospitals, and factories in the territory of the former Soviet Union.[35] "The psychological impact on the Turkish people of seeing independent states emerge in a region which we consider to be our ancestral homeland would be difficult to describe to foreigners," Ambassador Akşin declared.[36] Turkish politicians were quick to capitalize on the sense of psychological exhilaration that filled the people. President Özal and Prime Minister Demirel began to speak grandiosely of a powerful new Turkic commonwealth of nations stretching from "the Adriatic and the Balkans to the Great Wall of China." With a combined population of some 120 million, and with Ankara serving as their natural leader, the Turkic world would emerge as a major force in the twenty-first century.

The idea of Pan-Turkism—or Pan-Turanism, as it is known in Turkey—had some following in the latter years of the Ottoman Empire, but was prudently shelved by the pragmatic Mustafa Kemal Atatürk, the founder of the modern, secular Turkish Republic in 1923. Under Atatürk's leadership, Turkey relinquished all ideas of empire and sought to develop good relations with all its neighbors, including the Soviet Union and Greece. Since then support for an empire has been limited to ultranationalists, such as retired Col. Alparslan Türkeş, leader of the outlawed right-wing National Action Party and more recently, until his death in 1997, of the Nationalist Labor Party. However, after the collapse of the Soviet Union and the emergence of the central Asian republics at the end of 1991, the creation of a "Turkic world" attracted respected intellectuals, such as Aydin Yalçin, who came out in support of the concepts of Pan-Turkism and Pan-Turanism.

In statements in the summer of 1992, Prime Minister Demirel stressed that Ankara's desire to establish close bonds with the "brotherly" Turkic peoples had nothing to do with imperial designs. "We are not after racist or expansionist ideas," he told parliament. "These are our brothers and all we want is to embrace them, to help them. No one should be worried or disturbed by this." Foreign Ministry officials likewise emphasized that Ankara's objective was "not to dominate but to cooperate."[37] It soon became clear that while the Central Asians welcomed closer ties with Turkey, they resented the patronizing tone of some Turkish pronouncements. Having finally freed themselves from domination by "Big Brother" in Moscow, they had no desire to come under the tutelage of their *Agabey* (older brother) in Ankara. The details of Turkey's relations with the Central Asian Republics, the troubles in the Balkans, and the continuing friction with Greece are beyond the scope of this article.[38]

When the new Demirel Government took office after the elections in November 1991, both the U.S. and Israeli diplomats reminded Foreign Minister Hikmet Çetin of his predecessor's promise to upgrade relations with Israel when progress toward peace was made. Columnist Yalçin Dogan reported that the idea appealed to both Demirel and Deputy Prime Minister Erdal İnönü, the leader of the Social Democratic Populist Party (SDPP), the junior partner in the new coalition government. Professor İnönü, the son of President Ismet İnönü, who had first recognized Israel in 1949, recommended that Ankara's relations with the PLO be upgraded at the same time. Taking these actions would enhance Turkey's opportunities to play a role in the regional peace talks.[39]

Advocates of the move advanced other arguments. (1) The Soviet Union and the Eastern Europeans had all restored full relations with Israel (broken off after the 1967 Arab-Israel war). (2) Muslim Azerbaijan had already concluded aviation and technical cooperation agreements with Israel, and Uzbekistan established relations shortly thereafter. (The other Muslim Turkic republics were also on the way to opening ties with Israel.) (3) China and India were about to establish relations with the Jewish state. (4) Israel had shown its readiness for peace by entering into talks with the neighboring Arab states on the basis of UN Security Council resolutions 242 and 338. (Israel had thus essentially fulfilled the conditions Ankara had set in November 1956 for upgrading of relations.) A "senior diplomatic source" in Ankara, noting that even the Soviet Union had upgraded its ties with Israel, expressed the view at the end of November 1991 that "we do not think full recognition [sic] of Israel would create a reaction in the Arab world, which has, after all, shaken hands with Israel in Madrid." (In fact, Turkey had extended de facto recognition to Israel in 1949 and de jure, or full, recognition in 1950.)

In the aftermath of Desert Storm, the Arab members of the anti-Saddam coalition, and other states as well, were appealing to the United States to launch a new initiative to resolve the Arab-Israeli conflict. In keeping with Özal's activist foreign policy, during an official visit to Moscow in March 1991, immediately after the Gulf War, he offered to host Arab-Israeli peace talks in Istanbul. He expressed the view that there could not be peace and stability in the Middle East unless the Palestinian issue was resolved. He also called on the Israeli government to accept the principle of land for peace.[40] The Turkish president repeated his offer when he met with U.S. Secretary of State James Baker in Ankara, noting that Turkey was well suited to serve as host since, he claimed, Ankara had good relations with all the countries involved.[41] According to Aziz Utkan of *Hürriyet*, in Baker's talks with Turkish officials he had asked Ankara for help in support of the U.S. initiative to convince the Arab states to lift the economic boycott against U.S. and other foreign firms dealing with Israel.[42]

On December 19, 1991, the Turkish government announced that it had decided to raise the level of the representation in Ankara of both "Palestine and Israel to embassy status," and it would also upgrade its legation in Tel Aviv to an embassy. Subsequently it was clarified that the Turkish ambassador to Tunisia would also be accredited to the "State of Palestine," since Tunis was then the headquarters of Yasir Arafat, chairman of the Palestine Liberation Organization, whom the Turks called "the Palestinian president." Turkey had established diplomatic relations with Israel in 1950, whereas the PLO had a low-level representative in Ankara since 1979.[43] Since Ankara already had diplomatic relations with Syria, Jordan, and Lebanon, the raising of Turkey's ties with Israel and the Palestinians to ambassadorial level meant that Ankara now maintained full diplomatic relations with all parties directly involved in the Arab-Israeli dispute.

The Turkish press prominently reported that Israel favored a more active Turkish role in regional affairs and that Israeli Prime Minister Yitzhak Shamir had discussed this with Baker. Adding support to these views was the statement by Eli Shaked, counselor of the Israeli embassy in Cairo, who had previously served in Turkey, that Turkey could make important contributions to the peace process through its relations with the Arab countries; it could do so by persuading them to recognize Israel's right to exist and to enter into direct negotiations.[44]

When Madrid was chosen as the venue for the peace talks and Turkey was not even invited to send an observer, many Turkish politicians and editorial writers expressed anger and disappointment.[45] Demirel, the leader of the opposition True Path Party, expressed "strong regret" at the "nonparticipation of Turkey, which is one of the most powerful countries of the Middle East, in this conference even as an observer." Nevertheless, he added, he wanted the conference to be successful.[46] Demirel pledged to do whatever he could to contribute to peace in the Middle East.

Demirel, whose True Path Party replaced Özal's Motherland Party as the leader in the October 1991 parliamentary elections, charged that it was "incompetence" by Motherland officials that had led to Turkey's exclusion.[47] The same charge was leveled by Col. Alparslan Türkeş the leader of the opposition right-wing Nationalist Labor Party. However, Türkeş urged that Ankara engage in an initiative to join the conference even if belatedly.[48] Former Prime Minister Bülent Ecevit, who now headed the small socialist Democratic Left Party, also expressed regret that Turkey was neither host nor participant. He attributed Turkey's failure "to realize its historical function" in the Middle East to its "following the United States" too slavishly in its foreign policy.[49]

Foreign Minister Safa Giray responded to the critics by pointing out that only "the directly concerned" parties in the Arab-Israeli dispute were participating in the first stages of the conference and that Turkey would be invited to take part in the multilateral track of the peace process.

In the foreign policy section of its program, the Demirel-led coalition government reaffirmed the importance of strengthening Turkey's ties with the United States and the European Community, asserted its willingness to contribute to peace in the Middle East (including the right of Palestinians to their own state and of Israel to live behind safe borders, and expressed concern for Turkish-speaking groups in Western Thrace and the republics in the Caucasus.

Turkey's Participation in the Multilateral Working Groups

Turkey attended the multilateral regional peace talks that were inaugurated in Moscow at the end of January 1992 and has also participated in the five specialized working groups dealing with refugees, regional economic development, the environment, water resources, and arms control and regional security. Many believe that it is in the area of providing surplus water resources to the water-short Palestinians, Israelis, and Jordanians that Turkey may make the greatest tangible contribution.

While the Turks indicated that they would be prepared to host subsequent sessions in Ankara or Istanbul, the offer was not accepted by the Arab delegates. Some officials in Ankara were reportedly privately relieved that the Turkish offer had been rejected; they feared that Arab delegates, led by Syria, might use the occasion to raise their own complaints against Turkey over the vast network of dams and irrigation projects it was constructing in southeastern Anatolia in the Euphrates and Tigris river basins. Some Turks believe that residual Arab resentment of four centuries of Ottoman rule explains the rejection of Istanbul or Ankara as a venue. A more plausible explanation, however, is that until the fall of 1993, after the signing of the Israel-PLO Declaration of Principles, the Arab states had opposed any meetings within the Middle East, which Israel had favored as a symbol of its formal acceptance into the region. After the Israel-PLO agreement broke the ice, the working group on refugees met in Tunis in October 1993 and the one on the environment met in Cairo in November 1993. Since then working groups—all with Israeli participation—have also taken place in Morocco, Qatar, Oman, and Bahrain.

The multilateral working group on Arms Control and Regional Security (ACRS), meeting in Washington in May 1993, demonstrated its recognition of Ankara's ability to contribute in a practical way to the reduction of tensions and the growth of confidence among the parties. The group selected Turkey to serve as "mentor" for a seminar on prenotification and exchange of information on military maneuvers and related subjects. Since it bordered on the Soviet Union, this was an area in which Turkey had gained expertise through its discussions in NATO and the Conference on Security and Cooperation in Europe. The seminar was held in Antalya in October 1993. More than forty countries participated, including most of the Arab states. Syria and Lebanon, its client state, stayed away, maintaining their policy of boycotting all the multilaterals.

Although Turkey participates in the multilateral negotiations not as a Middle Eastern state but as an "extraregional" state (like the United States, the Europeans, Russia, Japan, and others), its geographic status as a state bordering the Arab world makes it more than merely an interested outsider. Alan Makovsky, a former U.S. State Department analyst for Turkey, points out that "Turkey's stake in Middle Eastern security—even a certain status as partly a Middle Eastern state—was implicitly acknowledged in the Conventional Forces in Europe (CFE) agreement of 1990. At its request, Turkey was granted a so-called 'exclusion zone' in the southeastern portion of the country that borders Syria, Iraq and Iran. Ankara was able to make this claim based on the fact that it has neighbors that are not part of the CFE regime. Within this exclusion zone, there are no limits on the troops and equipment that Turkey is allowed to deploy."[50]

Indeed, in the course of continuing war against the Kurdistan Workers Party guerrilla forces, Ankara has several times ordered its planes and even ground forces across the border into northern Iraq in hot pursuit of PKK rebels. One of the longest of these excursions was a six-week-long massive air and ground campaign in the spring of 1995, which was viewed sympathetically by Washington but aroused much criticism from many of Turkey's NATO allies in Western Europe. Although Ankara has frequently protested to Damascus and Teheran about their alleged support for the PKK, Turkish armed forces have thus far not crossed the borders with Syria and Iran. There have been frequent press comments in Turkey, however, suggesting that Turkey should attack PKK bases in neighboring countries as Israel had done to Hizbollah and Palestinian guerrillas in the Syrian-controlled Bekaa valley in Lebanon. While he was in opposition as leader of the Motherland Party, Mesut Yilmaz was heard to criticize Prime Minister Çiller for not taking a tough enough policy toward Syria and Iran. He pointedly noted that Turkey's control of water resources and vital trade routes were tools that Ankara could utilize in pressuring its neighbors to stop their hostile activities.

Ankara Confident of U.S. Support but Skeptical about Europeans' Reliability

Turkish-U.S. strategic relations have remained strong, despite occasional Congressional criticism of Turkey over its handling of the Kurdish problem and the persistent allegations of human rights abuses by the Turkish military and police. However, the failure of the Western Europeans to come to the aid of the Bosnian Muslims (whose relatives in Turkey constitute an important domestic constituency for Turkish politicians), as well as the reluctance of Turkey's NATO allies to promise to aid Turkey should Iraq attack, has reinforced Turkish skepticism about NATO's willingness to defend it in case of aggression coming from the Middle East rather than from Moscow. Put more crudely, the feeling is that the Christian states of Europe were not prepared to see their soldiers die to help Muslim Turks counter a non-European attack by an Arab or Iranian Muslim neighbor. The Turks suspected that the anti-Muslim bias that had delayed Turkey's admission into NATO until 1952 was still a factor in the difficulties in obtaining approval of the Customs Union with the European Union in 1995,[51] and the continuing reluctance to admit Turkey to full membership in the European Union.

Therefore, Makovsky concludes, the need to seek Middle Eastern solutions to its Middle Eastern problems emerged as an important incentive to Turkish policy makers in pursuing ties with Israel. He notes that good relations with Israel have already paid a handsome dividend to Turkey in its relations with Western Europe. Israeli diplomats were very active in lobbying for approval of the Customs Union with Turkey by the European Parliament in December 1995, over the opposition by Greece and by some European socialists upset by Turkey's Kurdish policy and record on human rights issues. The socialists were believed to hold the balance of power in what was expected to be a close vote. Drawing on his good Socialist International contacts, Israeli Prime Minister Peres telephoned leading European socialists in Spain, Germany, and Britain to lobby on Ankara's behalf. Turkish Prime Minister Çiller sent Peres a personal note of thanks for his successful efforts.[52]

Turkish, Israeli, Egyptian Cooperation in Tourism

Turkish Minister of Tourism Abdülkadir Ateş was among those who in 1991 urged that the level of relations with Israel be raised quickly, in the hope that this would stimulate travel to Turkey by Jewish tourists from the United States, Western Europe, and Israel. A special attraction would be major events to be held in Istanbul and elsewhere during 1992 by the Turkish government and the Quincentennial Foundation to mark the welcome given by Sultan Beyazit II to the Jewish refugees expelled by Spain in 1492.[53] In June 1992 Ateş went to Israel and concluded a tourism cooperation agreement. This was reportedly the first official visit to Israel by a Turkish cabinet minister in more than twenty years.[54] At the beginning of 1994, Turkey, Israel, and Egypt established an eastern Mediterranean tourist authority. Minister Ateş told me in January 1994 that he had tried to broaden the agreement to include Syria as well, but his efforts were rejected by Damascus, which refused even to discuss potential cooperation with Israel until Israel had formally agreed to withdraw from the Golan Heights.[55]

Turkish-Israeli relations reached a new height when President Chaim Herzog came to Istanbul in mid-July 1992. Initially billed as a "private" visit by the Israeli head of state to participate in the gala dinner of the Quincentennial Foundation, Herzog's trip quickly assumed all the trappings of an official visit. Not only did both President Özal and Prime Minister Demirel join with Herzog in speaking at the dinner at the Dolmabahçe Palace, but Herzog had lengthy separate meetings with both, and he was interviewed on state television. The visit received generally favorable comment in the Turkish media. At a joint press conference following their meeting, Demirel noted that Turkish-Israeli relations were gradually improving and declared that "further development of bilateral relations would be in the interests of the region and the world." He added that participation of all regional countries in the Middle East peace conference might lead to better results. (It was not clear whether this was a veiled criticism of Syria for its failure to attend the multilateral sessions or simply an appeal for a greater role for Turkey.) For his part, Herzog underscored that Turkey was an important country in the region and stressed that it could play a role in the Middle East peace conference.[56]

The Islamist Welfare Party Denounces Ties with Israel

The only reported criticism came from Iranian television and from a demonstration by Turkish Islamic fundamentalists at the Beyazit Mosque in Istanbul on Friday, July 17. The demonstrators—variously estimated at seven hundred to two thousand—burned American and Israeli flags, carried placards saying "The intifada will continue until Israel is destroyed," and shouted "Allah is Great" and the Turkish "dictators of laicism [secularism] are the puppets of the Jews."[57] During the mayoral election campaigns in 1994 and the parliamentary election campaign in 1995, Welfare Party leader Erbakan said the choice was between support for "Greater

Turkey" and "Greater Israel." He has also accused Prime Minister Çiller of being "Israel's puppet."[58] He included Jerusalem together with Bosnia and Nagorno Karabakh as Islamic places that he would liberate but adopted a more cautious policy when he became prime minister in 1996.

During the intifada the Welfare Party organized major anti-Israeli demonstrations in Istanbul, Konya, and Diyarbekir. The one in Istanbul on March 20, 1988, drew an estimated ten thousand to twenty-five thousand participants, including Iranian, Saudi, and PLO officials. The Israeli flag was burned and anti-Jewish as well as anti-Israeli slogans were shouted by the conservative Islamic crowd. The utilization of the Palestinian cause to rally support for pro-Islamic groups aroused concern among Turkey's secular elite.[59] The meddling of Iranian Islamic fundamentalists has also been a continuing source of annoyance for Turkey's secular elite. When informed that the Iranian ambassador to Turkey had participated in an anti-Israeli and pro-Islamic demonstration in the religiously conservative city of Konya, Foreign Minister Mesut Yilmaz declared his actions "contrary to diplomatic practice and protocol."[60]

The struggle continues. In February 1997, several hundred persons jammed a hall in Sincan, a working-class town twenty-five miles from Ankara, to celebrate "Jerusalem Day," an annual holiday proclaimed by Khomeini. The host was the mayor, and the guest of honor was Mohammed Reza Bagheri, the Iranian ambassador, who was greeted with chants of "Down with Israel! Down with Arafat!" Ambassador Bagheri delivered a fiery speech, calling on his audience to struggle for reimposition of the Sharia. As a clear warning that their patience was again wearing thin, the army ordered a column of tanks to roll through Sincan's streets. The mayor was detained for interrogation, and the Iranian ambassador was asked to return home.

As will be explained, Erbakan's days as prime minister were numbered. The National Security Council, headed by the president and dominated by the military, presented Erbakan on February 28, 1997, with twenty-two demands to cancel the pro-Islamic policies that he had been advocating in education and other areas of public policy. When he resisted, the military—supported by President Demirel and the secularist elements of the population—in effect forced Erbakan in June to hand in his resignation as prime minister.

Mrs. Çiller tried in vain to create a new coalition government with herself as prime minister, suggesting speeding up the rotation envisioned in her original agreement with Erbakan. But defections from her True Path Party, hastened by the continuing stench of scandal surrounding her, and widespread disillusionment with the failure of the Erbakan-Çiller government to meet the country's pressing economic problems or end the Kurdish insurgency of the PKK resulted in her failure. Erbakan said he looked forward to returning to power with an absolute Welfare Party majority after new elections. Following protocol, President Demirel asked Yilmaz rather than Çiller to try to set up a new prosecular coalition government without the Islamists. He succeeded in so doing.

One of the first acts of the new government, on July 18, 1997, was to give final approval to implementation of the free trade agreement concluded with Israel in 1996 during Demirel's visit. Despite Erbakan's reluctance, the agreement had received approval by the Turkish parliament but had not yet been put into force. The agreement foresees the creation of a free trade zone by the end of the century, by which time Turkish officials expressed the hope that bilateral trade would quadruple to $2 billion annually. Sources in Ankara reported that the new government's speedy move to enact the trade accord during its first week in office signaled its determination to expand ties with Israel.

We now consider details of the rapid development of Turkish-Israeli relations since the Oslo agreement of September 1993.

High Level Turkish-Israel Visits Become Routine

When Turkish Foreign Minister Hikmet Çetin arrived in Jerusalem in November 1993, he noted that this was the first official visit by a Turkish foreign minister, adding that he was "delighted to have made this trip." Çetin had twice postponed his voyage, which was originally scheduled for June. The first delay was attributed to Turkish domestic politics. On that occasion, only days before his planned arrival, the Turkish Embassy in Tel Aviv called to inform those who had been invited to attend a luncheon in his honor at the Jerusalem Hilton that the foreign minister had to remain in Ankara because his presence was necessary when the new coalition government was to be voted upon by the Turkish parliament. Çetin, who is of Kurdish origin, was a prominent leader of the Social Democratic Populist Party (SDPP), the junior partner in the coalition then led by Prime Minister Çiller.[61]

The foreign minister's trip was rescheduled for mid-July, but when he arrived in neighboring Jordan, the Israel Defense Force was in the midst of large-scale punitive raid into southern Lebanon, in retaliation for a wave of terrorist and rocket attacks on northern Israel. Fear of the impending Israeli attack, dubbed Operation Accountability, reportedly prompted some 300,000 Lebanese to flee their homes temporarily. The Israeli action was intended to drive home the message that the southern Lebanese would not be secure in their own homes if they did not stop attacks that had made Israelis feel unsafe in theirs. Sensitive to Arab reaction as well as to domestic public opinion, the Turkish foreign minister decided at the last minute to cancel his visit to Israel. Opinion in the political circles in Ankara was divided as to whether or not this second cancellation was wise, especially since the foreign minister and his team were already en route. Among the arguments for postponing the trip to a more opportune time was that Çetin, personally, and the SDPP as a political body had long been active in championing human rights in general and Palestinian rights in particular.

The two postponements of Çetin's visit illustrate the extent to which Turkish-Israeli relations can be affected by domestic developments in Turkey and by the Arab-Israel conflict. (There were reports that after Israel once again launched operations against suspected Hizbollah bases in Lebanon in April 1996, Ankara delayed implementation of some recent Turkish-Israeli agreements. However, when the UN General Assembly adopted an unbalanced resolution condemning Israeli attacks on civilians and demanding compensation, Turkey together with most European states abstained, whereas in the past Ankara would have voted with the Arab states in criticizing Israel. Only the United States and Israel voted against the resolution.)[62] By the time Çetin finally arrived in Israel in November 1993, the prospects for peaceful resolution of the Arab-Israel conflict had dramatically improved. At a White House ceremony on September 13 the Palestine Liberation Organization and the State of Israel had exchanged letters of mutual recognition and signed the Declaration of Principles on Interim Self-Government Arrangements. At the prodding of President Bill Clinton, Israeli Prime Minister Rabin shook the outstretched hand of PLO Chairman Arafat. With considerably less fanfare, on the following day at the State Department, Israeli and Jordanian officials signed a common agenda for negotiations designed to "culminate in a peace treaty." (The Israeli-Jordanian peace treaty was signed a year later, on October 26, 1994, at the Arava border crossing.)

"President Arafat" Officially Welcomed in Ankara

These positive developments in 1993 were warmly welcomed by Ankara. "President Arafat" was officially received by Demirel at the presidential residence, and the Turkish president reiterated Turkey's support for the peace process in general and the Palestinian people in particular. Arafat expressed the hope that both leaders would soon be able to pray together in Jerusalem. Thus Ankara demonstrated that its improved relations with

Israel were not at the expense of the Palestinians. In November 1993, in a statement summarizing the "comprehensive discussions" on regional and international issues he had in Israel with both President Ezer Weizman and Foreign Minister Shimon Peres, Foreign Minister Çetin said, "We believe that a new order is emerging in the Middle East." Although it was not possible to predict accurately what form it would take, he said, "We are resolved to collaborate in the creation of a new Middle Eastern order."

He noted that both Turkey and Israel shared a belief that, in the aftermath of the bipolar order and the Cold War, "terrorism has become one of the most pressing issues facing the world" and that "the struggle against terrorism is important for the peace and security of the region." In a scarcely veiled allusion to Damascus's support for radical Palestinian and anti-Turkish groups operating out of Syria and the Syrian-controlled Beqaa Valley of Lebanon, the Turkish foreign minister declared, "The Middle East should not be a region where some territories are available for the free training and movement of terrorists." He also said that he was able "to observe, with pleasure, that both our countries have the same approach to these issues."[63]

Turkish-Israeli Antiterrorist Action Excludes Kurdish Issue

While ready to condemn terrorism in general terms, Weizman and other senior Israeli officials scrupulously avoided getting drawn into the Turkish-Kurdish controversy. The antiterrorism agreement signed during Prime Minister Çiller's visit in November 1994 was cast in general terms. It limited cooperation to an exchange of intelligence—for example, to more effectively track and eliminate outside funding—from Saudi Arabia, Iran and, other sources—for radical Islamic fundamentalist groups. Enforcement action was to be taken by their criminal justice officials, not by military action. There were several good reasons for this. Israeli officials made it clear that Jerusalem had enough enemies in the region without adding the Kurds to the list.[64] Moreover, they recalled that Israelis owed a debt of gratitude to the Kurds of Iraq, who had helped smuggle out Iraqi Jews to safety after the public hangings of eleven Jews in Baghdad in 1969 on trumped-up charges of espionage.

Another important factor in Israeli reluctance to become involved was the difficult and sensitive negotiations taking place between Israel and Syria. Jerusalem and Ankara may have long shared a negative view of Hafez al-Assad and his regional ambitions, but the Israeli negotiators were careful to avoid giving the Syrian leader the impression that the improvement in Turkish-Israeli relations meant that the two countries were "ganging up on him" in an alliance designed to squeeze Syria in a pincer movement.[65] Conversely, Israeli diplomats dismissed as unwarranted Turkish fears that a Syrian-Israeli peace agreement would free Damascus to pursue its anti-Turkish activities more vigorously, or that Israel might use its influence in Washington to seek U.S. pressure on Turkey to provide more water to Syria from the Euphrates. Turkish-Syrian relations were embittered by Syrian demands that Turkey increase the guaranteed quantity of water flowing in the Euphrates across the border into Syria from five hundred cubic meters per second. Despite formal Turkish-Syrian agreements and despite President Assad's personal pledge to Demirel in January 1993 to outlaw PKK's activities against Turkey, Turkish officials remained convinced that the Syrians were continuing clandestine help to the PKK, both to disrupt the schedule of the large-scale Southeast Anatolia Development Project (known by its Turkish acronym as GAP) by fomenting unrest in southeastern Anatolia and to strengthen Syria's hand in the water talks.[66]

David Granit, Israel's ambassador in Ankara in 1994, told me that he had tried to reassure the Turks by noting that a peace treaty between Israel and Syria would signify that Assad had made a strategic decision to change his fundamental policy toward his neighbors. He noted that President Clinton and Secretary of State Warren Christopher had made it clear to Assad that Washington would not agree to remove Syria from its lists of terrorist-supporting and drug-trafficking states, nor would Israel agree on any withdrawal, unless Syria ceased supporting groups hostile to its neighbors and agreed to resolve all its disputes by peaceful means.[67]

However, shortly after Prime Minister Rabin's assassination in November 1995, Prime Minister Peres decided to make a major effort to achieve an early breakthrough in negotiations with Syria. His response to a question from a Turkish reporter at a National Press Club briefing in Washington in December 1995 was perhaps indicative of his determination not to permit Turkish concerns to complicate the issues Israel faced with Syria. Asked whether Turkey would insist that Syria expel the PKK as part of a peace agreement and whether there had been any contact between Turkey and Israel on that issue, Peres acted baffled. He asked, "I am sorry, where did Turkey come into the story? . . . I wouldn't like to speak about a situation which I am not sure I am fully aware of. . . . As far as we are concerned, there are ten refusal [that is, Palestinian rejectionist] organizations in Syria, and we say repeatedly that Syria must put an end to it."[68]

This statement was followed by press reports in Turkey that Peres allegedly planned to send one of his key aides to Turkey to convince the Turks to provide more Euphrates water to Syria, as a contribution to the peace process. After the reports, Ankara dispatched Deputy Foreign Minister Onur Oymen on an urgent mission to Jerusalem to convey the Turkish concerns to Israeli leaders, and Oymen reportedly received assurances along the lines of those given in 1994 by David Granit, Israel's ambassador in Ankara. Although both Jerusalem and Washington denied that Israel or the United States was putting pressure on Turkey, American and Israeli officials confirmed that in the American-brokered Israeli-Syrian talks held at the Wye Plantation in Maryland early in 1996, the Syrians had linked the two water issues. The Israeli delegation had stressed that Israel could not afford to relinquish any of the headwaters of the Jordan River flowing into Israel from sources in the Golan Heights and Southern Lebanon. The Syrian delegation reportedly responded that Damascus was sympathetic to Israel's water needs, but it could not justify to the Syrian public any concessions to Israel on the Jordan headwaters, unless Israel and the United States demonstrated greater sympathy for the Syrian people's demands for additional supplies of water from the Tigris and Euphrates.[69]

Presumably, the Turkish concerns were also raised at the highest level when President Demirel paid a state visit to Israel in March 1996. There he participated with twenty-nine other world leaders hastily convened by President Clinton in the Sharm-el-Sheikh "Summit of the Peacemakers," called to show support for the Israelis in the face of a series of four suicide bombings by Palestinian Islamic extremists. The public display of solidarity by Turkey for Israel in the struggle against terrorism in the region was in marked contrast to the conspicuous refusal of Syria to participate in the antiterrorist gathering.

Alluding to Syria's absence, Demirel said he wished that all the invited states had attended. Clearly with Syria in mind, Demirel noted that "the existence of countries which give shelter to terrorists and provide them with training facilities makes it harder to effectively combat terrorism."[70] The difference between the Turkish-Israeli and Syrian views had been made pointedly clear in November 1995, during a debate on the wording of the condemnation of terrorism in the final communique of the Euro-Med conference in Barcelona, which all three countries attended. Syrian Foreign Minister Faruq as-Sharaa complained, "Israel and Turkey insist on defining resistance movements as terrorist as well. In citing excuses such as the PKK and the opposition movement in Southern Lebanon, respectively, Israel and Turkey attempt to present all armed movements as terrorism. Syria cannot accept this."[71]

The Syrian-Israeli talks in Maryland were broken off following the wave of suicide bombings in Israel in March 1996. The defeat of Shimon Peres and the election of Likud leader Banjamin Netanyahu as Prime Minister in the May 1996 elections in Israel postponed negotiations with Syria indefinitely. The Likud is officially committed to retaining control of the Golan Heights, while Assad has been adamant in demanding their return. The congressional elections of November 1994, which gave the Republican Party control of both houses, resulted in harsh criticism of Syria's obstructive policies by Republican leaders. In spring 1996 the Clinton administration intensified efforts, during Secretary of State Warren Christopher's shuttle diplomacy, to bring about a ceasefire in Lebanon and to restart high-level Syrian-Israeli negotiations. Nevertheless, State Department reports to Congress continued to include Syria among the terrorist-supporting and drug-trafficking states. Such states are barred from receiving U.S. aid.

Water Disputes Continue to Trouble Turkish-Arab Relations

In the January–February 1996 issue of its bimonthly newsletter, the Turkish Embassy in Washington reiterated the charge that "in an attempt to secure endless concessions" from Turkey on the Euphrates and Tigris water issue, "Syria is providing a haven for the PKK and is supporting its terrorist activities." It noted that Turkey was in fact supplying Syria with an average of five hundred cubic meters per second, and that Ankara had repeatedly proposed to Syria and Iraq a plan for joint inventory of their land and water resources as the first step in achieving an equitable, rational, and optimum utilization of water resources in the Euphrates-Tigris basin. The Turkish Embassy report concluded, "In order to have a meaningful dialogue with Turkey, Syria must first stop supporting PKK terrorism."[72] Whereas Syria and Iraq fear that massive GAP dams and irrigation projects will sharply reduce the quantity and degrade the quality of water in the Euphrates and Tigris, Turkish-Israeli technical cooperation may help allay these concerns. On June 27, 1995, in Ankara, Israeli Minister of Agriculture Ya'acov Tsur and Turkish Minister of Agriculture and Rural Affairs Rafaiddin   ahin signed a cooperation agreement in the agricultural field. Israel will set up exhibition centers in several districts in Turkey. The centers will exhibit Israeli irrigation methods as well as methods to develop new varieties of vegetables. Israel has agreed to send a delegation of agriculture specialists to train the Turks on water-saving techniques. The specialists will also provide know-how on improving the health of livestock and improving plant growth. Tsur said Turkey is interested in upgrading the quality of its crops in an attempt to increase agricultural exports.   ahin said Turkey has abundant water sources, but in many parts of the country there is a shortage, mainly because of farmers' inadequate irrigation methods. According to a *Financial Times* (London) special report on Turkey in June 1996, Israeli technical assistance was beginning to have a positive impact on farming in the newly irrigated Harran plains of the GAP region. "Pilot projects by Israeli experts produce nearly twice as much cotton per hectare with half the water that local farmers use."[73]

Turkey's Practical Contribution to Peace

Whereas it is a cause of friction with its Arab neighbors, Turkish water may help lubricate the Arab-Israeli peace process. In 1994 Foreign Minister Çetin reiterated Ankara's position that "as part of the peace process," Turkey was prepared to supply water to Israel and its Arab neighbors from sources on the southern coast of Anatolia, "such as the Manavgat, Ceyhan and Seyhan Rivers." He expressed doubts that lasting peace between Israel and Syria, Jordan, and the Palestinians could be achieved without the addition of Turkish water supplies.[74] A similar comment was made by Prime Minister Çiller during her visit to Israel in November 1994. Noting that a pipeline from the Ceyhan or Seyhan Rivers "could supply both Israel and Syria," Çiller stressed, "But first we need peace." Adnan Abu Odeh, recently Jordan's ambassador to the UN, believes that Turkey's valuable contribution to Arab-Israeli peace is not limited to supplying desperately needed water to Jordan. The ambassador has been a close adviser to King Hussein and an active advocate of peace with Israel and of efforts to develop a modern, democratic Jordanian society. Citing Turkey as a Middle Eastern country with a well-established multiparty political system that was "more on the secular side," he said Turkey's involvement in regional projects would indirectly help other countries move closer to secularism. This would help promote peace, Ambassador Abu Odeh declared, because "militant Islamic rejectionism is the greatest threat to the Mideast peace process."[75]

When he was Israeli foreign minister, Peres stated that "our response to the Turkish offer is positive." If suitable arrangements could be worked out, in terms of price and assured supply, Israel was prepared to purchase water from Turkey.[76]

During Çetin's visit to Israel, which he said marked "a new phase in the mutually beneficial cooperative relations of the two nations," an agreement outlining the framework of bilateral relations and a cultural agreement were signed, and work was begun on various economic cooperation agreements, including one dealing with elimination of double taxation, another on encouragement and protection of investments, as well as an agreement in principle on a free trade agreement. These were finally signed during President Demirel's visit in March 1996. Turkey was eager to benefit from Israel's free trade agreements with the European Union and with the United States. Temel Iskit, a senior Turkish Foreign Ministry official, said that the Turkish-Israeli free trade agreement was intended as the first of a series linking Mediterranean countries to the EU. "Israel has the strongest relationship with the EU and the most trade, so therefore we decided to start with them." An Israeli official pointed out that both countries had market-oriented economies that were complementary in nature.[77]

Turks Visiting Israel Meet Palestinian Leaders

Çetin also crossed into East Jerusalem and met with Palestinian leaders, who expressed their gratitude for Turkey's steady support of the Palestinian cause, and he pledged continued Turkish help. He noted that Faisal Husseini, the leader of the Palestinian delegation, had welcomed him as the first Moslem foreign minister to visit East Jerusalem since 1967.[78]

In November 1994 Prime Minister Çiller had caused political furor in Israel when she paid a similar visit to Palestinian leaders at Orient House, the de facto PLO headquarters in east Jerusalem, and the Palestinians barred Israeli security forces from entering the building. Jerusalem Mayor Ehud Olmert, of the Likud Party, called for closing down Orient House, arguing that the Israel-PLO agreement barred Palestinian political activity in Jerusalem during the interim period. While the Rabin government was embarrassed by the action, Turkish officials noted that European and U.S. officials had also met with Palestinians at Orient House. (Çiller had earlier paid tribute to the Jewish victims of the Holocaust by visiting Yad Vashem.) At the Israeli cabinet meeting to discuss the issue of the Orient House visit, Education Minister Amnon Rubinstein of the dovish Meretz Party said that Çiller's visit should be understood as necessary, "given that she is prime minister of a predominantly Moslem country."[79]

On Saturday, November 5, 1994, the usually bareheaded Turkish prime minister donned a colorful scarf to tour the Haram as-Sharif (the Temple Mount), to meet with Muslim leaders, and to participate in noon prayers at the al Aksa mosque. She met with the mothers of Palestinians under Israeli detention and also with Jerusalem's PLO-appointed mufti, Ikrema Sabri. "Her visit means to us that the Moslems are one family," Sabri said. "She respects Islamic principles. When she came to the mosque, she covered her head."[80] (Apparently in deference to growing conservative Islamic sentiment among the voters back home, the fervently secularist Turkish prime minister responded to a champagne toast by Prime Minister Rabin by raising a glass filled with orange juice.)

After meeting in Gaza with Arafat, whom she referred to as "president of Palestine," Prime Minister Çiller declared that improving the situation of the Palestinians in Gaza "should be a priority for the whole world."[81] Çiller reiterated Turkey's pledge of $52 million in loans for Palestinian development, of which $25 million would be paid in 1995. She noted that the projected $2.2 billion in international aid was not yet being made available because of the absence of specific projects. Pointing out that Turkish construction firms had gained much experience dealing with the World Bank and the Arab world, she added, "Maybe we, as a Muslim country, can be a catalyst. If they want us, we can provide experts so that they can set up the projects." A spokesman for Palestinian Planning Minister Nabil Sha'ath welcomed the offer, calling it "very positive, especially in developing housing projects."[82]

During 1994 and 1995 Turkey maintained a high profile in its support for Palestinian-Israeli peace efforts. For example, Foreign Minister Çetin participated in the signing ceremony in Cairo on May 4, 1994, when Israel turned over administration of Gaza and Jericho to the Palestinian Authority. President Demirel issued a statement calling this a "turning point that gives hope in the Middle East" and reiterated that "Turkey is determined to continue her support for the rapid development of the Middle East Peace Process in a positive direction."[83] On July 8, 1994, Prime Minister Çiller spoke at the Paris ceremony at which Rabin, Peres, and Arafat received the UNESCO Peace Awards. In her speech she congratulated the three for their "courage and determination," which she said should serve as an example to leaders in other strife-torn regions of the world. Noting Turkey's historical and current ties with both Israelis and Arabs, she emphasized that Turkey supported "dialogue and tolerance" as the way to promote peace.[84] In September 1995, Turkish Foreign Minister Erdal İnönü flew to Washington to attend the White House signing of Oslo II.

Turkey and Israel Seek to Lead CSCME

As noted earlier, at a joint press conference in Ankara with visiting Foreign Minister Shimon Peres on April 11, 1994, Çetin announced that "Turkey has agreed with Israel to shoulder the leadership" in setting up the Conference on Security and Cooperation in the Middle East (CSCME), to be modeled on the CSCE.[85] Among its objectives would be to discuss and defuse threats to peace and stability in the region, including the escalating missile race, as well as to foster economic and technical cooperation. Turkey and Israel hope to draw in Egypt, Jordan, Morocco, Tunisia, and other moderate Arab states, which increasingly see the terrorism of Islamic fundamentalists and other radical groups as a major threat to regional stability.[86] The idea of extending the geographic scope of the Organization (formerly the Conference) on Security and Cooperation in Europe to the countries bordering on the Mediterranean has long had Italian support. At a conference on the future of the CSCE organization in Washington on September 26, 1994, John J. Maresca, a former U.S. ambassador to the CSCE and special U.S. negotiator on the Armenian-Azeri dispute over Ngorno-Karabakh, suggested that since the countries of the Caucasus and Central Asia had become members of the CSCE, the organization had "an unusual opportunity to help in the process of bridging the gap between the Judeo-Christian West and the Muslim East." However, such bridge building required a "mental change" in the Euro-centric thinking of the veteran members.[87]

Within Turkey, the idea of a CSCME—to include the countries of the Middle East and the Central Asian republics—has long been championed by Erdal Inönü, the recently retired leader of the SDPP. In June 1994 Inönü, as chairman of the Grand National Assembly's foreign relations committee, led a multiparty Turkish parliamentary delegation to Israel, at the invitation of the Knesset, and continued the discussions on regional cooperation with his Israeli counterparts.[88]

Expanding Turkish-Israeli Economic Cooperation

In early June 1994, Shimon Shetreet, the Israeli minister of economics and planning, led a seventy-person delegation of Israeli business representatives to explore investment opportunities in Turkey's defense, security, transport, and irrigation sectors. After meeting with the Israelis, Turkish Minister of Economy Aykon Dogan told reporters that the great and rapidly growing number of Israeli tourists was helping boost Turkey's foreign exchange revenues. He said that Turkey hoped that the projected free trade agreement would lead to an expansion of bilateral Turkish-Israeli trade, which he said had totaled $201 million in 1993. (Israeli statistics place the total at $227 million, of which $135.1 million represented Israeli exports [mainly chemicals, agricultural equipment, plastics, and medical equipment and optics], while $92 million represented imports from Turkey, mainly plants and vegetables, mineral products, yarns, fabrics, and textiles.) Dogan added that the two countries were also discussing possible joint ventures in the Central Asian republics.[89] At the time of the signing of the Turkish-Israeli free trade agreement, Turkish and Israeli officials expressed the hope that bilateral trade, which had grown from slightly more than $100 million in 1990 to $363 million in 1995, would further increase to the level of $1 billion to $2 billion by the year 2000.[90]

Turkish-Israeli-U.S Cooperation in Central Asia

Since the breakup of the Soviet Union, the United States has urged the Muslim republics of Central Asia, most of whom are Turkic-speaking, to choose secular Turkey rather than the fundamentalist Islamic Republic of Iran as their model for economic and political development. President Bush and Secretary of State Baker also actively encouraged efforts by Turkey to play a role in the region.[91] Israel, which has pioneered water-saving technologies, such as drip irrigation, has helped the Turkic republics bordering the ecologically endangered Aral Sea in conserving water and improving yields. Israeli projects have reportedly multiplied tomato yields sixfold in Kazakhstan and increased cotton output by 30 percent in Uzbekistan while reducing water consumption by two-thirds.[92] The United States has created a framework to support Turkish-Israeli cooperation in joint ventures in construction, agricultural technology, rural development, and other fields in the Central Asian Republics.

Promoting Peace through Regional Economic Development

Recognizing that conditions of desperate poverty and privation are breeding grounds for extremism, Çiller began her November 1994 Middle East tour by heading a two-hundred-member Turkish delegation to the Middle East and North African economic summit in Casablanca at the end of October. In her address to the plenary she stressed the need for building economic interdependencies among the nations of the area and proposed a variety of regional economic institutions—including a regional development bank, a confederation of chambers of commerce, a tourism advisory board, and an intergovernmental body to examine megaregional projects. Such projects would emphasize the interconnection of regional communication, transportation, and energy systems. Çiller said, "Turkey can play an important role in the new architecture of the Middle East . . . due to its geostrategic location and its involvement in various regional organizations."[93]

In Israel Çiller noted that while in Casablanca she had found "a will to cooperate, but we had no concrete projects." She ticked off a list of possible Turkish-Israeli bilateral projects, including improved fiber optic communications; allocation of a Turkish communications satellite channel to Israel; Mersin and Iskenderun port development to streamline handling of perishable fruits and vegetables; formation of multinational air and maritime companies; cooperation on power station construction; cooperation in expanding tourist facilities in Turkey; connection of Israel to the international electricity grid; establishment of joint construction companies; and investment by Israel in agricultural, industrial, and community development projects in Turkey's Southeastern Anatolia Project (GAP).[94]

She gave special emphasis to cooperation with Israel on various water-related projects. In the mid-1980s the late President Özal had proposed the "Peace Water Pipeline," a $21 billion project to bring water from the Seyhan and Ceyhan Rivers via two pipelines to eight Arab states and to Israel as well, once peace was achieved. The project never got off the ground. The Saudis contended that gas-fueled desalination would be cheaper and neither they nor the other Gulf states were willing to be vulnerable to the possibility that one of their upstream neighbors might turn off the tap.[95] Since Madrid, senior Turkish officials, including President Demirel and Prime Minister Çiller, have expressed support for a shorter pipeline (estimated at $5 billion) to convey Turkish water to Syria, Jordan, Israel, and the Palestinians. However, Syria—through which any pipeline would have to go—has refused to attend any of the multilateral committees, demanding that Israel make a commitment to total withdrawal from the Golan Heights before Damascus would even consider discussing any regional cooperation with Israel. Noting that such a pipeline "could supply both Israel and Syria," Çiller stressed during her visit to Israel, "but first we need peace."[96]

Turkey and Israel have also discussed a project to transport annually some 250 to 400 million cubic meters of surplus water from the Manavgat River, which flows into the Mediterranean near Antalya, directly to Israel, Cyprus, the Aegean Greek islands, and other neighboring countries via barges or giant plastic balloons called Medusas, still in the development stage. The water could help meet the needs of Palestinians, Jordanians (who face a growing domestic water shortage), and Israelis.

Work has been proceeding on the water export system project in Turkey, but large-scale feasibility studies on the Medusa bags have yet to be undertaken and important issues remain to be resolved. These include the cost of importing Turkish water relative to desalination of brackish and sea water, construction of terminals and storage facilities, a long-term Turkish supply commitment for ten to twenty years, and the financing and corporate structure for the venture.[97]

As noted, while serving as foreign minister, Peres had long been a strong supporter of water imports from Turkey as part of his broader objective of developing an integrated Middle East. In speeches he has pointed out that the European Union began with only limited cooperation by two longtime enemies, France and Germany, in the fields of coal and steel. He has voiced hopes that a peaceful Middle East could grow out of similar cooperation in the fields of tourism and water resources.

During her trip to the Middle East and North Africa in 1994, Prime Minister Çiller also acknowledged that progress would come step by step, beginning with Turkish-Israeli projects. "Then we can come up with interlinking institutions for the whole area. Egypt can be included, likewise Jordan. We can open up further, if more countries are willing to take part."[98] During her visit to Jerusalem in November 1994, Prime Minister Çiller summed up Ankara's vision of Turkey's growing regional role: "If you want the peace process to continue, economic cooperation is the only way to sustain it. We have a key position in the Middle East and we want to live up to our responsibility."[99]

Speaking for the Clinton administration, Marc Grossman, the U.S. ambassador to Ankara, has expressed U.S. support: "We will expand our cooperation on regional issues. Turkey makes an important contribution to the Middle East Peace Process. . . . There is great potential in the U.S.-Turkish-Israeli assistance program in Central Asia." He said that Washington and Ankara shared basic values and interests: "Turkey's success as a democratic, secular, Islamic state in a volatile region is crucial."[100]

In Jerusalem, as in Washington, there is strong concern that the Turkish government and multiparty democratic institutions effectively address the country's current economic and social challenges. It is clearly in the interest of the Western European democracies as well that the Turkish people reject the appeals of fundamentalism and extremism.

On July 2, 1997, shortly after he had succeeded in putting together a new coalition of secularist parties, Prime Minister Mesut Yilmaz charged that the Welfare Party had "incited fundamentalism" and reassured members of his Motherland Party at a meeting in Parliament, "Our government will give fundamentalism no breathing space."[101] A further hopeful sign that Turkey is returning unambiguously to its traditional pro-Western orientation was the inclusion in the cabinet as deputy premier of the staunch secularist former prime minister Bülent Ecevit, whose Democratic Left Party has been given the foreign ministry portfolio. This should end, at least for the foreseeable future, the strange spectacle of the previous twelve months, when Turkey had, in effect, pursued two contradictory foreign policies. One was that of Premier Erbakan, who demonstrated his high priority on expanding Turkey's ties with the Islamic world by rushing off to embrace and conclude major economic deals with the leaders of Iran and Libya—

going so far as to declare Muammar Qadhaffi to be a victim of U.S. terrorism while snubbing the European Union, seeking to derail or delay planned Turkish-Israeli cooperation, and even rebuffing the overtures of Israeli Prime Minister Benjamin Netanyahu for a meeting. The other was that of Foreign Minister Çiller, who tried to pursue Turkey's traditional priorities of improving relations with the United States and seeking entry into the European Union. She also worked to expand Turkey's ties with Israel, which she had explicitly described as a "strategic relationship."[102]

The Turkish defense establishment was also eager to develop its ties with the Jewish state, not only in defense industry projects and weapons production but also in joint training exercises of air force and naval personnel. "The operational Israeli flights in Turkish airspace will continue," Turkish Defense Minister Turhan Tayan declared on his first visit to Israel on April 30, 1997, contradicting Erbakan's statements that they would be postponed indefinitely. Brushing aside Arab and Iranian protests over the Turkish-Israeli defense cooperation agreements, Tayan insisted that "in the cooperation between us, we are not working against third parties." He went on to declare, "Turkey places great importance on these relations and I believe that the cooperation between us will add to stability in the region and advance the peace process."[103]

The secular Turkish and Israeli leadership were also brought together by a shared concern over the hostile policies of neighboring Syria and Iran. The Turkish defense establishment was incensed over continuing Syrian support for the PKK and Iranian nuclear ambitions and Islamist meddling in Turkey. Among the other areas of shared concern in Washington, Ankara, and Jerusalem has been mounting evidence that Syria and Iran are obtaining advanced intermediate and long-range missiles and actively developing their chemical and biological warfare arsenals, that Teheran is seeking to obtain a nuclear option, and that Baghdad is still attempting to conceal its unconventional weapons from UN inspectors. A sign of American support for the burgeoning Turkish-Israeli strategic relationship was the report in May 1997 that units of the U.S. Sixth Fleet planned to participate with Turkish and Israeli naval forces in joint search and rescue maneuvers. Israel Defense Minister Yitzhak Mordechai told Tayan that he welcomed the idea.[104] The close Turkish-Israeli military cooperation demonstrated its usefulness when, in response to an urgent appeal from the Turkish defense establishment, two Israeli Air Force helicopters and an airplane helped to extinguish a raging fire that had destroyed a munitions factory in Kirikkale, east of Ankara. Mordechai noted that in undertaking this dangerous humanitarian mission on behalf of a friendly country, Israel had "provided demonstrative proof that Turkish-Israeli cooperation was of a humanitarian and friendly character and was not motivated by other factors."[105]

Now that the prime minister, the foreign minister, and the military leadership in Ankara once again have more or less similar world-views, the basic question remains: Will Turkey be able to play the positive role its leaders envision in the region? Much will depend on continued progress in the Arab-Israel peace process and on the Turkish government's stability and its success in tackling the country's serious internal problems. These include double-digit inflation (over 80 percent in 1996), inefficient state-run enterprises, the costly war with the PKK, ethnic and religious tensions, and the questions of respect for human rights and treatment of cultural pluralism. Finally, if the secular parties can demonstrate a genuine commitment to ending corruption within their own ranks and promoting social justice, then the populist, Islamist Welfare Party will lose much of its popular appeal.

If Turkey manages to put its own house in order, it will be able to play a more effective and constructive role in the region. Benefiting from the breakthrough in Palestinian-Israeli relations achieved in Oslo, Turkey, acting in partnership with the United States, Israel, Jordan, and the Palestinian Authority, may help bring about a more stable and prosperous Middle East.

Notes

1. For developments in the earlier period, see George E. Gruen, "Turkey, Israel and the Palestine Question, 1948–1960: A Study in the Diplomacy of Ambivalence," Ph.D. dissertation, Columbia University, 1970; for developments in the 1970s and 1980s, see Gruen, "Turkey's Relations with Israel and Its Arab Neighbors"; for developments up to 1990, see Gruen, "Turkey between the Middle East and the West."

2. George E. Gruen, "Turkey's Growing Regional Role," *Near East Report*, June 27, 1994, 116.

3. For a critical analysis see Daniel Pipes, *Syria beyond the Peace Process*, esp. chap. 5. The acronym PKK stands for Partiya Karkeren Kurdistan, the Kurdish name of the Kurdistan Workers Party.

4. Ambassador Goldberg reiterated these views at the international conferences of the World Organization of Jews from Arab Lands in Washington in October 1987 and in London in November 1989. See George E. Gruen, *The Other Refugees: Impact of Nationalism, Anti-Zionism and the Arab-Israel Conflict on the Jews of the Arab World*, 10.

5. Ben-Gurion memorandum to Eisenhower of July 22, 1958 quoted in Moshe

Ma'oz, *Syria and Israel: from War to Peace-making* (London: Oxford University Press, 1995), p. 69.

6. See the sources listed in note 1.

7. Amikam Nachmani, *Israel, Turkey and Greece*, 74–76. This personal cooperation came to an end in 1960 when the military overthrew the Menderes government and imprisoned, tried, and executed him.

8. Personal communications to the author.

9. For example, in a statement to the Egyptian newspaper *Al-Ahram* in August 1993, Prime Minister Tansu Çiller declared that it would not be possible to attain peace and security in the region "without a just and durable solution to the Palestinian problem based on UN [Security Council] resolutions 242 [of 1967] and 338 [of 1973] and provision of the legitimate rights of the Palestinian people" (quoted in Turkish paper *Milliyet*, August 23, 1993).

10. George E. Gruen, "Ambivalence in Ankara," *Jerusalem Post*, July 27, 1979.

11. John Barham dispatch from Ankara, "Turkey, Israel to scrap barriers," *Financial Times* (London), March 12, 1996.

12. Leslie Susser, "Syria fears Israeli-Turkish joint air maneuvers and intelligence cooperation," *Jerusalem Report*, May 2, 1996, 6.

13. "Turkey and Israel to Cooperate on Security: Common Threats to be Met with Complementary Capabilities," report of a briefing by General Bir at a meeting of the Jewish Institute for National Security Affairs (JINSA) in Washington in March 1996, *JINSA Security Affairs* 19, no. 1 (February-March 1996): 1,12.

14. UPI dispatch from Ankara, April 17, 1996.

15. UPI dispatch from Cairo, April 23, 1996. The *Jerusalem Report*, May 2, 1996, stated that Turkish Defense Minister Ortan Sungurlu, who in early April had said his country agreed to allow Israeli pilots to train in Turkish airspace because Israel's was so narrow that planes "leave it almost as soon as they take off," revised his statement after vigorous protests from Syria, Egypt, and Iran. "Claiming he'd been confused, Sungurlu said there was no agreement for Israeli pilots to train in Turkey." It subsequently became clear that the second quote was inaccurate and possibly designed to deflect Arab opposition.

16. Robert Pear, dispatch from Washington, and AP dispatch from Nicosia, *New York Times*, November 17, 1988. For additional details on this period, see Gruen, "Turkey Between Middle East and West," 412–17.

17. Dispatch from Jerusalem, *New York Times*, November 17, 1988.

18. George E. Gruen, memorandum of March 2, 1989, on "AJC Meetings in Ankara, Turkey," in AJC files.

19. Henri J. Barkey, "Reluctant Neighbors: Reflections on Turkish-Arab Relations," cited on 10.

20. Alan Makovsky is a former U.S. State Department Turkish affairs analyst, currently at the Washington Institute for Near East Policy. Citation is from his draft chapter on "Turkish-Israeli Relations: A Turkish 'Periphery Strategy'?" in a forthcoming book by the U.S. Institute of Peace on Turkey and the Middle East.

21. In an opinion column welcoming and "applauding" the Demirel government's decision to improve Turkish-Israeli political relations, M. Orhan Tarhan cites the sharp decline in Turkish exports to the Arab countries and the reduction in construction contracts as one of the key reasons for not being concerned with Arab reaction. He also expresses annoyance that Kuwait did not favor Turkish companies in awarding contracts for postwar reconstruction (*Turkish Times*, June 15, 1992).

22. This figure was given by President Süleyman Demirel on March 28, 1996, during his visit to the United States in his policy forum meeting at the Washington Institute and published in the institute's *Policywatch* 193, April 3, 1996.

23. Interview with Emre Gönensay, Ankara, September 21, 1992.

24. Republic of Turkey, Prime Ministry, State Institute of Statistics, *Monthly Economic Indicators* (June 1992), export and import figures for 1990, 1991, and January–April 1990, 1991, and 1992, 27–34. In 1990 Iraq was the chief supplier of oil to Turkey. Saudi Arabia, Libya, and the U.A.E. filled the gap after Turkey closed the pipelines from Iraq in compliance with the UN sanctions.

25. This is the assessment of Alan Makovsky, in the chapter cited.

26. Quoted by Refat Kaplan in "Two parties take turns governing Turkey," *Washington Times*, March 7, 1996.

27. Henri Barkey, "Turkey, Islamic Politics, and the Kurdish Question." Barkey, an international economist and political scientist, describes Refah as "an obscurantist party with a simplistic and even absurd message, heavily laden with anti-Semitism," 46.

28. Celestine Bohlen, "2 Turkish Parties Agree on Freezing Out the Islamic Forces," *New York Times*, March 4, 1996; Sabri Sayari, "Election Results a Mixed Blessing for Turkey's Islamists," in Council on Foreign Relations, *Muslim Politics Report* 6 (March/April 1996): 1, 3, includes a table showing the 1987, 1991, and 1995 election results and the growing strength of the Refah Party.

29. Quoted by Edward Mortimer in "A marriage of convenience," a lengthy comment and rather pessimistic analysis of the new government's "shaky parliamentary base" and the difficulties it faces in tackling urgent reforms, *Financial Times* (London), March 13, 1996.

30. Quoted in an interview with Ecevit at Ben Gurion Airport by Nina Tarablus of the Turkish-language Jewish weekly *şalom* (Istanbul), "Bulent Ecevit: "Bariş sürecinin sonuca ulaşilmasinda Türkiye'nin büyük yarari var" [Turkey will derive great benefit from the successful conclusion of the peace process]. *şalom*, April 19, 1995, 7. A photo of the Ecevit's visit to Yad va-Shem, the Holocaust memorial, during what the paper headlined Ecevit's "historical Israeli visit" was featured on page 1 of the paper, and his visit to the Atatürk Forest planted by Turkish Jewish immigrants to Israel was on page 10. Mrs. Ecevit's influential role has been compared to that of Hilary Clinton.

31. Reuters dispatch from Ankara, April 24, "Turkey to Investigate Çiller," *New York Times*, April 25, 1996. Similar allegations had earlier been made against relatives of the late President Özal, thus strengthening the Welfare Party's electioneering posture as the only major party not tainted by corruption. There have, how-

ever, been allegations that Erbakan registered party property in his own name, and questions were raised as to whether the money raised by Refah ostensibly for Bosnian relief actually reached its intended beneficiaries.

32. Celestine Bohlen, "Islamic Party Gets Second Chance to Form Coalition in Turkey," *New York Times*, June 8, 1996.

33. Suna Erdem, "Turkey's Islamists preen for power, blast Jews," Reuters dispatch from Istanbul, May 21, 1996.

34. See Seyfi Taşhan, "Turkey from Marginality to Centrality," in Turkish Foreign Policy Institute's *Diş Politika: Foreign Policy* 16, nos. 3–4 (1993): 1–12; text of lecture given by Taşhan, director of the institute, before the Royal Institute of International Affairs, London, January 13, 1992.

35. Figures provided by Turkey's ambassador to the UN, Mustafa Akşin, in an address at Columbia University on November 6, 1992. Copy of unpublished text provided to the author by Ambassador Akşin.

36. Ibid.

37. Quotations cited by Sami Kohen in his article "Contacts with Central Asian States a Foundation for 'Pan-Turkism,'" *Washington Report on Middle East Affairs*, August/September 1992, 17–18.

38. See George E. Gruen, "Turkey's Emerging Regional Role," *American Foreign Policy Interests* 17, no. 2 (April 1995): 13–24.

39. Dogan column, "First Assault in Foreign Policy," *Milliyet*, November 30, 1991.

40. Dispatch from Moscow, *Cumhuriyet*, March 13, 1991.

41. For his part, Baker was seeking to enlarge the coalition of Moslem states supportive of the peace process.

42. Utkan reports in *Hürriyet*, March 14, 17, 1991.

43. For the circumstances leading to the Turkish decision to permit the opening of the PLO office in 1979—fifteen years after the creation of the PLO—see George E. Gruen, "Ambivalence in Ankara," *Jerusalem Post*, July 27, 1979, 6–7. The PLO representative has had full diplomatic immunity, although his status as "resident representative" was the equivalent of a chargé d'affaires. (James W. Spain, *American Diplomacy in Turkey* [New York: Praeger Special Studies, 1984], 63–66, 181–82.) This was the same rank as the Israeli head of mission after Turkey reduced the level of representation in 1956. The Ministerial Council's resolution of December 20, 1991, to upgrade relations was published in the *Resmi Gazete* (official gazette) on December 31, 1991 (Anatolian News Agency dispatch from Ankara, *Milliyet*, January 1, 1992). Fuad Yassin, the PLO resident representative, presented his credentials as ambassador to President Özal on March 3, 1992, and Uri Gordon, the Israeli representative, did so two days later.

44. "Turkey Talked about in Israel—Israel Asked Help from the Turkish Government," *Sabah*, March 13, 1991. Shaked's statement to the semiofficial Anatolian Agency was reported in the *Turkish Daily News* and several major Turkish-language papers, March 13, 1991. Shaked had previously served as chargé in Ankara and consul in Istanbul.

45. Typical was the front-page headline: "Here is the Table, Where Are We?" in

the major daily, *Milliyet*, October 30, 1991. See, for example, the column by Metin Toker, who blamed Özal and his grandiose foreign policy initiatives for unrealistically raising the Turkish public's expectations, *Milliyet*, October 21, 1991.

46. Report of Demirel's press conference in *Tercuman, Turkiye and Gunaydin*, October 25, 1991.

47. Demirel press conference, *Turkish Daily News*, October 31, 1991.

48. Before the 1980 military coup, Türkeş had headed the ultraright Nationalist Action Party, and in 1991 he was a parliamentarian elected on the Welfare Party slate. He died in 1997.

49. Ecevit press conference, reported in *Hürriyet*, October 29, 1991.

50. Makovsky, "Israeli-Turkish Relations: A Turkish 'Periphery Strategy'?" forthcoming.

51. Gruen, "Turkey's Emerging Regional Role," 14–16.

52. The secret behind-the-scenes Israeli efforts were revealed by a Euro-Parliamentarian who complained about international lobbying on behalf of Turkey and cited specifically Peres's phone calls. The story was cited in the Turkish press and confirmed by Turkish officials.

53. Former Foreign Minister Vahit Halefoglu publicly advocated the immediate upgrading of relations with Israel to ambassadorial level, adding that there had been no negative Arab reaction when he undertook practical steps in 1987 to expand and improve relations with Israel. Interview with German Radio quoted in *Tercuman*, November 4, 1991. In an interview with the semiofficial Anatolian News Agency, Israeli Ambassador Gordon reported that about 160,000 Israel tourists had visited Turkey during 1992 and had spent $250 million. (Text in *Sabah*, March 15, 1993.) In addition, a disproportionate percentage of U.S. tourists to Turkey were Jewish.

54. The text of the tourism agreement was published in the *Resmi Gazete* (official gazette) on September 11, 1992.

55. Interview in New York City, January 25, 1994. See also Gruen, "Turkey's Growing Regional Role," 16.

56. Text broadcast on Turkish TV, 1600 GMT, July 17, 1992.

57. George E. Gruen, "Turkey's Potential Contribution to Arab-Israel Peace," *Turkish Review of Middle East Studies* (Istanbul) 7 (1993): 193.

58. "Erbakan: Çiller Israil'in figurani," *Cumhuriyet*, November 7, 1994.

59. Ilnur Çevik, editor of the *Turkish Daily News*, in his column on March 22 charged that persons who had "never lifted a finger for Palestinian rights" were cynically exploiting the current anti-Israeli sentiment to gather support for their real but illegal objective, "the creation of Islamic rule in Turkey." Erbakan, an engineer by training, had long appealed to conservative voters by combining a call for return to traditional Islamic values with an emphasis on modern technology to industrialize rural areas. He had called for creation of an Islamic Common Market, and he blamed "international Zionism" for Turkey's economic problems. From 1972 to 1980 he had led the National Salvation Party (NSP). Many observers believe that

the September 6, 1980, "Jerusalem Liberation Day" rally organized in Konya by Erbakan's NSP was the final straw that prompted the Kemalist army officers to seize power and end the fractious and ineffective coalition government. In the 1980 Konya rally, the NSP demonstrators called for restoration of the caliphate, refused to sing the Turkish national anthem, carried anti-Semitic signs, and burned the Israeli, American, and Russian flags. Pro-Western Turkish officials regarded it as ominously significant that these were the flags of the "two Great Satans and the Little Satan" being reviled by the Khomeini regime that in the previous year had established an Islamic republic in neighboring Iran.

60. Sam Cohen, dispatch from Istanbul, *Jewish Chronicle* (London), April 22, 1988.

61. Since I was in Israel at the time, Turkish Ambassador Onur Gökçe had invited me to the luncheon, and his secretary called sheepishly to explain the sudden cancellation of the trip.

62. Reuters dispatch from the United Nations, April 25, 1996. The vote on the resolution, which also called for Israel's withdrawal from all Lebanese territory was 64 in favor, 2 against, and 65 abstentions.

63. Foreign Minister Hikmet Çetin, "A Statement on His Visit to Israel," *Focus on the Turkish World* (official publication of the World Turkish Congress [New York]), March 1994, 9–10.

64. David Makovsky, "Turkish PM arrives today seeking closer cooperation," *Jerusalem Post*, November 3, 1994.

65. Comments by Ambassador Itamar Rabinovich at the Association of Israel Studies Conference, Gratz College, Philadelphia, June 12, 1994. Rabinovich, a Middle East scholar, was Israel's ambassador to the United States from 1992 to 1996 and was chairman of the Israeli delegation in the bilateral peace talks with Syria.

66. For details see George E. Gruen, "Recent Negotiations over the Waters of the Euphrates and Tigris," International Water Resources Association, *Proceedings of the International Symposium on Water Resources in the Middle East: Policy and Institutional Aspects,* University of Illinois at Urbana-Champaign, October 24–27, 1993 ("Pre-Symposium Proceedings," 100–108); George E. Gruen, "International Regional Cooperation—Preconditions and Limits," proceedings of international conference, Ankara, October 4–8, 1993, *Water as an Element of Cooperation and Development in the Middle East,* ed. Ali İhsan Bağiş (Ankara: Hacettepe University and Friedrich-Naumann-Foundation, 1994), 263–87. See also Gruen, "Turkey's Potential Contribution," 199–201.

67. Conversation with the author, Ankara, October 17, 1994.

68. National Press Club, "Afternoon Newsmaker with Israel Prime Minister Shimon Peres," December 12, 1995, Federal News Service Transcript, 5.

69. Personal conversation by the author with U.S., Turkish, and Israeli officials in Washington, May 7–10, 1996. *The Jerusalem Report* reported in March that Dennis Ross, the U.S. Middle East peace talks coordinator, was preparing to fly to Turkey to work out a deal under which Turkey would guarantee additional water to Syria, whereas Syria would stop all support for the PKK and other hostile elements and

would permit uninterrupted flow of Jordan water to Israel. When asked in May 1996, Ambassador Ross declined to comment on this report.

70. "Demirel: 'Terrorism has become a global concern,'" dispatch from Egypt, March 13, *Turkish Times*, March 15, 1996.

71. Interview in *as-Safir* (Lebanon), November 20, 1995.

72. "Turkey urges Syria and Iraq to discuss plan to share water resources," *Turkey Today* (Washington) no. 154 (January/February 1996): 4. The official Turkish proposal is detailed in Republic of Turkey, Ministry of Foreign Affairs, Department of Regional and Transboundary Waters, "Water Issues between Turkey, Syria and Iraq," January 1995. Syria and Iraq (which don't agree on much else) met in Baghdad in early July 1995 to coordinate their demand that Turkey increase the guaranteed quantity of water in the Euphrates across the border into Syria from 500 to 693 cubic meters per second, or from roughly half to about two-thirds of river's average annual flow (ca. 1,050 cubic meters per second). On October 12, 1995, Ankara again officially warned Damascus to curb cross-border attacks from Syria because of the obvious "damage that such incidents do to Turkish-Syrian relations." In December 1995 Syria and Iraq managed to enlist the support of the Arab League, including Egypt and Saudi Arabia, in their water protests against Turkey.

73. John Barham report from Gaziantep, "The Southeastern Anatolia Project: Irrigation transforms area's prospects," *Financial Times Survey* (Turkey), June 3, 1996, 4.

74. Personal communication to the author, New York City, September 28, 1993.

75. Discussion with the author, New York City, July 21, 1992. For details of plans to bring Turkish water to Jordan and its neighbors, see Gruen, "Turkey's Potential Contribution to Arab-Israel Peace," 179–214, esp. 194–211. The strength of the pro-Islamic deputies in the Mejlis is only about half their number a few years ago, and the Jordanian-Israeli peace treaty of October 26, 1994, was approved by a substantial majority. The *Jordan Times* reported that the Islamic Action Front "bitterly criticized" the visit to Amman of a delegation from the Israeli Knesset, which was warmly received by the king (quoted by Liat Collins, "MKs do dinner in Amman," *Jerusalem Post International Edition*, February 18, 1955, 11).

76. Personal communication, New York City, September 28, 1993.

77. John Barham dispatch from Ankara, "Turkey, Israel to scrap barriers," *Financial Times*, March 12, 1996.

78. Çetin, "A Statement on His Visit to Israel," 10.

79. Bill Hutman, Dan Izenberg, and David Makovsky, "Rabin: I don't have majority to pass Orient House bill," *Jerusalem Post*, November 7, 1994. See also the critical editorial "Credibility on Jerusalem," *Jerusalem Post*, November 6, 1994.

80. "Çiller: Gaza should be world priority," *Jerusalem Post*, November 6, 1994.

81. Ibid.

82. Eric Silver, "Middle East Interview: The Ottoman Empress," *Jerusalem Report*, December 1, 1994, 20–21.

83. "Demirel: 'The agreement is a hopeful turning point,'" *Newspot* (Ankara), May 13, 1994, 3.

84. Prime Minister Çiller:"Turkey is the friend of both Arabs and Israelis," ibid., July 8, 1994, 1.

85. Ankara, Turkish National News Agency, in English, 1540 GMT, April 11, 1994, in BBC Summary of World Broadcasts, April 15, 1994, part 4, Middle East, ME/1972.

86. Gruen, "Turkey's Growing Regional Role," 116.

87. Cited in *The Future of the Conference on Security and Cooperation in Europe: A United States Institute of Peace Roundtable* (Washington, DC: 1995), 66.

88. Gruen, "Turkey's Growing Regional Role," 116.

89. "Turkey and Israel Negotiate Free Trade Accord," Istanbul, June 3, 1994, Reuters European Business Report. Israeli statistics provided to the author by the Israeli Consulate, Istanbul, October 1994.

90. Barham (see n.11).

91. For details of Turkish relations with Central Asia and U.S. policy see Gruen, "Turkey's Emerging Regional Role."

92. Clyde Haberman, "Israel Builds Ties to Ex-Soviet Muslim Lands," *New York Times*, May 2, 1993.

93. "Çiller Attends Middle East/North Africa Economic Summit," *Turkey Today*, no. 146 (September/October 1994): 3.

94. "Prime Minister Ciller Visits Israel, Egypt," ibid., 1.

95. Gruen, "Turkey's Potential Contribution to Arab-Israel Peace," 197–99.

96. Silver, op. cit., 21.

97. See George E. Gruen, "Contribution of Water Imports to Israeli-Palestinian-Jordanian Peace," proceedings of the First Israeli-Palestinian International Academic Conference on Water, Zurich, December 10–13, 1992, *Water and Peace in the Middle East*, J. Isaac and H. Shuval, eds. (Amsterdam: Elsevier Science Publishers, 1994), 273–88; and Gruen, "International Regional Cooperation—Preconditions and Limits," 270–84. For further details of the Medusa bag project, see James A. Cran, "Medusa Bag Projects for the Ocean Transport of Freshwater in the Mediterranean and the Middle East," abstract for presentation at the Eighth World Water Congress, Cairo, November 21, 1994 (11 pages, mimeographed). Copy provided to the author by Mr. Cran, president of the Medusa Corporation, Calgary, Canada. In a telephone conversation with the author on May 3, 1996, Mr. Cran said that the German government had recently expressed interest in conducting a feasibility study. He added that he had been told that Mrs. Çiller had offered to supply Israel with 150 million cubic meters of water per annum at a cost of $1.00 per cubic meter f.o.b., that is, not including the cost of transport to Israel. This offer was reportedly rejected by Israel as economically unrealistic under present circumstances.

98. Silver, op. cit., p.21.

99. Ibid., 20.

100. Text of Ambassador Grossman's speech to the American Turkish Council on January 19, 1995, in *Newspot*, February 10, 1995, 2.

101. Reuters dispatch from Ankara, July 2, 1997.

102. Interview with the *Jerusalem Post*, November 4, 1994.

103. Agence France Presse dispatch, Tel-Aviv, April 30, 1997.

104. Reuters dispatch from Ankara, May 1, 1997.

105. Quoted in a statement released by the Israel Defense Forces media coordinator, July 6, 1997. UPI reported from Ankara on July 4 that, when local fire brigades were unable to put out the fire, Turkish officials feared that it would spread to a depot where hundreds of bombs were kept and that, if they were set off by the fire, the devastation would equal that of a major earthquake of seven on the Richter scale.

8: Iraq after the Gulf War

The Fallen Idol

Phebe Marr

Iraq's position has declined dramatically in the six years since the Gulf War, domestically, regionally, and internationally. While Saddam Hussein's defeat and the damage inflicted by the Gulf War explain some of the dramatic decline in Iraq's fortunes, much also springs from the way in which the Iraqi leadership has handled its crisis and the reaction of the international community—and particularly the U.S.—to its policies. A severe sanctions regime, originally meant to achieve compliance with ceasefire regulations, has now eroded the economy, the society, and the institutions of state, while Iraq's regional and international isolation has continued. This persistent stalemate and Baghdad's worsening situation were probably the main factors behind Iraq's acceptance of UN resolution 986, allowing a temporary sale of oil for food in May 1996. However, this resolution is unlikely to end the current standoff, or to improve Iraq's domestic situation significantly, unless Iraq changes its behavior dramatically. Whether such a change is possible under the current leadership is at best questionable and at worst a contradiction in terms. What explains the current impasse? And what lies ahead for Iraq?

The Postwar Settlement and Its Impact

Several important outcomes of the Gulf War have helped shape this impasse and the regional environment in the Gulf. The first lies in the ceasefire terms and the way in which the international community decided to enforce them. Rather than leaving troops on the ground in Iraq (a costly measure), the coalition decided on maintaining an array of economic sanctions, including the oil export embargo, as the chief mechanism to achieve compliance. The compliance has been slow and grudging and, much to the surprise of most observers, the full sanctions regime is still in effect almost seven years after the war's conclusion. Even if UN resolution 986 (food for oil) is renewed periodically, it does not annul the original sanctions regime, which leaves control of Iraq's oil flow in international hands.

A second important outcome was the failure of the spontaneous 1991 rebellion in Iraq to unseat Saddam Hussein and his regime. Whether there might have been a different outcome had the coalition fought longer, ended the war on different terms, or rendered more support to the Shi'ah and Kurdish rebels cannot now be known.[1] What is clear is that the remnants of Saddam Hussein's army, especially those held back in Baghdad, turned against the rebels and brutally ended the uprising. As a result, Saddam Hussein and his regime survived but in a weakened state.

A third, unintended outcome of the war was the flight of some 2 million Kurds from northern Iraq into Turkey and Iran. To relieve their parlous plight, several coalition countries, notably the United States, Britain, France, and Turkey,[2] established a secure zone for the Kurds in northwest Iraq; undertook a massive and largely successful humanitarian effort to repatriate homeless Kurds, and created a no-fly zone (NFZ) north of the 36th parallel in Iraq to protect them from attack by the Iraqi government. Not long after, Saddam himself withdrew his own troops from a zone stretching from the Syrian border near Peshkhabur to the Iranian border near Khanaqin, leaving the inhabitants within this region to govern themselves. A similar NFZ was later established below the 32nd parallel in the south (later extended to the 33rd parallel) to monitor Iraq's treatment of the Shi'ah, but Saddam did not withdraw his troops from this region, leaving the central government in control on the ground. These zones have weakened but not destroyed Iraqi sovereignty over its territory.

Last, the survival of Saddam Hussein, his continued challenges to the coalition, and his slowness in complying with ceasefire provisions, have led the United States and its coalition partners to maintain a more substantial forward military presence in the Gulf than was the case before the war.[3] The presence is designed in part to deter a land-based Iraqi attack on Kuwait and, along with the sanctions regime, to contain and if possible diminish Iraq's military power. The presence, too, shows every sign of remaining in the Gulf as long as the West sees a potential future threat from Iraq.

The net result of these four outcomes is that Saddam Hussein is still in power almost seven years after the war and has still not fully complied with the ceasefire resolutions put into effect at the war's end. Trade sanctions, an oil embargo, NFZs, and other measures taken to "contain" Iraq have had some effect in weakening the regime, but they have weakened society and its population far more. And the United States, with its substantial forward presence in the Gulf, now finds itself thrust into the position of chief architect and guardian of Gulf security. How long is this situation likely to last? Is there any way, short of a change of regime in Baghdad, that it can be ameliorated? Can Iraq change its regime or, if not, is Saddam Hussein likely to change course sufficiently to satisfy the West and permanently remove these restrictions? And what lies ahead for Iraq, in any case?

While there are no definitive answers to these questions, an examination of events since the end of the Gulf War provides some clues to the future. The record of the regime and the response from the West since 1991 are fairly well established and have settled into a pattern with some fairly clearly defined characteristics: (1) Iraq's intransigence in complying with UN resolutions and the resulting continuation of sanctions; (2) the cumulative economic, social, and political toll of the sanctions regime on Iraq; (3) the survival of the regime despite a gradual shrinkage of its domestic support base; (4) the erosion of state institutions and national cohesion, and (5) Iraq's continuing isolation regionally and for the most part internationally.

Iraqi Intransigence in Meeting Ceasefire Requirements

In the immediate aftermath of the war there was some hope in Baghdad and elsewhere of a different outcome to this saga. Shortly after a cessation of hostilities in March 1991, Saddam Hussein promised an election and a multiparty system, and on March 23 he appointed a new cabinet with Sa'dun Hammadi as prime minister. Hammadi, a pre-Saddam-era Ba'thist with a Ph.D. from a U.S. university, a Shi'ah with some support in that community, and a man considered to have a better understanding of the West than most Ba'thists, was widely expected to introduce some modest political reforms and possibly to take a more conciliatory position on UN resolutions. On April 3, the main ceasefire resolution, 687, was passed by the UN, laying out requirements for Iraq in return for which the oil embargo would be terminated. These included recognition of Kuwait's sovereignty and a newly demarcated border with Kuwait; accounting for or returning more than six hundred Kuwaitis detained during the occupation; and returning Kuwaiti property stolen during the war. Most important were the provisions in paragraph 22, which requires the dismantling and destruction of Iraq's WMD (weapons of mass destruction) and missiles (over 150 kilometers in range) and the establishment of an intrusive monitoring system to prevent their reintroduction. Paragraph 22 also states that "the prohibition against the import of commodities and products originating in Iraq [oil] . . . shall have no further force" if Iraq fulfills the WMD provisions.[4] This does not apply to trade sanctions on Iraq.

Hope for compliance and a reasonably rapid end to the oil embargo soon came to an abrupt halt, however, when it became apparent that the UN did, indeed, intend to enforce the ceasefire provisions, especially those relating to Iraq's weapons of mass destruction. In May, UN weapons inspections began in Baghdad, drawing the first of many Iraqi challenges to the new inspection regime. Starting with the very first inspectors, Iraq tried to rein in the inspection rights of the UN Special Commission (UNSCOM), to use harassment tactics, and to limit its access. In June, 1991, when inspectors chased a vehicle removing items from a nuclear site, shots were fired at them. In September an even more serious incident occurred. The nuclear inspection team was prevented from removing documents from a site, and the next day it was detained in a parking lot for four days.[5] Finally, on September 14, Sa'dun Hammadi was removed as prime minister, and with him went any immediate hopes for reform or conciliation. While some groups inside the Ba'th Party leadership, especially those in the Ministry of Foreign Affairs, continued to favor reform and some cooperation with the UN as the most rapid avenue to recuperation, they consistently lost out to hard-liners, convinced they could achieve their aims with minimal concessions. Chief among them was Saddam Hussein, who adopted a different strategy, which he has followed with remarkable consistency.

Saddam's Hard-Line Strategy

This strategy has had several facets. One can be described as "intransigence and proportionality."[6] Iraq would comply with UN resolutions minimally and only when compelled to do so. Meanwhile, it would demand proportional concessions for its compliance, negotiating every step of the way in the hope of wearing down its adversaries and avoiding some of the ceasefire conditions. While this policy has, in fact, led to gradual compliance, it has prolonged the process well beyond original expectations; proportional concessions have not been forthcoming, and compliance is still not complete.

A second facet has been the attempt to divide the international coalition arrayed against Iraq, by encouraging some members, notably the French and the Russians, to break ranks in return for lucrative business opportunities and repayment of debt once sanctions are removed. While these tactics have caused some strains in the coalition, with some members more willing to ease sanctions and "encourage" Iraq than others, there is virtually universal agreement that the oil embargo should not be fully lifted until Iraq has complied with the WMD provisions in chapter 22 of UN resolution 687. The United States has gone further, claiming that it would not vote for a lifting of sanctions until Iraq has satisfied "all relevant resolutions," presumably including UN resolution 688, which holds that Iraq must cease repressing its people and ensure human and political rights for Iraqi citizens.[7] Pressure from allies has led to the passage of UN measures to provide relief to the Iraqi population, such as resolutions 706, 712, and now 986.[8] But these are temporary though renewable measures that leave the main sanctions provisions intact.

Third, Saddam has attempted to reduce Iraq's isolation within the region, having only marginal success. While Iraq remains an Arab League member and some regional states have full diplomatic representation in Baghdad (Oman, the UAE, Jordan), Iraq has been excluded from key Arab summit meetings, and Saddam's image in the region has diminished, as he has rejected UN resolutions designed to help the Iraqi population and has dealt with his opposition in an ever more brutal manner. His acceptance of resolution 986 was designed, in part, to improve that image. Finally, Saddam has manipulated the suffering of the Iraqi population to get international relief from sanctions, but he has seen to it that his family and his supporters are well taken care of.[9]

Of all these efforts, it is the policy of WMD intransigence that has probably been most damaging. The attempt to evade compliance began early. In the course of 1992, Iraq several times attempted to block inspections. The most dramatic confrontation between Iraq and the UN took place in July 1992, when a UN team, led by David Kay, an American, was detained in the parking lot of an Iraqi building and denied entrance for inspection for seventeen days.[10] In January 1993 minimal cooperation came to a standstill when Iraqi officials announced that Iraq would cease to cooperate with weapons inspectors and insisted that UNSCOM use Iraqi flights.[11] Iraq claimed that UNSCOM inspections were too intrusive, were a violation of sovereignty, and went beyond UN mandated procedures. They also challenged U.S. flights over the NFZs. Finally, this intransigence precipitated attacks on Iraqi targets in north and south Iraq and in Baghdad by the United States, Britain, and France, with one unfortunate consequence. On January 17, a cruise missile from a U.S. ship accidentally hit the Rashid Hotel in Baghdad, causing a number of civilian deaths. This crisis did bring about renewed cooperation from Iraq, but it did not last long. In April 1993 Iraqi security forces made an attempt to assassinate former President Bush during a trip to Kuwait, and the United States retaliated against Iraq again.

This time the United States struck Iraq's intelligence facilities in Baghdad, again killing several civilians by accident, including one of Iraq's leading artists. In June Iraq stonewalled once again, refused to install cameras in facilities designated by inspection teams for monitoring WMD, although it relented in July. Meanwhile, the Iraqi government had rejected UN resolutions 706 and 712, which proposed a temporary oil sale to relieve Iraq's humanitarian crisis but with intrusive supervision by the UN to assure appropriate distribution.

By 1994 UNSCOM and the International Atomic Energy Agency (IAEA), the two agencies charged with destroying Iraq's WMD and monitoring compliance with the ban on future production, had made some headway. Iraq's chemical weapons (CW) facilities and its nuclear plants had been dismantled, and most of its long-range missiles (SCUDs) had been accounted for, although there were some questions raised over what, if any, weapons remained.[12] However, there was as yet no accounting for Iraq's presumed biological weapons program. Without such an accounting, there could be no consideration of removing the embargo.[13] Nor had Iraq fulfilled other ceasefire requirements, such as recognition of Kuwait or accounting for over six hundred Kuwaitis who had disappeared during the occupation. Building on the progress to that point and invoking the concept of proportionality, Iraq began demanding UN discussions on lifting the oil embargo.

When no such discussions appeared to be forthcoming, Saddam Hussein decided to precipitate another crisis with the West. On October 5 he announced a deadline of October 10 for a lifting of the oil embargo as a condition for further cooperation, and he sent two divisions from the north to Basra and the Kuwaiti border. In the face of this potential threat to Kuwait, the coalition responded with a substantial movement of U.S. naval and air assets to the Gulf to deter any cross-border action. This October standoff achieved at least one Iraqi aim. It precipitated a visit of the Russian foreign minister, Andrei Kozyrev, to Baghdad, the first visit of such an important foreign minister since the Gulf War, and drew international attention to Iraq's humanitarian plight. However, Iraq's action also alarmed many in the West, where it was depicted as an indication of Iraq's bellicose intentions. On balance, there was one positive result of the "October surprise." After prodding from Russia and France, Iraq finally recognized Kuwaiti sovereignty and accepted the newly drawn border with Kuwait, a substantial concession on its part and one that put it closer to UN compliance. But Iraq's high-risk challenge was also costly. Under U.S. leadership, the UN passed resolution 949, which put further restrictions on Iraq's sovereignty. Under this resolution, Iraq is compelled to keep its best forces, the

Republican Guards, north of the 32nd parallel, further weakening its sovereignty and its control over the Shi'ah south.[14]

This particular cycle of intransigence was broken in spectacular fashion in August 1995, with the defection to Jordan of Saddam's son-in-law, Hussein Kamil, the administrative mastermind behind much of Iraq's WMD program. Uncertain of how much information Hussein Kamil would reveal to the West, the Iraqi government itself released a treasure trove of information on its WMD programs. This episode and an investigation of the documents released have profoundly affected the international community's perception of Iraq's compliance with UN resolutions and diminished even further UN willingness to trust the regime's assurances. The documents revealed the previous existence of an extensive biological weapons program that had progressed far enough to allow the emplacement of a number of BW warheads on missiles targeted on Israel, Saudi Arabia, and U.S. forces during the Gulf War. They also indicated discrepancies in the information previously given to UNSCOM and the IAEA on Iraq's WMD, necessitating the reopening of files on CW, NW, and missiles. Compounding these revelations, in March 1996 UNSCOM discovered attempts by Iraq to import and hide missile components prohibited under the sanctions regime, further damaging Iraq's already tarnished credibility.[15] These events clearly set back any prospects for an early end to the oil embargo.

U.S. Intransigence

Iraq's intransigence has been fully reciprocated by the United States, which has taken the lead in coalition policy toward Iraq. While there is little doubt that both the Bush and Clinton administrations would have preferred another regime in Baghdad, Iraq's prompt compliance with key UN ceasefire provisions would probably have compelled some easing of the oil embargo long ago. Early challenges by Iraq to the inspection regime, refusals to cooperate, and threats to coalition personnel gradually have hardened U.S. attitudes and policies. Intransigence in Baghdad was met with increased intransigence in Washington. Under the Bush administration, relations between Washington and Baghdad were highly personalized, and some of Saddam's challenges in 1992—and his attempted assassination of Bush in 1993—could be read as vendettas. With the advent of the Clinton administration in 1993, Baghdad hoped for an easing of this position, but the only change was cosmetic. Early in its tenure, the Clinton administration attempted to depersonalize the policy. In March 1993 Secretary of State Christopher stated that U.S. policy was aimed at full compliance by Iraq with all relevant UN resolutions, including UNSC resolution 688, specifying that

Iraq should cease repression of its population. He specified, however, that, in the U.S. view, Saddam could not fulfill these obligations and still remain in power; consequently, these requirements were widely interpreted as being synonymous with a U.S. desire to see him gone without officially calling for his overthrow. This policy was reinforced in the second Clinton administration by Secretary of State Albright in a speech in which she claimed that "Saddam's intentions will never be peaceful and, for these reasons, our policy will not change. It is the right policy."[16] Notwithstanding these nuances of policy, international pressure from U.S. allies would have made continuation of the oil embargo difficult had Baghdad rapidly complied with the key provisions of UN resolution 687. As Baghdad's reluctance to comply became increasingly evident, along with its concealment of information, attitudes in Washington—and other world capitals—hardened, making intransigence the U.S. policy as well. The result by the end of 1995 was a stalemate on both sides, increasingly difficult to break.

It was this stalemate and Iraq's conclusion that the oil embargo would not soon come off that may finally have persuaded Saddam Hussein to accept UNSC resolution 986. This resolution provides for the sale of $1 billion worth of Iraqi oil over ninety days, renewable under conditions of good behavior. Iraq's government does not get control of the funds, however, which are retained in an escrow account to be paid out for food and medicine. Their distribution in Iraq is to be monitored by UN inspectors to prevent diversion to the government and its supporters. Negotiations on the technicalities of its operation, which began in February 1996, ended in May, but only after tough restrictions imposed by the United States and Britain closed potential loopholes.[17] Baghdad's acceptance of 986 was regarded as a victory for the Iraqi contingent who had urged this action as the first step toward the removal of sanctions. In one sense, the adoption of 986 can be expected to ease pressure on the coalition to end the full sanctions regime until Baghdad has fully complied with all resolutions to its satisfaction.

The Economic and Social Toll of Sanctions

The result of continuing sanctions has been a gradual decline of Iraq's economy and society, although measurement of the physical and human damage is difficult. Some of this damage, of course, was afflicted by wars—the Iran-Iraq War, the Gulf War, and the rebellion. Whatever the origin, the damage can be seen in several areas. Most significant has been the impact on Iraq's human resources.

Human Damage

Estimates of war casualties have been controversial, but as the dust has settled over these events, the numbers have been revised downward. Losses in the Iran-Iraq war have been estimated at 135,000 to 150,000 killed, roughly 4 to 5 percent of the military-age population.[18] Accurate figures for the Gulf War are hard to come by and estimates range widely, but recent articles indicate that the earlier U.S. government estimate of 100,000 may have been greatly inflated. According to some, battle losses may have been as low as 10,000 to 20,000.[19] The number of those killed in the 1991 rebellion may equal or exceed this total, and thousands more probably died in the Kurdish exodus to the mountains.[20] However, even the maximum for the cumulative death toll in these events would probably not exceed 100,000. Including the toll taken by the Iran-Iraq war, Iraq may have lost about 6 to 8 percent of its military-age population. By any standard, this is a significant depletion of its workforce, and it will take a serious toll on Iraq's future capacity to produce. However, it must be remembered that Iraq also had a high fertility rate (5.8) prior to the Gulf War.[21] Although this may have declined somewhat under the impact of sanctions, Iraq can be expected to replenish its population fairly rapidly once sanctions are eased.

Even more serious in sapping Iraq's strength has been the steady emigration of its population, particularly of its substantial, well-educated middle class. This outflow cannot be attributed solely to the Gulf War. The exodus started in the late 1950s, after the first of a series of coups in Baghdad, which brought a decade of instability and increasingly repressive regimes. After a brief respite of prosperity in the 1970s, Iraq then suffered nearly a decade of war in the 1980s. There is little doubt that emigration has accelerated since the Gulf War. Today, Iraqis outside the country probably number between 1 million and 2 million, about 5–10 percent of its population. This exodus has not only depleted Iraq's skills, but by depriving the country of its most Westernized and sophisticated elements, it has also stunted the capacity for reform and for making the accommodations necessary for Iraq's recuperation. Iraq's diaspora, especially those in Western capitals, are, by training and exposure, better equipped to understand the emerging global environment and the kinds of domestic changes Iraq will have to make to adjust to it. Those left behind, in an increasingly isolated milieu, appear to be ever more out of tune with the currents of economic and political reform likely to shape the world in the twenty-first century.

Physical Damage

The damage done by the Gulf War to Iraq's physical plant was also substantial. It is estimated that the coalition destroyed substantial portions of its oil and gas facilities; its electrical and telecommunications grid; and its transportation facilities, including rail lines, roads, and bridges. However, in a remarkable tribute to the energy and stamina of Iraq's workforce, much of this damage was repaired within two years of the war's end. In Baghdad there are few remaining traces of war damage. However, much of this repair has been based on cannibalization of spare parts from other structures and may not hold up well over the long run. Maintenance, in the absence of spare parts, has become a severe problem. Outside of the capital area, especially in the south, reconstruction is less complete, partly because of neglect and partly because damage there was more extensive. In the north, the population suffered under a double embargo (the one imposed by the UN on Iraq and the other imposed by Saddam Hussein on the Kurdish area). In the summer of 1996, Saddam removed his embargo, although many constraints on internal trade remain. Both bans have hampered development. However, outside humanitarian aid to the north has helped sustain this region and has produced a modest revival of agriculture and animal husbandry.

Early in the sanctions regime, Iraq instituted a rationing system designed to cope with food shortages. Some food has been imported since the start of sanctions and is available on the market, but usually at prices beyond what ordinary citizens can afford.[22] Meanwhile, the ration system has favored the regime's supporters and kept control of food distribution in the regime's hands. However, the system did succeed in getting essential foodstuffs to the population, although the amounts had to be consistently lowered as time went on. In 1993 rations covered 1,800 calories a day, by 1995, after rations had been cut, about 1,150.[23]

By the middle of the decade, sanctions had begun to take an ever more serious toll on Iraq's economy and its population. Iraq's productive sectors were in continuous decline. Agricultural production suffered from a paucity of spare parts for agricultural machinery, a scarcity of seeds and fertilizers, and poor maintenance of irrigation systems. Instability in the countryside, both north and south, hampered production in irrigated and rain-fed areas. The massive draining of the marshes in the south, ostensibly to expand agriculture but in reality to control rebels, resulted in a loss of population and affected agricultural areas. In the north, the regime's earlier razing of villages under the "anfal" campaign against the Kurds destroyed much livestock and cropland, which only slowly came back to life.[24] In areas under its control, the government tried to encourage agricultural production by raising food prices, with some success. Farmers, usually among the poorest element of the population, benefited from scarcity. Nevertheless, Iraq was not able to feed itself. The government claimed to be spending as much as $600 million to $700 million a year of scarce foreign exchange on food imports.[25]

Industry suffered even more. Heavy industry (iron, steel, aluminum) was badly hampered by sanctions, but consumer industries continued to produce some goods. In 1994 industrial production was reported to be about 60 percent of prewar capacity; by 1995 it was estimated by one observer to be less than 50 percent.[26] The oil industry has received the lion's share of capital and attention, although some of the pumping, pipeline, and export facilities need further repair. Western oil analysts estimate, however, that Iraq could reach its prewar 3.2 million barrels-per-day production within fourteen months if the oil embargo were lifted completely and could probably reach the Iraqi goal of 6 million barrels per day in five to eight years. Both estimates, however, depend on a favorable investment climate, likely to be lacking.

Damage from Inflation

The chief impact of sanctions, however, has been financial—a gradual but dramatic drop in the value of the dinar, culminating by 1995 in runaway inflation. Prior to the Gulf War, one dinar (ID) had been worth slightly over three dollars. By early 1993 one U.S. dollar would buy 50 dinars; by 1994, ID500–700; and by 1995, ID1,500 to ID2,000.[27] But as it became apparent that the oil embargo would not soon come off, expectations plummeted and so too did the dinar. The government contributed to the problem by printing its own cheap currency. The plunge was not helped by government attempts to intervene directly in the economy by taking draconian measures to shore up the dinar. In July 1992 the government executed forty merchants accused of cheating on prices, but the dinar continued to fall. In May 1993 the government again attempted to punish speculators by temporarily closing its border with Jordan and removing from circulation the 25-dinar note, substituting its own cheaper notes. This measure temporarily reduced the amount of currency in circulation, but it hurt Jordanian merchants, who lost millions of Iraqi dinars, and further depressed trade. In January 1994 the government executed an additional thirty merchants and currency dealers it accused of fraud, and in May it introduced harsh measures for theft, including amputation of a hand. In June it clamped down on imports, banning more than three hundred items, to secure hard-currency assets. These acts did little to stem inflation. Finally, in September 1994, rations were cut by 40 percent, while prices of sugar and flour doubled.[28] The worst inflationary point was reached in August 1995, shortly after the defection of Hussein Kamil and his entourage to Jordan, when the value of the dinar temporarily fell to 3,000 dinars per dollar.

This runaway inflation and the government's inability to control it was probably a contributory factor in persuading Saddam to consider measures he had rejected before. In January 1996 Iraq finally announced that it would negotiate with the UN on resolution 986. Very soon after the start of negotiations, hopes rose in Baghdad for an end to the sanctions ordeal and the dinar made a remarkable recovery. Within weeks, it had risen to ID 300 to the dollar. Although it fluctuated between 300 and 800 ID to the dollar throughout the spring of 1996, the rapid recuperation of the dinar brought into circulation thousands of hidden dollars, which were soon snapped up by the government, giving the regime a windfall and a cushion of hard currency to help it withstand the crisis. It also pointed to a certain resilience in the Iraqi economy not hitherto suspected. These events benefited the lower classes, who could now afford food at cheaper prices, but hurt merchants and speculators who had bet on continued inflation. Such fluctuations indicated that rampant inflation was a problem the regime could ignore only at its peril.

Social Costs

Rampant inflation has wreaked social havoc on Iraq's middle class, the backbone of the regime and the state. Most of Iraq's educated professionals work for the government and live on fixed incomes. Government salaries have been raised several times in the last few years, but they have not kept up with inflation. To make ends meet, these Iraqis have depleted their savings and many have resorted to selling assets accumulated over a lifetime, including their household furniture. Joblessness is rife, with high unemployment among Iraq's growing population under twenty. Crime, once virtually nonexistent, is now rampant. Thefts, even by police, are common as Iraq's social cohesion erodes. Sanctions have also taken a toll on health. While statistics must be scrutinized with care, malnutrition, especially among children, is spreading, while deaths are rising due to lack of medicine.[29] However, the international community has pointed out that whatever food and medicine enters the country is disproportionately distributed among the regime's supporters and often fails to reach the vulnerable sectors of the population.

In the course of 1997, resolution 986 was gradually put into effect, with much haggling between Iraq and the UN over its implementation. If consistently renewed, it will help ease Iraq's situation, but even if oil begins to flow more steadily, Iraq's recuperation will be slow. Under this resolution, the UN will demand payment of reparations for victims of Iraq's aggression against Kuwait, which will take up to 30 percent of any oil sales, and up to an additional 10 percent is expected to go to pay the costs of the UN weapons inspection team. Iraq, through its several wars, has accumulated a debt to Europe and other industrial nations of at least $80 billion, which will have to be repaid, probably through discounted oil prices.[30] Meanwhile, Iraq's intransigence has produced a profound distrust of Sad-dam's regime, especially in Washington and London, that is not likely to give Iraq full control of its economic resources as long as the regime governs in Baghdad. This policy has been clearly articulated by spokesmen of the second Clinton administration.[31]

Erosion of the Regime's Political Base

War, rebellion, and sanctions have also taken a toll on the regime's support base, but not yet sufficiently to dislodge it. The rebellions of 1991 were too diffuse and disorganized, both in the north and the south, to overthrow the regime. Moreover, they were hurt by the lack of effective Western support. In the south, the perception that rebels were increasingly led by Shi'ah elements interested in installing an Islamic republic in Baghdad helped cement support for the status quo among military units, who might otherwise have revolted; they turned on the rebels and put the uprising down. In the north, the Kurds were too weak to keep control of cities and towns in the face of a sustained military attack by regular army forces. The massive Kurdish flight to the mountains was the result. This was followed by the establishment of a no-fly zone in the north and an eventual withdrawal of Iraqi forces and administration from a wide swath of territory north of Kirkuk. Patrolled by coalition forces and supplied with humanitarian aid, this northern region has remained for the most part outside Iraqi government control.

Since 1991 Saddam has gradually regrouped; he strengthened his security forces in Baghdad—military and political, ruthlessly eliminated dissidents, and extended his control over the south. His strategy has been to draw the wagons round: to raise the price of dissent to unacceptable levels and to wait out his adversaries, conceding only when he feels circumstances threaten his political survival. In assessing the regime's potential longevity, the question is whether the constraints arrayed against the regime, including sanctions, will be sufficient to cause its collapse, or whether an easing of sanctions, already begun, will give the regime enough relief to prolong its life indefinitely. No clear answers can be given, but the survival of the regime through almost seven years of drastic sanctions and international isolation indicates how difficult it will be to unseat it.

Two broad strategies for the regime's removal have emerged. The first is a strategy of the periphery, which focuses on establishing an opposition movement in the liberated areas of the north and encouraging defections from areas under government control, thus weakening the regime and building up an alternative opposition cadre in the north.

In the first few years after the war, this strategy gained momentum with the establishment in the north of the Iraq National Congress (INC), an umbrella opposition group consisting of the two major Kurdish parties—the Kurdish Democratic Party (KDP) and the Patriotic Union of Kurdistan (PUK), liberal secularists, ex-Ba'thists, and some of the Shi'ah Islamists. Ahmed Jalabi, a Western-educated Shi'ah was the movement's executive director. INC fortunes reached a peak after the Kurdish election in May 1992 and the subsequent formation of a Kurdish regional government, dominated by the two Kurdish parties. These events gave some hope that the northern enclave could establish a more democratic government on Iraqi soil. But the experiment was undermined in May 1994 when fighting broke out between the two Kurdish parties, ending the nascent "democratic" experiment and along with it cooperation between the two strongest groups in the INC.[32] In August 1996, Saddam's forces attacked Irbil, a key city in the "liberated" zone, capturing scores of INC members and putting an end to the remaining INC apparatus in the north. Many INC supporters took refuge in the United States and elsewhere. In the wake of this disaster, the future of the INC and its opposition components is uncertain. Shi'ah components of the opposition have also mounted sporadic attacks on government forces in the south, but this wing of the opposition movement has been weaker than its collaborators in the north. Moreover, southern territory is still under control of Saddam's ground forces, limiting what the opposition can do inside Iraq.

A second strategy has focused on Iraq's "center," roughly defined as Baghdad and the territory north to Mosul and west to the Syrian border. While this area is dominated by Sunni inhabitants presumed more sympathetic to a Sunni-dominated regime, it also contains substantial Shi'ah and some Kurdish inhabitants. The "centrist" strategy presumes that the demise of the regime can come only through some action in Baghdad—be it a coup, an assassination attempt, or a military putsch—undertaken by those with access to power. Interest in this strategy revived as reports began to surface of failed coup attempts or plots in the ranks of the military and the party, indicating disaffection close to the seat of power.

These reports began as early as 1992, when ninety officers accused of a failed plot against the government were executed; most were members of the Jubur tribe. In November and December of 1993, more plotting was uncovered. This time a number of people from Mosul and Tikrit, including Jasim Mukhlis, a Takriti from a good family close to the regime, were executed. A year later, in December 1994, the government arrested Mazlum al-Dulaimi, an air force general and a member of one of the key tribes in the regime's security apparatus.[33] In the same month, Major General Wafiq al-Samarra'i, a former senior military intelligence officer, defected and took refuge in the north; in March 1995 he attempted to orchestrate a military coup, which failed. The most serious unrest, however, was the trouble stirred up among the Dulaim tribes in May 1995, when the mutilated body of Mazlum al-Dulaimi was sent home for burial. This event caused an uprising in Ramadi, a city in the heart of regime territory, that had to be put down by force. By July 1995 a number of Dulaimi dissidents had been executed, weakening support for the regime among this group as well.[34]

Even more damaging to the regime than these events, however, have been splits within Saddam Hussein's extended family itself. It is on this group that Saddam has relied in staffing the highest levels of his security apparatus. The divisions have been apparent for some time, particularly between his sons and collateral family clans: the Ibrahims (half-brothers from his mother's second marriage) and the Majids (cousins on his father's side). His own sons, Udayy, the elder, and Qusayy, the younger, have been put in key security positions as he grooms them for succession, but they have also proven to be divisive factors. Both are ambitious and anxious for their place in the sun; Qusayy is quiet and operates behind the scenes, but Udayy is unreliable, flamboyant, and brutal. In August 1995 he was responsible for a gangland-style shootout with Wathban, Saddam Hussein's half-brother and a former minister of interior, in which Wathban was severely wounded. That episode may well have permanently alienated members of Wathban's group, which includes Barzan, the regime's representative in Geneva.

The Hussein Kamil Defection

There is no doubt, however, that the most serious blow to family unity and to the regime was delivered by the Majid clan. On August 8, 1995, Hussein Kamil al-Majid, former chief administrator of Iraq's WMD program and

Saddam's son-in-law, defected to Jordan with his brother Saddam Kamil, also married to one of Saddam's daughters. Both daughters accompanied their husbands, causing Saddam an acute loss of face in Baghdad. On August 11, at a press conference in Amman, Hussein Kamil publicly called for the regime's overthrow and put himself forward as a replacement. His defection marked a turning point for the regime in several ways. First, it led the regime to reveal documents on its WMD program that showed its deception and that had the effect of delaying the removal of sanctions. Second, it embarrassed the regime and tarnished its image abroad. Third, it removed a key pillar of the regime and further narrowed its base. Nevertheless, even this shock did not prove fatal.

Whatever Hussein Kamil's expectations may have been, it soon became apparent that he would not be joined in his call for the regime's overthrow by exile opposition leaders, who regarded him as part of the problem, not part of the solution. In time, his disillusionment led to an even more startling denouement to this drama. On February 20, 1996, the world learned that Hussein and Saddam Kamil and their wives had returned to Iraq. Apparently suffering from acute isolation, Hussein Kamil had negotiated terms for his return, evidently believing that a pardon from Saddam and the Revolutionary Command Council (RCC) would protect his life. That proved ephemeral, and on February 23 he and other members of his family, including his father and sister, were killed in another shootout in Baghdad, said by the regime to have been carried out by members of his own family seeking revenge for his disgrace. That event, while not entirely unexpected, further damaged the regime's image abroad. Moreover, it has probably permanently alienated many members of the Majid clan who cannot now be entrusted with security posts. By any measure, there has been a dramatic reduction in Saddam's support base in the key institution on which he relies for security, his extended family. The family's vulnerability—and unpopularity—was further dramatized by the failed assassination attempt on Udayy in December 1996, which seriously wounded the president's son and may have sidelined him permanently as a potential pillar of the regime.

Despite these signs of eroding support, however, the centrist strategy has also failed to unseat the regime. There are probably at least three reasons why. One is the pervasiveness of Saddam's security system. Access to Saddam is tightly controlled, and a multitude of informers lace the government's apparatus, making a centrist strategy difficult to execute. A second reason lies in fear of the punishment that awaits perpetrators of failed attempts, often involving family members as well. Third is the fear that should the strategy succeed, the regime's demise would be followed not by a better regime but by civil disorder and chaos, in which retribution would be visited on all connected with the regime. Saddam has played on these fears to sustain his political life.

In the aftermath of Hussein Kamil's defection, Saddam took steps to control the damage. In October 1995, in an attempt to shore up his claim to legitimacy, Saddam conducted a plebiscite on his presidency; with 99.6 percent of the vote, he was installed for another seven years. This was followed, in March 1996, by an election for a new parliament, which took office in April. Non-Ba'thists were permitted to run for office, but only if they espoused the party's principles. These measures eliminated any latent opposition. Meanwhile, as discussed later, Saddam has increasingly turned to tribal groups to keep law and order in the countryside. While these steps have temporarily shored up the regime's position in Baghdad, they indicate a regime on the defensive, with an ever-shrinking base of support on which to rely.

Erosion of State Institutions and National Cohesion

The weakening of Saddam Hussein's regime has been accompanied by a progressive erosion of state institutions and national cohesion. Evidence of this decline can be seen in several institutions. One is the military, the backbone of domestic security, which has been increasingly weakened by war and sanctions. When Saddam Hussein embarked on his occupation of Kuwait, the Iraqi army was close to 1 million men. In 1996, after several reorganizations, it was estimated at about 350,000. By any standards, this has been a substantial downsizing. In terms of equipment, Iraq has been able to salvage from the Gulf War about 40 percent of its tanks, armored personnel carriers, and artillery pieces. Its air force suffered greater losses, as more than 100 of its best planes were flown to Iran, but it still has about 350 aircraft, many of them aging.[35] While this is still a sizable military by Gulf standards, Iraq's forces have shown serious weaknesses on a number of fronts.

First is organizational fragmentation; Iraq's forces are recruited for several different kinds of armies. The regular army consists mainly of infantry, with some mobile and mechanized units. The regular army is the oldest independent institution in Iraq, dating back to the inception of the Iraqi state in 1920; as such, it has always represented a challenge to the regime. Not surprisingly, this force bore the brunt of the Gulf War, and its ranks have subsequently been thinned by demobilization and desertion. In contrast to the regular army, the crack Republic Guard units were originally recruited to protect the regime. Greatly expanded during the Iran-Iraq war, they have since become the backbone of Iraq's armed forces. These units are usually more carefully recruited and trained and are given special treatment to assure their loyalty. However, there is evidence that the economic sanctions and regime purges have taken a toll on this force as well. Its ranks, too, have been depleted, in part by desertions and in part by arrests and executions of disloyal officers. Its status as an elite unit has gradually been degraded by a shortage of funds, and it may now be only slightly better off than the regular army. The key force protecting the regime, a special forces unit of about twenty thousand members, is still assumed to be in good condition and loyal to the regime.[36]

In addition to these regular forces, a new irregular militia, the fidayyin al-Saddam, was created in October 1994 and put under the authority of Saddam's two sons. It is hardly a fighting unit, and its main function is assumed to be one of watching the regular military and performing security functions. These divisions within the military—and even more, the regime's distrust of the military—limit its effectiveness and unity of command. But the regime's precautions also help assure against coups. The most important factor in the military's degradation is morale, which is declining, especially among foot soldiers whose physical conditions are poor and getting worse. The seriousness of defections can be seen not only in the repeated military reorganizations but also in the draconian measures, such as amputation of defectors' ears (now discontinued), taken to discourage them.

The second key institution of state, the Ba'th Party apparatus, has also been in decline. Its ranks in the south were badly thinned during the rebellion, when many were attacked and killed. Others apparently defected from the party and joined the rebels. Most debilitating of all has been Saddam's own policy of putting relatives in key party posts, permanently undermining party discipline and ideological cohesion. The party functions basically as an arm of the regime in administering the state. At this level, however, it is still a viable institution. Evidence of its effectiveness has been displayed on numerous occasions. One was its ability to conduct elections for Saddam's presidency and for parliament. Second is the rationing system, which the party helped organize and which still feeds much of the population, thereby keeping it under control.

The bureaucracy is another institution that has been eroded by sanctions. Middle-class professionals at all levels except for the very top now are forced to hold several jobs to make ends meet, thereby neglecting the public's work. Rising crime rates and the inability (or unwillingness) of police to keep order are clear signs of bureaucratic decay and social erosion.

The Emergence of Tribalism

Nothing has been more indicative of institutional erosion than the reemergence of tribalism. While this trend was in evidence as early as the Iran-Iraq war, its manifestations since the Gulf War have been striking. In the countryside, Saddam has leaned ever more heavily on tribal leaders to maintain law and order, a reflection of the weakness of his central government and party bureaucracy. More important is the extent to which his military and security forces have become penetrated, at upper levels, by tribal members. It is not that tribal leaders control the military, but that appointments to most key posts have gone to members of well-known (mainly Sunni) tribes. Recruitment to military academies has been increasingly done on a tribal basis. Members of the Shammar, the Jubur, the Ubaid, and other tribal groups are also to be found in key security posts, raising questions about whether their primary loyalty is to the state—or to tribe and kin. It must be acknowledged that such tribal recruitment is a double-edged sword. The frequency of coup plots, reportedly based on tribal affiliations, indicates that such a policy can backfire.

By 1996 a conscious tribal policy had emerged. In May 1996 it was announced that recruitment to military academies for the following year would be limited to members of certain Sunni tribes.[37] In the same month, after a trip through some tribal areas, Saddam publicly supported a program of administrative decentralization on tribal lines. Among the steps envisioned was the return of previously confiscated land to tribal leaders, an action that would reverse decades of land reform. Even more significant, Saddam appeared to condone the restoration of tribal codes of justice to tribal areas, a system that would turn the clock back to the days of the British Mandate. And he urged the formation of tribal councils with direct access to the central government to administer provincial areas. If actually brought to fruition, such steps would undermine the highly centralized administration of the Ba'th regime and undercut the very foundation of the state itself.[38]

Erosion of National Cohesion

A weakening of state institutions has been accompanied by a similar erosion of national cohesion. Iraq's territorial integrity has been greatly diminished in the north by the government's lack of control over Kurdish areas. While the fiction of Iraqi sovereignty is maintained, a power vacuum has in fact developed in the north, as the struggle for power between two powerful Kurdish leaders, Masud Barzani, head of the KDP, and Jalal Talabani, leader of the PUK, continued.[39] While numerous ceasefires were arranged, they have been continuously breached. Barzani's forces controlled the lucrative truck traffic from Baghdad north to Turkey that passes through Zakhu. In mid-1995 "customs dues" on this traffic was estimated to be yielding $ 4.5 million a month.[40] Until August 1996, Talabani's forces controlled the city of Irbil, the Kurdish political capital, and Sulaimaniyya, its cultural and intellectual center. The collapse of a centralized government in the north has allowed outside elements to intrude across the border. The Kurdish Workers' Party (PKK) of Turkey, at war with the Turkish government, has established a presence in northern Iraq that no one has been able to dislodge. Iranian influence has also penetrated the region as Kurdish religious parties influenced by Iran have gained a foothold in territory near the Iranian border. By mid-1996 representatives of the Iranian government were reported to be situated in a number of Kurdish cities in the north, while Tehran competed with the United States in efforts to mediate the Kurdish dispute and keep U.S. influence out.[41] Meanwhile, Turkish influence also expanded in the north, in part through its participation with the coalition in monitoring the secure zone and in providing humanitarian aid, but also through frequent military incursions across the border to control the PKK.

In August 1996, dramatic events changed the situation in the north. An incursion of Iranian forces inside Iraqi territory, initially designed to deter cross-border attacks by Iranian Kurds, left a significant cache of arms in the hands of the PUK, strengthening their forces in the north. Barzani responded by turning to Saddam Hussein for help in confronting the PUK, and on August 31, Iraqi government forces, together with those of Barzani, occupied Irbil and expelled the PUK from this city, effectively ending the INC operation, supported by the United States, in the north.

The United States responded to this Iraqi incursion by insisting on a withdrawal of Iraqi troops from Irbil; by extending the no-fly zone in the south to the 33rd parallel, bringing U.S. aircraft to the suburbs of Baghdad; and by bombarding air defense installations in the extended zone. Iraqi troops were withdrawn to the outskirts of Irbil, but the north remained effectively partitioned between the forces of Barzani in the northwest and Talabani in the southeast. Subsequent efforts by the United States brought an uneasy ceasefire between the two groups but no fundamental change in the situation. A major incursion of Turkish troops into the north, in the spring of 1997, in pursuit of the PKK, revealed the continuation of a power vacuum.

By October the crisis had died down but it left a fluid situation in the north. Saddam removed the previously established embargo on the north, potentially opening the area to trade and commerce from central Iraq. The cooperation between Barzani and the Baghdad government also opened the door to an intrusion of the Iraqi government, particularly its security apparatus, in the north. The exodus of the small contingent of allied military representatives (the Military Coordination Committee) that had been patrolling the northern secure zone removed the Western ground presence from the zone. While the extended no-fly zone strengthened allied control over the south of Iraq, Saddam's position in the north was improved. His challenge also revealed fissures in the allied coalition arrayed against him, since Iraq's neighbors, notably Turkey and Saudi Arabia, demurred in allowing their territory to be used in air strikes, and France ceased participation in the northern no-fly zone.

In the south, Iraqi government control has been maintained on the ground, but much of the Shi'ah population remains bitter and alienated as a result of its failed rebellion and the brutality by which it was put down. Organized Shi'ah opposition has gone underground or abroad, mainly to Iran. While no confirmed figures exist, between 250,000 and 1 million Iraqi Shi'ah may reside in Iran; the actual figure could approach 600,000.[42] Two Shi'ah groups, both committed to the establishment of an Islamic state, have some influence in the south. One is the Da'wah, an indigenous movement that originated in the mid-1950s and was led by the revered Iraqi cleric Muhammad Baqr al-Sadr, executed by the regime in April 1980. It has been greatly reduced by Ba'th persecution. The other is the Supreme Assembly for the Islamic Republic in Iraq (SAIRI), an umbrella group led by a cleric, Muhammad Baqr al-Hakim, who resides in Tehran. How much support they have among Shi'ah inside Iraq cannot be determined, but it is probably not a majority.[43]

Sporadic insurgency continues in the south, making some roads unsafe after dark. The dissidents and army deserters in the marshlands on the border with Iran have been gradually brought under control by draconian government measures, including drainage of much of the marshland area. Even educated Shi'ah, however, constitute a disaffected group, resentful of the fact that they do not have a voice in government commensurate with their numbers. While few Shi'ah groups express a desire for separatism—most want a majority role in government—their dissatisfaction with the regime has greatly weakened national cohesion and the sense of Iraqi identity. Alienation of substantial numbers of Shi'ah and Kurds will make restoration of that identity more difficult—but not impossible—to achieve in a post-Saddam Iraq.

Iraq's Alternative Futures

Given these trends, what does the future hold for Iraq? Three alternatives appear possible. One is that continued pressure on Iraq from the international community, through sanctions, no-fly zones, and isolation, will eventually produce a change of regime. How this might come about is highly speculative. Splits in the family could cause the regime to self-destruct, or those close to the center of power might finally take action to unseat it. The sooner this occurs, the faster Iraq's recuperation can begin. A successor regime will most likely be drawn from elements now identifiable inside Iraq—the military, dissident Ba'thists, technocrats, educated bureaucrats, and, in the new tribal environment, kinship groups with ties to the military. These groups may turn to outside opponents of Saddam for help, soliciting support especially from the United States and the West, but this will depend on the composition of the group that emerges as successor. Whether the first attempt at change will be successful in garnering enough support to maintain stability is a major question. Should a new regime fail to accommodate Iraq's various communities, or fail to meet appropriate demands from the international community, Iraq could start down a slippery slope of instability and collapse.

A second and more likely alternative lies in the continuation in power of Saddam Hussein. His political longevity over time cannot be dismissed; it may have been strengthened by the collapse of the opposition in the north of Iraq and the erosion of Western influence there. Given the intransigence that has become a hallmark of his policy, little change can be expected in his long-term goals or behavior. Under this scenario, Iraq is likely to get sufficient outside help to limp along, but it is unlikely to be able to regain full sovereignty over its resources and territory or to recuperate fully.

A third alternative is the least likely but still possible. If the current regime remains in power too long or if a successor regime fails to establish itself in a reasonable period of time, Iraq could join the ranks of "failed states." This would probably involve not a clear ethnic and sectarian division into Kurdish, Arab Sunni, and Arab Shi'ah principalities but an erosion of control by the central government over outlying areas, along with increased local authority by various tribal, clan, and militia leaders. The situation in the north of Iraq provides a glimpse of what could happen in this case. Such an outcome would open the door to increased outside interference inside Iraq, as all of its neighbors competed for influence and attempted to prevent the dominance of rivals.[44]

Iraq's International Role

Regardless of which outcome occurs, Iraq is not likely to play a significant role in regional affairs over the next decade. If there should be a regime change, Iraq's long-term future would be more hopeful, but such an outcome poses a high risk. A new regime that rapidly secured its footing and acquired a measure of international support could begin to address Iraq's international and domestic problems. But even this "best case" scenario would necessitate a period of recuperation, payment of debts, and fundamental reform of domestic structures. Such a project would preclude a vigorous regional role. Moreover, such a smooth transition is highly unlikely. More probable is a period, perhaps a long period, of turbulence and instability as Iraq settles its domestic problems, including who will govern and how. In a "worst case" scenario, Iraq could descend to the level of a failed state.

The other alternative is equally debilitating. Should Saddam Hussein remain, no full regional integration of Iraq is likely, even if sanctions are eased. Under such circumstances, the current stand-off between Iraq and the United States is likely to persist well into the twenty-first century, although its parameters may change. Within the region, there has been a shift of attitude since Hussein Kamil's defection and his subsequent brutal extinction. King Hussein of Jordan has distanced himself from the regime, though not the country, and most regional leaders are unwilling to embrace Saddam.[45] Among GCC states, Kuwait and Saudi Arabia remain firmly opposed to Saddam Hussein, although they are also worried about the kinds of instability that might ensue with his departure. Iran, while unwilling to see a pro-Western regime in Baghdad, is not likely to cooperate in keeping Saddam in power. However, Turkey, which expects to benefit from opening its oil pipeline and would like to have better control of its borders with Iraq, is caught on the horns of a dilemma. It must be sensitive to U.S. and Western concerns over strengthening contacts with Saddam and hence is not likely to pursue this option. Rather, it is strengthening its military hold over the north.

Despite the anti-Saddam trend, Baghdad has made some inroads in restoring regional ties, especially among some GCC states like Qatar, Oman, and the UAE, where humanitarian concern for Iraqis and anxiety over Iran is strong. Egypt has opened an office in Baghdad but has not restored full diplomatic relations. This tendency was given a boost by Saddam's attack on Irbil and his acceptance of resolution 986, which has allowed a modest flow of oil. Companies are again seeking business in Iraq, and some countries in the region are positioning themselves to accommodate a situation that seems likely to continue. But most regional states are likely to hesitate before exchanging relations with Iraq for those with the United States. If the United States remains firmly committed to its current policy of containment and isolation, Iraq's regional role will remain constrained.

In Europe, several countries are positioning themselves to do business with Iraq in a post-sanctions period, including France, Russia, Italy, and Spain. Implementation of resolution 986 has increased speculation about an early end to sanctions. But none is willing to breach the sanctions regime or to vote for removal of the oil embargo before Iraq satisfies its requirements under UN resolution 687 on weapons of mass destruction. That point has not yet been reached. If Iraq meets the requirements, the United States is certain to face increased pressure to remove the oil embargo. However, given domestic U.S. attitudes toward the regime in Iraq, this pressure will probably be resisted. However, the costs to the United States of this policy will rise.

One cost, as the events of the summer of 1996 revealed, will be a widening split in the coalition over Iraq as some Europeans—and some Gulf states—seek to accommodate Baghdad. Another might be a closer alliance between Russia and Iraq. Foreign Minister Yevgeny Primakov may well try to revisit his earlier policy of "moderating" Iraq and bringing into being a loose alliance of Middle East countries, to include Iran, Iraq, and Syria, as a counterbalance to U.S. influence.[46] France and southern European countries such as Italy and Spain may benefit from the modest market that is likely to emerge in Iraq as sanctions are eased. If Saddam Hussein remains, Iraq will probably get enough oil income from an easing of sanctions to prevent starvation and collapse but not enough to recuperate fully, much less play any significant regional role. In this case, the erosion of Iraqi society and institutions will continue, in slow motion, with more serious consequences for Iraq—and the region—over the long term.

Notes

The views expressed in this chapter are those of the author and do not represent the position of the National Defense University, the Department of Defense, or the U.S. government.

1. The judiciousness of the war's end has been vigorously debated by scholars and the policy community and need not be reviewed here. Among the best expositions of various viewpoints, including those who feel the war should have been carried further or ended differently, are Bernard Trainer, *The Generals' War: The Inside Story of the Conflict in the Gulf* (Boston: Little Brown, 1995), and Laurie Mylroie, *The Future of Iraq* (Washington: The Washington Institute for Near East Policy, 1991). One of the best expositions of the uprisings and their failures is Faleh Abd al-Jabbar, "Why the Uprisings Failed," *Middle East Report* (May/June 1992), 2–14.

2. The Netherlands was originally involved in Operation Provide Comfort but later withdrew.

3. This military presence now includes a U.S. naval component (reorganized as the Fifth Fleet), headquartered in Bahrain, that regularly includes a battle carrier group; a maritime intercept operation enforcing the UN sanctions regime on Iraq; and a Marine Expeditionary Force with pre-positioned equipment in the Gulf. In addition the United States has an air wing, currently conducting Operation Southern Watch in southern Iraq, under the command of a joint task force in the Gulf and forward-deployed patriot batteries. Although the United States has no permanent ground troops stationed in the Gulf, it is in the process of pre-positioning equipment for three brigades in or near the Gulf to be flown in if there is a crisis. In addition, the United States and its allies are conducting more frequent exercises in the Gulf. Through security assistance and training programs and sales of U.S. equipment, the United States has greatly improved its ability to mount a more rapid defense of the region should that be necessary.

4. UNSC resolution 687 (April 3, 1991), cited in United Nations, *The United Nations and the Iraq-Kuwait Conflict, 1990–1996* (New York: Department of Public Information, United Nations, 1996), 193–98.

5. Tim Trevan, "UNSCOM Faces Entirely New Verification Challenges in Iraq," *Arms Control Today* 23, no. 3 (April 1993): 11–13.

6. Saad al-Bazzaz, "The Iraqi Model: Hostage of the Future" (unpublished paper).

7. UNSC resolution 688 (April 5, 1991), cited in United Nations, *Iraq-Kuwait Conflict*, 199.

8. UNSC resolution 706, adopted August 1991, permitted Iraq to sell $1.6 billion in oil over six months; resolution 712 stipulated that some of that money was to pay compensation for losses afflicted by Iraq on others through its occupation of Kuwait, and some was to pay the expenses of the UN inspection mission in Iraq. The distribution of humanitarian aid was to be monitored by the UN. UNSC resolution 986 permitted the sale of $1 billion in oil over ninety days, renewable for another ninety days, for food and medical goods, with distribution also to be monitored by the UN. UNSC resolution 706 (August 5, 1991), United Nations, *Iraq-Kuwait Conflict*, 285–86; UNSC resolution 712 (September 19, 1991), ibid., 308–9; UNSC resolution 986 (April 14, 1995), ibid., 754–56.

9. Ambassador Madeleine Albright, U.S. representative at the UN, has photographs of fifty palaces and luxury residences built by Saddam Hussein for himself and his supporters, costing an estimated $1.5 billion. Members of the family enrich

themselves by importing scarce goods and reselling them at high prices. Testimony by Madeleine Albright before the Senate Foreign Relations Subcommittee on the Near East and South Asia, reported in the *New York Times*, August 4, 1995, A7.

10. Trevan, "UNSCOM Faces New Challenges," 13.

11. Ibid., 12.

12. At the time the United States raised some questions about the accuracy of UNSCOM's accounting of SCUDs. Kenneth Katzmann, "Iraqi Compliance with Cease Fire Agreements," CRS report to Congress, April 17, 1995 (Washington: Congressional Research Service), 1–4.

13. See "Eighth Report of the UN Secretary General on the Status of the Implementation of the Plan for the Ongoing Monitoring and Verification of Iraq's Compliance with Relevant Parts of Section C of Security Council Resolution 687, 11 October 1995," cited in UN, *Iraq-Kuwait Conflict,* 781–86. For the report's review of Iraq's intransigence, see Boutros-Ghali, Introduction, 3–119.

14. UNSC resolution 949 (October 15, 1994) demanded the withdrawal of the forces that had been moved south and disallowed their redeployment there (United Nations, *Iraq-Kuwait Conflict,* 694). The United States and Britain have interpreted this resolution to mean that Iraq may not move its Republican Guard units into the region below the 32nd parallel, and they are enforcing this interpretation.

15. The conclusion to the secretary general's report to the UN on UNSCOM's activities in October 1995, following Hussein Kamil's defection, claimed that Iraq had been "concealing proscribed activities," forcing the commission to revise earlier reports; that "Iraq has been misleading the Commission by withholding information"; that it had provided "incorrect information"; and that the commission "has detected and identified a hitherto secret offensive biological weapons program . . . including the filling and deployment of missile warheads and aerial bombs with agents" (Secretary General, "Report . . . on the Status of . . . Verification of Iraq's Compliance with . . . Resolution 687," October 11, 1995, cited in United Nations, *Iraq-Kuwait Conflict,* 789–90).

16. Such statements were first made during a sanctions review process at the end of March 1993 and have been reiterated many times since. See statements by Madeleine Albright and by Dee Dee Myers, White House spokesperson, cited in the *Washington Post,* March 30, 1993, A17, A20; *Washington Post,* March 27, 1993, A1. Secretary of State Christopher also made the statement in a TV interview, quoted in *al-Hayat* and translated in *Mideast Mirror,* March 29, 1993. Madeleine Albright reiterated this position in a major foreign policy address at Georgetown University on March 26, 1997, and it was reiterated in a speech by Bruce Reidel, senior director for the Middle East on the National Security Council, at a Middle East Institute conference on Iraq, Washington, May 27, 1997.

17. Informal communication to the author from State Department officials.

18. Phebe Marr, "Iraq's Future, Plus Ça Change . . . or Something Better?" in Ibrahim Ibrahim, ed., *The Gulf Crisis: Background and Consequences* (Washington: Georgetown University Press, 1992), 49.

19. John G. Heidenrich, "The Gulf War: How Many Iraqis Died?" *Foreign Policy* 90 (Spring 1993): 123.

20. Estimates vary widely, but the toll for the rebellion has been put at 20,000 to 100,000. The latter estimate is very high. Tehran estimates that fighting in Najaf and Karbala, where most of the deaths occurred, took 12,000 to 16,000. The number of Kurds who died in the exodus to the mountains is estimated at 15,000 to 30,000. Abbas al-Nasrawi, *The Economy of Iraq* (London: Greenwood Press, 1994), 120.

21. Economist Intelligence Unit (EIU), *Iraq: Country Profile, 1995/1996* (London: EIU, 1996), 7

22. For example, a basic food "basket" for a family of six that cost between ID66 and ID100 before the Gulf War cost more than ID1,000 in August 1991 and ID5,400 in June 1993. Monthly wages in mid-1993 ranged from ID250 for an unskilled worker to ID775 for a senior civil servant. Sarah Graham-Brown, "The Iraq Sanctions Dilemma: Intervention, Sovereignty, and Responsibility," *Middle East Report* (March/April 1995), 11.

23. Ibid., 10.

24. The anfal campaign refers to the operation of the Iraqi government beginning in February 1988 and ending in September 1988 that demolished Kurdish villages and killed up to 100,000 Kurds. The term *anfal* comes from the Qur'an, where it means "spoils of battle," an attempt to provide a religious justification for this massacre. Michael Gunter, "A *de facto* Kurdish State in Northern Iraq," *Third World Quarterly* 14, no. 2 (1993): 296. For a complete account, see Middle East Watch, *Genocide in Iraq: the Anfal Campaign against the Kurds* (New York: Human Rights Watch, 1993).

25. *Financial Times* (London), October 23, 1994, cited in Graham-Brown, "The Iraqi Sanctions Dilemma," 9.

26. EIU, *Iraq: Country Profile, 1994/1995* (London: Economist Intelligence Unit, 1995), 13; James Placke, testimony before the Senate Committee on Foreign Relations, Subcommittee on Near East and South Asian Affairs, March 2, 1995 (Washington: U.S. Government Printing Office, 1996), 63.

27. EIU, *Iraq: 4th Quarter, 1995* (London: Economist Intelligence Unit, 1995), 16; *Iraq: 3rd Quarter, 1995* (London: EIU, 1995), 6–7.

28. Graham-Brown, "The Iraqi Sanctions Dilemma," 10.

29. UN Food and Agriculture Organization (FAO), Report, July-August 1995 (unpublished). The report cites an eightfold increase in infant mortality since 1989 and an average of over 100,000 deaths a year from malnutrition since the start of sanctions. However, these figures were obtained from the Iraqi government, and the FAO report indicates that they could not be independently confirmed. U.S. government sources believe these figures to be too high and lacking credibility owing to the source.

30. EIU, *Iraq: Country Profile, 1994/1995,* 32; Abbas al-Nasrawi, *The Economy of Iraq,* 108.

31. Secretary of State Madeleine Albright, speech, Georgetown University, March

26, 1997; senior director, Near East/South Asia Affairs, National Security Council, Middle East Institute conference, May 27, 1997.

32. For a good account of the two-party rivalry, see Michael Gunter, "The KDP-PUK Conflict in Northern Iraq," *Middle East Journal* 50, no. 2 (Spring 1996): 225–41. See also KDP, "What happened in Iraqi Kurdistan, May, 1994," report of the KDP Research Department, June 1994, and PUK, "Iraqi Kurdistan: A Situation Report on Recent Events," report of the PUK Foreign Relations Committee, February 1995.

33. On these tribal politics, see Rend Rahim Francke, "Inside Iraq: Race to the Finish Line," *Middle East Insight*, May–August 1994, 38–39.

34. EIU, *Iraq: 3rd Quarter, 1995* (London: EIU, 1995), 6–7.

35. Anthony Cordesman, "Iran and Iraq: Strategic Developments in the Gulf: A Graphic Summary" (unpublished paper, 1995).

36. Ibid.

37. *Al-Sharq al-Awsat* (London), May 10, 1996, 2.

38. Ibid., May 15, 1996, 2.

39. For a discussion of the breakdown of the Kurdish regional government in the north, see "Human Rights Abuses in Iraqi Kurdistan since 1991," Amnesty International report, February 1995; Gunter, "The KDP-PUK Conflict in Northern Iraq."

40. Gunter, "The KDP-PUK Conflict," 237.

41. Information conveyed to the author by Kurdish representatives in northern Iraq.

42. "Iraq: Down but Not Out," *Economist* (London) April 8, 1995, 23.

43. On the Shi'ah opposition, see Kenneth Katzman, "Iraq's Opposition," CRS report for Congress, April 19, 1993 (Washington: Congressional Research Service).

44. For an exposition of this view, see Laura Drake, "Implosion of Iraq," *Middle East Insight* 12, no. 3 (March/April 1996): 24.

45. EIU, *Iraq: 1st Quarter, 1996* (London: EIU, 1996), 9–10.

46. Robert O. Freedman, "Courting Baghdad," *Middle East Insight* 12, no. 3 (March/April 1996): 51–53.

9: Iran since the Gulf War:

Shaul Bakhash

The Iraqi invasion of Kuwait and the Gulf War that followed coincided with a moment of potentially significant change in the direction of the Islamic Republic. Iran's own devastating eight-year war with Iraq had come to an end in 1988. In 1989, Ayatollah Khomeini, who had led the revolution that overthrew the monarchy, passed away. For a decade, in his role as *faqih*, or spiritual guide, he held the highest constitutional office in the country and dominated Iran, its policies and its politics. Just before Khomeini's death, the constitution had been amended, abolishing the post of prime minister, vesting executive powers in the previously ceremonial office of the president and creating a more centralized state system. Khomeini was succeeded as spiritual guide by Ayatollah Ali Khamenei, a cleric who lacked Khomeini's charisma, prestige, scholarly standing, and religious authority. This weakness of political-religious authority at the apex of power predictably had important implications for Iran's foreign and domestic policies.

On the other hand, the new president, Ali-Akbar Hashemi-Rafsanjani, formerly speaker of the Majlis, or parliament, was an astute politician who had a clearer idea where he wanted to take the country. Rafsanjani set himself four goals for the post-Khomeini period: to end Iran's isolation and integrate Iran into the international community; to begin the work of post-war reconstruction by harnessing both public and private sector resources and both domestic and foreign investment; to rationalize the administration by reining in the revolutionary organizations and placing technocrats in key ministerial and economic posts; and, finally, to mollify the middle and educated classes and the young by easing up on state controls on social and cultural (but not political) life.

Progress was made in each of these areas. But by 1996 every one of Rafsanjani's programs was in trouble, and Iran, as usual, seemed a tangle of contradictions. Foreign policy was characterized by both radicalism and pragmatism, economic policy by an erratic mixture of state control and private sector initiative, and politics by both severe repression and a fairly vigorous press and parliament. State control was eased in the social and cultural spheres, but there were repeated attempts to dictate the dress women wore and the music, films, television, and art available to the people. Iran's diplomats worked patiently to repair fences abroad, even as agents of Iran's secret service funded assassinations and acts of terrorism outside Iran's borders.

These contradictions were an accurate reflection of the nature of the regime. Nearly two decades after the revolution, a great deal of normalization had taken place, but the regime still found it difficult to shed its revolutionary past. A divided leadership of ideologues and pragmatists, radicals and moderates, advocates of state and private sector primacy in the economy competed over the direction of policy. The state was both highly centralized and a conglomerate of quasi-independent fiefdoms that did not work in harmony. The government was overstaffed, inefficient, unrepresentative, and corrupt, and it could not come up with a set of policies that would at once satisfy traditional and modern, Western-oriented and Islamic, secular and religious, moderate and revolutionary elements in the population. In foreign policy, Iran's leaders entertained ambitions for a regional and international role far exceeding Iran's resources and had to resort to both conventional diplomacy and unconventional means to achieve it.

Foreign Policy

The Gulf crisis of 1990–91 yielded Iran immediate benefits.[1] Saddam Hussein was forced to evacuate Iranian territory that Iraq had continued to occupy after the 1988 ceasefire. The war broke Iraq's military machine and greatly weakened a better-armed and menacing enemy. During the crisis, Iran acted out of national interest when it refused to acquiesce in the Iraqi annexation of Kuwait. But Rafsanjani enhanced his reputation as a pragmatist by siding, in effect, with the aims of the U.S.-led alliance. He consolidated his position at home by facing down a radical faction in the Majlis that urged an alliance with Iraq against the United States. Rafsanjani used the cover of the war to resume diplomatic relations with Saudi Arabia, Egypt, and Morocco—all domestically controversial measures. At the end of the war, Iran again showed restraint in the limited aid it extended to fellow Shi'ites when Saddam Hussein brutally crushed an uprising in south-ern Iraq and by standing by even as Iraqi troops bombarded Shi'ism's ho-liest shrines in Najaf and Karbala.

After the war, Iran continued to support Islamic movements distant from its own borders, in Lebanon and, as the opportunity arose, also in Sudan, the West Bank, and Bosnia. However, along its own borders, Iran attached priority to stability and order and sought good relations with neighboring states. It did not attempt to stir up Islamic sentiments in the newly independent states of Central Asia and the Caucasus. It tried to mediate differences between Armenia and Azerbaijan. Concerned lest the creation of a zone under U.S. and allied protection in northern Iraq en-courage Kurdish separatism and lead to the breakup of the country, Iran joined Syria and Turkey in reaffirming a commitment to Iraq's territorial integrity. The government worked assiduously to improve relations with then-secular Turkey, with Saudi Arabia, Kuwait, and the Persian Gulf states. Iran, for example, remained highly critical of the U.S. military buildup in the Gulf, but its criticism of Kuwait for the military basing agreement it signed with Washington was muted. Iran was unalterably opposed to the Arab-Israeli peace process and the terms of the Israeli-Palestinian settle-ment. But it did not criticize the Gulf states for their approval of the peace process and remained silent when Oman and Qatar established diplomatic relations with Israel. It refrained from making an issue of claims of dis-crimination by Pakistan's Shi'ite community and took care not to become enmeshed in the Indian-Pakistani dispute over Muslim Kashmir.

As a counterweight to the United States, with which relations remained strained, Iran deliberately set out to cultivate relations with other major powers, including Russia, China, Japan, Germany, and France. This policy paid dividends. Iran secured sources of arms, industrial goods, credits, and occasional diplomatic support; and the relationships it developed with these countries proved durable, even in face of considerable U.S. pressure on its NATO allies and Russia and Japan to join the United States in com-prehensive trade sanctions against Iran.

The end of the Gulf War saw no improvement and in fact witnessed a deterioration in Iran-U.S. relations. Several factors were responsible. After the war, Iran expected to be reintegrated into the international community, to be able to buy Western arms, and to play a role in postwar defense ar-rangements for the Persian Gulf. However, for a variety of reasons, U.S. suspicions of the Islamic Republic persisted, and Iran was excluded from postwar discussions on Persian Gulf security, even as two outside states, Syria and Egypt, were invited to join the Arab states of the Gulf in contributing to Gulf defense. Although its military had been ravaged by eight years of war with Iraq, Iran continued to be denied Western weapons, even as Saudi Arabia, Kuwait, and other Persian Gulf states undertook a massive armaments program. Iran responded to a statement in President Bush's 1989 inaugural address that "goodwill begets goodwill" by interceding with its Hizbollah protégés to secure the release of American hostages in Lebanon. But, at least from Tehran's perspective, the United States did not reciprocate.

America's huge postwar military presence in the Gulf was also problematic for Iran. Acquiescence in this military presence went against the grain of the ideology of the Islamic revolution. The U.S. presence, moreover, bolstered the weight of Saudi Arabia, one of Iran's traditional rivals for supremacy in the Persian Gulf; afforded the Gulf emirates a shield against Iranian pressure; and fueled anxieties in Tehran that the United States intended Iran harm and was plotting against its territorial integrity. When in 1992 Iran attempted to bolster its presence on Abu Musa, a Persian Gulf island over which Iran and Sharjah (by then part of the United Arab Emirates) exercised a shared sovereignty in an unsettled dispute, the UAE chose to revive Arab claims to all of Abu Musa and the Tunbs, two other islands the shah had seized in 1971. The United States supported the UAE claims.

Another point of contention between the United States and Iran was the Islamic Republic's attempt to modernize and refurbish its military.[2] Iran found itself, at the end of its own war with Iraq, with its military capability greatly reduced in relation to that of its neighbors. Instability was endemic along Iran's borders with Afghanistan and the former Soviet Republics in Central Asia and the Caucasus. Iraq remained a better-armed and threatening neighbor. The U.S. navy was a looming military presence. Iran was ambitious to play a dominant role at sea and in Persian Gulf and Middle East affairs. A projection in 1992 by CIA Director Robert Gates that Iran had launched a five-year, $10 billion armaments program[3] proved greatly exaggerated. In fact Iran's acquisition of conventional arms, in terms of aircraft, tanks, naval craft, and artillery remained modest.[4] However, the United States was alarmed by evidence that Iran had developed a chemical weapons capacity, was working on biological weapons, and was seeking to acquire nuclear weapons. Iran purchased short- and medium-range missiles from China and North Korea capable of reaching population centers on the Arab side of the Gulf and was helping fund the long-range North Korean Nodong-1 missile with a 1,300-kilometer range, thus theoretically capable of reaching population centers in Israel. The development of the Nodong had run into technical and financial difficulties. But the potential combination, in Iran's hands, of a long-range missile and a nuclear or biological-chemical weapons capacity, along with concern regarding Iran's support for radical Islamic movements abroad and opposition to the Arab-Israeli peace process, led the United States to oppose almost all aspects of Iran's rearmament program.

Iran's propensity to support radical Islamic movements abroad was also a source of friction with the United States, Israel, Egypt, and, to a lesser degree, with the European states. Iran was the chief sponsor of Hizbollah, the radical Shi'ite movement in Lebanon. A contingent of Iranian Revolutionary Guards had been stationed in the Bekaa Valley since the early 1980s. Iran provided funds and training for Hizbollah's armed contingents. With Syrian collusion, Iran also supplied the arms that the Hizbollah used against the Israeli-supported forces in Israel's security zone in Southern Lebanon. These weapons were also used to shell Israeli settlements across the Lebanese border. In 1993 and again in 1996, Israel responded to such attacks by heavily bombarding Southern Lebanon. On both occasions, there was evidence that Iran had transferred planeloads of arms to Hezbollah through Damascus airport. Iran supported a network of schools, clinics, day-care centers, mosques, and seminaries that catered to the Shi'ite community in Lebanon and thus managed to emerge as a major player in Lebanon's politics.

In the early 1990s the Islamic Republic had moved with alacrity to support the "Islamic" government that had seized power in the Sudan, despite the damage this did to its fragile relations with Egypt, which had been reestablished with much difficulty after a ten-year break. The Islamic Republic adopted an uncompromisingly hostile posture toward the Arab-Israeli peace talks and the Palestinian-Israeli agreement of September 1993, taking the view that the Israeli state was illegitimate and that the Palestinian people should have an unconditional right of return to their "usurped" homeland. Iran was alleged to be assisting the Islamic movements, Hamas and Islamic Jihad. These movements were opposed to the peace process and were implicated in bombings in Tel-Aviv and Jerusalem in 1995 and 1996 that cost many Israeli lives. In 1994 Iran began deliveries of arms to the Muslim forces in Bosnia. (Although such arms deliveries were banned at the time, the United States was aware of the "surreptitious" deliveries and turned a blind eye to them.)

Iran's support for Muslim causes outside its own borders served a number of purposes. It satisfied the aspirations of the radical faction within the ruling group, which argued for export of the Islamic revolution, support for Islamic movements abroad, and confrontation with the United States. It helped bolster the claims of the Islamic Republic, and of its spiritual guide, to be leaders of a worldwide Islamic awakening that would revitalize the Islamic world; provide an alternative model to Western cultural values, materialism, and hedonism; and end the domination of the Muslims by the United States and the world powers. Islam was a convenient vehicle for the extension of Iranian influence, whether in Lebanon, Bosnia, or Africa. It served as a means of leverage against the United States and other great powers. If Iran often cast itself in the role of spoiler, whether in the Sudan or Lebanon, this was a way of reminding Washington that, if the United States opposed Iranian interests, the Islamic Republic was capable of reciprocating by undermining American interests and America's friends. By rhetorically championing populist Muslim causes and the interests of the "disinherited," the Islamic Republic sought to identify with the masses rather than with ruling elites of regional countries and to distinguish itself from conservative, status quo powers, like Saudi Arabia, which also spent heavily on Muslim causes.

Thus Iran's opposition to the Arab-Israeli peace process served—or so Iran's leaders imagined—to identify Iran with the Palestinian masses and the Palestinian diaspora, distinguished the Islamic Republic from the supposedly pliant Arab states that had acquiesced in a U.S.-sponsored pro-Israeli peace plan, served as a reminder that Iran could play the role of spoiler on issues of great moment to America, and helped enhance the standing of the regime and of Khamenei with constituencies at home.

The radical, Islamic strain in Iran's foreign policy stemmed in part from the problems faced by Khamenei in exercising the role of faqih, or spiritual guide. As noted, strictly speaking, Khamenei lacked the religious seniority and scholarly standing implicit in the office. The constitution required the spiritual guide to be both a faqih, a fully qualified Islamic jurist, and a *marja'*, one of the "sources of emulation," to whom Shi'ites look for guidance on religious and other matters. At the time of his succession, Khamenei did not qualify on either score. He was simply "promoted" to the rank of faqih. The constitution was amended to allow him to take up the office of spiritual guide without qualifying as a marja'. This implied a separation of the political and religious leadership of the community—roles that Khomeini had combined in his person. Khamenei's claim to the office of spiritual guide was not universally acknowledged by Iran's other leading senior clerics, and although these reservations were rarely publicly articulated, reminders of Khamenei's problem were all too common. Ayatollah Abol-Qassem Kho'i, the senior living marja', died in 1992. His death was followed in short order by the death of Kho'i's successor, Mohammad Reza Golpaygani in 1993 and then of Golpaygani's successor, Ayatollah Araki, in 1995. Each occasion was an embarrassing reminder that the spiritual guide of the Islamic Republic was not also *the* senior source of emulation (or at least one of the sources) for all Shi'ites.[5] Khamenei took up the cause of Muslims in Bosnia and the Sudan, of Palestinians on the West Bank and in the diaspora, and he championed other Muslim causes to bolster his credentials, both at home and abroad, as a fitting successor to Khomeini's mantle.

Revolutionary ideology, in combination with radicals at home who were ready to denounce any sign of moderation on sensitive issues as an abandonment of revolutionary principles, made striking a more moderate foreign policy pose difficult in other ways. In his attempt to build bridges with European states, Rafsanjani tried on a number of occasions to explain away the *fatwa*, or decree, issued by Ayatollah Khomeini before his death, calling for the death of the writer Salman Rushdie because his novel *The Satanic Verses* was deemed an insult to Islam. The decree became a serious problem in Iran's relations with the European Community, but no official in Iran dared renounce it or suggest that it had been withdrawn. Discussions between Iran and the Europeans in 1992 led to a declaration by Iran that it would respect international law in this matter, implying that Iran would not attempt to assassinate Rushdie. Almost immediately, 180 deputies in the Majlis signed a letter affirming that Khomeini's edict remained in effect. In 1994 Iran promised the Europeans it would put in writing an undertaking not to kill Rushdie. But at the last minute, Iran's representative refused to put his signature to the document.

Iran was also implicated in assassinations of Iranian dissidents abroad and in acts of terrorism—indications that some elements in the Iranian leadership continued to have difficulty shedding their revolutionary, clandestine past; that violence continued to be seen as a useful instrument of policy; and that Iran's state security apparatus enjoyed considerable freedom of action. Prominent and less well-known Iranian opposition figures were killed in Paris, Berlin, Vienna, Istanbul, Switzerland, and other countries. Although Iran denied responsibility, in March 1996 the German federal prosecutor issued a warrant for the arrest of Iran's minister of intelligence (state security), Ali Fallahian, for involvement in the 1992 assassination at the Mykonos Restaurant in Berlin of Sadeq Sharifkandi, the secretary general of the Kurdish Democratic Party of Iran, and three others. In April 1997, a German court found an Iranian and two Lebanese guilty of the Mykonos assassinations and also implicated Iran's highest authorities in the plot. Also in March 1996, Belgian police at Antwerp boarded an Iranian ship, the *Kollahduz,* headed for Germany and found on board mortar shells, a rocket launcher, and 125 kilos of TNT. Agents of Lebanon's Hizbollah were believed responsible for at least one of two bombing incidents, in 1992 and 1994, at the Israeli Embassy and at a Jewish cultural center in Buenos Aires, which together took more than one hundred lives. The evidence was circumstantial, and Iran was not directly involved. But Iran was a major sponsor of Hezbollah.

Both the United States and its allies took the view that Iran had to be persuaded to change its behavior. The Europeans favored "critical dialogue," believing that engagement would strengthen the hand of more moderate elements in Iran. The United States took the view that Iran's unacceptable behavior on a number of key issues—acquisition of nuclear arms and weapons of mass destruction, terrorism, support for radical Islamic movements that undermined friendly regimes, and opposition to the Arab-Israeli peace process—would change only under pressure, by "containing" Iran and denying it arms, trade, markets, technology, and credits.[6]

The United States and Sanctions Policy

A U.S. ban on the export to Iran of dual-use technology that had been in place since 1984 limited the amount of American exports to Iran following the Gulf War. In 1993, for example, the United States refused to permit Boeing to sell Iran twenty 737–400 passenger jets in a deal worth some $750 million. The United States also sought to persuade its European allies and Japan to join it in more comprehensive sanctions against Iran and to deny Iran commercial credits; Russia and China to deny Iran nuclear reactors and weaponry; and international lending bodies to deny Iran loans. This U.S. campaign was only partially effective. In the years immediately following the Gulf War, the World Bank extended some $750 million in loans to Iran for irrigation, electrification, family planning, and earthquake reconstruction projects. But U.S. opposition effectively prevented further World Bank credits to the Islamic Republic. U.S. opposition was also decisive in excluding Iran from a multinational consortium to develop newly independent Azerbaijan's Caspian Sea oil fields. Iran's 5 percent share in the $7.5 billion project went to Exxon. The United States, bolstered by the efforts of Turkey and Russia, which sponsored competing pipeline projects, helped ensure that pipelines carrying Azerbaijan's oil would not pass through Iran until 1997. The United States also opposed preliminary proposals to use Iran as the transit route for pipelines carrying natural gas from Turkmenistan to Turkey and Europe.

Elsewhere, the United States met with only limited or no success. Japan agreed to delay providing the second, $500 million tranche of a loan for a hydroelectric power dam on the Karun River, but it refused to abandon the project or curtail trading with Iran. Russia agreed in 1995 that it would not sign new arms agreements with Iran but insisted on completing deliveries of weapons already purchased and agreements to supply Iran with two nuclear power stations. China continued to provide Iran with weaponry and nuclear and military technology. The European states, led by Germany, conducted a substantial trade with Iran and agreed to reschedule loans when Iran faced a foreign exchange crunch in 1993–94.

The limited success of the United States in securing international cooperation for a sanctions policy against Iran increased pressure on the Clinton administration to tighten its own sanctions program. America's European allies pointed out that U.S. oil companies were the primary purchasers of Iranian oil, taking about 25 percent, or up to $4 billion worth, of Iran's annual exports. Bills were making their way in Congress for comprehensive trade sanctions against the Islamic Republic. Concerned about the potential acquisition by Iran of long-range missiles and nuclear weapons and about Iran's role in supporting opponents of the peace process, Israel also argued for stronger U.S. action. In March 1995 the America Israel Public Affairs Committee issued a study arguing for comprehensive sanctions and lobbied Congress to enact them.[7]

When the U.S. oil firm Conoco signed a $1 billion agreement in March 1995 to help develop two Iranian offshore fields near Sirri Island in the Persian Gulf, President Clinton signed a presidential order that barred U.S. companies from investing in Iran's oil industry and thus forced Conoco to cancel the deal. In April the president signed an order banning all U.S. trade with Iran. Although the administration had initially advised against a secondary sanctions bill under consideration in Congress, in 1996 Clinton signed a bill requiring the president to impose a range of secondary sanctions against foreign firms investing over $40 million in the Iranian oil and gas industry. These sanctions bills hurt Iran, but the damage was limited. Iran remained a significant market for exports and investments.

America's allies resented U.S. attempts to dictate trade and foreign policy. Iran had resources of oil and gas that other countries wanted, and it was able to offer incentives (to Turkey and Turkmenistan, for example) that tempted governments to circumvent U.S. sanctions. Thus, European allies of the United States indicated that they would fight the secondary sanctions law. Total, the French firm that promptly signed with Iran the offshore oil deal that Conoco had canceled, insisted it would go ahead with its Iranian project. In August 1996 Turkey, another close U.S. ally, signed a deal to purchase over $20 billion worth of natural gas from Iran over a 20-year period, while German institutions extended new credits to Iran. The economic difficulties that Iran began to experience in 1993–94 stemmed more from domestic mismanagement than from U.S. sanctions policy.

Economic Policies and Problems

Before his death in 1989, Khomeini had already given his approval for a five-year development plan (1989–94) which, controversially, provided for a larger share in the economy for the domestic and foreign private sectors and allowed the government to borrow up to $27 billion abroad for development projects. President Rafsanjani, assisted by technocrats like Finance Minister Mohsen Nourbakhsh and Central Bank governor Mohammad Adeli, used the plan as the basis to move Iran away from a state-controlled war economy and to begin economic liberalization and postwar reconstruction.[8] In 1991 the government reduced multiple exchange rates from seven to three. In March 1993 it further rationalized exchange rates, announced a new "floating" rate for the Iranian rial that was closer to real market rates, and declared full convertibility of the rial. Import and foreign currency controls were eased, and banks were given greater autonomy to lend and open letters of credit. In principle, importers were allowed all the foreign exchange they needed. Price controls were lifted, and state subsidies for essential goods were reduced and limited to five items instead of the previous seventeen. With the end of the war, rationing was no longer necessary. Other prices, way out of line with true costs, were also adjusted. Telephone and electricity rates were raised, air fares for international flights on the national carrier were increased by 800 percent, and in March 1995 fuel prices were doubled.

New regulations permitted foreign investors equity participation of up to 49 percent in joint ventures, with foreign majority control promised in future legislation. Free trade zones were established on the islands of Qeshm and Kish in the Persian Gulf. Several hundred government factories were slated for privatization, partly through sale of shares to the public. The stock exchange was reopened in 1989, and although the volume of shares traded remained light in relation to the size of the economy, activity was nevertheless brisk. The government promised to reduce its own role in the economy; at the time, only 3 percent of all investments were being made by the private sector. The five-year plan, nevertheless, foresaw an ambitious government investment program in petrochemicals, gas, steel, machine tools, electrification, and automotive and other industries. Fueled by rising imports, large government spending, and private sector investment in construction and light industry, the real GDP grew by more than 10 percent in each of the years 1990–91 and 1991–92.

The liberalization program, however, soon ran into difficulties. Privatization stalled. The huge parastatal organizations, like the Foundation for the Disinherited and the Martyrs' Foundation, and the Ministries of Industry and Heavy Industry proved unwilling to give up the hundreds of expropriated industries and enterprises that they controlled. Inefficient, overstaffed state enterprises could not be sold off until they were made profitable. Only fifty-five companies went on the stock exchange between 1989 and 1994. Government efforts to persuade monarchy-era Iranian businessmen abroad to return and invest in Iran were hampered by the memory of past confiscations, continued uncertainty regarding the security of private property, unhelpful laws and regulations, the arbitrariness of the courts, bureaucratic red tape and, after 1993, concerns over the stability of the rial.

The easing of import and currency restrictions led to a rush of imports, which increased from $14.7 billion in 1989–90 to $27.4 billion in 1991–92. Foreign exchange reserves were depleted. Iran, which through the eight years of war with Iraq had done minimal foreign borrowing, quickly ran up a short- and medium-term foreign debt of nearly $30 billion and by spring of 1993 was unable to meet its repayment commitments. The government managed in 1993–94 to reschedule about $12 billion of debt, signing nineteen agreements with creditor countries, primarily Japan, Germany, and other European states. But debt servicing, estimated at $4.6 billion in 1995 and $4 billion to $6 billion each year through 1999, was expected to eat up some 25–30 percent of foreign exchange earnings, a heavy drain on resources.[9]

Severe retrenchment was inevitable.[10] Imports were sharply cut and by 1994–95 stood at under $13 billion, or less than 50 percent the level of three years earlier. Credit to the private sector was restricted. In 1994–95 many factories operated at only 50 percent capacity due to the lack of spare parts and raw materials. The money supply more than doubled in the 1989–94 period, and even during the budget squeeze the government in 1995–96 projected a 40 percent increase in spending over the previous year. Continued deficit spending contributed to severe inflation which, at official rates, stood at 35 percent in 1994–95 and around 50 percent in 1995–96. Nonofficial inflation estimates were higher. The foreign exchange squeeze, considerable liquidity in private hands, panic buying of the dollar, and government mismanagement led to a rapid erosion of the value of the rial, which plummeted on the open market from the officially announced rate of 1,625 to the dollar in 1993 to 4,000 rials to the dollar in January 1994—a depreciation of nearly 60 percent. (The value of the rial fell to more than 7,000 rials to the dollar on the open market in the wake of the new and comprehensive trade sanctions announced by President Clinton in April 1995, but this proved a temporary setback, and the rial reverted to around 4,000 rials to the dollar later that year.) The start of the second five-year development plan was postponed by a year.

The economic liberalization program began to unravel. Multiple exchange rates once again became common. A ban was imposed on the import of luxury or non-essential items. A decline in non-oil export earnings resulted from the requirements that exporters sell their foreign exchange earnings to the government at the new official rate of 3,000 rials to the dollar (set in the spring of 1995 following the free fall of the rial in the wake of the U.S. trade ban). Contrary to its avowed commitment to free market principles, in spring 1995 the government launched a crackdown against overpricing by merchants and retailers, and the president announced plans for a network of one thousand government retail stores to compete with the private sector and provide goods at cheaper prices.

Economic hardship led to severe riots in Mashad, Arak, and Shiraz in 1992. Urban unrest erupted in Qazvin in 1994, and although the Qazvin disturbances were rooted primarily in local and provincial politics, they reflected the antigovernment sentiments that seethed just below the surface. More ominously for the government, regular army and Revolutionary Guards units in Qazvin gave notice they would not again fire on crowds to quell civil disorder,[11] leading the government to rely increasingly on the paramilitary *basij*, until then a poorly trained and poorly equipped auxiliary force. When rioting again broke out, this time over inadequate municipal services and higher bus fares in two working-class districts near Tehran in April 1995, it was the basij that were brought in to curb the unrest; several demonstrators were killed.

The government responded to these signs of popular discontent by expanding and beefing up the basij and the secret police apparatus. In 1995–96 the Majlis approved a new security law that provided for sentences of up to ten years for any two or more persons forming an organization at home or abroad that threatened national security; the same sentences would be imposed on anyone who belonged to illegal groups, engaged in propaganda against the Islamic Republic, passed confidential information to third parties, or insulted the country's spiritual guide. These measures came on top of the campaign that began in 1992 against the Western "cultural onslaught," growing restrictions on press and intellectual freedom, and periodic crackdowns against women who violated the Islamic dress code.

Politics

In the immediate post-Khomeini period, Rafsanjani initially scored successes in the political sphere also. By a kind of constitutional gerrymandering, the president managed to exclude the leading figures of the radical faction from the 1992 parliament. Among those not elected were Mohammad Khoeniha, the mentor of the students who seized the American embassy and took U.S. diplomats hostage in 1979; Sadeq Khalkhali, the notorious "hanging judge"; Farkhr ad-Din Hejazi, a rabble-rousing cleric; Mehdi Karrubi, speaker of the outgoing "radical" parliament; and Ali-Akbar Mohtashami, who helped forge Iran's ties with Lebanon's Hizbollah when ambassador to Damascus in the early 1980s. Mohtashami had also secured the election of a large radical bloc to the third Majlis (1988–92) when he was interior minister, and he had urged an Iranian-Iraqi alliance against the United States when he was a member of parliament following the Iraqi occupation of Kuwait. Rafsanjani himself was reelected to a second four-year term as president with a comfortable, if reduced, margin in 1993. He was able to place his own men in key economic posts and to get his protégés elected to parliament. For example, Raja'i-Khorasani and Hasan Ruhani played key roles as foreign policy spokesmen in the Majlis.

The easing of social and cultural controls that occurred in the post-Khomeini period was evident in various areas.[12] Women were able to appear in public in more brightly colored headscarves and to show a bit of hair as well as wearing nail polish and lipstick. Young men and women could not openly socialize on university campuses but found an opportunity to mix, always under the watchful eyes of the "morals police," on picnics and walks along the hills above Tehran where they went on Fridays. The authorities tolerated a brisk underground trade in videocassettes of Hollywood films. Satellite dishes, which permitted Iranians to tune in to CNN and Baywatch, proliferated. Iranian directors made films that hinted at social criticism and won prizes at international film festivals. Mozart and Beethoven returned to the concert halls and Chekhov, Shakespeare, and Arthur Miller to the theaters.

Newspapers speaking for the political opposition were not permitted. For example, the Iran Liberation Movement, a liberal, centrist opposition group, was barely tolerated and was not allowed to publish its newspaper. However, newspapers published by men of the regime reflected a range of opinion, and Khoeniha's *Salaam* sniped at the government from the left, while *Resalat* sniped at it from the right. More significant was the proliferation of independent women's journals, such as *Zanan*, and literary and intellectual journals such as *Kiyan, Goftegu, Gardun, Iran-e Farda,* and *Kelk.* Such journals addressed issues relating to women's rights and their problems. On the pages of the intellectual journals a guarded but lively debate took place on current politics and on such issues as civil society, the place of religion in public life, and the relationship between religion and democracy. *Kiyan,* the most influential of these journals, each month carried an article by the Islamic thinker and philosopher Abdol-Karim Soroush. Soroush, trained in both Western and Islamic philosophy and able to engage clerical scholars on their own ground, argued for an Islam that was pluralistic, tolerant, open to change and interpretation, and compatible with democracy. Soroush avoided issues of current politics. But by arguing against the clerical monopoly over the interpretation of the sources of Islamic law, ethics, and theology and against clericalism as a profession—clerics, he said, should work for a living like everyone else—he implicitly challenged the clerical domination of the state and the clerics' claim to a mandate to rule. He gained a large following among university and seminary students and, in time, among the secular intellectuals as well. Cassette tapes of Soroush's lectures were widely circulated.

The extent of this opening up in the cultural and social sphere should not be exaggerated. Politics remained restricted to the rival factions of the ruling circle, and opposition political parties were not permitted. Elections were controlled. Crackdowns by the morals police, especially in matters of women's dress, were erratic but frequent. Officially sanctioned club-wielding bully-boys were always available to break up public gatherings of which the government did not approve. Arbitrary arrests continued, and in political matters there was no such thing as an independent judiciary. The secret police was a pervasive and menacing presence. As the suppression of urban unrest in 1992 and 1995 indicated, the government was ready to crush any serious challenge to its authority. Nevertheless, a space opened up that artists, film directors, publishers, writers, and intellectuals were able effectively to exploit.

Even this limited liberalization, however, ran into trouble. Rafsanjani had succeeded in excluding the radicals from the fourth Majlis, but he ended up with a parliament dominated by social conservatives from provincial constituencies. These deputies bristled at the easing of the dress code and of controls over the content of films, books, and magazines. Disaffection with the regime was widespread, its popular base narrow. The urban riots of 1992 led the ruling group to fall back on what it considered to be its core constituency in the Revolutionary Guards, the revolutionary committees, the basij, the Islamic committees at places of work, the families of "martyrs" and similar groups. Elements in the regime reverted to populist, Islamic, and conservative slogans and to attacks on supposedly corrupt Western values and Westernized intellectuals. The Ministry of Islamic Guidance, which set cultural policy and funded artistic activities, came under attack for allegedly liberal policies in regard to film, theater, art, and publications. In order to bolster his weak position at home, the spiritual guide, Khamenei, led the campaign against the so-called Western "cultural onslaught" and, without citing the ministry by name, pointedly asked why dedicated Muslim youth loyal to the revolution were not given an opportunity to direct films and plays and hold art exhibitions.

In 1992 parliament forced the resignation of the minister of Islamic guidance, Mohammad Khatami (who was to be elected president of Iran in 1997). Under new management, the ministry adopted a more restrictive policy in the production of film, theater, and books and magazines. In 1994 the Majlis authored a harshly critical report of television broadcasting that led to the resignation of Rafsanjani's brother as head of the state-controlled radio and television networks. The following year the Majlis also passed a law banning satellite dishes, although the government was able to enforce it only fitfully. There was a crackdown against the press and several newspapers and journals were suspended or closed down.[13] The editor of *Salaam* spent three months in jail in 1993. *Jahan-e Islam* was shut down in February 1995. *Payam-e Daneshju*, a newspaper that had alleged irregularities at the Foundation for the Disinherited, was suspended for three months in August 1995. In the following year the newspaper was shut down and its editor put on trial for reporting on the business activities of members of the Rafsanjani family. In January 1996 Abbas Maroufi, editor of the intellectual journal *Gardun*, was sentenced to thirty-five lashes and six months in jail. His license to publish was revoked and he was banned from engaging in any form of journalism for two years. Maroufi managed to go abroad before being sent to jail.

In November 1994 Ali-Akbar Saidi-Sirjani, a well-known essayist and satirist, who had been arrested on fabricated charges of spying, homosexuality, and drug use, died while in police custody. In 1996 Ahmad Mir-Alai, a writer and translator, was found dead on a street in his hometown of Isfahan—a death that rumor among the intelligentsia also attributed to the security authorities. Acts of random violence began to occur. In August 1995 club-wielders attacked the offices of the publisher of a novel deemed disrespectful of Islam. Forty publishers addressed a letter to the government, asking for protection. Three months later, a bookstore near Tehran university was torched, presumably for carrying objectionable literature. In May 1996 club-wielders attacked two movie theaters, setting one on fire. A gang beat up women cyclists on a cycle path in a Tehran park.

Gangs of club-wielders were not a new phenomenon. They had been deployed by the clerics in political struggles in the early years of the revolution and continued to be used to break up political meetings into the mid-1980s, when opposition political activity virtually ceased. But these gangs were conveniently anonymous. They appeared, did their disruptive work, and disappeared; no one took responsibility for them. The club-wielding gangs that reemerged in 1995 were different. They proudly proclaimed their identity, calling themselves the Ansar-e Hezbollah, or the Helpers of the Party of God. They produced spokesmen and issued press releases justifying their actions. The Ansar were also publicly championed by Ayatollah Ahmad Jannati, a prominent senior cleric. Jannati defended the Ansar attack on the Tehran publishing house and the group's other actions on the grounds that devoted Muslims were required to act when the government did not perform its duty to prevent corruption and un-Islamic activities.

In 1996 Jannati caused consternation among university faculties by taking up and reiterating Khamenei's earlier call for the Islamization of the universities. In the early years of the revolution, a similar campaign for university Islamization had led to a purge of university faculty and tampering with the university curriculum. Jannati was a member of the Council of Guardians, a body of senior Islamic jurists and experts in Islamic law that, like the U.S. Supreme Court, was empowered to strike down legislation it deemed in violation of the constitution or Islamic law. As a protector of the constitution and Islamic law, the Council of Guardians was regarded as neutral and above politics. During his lifetime, Ayatollah Khomeini at times sought to shape the Council of Guardian's decisions, but in general respected its independence. The involvement of Ayatollah Jannati in openly partisan politics was a sign that a politicization of the Council of Guardians was taking place on Khamenei's watch.

The Ansar-e Hezbollah were also utilized in an attempt to silence Soroush. In October 1995 members of the group prevented Soroush from delivering a lecture at Tehran University and physically attacked him. A few weeks later they again attacked Soroush and prevented him from speaking at Isfahan university. In the following year, they threatened to break up a meeting Soroush was to address at Amir Kabir University in Tehran, leading him to cancel the lecture altogether. These attacks did not entirely cow the intellectual community. In October 1994, 134 writers and intellectuals signed a cautiously worded declaration in defense of freedom of the pen. The following year 214 film directors, screenwriters, and others involved in the cinema signed a letter to the authorities criticizing state interference in the film industry. Soroush was prevented from speaking publicly, but he continued to write and *Kiyan* to publish his articles. Nevertheless, by the spring of 1996 liberalization appeared to have suffered a decided setback. The elections for the fifth Majlis took place in this uncertain environment.

Contradictory Signals: The 1996 Parliamentary Elections

The 1996 parliamentary elections helped focus attention on the foreign policy and the political and economic choices before the country. The first round of balloting was held in March, with candidates receiving at least 30 percent of the vote going on to a second round in April. In addition to a large number of independents, the elections were contested by four loosely organized movements.

The Association of the Combatant Clerics of Tehran was the largest and best known of these groups. An organization of leading middle-rank and senior clerics that went back to the early years of the revolution, the Combatant Clerics and their supporters were led by the Majlis speaker, Ayatollah Ali-Akbar Nateq-Nuri, and had dominated the outgoing fourth Majlis. Socially conservative, the Combatant Clerics had led the campaign to ban satellite dishes and establish stricter controls over television, films, and journals. The Combatant Clerics were associated with free market policies, in the sense that the group had close links to the bazaar merchants, traders, and shopkeepers. But the group also displayed suspicion of foreign investment and large industrial interests and viewed themselves as defenders of the "barefoot" and the poorer classes.[14] In this role, they limited Rafsanjani's subsidies-cutting program and in 1993 rejected the reappointment of Mohsen Nurbakhsh, one of the architects of Rafsanjani's free market policies, as minister of finance.

The fourth Majlis at times had also been fiscally more conservative (and, some would argue, fiscally more responsible) than the government. For example, the Majlis insisted on more realistic oil revenue projections in the 1994–95 budget and required the government to limit deficit spending in the 1995–96 fiscal year. In 1996 the Majlis undertook an investigation of the Foundation for the Disinherited and issued a critical report. The foundation acted largely independently of the state and provided little information on its administration of some four hundred mostly expropriated enterprises. Though not a formal opposition, as it cooperated with the government on most issues, by 1996 the majority bloc in the fourth Majlis nevertheless emerged as a sometimes obstructionist and rival center of power to Rafsanjani's government. Speaker Nateq-Nuri, the leader of the Combatant Clerics, made no secret of his desire to succeed Rafsanjani as president.

The Servants of Construction were a newly formed group of senior civil servants, primarily technocrats, closely associated with President Rafsanjani. The group announced its existence in a manifesto issued in January 1996, only three months before the balloting. The sixteen signatories included ten cabinet ministers, four deputies to the president, the mayor of Tehran, and the governor of the Central Bank. The manifesto, skimpy on details, nevertheless constituted a strong endorsement of the programs and legacy of Rafsanjani, and it emphasized the need for investment, economic development, and technocratic skills. The Servants of Construction clearly represented a bid by Rafsanjani and his lieutenants to secure strong representation, perhaps a majority, for the government's program in the new Majlis and to keep Rafsanjani's policies alive after Rafsanjani stepped down as president at the end of his second (and final) term. A new newspaper, *Bahman*, edited by a deputy to the president, was launched to promote the group's ideas. There was even talk of transforming the Servants of Construction into a political party.

The Coalition of the Imam's Line represented four radical Islamic groups, of which the Mujahedin of the Islamic Revolution, led by Behzad Nabavi, a former minister of heavy industry, was the most prominent. The Imam's Line coalition opposed privatization and emphasized social justice, more equal distribution of wealth, state control of the economy, and continuation of rationing and subsidies. In foreign policy, it argued for export of the revolution, support for Islamic movements abroad, and confrontation with the United States.

The Society for the Defense of Islamic Values was a small group put together by Mohammad Rayshahri. A cleric, former judge of the Revolutionary Courts, and a former minister of intelligence (state security), but now out of office, Rayshahri hoped to ride his newly organized group back to political power. Its policies were similar to those of the Combatant Clerics.

The elections were by no means free. The Council of Guardians, authorized to supervise elections, vetoed the candidacy of some 40 percent of more than five thousand would-be candidates. While a majority of these were unknowns with little chance of being elected, the Council of Guardians barred the candidacy of many prominent local and national figures and political groups. It disqualified members of the Iran Liberation Movement from running. The organization of radical clerics associated with Mohtashami, Karrubi and Khoeniha, having been excluded from the fourth Majlis, chose not to contest the elections at all. During and after the balloting, the Council of Guardians nullified the elections in fourteen constituencies, comprising twenty-two seats. In most of these, supporters of Rafsanjani were the favored candidates. In Isfahan the council vetoed the candidacy of Hasan Kamran, a popular but radical parliamentary deputy. When his wife, Nayereh Akhavan, ran in his place and secured the largest number of votes, the council canceled the Isfahan ballot altogether. In Saveh, the council nullified sufficient ballots to throw the election from a Rafsanjani supporter to a conservative. In Ardabil, candidate Gharibani's credentials were not approved, but he nevertheless secured 140,000 votes.

Nevertheless, among the circumscribed group of individuals and factions in the ruling hierarchy allowed to participate, an energetic competition took place for seats, control over the next Majlis, and, implicitly, over the direction of government policy. The main contest was between the Combatant Clerics and the Rafsanjani technocrats. Associated, at least implicitly, with free market policies and a more moderate foreign policy, the Rafsanjani technocrats appeared to offer voters a choice and lent to the elections a special significance. The Combatant Clerics were sufficiently disturbed by the appearance of the Rafsanjani group to launch a concerted campaign to discredit them. Some 130 members of parliament addressed a letter to the spiritual guide suggesting that he ban electioneering by senior government officials as constituting an improper use of state facilities. Khamenei declined to oblige, but at the suggestion of the Council of Guardians the ten cabinet ministers withdrew from the group. The Servants of Construction were accused of wishing to abandon revolutionary principles, readiness to sacrifice Iran's independence for the sake of economic development, and insufficient dedication to the principle of *velayat-e faqih*, the Shi'ite doctrine in whose name supreme authority in the Islamic Republic was vested in the clergy and ultimately in the faqih, spiritual guide, or Islamic jurist. Nateq-Nuri warned on February 12 against those who favor "ties with the United States, non-interference in the Palestinian issue and the struggle against the Zionist regime, and giving up the issue of Salman Rushdie." He called on the Revolutionary Guards to defend the country against the liberal menace.[15] The commander of the Revolutionary Guards referred on April 12 to the "cancerous tumor" of liberalism in Iran and called for the election of candidates committed to Islam and to the concept of rule by the Islamic jurists.[16] The Rafsanjani technocrats had never publicly espoused the policies attributed to them regarding ties with the United States, Israel, and the Rushdie issue. The accusation, however, reflected what was supposed to be the hidden agenda of the Rafsanjani group and was Nateq-Nuri's way of mobilizing the "revolutionary" constituency against them.

Candidates associated with the Servants of Construction appeared to do well in the first round of balloting. This perhaps led Khamenei, on the eve of the second round, to denounce candidates who emphasized technical skills more than religiosity. He warned against the election of candidates "whose radios are tuned to the powerful transmitters of the United States and the West" and said that if candidates inspired by the West managed to get into the parliament, "the nation . . . will stretch its hand . . . and throw them out."[17]

The attempt of the Rafsanjani group to break the hold of the conservative clerics over the Majlis did not succeed. The Combatant Clerics won the bulk of the 30 seats in the capital, Tehran, the country's most important constituency, and an overall majority in the Majlis. Nateq-Nuri was re-elected speaker with 146 votes (out of 240 cast) against 92 for Abdollah Nuri, the candidate of the Servants of Construction. The Rafsanjani technocrats' bloc was even smaller than this division suggested, since Abdollah Nuri's 92 supporters included a bloc from the Imam's Line coalition, who could not be counted on to vote with the Servants of Construction on all issues. Deputies associated with the Combatant Clerics won elections for the other principal offices in the new Majlis as well. *Bahman*, the unofficial organ of the Rafsanjani parliamentary group, suspended publication. At the same time, the Servants of Construction, themselves part of the ruling group, were not about to alter radically the direction of Iran's domestic and foreign policy, but gradually to shift it. They could not have done so without agreement of the spiritual guide and powerful figures in the clerical hierarchy and other major institutions.

Nevertheless, the 1996 parliamentary elections were not without significance and underlined both the possibility and the difficulty of change. The elections indicated that debate about the direction of domestic and foreign policy was still taking place within the ruling group—albeit within a narrow range. The campaign suggested to the public that there were choices to be made, however small, over the direction of policy. The elections brought to Majlis an articulate faction that might be willing to argue for these policy alternatives. On the other hand, the election results also were an accurate mirror of the divisions within the Iranian leadership. They suggested that the forces of what might be termed continuity

—of divided leadership and conflicting policies and purposes described here—were still stronger than the forces of change.

The People Speak: The Presidential Elections of 1997

Further signs of divided leadership were evident in the presidential elections in May 1997. The Council of Guardians approved only four candidates from a much larger field. The election was therefore a competition among members of the ruling elite. But within these restrictions, the campaign was vigorous. The election was primarily a contest between the Majlis speaker, Nateq-Nuri, and the former minister of Islamic guidance, Mohammad Khatami. Against all expectations, clear differences emerged between them. They campaigned seriously and worked hard for votes.

Nateq-Nuri, universally dubbed the conservative candidate by the Iranian media, was considered the front-runner. His clerical organization controlled the majority of the seats in the Majlis. He was supported by the bazaar and was endorsed by almost all the senior, politically active clerics, by the commander of the Revolutionary Guards, by the foreign minister and other officials, and, indirectly, by a majority of members of the Council of Guardians. He was also supported by several of Khamenei's personal representatives in major provincial capitals and, implicitly, by the spiritual guide himself. On the eve of the balloting, in what was widely read as a reference to Khatami, Khamenei remarked that Iranians would not vote for a candidate "lenient toward America."

Khatami was supported by the Servants of Construction, the Coalition of the Imam's Line, and a loose association of radical clerics. This was a disparate coalition, but Khatami ran a campaign that galvanized the public. He stressed the need to respect the constitution, strengthen civil society, and enforce the rule of law. He said the government should not interfere with what Iranians did in the privacy of their homes. He paid special attention to the problems of women and youth. Although he did not challenge the principle that ultimate authority rested with the spiritual guide, he said power should not be the monopoly of one group (presumably the clergy). He said he did not approve of American popular culture but remarked that in the modern world it was impossible to block out satellite television programs and the internet. He said Iranians could learn a great deal from Western civilization, whose culture was dominant in today's world. In a clear reference to the harrassment of the intelligentsia, he said intellectuals had the right to personal security.

Khatami excited the electorate sufficiently that 90 percent of eligible voters went to the polls. He culled 70 percent of the vote, securing 20 million votes to Nateq-Nuri's 7 million. His support was wide as well as deep. He did especially well among women, the young (those over fifteen are allowed to vote), the intelligentsia, and the modern middle classes. But while he won large majorities in major urban centers, he won also in small towns and rural areas, a clear indication that he got votes from traditional and religious households.

Khatami's election appeared to be an overwhelming mandate for change, a repudiation of official mismanagement and corruption, and a demand for the rule of law, personal freedoms, and improved economic opportunities. These were themes that Khatami himself had emphasized, but whether he would succeed in overcoming resistance to change and transforming his mandate into effective programs remained to be seen.

Notes

1. Iran's foreign policy during the Gulf war and in the immediate postwar period is covered in greater detail in Shaul Bakhash, "Alternative Futures for Iran: Implications for Regional Security," in Geoffrey Kemp and Janice Gross Stein, eds., *Powder Keg in the Middle East* (Washington: American Association for the Advancement of Science, 1995), 87–108.

2. For an alarmist account of Iran's armaments program, see Patrick Clawson, *Iran's Challenge to the West: How, When, and Why*. For a more balanced view, see Shahram Chubin, *Iran's National Security Policy: Capabilities, Intentions & Impact*.

3. Robert Gates, testimony before the Defense Policy Panel and the Department of Energy and Defense Nuclear Facilities Panel of the House Armed Services Committee, March 27, 1992.

4. For details of Iran's arms acquisitions, see Michael Eisenstadt, "Deja Vu All Over Again: An Assessment of Iran's Military Build-Up," in Patrick Clawson, ed., *Iran's Strategic Intentions and Capabilities* (Washington: National Defense University, Institute for National and Strategic Studies, 1994), 93–151, and Michael Eisenstadt, testimony before the House International Relations Committee, November 9, 1995. In his testimony before the House International Relations Committee, Eisenstadt noted that Iran's arms purchases were running at around half the level of earlier projections and that Iran "has acquired only a fraction of the items on its military wish list." He argued, however, that Iran remains a threat to U.S. interests and to America's allies in the Gulf due to its chemical and biological weapons capacity and its ability (though limited) to disrupt Persian Gulf sea traffic. Press reports in 1994 also cited Pentagon estimates that Iran had spent $800 million rather than the anticipated $2 billion on arms in 1993. See Elaine Sciolino, "Iran's Difficulties Lead Some in U.S. to Doubt Threat," *New York Times*, July 5, 1994.

5. The problems surrounding the succession to the office of spiritual guide are discussed in Shaul Bakhash, "Iran: The Crisis of Legitimacy," in Martin Kramer,

ed., *Middle Eastern Lectures: Number One* (Tel-Aviv: Moshe Dayan Center for Middle Eastern and African Studies, and New York: Syracuse University Press, 1995), 99–118.

6. U.S. policy toward Iran under the Clinton administration was spelled out frequently by administration officials. See, for example, Anthony Lake, "Confronting Backlash States," *Foreign Affairs* 73 (March-April 1994); Peter Tarnoff, under secretary of state, and, separately, Bruce Reidel, deputy assistant secretary of defense, testimony before the House International Relations Committee, November 9, 1995; Tarnoff, testimony Before Senate Banking Committee, October 11, 1995; and John Gannon, CIA deputy director for intelligence, statement on sanctions against Iran before Senate Committee on Banking, Housing and Urban Affairs, October 11, 1995.

7. See "Comprehensive U.S. Sanctions against Iran: A Plan for Action," America Israel Public Affairs Committee report, March 29, 1995.

8. Accounts of Iran's economic liberalization program can be found in the following sources: "Iran's Top Banker" (an interview with Central Bank Governor Mohammad Adeli), *US-Iran Review,* May 1993; Masoud Kavoossi, "Iran's Open Door to Foreign Investors," *US-Iran Review,* July 1993; Masoud Kavoossi, "Iran's Economy: An Assessment," *US-Iran Review,* January 1994; "Minister of Economy Sees Great Potential for Iran's Future," *Iran Business Monitor,* June 1993; "Currency Market Development," *Iran Business Monitor,* July 1993.

9. Figures on Iran's debt and projections of its debt refinancing burden, can be found in an unpublished report by Firuz Vakil, "Iran: Debt Free to Debt Ridden: A Problematic Transition," Lazard Freres, May 1, 1996; and in "How Western Credits Underwrite Iran's Mullahs: Iran Report No. 4," America Israel Public Affairs Committee report, February 20, 1996. Both draw their figures from the Institute for International Finance, Islamic Republic of Iran, Country Report, October 25, 1995.

The deputy governor of Iran's Central Bank, Ahmad Azizi, however, in an interview in 1996 gave much lower figures for Iran's external debt and a much rosier picture of Iran's debt-servicing burden. He calculated Iran's total external debt as of March 1995 at $25.3 billion and claimed that Iran had paid $5.5 billion of this debt in the 1994–95 fiscal year. He projected a further repayment of $6 billion in the year ending March 1996; $4.3 billion in 1997; $3.8 billion in 1998; and $2.6 billion in each of the two following years, leaving Iran free of the existing foreign debt by March 1999. See "Foreign Debt Drops to $17 billion, " *Iran Business Monitor,* February-March 1996.

10. The discussion of economic retrenchment that follows is based, in part, on the following: "Iran: Revolutionary Culture Faces the Music," *Middle East Economic Digest,* February 11, 1994; Bahman Komali-Zadeh, "Officials Discuss Inflation, Ways to Curb Money Supply," *Iran Business Monitor,* April 1994; "Iran: An Economy in Disarray," *Middle East,* December 1994; Peter Waldman, "Iranian Revolution Takes Another Turn, But Where Is It Going?" *Wall Street Journal,* May 11, 1995; Bahman Komali-Zadeh, "Bigger Deficit Feared as Gov't. Ups Spending 40%," *Iran Business Monitor,* July 1995; Ali Jafari, "Fixed Rate Exchange Policy May Slow Exports," *Iran*

Business Monitor, July 1995; and Masoud Kavoossi, "Iran's Economy in Transition," *Middle East Insight* (Special Edition: Iran), July-August 1995.

11. It was widely rumored at that time that the army and Revolutionary Guard put the government on notice, after the Qazvin riots, that they would not again order their troops to quell civil disorder; the situation was reported in some detail in the *Economist*. See "Don't Count on Us, Ayatollah," *Economist*, August 27, 1994. See also reference in Elaine Sciolino, "Fear, Inflation and Graft Feed Disillusion among Iranians," *New York Times*, May 30, 1995.

12. An overview of the effects of eased controls can be found in Robin Wright, "A Tehran Spring," *New Yorker*, June 22, 1992, and Robin Wright, "Testing the Limits of Cultural Freedom," *Civilization*, March-April 1995.

13. The description of the crackdown on press and artistic activity that follows is partly covered in Sciolino, "Fear, Inflation and Graft Feed Disillusion Among Iranians," and Robin Wright, "Dateline Tehran: A Revolution Implodes," *Foreign Policy* no. 103 (Summer 1996): 161–74. The suppression of civil rights is covered in some detail in "Iran: Power vs Choice: Human Rights and Parliamentary Elections in the Islamic Republic of Iran," a report by Human Rights Watch/Middle East, March 1996.

14. Suspicion of big business, however, did not prevent several prominent clerics from participating as silent partners in large business enterprises.

15. Associated Press, April 1, 1996, citing Iranian newspapers.

16. Islamic Republic News Agency (IRNA), April 12, 1996.

17. *Ettellaat*, international edition, April 18, 1996, 2.

10: The Arabian Peninsula

F. Gregory Gause III

In the five years since the Gulf War of 1990–91, political energies in the states of the Arabian Peninsula—the six states of the Gulf Cooperation Council (Saudi Arabia, Kuwait, Bahrain, Qatar, the United Arab Emirates, Oman) and Yemen—have been focused inward. While a number of important foreign policy issues remain, Desert Storm to a great extent "settled" external security issues in the peninsula for the near-term future. A combination of domestic issues—some predating the Iraqi invasion of Kuwait, some caused or exacerbated by the Gulf crisis, some unrelated to the events of 1990–91—have risen to the top of the political agenda. Demands for greater popular participation in political life and evidence of political opposition are increasingly prevalent in the Gulf states as governments are being forced to cut back on state welfare benefits to citizens. Yemen has yet to consolidate the unity it achieved in May 1990, suffering a brief civil war in the summer of 1994 and continuing political and economic difficulties.

The challenges faced by the GCC states are sufficiently analogous, and the structure of their political economies sufficiently similar, that they will be treated as a group in this chapter. The Republic of Yemen, the only non-monarchical regime on the Arabian Peninsula, faces similar economic and political problems, but in a much different context. It is treated separately at the end of the chapter.

The Political Economy of Relative Scarcity in the GCC States

Between 1980, the high-water mark of world oil prices, and 1991, the conclusion of the war to liberate Kuwait, the GCC governments experienced an enormous decline in their financial reserves. Saudi and Kuwaiti reserves, each estimated at over $100 billion in the early 1980s, had fallen to around $30 billion, if not lower, by 1994.[1] The Gulf War, which was funded largely by Kuwait and Saudi Arabia, was a major cause of the depletion of these reserves, but it was not the only cause. During the 1980s world oil prices declined precipitously, from their 1980 high of nearly $38 per barrel (for West Texas Intermediate Crude, averaged over the year), to $15 per barrel in 1986. Prices recovered somewhat in the late 1980s, spiked to about $25 per barrel during 1990 with the Gulf crisis, and have settled back down to the $17–19-per-barrel range in the last few years. It should be noted that oil produced in the GCC states fetches a lower price on the market than West Texas Intermediate, which is an industry benchmark. For its 1995 budget Saudi Arabia estimated, conservatively, that its oil would be sold at an average price of $14 per barrel.[2]

All the GCC states saw their government revenues fall substantially during the 1980s. However, the states continued to maintain, and even to increase, government spending. They funded at least part of the deficits they accrued by spending down their financial reserves. Meanwhile, the GCC states, particularly Saudi Arabia and Kuwait, provided Iraq with "loans," grants and oil sales on the Iraqi account estimated to be around $40 billion during its war with Iran from 1980 to 1988.[3] The financial burdens of the Gulf War thus came at a time when the GCC states were already drawing down their financial reserves. Estimates of Kuwaiti expenditures during and immediately after the Gulf crisis range as high as $65 billion; the International Monetary Fund estimated the direct costs of the Gulf War for the Saudis at $55 billion, a figure that Saudi officials have not challenged. The Saudis were able to take advantage of the removal of Iraqi oil from the world market by increasing their production by about 3 million barrels per day (bpd) in 1990, an increased level of production that they have maintained since. However, Saudi government revenues in 1996 are estimated to be more than 200 billion Saudi riyals (approximately $53 billion) less than revenues were in 1980. The costs of the Gulf War for the other GCC states were much less but hardly negligible.[4]

The bottom line for the GCC states is that the past decade has removed the margin of financial safety they previously enjoyed. They now have to live within their means. Those means remain extensive but are no longer limitless. Moreover, they face the demands of rapidly increasing populations that have become accustomed to welfare states constructed in the 1970s, a time of much smaller populations and greater resources. Population growth rates in all the GCC states have been, for the last two decades, among the highest in the world. While the rate of population increase has recently been brought down, each of the GCC states is projected to double its current population within forty years if current growth rates are sustained.[5] While some of this growth has come from immigration, a large portion of it is accounted for by high birth rates and longer life expectancies.

The strains placed on the GCC states' welfare systems by burgeoning populations are manifold. Longer life expectancies mean greater health care costs. High birth rates mean more schools. Larger populations mean greater demand for water, electricity, and telephone services, all of which are heavily subsidized in these states. More school graduates mean greater demand for jobs, particularly in the public sector, which for the past two decades has absorbed almost all the citizen (as opposed to foreign labor) workforce in these countries. These demands are occurring at a time when there is just not as much money available to these governments as in the past. The long-term political consequences of this fiscal squeeze are very serious. For more than two decades (longer in the cases of older oil states, like Kuwait and Bahrain), the GCC governments have maintained a clear political bargain with their populations: the state provides jobs, goods, and services without taxation to the people, and the people remain loyal to (or quiescent about) their rulers. If the state cannot deliver on its part of the bargain, more of its citizens might feel free to ignore their part.[6]

The GCC states have taken, or have talked about taking, a number of steps to confront their fiscal problems. The most obvious step is to cut government expenditures and to raise government revenues. All have talked about this, but few have acted decisively. Saudi Arabia has gone the furthest. In 1994 it reduced the government budget by 19 percent and in 1995 by a further 6 percent. It decreased subsidies on a number of consumer products, including gasoline and electricity, and raised the price of foreign worker permits and visas. Agricultural subsidies have also been reduced.[7] Still, analysts estimate that the 1995 Saudi budget deficit was slightly higher than forecast, despite oil earnings $3.7 billion to $4.0 billion higher than earlier government forecasts based on conservative projections of oil prices.[8] The Saudis used this cushion to pay off the remainder of their government debt to foreign lenders and to begin to make good on late payments to local contractors.[9] The 1996 Saudi budget forecast a deficit of nearly $5 billion, more than 12 percent of the total budget.[10] Even with a concerted effort, controlling spending is proving a difficult task for the Saudis, particularly as payment will come due in the next five to ten years for a number of big-ticket purchases (such as a new fleet of domestic aircraft for Saudia, the national airline, purchased from Boeing and McDonnel-Douglas).

Other GCC states have not taken even the initial cost-cutting steps that

Riyad has pursued. Qatar's projected budget deficit for 1995–96 is nearly $1 billion, in a budget of $3.5 billion.[11] The Kuwaiti 1995–96 budget has a deficit of $5.3 billion; the government promised to address the deficit in a new five-year plan that has yet to be published.[12] Bahrain's combined budget deficit for 1995–96 is projected to be 72 percent higher than in the 1993–94 period.[13] While increased oil production has reduced Oman's projected 1995 deficit, the government does not foresee a balanced budget until the year 2000, according to the recently adopted five-year plan.[14]

The difficulty in cutting budgets is more political than economic. Reduced government spending translates directly into economic costs for citizens, in terms of fewer state jobs and state contracts, reduced subsidies, and cuts in services. Given the experience of Desert Storm and the pressure from the United States to build up their military forces with purchases of American arms, major cuts in defense spending are unlikely. Raising revenues through taxes could increase demands for greater popular participation in government. None of the GCC states are willing to go very far in these directions. Thus the governments have been exploring ways to deal with the fiscal crunch that avoid these political costs.

Both Kuwait and Oman have relied on foreign loans to help fund deficits, but both are now approaching the limits of international creditors' willingness to extend new loans. The Kuwait Investment Authority, which oversees the state's foreign investments, told the Kuwaiti parliament in January 1996 that official reserves had fallen to about $47 billion, from $117 billion before the Iraqi invasion, and that the state's foreign debt was approximately $30 billion. Officials of the investment authority said Kuwait could shortly become a net debtor unless action were taken to reduce government budget deficits.[15] Saudi Arabia has funded its deficits largely through domestic borrowing, using techniques perfected by the U.S. Treasury—selling government bonds to state social security funds and to local banks. Its domestic debt levels are, according to analysts, between 60 percent and 80 percent of GDP, a manageable but somewhat high figure by world standards.[16] Bahrain has sought and received assistance from some of its neighbors, particularly Saudi Arabia, as Riyad has recently given Bahrain a larger share of an offshore oil field that the two states have jointly developed.[17] But none of these expedients can be relied upon indefinitely.

One policy option aimed at lessening the economic burdens on the state that has attracted increasing attention among the GCC leadership is privatization. Privatization holds out the promise of allowing the state to shift many of the economic responsibilities it assumed during the 1970s and 1980s, like job creation and maintaining many inefficient companies, to the private sector. Privatization should also increase the amount of investment in the countries' economies, both from local capitalists and from abroad, allowing for greater economic growth. A number of GCC states have adopted the rhetoric of privatization; some have even begun to take steps in that direction.

Oman has been the most aggressive of the Gulf states on the privatization issue. It has adopted a five-year plan calling for the sale of a number of state assets and legal changes to encourage foreign investment in its oil and gas industries, hoping to increase revenues in the long term.[18] Qatar has also been inviting multinational companies back into the oil and gas sectors, has aggressively pursued international financing tied directly to the development of its offshore gas deposits, and has taken the first steps to set up a stock exchange as a possible prelude to privatizing some parts of state-owned companies.[19] In the other GCC states there is more talk of privatization than action. Kuwait has auctioned its stake in the National Industries Company, the largest industrial firm in Kuwait outside of the oil sector, and is setting up a private sector company to own and manage gasoline stations belonging to Kuwait National Petroleum Company.[20] Leaders in both Saudi Arabia and Kuwait have spoken publicly about privatizing their national airlines.

The hesitations about pursuing privatization more aggressively are, once again, more political than economic. First and foremost, privatization means a loss of at least some measure of control over the economy. The GCC regimes, having spent the last three decades consolidating their dominance of their economies, are reluctant to give that up. Real privatization means higher prices. If privatization is to relieve economic burdens on the state, it means an end to subsidized inputs and controlled prices. Real privatization would also mean a wrenching transformation of the Gulf business environment—the rewriting of commercial codes, the elimination of sweetheart deals between private businesses and powerful members of the ruling families, and the opening of the Gulf economies to greater competition domestically and internationally. It is not clear that Gulf business elites would greet such changes enthusiastically. Finally, and most explosive politically, real privatization would mean increased citizen unemployment. In the GCC, citizen members of the workforce are overwhelmingly concentrated in government service and the state economic sector; foreign labor dominates the private sector. Privatized companies would presumably look to improve efficiency and boost profits by reducing their payrolls.[21]

The unemployment issue has risen to the top of the political and economic agendas in a number of GCC states. Bahrain saw an upsurge in social unrest during 1995, to be discussed in more detail later, that is at least partially attributable to the very high levels of unemployment among Bahrainis, estimated to be as much as 15–20 percent of the citizen workforce. Saudi Arabia and Oman are also beginning to face problems in employing recent school graduates.[22] The answer to the problem of citizen unemployment in countries with hundreds of thousands (in Saudi Arabia, millions) of foreign workers seems obvious—kick at least some of the foreigners out. Unfortunately for the Gulf rulers, the issue is not that simple. Foreign workers are cheaper for employers than citizen workers. They accept lower salaries and fewer fringe benefits; they are easier to control because their status in the country depends completely upon their employer renewing sponsorship of their visas. At a time when the GCC governments are talking about the private sector assuming a greater role in the economy, it is difficult to impose increased labor costs upon it.

The related economic issues of government spending, privatization, and unemployment have no easy answers. But it is increasingly clear that not taking steps to address them now will only exacerbate them in the future. There is no *deus ex machina*, like drastically higher oil prices, that will allow the Gulf states to avoid hard political and economic choices. Those choices have to be made in a changed political environment, where there are greater public demands for political participation and serious manifestations of opposition to the ruling regimes.

Political Demands and State Responses in the GCC States

Desert Storm initiated a period of intense political activity in the GCC states. The crisis itself was a major cause. The military and ideological challenge presented by Saddam Husayn, the massive presence of U.S. and other coalition forces, and the intense focus of the world media all combined to open up a small bit of political space in countries whose rulers had assiduously worked to depoliticize their populations and suppress any manifestations of opposition activity. Citizens of the GCC states demanded to know why the billions their governments had spent on defense had not provided the capacity to defend themselves. The governments needed to show the world that their citizens were loyal and supportive, and they thus were obliged to tolerate greater openness. The crisis itself politicized people who had previously been content to remain on the sidelines of public life.

The crisis was not the only impetus to greater political activity in the GCC states. The steady decline of oil revenues in the 1980s deflated the region's economic boom, calling into question the tacit bargain of political quiescence for economic benefits that the GCC regimes had made with their citizens. The end of the Iran-Iraq war in 1988 removed the security rationale that governments had used to justify closed political systems. In fact, before the Iraqi invasion in August 1990, Kuwait had witnessed a public campaign aimed at pressuring the ruler to restore the elected Kuwaiti parliament that had been suspended in 1986. But it was the Gulf crisis of 1990–91 that opened up the possibility of more active political life in all the GCC states.

Throughout most of the GCC states, the most widespread manifestation of new political activism, during and immediately after the crisis, was the circulation of petitions. In Kuwait, Saudi Arabia, Bahrain, and Qatar, citizens of various political inclinations addressed requests to their rulers for more responsible government and greater popular participation in decision making. The nature of the demands differed from country to country. In Kuwait and Bahrain, the call was for restoration of constitutions that mandated elected legislatures. In Saudi Arabia and Qatar, there were more modest requests for an end to arbitrary practices, more freedom of speech, and more formal avenues of consultation between the government and the people. In Saudi Arabia, petitions reflected different political agendas, with ad hoc groups of liberals, Islamists, and members of the minority Shi'i population all proposing their own reform recommendations to the rulers.[23]

The Gulf regimes reacted to these displays of public involvement in politics with differing degrees of flexibility. Kuwait, whose ruling family was the most damaged by the 1990–91 Gulf crisis, restored the 1962 constitution that the ruler, Shaykh Jabir al-Ahmad Al Sabah, had suspended in 1986. In October 1992 elections to the Kuwaiti parliament were held. A number of organized political factions, including three Islamic groups and a liberal coalition, participated in a vigorous and open campaign. Thirty-three of the fifty victorious candidates were identified with the various groups that had pushed the government to restore constitutional life. The largest ideological bloc was the Islamists, but they were divided along sectarian (Shi'i and Sunni) and organizational (Muslim Brotherhood and *salafi*-Wahhabi) lines. (The term *salafi* is used in the Gulf countries and Saudi Arabia to signify Islamic movements that take their inspiration from the Saudi Wahhabi tradition.)

The Kuwaiti parliament has played an active role in monitoring government policy, bringing to light financial scandals (including one involving members of the Al Sabah family), and has provided a forum for debate of major issues.[24] It also extended the franchise to more Kuwaitis, increasing the size of the electorate for the 1996 elections by approximately 20 percent, though it did not, as some expected, give Kuwaiti women the right to vote.[25] The parliament was less successful in grappling with the financial pressures facing Kuwait, adopting budgets with large deficits and voting to ease repayment schedules on debt relief programs adopted immediately after liberation.

On March 1, 1992, King Fahd of Saudi Arabia issued three royal decrees codifying and changing important elements of the Saudi political system. One decree promulgated the "Basic System of Government," a constitution-like document. The Basic System reiterated the unwritten bases of Saudi rule: the monarchical nature of government, with rulership residing in the Al Sa'ud family; the Islamic law basis of the legal system; the centrality of the king in executive and legislative matters. It also set out formally a number of rights of citizens to be observed by the government.[26] Formal safeguards against arbitrary government action are included in the Basic Law, but it is not clear either from the text or from the first years of its operation how citizens can appeal for redress of grievance against the state.

The second Saudi decree established the Consultative Council (*majlis al-shura*). The council, appointed by the king, reviews legislation proposed by the Council of Ministers, can recommend amendments and new laws to the Council of Ministers, and can question ministers about the operation of their ministries. It has no legislative power; it is purely consultative. King Fahd appointed the sixty members of the first Consultative Council in August 1993. The council's deliberations are not open to the public, so it is difficult to assess what effect, if any, it has had on the conduct of government business. While the council is clearly limited in powers, its establishment represents an important innovation in Saudi politics—the first acknowledgment of the right of people outside the ruling family to institutionalized access to the decision-making process.

The third Saudi royal decree of March 1992 mandated greater autonomy for the kingdom's fourteen provincial governors on spending and development priorities and established regional consultative councils. The king appoints provincial governors; all fourteen current governors are members of the Al Sa'ud family.[27]

In November 1990 Sultan Qabus of Oman announced the establishment of the Consultative Council, appointed by the sultan from candidates nominated through indirect election on a provincial basis. Given the lack of any public political pressure for change in Oman, the decision caught most observers by surprise. Like its Saudi counterpart, the Omani council can only recommend; it has no formal legislative power. Unlike the Saudis, however, the sultan has allowed its deliberations to be open to the public.

The council has called ministers on the carpet for public questioning, a show enjoyed by politically aware Omanis. In November 1994 members of the new council (the councils have four-year terms) were chosen by the sultan after provincial indirect elections. Two women entered the new council, and its membership was expanded from fifty-nine to eighty members by granting more populous governates two members rather than one.[28]

In December 1992 Shaykh 'Isa Al Khalifa of Bahrain established the Consultative Council along the lines of its Saudi counterpart. Thirty members were appointed, evenly divided between Sunnis and Shi'is. Unlike the situation in Saudi Arabia and Oman, the Bahraini council does not have the same character of being a step forward, for Bahrain had an elected parliament with real legislative powers that was suspended in 1975. The campaign for restoration of the Bahraini constitution and the legislature continues to dominate political debate in the small island country, and is discussed in more detail later.[29] Neither Qatar nor the United Arab Emirates adopted similar institutional innovations, though the new amir of Qatar recently suggested that he may permit elections to municipal councils.[30] It should also be noted that in both Bahrain (June 1995) and Saudi Arabia (August 1995) there were cabinet shakeups, and a number of new faces entered both governments in technocratic ministries. Ruling family members held on to the most important positions in both cases.[31]

With the exception of Kuwait, the institutional changes adopted by the Gulf states since Desert Storm share a number of characteristics. They are limited—no real legislative power for the councils, no direct elections of members. They are meant to give the appearance of greater public input into politics while maintaining the firm control of the governing elites. They may in the future develop into more substantial checks on executive authority, having independent legislative power and direct relationships with popular constituencies, but that day is not here yet. It is also clear that the appointment of these councils has not mollified important elements of political opposition to the regimes that have emerged in public since Desert Storm.

Political opposition has been the most widespread and public in Bahrain. Demonstrations and acts of violence began in December 1994 with the arrest of Shaykh 'Ali Salman Ahmad Salman, a Shi'i preacher in a large Manama mosque. The arrest led to more than two weeks of confrontations between his partisans and the security forces in a number of villages outside Manama and occasionally in the capital city itself. Estimates of those arrested and those killed during the clashes differ widely. Opposition groups claimed that ten people died and more than fifteen hundred were arrested. The government announced one death—of a policeman confronting protesters—and refused to give the number of those arrested, though anonymous government sources later put the number of those detained at around four hundred.[32] These disturbances occurred at a particularly embarrassing time for the Bahraini government, as it was hosting the annual Gulf Cooperation Council summit. The seriousness of the disturbances led the government to deport Shaykh 'Ali Salman and three other Shi'i clerics to Iran in January 1995.[33]

The disturbances in Bahrain have a number of causes. Unemployment is a serious problem in the country, particularly among younger Bahrainis. Outside analysts put the unemployment rate as high as 15 percent, though the government contends that it is in the single digits.[34] Most of the violent demonstrators are young men. Sectarian tensions also play a role. The most serious disturbances have been concentrated in Shi'i neighborhoods and villages. The Shi'i majority on the island has historically chafed under the rule of the Sunni Al Khalifas, who have been very skillful in framing political dissent in sectarian terms to divide potential opposition movements. Some Bahraini Sunnis sympathetic to the cause of political reform have been put off by the violence in Shi'i communities.[35]

But economic distress and sectarian tensions alone do not explain the political unrest in Bahrain. Since Desert Storm there has been an active movement, cutting across sectarian lines, to push the government to restore the Bahraini constitution and reestablish the elected legislature prorogued in 1975. The 1992 petition in this regard has been followed by a similar petition composed in 1994. Opposition sources report that it has received thousands of signatures. There were reports of another petition addressed to the amir making the same demands in October 1995 and of an April 1995 petition signed by three hundred prominent Bahraini women calling on the authorities to seek a political solution to the unrest.[36]

This mix of economic, political, and sectarian grievances has kept alive discontent in Bahrain through 1995 and into 1996. Sporadic outbreaks of violence occurred in the spring and summer of 1995. The regime sought to contain the unrest through a mix of security measures and political gestures aimed at the dissidents, including the release of people detained at various stages of the unrest and entering into talks with opposition leaders, particularly Shi'i community leaders.[37] However, unrest flared again in December 1995 and January 1996. In response, the government arrested eight leading Shi'i figures and obliquely threatened to declare martial law unless order was restored.[38] A special state security court was formed in 1996 to try those accused of violent opposition to the government; that court passed a number of death sentence and, as of July 1996, had convicted 128 Bahrainis of various crimes.[39] The most recent unrest was not as widespread as that of late 1994 and early 1995, and normal life in Manama, the capital, was not substantially disrupted except for two bombs set in downtown hotels. Arson attacks continue; the most serious took the life of seven Bangladeshi guest workers in March 1996, when a Molotov cocktail was thrown into a restaurant frequented by foreign workers.[40] The continuing inability of the government to either snuff out the violence or appease the opposition means that tensions will continue in Bahrain.

In none of the other Gulf states was political opposition as public and sustained as in Bahrain. But in both Saudi Arabia and Oman, the regimes very publicly cracked down on Islamic political activists. Islamists in Saudi Arabia began to assert themselves immediately after the Gulf War, sending a brief petition to the king that carried more than four hundred signatures, including those of very senior clerics; the petition called for reform in a number of areas and for more stringent application of Islamic law. Later, in 1992, more than one hundred activists signed a 46-page "memorandum of advice" to the king. The "memorandum" was blunt in its tone and detailed in its critique of nearly every aspect of Saudi political life, written from a strict Wahhabi Islamist perspective. In May 1993 six Saudi Islamic activists announced the formation in the kingdom of the "Committee to Defend Legitimate Rights" (*lajnat al-difa' 'an al-huquq al-shar'iyya*), calling on citizens to contact them with complaints about injustices.

The regime reacted harshly to this move, arresting some of those involved and removing others from their government jobs. The spokesman for CDLR, Muhammad al-Mas'ari, a physics professor at King Saud University in Riyad, escaped from the country and set up shop in London. From there, his faxes, e-mails, and press releases about the kingdom have so angered the Saudis that they put heavy pressure on the British government to expel him. As of January 1996 the British decision to deport him to the small Caribbean state of Dominica was being appealed. Riyad also took the rare step in April 1994 of revoking the Saudi citizenship of 'Usama bin Laden, a member of one of the kingdom's leading merchant families. Bin Laden was an active member of the *mujahidin* who fought the Soviets in Afghanistan, and he has continued from his headquarters in Sudan to support the overthrow of Middle Eastern governments, including the Saudi government, that he deems insufficiently "Islamic."[41]

A sign of the seriousness with which the Saudi regime viewed its increasingly vocal Islamist critics was the official acknowledgment of the arrest in September and October 1994 of 157 people, including two prominent Islamists, Salman al-'Awda and Safar al-Hawali, who had organized demonstrations in Burayda, a city about 250 miles northwest of Riyad. Opposition sources put the number of arrests during that period at well over a thousand. The Saudi Interior Ministry took the unusual step of giving a detailed account of its case against al-'Awda and al-Hawali, accusing them of planning actions to foment chaos in society and having contacts with "notorious groups" abroad. The statement said that the two had been under investigation by the Committee of Senior 'Ulama for over one year and had refused the opportunity to recant their statements and promise not to engage in public preaching. In October 1994 a total of 130 of those arrested were released, but al-Hawali and al-'Awda remained in custody as of January 1996.[42]

The regime followed up the arrests with moves to reassert government control over the Saudi religious establishment and signals that it would not tolerate Islamist dissent. In early October 1994 King Fahd established two new committees to oversee Islamic activities in the kingdom. The first, the Supreme Council of Islamic Affairs, is headed by Prince Sultan, the minister of defense, and includes other senior members of the government and the ruling family. The second, the Council of Proselytization and Guidance (al-da'wa wa al-'irshad), included a number of senior functionaries in the religious establishment. It was charged with planning and oversight responsibilities for proselytization activities and for all matters relating to mosques, including personnel and promotion issues.[43] In August 1995 the Saudi government publicly announced the execution of a Saudi Islamic activist accused of attacking an officer of the security services. Both the publicity given to this case and the regime's contention that the man had received his instructions from the CDLR in London were unusual for a government that prefers to keep its political business out of the public eye.[44] But the Saudi hard line could not prevent the November 1995 bombing of an office in Riyad used by a U.S. training mission attached to the Saudi National Guard, killing five Americans and two others and injuring scores. Two previously unknown Islamist organizations claimed responsibility.[45] The Saudi authorities were also unable to prevent the June 1996 bombing of the Kobar Towers residence of U.S. airmen that killed nineteen Americans.

The Omani government in August 1994 revealed that in June it had arrested over two hundred people implicated in a plot organized by the Muslim Brotherhood to overthrow the government. Among those arrested were a former Omani ambassador to the United States, a former commander of the Omani Air Force, and two undersecretaries of government ministries. A number of those arrested were sentenced to death, but the sultan commuted those sentences to imprisonment of various durations, then in November 1995 pardoned all those involved.[46] In neither Qatar nor the United Arab Emirates did public manifestations of Islamic opposition activity emerge, and in Kuwait the three Islamic groups that contested the 1992 elections prepared to contest the 1996 parliamentary elections.

Politics at the Top: The Ruling Families and the Governing Elites

The combination of difficult economic issues and newly vocal publics present the Gulf leaders with a new set of constraints in their decision making, but power still resides almost exclusively at the top of these political systems. The direction they take on these issues depends upon the decisions made by the senior members of the ruling families. Their political stability will be affected more by the ability or inability of the ruling families to manage their own internal tensions than by the increasingly serious social problems they face. If the families hang together, they probably have the financial and coercive resources (along with the support of important foreign actors) to stand up to domestic opposition. If the solidarity of the ruling group falls apart, the political field will open up as rival family factions seek support in the military and from society. It is at that point that revolutionary political change could occur.

In the years since Desert Storm, there has been only one case of serious intrafamily political squabbling, in Qatar. After an extended period of tensions between the amir, Sheikh Khalifa bin Hamad Al Thani, and his son the crown prince, Hamad bin Khalifa Al Thani, the crown prince in June 1995 staged a palace coup while his father was overseas. With the support of a number of his brothers and other prominent members of the Al Thani family, he declared himself amir. Hamad had been a controversial figure in the GCC, seen by many as the source of Qatar's maverick foreign policy, which sought good relations with Iraq and Iran while antagonizing Saudi Arabia on border issues. He quickly received the recognition of the United States and of the other GCC states, however, and it appeared that the transition in Qatar would be relatively simple.[47]

However, by early 1996 it seemed that the Qatari leadership issue, which had looked settled, might be reopened. Sheikh Hamad staged a very public boycott of the closing ceremonies of the GCC summit in December 1995, after his candidate for secretary general of the organization was not accepted. That behavior, along with his very public courting of Iran, Iraq, and Israel, appears to have rubbed a number of his neighbors the wrong way. His deposed father, who has asserted from the moment of the coup that he remains the rightful ruler of Qatar, staged a very public tour of the region in December 1995 and January 1996. He was received by the rulers in all the other GCC states, Egypt, and Syria, and he seemed to be organizing regional support for his return to power. In February 1996 Qatari authorities announced that they had uncovered a plot to destabilize the government and bring Sheikh Khalifa back to power. The former amir denied his involvement in the alleged coup but said that it reflected popular support in Qatar for his return. Whether he can successfully dislodge his son remains to be seen, but the tensions within the ruling family in Qatar have now spilled over into the GCC as a whole, with Qatar accusing some of its GCC allies of abetting Sheikh Khalifa's effort to return to power.[48]

Other leadership issues in the GCC states have been handled with a minimum of public fuss, but they do highlight the centrality of the top man in all these regimes. Saudi Arabia's King Fahd suffered what diplomatic sources reported was a mild stroke in December 1995, and on January 1, 1996, he temporarily transferred executive powers to Crown Prince 'Abdallah.[49] Some have speculated that this move is the beginning of a gradual transition to 'Abdallah assuming the kingship. While 'Abdallah is believed by many Saudi observers to be temperamentally less partial to the United States than his half-brother the king, every indication was that the transfer of authority would not lead to changes in Saudi policy. Sultan Qabus of Oman was involved in a serious auto accident in September 1995, in which his long-time deputy prime minister, Qays al-Zawawi, was killed. The sultan himself escaped without serious injury, but the incident highlighted the uncertainly of succession issues in Oman. The sultan has no sons and has not appointed a crown prince.[50]

Succession is not the only political issue related to the ruling families in the GCC states. Economic austerity has brought with it an increasing focus on the finances of the rulers themselves. Opposition groups like the Committee for the Defense of Legitimate Rights in Saudi Arabia and the Bahrain Freedom Movement highlight stories (impossible to confirm for outsiders) about ruling family members muscling in on local businessmen, collecting outlandish commissions on state contracts with foreign companies, and generally not assuming their share of the burdens in the current round of economic belt-tightening. With the ruling families in all the GCC states growing in size, and with the end of the days of unlimited government employment opportunities for family members, the relationship between the families and the business communities becomes a more difficult issue to manage. The unstated bargain in most of the states—that the families would run politics and take their cut of the oil money but leave the private sector to others—is under increasing pressure. The general issue of the economic role of the families, both regarding their share of public funds and their relationship to the business community, will take on increasing importance.[51]

Foreign Policy

Since the end of the Gulf crisis of 1990–91, foreign policy issues have played a less central role in the politics of the GCC states. Security issues were, at least for the time being, basically settled by Iraq's defeat and the demonstrated willingness of the United States to assure militarily their defense. All of the GCC states reaffirmed in a much more public way than in the past their security links with Washington, through formal agreements, arms sales, and the increased presence of U.S. forces and pre-positioned equipment in the region. All the GCC states also expressed public support for the Arab-Israeli peace process that restarted with the Madrid conference of 1991 and accelerated with the Israeli-PLO agreement of 1993 and the Jordanian-Israeli peace treaty of 1994. All participate in the multilateral talks set up at Madrid, with Oman, Qatar, and Bahrain hosting meetings of various multilateral committees.

With the exception of a few serious bilateral disputes within the GCC, the differences between and among GCC states on foreign policy issues have been more disagreements over timing, emphasis, and nuance than over fundamentally divergent views of basic interests. But it also must be noted that, after the crises of the 1980s and early 1990s, the GCC seemed to lose a certain amount of cohesion. With no immediate threat on the horizon, the incentives for cooperation on military and security issues disappeared. Nagging bilateral disputes rose to prominence. Differences in emphasis stymied efforts to reach common positions on regional issues.

An ambitious plan, put forward by Sultan Qabus of Oman immediately after the Gulf War, to form a unified GCC military force of 100,000 men was shelved by the GCC leaders. Each of the countries negotiated bilaterally its own security agreements and arms deals with foreign powers. The rhetoric of economic integration, part of the GCC agenda since the founding of the organization in 1981, has not been matched by deeds. The GCC, however, is hardly moribund. There was movement in 1995 toward unification of tariff systems, a necessary step in negotiations with the European Community for a GCC-EU trade agreement, and for construction of the joint electricity grid, though in neither case by January 1996 was agreement complete.[52] Plans have been mooted to expand the Peninsula Shield force, a joint GCC unit stationed near the Saudi-Kuwaiti border, and cooperation on air defense matters has been achieved.[53] Still, given the experiences of 1990–91, progress on GCC cooperation has been limited.

The most serious bilateral tensions within the GCC have been those between Bahrain and Qatar, and between Qatar and Saudi Arabia. The Bahraini-Qatari territorial dispute over ownership of the Hawar Islands (between the two countries), pushed to the background by the larger issues of the previous years, reemerged. Qatar took the case to the International Court of Justice, despite Bahraini refusal to recognize the court's jurisdiction. The matter as of January 1996 was still before the court and was the occasion for frequent verbal sniping between Doha and Manama. The Saudi-Qatari dispute, over implementation of a border agreement signed in 1965, flared in October 1992 with a skirmish that left two dead on the Qatari side and one dead on the Saudi side. While mediation by President Mubarak of Egypt (not, it should be noted, other GCC members) smoothed the incident over, tensions between Doha and Riyad remain. The accession of Sheikh Hamad to rulership in Qatar will likely exacerbate difficulties, since many in Riyad hold him responsible for Qatar's more aggressive foreign policy of recent years.[54] His boycott of the final session of the December 1995 GCC summit did nothing to endear him to his fellow rulers, and the new tensions over the purported coup attempt in Qatar in February 1996 further cloud the prospects of GCC cooperation in the future.

The GCC states have differing interpretations of the way to deal with the regional aftermath of the Gulf War. Kuwait and Saudi Arabia see Iraq as a continuing military threat. The return of Iraqi oil to the world market would also reduce their revenues at a time when both face serious fiscal problems. The other states, further down the Gulf, less affected by the war, and less vulnerable to an Iraqi return to the oil market, have signaled a greater willingness to rehabilitate Iraq, if only as a balance again Iran. Bahrain and the UAE both see Iran as a serious threat: Bahrain because it blames Iran for stirring up Shi'i unrest and the UAE because of its dispute with Iran over Abu Musa and the Tunbs Islands. Qatar and Kuwait, on the other hand, court Iran. Saudi Arabia is leery of Iranian intentions, on both strategic and ideological grounds, but pursues formal and correct relations with Teheran. None of the GCC states expressed support for Washington's policy of "dual containment" against Iran and Iraq, despite the close security ties between them and the United States.

Immediately after the Gulf War, the GCC states signed the Damascus Declaration with Egypt and Syria, establishing what seemed to be a formal security organization. But immediately thereafter they backed away from the more far-reaching interpretations of the agreement, which foresaw the permanent stationing of Egyptian and Syrian forces in the Gulf.[55] Good relations are maintained by all the states with both Cairo and Damascus, but not nearly on the level envisaged by some in 1991. While most of the lower Gulf states have been willing to forgive and forget in regard to those Arab states seen as backing Saddam in 1990—Jordan, Yemen, the PLO, Tunisia, and Algeria—Kuwait has steadfastly refused any reconciliation with the PLO and only moved to improve ties with Jordan toward the end of 1995. Saudi Arabia has mended its fences with the North Africans, and under U.S. prodding has agreed to provide financial aid to the new Palestinian Authority in the West Bank and Gaza. Both Yasir Arafat and King Hussein have been received in Riyad, but relations between the Saudis and those leaders remain cool. It was not until late 1995 that Riyad agreed even to send a new ambassador to Jordan.[56] Saudi Arabia took the lead in supporting the breakaway Southerners in the Yemeni civil war of 1994, while Qatar and Oman were more supportive of the unified Yemeni government in San'a.

All the GCC states support the Arab-Israeli peace process. In September 1994 they agreed as a group to lift the secondary and tertiary boycotts on economic dealings with Israel, while leaving in place the boycott on direct dealings with Israeli companies until the Syrian and Lebanese negotiations are completed.[57] But once again they differ in terms of degree and emphasis. Qatar and Oman have been the most open in their dealings with Israel. Qatar gave the go-ahead to Enron, a Houston-based gas company developing part of Qatar's extensive gas reserves, to negotiate the sale of Qatari gas to Israel. Qatar's foreign minister also met with Israeli Foreign Minister Shimon Peres in London in September 1993.[58] Oman hosted a visit by the late Prime Minister Yitzhak Rabin in December 1994, and in January 1996 signed an agreement with Israel to allow each state to establish a trade office in the other.[59] Both, along with Bahrain, sent representatives to Rabin's funeral in Israel. Kuwait, the United Arab Emirates, and Saudi Arabia have been more cautious in their dealings with Israel, both to avoid antagonizing Syria and, in the Saudi case, in response to domestic public opinion.

Even in relations with the United States, closer since the Gulf War for all the states than ever before, there are some differences in approach. Kuwait and Qatar have signed new security agreements with Washington, agreeing to pre-position U.S. military equipment in their countries. Bahrain remains (since immediately after World War II) the headquarters of the U.S. naval forces in the Gulf, recently expanded and reorganized as the Fifth Fleet of the U.S. Navy.[60] Oman has an access-to-local-facilities agreement with the United States dating to the late 1970s. The United Arab Emirates, on the other hand, seems to be cultivating closer relations with European powers on arms acquisitions and training issues. Saudi Arabia has been reluctant to sign a formal security agreement with the United States and to agree publicly to pre-position American equipment in the kingdom.[61] These differences, once again, pertain to the details of what is a very strong relationship between each of the GCC states and the United States.

The Other End of the Peninsula: The Republic of Yemen

While not nearly as central to world interest as its oil-rich neighbors on the Arabian Peninsula, Yemen cannot be forgotten in the regional political picture. Its total population is greater than the combined citizen populations of the GCC states. It occupies the only part of the peninsula that can sustain agriculture on a large scale. It is the only nonmonarchical regime on the peninsula. It faces many of the same economic and political problems that its neighbors do, but in very different circumstances. While an oil-producing country (approximately 300,000 barrels per day in 1995), its revenues are much less than those of its neighbors and its population much larger. It has gone further than the other peninsula states in developing electoral political institutions but faces serious problems in stabilizing and integrating its political life.

The years 1990–95 were extremely eventful in Yemen. In May 1990 the former states of North Yemen (Yemen Arab Republic) and South Yemen (People's Democratic Republic of Yemen) agreed to end two decades of conflict and tension between them by uniting into the Republic of Yemen. Unity had been on the political agenda in both Yemeni states since the 1950s, when the imamate ruled in the North and the British were the colonial masters in the South.[62] However, the end of the Cold War (the Soviet Union had been the South's major ally) and the chance to jointly develop oil resources near their border brought the two sides together. The resulting political structure—an uneasy amalgam of the military regime of 'Ali 'Abdallah Salih, president of North Yemen, and the Yemeni Socialist Party, which had governed the South—was hardly a model of efficiency or clarity. But both sides seemed committed, at the beginning, to making it work.[63]

The new Republic of Yemen had the misfortune of facing a major international crisis almost immediately upon coming into existence. The Iraqi invasion of Kuwait forced the new government to make a historic choice. The importance of the choice was magnified by the fact that, by chance, Yemen held the Arab seat on the U.N. Security Council during the crisis. In the end Yemen refused to support the dispatch of coalition forces to Saudi

Arabia. For the Saudis, this stand by a country to which it had given substantial amounts of aid was tantamount to a stab in the back, and the Saudis reacted harshly. In the fall of 1990 the Saudis forced hundreds of thousands of Yemeni guest workers in the kingdom to return to Yemen, severely reducing Yemen's major source of foreign exchange—workers' remittances.[64] The returnees exacerbated a serious unemployment problem in the country and strained the already inadequate public services provided in San'a, the capital. The economic problems caused by the Gulf War contributed to a marked increase in crime, both in San'a and the tribal countryside, and increased the tensions between the uneasy partners in the coalition government.

Everyone in Yemen looked to the country's first democratic parliamentary election, in April 1993, to clarify the political picture. A vigorous and open campaign preceded the poll, with newspapers publishing rival party platforms and candidates holding rallies to bring their message directly to the voters. International monitors pronounced the elections free and fair, though Yemenis complained of intimidation, interference, and vote rigging by the two ruling parties—President Salih's General People's Congress and the Yemeni Socialist Party. Of the 301 seats at stake, the GPC won 124 directly and perhaps 30 more as independents joined the grouping. The YSP won 56, all in the areas of former South Yemen. The Reform Party, an amalgam of tribal, Islamist, and business interests, won 62. A coalition government of the three parties was then formed.[65]

Far from settling the political tensions, the elections exacerbated them. Violent incidents, particularly attacks on YSP members, increased. The head of the YSP, 'Ali Salim al-Bayd, who had been president of South Yemen and who was now vice president of the united state, refused to come to San'a to assume his duties, remaining in Aden, the capital of the former state in the South. The military forces of the former states, which had not been integrated into a single command structure, began to square off in hostile confrontations. In April 1994 war erupted, initiated by forces loyal to Salih and supported by tribal and Islamist groups in the Reform Party. Elements of the YSP, led by al-Bayd and supported by other Southern groups (ironically, groups with which the YSP in the past had been at daggers drawn), declared the South an independent state and sought international recognition. Saudi Arabia supported the breakaway state diplomatically, and, if opposition reports are correct, with arms also, but did not recognize it.[66] The fighting ended in July 1994, when forces of the unified state occupied Aden and Mukalla, the two strongholds of the separatists.[67]

Since the end of the civil war, Salih and the Reform Party have governed Yemen in an uneasy coalition. The state faces serious economic problems, including persistent budget deficits and the political difficulties in implementing structural adjustment policies mandated by the International Monetary Fund.[68] Relations with Saudi Arabia have improved somewhat. The two sides agreed in February 1995 to renew their existing border agreement (dating from 1934) and to explore ways to demarcate the large sections of the border that have not been defined.[69] The various border committees set up in that agreement have been meeting regularly. However, reports persist of occasional armed clashes along the border, and many in Riyad undoubtedly have not yet forgiven 'Ali 'Abdallah Salih for his stand during the Gulf War.

Conclusion

The focus of political energies in all the states of the Arabian Peninsula has shifted from the foreign policy realm, which was dominant from the 1970s through the Gulf War of 1990–91, to domestic affairs. The outside world is still important. The future of Iraq, tensions within the GCC, Iran's relations with the peninsular states, the future of the Arab-Israeli peace process, and relations with the United States all remain on the foreign policy agenda. However, the most important political issues facing peninsular states today revolve around the twin challenges of managing economic change and responding to increasing popular demands for greater political participation. How the states resolve those challenges will determine the nature of their politics as they enter the twenty-first century.

Notes

1. It is extremely difficult to find accurate and official figures on the liquid reserves of the Saudi government. *Middle East Economic Survey*, January 25, 1993, B3, puts usable Saudi government reserves at $7.1 billion at the end of October 1992, though other analysts involved in Gulf financial matters put the figure much higher, closer to $20 billion. The *New York Times* published a two-part series on the Saudi financial situation (August 22, 1993, 1, 12; August 23, 1993, 1, A6) in which they quoted an unnamed Saudi official as estimating the country's liquid reserves at $7 billion. In a response to these articles, the Saudi finance minister, Muhammad Aba al-Khayl, wrote that the kingdom had a $20 billion hard currency fund to support the national currency, and that Saudi banks had hard currency assets in excess of $15 billion. Part of Aba al-Khayl's response was published as a letter to the editor in the *New York Times*, August 26, 1993, A18. The full text of the letter can be found in *Middle East Mirror*, September 2, 1993, 20–22. Al-Shal Consultancy, a respected Kuwaiti economic analysis firm, put Kuwaiti foreign reserves at $35 billion and Ku-

waiti foreign debt at $30 billion at the end of 1994. See al-Shal reports in *al-Hayat*, January 28, 1995, 9; and February 25, 1995, 9.

2. Oil price figures taken from British Petroleum, "BP Statistical Review of World Energy," June 1994. The Saudi estimate of $14 per barrel is from "Saudi sets $40 billion 1996 budget, deficit $4.93 billion," Reuters (on-line), January 1, 1996.

3. These numbers are very rough estimates, since none of the governments involved released a full accounting of their financial relations during the Iran-Iraq war. For a careful investigation of this issue, see Gerd Nonneman, *Iraq, the Gulf States and the War*, 95–104.

4. See F. Gregory Gause III, *Oil Monarchies: Domestic and Security Challenges in the Arab Gulf States*, 147–48, for war expenses figures. A number of the themes discussed here are developed at greater length in this book. On the Saudi 1996 budget, see "Saudi sets $40 billion 1996 budget, deficit $4.93 billion," Reuters (on-line), January 1, 1996. On the economic consequences of the Gulf War in general for the Middle East, see Yahya Sadowski, *Scuds or Butter? The Political Economy of Arms Control in the Middle East*.

5. For longitudinal data, see *Demographic Yearbook—1991* (New York: United Nations, 1992), table 1, p. 103, table 3, pp. 106–11. For most recent data, see *1995 World Population Data Sheet* (Washington: Population Reference Bureau, 1995).

6. There is a substantial scholarly literature on the unique political economy of these kinds of states, called *rentier* or *distributive* states, where the government gets its revenue not from taxing its citizens but directly from the world economy through the sale of oil. See Jacques Delacroix, "The Distributive State in the World System," *Studies in Comparative International Development* 15 (1980); Hazem Beblawi and Giacomo Luciani, eds., *The Rentier State*; Jill Crystal, *Oil and Politics in the Gulf: Rulers and Merchants in Kuwait and Qatar*; Khaldun Hasan al-Naqeeb, *al-mujtama' wa al-dawla fi al-khalij wa al-jazira al-'arabiyya* (Beirut: Markaz Dirasat al-Wahda al-'Arabiyya, 1987). Some important work has recently been done questioning some of the conclusions of the earlier rentier literature. See particularly Kiren Aziz Chaudhry, "The Price of Wealth: Business and State in Labor Remittance and Oil Economies"; idem., "Economic Liberalization in Oil-Exporting Countries: Iraq and Saudi Arabia," in Iliya Harik and Denis Sullivan, eds., *Privatization and Liberalization in the Middle East* (Bloomington: Indiana University Press, 1992); and Eric Davis, "Theorizing Statecraft and Social Change in Arab Oil-Producing Countries," in Eric Davis and Nicolas Gavrielides, eds., *Statecraft in the Middle East* (Miami: Florida International University Press, 1991).

7. *al-Hayat*, January 3, 1995, 1, 4; *New York Times*, January 3, 1995, A3; "Saudi wants to quickly balance budget," Reuters (on-line), January 9, 1995; Christine Hauser, "Saudi Arabia cuts back desert wheat farms," Reuters (on-line), July 2, 1995.

8. Ashraf Fouad, "Saudi 1995 budget deficit slightly above target," Reuters (on-line), January 15, 1996.

9. Diana Abdallah, "Saudi economy healthier, but more challenges ahead," Reuters (on-line), June 11, 1995.

10. "Saudi sets $40 billion 1996 budget, deficit $4.93 billion," Reuters (on-line), January 1, 1996.

11. Youssef Azmeh, "Qatar confident after loan deal for huge gas field," Reuters (on-line), June 19, 1995.

12. *al-Hayat*, August 23, 1995, 1, 6.

13. "Drop in oil income to raise Bahraini budget gap," Reuters (on-line), November 30, 1994.

14. "Oman narrows budget deficit," Associated Press (on-line), January 15, 1996.

15. William Maclean, "Kuwaitis angry at asset fall, weigh deficit cut," Reuters (on-line), January 18, 1996.

16. Personal communications with financial analysts in Saudi Arabia and the United States.

17. "Drop in oil income to raise Bahraini budget gap," Reuters (on-line), November 30, 1994; Agence France Presse (on-line), November 28, 1995.

18. Randall Palmer, "Oman may be overdoing expansion, economists say," Reuters (on-line), January 19, 1995; *al-Hayat*, June 23, 1995, 1, 6; United Press International (on-line), December 27, 1995.

19. Youssef Azmeh, "Qatar confident after loan deal for huge gas field," Reuters (on-line), June 19, 1995; "Qatar issues law to establish stock exchange," Reuters (on-line), July 3, 1995; Hilary Gush, "Qatar bourse seen soon, privatisation later," Reuters (on-line), July 12, 1995.

20. "Kuwait auctions share of industrial concern," Reuters (on-line), June 22, 1995; "Kuwait outlines petrol station privatisation," Reuters (on-line), September 11, 1995.

21. For an extensive discussion of the privatization issue in a theoretical context, see Kiren Aziz Chaudhry, "The Myths of the Market and the Common History of Late Developers." For an informed treatment of this issue and more general economic dilemmas facing the GCC states, see Vahan Zanoyan, "After the Oil Boom: The Holiday Ends in the Gulf," *Foreign Affairs* 74, no. 6 (November/December 1995): 2–7.

22. Bahraini officials are considering doubling the cost of work permits and renewals of such permits for foreign workers, in the wake of serious social unrest on the island at the end of 1994 and the beginning of 1995. "Bahrain might raise work permit fees for foreigners," Reuters (on-line), September 23, 1995. Saudi Interior Minister Prince Na'if ibn 'Abd al-'Aziz, whose country increased the cost of foreigners' work permits at the beginning of 1995, told the Saudi Press Agency that "replacing the expatriate work force by Saudi nationals is a strategic goal of the state." "Saudi to replace expatriates by Saudis, Minister says," Reuters (on-line), July 20, 1995.

23. For a full discussion of the "petition fever" in the Gulf during 1990–92, see Gause, *Oil Monarchies*, 78–101.

24. For a more detailed account of the 1992 Kuwaiti elections, see Gause, ibid., 101-5.

25. *al-Hayat,* July 13, 1995, 5.

26. For an extensive and very critical review of the Basic System, see Middle East Watch, "Empty Reforms: Saudi Arabia's New Basic Laws," May 1992.

27. For a discussion of the royal decrees, see Gause, *Oil Monarchies,* 105–12.

28. On the second Omani Council, see *al-Hayat,* November 21, 1994, 1, 4; and November 27, 1994, 4.

29. For a discussion of the Omani and Bahraini Councils, see Gause, *Oil Monarchies,* 112–16.

30. "Qatar's Emir Eyes Democracy," Associated Press (on-line), November 14, 1995.

31. On the new Bahraini cabinet, see *al-Hayat,* June 27, 1995, 1, 6; on the new Saudi cabinet, see *al-Hayat,* August 3, 1995, 1, 6.

32. Opposition accounts of the events in Bahrain can be obtained from the monthly publication of the Bahrain Freedom Movement, the London-based Bahraini opposition group. The publication, *Voice of Bahrain,* is published in English and Arabic versions. It can be obtained from the Bahrain Freedom Movement's Washington address (P.O. Box 987; Washington, D.C. 20044) or via e-mail at 100542.1623@compuserve.com. For a discussion in English of the beginnings of the recent disturbances from the opposition point of view, see *Voice of Bahrain,* no. 37 (January 1995), and no. 38 (February 1995). Human Rights Watch/Middle East reported in December 1994 that two people had died in the first weeks of the disturbances and many had been seriously injured. See "Widespread Arrests of Pro-Democracy Activists in Bahrain," Human Rights Watch/Middle East press release, December 19, 1994. For government statements on the beginnings of the disturbances, see "Bahrain protesters kill policeman—ministry," Reuters (on-line), December 17, 1994; *al-Hayat,* January 13, 1995, 1, 4, and January 16, 1995, 1.

33. *al-Hayat,* January 23, 1995, 1, 4.

34. The minister of labor and social affairs said the unemployment rate, which had been as high as 13.8 percent in 1993, had been brought down below 5 percent in 1995; Agence France Presse (on-line), November 28, 1995. The U.S. Embassy in Manama published an economic analysis of the country for 1996 that put unemployment at 15 percent. Christine Hauser, "Bahrainis hope all roads lead to jobs," Reuters (on-line), January 22, 1996.

35. See the editorial by Bahraini newspaper columnist Hafedh al-Shaykh, "al-bahrayn: shay'un min al-musarah ghayr ma'huda" (Bahrain: Some unusual straight talk), *al-Quds* (London), April 20, 1995.

36. For an English-language text of the 1994 petition, see Bahrain Freedom Movement, *Voice of Bahrain,* no. 35 (November 1994). For a report on the October 1995 petition, see Agence France Presse (on-line), October 14, 1995, and Bahrain Freedom Movement, *Voice of Bahrain,* no. 47 (November 1995). On the April 1995 women's petition, see the October 12, 1995, press release of Human Rights Watch/Middle East, "Bahrain: Harassment of Pro-democracy Women Activists."

37. "Bahrain seeks reconciliation with Shi'ite foes," Reuters (on-line), September 5, 1995.

38. *al-Hayat*, January 20, 1996, 1, 6; "Bahrain army ready to put end to Shi'ite unrest," Reuters (on-line), January 20, 1996; "Bahrain arrests eight opposition leaders," Reuters (on-line), January 22, 1996.

39. "Bahrain court sentences three to death," United Press International (on-line), July 1, 1996; "Bahrain jails nine for planting bomb, leaflets," Reuters (on-line), July 9, 1996.

40. "Seven Die in Bahrain Attacks," Associated Press (on-line), March 14, 1996.

41. For discussion of the upsurge in Islamic political activism in Saudi Arabia, see Gause, *Oil Monarchies*, 31–40, 96–97; and R. Hrair Dekmejian, "The Rise of Political Islam in Saudi Arabia," 627–43. On the deportation proceedings against al-Mas'ari, see Gerrard Raven, "Britain orders Saudi dissident to leave," Reuters (on-line), January 3, 1996.

42. For the Saudi Interior Ministry statement, see *al-Hayat*, September 27, 1994, 1, 4. For the official announcement of the number of those arrested and the release of the 130, see *al-Hayat*, October 17, 1994, 3. For an opposition account of the incident, including the claims of thousands of arrests, see Committee for the Defense of Legitimate Rights (London), communique no. 20, September 18, 1994. Anonymous Western diplomats put the number of arrests during this period between four hundred and five hundred. "Hundreds Arrested in Riyadh," Associated Press (on-line), September 19, 1994.

43. *New York Times*, October 6, 1994, A5; "Saudis Create Muslim Councils," Associated Press (on-line), October 8, 1994; *al-Hayat*, October 9, 1994, 4.

44. *al-Hayat*, August 13, 1995, 1, 6. For the CDLR's response to the execution, see its detailed press release "Saudi judicial murder marks beginning of new stage in the confrontation between the regime and its opposition," London, August 13, 1995.

45. "Bomb suggests Saudi opposition," Associated Press (on-line), November 14, 1995. For a general, and very critical, discussion of recent politics in Saudi Arabia and the emergence of the Islamist opposition, see Alain Gresh, "The Most Obscure Dictatorship," *Middle East Report* no. 197 (November-December 1995), 2–8.

46. *al-Hayat*, August 29, 1994, 1, 4; September 5, 1994, 1, 4; November 13, 1994, 1, 4; "Oman pardons political prisoners," Reuters (on-line), November 5, 1995.

47. *al-Hayat*, June 28, 1995, 1, 6; see also the reporting on Qatar in Reuters (on-line), June 28, 1995, and United Press International (on-line), June 27, 1995.

48. Steven Swindells, "Qatar's new ruler consolidates power," Reuters (on-line), January 10, 1996. On the Qatari coup attempt, see *al-Hayat*, February 22, 1996, 1, 6; February 26, 1996, 1, 6; February 29, 1996, 1, 6; and March 1, 1996, 1, 6.

49. Carol Giacomo, "U.S. medical team said sent to treat Fahd stroke," Reuters (on-line), December 4, 1995; "Saudi king delegates authority," Associate Press (on-line), January 1, 1996.

50. "Oman deputy minister dead, sultan unhurt in crash," Reuters (on-line), September 12, 1995; *al-Hayat*, September 17, 1995, 1.

51. Corruption is one of the most talked about but most difficult to document issues in the politics of the GCC states. A number of books purport to demonstrate

the financial and moral peculations of ruling family members. One of the most recent is Said K. Aburish, *The Rise, Corruption and Coming Fall of the House of Saud.* Aburish's work, like most of the others in this vein, does not contain reference notes or supporting documentation. But without a doubt, ruling family members have benefited financially from their political position in all these countries.

52. Reuters (on-line), October 24, 1995, and October 26, 1995. Both reports from the biannual meeting of the GCC finance and economy ministers.

53. Ashraf Fouad, "Gulf Arab military integration gains steam," Reuters (on-line), January 21, 1996.

54. See Gause, *Oil Monarchies,* 130–32 for a discussion of these two disputes.

55. Ibid., 132–37.

56. "Saudi to send first envoy to Jordan in five years," Reuters (on-line), November 8, 1995.

57. *New York Times,* October 1, 1994, 1.

58. Ashraf Fouad, "Qatar says Enron can sell gas in Mediterranean," Reuters (on-line), March 13, 1995.

59. *al-Hayat,* January 28, 1996, 1.

60. "U.S. to create 5th Gulf fleet," Associated Press (on-line), June 29, 1995.

61. Gause, *Oil Monarchies,* 140–43; Charles Aldinger, "Saudis decline to base U.S. arms," Reuters (on-line), November 4, 1994.

62. For background on Yemeni politics, see Robert Burrowes, *The Yemen Arab Republic: The Politics of Development, 1962–1986;* Helen Lackner, *PDR Yemen;* Robin Bidwell, *The Two Yemens;* and F. Gregory Gause III, *Saudi-Yemeni Relations: Domestic Structures and Foreign Influence.*

63. On the politics of unification, see Charles Dunbar, "The Unification of Yemen: Process, Politics and Prospects."

64. See *New York Times,* November 28, 1990, 14; and *al-Hayat,* September 21, 1990, 1, for accounts of the changes in Saudi labor policy that forced the return of the Yemeni guest workers.

65. Sheila Carapico, "Elections and Mass Politics in Yemen"; Renaud Detalle, "The Yemeni Elections Up Close."

66. Committee for Defense of Legitimate Rights (London), communique no. 9, "Saudi Role in the Yemeni Crisis," May 28, 1994.

67. For accounts of the war, see Michael Hudson, "Bipolarity, Rational Calculation and War in Yemen"; David Warburton, "The Conventional War in Yemen"; Sheila Carapico, "From Ballot Box to Battlefield: The War of the Two 'Alis." All three of the authors were in Yemen during the war.

68. Assem Abdel-Mohsen, "Yemen cabinet approves budget, cuts down deficit," Reuters (on-line), January 14, 1996.

69. *al-Hayat,* February 26, 1995, 1, 4; February 27, 1995, 1, 4.

PART III

North Africa

11: North Africa in the Nineties

Moving Toward Stability?

Mary-Jane Deeb

The Maghrib has undergone some important changes, both political and economic, in the first half of the 1990s. Algeria, Morocco, and Tunisia have all had multiparty elections and have undertaken major economic reforms. Although the regimes of the Maghribi states, including Libya, have faced a strong Islamist opposition, it was only in Algeria that this opposition turned into a civil conflict that could have destabilized the whole region. Finally, the Maghrib has moved closer to the European Union (EU) economically, which could have significant implications for the future stability of the region.

Political Developments and Political Reforms

Each country of the Maghrib has fared differently in political terms. Algeria descended into chaos as a civil war of enormously destructive proportions engulfed it in the past four years. By contrast Morocco and Tunisia went through a relatively calm period of multiparty elections and majority support for the economic policies and political choices made by their governments. Libya did not fare well, with tribal uprisings and an attempted coup in 1993.

Algeria

In Algeria, it was Shadhli Bin Jadid, president from 1978 to 1992, who started the process of political and economic reforms in the mid-1980s. He liberalized the economy, encouraged privatization, opened the country to limited foreign investment, and supported domestic private investment. He appointed a number of prime ministers like Muhammad Sharif Messadia, Mawlud Hamrush, and Sid Ahmad Shazali, rather than retain the powers of this office, as his predecessors had done. By 1987 he had moved away from socialism and adopted a free market approach to the economy. That same year he allowed the Algerian League of Human Rights to be formed and various independent political organizations, critical of the government, to operate freely. Despite these reforms there was deep dissatisfaction in the country, and major strikes and riots broke out in October 1988. The military was used to put down the riots and hundreds were killed in the ensuing confrontation.

As a result of that crisis, Bin Jadid introduced further reforms. In February 1989 a new constitution was drafted by the National People's Assembly and approved by a national referendum. The constitution no longer maintained that Algeria was socialist or a one-party state; it separated religious institutions from the state and allowed the formation of political associations. It also abolished the restriction that limited candidacy for parliament to members of the Front de Liberation Nationale (FLN), and it allowed candidates from different parties to compete for parliamentary seats. Electoral districts were created on the basis of a proportional representation system. A seat was won by a simple majority of the vote. Nationally, if no party won a majority, then the one with the highest number of votes was awarded 51 percent of the seats. The rest were divided among the parties that had received at least 7 percent of the total vote, in proportion to their winnings. In 1991 the National People's Assembly increased the number of seats to 430 from 261, which had been in force since 1976.

Political parties were subsequently legalized by new legislation, and over fifty parties were formed in the following two years. In June 1990, the first free and fair local elections in Algeria's postindependence period took place. The Front Islamique du Salut (FIS), or Islamic Salvation Front, got the lion's share of the vote, spelling the demise of the FLN.[1] This organization comprised a number of militant Islamic groups opposed to the government of Bin Jadid. In July 1991, Bin Jadid resigned as secretary general of the FLN, which had broken up into several factions following the elections.

National elections were held in December 1991 (table 11.1). More than fifty political parties participated, but the FIS was the clear winner in the first round. Two hundred seats had to be decided in the second round of the elections, set for January 16, 1992. It was apparent that the FIS would win again, and by more than the two-thirds majority needed to transfer parliamentary powers from the Bin Jadid regime to the Islamist opposition. The military, headed by the minister of defense, Major General Khalid Nizar, fearful of such a transfer of power, called for the suspension of the second round of elections and the resignation of the president. Shadhli Bin Jadid resigned on January 11, 1992.

The military then created an advisory council (the High Security Council) headed by Nizar and another major general, Larbi Bil Khayr. The council took power, voided the December 1991 electoral results, and suspended all political institutions. It then created another council, the High Council of State, headed by an old independence leader, Muhammad Boudiaf, who had been in exile in Morocco for over thirty years, to act as a transitional government.

To protest such policies, Islamists fought back in mass demonstrations and acts of violence against government forces. A state of emergency was imposed, the National Assembly was suspended, the FIS was banned, and local and municipal assemblies controlled by Islamists were dissolved. There were mass arrests and imprisonment of FIS leaders. The country fell into a state of civil war as Islamists began a campaign of assassinations and violence, first against government forces, then against civilian targets. The government responded with ruthless military force. On June 29, 1992, Boudiaf was assassinated, allegedly by a member of the military. By 1993 more radical Islamist groups such as the Islamic Armed Group (GIA) had emerged, and the casualties of the civil war rose to an average of five hundred a week. It is estimated that over 60,000 Algerians have lost their lives between 1992 and 1997.

Table 11.1. Electoral results in Algeria (December 26, 1991, first round)

Party	Votes	% of vote
FIS (Front Islamique du Salut)	3,260,222	47.3
FLN (Front de Libération Nationale)	1,612,947	23.4
FFS (Front des Forces Socialistes)	510,661	7.4
Hamas (Mouvement de la Société Islamique)	368,697	5.3
Independents	309,264	4.5
RCD (Rassemblement pour la Culture et la Democratie)	200,267	2.9
MNI (Mouvement de la Nahda Islamique)	150,093	2.2
MDA (Mouvement pour la Democratie en Algérie)	135,882	2.0
PRA (Parti du Renouveau Algerien)	67,828	1.0
PNSD (Parti National pour la Solidarité et le Developpement)	48,208	0.7
PSD (Parti Social Democrate)	28,638	0.4
MAJD (Mouvement Algerien pour la Justice et le Developpement)	27,623	0.4
Others	177,389	2.5

Source: Journal Officiel de La Republique Algerienne Democratique at Populaire, 4 January, 1992. Quoted in Arun Kapil, "Algeria," in Frank Tachau ed., *Political Parties of the Middle East and North Africa* (Westport: Greenwood Press, 1994), 26

Since January 1992 Algeria has not had a working parliament. A consultative body called the National Consultative Council was created in February 1992 to act in its place and legislate. In 1993 a five-member High Council of State was created to govern the country until the end of the year. It then turned over its powers to a National Transitional Council of two hundred members, which became the new government of transition. The council represented certain professional associations and business groups but did not include Islamists or members of major political parties such as the FLN or the Front of Socialist Forces (FFS). In January 1994, Liamine Zeroual was appointed president by the military leaders, and he then chose a prime minister to head the transitional council.

On November 16, 1995, Algeria held national presidential elections. There were four candidates: Liamine Zeroual, the acting head of state; Mahfudh Nahnah, president of the moderate Islamist movement, Mouvement de la Societe Islamique (Hamas); Sa'id Sa'adi, general secretary of the primarily Berber Rassemblement pour la Culture et la Democratie (RCD); and Nur al-Din Boukrouh, president of the Parti du Renouveau Algerien (PRA). The turnout was very high: 74.92 percent of registered voters participated, and the elections were seen by most as free and fair. Zeroual won by a comfortable majority of 61.3 percent. Nahnah received 25.3 percent of the vote; Sa'adi, 9.2 percent; and Boukrouh, 3.7 percent.[2] Those elections strengthened Zeroual and weakened the FIS and the other Islamist groups. Zeroual is perceived as a moderate who wants to negotiate with the Islamists to put an end to the conflict.

In June 1997, legislative elections were held in Algeria. They were monitored by observers from the United Nations, the League of Arab States, and the Organization of African Unity. Forty-one parties competed for 380 seats. The RND, the government party, won 156 seats and its close ally, the FLN, won 64. Two Islamist parties, Al-Nahda and Hamas, won together 103 seats, and the Berber-based parties, the RCD and the FFS, won 19 and 20, respectively.

After five years of violence and the death of an estimated 60,000 people,[3] there appears to have been a reassessment of the situation in Algeria reflected in its 1997 legislative elections. Whereas in 1991 voting for the FIS was not merely an expression of support for Islamists but also a protest vote against government policies, Algerians were more careful how they cast their votes in 1997. First, more Algerians went to the polls: in 1991 just over 50 percent of eligible voters, in 1997 over 65 percent. The results show that support for radical Islamist groups had declined and that people wanted the restoration of law and order when they voted overwhelmingly for the RND. Also in contrast to the 1991 elections, all parties seemed intent on becoming part of the political process, and the government appeared ready to share power, at least to some degree. Thus while the electoral law prohibited the participation of parties that promoted a religious, regional, or ethnic agenda, religious and ethnic parties were included in the elections. Al-Nahda and Hamas between them received most of the Islamist vote with FIS supporters voting heavily for Hamas, and the RCD and FFS receiving the Berber vote in regions such as Tizi Ouzou that are heavily populated by Berbers. (These observations on the 1997 elections are based on the author's presence as a United Nations delegate in Algeria in June 1997.) After the elections and as a conciliatory gesture toward the Islamists, the government released two major FIS leaders, 'Abassi Madani and 'Abd al-Qadir Hashani. In turn, Madani made declarations condemning violence. They were later returned to prison.

Overall this new legislature may become a forum wherein all major opposition forces are represented (with the exception of the most radical Islamist groups) and where a dialogue can take place between the government and the various opposition parties. On the other hand, that legislature may not be effective because it is only one of the two legislative chambers of the Algerian parliament. The members of the other chamber are either appointed or indirectly elected. Furthermore, the revised Constitution of 1996 has given enormous power to the president, and the military is still the most powerful institution in Algeria.

Morocco

The most recent elections in Morocco were held in June 1993. The major opposition parties closed ranks and formed the National Front in 1992 to contest government policies and to demand electoral reforms, guarantees of fair elections, the lowering of the minimum age for voting, and greater powers for the legislature. King Hasan then proposed amendments to the constitution to meet some of the demands of the National Front. This resulted in the fairest and most representative elections in Morocco since its independence. The National Front included the Istiqlal, Union Nationale des Forces Populaires (UNFP), Union Socialiste des Forces Populaires (USFP), Organisation de l'Action Democratique et Populaire (OADP), and Parti du Progres et du Socialisme (PPS). A new party was also formed in 1991, the National Popular Movement (MPN), representing rural, Berber, and pro-monarchy tendencies.[4]

The parliament of 1993 had 333 deputies, 222 of whom were directly elected by popular vote, and 111 indirectly elected by electoral colleges of local officials still primarily loyal to the king. Twelve parties and two trade unions participated, with the pro-government party, the Union Constitutionelle (UC), winning 54 seats, the USFP 52, the rural Berber Mouvement Populaire (MP) 51, the Istiqlal 50, and the supporters of King Hasan, the Rassemblement National des Independents (RNI), 41. In addition to the organizations that had participated in the 1984 elections, three other parties were included in 1993: an old nationalist party, Parti Democratique de l'Independence (PDI); the leftist Berber intellectuals' Parti de l'Action (PA); and the Mouvement Populaire National (MPN), another rural Berber party (table 11.2).

Politically, the 1993 elections may have been the freest yet in Morocco's history and also the most inclusive. Although by no means a democracy yet, since the king is the final authority on all things, it has certainly become a much more pluralist society, in which political participation has increased significantly. Islamist groups, however, cannot form political parties and run in elections, although their candidates can do so if they run as independents. 'Abd al-Salam Yasin, the head of the most influential Islamist group in Morocco, the Association for Justice and Charity, has been

Table 11.2. Seats in Moroccan Parliament based on electoral results (1984 and 1993)

	1984	1993
Progovernment		
Mouvement Populaire	31	33
Rassemblement National des Independents	38	28
Union Constitutionelle	55	27
Movement National Populaire	—	14
Parti National Democratique	15	14
Total	139	116
Opposition		
Union Socialiste des Forces Populaires	34	48
Parti Istiqlal	23	43
Parti du Progrès et du Socialisme	1	6
Opposition pour l'Action Democratique et Populaire	—	2
Total	58	99
Other		
Parti Democratique pour l'Independence	—	3
Parti de l'Action	—	2
Independent (no party allegiance)	—	2

Source: Government of Morocco, quoted in Mark A. Tessler et al., "The Kingdom of Morocco," in David Long and Bernard Reich, eds., *The Government and Politics of the Middle East and North Africa* (Boulder, Col.: Westview Press, 1995), 381.

under house arrest since 1989. The estimated number of supporters and sympathizers of Islamist groups range from 3 million to a few thousand, and the number of Islamist associations is estimated at around fifty.[5]

Their welfare activities are banned, as well as their proselytizing. In 1992, riot troops cracked down on Islamist students at the University of Rabat, and many were arrested and remain behind bars.

Unlike the case in Algeria, Islamists in Morocco have had a difficult time mobilizing support against the monarchy. The skillful manner in which the king has played up his Commander of the Faithful role and his descendance from the Prophet Muhammad, and the gradualist approach he has taken to introducing change in a very traditional Moroccan society, have certainly been factors that have prevented those movements from becoming more popular.

Tunisia

Since its inception the National Assembly in Tunisia has been completely dominated by the Neo-Dustur party (and its various manifestations, the Parti Socialiste Destourien, or PSD, and, since 1988, the Rassemblement Constitutionel Democratique, or RCD). In 1988 the National Assembly passed a somewhat restrictive law prohibiting the formation of political parties on the basis of religion, ethnicity, or region. Legally recognized parties were authorized to collect dues from their members and to manage their offices. On all other matters, including meetings outside their headquarters, they were required to ask permission from the Ministry of Interior. Parties that were legalized and that participated in the 1994 elections included the RCD, Mouvement Socialiste Democratique (MDS), Mouvement pour le Renouveau (the old Tunisian Communist Party), Parti de l'Union Populaire (PUP), Rassemblement Socialiste Progressif (RSP), Parti Social pour le Progres (PSP), and Union Democratique Unionioniste (UDU). On the other hand, organizations such as the Islamist Al-Nahda movement were not legalized, because of their religious platform. They therefore could not run as a party in the national elections, although they could send candidates to run but only as independents.

In December 1993, the National Assembly passed amendments to the electoral law of 1988. The majority list voting system was modified by a system of proportional representation. Of the 163 seats, 19 were allocated proportionately to slates that did not win a majority. In the national elections of March 1994, Tunisians were asked to vote for the president and the National Assembly. Zayn al-'Abdin Bin 'Ali, the only presidential candidate, won with 99.91 percent of the vote, while the RCD won with 97.73

percent of the total vote. The other six parties and the independents shared among themselves 2.27 percent of the vote, of which half went to the MDS. They also shared the nineteen parliamentary seats allotted to them by virtue of the 1993 amendment of the electoral law (table 11.3).

It is clear that this multiparty system is not functioning as it should. Some of the reasons for those skewed electoral results may be found in some of Tunisia's electoral laws. For instance, when Munsif Marzuqi, the ex-president of the Tunisian League of Human Rights (LTDH), attempted to run as an alternative candidate for the presidency, he found he was ineligible. His candidacy could not be supported (according to the law) by thirty members of parliament or heads of municipal councils. The reason for this was that all mayors in Tunisia, except for one, were members of the RCD, and all 1989 National Assembly deputies were also RCD members, and supporters of Bin 'Ali.[6]

Another reason for the poor showing of the political opposition is that some of the parties (namely, the RSP and PSL) were relatively new and had very weak political bases of power to start with. They were able to present their lists of candidates in fewer than a third of the twenty-five electoral districts.

The more established parties such as the MDS fell victim to Bin 'Ali's strategy of coopting into the RCD or the government cadres from the opposition parties. Feuds among the party leaders, unclear platforms, lack of funds, and little access to the mass media contributed further to their dismal showing at the polls.

Table 11.3. Results of the legislative elections in Tunisia, March 20, 1994

Parties	% of total vote	Seats
RCD (Democratic Constitutional Rally)	97.73	144
MDS (Socialist Democratic Party)	1.08	10
Ijtihad Movement	.39	4
UDU (Union for Democratic Unity)	.32	3
PUP (Party of Popular Unity)	.29	2
RSP (Socialist Rally of Progressive Unity)	.06	0
PSL (Social Liberal Party)	.06	0
Independents	.03	0
Total	100.00	163

Source: Based on Denoueux, "Tunisie: les elections presidentielles et legislatives, 20 Mars 1994," 49–72.

By contrast the RCD had a clear platform, a vast network of professional associations, rural cooperatives, and labor syndicates that supported it. Since 1988 it had brought in new and younger cadres, technocrats who knew how to run a media campaign. Furthermore, Bin 'Ali's message of ensuring the security of the state was very powerful indeed, as Tunisians watched with deep concern the events unfolding in Algeria. No other party could begin to deal with this issue. Finally, the turnout at the polls was extremely high: 95 percent of eligible voters turned out, with women overwhelmingly supporting Bin 'Ali and his party.[7]

Libya

On January 21, 1992, the UN Security Council unanimously adopted Resolution 731, implicating Libyan government officials in the blowing up of Pan Am flight 103 and the French UTA flight 77. The resolution demanded that the Libyan government "respond effectively" to requests by the United States, Great Britain, and France "to cooperate fully in establishing responsibility for the terrorist acts." When the Security Council determined that Libya had *not* responded effectively to those requests, it passed Resolution 748 in April 1992, with 10 votes in favor and 5 abstentions. The resolution banned flights to and from Libya; prohibited the supply of aircraft, aircraft parts, or craft maintenance, and the sale or transfer of military equipment of any kind; and decided that all states should significantly reduce diplomatic personnel and staff in Libyan embassies.[8] The sanctions have been renewed several times.

Undoubtedly, the sanctions have had a punitive impact on the Libyan economy, making the transfer of goods and the movement of people more difficult and time consuming. There is also no doubt that Qadhdhafi has tried every means to have the embargo lifted except turning over to the United States or the UK the two men accused of involvement in the explosions. In seeking to have the sanctions lifted, Qadhdhafi addressed the issue of terrorism. In response to Resolution 731, Qadhdhafi reportedly ordered the closing down of Abu Nidal's offices in Tripoli in April 1992, and a month later the People's Committee for External Liaison and International Cooperation issued a statement formally renouncing terrorism.[9] There have been no reports of acts of international terrorism carried out by the Qadhdhafi regime since then.

There has been unrest in the country since the sanctions were imposed, although that may have nothing to do with the sanctions. A reported coup attempt in October 1993, led by a colonel with the assistance of certain army units, was foiled. Fifteen hundred people were arrested and hundreds executed. This led to new cuts in the military, shifts of military units from one area to another, and the appointment of members of Qadhdhafi's tribe to sensitive posts within the military.[10] In March 1995, there was tribal unrest in Cyrenaica and in the Jufrah region, some 150 miles from Sirte. There were again major clashes between the tribes and the security forces, and reports of casualties.

The Qadhdhafi regime, just like those of Mubarak, Bin 'Ali, or Zeroual, is perceived by militant Islamic movements as a regime that is too secular and that has become anti-Islamic. As in other countries of North Africa, the Islamic opposition in Libya has called for the overthrow of the regime and its replacement by an Islamic government.

In reaction Qadhdhafi has taken the same stand as the other North African leaders, namely, denouncing the movements in no uncertain terms, cracking down on the various movements, and also trying to appeal to his people by playing the Muslim leader. Until the late 1980s the major Islamic opposition included the Muslim Brothers (the *Ikhwan*), the Hizb al-Tahrir al-Islami, the Islamist wing of the National Front for the Salvation of Libya, and the Jihad al-Islami. Now, however, Islamic groups appearing on the scene have names more familiar in the Egyptian or Algerian contexts than in Libya, including Takfir wal-Hijra, al-Tabligh, and al-Jama'a.[11] The significance of this is that the Arab leaders of North Africa have closed ranks against the Islamic opposition and ipso facto have included Qadhdhafi in their ranks. They share information on those groups and are cooperating to limit their activities in North Africa.

In August 1995, before the signing of Oslo II, Qadhdhafi undertook a major propaganda exercise concerning the expulsion of some 35,000 Palestinians working in Libya. The intent was, supposedly, to demonstrate that the peace agreements between the Israelis and the Palestinians did not meet the needs of the Palestinian people and ought, therefore, to be rejected by the Arab states. What was not advertised was the fact that Libya had been expelling foreign workers since 1994, starting with the Thais, then sub-Saharan Africans in May 1995, Somalis in June 1995, Egyptians in August, and finally 70,000 Sudanese in December 1995. Repatriation of more Sudanese took place in 1996.[12] It is clear that those mass expulsions of foreign workers had little to do with the peace process, but reflected the inability of the Libyan government to provide work, housing, health care, and other services to 2.5 million foreign workers and their families. In fact, the Tripoli news agency JANA reported that "the main reason for dispensing with foreign workers is care for [the] public interest . . . with regard to

... food, health, environment and security. ... The humanitarian condition of those workers attracted ... attention as well. While we considered them our guests, we were ashamed when they slept in the streets or when they worked at menial tasks."[13]

The other reason for expelling foreign workers was that some of them—especially the Sudanese, the Egyptians, and some of the Palestinians—had links with Islamic groups in their home countries and were providing support for Islamic opposition groups in Libya.

The Maghrib and the Peace Process

The rule of thumb about the Arab world and the peace process is that the regimes in power support the peace process, while the Islamic opposition groups reject it. Those in power support the peace process for a variety of reasons, but primarily because the cost of the conflict has been too high and support from the West, particularly the United States, the only remaining superpower, is conditional, in part at least, on a peace settlement. The Islamists reject peace with Israel because they see it as giving sovereign rights over a piece of the land of the Islamic Umma to non-Muslims. One notable exception to this rule has been the Libyan regime.

Libya

Qadhdhafi has always been in the vanguard of those who denounced Israel and supported the Palestinian cause. The years did not mellow him, and he strongly denounced Arafat and the Declaration of Principles of September 1993. He also expressed his disapproval of the Oslo II agreements of September 1995. Having said that, there are a number of regional and domestic issues that may soften his position on the peace process and make him less adamant against recognizing a two-state solution promoted by the Palestinians.

On May 31, 1992, a group of around two hundred Libyans crossed from the Rafah area into Israel to visit Muslim holy places on the occasion of 'Id al-Adha. Egyptian authorities and the Israeli Tourism Ministry helped coordinate the visit. Concomitantly Qadhdhafi invited Libyan Jews who lived in Europe, Israel, and the United States to visit Libya. Rafael Felah, head of the World Association of Jews from Libya, claimed that the visit was planned in mid-February, when he visited Qadhdhafi.

On the other hand, the pilgrims claimed that they had come because Saudi Arabia had refused to allow them to fly directly from Libya to Riyadh and so chose to go on pilgrimage to Jerusalem instead. An Israeli businessman, Yaaqov Nimrod, cooperating with Saudi businessman 'Adnan Khashoggi, apparently was also involved in planning this episode and made statements to the effect that Qadhdhafi would visit Israel within a year.[14]

Although this visit was probably a ploy to use Israeli goodwill to help lift the UN sanctions imposed on Libya,[15] and to improve Libya's image in the West, it demonstrates that even Qadhdhafi, the most radical of North African leaders, is willing, provided his interests are served, to deal with Israel, and would probably eventually even recognize its right to exist.

Qadhdhafi today is less willing to support Islamic groups anywhere in the Middle East because of their links to the Libyan Islamist opposition. Those Islamist groups also oppose the peace process. So although Libya is officially against the Oslo agreements, it is in no position to support the opponents of the peace process. Those include all Palestinian Islamic groups, such as Islamic Jihad and Hamas, and also those in Egypt, Algeria, Tunisia, and elsewhere. Furthermore, Libya has relied on states such as Egypt and Morocco to intercede with the United States and the United Nations to lift the sanctions on Libya. Both Egypt and Morocco are staunch supporters of the peace process and are engaged in fighting Islamic organizations in their midst. They have exerted pressure on the Libyan regime to moderate its stand.

At the UN in October 1995, Libya's foreign minister, 'Umar al-Muntasir, addressed the General Assembly and argued for the lifting of the sanctions against Libya, saying it was innocent of the bombing of Pan Am 103. He then addressed the issue of Israel and the Palestinians. He criticized Israel's nuclear threat to the region, its policies in Lebanon and the Golan Heights, and its confiscation of Palestinian land. He also talked about Libya's "effective contribution toward resolving many regional disputes by peaceful means"[16] but never addressed the peace process or the Oslo II agreement. Having followed Libyan rhetoric for years, I would say that this demonstrates a definite change in tone: first, because the Oslo agreements were not criticized in this international forum, and second, because al-Muntasir spoke of using "peaceful" means to resolve regional disputes.

Tunisia

Tunisia has never taken the lead in the peace process. It has followed other states in North Africa. Since 1993, the Tunisian government has gone out of its way to show its support for the peace agreement. It has invited delegations of Tunisian-born Jews to visit Tunisia, encouraged tourism of Israelis to Tunisia, hosted conferences with Tunisian Jews in Paris at UNESCO, and held major events in Washington in 1993 around the theme of Jewish culture in Tunisia. Tunisian officials also like to remind Westerners that it was Bourguiba who first talked about peace with Israel in 1965, and he was boycotted by Arab states all over the region for having made that statement publicly.

On the day of the signing of the Oslo II agreements, the Tunisian Foreign Minister Habib Bin Yahya agreed to speak on Israeli television, the first time ever by any high-ranking Tunisian official. He stated, "To the Tunisian-born Jewish community, [I wish] to tell them that Tunisia, the land of peace, which stood for dialogue and moderation, is playing the same role and is committed to achievement of peace, a comprehensive peace and the sooner the better, because I think time is of [the] essence for everybody."[17]

When the foreign minister was asked what role Tunisia was playing in the peace process, he admitted that it was a very discreet role, "a catalytic role with the Palestinians."[18] He also said that he had been personally involved in the last stage of the Taba negotiations and suggested that Tunisia could play a role in the negotiations with Syria and Lebanon.[19]

Tunisia has also opened "interest sections" in the Belgian embassies in Tunis and Tel Aviv in 1994. Although not embassies because there is no peace treaty yet between the two states, this is a way of normalizing relations gradually until such treaties are finally signed.

Algeria

The official Algerian position, although positive, has been cool. The government of President Zeroual supported the Palestinian-Israeli agreement with some reservations. The official statement by the spokesman of the Foreign Ministry, after the signing of the Oslo II agreement in September 1995, was that "Algeria considers the agreement a step aimed at achieving the constant national rights of the Palestinian people, particularly their right in establishing their independent state with Holy Jerusalem as its capital."[20]

This statement is not very supportive of the Oslo II agreements: first, because neither the head of state nor the minister of foreign affairs made it; second, because the statement mentions only the Palestinians and Palestinian rights, and Israel is not mentioned at all; and third, because the emphasis is placed on Jerusalem, although the issue of Jerusalem was not part of the negotiations. The explanation for this cool support lies in the domestic situation of Algeria. While the Algerian leadership wishes to accommodate the West, work out its relations with Israel and follow in the footsteps of Egypt, Jordan, and Morocco, it has to contend with the Islamist groups within its territory. Those groups, like their counterparts throughout the region, have rejected unconditionally the peace accords. In order not to further alienate the Islamists, the Algerian leaders have had to toe the line in supporting the accords while doing it for all the "right" reasons. In other words, they have to be seen as supporting the peace process for the sake of the Palestinians and for the sake of Islam, to ensure that Jerusalem remains in the hands of Muslims and is not lost to the Israelis.

Morocco

King Hasan II of Morocco has always supported peace negotiations with Israel, and he had secret meetings with Israelis long before Sadat went to Jerusalem. In the summer of 1977, Hasan hosted a secret meeting of Moshe Dayan and Hasan al-Tuhami, a prominent Egyptian and a special envoy of Sadat in Morocco, to discuss Egyptian-Israeli relations. In July 1986, King Hasan met publicly with Prime Minister Shimon Peres at Ifrane in the Atlas mountains of Morocco. He was only the second Arab leader, after Sadat, to meet officially with an Israeli head of state. Syria broke its diplomatic relations with Morocco because of that meeting. Hasan has continued to promote better relations with Israel in the Arab world. He has tried to persuade the Saudis to develop ties with Israel. A day after the signing of the DOP in September 1993, Hasan welcomed Israel's prime minister, Yitzhak Rabin, to Rabat to show his support for the peace accords.

In October 1994, Morocco hosted the Casablanca Economic Conference for the Middle East, which brought together 2,500 people—900 government officials and 1,600 businessmen from the Arab world, Israel, Europe, and the United States. It was the first time that an Arab country had included Israel as a full partner in a discussion that was not about finding a solution to the Arab-Israeli conflict but about planning for regional economic growth and development in the region. In his opening speech the king said, "This original conference has been convened to consolidate the pillars and to provide peace with the means to become widespread, durable and inclusive of the entire region, so that everyone can live in tranquillity and quietness, preserve dignity, and respect sovereignty."[21] In September 1994 Morocco announced that it would have official ties with Israel at the level of liaison offices in Rabat and Tel Aviv but has not yet signed a peace treaty with Israel.

Economic Developments and Economic Reforms

Relative to other parts of the Arab world, Morocco, Tunisia, and even Libya appear to be doing better, while Algeria is not faring too well, primarily because of its domestic political crisis.

Economic reforms were introduced gradually in Morocco in the 1980s but remained fairly consistent for a decade. They included deficit reduction, trade liberalization, financial market development, structural reforms in pricing, and incentives for private investment. Morocco is not an oil exporter and therefore could not rely on a significant rent to finance its public sector. Instead it chose to create low-wage jobs in export-oriented industries and gave investors incentives to create jobs rather than substitute technology for labor.

Some of the major World Bank economic indicators show that those policies were successful. In the 1990s Morocco had a higher growth in incomes, in exports, and in jobs than during the 1980s. In 1991 Morocco's unemployment rate was 12 percent, not much higher than unemployment in France today.[22] A decade earlier, experts had estimated that unemployment ranged from "20 to 30 percent in the cities and probably averages 40 percent in the rural areas."[23] Exports rose from $2.145 billion in 1985 to over $4 billion in 1994, and GNP per capita rose by approximately 20 percent during that period. The GDP also rose from $14.7 billion in 1981 (in 1981 dollars) to $26.635 billion in 1993 (in 1987 dollars).[24] On the negative side, however, the total debt increased from $16.526 billion in 1985 to $22.096 billion in 1994 (in 1987 dollars) (table 11.4).

In Tunisia, the picture is even brighter. Structural adjustment reforms were adopted early in 1985, after its external current account deficit reached a record level of 10 percent of GDP, and disposable foreign exchange reserves dwindled to nothing.[25] In order to meet its financial obligations,

Table 11.4. Economic indicators in Morocco (in $ millions)

Indicator	1990s	1980s
GDP	$26,635 (in 1993)	$14,780 (1981)
GNP per capita	$1,040 (in 1993)	$860 (1981)
Military spending	$692 (in 1992)	
(proportion of GNP)	4%	6.1%
Total debt	$22,096 (1994)	$16,526 (1985)
Balance of trade	-$3,108 (in 1994)	-$1,716 (1985)
Exports	$4,036	$2,145 (1985)
Imports	$7,144	$3,861 (1985)
Average rate of inflation	6.6% (1980–93)	6.6% (1980–93)

Sources: World Bank, *World Development Report 1983: World Economic Recession and Prospects for Recovery* (New York: Oxford University Press, 1983); World Bank, *World Development Report 1995: Workers in an Integrating World* (New York: Oxford University Press, 1995); *Claiming the Future: Choosing Prosperity in the Middle East and North Africa* (Washington, D.C.: The World Bank, 1995).

Tunisia turned to the IMF for help and received $180 million in standby credit provided it started a major structural adjustment program. The program worked so well that Tunisia has a higher growth in exports, job creation, and income per capita than any other country in the region. According to World Bank data, GDP growth per capita for the period 1990–94 was 2.10 percent; the average rate of inflation hovered around 6 percent during the period 1984–94, and the non-oil exports growth rate, for the same period, was 10.5 percent.[26] Foreign direct investment more than doubled to $200 million between 1990 and 1993,[27] largely because of the economic and tax incentives Tunisia offered foreign investors. Poverty was reduced almost by half in the last decade, and today Tunisia has one of the lowest rates of poverty in the world.[28] Unemployment, however, remains relatively high, at 16 percent in 1993, but social services provided by the state ensure that people do not fall between the cracks (table 11.5).

An article that appeared in the French *Marches Tropicaux et Mediterraneens* in August 1995 on Libya's economy argues that since the country's economic and financial activities are based on petroleum revenues, and those have not been significantly affected by the UN sanctions, then the economy is in relatively good shape.[29] The article uses a number of indicators to support this thesis:

1. Libya has a very small external debt (mostly to Turkey, India, South Korea, and Russia), $4.34 billion or 18 percent of GNP, and services it at the rate of $765 million a year, or 10 percent of its export revenues.

2. Although until 1986 Libya's balance of trade sheet always showed a surplus, often exceeding $3 billion, it has since shown a small deficit, due to the fall in the price of oil. The deficit has risen to $1.7 billion in the past year, but that is not serious enough to cause concern.

3. Although there has been a decrease in its international reserves between 1993 and 1994, this has been due to the decline of oil exports and to capital transfers from Eurobanks to Bahrain banks, starting in 1992. The reason for the transfer is that Libya fears expanded UN economic sanctions and a European freeze of its foreign accounts.

Libya also continues to invest in Europe through its holding company Oil Investments International Company (Oilinvest). It was set up in 1988 and registered in Curaçao with a capital of $450 million. Libya has invested in Italy, Germany, and Switzerland, and is expanding its activities in Spain

Table 11.5. Economic indicators in Tunisia (in $ millions)

Indicators	1990s	1980s
GDP	$12,784 (1993)	$7,100 (1981)
GNP per capita	$1,720 (1993)	$1,420 (1981)
Military spending	$355 (1992)	3.9%
Total debt	$9,495 (1994)	$4,884 (1985)
Balance of trade	-$1,926 (1994)	-$1,012 (1985)
Export	$4,638 (1994)	$1,729 (1985)
Import	$6,564 (1994)	$2,741 (1985)
Average rate of inflation	7.1% (1980–93)	7.1% (1980–93)

Sources: World Bank, *World Development Report 1983: World Economic Recession and Prospects for Recovery* (New York: Oxford University Press, 1983); World Bank, *World Development Report 1995: Workers in an Integrating World* (New York: Oxford University Press, 1995); *Claiming the Future: Choosing Prosperity in the Middle East and North Africa* (Washington, D.C.: The World Bank, 1995).

and France. The company owns 2,730 service stations and gasoline distribution centers in Europe and a number of refinery plants in Italy and Switzerland.[30]

International transport of people and goods has been directly affected by the UN sanctions. It has become more expensive and more difficult. Tens of thousands of Libyans used to fly to the Arab world and Europe on holidays or on pilgrimage and now have to use other means of transport. Because of the increased demand, land and sea transport has more than doubled in price. So has the price of some goods that were imported by air. Military spending has declined, as it has become very difficult for Libya to import military hardware or even spare parts for its military arsenal.

In terms of its overall economic situation, Libya has a relatively high per capita income of $5,700 and an estimated GDP of around $27.2 billion (1992 figure) for a small indigenous population of 5.2 million. The economy, however, is dependent for most of its revenues on earnings from the export of crude and refined oil and oil products. Those earnings fell from $11 billion in 1990 to approximately $7 billion in 1995.[31] Libya is also importing 75 percent of all its food needs, which represent 16 percent of its total imports. To improve agricultural production, the government in the 1980s undertook a $25 billion project to create an enormous pipeline for underground water (the Great Man Made River), which is beginning to irrigate agricultural crops on the coastal region of Libya. This, however, has not made Libya less dependent on imports for its basic food needs.

In Algeria major economic reforms were introduced in 1990–91, in the form of new legislation passed to encourage foreign investment, international trade, and joint ventures. One such law, the Law on Money and Credit of April 1990, liberalized Algeria's foreign investment code and allowed unrestricted joint ventures between private Algerian firms and foreign companies. In the hydrocarbon sector, however, foreign companies were limited to joint ventures with Sonatrach, the state-owned oil company. The new law formalized the legal framework for investment and permitted the repatriation of profits. Finally, the law prohibited multiple exchange rates, and the government devalued the Algerian dinar by almost 100 percent in a six-month period from the winter of 1990 to the spring of 1991.

Privatization was encouraged as early as the mid-1980s. In the agricultural sector, for instance, state farms were sold to the private sector, and land that had been collectivized in the 1970s was returned to individual farmers. Restructuring of the industrial sector achieved some success: stories such as that of the Societe Nationale de Constructions Mecaniques, a manufacturer of agricultural equipment, which was completely decentralized and became very productive, are not infrequent.[32]

The small-business sector was also encouraged and appears to be doing well. In 1993, there was a 2 million housing unit shortage in Algeria, and the problems in that sector were critical. Private firms were encouraged to work with government agencies to provide prefabricated construction materials and introduce new techniques to help meet the rising demand.

Algeria's oil reserves are expected to be depleted within three decades. Its significant gas reserves of an estimated 3,200 billion cubic meters, on the other hand, are expected to last for more than sixty years at 1992 production levels. Algeria has therefore restructured its state-owned oil and gas company, Sonatrach, and increased its exports of natural gas to Europe and to the United States. It liquefies natural gas and transports it through the existing trans-Mediterranean pipeline to Spain.

Trade relations with Western countries, especially the United States, improved significantly in the 1990s. US imports from Algeria rose to $2.6 billion in 1990. American companies signed multimillion-dollar contracts with Algerian companies, as did French and Italian firms. Pfizer signed a $27 million contract to build a pharmaceutical plant outside Algiers in 1990, and Occidental signed a $32 million oil exploration and production contract with Sonatrach in 1991. Forty percent of Algeria's imports in the 1990s came primarily from the European Union, while only 2 percent came from the countries of the Arab Maghribi Union.[33] One-third of its imports were foodstuffs, 10 percent were consumer goods, and the rest were industrial and semifinished products.

Tourism as a source of foreign exchange has been encouraged only since 1989. Foreign companies such as Hilton and the French Sofitel were allowed to open large tourist hotels in the early 1990s. A number of state-owned hotels became autonomous and had to run their business on a strictly commercial basis. The Algerian political crisis, however, has all but destroyed the budding tourist industry.

The Algerian foreign debt has been a major problem. Throughout the 1980s it kept growing. In 1980, Algeria's external debt was $19.365 billion, and it rose to $25.757 billion by 1993.[34] Between 1980 and 1989, the debt service ratio increased from 25 percent to 95 percent of export earnings,[35] leaving little or nothing to spend on internal development. In 1994, due to debt restructuring and cautious fiscal policies, those figures began to improve.

The Algerian crisis, however, has put a halt to a number of projects and has undermined not only the economic reforms but the confidence of foreign investors. It is not clear yet what the cost of the crisis is to the domestic Algerian economy and to private individuals, but it is certainly very high. The political crisis has only exacerbated the economic conditions in Algeria today (table 11.6).

Table 11.6. Economic indicators in Algeria (in $ millions)

Indicator	1990s	1980s
GNP per capita	$1,780 (in 1993)	$2,140 (1981)
GDP	$39,836 (in 1993)	$41,830 (1981)
Military spending	$1,59 (in 1992)	
(proportion of GNP)	2.7%	
Total debt	$27,225 (in 1994)	$18,260 (1985)
Balance of trade	-$972 (in 1994)[a]	$2,212 (1985)
Exports	$8,890 (in 1994)	$12,975 (1985)
Imports	$9,862 (in 1994)	$10,763 (1985)
Average rate of inflation	13.2% (1980–1993)	13.2% (1980–1993)

a. The balance of trade was positive in 1990, 1991, 1992, and 1993, when Algeria imported less than it exported.

Sources: World Bank, *World Development Report 1983: World Economic Recession and Prospects for Recovery* (New York: Oxford University Press, 1983); World Bank, *World Development Report 1995: Workers in an Integrating World* (New York: Oxford University Press, 1995); *Claiming the Future: Choosing Prosperity in the Middle East and North Africa* (Washington, D.C.: The World Bank, 1995).

The European Union and the Maghrib

In the mid-1970s the European Economic Commission became very actively involved in developing a zone of economic prosperity and political stability in the Mediterranean region. The approach it adopted then was based on the principle of linking the liberalization of trade with aid for development. The dominant concept was that developing countries needed the markets of the industrialized nations for their products while simultaneously needing to protect their own infant industries from competition from Western countries.[36]

When this classical development model failed to achieve its objectives, the European Union (EU) in the late 1980s and early 1990s designed a new set of agreements with the southern countries of the Mediterranean. The ultimate objective of those agreements remained the same: creating a zone of stability and prosperity around the Mediterranean. What changed was the means to achieve that goal. The agreements were bilateral between the EU and individual countries on the southern shores of the Mediterranean. To date, these agreements have been signed with both Tunisia and Morocco.[37]

The 1990s agreements focus on the liberalization of external trade in order to create a free trade zone in the Mediterranean. Under the 1970s agreements most Maghribi industrial products had duty-free access to the EU, while EU-manufactured products were subject to high tariffs when they entered Maghribi countries. There were preferential agreements with the EU for agricultural products from the Maghrib. The 1990s agreements stipulate that all trade barriers for EU industrial products entering Tunisia or Morocco be removed within a maximum period of twelve years. Tariffs on 40 percent of Tunisia's imports must be lifted within the next five years, while tariffs on 45 percent of Morocco's imports from the EU must be lifted in the next three years.[38]

The second part of those 1990s agreements includes strong incentives to encourage the states of the southern Mediterranean, namely, financial aid. For the period 1991–96 the European Investment Bank allocated $5 billion to the Mediterranean countries, $2 billion of which went to the Maghrib, half in the form of loans and half in the form of grants. The EU is increasing the aid for the period 1995–99 to $12 billion, divided in the same proportion between loans and grants.[39] The third element of those EU-Mediterranean agreements includes a political partnership to promote democracy, the rule of law, and the protection of human rights, in order to promote peace and stability in the region.

To achieve those goals the EU and the states on the southern shores of the Mediterranean agreed to meet on a regular basis and start a dialogue on economic and political matters. The first such meeting took place in Barcelona on November 27–28, 1995, when twenty-six countries, the Palestinian Authority, and the European Commission met for a two-day conference. The document produced at the end of the conference, the Barcelona Declaration, was made up of two parts: a set of resolutions and an annex called the work program. The annex defined the specific measures that needed to be taken in order to achieve the resolutions.

According to the Barcelona Declaration, the ultimate goal is to establish a "partnership" between the countries of Europe and those of the Mediterranean to transform "the Mediterranean basin into an area of dialogue, exchange and cooperation guaranteeing peace, stability and prosperity [that] requires a strengthening of democracy and respect for human rights, sustainable and balanced economic and social development, measures to combat poverty and promotion of greater understanding between cultures."[40]

To achieve those very ambitious objectives, the work program included numerous measures that ranged from preventing and combating terrorism to establishing a Middle East zone free of weapons of mass destruction, settling disputes by peaceful means, removing all trade and nontrade barriers on manufactured goods (but not on agriculture produce), structural adjustment reforms, the protection of intellectual property rights, development of efficient systems of telecommunications and information technology and protection of the environment.[41]

Conclusions

The Maghribi countries appear to be moving slowly toward developing more open and more liberal political systems in the 1990s. The three major powers, Morocco, Algeria, and Tunisia all held elections that were among the freest since their independence. The outcomes of those elections, however, were unexpected in at least two of the three countries. The Algerian legislative elections brought the Islamists to center stage: first, when they appeared to win the elections, then when the second round of elections was annulled, and finally, when the Algerian crisis, described by some as a civil war, erupted. In Tunisia, the elections demonstrated that the existing multiparty system was extremely weak, and the outcome, namely, the overwhelming victory of the dominant state-supported party, gave the impression that Tunisia was really moving back to an authoritarian, one-party type of political system. Only in Morocco did the elections hold no surprising outcome, although the power of the monarchy remains undiminished. If the Islamist threat is contained, then the process of democratization in North Africa is underway. If Islamists get the upper hand, then we may see a period of instability in the Maghrib.

Economically, the Maghrib has made significant progress in the 1990s. Structural adjustment programs encouraged by the World Bank, the IMF, and Western nations have begun to show positive results, especially in the cases of Tunisia and Morocco. Civil strife in Algeria has been the major obstacle to that country's economic development, despite its attempt at restructuring the economy and creating incentives for foreign investment. As long as security concerns exist, it is unlikely that much foreign or domestic investment will take place.

Overall, the political and economic prospects for the Maghrib in the 1990s are much more encouraging than they seemed a decade earlier. Domestic and regional developments, however, including the direction the Islamist movements will take, as well as the outcome of the peace negotiations on the remaining issues including the final status of Jerusalem, may affect those positive trends.

Notes

1. For a discussion of those elections, see Robert Mortimer, "Islam and Multiparty Politics in Algeria."

2. *Le Monde,* Paris, November 19–20, 1995, 4.

3. See Robert Mortimer, "Islamists, Soldiers and Democrats: The Second Algerian War."

4. For an excellent overview of parties in Morocco see Frank Tachau, ed., *Encyclopedia of Political Parties in the Middle East,* 387–421.

5. See report on Morocco by Marvin Howe, "Morocco Is Not Algeria, but Is It Heading in the Same Direction?"

6. See Guillain Denoueux, "Tunisie: les elections presidentielles et legislatives, 20 Mars 1994," 52–53.

7. Ibid., 49–72.

8. *New York Times,* April 1, 1992, A-12.

9. *FBIS-NES,* May 14, 1992, 12.

10. See "Libya, Critical Period Ahead: Will Foreign Investment in the Oil Sector Save the Government?," Petroleum Finance Company, Ltd., *Country Report,* December 1995, 12.

11. *FBIS-NES,* May 5, 1993, 16.

12. "Libya, Critical Period Ahead," 6.

13. Quoted in *FBIS-NES,* October 4, 1995, 33.

14. *New York Times,* June 3, 1993, A 10; also *Washington Post,* June 1, 1993, A 13.

15. See Joel Greenberg, "In an Overture to an Enemy, Libyan Pilgrims Visit Israel," *New York Times,* June 1, 1993, A3.

16. *FBIS-NES,* October 5, 1995, 21.

17. *FBIS-NES,* October 3, 1995, 37.

18. Ibid.

19. Ibid., 38.

20. FBIS-NES, September 29, 1995, 16.

21. FBIS-NES, Special Supplement on the Casablanca Conference, November 1, 1994, 2.

22. See *Claiming the Future: Choosing Prosperity in the Middle East and North Africa* (Washington, D.C.: World Bank, 1995), 54.

23. See Mark A. Tessler and John P. Entelis, "The Kingdom of Morocco," in David Long and Bernard Reich, *The Government and Politics of the Middle East and North Africa,* 3d ed. (Boulder, Col.: Westview Press, 1995), 397.

24. *Claiming the Future,* 107.

25. See Abdelsatar Grissa, "The Tunisian State Enterprises and Privatization Policy," 121.

26. *Claiming the Future,* 10.

27. Ibid., 19.

28. Ibid., 58.

29. The French-language article was translated and reproduced in *FBIS-NES,* September 15, 1995, 25.

30. Ibid., 28.

31. "Libya, Critical Period Ahead," 4.

32. Helen Chapin Metz, ed., *Algeria: A Country Study,* 150.

33. Ibid., 168.

34. World Bank, *World Development Report 1995: Workers in an Integrating World* (New York: Oxford University Press, 1995), 201.

35. Ibid, 171.

36. For a discussion of the 1970s ECC-Maghrib agreements, see William Mark Habeeb, "The Maghribi States and the European Community."

37. For a discussion of those agreements see Bertin Martens, European Commission, Directorate-General, Economic Financial Affairs, "The European Union and the Maghreb," paper delivered at the Middle East Institute and World Bank Conference, "MENA: Regional Prospects for Economic Development," Washington, D.C., November 20, 1995.

38. Ibid.

39. Ibid.

40. Text of the "Barcelona Declaration Adopted at the Euro-Mediterranean Conference (27 and 28 November 1995)," Barcelona, November 28, 1995, 3.

41. Ibid., 5–7.

12: The Sudan

Militancy and Isolation

Ann Mosely Lesch

The Sudan, a pivotal country in northeast Africa, lies astride the Nile River, adjoins the Red Sea, and juts into East and Central Africa. Its endemic political instability affects its neighbors and impacts on governments that seek access to or domination of those strategic waterways. The country is isolated internationally, wracked by civil war, and impoverished economically. The foreign and domestic policies adopted by its highly ideological regime have intensified its isolation. The country is caught in a vicious cycle, since that isolation has been used by the regime to justify and further harden its policy line.

The Sudan has been ruled since June 30, 1989, by military and security officers in conjunction with the National Islamic Front (NIF). It is a tightly organized political movement that seeks to enforce its particular Islamist ideology on all aspects of the citizens' lives. In its rigorous Islamizing drive, it seeks to overcome the heterogeneity of the society and to silence opposition.

The Sudan is the largest country in Africa, covering a million square miles. Its 26 million residents, scattered across that wide expanse, derive from a complex mix of ethnic groups. Arabic culture and ethnicity predominate even though a majority of the population is African in self-identification: Nubian, Fur, Nuba, Beja, Dinka, Shilluk, and numerous other groups in the far south. More than 70 percent of the citizens are Muslim by faith, including non-Arab peoples such as the Nubians, Fur, and Beja. Most southerners adhere to traditional African religions and perhaps 6 percent of the total populace is Christian, most of whom converted to Christianity during the Anglo-Egyptian condominium over the Sudan (1898–1956).

The politicization of ethnicity affects both internal politics and foreign policy.[1] The non-Arab peoples are marginalized politically, since the central government is controlled by (and predominantly benefits) the Muslim Arabized peoples of the Nile Valley around Khartoum, the capital city. The two major political movements are the Umma Party, which is supported by the quasi-religious Ansar (Mahdiyya) movement, and the Democratic Unionist Party (DUP), led by the Khatmiyya brotherhood. Fur and Nuba in the west, Beja in the east, and Nubians in the far north have some political and cultural influence insofar as they adopt Arabic in their discourse, are largely Muslim by religion, and link themselves to Umma or the DUP.

The residents of the south are doubly disadvantaged since they are non-Arab and largely non-Muslim. The British kept the south isolated from the north but then compelled that region to unite with the north when the country gained independence in 1956. Southerners are angered by central governments' measures to Arabize their education and administration, restrict Christian churches, denigrate traditional religions, and promote the spread of Islam. They consistently seek a federal system that would accord them political self-rule, including autonomous powers over education, the economy, and internal security. Considerable devolution of power took place from 1973 to 1983 under the Addis Ababa Accord of 1972, which ended seventeen years of civil war. But President Ja'far Numairi undermined that inclusive policy in 1983 when he stripped the region of its autonomy and instituted Islamic law (*Shari'a*).

Forced religious and linguistic homogenization caused a violent reaction. The south rose up again in rebellion, led by the Sudan People's Liberation Movement (SPLM), which demanded a secular constitution, the restructuring of power in Khartoum, and autonomy for marginalized peoples. Moreover, widespread dissent in the north led to a civil uprising in April 1985 that forced Numairi from power. Although a parliamentary system was instituted in the north, the civil war continued to rage in the south.

When northern political forces were on the verge of convening a constitutional conference that would address the SPLM's demand that a secular political system replace the Shari'a-based constitution, NIF and a small group of military allies seized power in 1989.[2] They closed the parliament, banned political parties and unions, and tore up the tentative accord with the SPLM. Brigadier General Umar Hasan Ahmad al-Bashir formed a fifteen-man Revolutionary Command Council (RCC) and a partly civilian Council of Ministers, in which NIF gradually assumed the dominant role. Under the state of emergency, the RCC banned any expression of political opposition and detained many politicians, union organizers, doctors, students, and army officers when they tried to organize strikes and demonstrations against the regime. The RCC also purged the armed forces, police, security services, judiciary, diplomatic corps, and civil service.

The government formed a Popular Defense Force (PDF), which now outnumbers the regular armed forces. Designed to reinforce religious zeal by leading the fight for "God" and "Islam" in the south, the PDF contains a mix of enthusiasts and press-ganged members. High school graduates are compelled to train in the PDF before they can enter the university; civil servants are required to undergo PDF training, which includes a heavy dose of religious indoctrination; and young men are rounded up to augment its ranks. The PDF is ill trained by military standards and has suffered heavy casualties fighting in the south.

NIF wields predominant influence in the government. Its leaders initially operated behind the scenes as advisers and hidden decision makers. However, even before the RCC dissolved itself in October 1993, NIF controlled the pivotal ministries of interior, justice, foreign affairs, education, culture, and social planning as well as most of the economic-oriented ministries. Most significantly, the second-in-command of NIF—Ali Uthman Muhammad Taha—became minister of social planning in July 1993 and foreign minister in February 1995.

Moreover, NIF adherents comprised the majority in the appointed Transitional National Assembly, which was formed in January 1992, and of the assembly elected in the spring of 1996. In line with NIF ideology, Shari'a law was applied to the north in 1991, with the south exempt from the punishments associated with only five of 186 articles. Christian institutions are restricted and virtually all foreign schools have been closed. Property and assets of the Khatmiyya order and the Ansar movement have been confiscated, including mosques. These measures seek to undermine the power of the movements and prevent adherents from assembling for religious holidays, since the movements often used those occasions to denounce the regime and call for the restoration of democracy. The closure of businesses for noon prayers on Friday, dress codes for women, and the ban on liquor are enforced by NIF's Guardians of Morality and Advocates of the Good. NIF's Revolutionary Security Guards interrogate and torture political dissidents in unofficial detention centers (known as "ghost houses") that are outside the control of the prisons authority.

NIF's leader Hasan al-Turabi (a former law professor who served as attorney general under Numairi) has not entered the government directly, although he became speaker of the assembly in 1996. There are, nonetheless, indications of tension between the military and civilian wings of NIF and also within the civilian wing. NIF civilians are wary of Bashir's occasional efforts to form local-level popular committees and councils, since those could dilute their control. Military officers find the PDF a hindrance on the battlefield, where its forces are ill prepared for combat. Some military and security officers criticize Turabi and Taha's enthusiasm for militant Islamist groups. When Sudanese security operatives were implicated in the attempt to assassinate Egypt's President Husni Mubarak in June 1995, for example, Bashir replaced the NIF stalwart who was minister of interior with a nonpolitical intelligence officer. Turabi responded by placing the ousted minister in charge of NIF's security organs.[3] Moreover, some of the less ideological civilian members of NIF criticize the economic policies that have undermined the economy and the hosting of militant Islamist groups, which has resulted in trade sanctions against the regime.

The economy is near collapse, caused by the high cost of prosecuting the war in the south and decades of mismanagement and corruption. Economic strictures have left the urban public with limited access to health care, social services, quality education, and affordable food. Drastic shortages of bread, fuel, and heating oil force the government periodically to stop distributing rations and to raise prices. By 1993 inflation ran at over 150 percent.[4]

The Civil War

Opposition is led by the Sudan Peoples Liberation Movement and Army (SPLM/SPLA) in the south and, in exile, by the National Democratic Alliance (NDA), which was formed in October 1989 by the fifty-one unions and twelve political parties that the regime had just banned. The NDA charter called for a campaign of civil disobedience that would topple the regime and reinstate democracy. In September 1990 the NDA was joined by senior military officers whom the regime had cashiered, who termed themselves the Legitimate Military Command. SPLM and NDA leaders sought to ally against the regime, but they had difficulty agreeing on the future form of government. The SPLM insisted that the government be secular, open equally to all citizens, and with substantial devolution of power to the deprived regions. In contrast, DUP and Umma still sought a political system that would be predominantly Muslim and Arab in orientation. Not until April 1993 did they agree with SPLM that "laws shall guarantee full equality of citizens on the basis of citizenship and respect for religious beliefs and traditions."[5]

By then, the SPLM had fractured into warring factions due to the loss of vital Ethiopian support when Mengistu Haile Mariam was overthrown in May 1991 and to the heightened perception that the NIF regime would never accord equal rights to the south. Important southern politicians and commanders revived the call for secession, viewing that as the only viable solution to the conflict. These strategic shifts were compounded by personal rivalries among commanders, tensions between Dinka and Nuer officers, and the authoritarian behavior of SPLM commander John Garang toward his rivals. The government played off the intrasouthern strife by arming anti-Garang factions and launching major military drives that enabled it to regain control over virtually all the towns and garrisons. SPLA retained toeholds on the Uganda and Kenya borders.

The government rejected both the call for secession and the demand for a secular political system. Negotiations held in Abuja, Nigeria, in 1992 and 1993 foundered on these issues. Subsequent mediation by East African presidents (Kenya, Uganda, Ethiopia, and Eritrea) through the Inter-Governmental Authority on Drought and Development (IGADD) also failed to break the impasse. In April 1996 the government attempted to reach its own peace agreement with dissident southern factions that it had been arming to fight the SPLA. A year later the government promised those factions that the south could have autonomy and self-determination, but those promises appeared hollow to most observers, since there was no firm timetable for a popular referendum and the factions controlled only a fraction of the territory within the south. The promise appeared designed primarily to set southerners against each other at a time when the armed forces and PDF were retreating on the ground.

The southern economy has been devastated and the society fragmented and dispersed. By 1990 the UN estimated that 3.5 million of the 5.5 million residents had fled their homes.[6] The majority of the population is scattered throughout the south, living in crude shantytowns in the north or in refugee camps in neighboring countries. Fighting has also engulfed the Nuba Mountains, where the government quells Nuba opposition by bombing and burning villages, forcibly removing Nuba to other regions, and bringing in Arab tribal groups to farm the land. Other non-Arab peoples in the north—notably the Ingessena, Fur, and Beja—also tend to be marginalized by the regime and have become engaged in conflicts with the armed forces and Arab militias.

By mid-1995, the opposition began to regain the initiative. In June, Eritrea hosted a meeting of the NDA that included the SPLM, all the major northern political movements, and two groups of military officers who opposed the regime.[7] They issued the Asmara declaration that called for the establishment of a democratic political system based on the separation of religion and state. Moreover, for the first time, the northern political forces not only conceded the south's right to self-rule but also formally acceded to the south's right to self-determination. These policies meant that, should the proposed new political system fail, the south could opt to secede and the north would not try to force it to remain within the Sudan. Eritrean President Isaias Afwerki allowed those exiled officers and Beja tribal forces to establish training camps on its territory. This move put some muscle behind the call for a popular uprising to overthrow the Khartoum government, institute an interim authority, and restore democracy on a nonsectarian basis. Partly in reaction to these threats, the government detained former Prime Minister al-Sadiq al-Mahdi for the fifth time, from May 16 to late August 1995; thousands of Ansar demonstrated on June 2 in protest, with the implied threat of violence if he were harmed. By then, some of the SPLM factions had patched up their differences and regained control over substantial territory in Equatoria, pushing back the overextended and under-supplied armed forces and PDF recruits. Public demonstrations in the capital and other northern cities in September 1995 underlined the citizens' opposition to the regime and to the escalating cost of living. Several students were killed in clashes with NIF security forces. Calls for the overthrow of the regime intensified during 1996, but al-Mahdi's presence as a hostage inside the capital city put brakes on those efforts. Al-Mahdi then escaped to Eritrea in December 1996, becoming the NDA's premier diplomatic envoy and freeing the NDA to expand its military operations inside the north. That intensification was marked by the movement of NDA forces in early 1997 to within virtual striking distance of the hydroelectric power plants at Damazin.

Islamic Militants

The government made a dramatic gesture in August 1994 by extraditing Illich Ramirez Sanchez ("Carlos") to France, at the request of the French government, which sought him for decades-old bombings. Khartoum hoped to prove it did not host terrorist groups and thus persuade the U.S. government to take it off the list of countries supporting terrorism. However, the government's effort to convince people that it had no idea that Carlos was living in Khartoum was unpersuasive. It became evident that he had lived there for a full year, under the protection of Turabi. Carlos had been given a Sudanese diplomatic passport after he arrived from Syria. He had enjoyed an active social life at clubs and hotels and maintained close ties to Sudanese businessmen.

Moreover, Khartoum was placed on the defensive by Islamists and radical groups abroad who feared that extraditing Carlos meant that others were at risk. Sudan received protests not only from the Popular Front for the Liberation of Palestine (PFLP), with which Carlos had been associated, but also from Islamic Jihad (Palestine), Hizbollah (Lebanon), Islamists in Afghanistan, and Iranian politicians.[8] Turabi responded that Carlos was a "criminal" rather than a "politically persecuted" person or a revolutionary, since he had no ideology and "sold himself to various customers."[9] Another NIF official stressed that Carlos could not be compared with an Afghani Muslim fighting against the atheist Soviet Union. He emphasized that Islamist groups are not terrorists but freedom fighters since they fight Israel and secular Arab leaders. He argued that it is the duty of an Islamic country to give shelter to any Muslim who is threatened because of his faith.[10]

The arrival of large numbers of militants was facilitated when the government altered its visa requirements in 1990 to allow Arabs to enter without requiring a visa. Moreover, the interior minister could grant Sudanese citizenship and passports to Arabs: reportedly 120 Arabs from Egypt, Algeria, Tunisia, Libya, Jordan, and Palestine gained Sudanese nationality in March 1994 alone.[11] Further changes in the nationalization law in June 1994 enabled the president to grant citizenship to non-Arab Islamists, such as those from Afghanistan or Africa.

Diplomats reported that more than 5,000 Islamist militants resided in Sudan by mid-1994, many of whom were placed in camps, farms, and construction projects in various places in the north. During the previous year several governments had dumped unwanted persons on Sudan: Iran dispatched Revolutionary Guards; Syria sent persons affiliated with the PFLP, Abu Nidal, and other militant Palestinian groups in August 1993 (including Carlos) so they would not cause embarrassment during its negotiations with Israel; and Pakistan expelled "Afghan-Arabs" whose presence as *mujahidin* in Peshawar on the Afghan border had become a political burden.

Funds for their travel and sustenance were covered, in part, by Saudi businessman Usamah Bin Ladin, who moved to Khartoum in 1992.[12] He employed many of them in the construction and agricultural projects undertaken by his company. The Sudan provided him with a passport in 1994 when the Saudi royal family stripped him of his citizenship. Bin Ladin also maintained an office in London, where he cooperated with the Islamist opposition to the Saudi regime, and he had ties to the (Islamist) Islah Party in Yemen. In early 1996, however, Khartoum asked Bin Ladin to leave the country, since his presence was exacerbating relations with the United States and Saudi Arabia. Angered at his forced departure, Bin Ladin has reduced his financial involvement in the Sudan, leaving several agricultural projects to languish.

An unusual insight into the government's policies toward Islamist groups was provided by Aldo Ajo Deng, a southern politician who had been deputy speaker of the Transitional National Assembly. He took political asylum in England in late 1993, after he concluded that NIF's dominance precluded the government from negotiating seriously with the SPLM; rather, the regime was determined to achieve a military victory in the south so that it could enforce its ideology throughout the country. Ajo maintained that support for Islamist groups had several aspects:[13] (1) secret training in mosques and private farms near Khartoum and Shendi, led by Iranian and Arab instructors and funded by Bin Ladin; (2) secret training programs for militants from Iran, Arab countries, and the Horn of Africa inside public training centers for the PDF that were located throughout the north;[14] and (3) six-month training programs for Sudanese security personnel in Iran.

In addition, according to Ajo, foreign policy was controlled by President Bashir through his International Friendship Council and by Turabi through his Popular Arab and Islamic Conference (PAIC). These organizations (rather than the non-NIF foreign minister) decided on the basic lines of foreign policy and maintained contact with Islamist groups around the world. They even arranged for shipments of weapons and ammunition for the Afghan-Arabs and other militants, Ajo claimed. During 1996, Khartoum's policy began to change—largely in reaction to UN sanctions—as it tried to distance itself from this transnational Islamism. Turabi's PAIC has not reconvened and controls on obtaining visas tightened. Nonetheless, the government's relations with most of its neighbors remain antagonistic.

Antagonistic Relationships

Internal and foreign policy issues are necessarily closely intertwined.[15] Sudan's strategic location on the Nile and the Red Sea and its position adjoining eight Arab and African countries make it vulnerable to incursion. Tribal and linguistic groups straddle the borders. Its territory provides sanctuary for citizens of neighboring countries who flee famine and warfare; conversely, Sudanese flee to neighboring territories when they face political or economic hardship at home. Guerrilla forces find haven and establish bases: southern Sudanese guerrilla movements seek sanctuaries and support from Eritrea, Ethiopia, Uganda, and Kenya; Eritrean and Ethiopian forces used bases in Sudan from which to attack and overthrow the government in Ethiopia in 1991 and win Eritrean independence; and political dissidents from Uganda and Chad have also used Sudan as a sanctuary, with support from the Sudanese government.

Current foreign policy concerns are intimately related to the civil war in the south, the NDA's opposition to the regime, and NIF ambitions to spearhead the spread of Islamist movements into East and North Africa. Most neighboring governments have therefore become increasingly antagonistic toward the Khartoum regime.

The Horn of Africa. The civil war in the south was inevitably a regional issue, affecting the neighboring countries of East Africa. The IGADD initiative was motivated by those governments' concern about stability on their borders, since intra-Sudanese conflicts spill over onto their lands and the Khartoum government supports antiregime dissidents. Uganda accuses Khartoum of arming and training the so-called Lord's Resistance Army and other regionally based guerrilla forces. Eritrea, Ethiopia, and Kenya argue that the Sudan aids underground Islamist groups in their countries. Sudanese troops also bomb or make incursions into their territories in pursuit of the SPLA.

Of Sudan's black African neighbors, only Chad, Zaire, and the Central African Republic (CAR) have been neutral or friendly. Khartoum helped Idriss Deby seize power in Ndjamena in December 1990, and the two regimes cooperate to suppress Fur unrest along the Sudan-Chad border. Officials in Zaire and CAR have been bribed by the Sudanese government to let Sudanese troops cross through their territory in order to encircle the SPLA.

Relations with Kampala are particularly tense, since the SPLA receives military and relief supplies through Uganda. The Sudanese air force has even occasionally bombed sites on the Ugandan side of the border, where SPLA fighters and more than 330,000 civilians have taken refuge.[16] Khartoum also supports Ugandan opposition forces and uses its embassy and Islamic missionary organizations to subvert the government of President Yoweri Museveni. As a result, Uganda closed the border and expelled Sudanese diplomats in April 1995. Although Libya and Malawi then mediated accords between the two governments, neither regime changed its behavior. Museveni even stepped up support for the SPLA in an effort to expel the Sudanese armed forces from the border zone.[17]

Although Khartoum provided sanctuary for Tigray and Ethiopian exile movements and helped the current Ethiopian government overthrow Mengistu in 1991, President Meles Zenawi is now concerned about Khartoum's Islamizing zeal. He criticizes the placement of PDF bases near the border and argues that NIF indoctrinates Ethiopian refugees and supports Ethiopian Islamists as well as the Oromo Liberation Front. By July 1994, there were frequent border clashes, and in March 1995 Zenawi declared that he would not hesitate to declare war against Sudan if it did not stop supporting Islamist groups in Ethiopia.[18]

Nonetheless, after the attempt to assassinate Egyptian President Husni Mubarak in June 1995 near the Addis Ababa airport, Zenawi delayed blaming Sudan until September, when he formally accused Khartoum of providing sanctuary to the perpetrators and furnishing them with logistical support, including false passports and seats on Sudanair flights to and from Addis Ababa.[19] Zenawi slashed Sudan's diplomatic representation, closed the Sudanese consulate on the border at Gambela, and expelled Sudan's Islamist relief organizations that allegedly provided cover for subversive operations.

A similar shift took place between Khartoum and Asmara. Sudan had strongly supported the seizure of power by the Eritrean Peoples Liberation Front in May 1991 and the self-determination referendum in April 1993. But on January 1, 1994, President Afwerki charged that Sudan supported cross-border raids by Eritrean Jihad, which received training at NIF/PDF camps.[20] The two governments exchanged accusations: in fall 1994 Sudan denounced Eritrea for allegedly training 3,000 Sudanese (Beja) fighters and Eritrea accused Sudan of training up to 700 members of Eritrean Jihad. Eritrea severed diplomatic relations with Sudan in December 1994; efforts by Yemen to mediate came to naught. As in the case with Uganda, the government subsequently shifted from covert to overt support for Sudanese opposition groups. In May 1995, Afwerki publicly embraced the Sudan Alliance Forces and the Beja tribal militia, and in June Eritrea hosted the meeting of the NDA and SPLA that endorsed the violent overthrow of the Khartoum government. Asmara then became the de facto headquarters for the NDA.

What began as an effort by the governments of Kenya, Uganda, Ethiopia, and Eritrea to resolve peacefully the SPLA-government fighting shifted to all-out confrontation with Khartoum when the Sudan rejected their proposals and continued to destabilize the regimes. Those states argue that Sudan seeks to support and spread Islamist political movements that will seize power throughout East Africa. Only Kenyan President Daniel arap Moi maintains the effort to mediate, even though Khartoum allegedly supports the opposition Islamic Party of Kenya, based in Mombasa. Khartoum, in turn, calls the actions by its neighbors part of a plot against its Islamist beliefs. NIF cadres argue that it is Sudan that is encircled by ideological enemies, not Sudan that launches offensive operations. The tension feeds their zealotry rather than making negotiations more likely.

Egypt. Sudanese-Egyptian relations are also antagonistic. Cairo's primary concern is to guard its southern flank and its access to the Nile. It seeks a regime in Khartoum that will maintain its strategic interests and, if possible, promote economic cooperation. Although Mubarak initially welcomed Bashir as a fellow military officer, he quickly began to criticize NIF influence. Sudanese sympathy for Iraq during the Gulf crisis widened the rift. Egyptian officials even threatened to attack Sudan should rumors of Iraqi missiles on its soil prove true.

Since 1991 the conflict has assumed multiple forms: (1) contested claims concerning the border, specifically related to the Hala'ib triangle and the Wadi Halfa area; (2) tensions over the two countries' Nile Valley relationship, including river transport, properties, and water allocation; and (3) the provision of sanctuary for political opponents. The conflict culminated in September 1995, when Mubarak annulled the appointment of a new ambassador to Khartoum, in the wake of Ethiopia's presenting evidence of Sudanese collusion in the attempt to assassinate Mubarak.

The border between Egypt and Sudan was established at the 22nd parallel in 1899 by the two (then British-controlled) governments. However, an agreement in 1912 accorded Sudan administrative control over the Hala'ib triangle, a 20,000-square-kilometer area along the Red Sea just north of the 22nd parallel, since the local population was similar to neighboring Sudanese groups and since the area was remote from populated areas in Egypt. The issue of sovereignty flared up briefly in 1958, but Sudan retained administrative control virtually without incident until 1991; the residents held Sudanese identity cards and voted in Sudanese elections.

Then in 1991 Sudan offered a concession to a Canadian company to prospect for oil in Hala'ib. Egyptian companies were already exploring manganese and mica deposits there, and Cairo argued that Sudan did not control the subsoil. Egypt also alleged that local residents were paid to smuggle arms and explosives from Sudan into Egypt to help Islamist militants in Upper Egypt. This argument was used to justify beefing up Egypt's security presence in the triangle.

Although an Egypt-Sudan joint committee met in October 1992 and called for maintaining the status quo, Egypt acted swiftly to dominate Hala'ib. Cairo sent 600 troops that month, which it increased to two brigades (10,000 men) in May 1993.[21] The government issued an ultimatum to Sudan to cease all civil and political activities in Hala'ib town. Egypt blocked Sudanese efforts to include Hala'ib in its new national census, issued Egyptian citizenship papers to residents, and registered them to vote in Egypt. In a flurry of activity, Egyptian ministries upgraded the port and road system, began to prospect for oil, allocated funds to reclaim land, built housing projects, introduced water desalinization units, established radio and TV facilities, recruited Egyptian teachers and medical personnel, and even brought in preachers from al-Azhar. In 1994, Egypt appointed a governor and completed its demarcation of the border along latitude 22 with the construction of sand embankments and barbed wire fencing. In January 1995, Egyptian forces besieged Sudanese police posts. In late June 1995—days after the attempt to kill Mubarak—Egyptian troops expelled the remaining Sudanese officials and policemen.[22] Khartoum has protested continuously to regional and international organizations and declared that it would accept binding arbitration or a decision by the World Court. But Egypt's prominent role in the Arab League, Organization of African Unity, and (through then Secretary-General Boutros Ghali) in the United Nations helped to ensure that those protests remained ineffective.

The issue of the Arqin bulge, near Wadi Halfa and Lake Nasser, similarly relates to territory that crosses the 22nd parallel as well as to Egyptian fears of infiltration by armed Islamist groups. Sudan complains that, since 1993, Egypt has reinforced observation posts within the bulge and blocked Sudanese fishermen from access to the lake. Cairo responds that security controls are required to prevent gun-running from Sudan.

This issue further relates to the overall deterioration in bilateral cooperation. Since 1993 the Sudanese government has confiscated nearly all of Egypt's property in the Sudan: seventeen schools, the Khartoum branch of Cairo University, and sixteen properties and thirty-three guesthouses used by irrigation officials, embassy officials, and public sector companies.[23] Sudan claims these are Sudanese properties whose leases have expired, but the timing indicates that these were largely responses to Egyptian actions in Hala'ib.[24]

Similarly, each side detains ferries that operate between Wadi Halfa and Aswan. When Egypt placed armed guards on steamers in fall 1994, Sudan suspended traffic on the heavily traveled Nile route to Egypt. Egypt retaliated by demanding the dissolution of the Nile Valley Authority for River Navigation, in an official letter in January 1995.[25] Sudan angrily retorted that if this seventeen-year-old joint venture were liquidated, Khartoum would demand that other joint projects be dissolved. In July 1995, Turabi even stated that Sudan might alter unilaterally the terms of the 1959 accord on sharing the Nile waters: when he claimed that changes could be lethal to Egypt, Cairo warned him not to play with fire.[26]

The governments harass each others' citizens. In March 1993, Sudan held hostage the head of the Egyptian community in Sudan after Egypt detained eight Sudanese on charges of terrorism.[27] Egypt arrested thirty-one other Sudanese in May as spies, and Sudan arrested twenty Egyptian engineers and project workers in late June and three more in November, including the headmaster of the Egyptian Embassy school in Khartoum. Ultimately, all were released or swapped for Sudanese held in Egypt. However, in August 1994, the harassment escalated when a Sudanese court convicted an Egyptian of prostitution and bribery, and security forces attacked Egyptian diplomats while they drove in Khartoum.[28] In retaliation, Egyptian security men attacked a Sudanese diplomat in Cairo as he got out of his car near his home.[29]

The government later seized the headquarters of the Egyptian community in Khartoum, including the compound in which thirty-three Egyptian teachers lived; cut off the water, electricity, and communications to the Egyptian embassy, consulate, and residences; increased surveillance of Egyptian diplomats; requested three Egyptian diplomats to vacate their residences; and declared two Egyptian diplomats persona non grata. These measures were taken in the wake of Sudanese accusations that the Egyptian embassy was involved in an alleged plot by the Umma Party to assassinate Bashir and Turabi.

This mutual harassment occurs in the context of each government's support, to a degree, for political forces that seek the downfall of the other regime. Egypt has long provided sanctuary to Sudanese exiles on condition that they not engage in actions against their government. It has hosted Numairi since 1985, allowed the SPLM to open an office, and let the parties affiliated with the NDA maintain a low-keyed presence. As many as 3 million Sudanese have received sanctuary in Egypt.

However, the Egyptian government has kept them under numerous restrictions. They cannot protest in public or operate a radio station. They must be cautious in their public statements. They are not granted official refugee status and therefore few of them can receive support from the UN High Commissioner for Refugees (UNHCR), even though many live in difficult circumstances. Only after the attempt to kill Mubarak in June 1995 did the government allow Sudanese exiles to demonstrate in Cairo and arrange for Mubarak to receive a delegation from the NDA. But other measures taken at that time—notably the new requirement that Sudanese must obtain visas in order to enter Egypt—harm the Sudanese opposition more than they hurt the Khartoum government. Mubarak is wary of the NDA's promise of self-determination to the south, fearing that southern secession would harm its interests along the White Nile.

Despite Cairo's relative caution, NIF and Bashir have asserted that Egypt actively seeks to overthrow their government by supporting the NDA and SPLM and has even planned to invade. Mutual threats during the Gulf crisis escalated to the point that Sudan claimed in the spring of 1993 that the NDA was about to invade, assisted by an Egyptian warship and twelve Egyptian military helicopters as well as by sabotage specialists in the Egyptian embassy.[30] Mubarak responded that no invasion was planned but that, if Sudanese troops approached Hala'ib or if foreign (Iranian) naval units were based in Port Sudan, Egypt would strike back.[31]

Khartoum reacted by closing the Egyptian consulates in Port Sudan and al-Obeid and preemptively shutting its own consulates in Alexandria and Aswan. A year later, in June 1994, Khartoum alleged that the Egyptian embassy was involved in a coup plot supposedly organized by the Umma Party.[32] In that context, as noted, the government harassed the embassy and expelled two diplomats.

The Egyptian government accuses Sudan of providing sanctuary to Islamists from Egypt. Specifically, it argues that they are trained in sabotage, assassination, and bombing on NIF-run farms near Khartoum. In November 1994 and March 1995, Egypt asked Sudan to extradite fifty-four persons wanted in Egypt on terrorism charges. Egyptian security clashed with a group that was carrying weapons across the border in November 1994 and uncovered a substantial arms cache in June 1995 in a village 200 kilometers north of the border.[33]

Egyptian officials said that arms transfers had accelerated after Turabi promoted cooperation between Jihad and al-Gama'a al-Islamiyya, the two main Egyptian Islamist groups. The head of al-Gama'a, Mustafa Hamza, was viewed as the key person who instructed these groups, from his hiding place in a training camp near Khartoum. Mubarak was quick to blame Hamza and NIF for the assassination attempt in June 1995. Although the government denied any involvement, Turabi hailed the "mujahidin who pursued the pharaoh of Egypt," Bashir fired the militant NIF minister of interior, and Hamza slipped out of the country to Pakistan.[34]

A joint Egyptian-Sudanese committee that is intended to resolve disputes met three times in 1992 and early 1993, and the Sudanese foreign minister, neurosurgeon Husayn Abu Salih, eagerly met his Egyptian counterpart at the UN and in Cairo until he was replaced by an NIF stalwart in February 1995. However, Egypt refused to send its foreign minister to Khartoum for meetings, showing its displeasure at Sudanese policies. Moreover, Abu Salih was often uninformed in advance of actions—such as the confiscation of Egyptian property—and the NIF-controlled press criticized him for his accommodating tone toward Cairo. Mubarak was willing to meet Bashir only on the sidelines of regional conferences, generally at the urging of intermediaries such as Yasir Arafat of the Palestine Liberation Organization (PLO), Mu'ammar Qaddafi of Libya, and King Hassan II of Morocco. When Ali Uthman Muhammad Taha became foreign minister in 1995 and strongly asserted Sudan's claim to Hala'ib as well as its Islamist agenda, Egyptian officials refused to hold bilateral meetings with him when he came to Cairo for Arab League sessions. Soon after, Mubarak annulled the appointment of a new ambassador to Sudan. Nonetheless, Egypt opposes the complete isolation of Sudan by the international community, on the grounds that such isolation could lead the regime to even more extreme actions.

North Africa. Khartoum has antagonized its Arab neighbors in North Africa. Tunisia recalled its ambassador in 1992 and Algeria broke diplomatic relations in 1993, based on allegations that Khartoum was supporting Islamist groups in those countries.[35] Tunisia was angry, in part, because Sudan had provided a diplomatic passport to the leader of al-Nahda, Rached Ghannouchi. Turabi's claims that he could mediate among the Islamic Salvation Front (FIS), the Islamic Armed Group (GIA), the Algerian government, and Paris failed to impress Algerian President Liamine Zeroual. Zeroual may also have been wary of the terms of the compromise that Turabi apparently proposed: forming a coalition between the Islamists and the armed forces, perhaps along the lines of the NIF-Bashir regime. Zeroual and the military commanders would view that as a way to enable FIS to seize power from within.

In fall 1994, Mauritania accused Sudan of smuggling in arms for subversive groups that planned to assassinate cabinet ministers.[36] Even the Moroccan king was irritated by Turabi's comment that he was not a good Muslim and "not qualified to judge who is Islamic and who is not."[37] Hassan II was also annoyed by Bashir's impolitic statements about Mubarak while the king was trying to ameliorate relations.

The relationship with Libya is particularly complex. Qaddafi has long championed unity with Sudan, in part to gain enhanced strategic access to neighboring Darfur province. His greatest successes came in March 1990, when the two countries signed a "Charter of Integration," and in December 1990, when dissidents from Chad swept into power in Ndjamena from their bases in Darfur.

Since then, relations have deteriorated. On a visit to Khartoum in 1991, Qaddafi criticized NIF and called on Bashir to rid himself of Turabi's influence. In 1992, Libya stopped supplying oil to Sudan. In March 1993, when Sudan faced an acute oil shortage, Bashir flew to Tripoli, where Qaddafi made tough demands—remove NIF, reach an accord with the NDA, and improve relations with Egypt—but did resume some oil shipments in May.[38] Soon, however, Qaddafi feared subversion by Islamist militants, some of whom were apparently trained in PDF bases in Darfur. He was especially jittery after armed Islamist militants clashed with Libyan security forces in Benghazi in September 1995. Qaddafi responded by trucking 50,000 Sudanese to the border and ordering 300,000 others to leave by 1996 and by removing the Libyan ambassador from Khartoum.[39] However, Bashir did not dare to protest these expulsions, since Libyan oil remained vital to the existence of his regime.

United States. The U.S. government maintained its distance from Bashir's regime from the start, partly because Congress had passed legislation requiring that aid programs be terminated when armed forces overthrow an elected government. Tensions mounted as Sudan sided with Iraq in the Gulf crisis and as the regime's hard-line stance on the south became increasingly apparent. A turning point came in July 1992, when security forces executed four southern Sudanese employees of the U.S. AID program and the European Community (EC) in Juba in the wake of an uprising supported by the SPLA. From then on, the United States sharply criticized the government's violations of human rights in the south, Khartoum, and the Nuba Mountains. Washington pressed for resolutions at the UN and urged the International Monetary Fund to expel Sudan. In August 1993, the U.S. State Department put Sudan on the list of countries that support terrorism, based on evidence that Islamist groups and individuals not only took sanctuary but were also being trained in Sudan.[40]

This tension culminated in the withdrawal of the U.S. ambassador and the American diplomats from Khartoum in February 1996, announced immediately after the UN Security Council had threatened sanctions against Sudan if it did not carry out Mubarak's request to hand over three Egyptian suspects to Ethiopia.[41] The U.S. suspension of diplomatic relations was related to concerns that Khartoum could not protect Americans against threats from extremist groups operating in the country, but its timing placed intense pressure on the regime.

The British ambassador was as outspoken as the U.S. ambassador in his criticism of the regime. His stance—when combined with a flap over protocol for the planned visit to Sudan of the Archbishop of Canterbury—caused Khartoum to expel him in January 1994 and to withdraw its own ambassador from London.[42] A new British ambassador did not arrive until April 1995.

Officials in Sudan attribute the tensions with the United States to Washington's seeking hegemony in the Middle East and the Horn of Africa: Sudan's assertion of its independence cannot be tolerated in the New World Order being created by the sole superpower. Moreover, Khartoum argues, Washington specifically opposes the Islamic civilizational choice adopted by Sudan—that is, the United States supports secession by the south and encourages measures by Egypt and Horn of Africa governments to weaken Khartoum. Officials even expressed concern in the early 1990s that the presence of UN peacekeepers in Somalia presaged a U.S. invasion through southern Sudan.[43] They found proof in calls from Washington for the establishment of internationally guaranteed "safe havens" for civilians in the south. Foreign Minister Taha emphasized that the regime would not make ideological concessions or be pressured by the United States.[44] Nonetheless, the quiet removal of Bin Ladin and Hamza from Sudan and statements by diplomats that stress that Sudan does not support terrorism indicate that fear of international sanctions has, in fact, persuaded the regime to modify its overt involvement with militant groups.

Pragmatic and Ideological Allies

The picture that emerges is one of severe isolation: Khartoum has antagonistic or at least mutually suspicious relations with most of the adjoining countries as well as with the United States and brought down UN sanctions on its head. Nonetheless, the government has managed to maintain several crucial alliances. Its strategic relations with Iran, Iraq, and Yemen are also encouraged by common Islamist or Pan-Arab values. Its relations are pragmatic with arms-selling China and Belarus. France has found strategic and economic benefits in the bilateral relationship. And Khartoum's new ties to Qatar are largely a function of both countries' tension with Saudi Arabia, which has treated the Sudanese regime as a pariah since the Gulf crisis.

Iran. The Iranian and Sudanese governments share an ambition to spread their brands of Islamist cultural and political revival internationally. Iran also sees strategic opportunities in Sudan, as their alliance places pressure on Egypt and Saudi Arabia and opens up opportunities to spread their ideology into Africa.

Iran already had cordial relations with Mahdi's government, including paying for weapons that Sudan purchased from China. Relations, however, have deepened substantially under the influence of Turabi, who seeks to bridge Shi'i-Sunni divisions and create a common Islamic international front.

Ties became particularly visible in the wake of a high-profile trip by

Iranian President Ali Akbar Hashemi Rafsanjani to Sudan in December 1992. Military and economic protocols were signed in January 1993.[45] The military protocol provided for Iranian air force pilots to train their Sudanese counterparts; for Iran's Defense Ministry to finance the purchase of advanced armaments from China, such as the nearly twenty ground-attack aircraft acquired in the fall of 1993; for Pasdaran (Revolutionary Guards) to train Sudanese militias and security forces; for the provision of intelligence and security equipment; for additional military and intelligence training in Iran, including the use of Pakistani instructors who were familiar with Chinese weapons; and for assistance in training the Sudanese navy in the Red Sea at Suakin and Port Sudan. The new Iranian ambassador, who had helped establish Hizbollah in Lebanon, was apparently involved in the Pasdaran activities. At present, Iranians as well as Afghanis and Pakistanis reportedly help to operate NIF-linked internal security forces. Many of the training programs and security operations were camouflaged by placing them under the cover of nongovernmental Islamist relief and cultural organizations.[46]

The economic protocol provided for Iran to supply oil to Sudan, partly free and partly on a barter basis. Khartoum, desperate for oil supplies, made an urgent request to Tehran in March 1993.[47] However, Iran has often failed to meet Sudan's demands for oil. Since the Iranian economy is cash-starved, the government generally insists on payment for oil, rather than extending credit that it knows can never be repaid. The government is also unable to fund ambitious projects, such as a highway connecting north and south Sudan. Nonetheless, Iran helps to finance Sudan's costly arms purchases from China, which indicates the priority that it places on its strategic access to the Red Sea and Horn of Africa.

Iraq. The Sudanese government consistently and vigorously defends Iraq's right to sovereignty over all its territory and airspace. Khartoum argues that Iraq has complied with the terms for UN sanctions and that therefore they should be lifted. It denounces U.S. air raids and diplomatic pressure on Iraq and calls for the withdrawal of foreign forces from the Gulf region. Bashir views the two countries as not only linked in Pan-Arabism but also linked as the target of imperialist powers because they reject Western hegemony.[48]

There is close cooperation in the fields of security, intelligence, and arms training. The Iraq-Sudan telecommunications agreement of January 1993 reportedly included security dimensions; soon after, Iraq apparently assisted Sudanese agents in deciphering French satellite and high-altitude photos taken above southern battlefields.[49] Iraq is also involved in irrigation projects and in providing expertise for oil drilling, mineral exploration, manufacturing, and transport. Iraqi experts have enhanced the capacity of the loading ramps and cranes at Port Sudan, although some argue that the real purpose for the Iraqi presence is construction of missile and radar defense systems, training the air force, and development of a secret airport nearby. Iraqi pilots and maintenance personnel are also responsible for the Iraqi airplanes that have been based near Khartoum since the Gulf crisis: they are used in the Nuba Mountains as well as the south.[50]

Yemen. Bashir strongly supports fellow-officer Ali Abdullah Salih, president of North Yemen since 1978 and president of the united country since May 1990. NIF supports the Islah Party, which is Islamist in orientation and has the third largest bloc in the elected assembly. Turabi reportedly encouraged Islah to align with Salih during the attempt by southern politico-military forces to secede in May–June 1994 and has allegedly provided advice as Islah seeks to deepen its influence in the southern province.[51] NIF hopes that the military-Islamist alliance in Yemen can lead to a government that resembles its own. Khartoum also argued that the secession must be opposed both because of the secular, socialist leanings of the southern political forces and because Muslim and Arab unity are essential in order to ward off foreign pressures.[52]

Some analysts argue that Sudan provided military aid to Yemen during the two months of civil war; they charge that the two Sudanese ships that picked up Sudanese from Hudaydah port had been sent primarily to deliver military supplies. The government, however, claimed that it provided only medical aid.[53] Nonetheless, Yemeni appreciation was shown when it supplied Russian-made helicopters to Sudan the next year. These helicopters were apparently seized during the fighting in the south of Yemen.[54]

The bilateral ties serve strategic purposes for both countries. They put further pressure on Saudi Arabia, which shares a porous border with Yemen and has been on bad terms with the Yemeni government since the Gulf crisis. The ties also outflank Eritrea, which faces a hostile Sudan to its west and a potentially antagonistic Yemen to its east.

China. The Chinese government has maintained economic relations with Sudan for decades, irrespective of the regime in power. It has constructed textile factories, highways, hospitals, and public buildings. As noted, al-Sadiq al-Mahdi purchased arms from China, utilizing Iranian contacts and funds.

By January 1994, when the Chinese foreign minister visited Khartoum, Beijing already contributed to two dam projects, energy development, and irrigation works.[55] It sought more contracts in construction, mining, agriculture, and commerce. A year later, the two governments agreed that China would help to establish five factories in Sudan,[56] and soon after that a joint company to drill for oil was established, at least on paper.[57]

Bashir's subsequent visit to China in August 1995 focused on continued arms purchases. Beijing sells not only high-technology weapons but also spare parts for aircraft. The U.S. and European Union arms boycotts have compelled Khartoum to rely on China for maintenance as well as for the parts themselves. These contracts are purely pragmatic for China, which is paid in hard currency by Iran for its military supplies to Sudan.

Other allies. Sudan's arms deals with Belarus are equally pragmatic. That former Soviet satellite sold ten Soviet-built bombers to Sudan in 1995, as a means of gaining hard currency.[58] The deal was financed by Qatar, the small Gulf state whose new ruler wishes to assert his independence from Saudi Arabia. Qatar also is the only country that currently provides oil to Sudan on credit, Iran and Libya being fully aware of Sudan's inability to pay for any oil, and none of the other Gulf states will even sell oil to Sudan.

France. Turabi used his cordial relationship with the socialist government in France to circumvent pressure from Washington and London as well as from the International Monetary Fund, which stopped assistance in 1986, and the European Union, which called in 1995 for a ban on arms sales to Sudan. The French interior ministry, headed by Charles Pasqua, maintained close ties with NIF security officers in order to secure Sudan's borders with Chad, Zaire, and CAR, countries with which France has long-standing strategic ties.[59] Paris shared Khartoum's antagonism for Museveni, who backed insurgent forces in Rwanda against the French-supported government. French and Sudanese security forces worked together closely. It has even been claimed that France supplied satellite photos to the army that facilitated its offensive against the SPLA and that France engineered the accords with Zaire and CAR that enabled the Sudanese army to outflank the SPLA in western Equatoria, using their territories.[60]

More broadly, the French government sought to reduce Anglo-American influence in the Horn of Africa and viewed economic and strategic ties with Sudan as a valuable means to make inroads into that area. Paris encouraged French companies to sell Airbuses, prospect for oil, mine for gold, work in construction, and export gum arabic from Sudan, often with officially encouraged financial underpinning from French banks.[61] Moreover, France opposed Sudan's expulsion from the IMF at a critical moment in April 1994 and played an important role in convincing the IMF to lift the ban on technical aid in the spring of 1995.

In August 1994, at the height of Turabi's efforts to convince the French that he could help to resolve the strife in Algeria, Khartoum, as noted, handed over Illich Ramirez Sanchez ("Carlos"), who was wanted for terrorist acts in France.[62] The Sudanese government hoped that this act would also serve as evidence that it did not want to harbor terrorists. Instead, the handover indicated the ease with which Carlos had lived for an entire year in Khartoum and revealed his close ties with Turabi, Sudanese businessmen, and NIF operatives. The security aspects of this bilateral relationship appear to have diminished since the changes in government in France, but Paris continues to seek to pursue its economic and strategic interests in Sudan.

Policies toward the Arab-Israeli Conflict

The Israeli-Arab conflict is distant geographically from the Sudan. In the past, its government has followed the direction set by Egypt. Sudanese troops fought on the Suez front, and Egyptian fighter planes were stationed in Sudan in the late 1960s in order to keep them out of range of Israeli Phantom jets. Later, Khartoum and Muscat were the only Arab capitals that supported Anwar Sadat's peace initiative in 1977–79. Sudanese governments also emphasized their sympathy for the Palestinian cause. While lacking resources to aid the PLO, Numairi permitted Palestinian forces to be stationed in Sudan after they were expelled from Lebanon in 1982, and Arafat has been a frequent visitor to Khartoum.

The current regime distances itself from the peace process, applauds Syria's tough negotiating stance, and articulates support for Islamist movements in Palestine and Lebanon. These actions can be seen as ways to exert pressure on Egypt, but they are also consistent with the regime's Pan-Islamist and Pan-Arab ideological positions. Turabi's emphasis on the importance of restoring the cohesion and strength of the Arab states in the wake of the highly divisive Gulf crisis resonates with Palestinians. But his criticism of their capitulation to U.S. and Israeli terms of negotiation causes complications with both Arafat and King Hussein of Jordan, since it implies fundamental criticism of their accords with Israel.

Turabi has sought to reconcile Fatah, the secularist backbone of the PLO, and Hamas, the leading Palestinian Islamist movement. As early as 1992–93, Turabi tried to mediate tension between Fatah and Hamas. He proposed that Hamas join the PLO in order to ensure unity among Muslims. Hamas was ready to join the PLO on condition that its members receive 40 percent of the seats on the Palestine National Council, a condition to which Arafat would not accede.

When Arafat and the Israeli government announced the Oslo accord in August 1993 and signed the Declaration of Principles (DOP) in September

1993, Sudanese officials and politicians issued contradictory statements. The foreign ministry immediately declared that Sudan supports whatever choice the Palestinians make.[63] The (non-NIF) foreign minister said he viewed the DOP as a first step toward Israel's according the Palestinian people their legitimate rights and toward Israeli withdrawal from the Golan and South Lebanon as well as the West Bank and Gaza Strip.[64]

However, President Bashir expressed reservations. His view was that, rather than being a first step, the agreement on Gaza and Jericho meant that Israel might never evacuate the rest of the territories and the Palestinians might never gain their self-determination.[65] He would prefer a plan that would accord Palestinians the right to establish their state. He also joined Syria in opposing Arab governments' normalizing relations with Israel before its forces withdraw fully from all Arab territories.

The NIF-affiliated speaker of the Transitional National Assembly adopted yet a different position. He argued that the Sudan must steer a middle course: it has the right to criticize the accords on principle, but it must not reinforce intransigence against them, since that would pour oil on a fire.[66] Its efforts should be devoted to preserving Islamic solidarity and reaching a constructive consensus.

The speaker's cautionary words may have been intended as a response to Turabi, who had denounced the DOP as "a peace and capitulation plan which conflicts with the Palestinian, Arab and Islamic principle rejecting Israel."[67] Turabi's Popular Arab and Islamic Conference (PAIC) rejected the DOP decisively during its meeting in Khartoum in December 1993.[68]

Nonetheless, Turabi sought to criticize the DOP without condemning Arafat. Turabi emphasized that he had a long-term friendship with Arafat, from the time when they were students together in Prague in the 1950s. Describing Arafat as "merely the mayor of a ruined city,"[69] Turabi maintained that "He was in a desperate situation. He has lost the support of Palestinian society to Hamas and he has lost the support of the Arab governments [since the Gulf crisis]. He has no financial or political support. He even lost European support, under pressure of the U.S. which is close to the Zionist movement. So he accepted anything. Poor man. . . . When you are trapped, you accept any compromise whatsoever."[70]

Turabi tried to bridge the gap between Arafat and Hamas, whose activists in Khartoum vociferously opposed the DOP. At the PAIC conference in December 1993, he sought (unsuccessfully) to forge a reconciliation among Fatah, Hamas, and Islamic Jihad, stressing the importance of unity of ranks and of avoiding dangerous infighting. Turabi resumed his efforts in October 1994, arguing that otherwise tensions could result in armed struggle on the streets of Gaza.[71] (Those fears were partly realized a month later when Palestinian police shot at Hamas supporters outside a mosque in Gaza City.) Nonetheless, Turabi's sympathies clearly lay with Hamas; he praised Hamas attacks in Tel Aviv and other Israeli cities as evidence that they were honorable freedom fighters who opposed Israeli illegitimacy.[72] He even declared that these attacks proved that the intifada had been resumed and escalated by the Islamist popular movements, whose principles remained firm.[73] In time, he concluded, a Saladin will reappear and restore Palestine and Jerusalem to their historic owners. Those were strong words, attacking the legitimacy of Arafat's rule and the wisdom of his negotiating approach.

Turabi appeared to backtrack in the fall of 1995, after the signing of further Israeli-Palestinian agreements that set the stage for legislative and presidential elections in the West Bank and Gaza Strip in January 1996 and for Israeli withdrawal from all the major cities of the West Bank except Hebron. The violent attacks by Hamas against Israelis during the spring and summer of 1995 had failed to block the negotiations and, in fact, may have accelerated the accord. This shift in the strategic situation necessitated a rethinking by Hamas of its stance vis-à-vis the Palestine National Authority (PNA).

Turabi hosted a meeting in October 1995 that brought Hamas leaders who lived in Gaza together with leaders in exile, in order to hammer out a common strategy.[74] The tendency among the four Hamas representatives from Gaza was apparently to reach an accord with Arafat in order to guarantee for themselves a role in the elected PNA and its bureaucratic institutions. This approach was contested, however, by other Hamas militants in Gaza as well as by the external wing of Hamas. In the end, no clear-cut agreement was reached within Hamas during its deliberations in Khartoum. Moreover, Turabi's offer to host reconciliation sessions between Hamas and Fatah was viewed with distrust by Arafat, who feared that Turabi would tend to support Hamas's conditions. Arafat preferred mediation by the Egyptian government, which strongly supported the peace process and was clamping down on its own Islamist movements.

Conclusion

The strong ideological stance upheld by the NIF government has contributed to its isolation internationally. Its repression of political freedom internally and its all-out prosecution of the war in the south have estranged most of the international community. Its support for dissident movements in neighboring countries has earned the animosity of those governments.

Its close ties with Iran and Iraq have been important for its armed forces, security apparatus, and economy but have induced further suspicion of its goals. Its call for Arab and Muslim unity has been based on terms that would lead to the overthrow of most Arab regimes and the spread of Islamic militancy in Africa. Efforts to mediate conflicts—as in the case of the Palestinian movements—have lacked credibility since the Sudanese mediator has been perceived as tilted toward the more radical parties.

As Sudan becomes increasingly isolated, its leaders become more strident in their declarations and more extreme in their actions. They fear attack by foreign opponents, whether Uganda from the south, Eritrea from the east, or Egypt from the north. They see these threats as evidence of the outside world's rejection of their religious commitment and of their assertion of an independent foreign policy.

Some members of the regime have been trying to break out of the vicious cycle in which the government is caught. They have called for a new approach toward the south that grants its people self-determination; they have sought to end international sanctions so that the country can rebuild its economy; they have insisted that the government no longer supports foreign Islamist groups; and they have suggested that participation in the political arena will be widened. Nonetheless, it remains unlikely that the regime can break out of this cycle. The leaders are too committed to their political ideology to restore genuine democracy and to support a pluralistic resolution of the war in the south. Their promise of self-determination appears intended more to split the southerners than really to risk the secession of that territory. And any loosening of their control over power in Khartoum would produce a popular uprising against them. Indeed, they appear to be creating a self-fulfilling prophecy: a coordinated movement by diverse domestic and foreign opponents to overthrow the regime. Otherwise, the regime is likely to continue in its course of attempting to destabilize neighboring governments and prosecuting the war at home, actions that reflect less their confidence in their cause than their desperation as their isolation increases.

Notes

1. Background on Sudanese ethnic tensions can be found in the author's "Confrontation in the Southern Sudan" and "Negotiations in the Sudan." For a brilliant analysis of the north-south relationship, see Francis M. Deng, *War of Visions: Conflict of Identities in the Sudan.*

2. For an analysis of the current regime, see the author's "The Destruction of Civil Society in the Sudan," in Augustus Richard Norton, ed., *Civil Society in the*

Middle East, vol. 2 (Brill Publishers, 1996). The problems that beset the elected government are addressed in the author's "The Parliamentary Election of 1986: Fatally Flawed?" *Northeast African Studies* 1 (1994): 2–3.

3. *Sudan Democratic Gazette* (London), no. 68 (January 1996): 7.

4. *The Middle East* (London), January 1993, 38.

5. Quoted in *Sudan Democratic Gazette* (London), May 1993.

6. Middle East News Agency (MENA), Cairo, October 21, 1989; *Sudan Update* (London), September 25, 1990.

7. *Africa Confidential* 36, no. 14 (7 July 1995): 3.

8. *Al-Sharq al-Awsat* (London), August 23, 1994 (*FBIS–NES–94–164,* August 24, 1994).

9. *Der Spiegel,* August 29, 1994 (*FBIS–NES–94–167,* August 29, 1994).

10. Dr. Ghazi Salah al-Din of the Foreign Ministry, Reuters, July 5, 1995 (internet).

11. *Al-Wafd* (Cairo), May 29, 1994 (*FBIS–NES–94–106,* June 2, 1994).

12. For a profile of Bin Ladin, see *Africa Confidential* 35, no. 18 (September 9, 1994): 8.

13. *Al-Ahram* (Cairo), January 17, 1994 (*FBIS-NES-94-015,* January 24, 1994); also *al-Sharq al-Awsat,* January 12, 1994 (*FBIS-NES-94-010,* January 10, 1994). Omdurman radio reported on January 12, 1994, ibid., that the TNA unanimously revoked Ajo's membership due to his recent conduct, which it considered a betrayal.

14. This was confirmed by other defectors, notably Muhammad Ahmad Abd al-Qadir al-Arbab, the minister of health and social affairs in Sennar province. Arbab said he was personally aware of foreign Islamists in PDF camps near the borders with Eritrea, Ethiopia, Egypt, and Libya as well as near Khartoum. Some of the foreigners, he claimed, were trainers, and others were being trained for operations against their home government, on the other side of the border. *Al-Sharq al-Awsat,* March 28, 1995 (*FBIS-NES-95-061,* March 20, 1995).

15. For background on Sudanese foreign policy, see the author's "A View from Khartoum," *Foreign Affairs* 65, no. 4 (Spring 1987) and "Sudan's Foreign Policy: In Search of Arms, Aid and Allies."

16. *Al-Sharq al-Awsat,* February 7, 1995 (*FBIS-NES-95-026,* February 8, 1995).

17. *Africa Confidential* 36, no. 15 (July 21, 1995): 3.

18. *Al-Hayat* (London), March 12, 1995, in *Sudan News and Views,* no. 6, March 16, 1995.

19. Foreign Ministry press release, September 1, 1995; for analyses of the diplomatic implications, see *Middle East International* (London) no. 508 (September 8, 1995) and *Middle East Times* (Cairo), September 10, 1995, 2.

20. Agence France Presse (AFP), January 4, 1994, in *Sudan Update* 5, no. 2 (January 17, 1994); *Africa Confidential,* January 7, 1994.

21. AFP, May 8, 1993 (*FBIS-NES-93-088,* May 10, 1993) and May 13, 1993 (*FBIS-NES-93-092,* May 14, 1993).

22. *Middle East Times,* July 16, 1995, 1; July 21, 1995, 11.

23. On the schools, see MENA, January 5, 1993 (*FBIS-NES* January 6, 1993), *Middle East Times*, January 12, 1993. On the properties, see Sudan News Agency (SUNA) May 23, 25, 26, 1994 (*FBIS–NES–94–102/103*, May 26/27, 1994).

24. Comment by Sudanese foreign minister Taha, *al-Sha'ab* (Cairo), March 28, 1995 (*FBIS-NES-95-067*, April 7, 1995).

25. *Al-Sudan al-Hadith* and AFP, January 29, 1995, in *Sudan Update* 6, no. 2 (February 6, 1995).

26. *Al-Ahram*, July 2, 1995, quoted in *Middle East Times*, July 9, 1995, 16; Turabi's warning, given to Lebanese radio, July 2, 1995 (*FBIS–NES–95–127*, July 3, 1995).

27. MENA, March 31, 1993 (*FBIS-NES* April 2, 1993).

28. SUNA, August 6, 1994 (*FBIS–NES–94–153*, August 9, 1994); Reuters, August 18, 1994 (internet).

29. Reuters, August 15 and 19, 1994 (internet).

30. Omdurman radio, April 23, 1993 (*FBIS-NES-93-079*, April 27, 1993); *Al-Hayat*, April 25, 1993 (ibid.).

31. *Egyptian Gazette* (Cairo), March 11, 1993; *Daily Telegraph* (London), March 15, 1993; Sudanese foreign minister's denial on Omdurman Radio, March 18, 1993 (*FBIS-NES* March 19, 1993).

32. MENA, June 20, 1994 (*FBIS–NES–94–119*, June 21, 1994); SUNA, June 21, 1994 (*FBIS–NES–94–120*, June 22, 1994); *al-Sharq al-Awsat*, June 27, 1994, interview with Egyptian Foreign Minister Amr Musa in *Sudan Update* 5, no. 12 (July 14, 1994).

33. *Independent* (London), November 22, 1994.

34. *Middle East International* no.505 (July 21, 1995): 11.

35. The Sudanese foreign minister expressed regret and astonishment at Algeria's action; Omdurman Radio, March 28, 1993 (*FBIS-NES* March 29, 1993).

36. BBC Radio (London), November 9, 1994 (internet).

37. *Le Figaro* (Paris), April 17, 1993; Turabi made the same criticism of Mubarak and King Fahd of Saudi Arabia in that interview.

38. Omdurman Radio, March 31, 1993 (*FBIS-NES-93-062*, April 2, 1993); *al-Sharq al-Awsat*, May 27, 1993 (*FBIS–NES–93–102*, May 28, 1993).

39. *New York Times*, September 10, 1995; Reuters, September 25, 1995 (internet).

40. AFP, August 18, 1993 (*FBIS–NES–93–159*, August 19, 1993); *Sudan Update* 4, no. 19 (September 3, 1993). The Foreign Ministry denied U.S. allegations; one version of its formal response was printed as a letter in *The Nation* (Bangkok), August 26, 1993 (*FBIS–NES–93–165*, August 27, 1993).

41. Voice of America, January 31, 1996, and State Department press briefing by Nicholas Burns on February 1, 1996 (internet).

42. See Sudan Embassy *Bulletin* (London), December 29, 1993, and *Daily Telegraph* (London), December 31, 1993, in *Sudan Update* 5, no. 1 (January 1, 1994); *Africa Confidential* 35 no. 1 (January 7, 1994): 2–3.

43. See, for example, Bashir's interview in *al-Quds al-Arabi* (London), December 8, 1993 (*FBIS–NES–93–236*, December 10, 1993).

44. His comments on his first meeting with the U.S. ambassador since becoming foreign minister; *al-Sharq al-Awsat*, March 19, 1995 (*FBIS-NES*-95-056, March 23, 1995).

45. *Indian Ocean Newsletter*, February 6, 1993, in *Sudan Update* 4, no. 12 (March 16, 1993).

46. *Africa Confidential* 34, no. 21 (October 22, 1993): 3.

47. MENA, March 26, 1993 (*Sudan Update* 4, no. 13, March 21, 1993), reported that Iran responded that it could provide fuel oil only if a European government served as a third-country guarantor; no guarantor was found, so Sudan did not receive any oil.

48. For example, interview with Bashir by the Iraqi News Agency (Baghdad), December 11, 1993 (*FBIS–NES–93–237*, December 13, 1993).

49. SUNA, January 3, 1993, in *Sudan Update* 4, no. 18 (January 16, 1993).

50. *Sudan Democratic Gazette* no. 68 (January 1996): 4. The article argues that, since November 1995, Iraq has been using chemical weapons in the Nuba Mountains as well as training Sudanese technicians in the handling of gas shells. These operations enable Baghdad to test their effectiveness; no-fly zones prevent the armed forces from testing their weapons on the Kurdish and Shi'ite populations inside Iraq.

51. *Al-Sharq al-Awsat*, May 12 and 13, 1994, in *Sudan Update* 5, no. 9 (May 20, 1994); *al-Wafd*, May 29, 1994 (*FBIS–NES–94–106*, June 2, 1994).

52. SUNA commentary, May 26, 1994 (*FBIS–NES–94–103*, May 27, 1994); Bashir statement, Omdurman Radio, June 21, 1994 (*FBIS–NES–94–120*, June 22, 1994).

53. Omdurman TV, May 27, 1994 (*FBIS–NES–94–104*, May 31, 1994); Omdurman Radio, July 5 and 6, 1994 (*FBIS–NES–94–129/130*, July 6/7, 1994); Yemeni Radio, July 10, 1994, in *Sudan Update* 5, no. 14 (August 30, 1994).

54. *Sudan Democratic Gazette* no. 68 (January 1996): 4.

55. SUNA, January 15 (*FBIS-NES*-94-011, January 18, 1994), 16 (ibid.), and 24, 1994 (*FBIS-NES*-94-016, January 26, 1994).

56. Reuters, January 23, 1995, in *Sudan Update* 6, no. 2 (February 6, 1995).

57. Omdurman Radio, June 13, 1995 (*FBIS–NES–95–115*, June 15, 1995).

58. *Sudan Democratic Gazette* no. 68 (January 1996): 4.

59. *Africa Confidential*, July 29, 1994.

60. *Middle East*, February 1995, 17–18.

61. *Africa Confidential* 35 no. 3 (February 4, 1994): 8; ibid., no. 15 (July 29, 1994): 8; *Middle East*, February 1995, 17–18.

62. *Africa Confidential* 35, no. 17 (August 26, 1994).

63. MENA, August 31, 1993 (FBIS–NES–93–168, September 1, 1993).

64. *Al-Sharq al-Awsat*, October 1, 1993 (*FBIS–NES–93–191*, October 5, 1993).

65. AFP, September 1, 1993 (*FBIS–NES–93–169*, September 2, 1993).

66. Interview with *al-Safir* (Beirut), December 7, 1993, in *FBIS–NES–93–240* (December 16, 1993).

67. *Al-Hayat*, September 30, 1993 (*FBIS–NES–93–191*, October 5, 1993).

68. *TransState Islam,* Spring 1995, 14–15.

69. *Le Republica* (Rome), November 3, 1994 (*FBIS–NES–94–214,* November 4, 1994).

70. *Le Nouvel Observateur* (Paris), August 25, 1994 (*FBIS–NES–94–166,* August 26, 1994).

71. *Al-Safir* (Beirut), October 18, 1994 (*FBIS–NES–94–206,* October 25, 1994).

72. Reuters, October 20, 1994 (internet).

73. *Al-Sha'ab* (Cairo), February 10, 1995 (*FBIS-NES-95-030,* February 14, 1995).

74. *Jerusalem Post,* October 8, 1995; *al-Quds* (Jerusalem), October 9, 1995 (internet).

PART IV

The Role of External Powers

13: U.S. Middle East Policy in the 1990s

Don Peretz

Since President Bill Clinton assumed office following George Bush in January 1993, U.S. policy in the Middle East has remained basically the same, with only slight modifications. Most State Department personnel responsible for the region stayed in office, and their statements about policy were identical to those of the previous administration. The assistant secretary of state for Near Eastern affairs, Robert H. Pelletreau, Jr., a career Middle East diplomat, described U.S. policy at a symposium of the Middle East Policy Council in May 1994 in these words:

> The prism through which we assess trends and conditions in the Middle East is the protection and advancement of U.S. national interests. These are, briefly: a just and lasting peace between Israel and its Arab neighbors, Israel's security and well-being, a security framework in the Gulf that assures access to its energy resources upon which we and other industrial nations continue to be dependent, non-proliferation of weapons of mass destruction, control of destabilizing arms transfers, promotion of political participation, and respect for basic human rights, ending state-supported and other forms of terrorism, promotion of economic and social development through privatization and market economies, encouragement of American business and investment opportunities.[1]

Notable in this, as in the policy statements of previous administrations, was the priority given to resolution of the Arab-Israel conflict and Israel's security.

Since its establishment in 1948 the well-being and security of Israel have been singled out as a major U.S. policy interest. Domestic as well as foreign considerations account for the great emphasis placed on this objective. Israel's supporters in the United States have included not only the American Jewish community but labor unions, Protestant evangelicals, and many in the U.S. security establishment. Thus both principal political parties, Republican and Democrat, have always included in their election platforms strong support for Israel.

U.S. Middle East policy was characterized by a fundamental contradiction after the late 1940s—how to maintain close and friendly relations with Arab nations whose oil has been crucial to the sustenance of Europe's economy while maintaining intimate relations with Israel, America's principal ally in the region. This contradiction was compounded by the Cold War between the Soviet Union and the United States, in which Moscow used the Arab-Israel conflict to its advantage by aligning itself with the Arabs against the Jewish state. Thus, despite its shortcomings, the Israel-PLO Declaration of Principles (DOP) signed in Washington, D.C., on September 13, 1993, constituted a significant accomplishment because it opened the way for removal of an irritant that had plagued U.S. policy makers for nearly half a century.

The Arab-Israel Conflict

During the Cold War era, resolution of the Arab-Israel conflict remained a primary U.S.objective, along with containment of Soviet influence in the region and maintaining free access by the West to Middle East oil. From 1947 until 1993 U.S. policy makers pursued this apparently elusive goal with little if any success. Efforts to limit weapons shipments to the region in the 1950s were subverted by Soviet armament of Egypt, Syria, and Iraq. The region became the world's leading importer of weapons and the scene of half a dozen major wars by the 1980s. Dozens of diplomatic endeavors, from the Lausanne Conference in 1949 to the Madrid Middle East Peace Conference in 1991, failed to end the conflict.[2]

Although the United States played a major role in achieving the 1979 peace treaty between Egypt and Israel, hope for wider regional agreements was frustrated when other Arab League members shunned Egypt for nearly a decade. Attempts to diminish regional tensions through functional efforts placing emphasis on cooperative economic development, resource planning, and water allocation did not prove more successful. The McGhee plan for regional economic development,[3] the Johnston and Clapp proposals for joint development of the Jordan River system,[4] and various schemes for Palestine Arab refugee rehabilitation—none have ever been implemented; all were undermined by political squabbles, especially by the continuing hostility between Israel and the Arab nations. U.S. efforts to bypass political disagreements through Arab-Israel regional cooperation in functional economic programs seemed to put the cart before the horse, since political agreement was a prerequisite to cooperation in any regional development scheme.

By the 1990s major changes in international affairs, especially within the Middle East, cleared away several obstacles to U.S. objectives in the region. The collapse of the Soviet Union brought to an end the economic, military, and diplomatic backing for Arab clients that had made the Middle East one of the most active fronts in the Cold War. Arab states, especially Syria, that had relied on Soviet assistance against Israel, were bereft of their chief ally; Syria sought to establish friendly ties with the United States by joining the alliance against Iraq in the second Gulf War and by softening its rhetoric against Israel.

The defeat of Iraq in the second Gulf War by the U.S.-led coalition established the United States not only as the dominant outside factor but also as the hegemonic power, uncontested by any other state either from within or from outside the area. The Soviet Union no longer existed, and the new CIS appeared to have neither resources, energy, nor inclination to challenge Washington's dominant role.

The war against Iraq had divided the Arab world into allies of the United States (the largest and most powerful Arab states, including Egypt, Syria, Saudi Arabia, and Kuwait) versus those either sympathetic to Iraq or neutral, having little if any economic, military, or political clout (such as Yemen, Libya, Sudan, and Jordan). This deep and blatant rift facilitated Washington's negotiations with each Arab state individually. There was no longer even the pretense of a united front against the West or, for that matter, against Israel. Cracks in the anti-Israel front became obvious even before the Gulf War when, state by state, Arab leaders began to ease the boycott of Egypt they had imposed after Camp David and the 1979 peace treaty.[5]

The end of Soviet anti-Western instigation, the deep divisions within the Arab world, and the establishment of U.S. hegemony created an environment conducive to new initiatives in U.S. policy on the Middle East. However, a negative factor in the new equation was the continuing rebellion, or intifada, by Palestinian Arabs against Israel in the occupied West Bank and Gaza. Although neighboring governments hesitated to give outright support to the intifada, it aroused the sympathy of "the street" throughout the Arab world. Continuation of the intifada threatened to become a destabilizing element that could undermine the gains achieved through the demise of Soviet influence and the victory over Iraq.[6]

Every American president from Truman to Bush had his own proposal for ending the Palestine conflict. Truman urged Israel to take back thousands of Palestinian Arab refugees; Eisenhower sent Eric Johnston to the region with a scheme for developing its water resources; Kennedy sent Joseph Johnson with a new refugee plan;[7] Nixon's and Ford's emissary, Henry Kissinger, spent months in shuttle diplomacy. Although Carter ended the conflict between Egypt and Israel, he failed to make progress on the question of Palestine. Finally, after many visits to the region, President Bush's secretary of state, James Baker, succeeded in persuading Israel, Syria, Lebanon, Jordan, and the Palestinians to join in negotiations at the Madrid Middle East Peace Conference in October 1991. However it is unlikely that Baker would have succeeded without the collapse of the Soviet Union, the Palestinian intifada, and Iraq's defeat.

While the negotiations initiated in Madrid were perceived as a breakthrough, it was only after two years that real progress could be claimed in resolving the Arab-Israel conflict. The Madrid process brought Israel and its principal remaining antagonists to the bargaining table, but little was accomplished in these contacts during the first two years.

The peace negotiations were divided into a set of bilateral talks, when Israel met separately with Syria, Lebanon, Jordan, and the Palestinians, and five multilateral meetings dealing with functional problems—water, refugees, environment, regional security, and economic development. The greatest achievement in the bilaterals was that the parties agreed to continue their discussions. Participants in each of the multilateral talks included over a score of nations, but they too did not reach any major substantive agreements, using their meetings for technical matters such as how to improve refugee quality of life, take stock of regional water resources, or devise schemes to monitor weapons placement.

Far more significant was the breakthrough in September 1993, when Israel and the Palestine Liberation Organization (PLO) signed the Declaration of Principles in Washington. Although the United States played little, if any, role in the secret diplomacy leading up to the DOP, once the agreement was signed, U.S. participation in the continuing peace process became vital. The role of American government intermediaries behind the scenes was as crucial in keeping the Israel-PLO negotiations on track as it was during 1977–79 in preventing collapse of the Israel-Egypt peace talks.[8]

Sponsoring negotiations between Israel and the PLO that led to withdrawal of the Israeli army and Palestinian elections in the West Bank and Gaza during January 1996 was one of the few diplomatic achievements in the first four years of the Clinton administration, often criticized for many of its other foreign policy initiatives. It appeared that more energy was devoted to resolving the Middle East conflict than to other critical international problems.

In efforts to complete the process following the DOP and the Israel-Jordan peace treaty, the Clinton administration made strenuous efforts to obtain an agreement between Israel and Syria. Secretary of State Warren Christopher engaged in shuttle diplomacy that brought him to Jerusalem and Damascus at least seventeen times. His visits to the Israeli and Syrian capitals far outnumbered those to other foreign cities, such as Moscow, Berlin, Beijing, London, Tokyo, or Paris. Some critics maintained that it showed disproportionate attention to an area far less vital to U.S. interests than Russia, China, or Japan.[9]

Credit for keeping the Middle East peace process alive must be given to Dennis Ross, the State Department's special Middle East coordinator, whose role as intermediary frequently prevented collapse of the negotiations. Ross, a hold-over from previous Republican administrations, with his extreme patience and personal persuasiveness provided the historical continuity required to keep the parties at the table when acrimony and bitter exchanges between Israelis and Arabs threatened to blow the peace process apart.

The State Department's dogged determination to achieve a settlement between Israel and Syria before the end of Clinton's first term in office led to a dispute over the role the United States might play in assuring Israel's security should it withdraw from the Golan Heights, captured from Syria in the June 1967 war. Both Israeli negotiators and U.S. intermediaries recognized that there could be no settlement without return of the Golan to Syria. The question was, under what conditions would Israel leave the Golan Heights without jeopardizing its own security?

When the United States indicated that it would be willing to provide some form of presence—to man early warning devices, to act as a trip wire in case of a Syrian advance into a demilitarized Golan, or as an observer force like the one in Sinai—the question became highly politicized in both Israel and the United States.[10] Those opposed to Israel's withdrawal strongly objected to any U.S. role in the Golan. In Israel the dispute was largely between the Labor governing coalition and the opposition Likud, with a few Laborites supporting the Likud position. In Washington, a pro-Likud constituency emerged, supported mostly by conservative Republicans in opposition to the Democratic Clinton administration.

A study for the Washington-based Center for Security Policy by several retired U.S. generals, admirals, and former high officials in previous Republican administrations concluded: "There is no mission or rationale for a U.S. peacekeeping force on the Golan that would justify the resulting costs and risks. Indeed, the net effect could be negative for Israel's security and regional stability, while the consequences could include the loss of U.S. lives and, possibly, a credibility-damaging retreat of the U.S. forces under terrorist fire. In any event such a deployment would increase the danger of direct U.S. involvement in a future Middle East war and undermine Israel's standing with the U.S. public as a self-reliant ally."[11]

The study calculated that the cost to the United States of sponsoring a peace settlement between Israel and Syria would be $12 billion for Israel alone, in addition to the $3 billion in aid Israel receives annually from the United States. The extra funding would include $7 billion for new weapons to strengthen Israeli forces against Syria, $3 billion to assure Israel access to water in the Golan region, and $2 billion to move Israeli settlers from the Golan.[12]

A report by a study group of the Washington Institute for Near East Policy had a different perspective. It recognized the need for a U.S. role in Golan peacekeeping to bolster "solid security arrangements between Israel and Syria." The report recommended that "if asked by Israel and Syria to do so, the United States should stand ready to participate in peacekeeping. In deciding to participate in peacekeeping arrangements, Washington will have to balance *possible* risks inherent in peacekeeping as well as the potential opportunities peace will create versus the *likely* risk of increased instability and perhaps even war should the Israel-Syria peace effort collapse."[13] The report cited the successful role of the multinational force established in Sinai following the agreement between Israel and Egypt as a possible model for the Golan.

The progress made following the DOP cleared the way for a peace treaty between Israel and Jordan and for recognition of Israel by several Arab states.[14] Morocco, Tunisia, Oman, Qatar, Bahrain, and Mauritania sent envoys to Israel or received Israeli diplomatic and trade representatives. Several states lifted the Arab League secondary boycott against Israel, and Arab and Israeli diplomats began to confer publicly at various international meetings. Even Syria, the last holdout in peace negotiations among Israel's immediate neighbors, softened its anti-Israel rhetoric, indicating that it too desired to join the peace process. There were even reports that Iraq's Saddam Hussein would not stand in the way of a final settlement.

Although the DOP appeared to greatly diminish the Arab-Israel conflict as an irritant in U.S. relations with the Arab world, many difficult problems still had to be negotiated in the final status talks between Israel and the Palestine Authority. They included the future of Jerusalem, the fate of nearly 3 million Palestinian refugees, and the status of Jewish settlements in the West Bank and Gaza.[15]

Dual Containment

While the Arab-Israel conflict was perceived by many as the most difficult aspect of U.S. Middle East policy, the U.S. government considered several other areas troublesome. With the decline of Soviet influence, some policy analysts and politicians raised the specter of militant Islamic nationalism, labeled by some "Muslim fundamentalism," as a threat to the West. Iraq and Iran were also cited as threats to U.S. interests, both charged with secretly developing nuclear, chemical, biological, or other unconventional weapons. Along with Libya, Sudan, and Syria, they were accused of supporting anti-Western terrorist groups. There was some recognition that economic and social conditions contributed to regional unrest and instability, but primary emphasis focused on the activities of regimes rather than the welfare of their populations.

In a recent conference, the U.S. assistant secretary for Near Eastern affairs, Robert Pelletreau, examined the impact of resurgent Islam on U.S. interests. He stated that in the foreign affairs community the term "political Islam" (referring to groups with a political agenda) rather than "Islamic fundamentalism" was preferable. The United States recognized that there were many legitimate, socially responsible Muslim groups having political goals. What the United States opposes is groups that operate outside the bounds of the law and that espouse violence to achieve their aims. The issue was underscored by the World Trade Center bombing in New York City and by what then Assistant Secretary Pelletreau stated were actions of Iran and Libya. As "a government, we have no quarrel with Islam. We respect it as one of the world's great religions and as a great civilizing movement . . . [but we] question certain features of the Islamic resurgence. . . . certain manifestations of the Islamic revival are intensely anti-Western and aim not only at elimination of Western influences but at resisting any form of cooperation with the West or modernizing evolution at home. Such tendencies are clearly hostile to U.S. interests."[16]

Iran was regarded as the chief instigator of anti-Western and anti-U.S. Islamic factions in various Middle Eastern countries, including Lebanon, Saudi Arabia, and Bahrain. Both Iran and Iraq became targets of a new U.S. policy called "dual containment" by the Clinton administration's National Security Council specialist on the Middle East, Martin Indyk (who later became U.S. Ambassador to Israel), a policy that occasioned some controversy.

According to Indyk, previous U.S. administrations had chosen either

Iraq or Iran to promote and protect American interests in the Gulf, first Iran under the shah and then, after the shah was overthrown by groups hostile to the United States, Sadam Hussein's Iraq.[17] The results of these previous policies were, Indyk stated, "less than good, to put it mildly. One might say disastrous in terms of what followed"—the 1979 revolution in Iran, the Iraq-Iran war, Iraq's 1990 invasion of Kuwait, and the Gulf War. Dual containment aims at achieving a balance of power in the region, favorable to the interests of the United States and its friends without depending on either Iraq or Iran. Recent developments affecting the Middle East—including the end of the Cold War and elimination of Soviet influence, the two Gulf wars, and the U.S.-led alliance against Iraq after its invasion of Kuwait—called for establishment of new security arrangements, according to Indyk. Such arrangements should make it easier for the United States to project its power and deal with threats to its interests. Dual containment, Indyk maintained, "does not mean duplicate containment. Our policies towards Iraq and Iran are not the same, because each regime presents different challenges to our interests, and we have developed policies to deal with the specific cases."[18]

A bulwark of dual containment has been the Gulf Cooperation Council (GCC), a U.S.-supported quasi-alliance of Saudi Arabia, Kuwait, Qatar, the United Arab Emirates, Oman, and Bahrain. The policy has involved positioning either U.S. military equipment or U.S. troops in Gulf states, including Saudi Arabia, Kuwait, Qatar, and Bahrain.

Economic boycott and blockade are also dual containment measures. However, their effectiveness is often frustrated by lack of cooperation from other countries. In 1995, when the Clinton administration ordered U.S. companies to halt commercial dealings with Iran, Teheran found other buyers for the 500,000 barrels of oil originally destined for U.S. clients. The Iranian government turned to multinational firms owned by Great Britain and France, Royal Dutch Shell and Total, to buy $3 billion to $4 billion worth of petroleum. U.S. attempts to persuade the Group of Seven and OPEC to join the embargo were also unsuccessful. Several OPEC oil ministers claimed that it was not solidarity with Iran that concerned them about U.S. sanctions, but a question of "who's next! . . . No one here is going to encourage, support or go along with this kind of economic war."[19]

Containment of Iraq is maintained through strict enforcement of U.N. Security Council resolutions imposing an embargo and blockade until Baghdad destroys its nonconventional weapons. In October 1994 a sudden buildup of Iraqi military forces near the border with Kuwait led President Clinton to send nine thousand U.S. troops to the region, but the crisis was soon defused when Saddam Hussein withdrew, claiming his soldiers had been engaged in maneuvers only. There was another minicrisis early in 1996 when the U.S. Defense Intelligence Agency suspected Iraq of preparing to send several armored divisions toward the Kuwaiti border. The United States responded on a relatively small scale compared with the reaction in 1994 because there was no conclusive evidence of an impending attack. Nevertheless, in response to Iraq's military position, the United States has maintained about 20,000 troops in the region, 14,000 of them naval personnel on thirty-five ships, part of the Fifth Fleet, to patrol the waters between the Suez Canal and the eastern Indian Ocean. Between 1990 and 1996 the Fifth Fleet intercepted some 22,000 ships in its mission to block trade with Iraq.[20]

According to some estimates, the Gulf accounts for $50 billion of the Pentagon's annual budget of $260 billion, nearly five times the amount paid by the United States for oil imported from the region. There seems to be little economic rationale for this large security expenditure. U.S. military presence in the Gulf has been of little, if any, benefit to American business. In 1994 there was a $1 billion trade deficit with the region, which imported only $10 billion of U.S. products. Two U.S. analysts have suggested that the European Union and Japan, whose trade is nearly four times America's, carry a far larger share of the containment burden.[21]

U.S. critics of dual containment believe that the Iranian threat has been greatly exaggerated. They were particularly concerned with the revelation early in 1996 that the U.S. Congress had appropriated $18 million for covert assistance to the opposition within and outside Iran. Teheran's response was to allocate $20 million to "combat United States terrorist activities and plots against Muslim nations, particularly the Islamic Republic of Iran."[22]

A clear distinction should be made between Iraq and Iran, the critics argue. Although regimes in both countries are hostile to the United States, possibilities of opening a dialogue with Iran are much more favorable. Iran is seen as a partially open, evolving society capable of change. Milton Viorst, a recent observer in Iran, wrote in *Foreign Affairs:* "The religious and secular elites [in Iran] are increasingly willing to contemplate pluralism and openness to the world, though most makers of the revolution remain obdurate and appeal to anti-Americanism to stir up the masses. Washington needs to listen to the new voices of Iran. . . . Given America's regional interests, permanent hostility toward Iran serves no purpose. . . . The Iranian government is reaching out. A decade from now, it will not necessarily be easier to respond."[23]

Russia, France, the Vatican, several U.N. agencies, and Arab states have criticized the sanctions on Iraq, partly for political and partly for humanitarian reasons. A 1995 survey by representatives of the U.N. Food and Agricultural Organization found that there was a steep rise in malnutrition among Iraqi youths as a result of the sanctions. The survey stated that as many as 576,000 Iraqi children may have died since the end of the Gulf War because of the Security Council's economic measures. The situation poses a challenge to "the moral, financial and political standing of the international community," the authors of the survey wrote.[24]

France, Russia, and China argued in the Security Council, where continuation of the sanctions must be reviewed every sixty days, that Iraq was about to comply with UN demands to eliminate its dangerous weapons systems and therefore should have the right to export its oil to world markets. The Arab League also expressed concern and urged the UN and Iraq "to reach a compromise" that would permit limited sales of Iraqi oil.[25]

Both the United States and Great Britain strongly disagreed, pointing to evidence that President Hussein had failed to comply with requirements for weapons destruction and that he was hindering the work of UN observers sent to monitor Iraqi disarmament.

According to the original UN resolutions, Iraq was permitted to sell some of its oil to purchase medical and other humanitarian supplies, but only under UN control. However, the embargo continued because Saddam Hussein resisted international supervision. By 1996 the desperate economic situation and threats of internal unrest seemed to soften his resistance, and Baghdad entered negotiations to discuss implementing a new U.S.-sponsored resolution permitting strictly supervised sales to finance purchases of food and medicine.[26]

Although Great Britain backed some dual containment measures, other European countries and China failed to support them. Both France and Russia continued their trade with Iraq and Iran. After the Gulf War Iran became a major buyer of Russian weapons including airplanes, tanks, submarines, and air defense systems. Moscow also negotiated the sale of nuclear reactors to Iran. Russia's relations with Iraq improved after the Gulf War and now include agreements on trade and economic development, with joint projects estimated at $12 billion.[27]

Middle East Oil

Next to Israel, Saudi Arabia and the Gulf states are probably the United States' closest Middle East allies. Saudi oil exports, by far the largest in the region, are vital for Western Europe's economy and important in the United States as well. Washington has established close military ties with Saudi

Arabia, which, as the site of Islam's two most holy cities, Mecca and Medina, carries great weight among other Islamic nations. Recent U.S. administrations have gone out of their way to facilitate trade between American business and the Saudis.

As the percentage of imported oil the United States needed increased from 37.2 percent in 1973 to over half the oil used in 1996, Saudi Arabia's importance grew; it now ranks second to Venezuela as a supplier of imported petroleum. Of the 62 million barrels of oil the world consumed daily in the early 1990s, 17 million came from the Middle East, and Saudi Arabia provided 8 million of that amount. The Saudis produced a third of OPEC's exports and OPEC contributed 37 percent of world production. With the world's largest reserves, it appears that Saudi Arabia will continue to dominate the international oil trade well into the twenty-first century.[28]

Despite its role as the world's largest oil producer and exporter, with the largest reserves, the recent decline in market prices has brought a reduction in Saudi Arabia's revenues just when it is experiencing a population explosion. As a result, per capita income plunged from $21,000 in 1981 to about $6,800 by 1996. Unemployment now looms as an impending crisis. The oil boom of the 1970s that brought great wealth to Saudi Arabia and other Gulf countries ended by the late 1980s. Rather than current account surpluses, the Gulf states have fallen into debt, according to Vahan Zanoyan. "Today, despite the investments of the last two decades, almost every economy in the group [Gulf states] faces more serious structural problems than before the oil boom of the 1970s. Furthermore, the political will to deal with such problems is less than it was before 1973."[29]

Although none of the Gulf regimes have faced an immediate threat, political and social unrest and overt opposition to rulers in several Gulf states have begun to cause concern. Vahan Zanoyan, a long-time observer of conditions in the Gulf, comments: "The most unmanageable risk facing American interests in the Persian Gulf is neither Saddam Hussein nor Iranian expansionism. Rather, it is the slow but sure decay of the economic and political structures of the United States' key allies. . . . Washington's obsession with external threats to friendly governments and direct threats to the continued flow of oil has blinded it to the end of these countries' 20-year holiday from politics and economics."[30]

The Middle East Arms Race

Until the 1990s U.S. policy heavily emphasized strengthening military ties with Saudi Arabia and the Gulf states. During the 1980s Saudi Arabia purchased $28.4 billion worth of spy planes, missiles, and other sophisticated

U.S. equipment, and several thousand U.S. military personnel were stationed there. The Saudi government provided $1 billion for CIA operations around the world during the 1980s, including support for Nicaraguan rebels after the U.S. Congress cut funding for the antigovernment forces. The Gulf war was a financial setback costing Saudi Arabia $55 billion (about the amount of the country's annual budget), according to the International Monetary Fund. Of that amount, $12.8 billion went directly to the United States. As a result of its recent economic plight, the country has been forced to reduce or eliminate a number of popular subsidies such as those on fuel, transportation, and food.[31]

The strong emphasis on military dimensions of achieving regional security results in a fundamental contradiction in U.S. Middle East policy. On the one hand, policy statements call for ending the Middle East arms race but, on the other, the United States continues to be a leading supplier of weapons to several countries in the area.

An initial attempt to limit the flow of arms was the May 1950 Tripartite Declaration signed by the United States, France, and Great Britain, in which they agreed to limit weapons shipments to the various parties in the Arab-Israel conflict. However, efforts to contain the arms race broke down in 1954 when Israel concluded a major arms agreement with France. As the Cold War intensified, the Soviet Union made deals with several Arab countries to provide them with weapons and military delegations to train their armies. The race escalated with the oil boom of the 1970s, when the Gulf states became major customers for both Soviet and Western weapons; they also provided funds for non-oil states like Egypt and Syria to participate in the arms race. By the end of the 1970s, the Middle East had become the world's largest importer of weapons. The Persian Gulf crisis in 1990–91 and the Iraq-Iran war before it greatly stimulated a high level of arms transfer agreements, especially with Saudi Arabia and the GCC nations threatened by Iraq's invasion of Kuwait and by Iran.[32]

In 1994 the Middle East still ranked highest in per capita military expenditures, according to the U.S. Arms Control and Disarmament Agency (ACDA). Arms expenditures amount to 20.1 percent of GNP and 54.8 percent of total government costs. The number of persons in military service per thousand was among the highest (13.5 compared with 7.4 for industrialized nations). According to ACDA, the Middle East share of world arms purchases rose from 35.9 percent in 1981 to 41.4 percent by 1991.[33]

Saudi Arabia was by far the leader between 1987 and 1994, when its arms transfer agreements totaled $75.9 billion. It alone was responsible for 29 percent of all developing world arms transfer agreements between 1991 and 1994, totaling $30.2 billion. The region's main suppliers were the United States and France, Russia, Britain, and Germany. Other major large purchasers were Egypt, Israel, Kuwait, Syria, United Arab Emirates, Iran, Qatar and Yemen, and Turkey.[34]

The Bush administration and the U.S. arms industry opposed even a temporary moratorium on arms sales despite Secretary of State Baker's statement to the House of Representatives Foreign Affairs Committee in February 1991: "The time has come to try to change the destructive pattern of military competition and proliferation in this region and to reduce the arms flow into an area that is already very over-militarized."[35] During the Gulf war and immediately afterwards, more than thirty bills relating to arms control were introduced in Congress, but the administration blocked them all.[36]

During 1991 and 1992, the five permanent members of the U.N. Security Council met several times to discuss limiting arms sales, but the talks broke down when China withdrew in protest against the U.S. sale of 160 F-16 warplanes to Taiwan. During this period Congress approved some $18 billion in weapons sales to the Middle East. The only law passed limiting arms exports was the Iran-Iraq Arms Non-Proliferation Act, prohibiting sales to the two countries.

In the 1992 presidential campaign, both George Bush and Bill Clinton said they approved the sale of three squadrons of F-15s to Saudi Arabia, claiming that production of these seventy-two warplanes by McDonnell-Douglas was a shot in the arm for the U.S. economy. Despite the Clinton administration's assertion that weapons proliferation is a serious threat, the United States remains a major supplier and financier of weapons in the region through the foreign assistance program, recently renamed the Prosperity and Democracy Act (Security Assistance has become Assistance for Promoting Peace and Democracy). Eighty-seven percent of total aid now labeled "Middle East Peace Assistance" is for military supplies to Egypt and Israel, with the rest going to Turkey.[37]

Between 1991 and 1994, America's principal Middle East customers were Saudi Arabia ($20.2 billion), Egypt ($4 billion), Kuwait ($3.9 billion), and Israel ($3 billion). In 1994, the United States also loaned Turkey $320 million to purchase U.S. weapons, including warplanes, tanks, and antipersonnel mines, used mostly in Ankara's war against its Kurdish population.[38]

In 1994, U.S. arms transfer agreements with developing nations decreased, mostly because clients had completed their purchase cycles and were absorbing equipment already acquired. Furthermore, Saudi Arabia, the largest client, was having severe budget difficulties. As a result the total value of U.S. arms transfer agreements with developing nations decreased from $15.4 billion in 1993 to $6.1 billion in 1994, the lowest level in real terms for eight years. The U.S. share of all such agreements fell from 60.5 percent in 1993 to 24.1 percent in real terms.[39]

Free Market Economies

Until 1985 the Middle East had a higher rate of growth than any other economic region except East Asia, mostly as a result of dependence on oil income. However, since the end of the oil boom and the decline of oil prices, the economies of the Middle East have increased by less than one-half of one percent, compared with Third World growth at an average rate of 3.4 percent during the same period. Many economists perceive this lack of growth as a crisis.[40]

Despite improvements in living standards during the 1970s and early 1980s—in terms of life expectancy, infant mortality rates, literacy, and education—the region now lags behind middle-income countries in many key indicators of social development. Life expectancy is four years less than in middle-income countries, infant mortality rates a third higher, adult literacy half as high, and enrollment of women in elementary and secondary schools about half that of middle-income nations.

In 1960 the per capita income of the seven major Middle East economies was higher than that of the four Asian tigers—Hong Kong, Korea, Singapore, and Taiwan—at $1,500 per person compared with $1,450. The current per capita level in the Middle East is $3,300, compared with $8,000 in the four Asian capitalist countries. In the Middle East much of the largesse from oil income was wasted in nonproductive investment, including military equipment; "productivity-driven economic growth has by-passed the Middle East and North Africa."[41] "The aggregate Arab economy today remains as undiversified as it was in the 1970s. Oil exports are still the exclusive economic engine of the region."[42]

As special assistant to the president and senior director for Near East and South Asian affairs in the National Security Council during 1993, Martin Indyk stated: "Our vision is of a peaceful, more democratic region focused on regional development. This is a new golden age for the region, where the potential that had been realized centuries ago can be realized again in cooperation with the West rather than against it. I really think that the region is ready for it and that a lot is now possible that wasn't possible a decade ago."[43]

Then Assistant Secretary of State for Near East Affairs Robert H. Pelletreau also listed "promoting democratization and pluralism, more open political and economic systems" and "ensuring fair access for American business to commercial opportunities in the region" among U.S. priorities.[44]

With the end of the Cold War and the greatly diminished intensity of the Arab-Israel conflict following the DOP, it was hoped that major obstacles to these objectives would be realized. Initial efforts during the early 1990s to start the process of regional development and democratization included economic summit meetings of government officials and business leaders at several international conferences, most notably, those in Casablanca, Morocco, during 1994 and in Amman, Jordan, in 1995. The United States also organized a pledging conference of thirty-five international donor countries and organizations in Washington during 1993 to raise $2.3 billion for assistance over a five-year period to the new Palestine Authority in the West Bank and Gaza.

By the end of 1995 the United States had committed only $47 million, approximately 25 percent of its 1994 and 1995 pledge amounts to assist the Palestine Authority. Controversies over administration of the funding between the donors and the Palestine Authority also blocked payment by most other contributors.[45] The results of the Casablanca and Amman conferences have yet to be determined. It will probably take decades before any realistic evaluation of programs for regional development are available because economic conditions have so deteriorated in recent years, because plans for regional development are so far from implementation, and because of increasing instability caused by poor economic conditions and unpopular governments.

Conclusion

Whether or not the United States attains its objectives in the Middle East will depend less on its foreign policy than on the course of internal economic, political, and social developments within the region. True, Washington can influence the pattern of these developments through, for example, encouraging or discouraging large expenditures for weapons, support for or censure of undemocratic regimes, and extending or withholding economic assistance to creative development programs.

U.S. public opinion and the role of influential lobbies are also an important factor. Since the Gulf War against Iraq, the region has receded from importance in public consciousness. According to a survey sponsored by the Council on Foreign Relations, both Europe and the Far East are more important. The general public rates Saudi Arabia along with Japan and Russia, followed by Kuwait and Mexico (tied), and Canada as vital U.S.

interests. The countries perceived as most vital among U.S. leaders are Mexico and Russia (tied for first), followed by Japan, China, Saudi Arabia, Canada, and Germany. Over half the public and four-fifths of the leaders would favor use of U.S. troops in case of an Iraqi invasion of Saudi Arabia, a higher figure than in the case of an Arab invasion of Israel, even though it is considered a key ally.[46]

The public shows increasing disenchantment with economic aid, preferring to decrease or altogether stop assistance to Egypt, the Palestinians, and Israel. Keeping aid to Israel at the same level is favored by 38 percent of the public, 9 percent favor an increase, and 44 percent want to decrease or stop it altogether. Among leaders, 45 percent favor maintaining the same level of aid, 50 percent favor decreasing or stopping it, and only 4 percent favor an increase.[47]

With the end of the Cold War, prospects for ending the Arab-Israel conflict, and growing opinion among leading Israelis that U.S. aid should be greatly diminished if not terminated altogether, the role of the powerful Israel lobby is likely to decline as an influential factor in U.S. Middle East policy. As the question of Israel becomes less important in internal U.S. politics, its high-ranking priority will also be lowered. Indeed, if the Arab-Israel conflict dissipates, the region as a whole is likely to become less significant in U.S. foreign policy, although continued U.S. dependence on oil will, most likely, keep the Persian Gulf high on the U.S. list of foreign policy priorities.

In sum, the United States has been basically successful in helping to broker a series of Israeli-Palestinian agreements—at least until the advent of the Netanyahu government—but its policy of "dual containment" against Iran and Iraq has met with less success, although the United States remains the primary defender of the Gulf Cooperation Council states. At the same time, while the United States has become more dependent on Middle Eastern oil and has sought to sell extensive armaments to the countries of the GCC, internal problems in these countries may cause increasing problems for the United States in the future.

Notes

1. *Middle East Policy (MEP)* 3, no. 2 (1994): 1.

2. The Lausanne Conference, April-September 1949, following the armistice agreements between Israel and Egypt, Jordan, Syria, and Lebanon, was the first attempt to discuss a comprehensive settlement of the Arab-Israel conflict, an attempt that failed. See Neil Caplan, *The Lausanne Conference, 1949: A Case Study in Middle East Peacemaking* (Tel Aviv: Tel Aviv University, 1993).

3. George C. McGhee, assistant secretary of state for Near Eastern, African and South Asian affairs, in 1949 proposed a plan for economic rehabilitation of the whole Middle East as the key to a peace settlement.

4. In 1963 Eric Johnston headed a mission sent by President Eisenhower to implement a plan for developing the Jordan River system involving Israel and the Arab riparian states. Gordon Clapp headed the U.N. Economic Survey Mission sent to survey possibilities of regional economic development in 1949.

5. The Camp David agreements signed by Israel and Egypt in 1978 preceded the 1979 Israel-Egyptian treaty of peace.

6. The intifada, or Palestine Arab uprising against Israel's occupation of Gaza and the West Bank, erupted in December 1987. It never officially ended but gradually petered out by the time the DOP was signed in 1993. See Don Peretz, *Intifada: the Palestinian Uprising* (Boulder: Westview Press, 1990).

7. Joseph E. Johnson, former president of the Carnegie Endowment for International Peace, was appointed by President Kennedy to explore practical measures for dealing with the Palestine refugee problem.

8. From the time of President Anwar Sadat's visit to Jerusalem in November 1977 to the peace treaty in 1979, President Jimmy Carter and his representatives were instrumental in preventing collapse of the negotiations.

9. See Michael Mandelbaum, "Foreign Policy as Social Work," *Foreign Affairs (FA)* 75, no.1 (January-February 1996): 17–32.

10. See statements by American officials indicating U.S. willingness to "help guarantee border security arrangements in support of an Israel-Syrian agreement," in *Supporting Peace: America's Role in an Israel-Syria Peace Agreement* (Washington, D.C.: The Washington Institute for Near East Policy (WINEP), 1994), 71–73.

11. *U.S. Forces on the Golan Heights: An Assessment of Benefits and Costs,* Center for Security Policy, Washington, D.C., October 25, 1994.

12. See article by Dov S. Zakheim, former U.S. deputy undersecretary of defense, in the *Washington Times,* January 5, 1996; *Middle East International (MEI),* no. 517 (January 19, 1996): 6.

13. *Supporting Peace,* 47.

14. The DOP of September 1993 was the first in a series of agreements between Israel and the PLO leading to an interim agreement signed in September 1995, providing for Palestinian self-rule prior to a final peace settlement.

15. Final status talks between Israel and the Palestine Authority were to begin in May 1996 and are to be completed by 1999. The increasing confrontation between the Netanyahu government and Arafat postponed the beginning of final status talks.

16. *MEP* 3, no. 2 (1994): 3.

17. Ibid., no. 1: 1–7.

18. Ibid.

19. *New York Times,* June 21, 1995.

20. *New York Times,* January 30, 1996; February 6, 1996.

21. Shibley Telhami and Michael O'Hanlon, "Europe's Oil, Our Troops," *New York Times*, December 30, 1995.

22. *New York Times*, December 26, 1995; *MEI*, vol. 516 (January 5, 1996): 9.

23. Milton Viorst, "The Limits of Revolution," *Foreign Affairs*, November/December 1995, 63–76.

24. *New York Times*, December 1, 1995.

25. *New York Times*, February 6, 1996.

26. *New York Times*, March 17, 1995; March 5, 1995; January 27, 1996. See also chap. 8 by Phebe Marr in this volume.

27. *MEI*, vol. 517, January 19, 1996, p.20. See also chap. 14 by Robert O. Freedman in this volume.

28. *New York Times*, April 3, 1994; April 24, 1995.

29. Vahan Zanoyan, "After the Oil Boom," *Foreign Affairs*, November/December 1995, 2–7. See also chap. 10 by F. Gregory Gause III in this volume.

30. Zanoyan, ibid.; see *Saudi Arabia: A Country Report—The Political and Economic Situation*, The Committee for the Defense of Legitimate Rights, London, November 22, 1994.

31. *New York Times*, August 13, 1993; August 22, 1993; January 3, 1994; January 30, 1996.

32. *Conventional Arms Transfers to Developing Nations, 1987–1994*, Congressional Research Service, Washington, D.C., August 4, 1995, 10.

33. Joe Stork, "The Middle East Arms Bazaar after the Gulf War," *Middle East Report*, vol. 197 (November/December 1995): 14–19.

34. *Conventional Arms Transfers*, 30.

35. Stork, 15.

36. Ibid.

37. Ibid., 19.

38. *Conventional Arms Transfers*, 30.

39. Ibid., 6.

40. *A Population Perspective on Development: The Middle East and North Africa*, World Bank, Washington, D.C., August 1994, 4.

41. John Page, "Regional Development Finance Institutions," in *Regional Economic Development in the Middle East: Opportunities and Risks*, The Center for Policy Analysis on Palestine (CPAP), Washington, D.C., December 1995, 8.

42. Atif Kubursi, "The Economics of Peace: The Arab Response," in *Regional Economic Development*, 39.

43. *Middle East Quarterly* 1, no. 1 (March 1994): 61.

44. *MEP* 3, no. 2 (1994): 1.

45. "PLO's Ability to Help Support Palestinian Authority Is Not Clear," U.S. General Accounting Office, *GAP/NSIAD–96–23*, November 1995.

46. John E. Rielly, ed., *American Public Opinion and U.S. Foreign Policy 1995*, The Chicago Council on Foreign Relations, Chicago, 1995.

47. Ibid.

14: Russia and the Middle East under Yeltsin

Robert O. Freedman

The Middle East policy of Boris Yeltsin's Russia has been, in its formulation and execution, far different from that of the Soviet Union toward the region. Soviet policy was ideologically influenced, if not driven, until the midpoint of the Gorbachev era. Russian policy under Yeltsin has been far more pragmatic, if far more disjointed, and has had a very different regional focus. This chapter deals first with the changed process and priorities of foreign policy making under Yeltsin. Then, after a brief overview of Russian policy in the latter part of the Gorbachev era, I turn to an analysis of Russian policy toward the "near abroad," which this chapter treats as a critical part of Russian policy toward the Middle East. Next, the chapter analyzes Russia's policy toward the Persian Gulf, now the most important regional area for Moscow, with particular attention to Iran and Iraq. The chapter also deals with the other two major partners of Russia in the Middle East, Turkey and Israel. Finally, some conclusions are drawn about the nature of Russian policy toward the Middle East in the Yeltsin era.

Russia's Foreign Policy-Making Processes and Priorities

Domestic Politics

In most democratic countries, domestic politics play a significant role in foreign policy. In Russia, a country that became democratic only at the end of 1991, domestic politics have become particularly central in foreign policy making, not only toward the Middle East but also toward the world as a whole. The following overview of the main thrust of Russian politics since 1991 focuses particularly on its effect on foreign policy making.

The effect on Russian foreign policy toward the Middle East is clearly illustrated by a shift from a strong pro-Western tilt in 1992 to a highly nationalist thrust in 1996, a process punctuated by the January 1996 replacement of Andrei Kozyrev by Yevgeny Primakov as foreign minister. During this period Yeltsin's foreign policy tacked with the political winds of Russia, particularly after the December 1993 Duma elections. Instead of openly confronting the new Duma, as he had its predecessor, Yeltsin chose instead to try to adapt to its highly nationalistic foreign policy priorities. He repeated this pattern of behavior when a still more nationalist, and this time communist-dominated, Duma was elected in December 1995.

Stage One: A Pro-American Approach. The first stage of foreign policy during Kozyrev's tenure covered the year 1992 and was clearly characterized as pro-American. Thus Russia joined in enforcing the sanctions against Iraq by dispatching two warships to the Persian Gulf; it supported sanctions against Libya (the Russian Embassy in Libya was attacked because of Russia's support of the sanctions); and Russia was an enthusiastic supporter of the Arab-Israeli peace process. As for the countries of the former Soviet Union—the "near abroad" in Russian parlance, where 25 million Russians lived—Kozyrev took the lead in calling for normal diplomatic relations. He discarded Moscow's old, imperial behavior—a change in attitude strongly supported by the United States. Only in the case of arms sales to Iran did Russia take a position markedly different from that of the United States.

By December 1992, however, Yeltsin's relatively free hand in foreign policy was being challenged by Russian parliamentary opposition, where three main groups vied for power. On the left of the political spectrum was the group of legislators who supported Yeltsin's pro-Western foreign policy—including good ties with Israel, sanctions against Iraq, and cooperation with the countries of the "near abroad"—along with Yeltsin's efforts to reform and privatize the Russian economy. In the center of the spectrum were the advocates of a "Eurasian" emphasis in foreign policy, shifting away from an exclusive focus on the United States and Western Europe in favor of good ties with the Middle East, China, and other areas of the world as well. This group also wanted much closer ties with the "near abroad," where Russia would retain a dominant position. On domestic policy, the Eurasianists favored reform but advocated a far slower process of privatization. Finally, on the right of the political spectrum was the combination of "old-line" communists and ultranationalists. Though differing on economic policy, they all wanted a powerful, highly centralized Russia that would (1) actively protect Russians living in the "near abroad"; (2) act like a major world power, as the Soviet Union had done; (3) adopt a confrontational approach toward the United States, which they saw as Russia's main enemy; and (4) renew close ties with Moscow's former

Middle East allies such as Iraq. Both communists and ultranationalists also advocated the reestablishment of Moscow's domination over the "near abroad."

Stage Two: A Move to the Center. With Duma opposition to his policies growing, Yeltsin fired his prime minister, Yegar Gaidar, a Western-style reformer, in December 1992, and replaced him with the centrist Viktor Chernomyrdin. One month later, Yeltsin openly broke with the United States by criticizing the renewed U.S. bombing of Iraq. During 1993 he also increased arms sales to Iran—including submarines—and took a stronger position on the protection of the Russians in the "near abroad," suggesting that Russia should have "special powers as guarantor of peace and stability there."[1] Moscow also intervened more openly in conflicts in the Transcaucasus—the Abhaz-Georgian and Azerbaizhan-Armenian wars—and the civil war in Tajikistan.

Despite these nationalistic moves, Yeltsin's conflict with Parliament increased, reaching the stage of armed confrontation in late September 1993, after he sought to dissolve the Duma. While Yeltsin won the confrontation, it was politically costly and appeared to make him more dependent than before on the Russian military. Consequently when, probably much to his surprise, an even more nationalistic and communist-influenced Duma was elected in December 1993, he chose to try to work with the new Parliament instead of openly confronting it. This brought about the third stage in his Middle Eastern policy, which was characterized by a further turn to the right.

Stage Three: Moving Toward the Right, 1994–95. One of the indicators of the rightward turn in Russian foreign policy was the steady rapprochement between Russia and Iraq. Not only were Russian and Iraqi government officials visiting each other regularly, but by the summer of 1994, Russian officials began to call for the lifting of sanctions against Iraq. In addition, Russia stepped up its arms sales to Iran during this period and for the first time took a position independent of the United States in the Arab-Israeli conflict.

As far as the "near abroad" was concerned, Russia stepped up its efforts to assert control. It limited the amount of oil it would permit Kazakhstan to send through Russian pipelines, and it actively worked against Azerbaizhan's efforts to maintain its economic independence by seeking to control its oil exports.

Perhaps the strongest signal of Yeltsin's turn to the right was his decision to invade Chechnya in December 1994. This ill-fated decision, perhaps aimed at securing control over the Baku-Grozny oil pipeline, was both an economic and military disaster. It led to the deaths of more than thirty thousand civilians, and it involved an ill-equipped, poorly trained, and poorly motivated Russian army in a prolonged and bitter war.

As far to the right as Yeltsin had moved in 1994, he was to move still further in 1995. Under his direction, Russia moved ahead with the sale of nuclear reactors to Iran in the face of bitter U.S. criticism. Yeltsin also stepped up Russia's efforts to lift the sanctions against Iraq. In the "near abroad," Russia adopted its toughest position to date. Yeltsin called for changes in the CFE treaty limitations on the stationing of military equipment in southern Russia. He also signed an edict that ominously called for Russia to ensure that the members of the Commonwealth of Independent States (CIS) pursue a "friendly" policy toward Russia, and called for the stationing of Russian Federation border guard troops in these countries.[2]

Despite this turn to the right, Yeltsin suffered a major defeat in the December 1995 Duma elections. This development led him to fire almost all of his reformist and overtly pro-Western government officials, such as Kozyrev, and to replace them with conservatives or Russianist nationalists like Yevgeny Primakov, who had long argued for an independent position for Russia in world affairs. These actions set the stage for Yeltsin's activist presidential election campaign. He sought to convince the Russian electorate that he was as nationalist and as faithful to Russian interests as his main rival, communist leader Gennady Zuganov, a strategy that was to prove successful, as Yeltsin was to be reelected as Russia's president in July 1996.

Discordant Voices in Russian Foreign Policy Making

While Yeltsin has set the overall tone for Russian foreign policy, a number of other autonomous or semiautonomous actors have been assertive in Russian policy toward the Middle East, as well as the "near abroad." They have tended to complicate Russian foreign policy making, particularly when a direct clash occurs between the independent actor and the Russian Foreign Ministry. Indeed this was one of the reasons Kozyrev was replaced as foreign minister by Primakov in January 1996, but it is not yet clear that Primakov has managed to assert control over the foreign policy making process in Moscow. The five key actors in Russian foreign policy appear to be (1) Yeltsin himself and the presidential office, (2) the Foreign Ministry, (3) Lukoil, Transneft, and the other energy conglomerates that have close ties to Prime Minister Chernomyrdin, (4) the Defense Ministry, and (5) the Atomic Energy Ministry.

Perhaps the leading example of independent foreign policy making in Russia is Lukoil. Owned in part by the U.S. oil company ARCO (which has been seeking to compensate for declining oil output in Alaska), Lukoil in 1994 came into direct conflict with the Russian Foreign Ministry. The Foreign Ministry claimed that none of the five Caspian Sea littoral states (Russia, Azerbaizhan, Iran, Kazakhstan, and Turkmenistan) could act independently in developing the oil resources in the Caspian Sea. Rebuffing the policy of the Russian Foreign Ministry, Lukoil signed an agreement with the Azerbaizhani international operating company to extract Azeri oil from the Caspian Sea, an action which explicitly recognized Azerbaizhan's right to extract oil in its sector of the Caspian.[3]

Lukoil in mid-March 1996 joined Chevron and Mobil in a consortium to build an oil pipeline from the Tenghiz field in Kazakhstan to the Russian oil port of Novorossisk. Kazakhstan, like Azerbaizhan, claims the right to extract oil independently from its sector of the Caspian Sea, and until March 1996 its efforts to market its oil had been stymied by Russian limits on its oil transshipments through Russian pipelines. Indeed, in February 1996 Primakov had reportedly visited Kazakhstan in an unsuccessful effort to persuade Kazakhstan to accept the Russian position on Caspian Sea oil. While Russia will still have influence over the oil shipments since the pipeline will go through Russian territory, the presence of major foreign contractors makes it less likely that the Kazakh oil shipments will be interfered with, thus giving Kazakhstan a greater degree of freedom of action vis-à-vis Russia.[4]

In commenting rather caustically on the lack of order in Russian foreign policy making, the Russian periodical *Kommersant* noted, "It is impossible to pursue an integrated foreign and foreign economic policy today [in part] because Russia's political and economic elite, including its ruling elite, not only is not consolidated, but has split into competing, hostile factions, groups and groupings that are openly battling each other. It would be simply foolish for our foreign partners not to take advantage of this circumstance at any talks with Moscow."[5]

Another example of an independent foreign policy actor is the Russian Defense Ministry. In both Chechnya and Tajikistan, it appears that the Defense Ministry was making its own policy, often at cross-purposes to that of the Foreign Ministry and the Office of the President. Yeltsin's National Security adviser, Yuri Baturin, interviewed after an early March 1996 trip to Tajikistan, was asked who had influenced the situation in Tajikistan—the Ministry of Foreign Affairs, the Ministry of Defense, or the Federal Border Service. He replied, "All of them. All the departments are in on the act. The problem is that there has been no single department to coordinate this work."[6] In addition, in apparent contradiction of the Duma's and the

Foreign Ministry's opposition to NATO expansion, Sergei Svechnikov, chairman of Russia's State Committee for Military-Technical Policy, stated in February 1996, "Our country is prepared in principle to cooperate with the East European countries in switching their army's weapons to NATO standards."[7]

Another major independent actor affecting Russian policy toward the Middle East has been the Russian Atomic Energy Ministry, led by Viktor Mikhailov. According to the available evidence, Mikhailov wanted to go considerably farther than Yeltsin in selling nuclear equipment to Iran, including, in a preliminary agreement, a gas centrifuge system that had the clear capability of enabling Iran to produce nuclear weapons.[8]

In sum, these discordant voices and actions of quasi-independent Russian policy makers have seriously complicated Russian policy in the near abroad and in the Middle East.

Regionalization of Russian Foreign Policy Priorities

In addition to the appearance of conflicting centers of foreign policy making, one of the most striking changes in Russian foreign policy is the shift in regional priorities from those of the Soviet Union. With the breakup of the Soviet Union, the newly independent states of Central Asia and the Transcaucasus became a central focus of Russian policy makers in Moscow. Given the ties of the states of both subregions to Turkey and Iran as well as to other Middle Eastern states, Moscow has tended to view its policy toward Iran and Turkey through the lens of their policies toward Central Asia and the Transcaucasus,[9] particularly as Russia, with mixed success, has sought to regain control over both regions.

If the "near abroad" regions of Central Asia and the Transcaucasus are the most important regions to Russia, the area next in importance is the Persian Gulf. In the oil-rich and strategically important region, Moscow has sought, not always successfully, to balance its policy among Iran, Iraq, and the Gulf Cooperation Council (GCC) states, whose relations among themselves have usually been marked by deep hostility.

The third priority of importance is the central Arab-Israeli zone, composed of Israel, Egypt, Syria, Jordan, Lebanon, and the Palestinian entity. During most of the Soviet period this region was of primary importance to Moscow, as the Soviet leaders sought to construct an anti-imperialist Arab unity based on Arab hostility to what the USSR called the "linchpin" of Western imperialism—Israel. In one of the major transformations of policy, Moscow now sees Israel as its closest collaborator in the region. Israel is Russia's major trading partner among these states and the 800,000 Israeli citizens originating in the former Soviet Union create a major cultural bond between Russia and Israel. In addition, as shown later, a close Russian-Israeli tie enables Russia to play at least a symbolic, if not substantially important, role in the Arab-Israeli peace process.

Finally, Turkey plays a special role in Russian foreign policy toward the Middle East. Not only is it Russia's major trading partner in the entire Middle East and increasingly a key actor in Middle Eastern politics, it is also seen as a challenger to Russia's position in the Transcaucasus and Central Asia.

In sum, Russia's regional priorities have shifted dramatically since the collapse of the Soviet Union, with Moscow's central focus on Central Asia and the Transcaucasus significantly affecting Russian policy toward the Middle East. Following is an analysis of Russian policy toward these regions, which Moscow calls its "near abroad."

Russian Policy toward Central Asia and the Transcaucasus

There are genuine Russian interests that influence foreign policy toward Central Asia and the Transcaucasus, which some Russian leaders call the "soft underbelly" of Russia. However, there are also Russians who wish to incorporate the area into the Russian Federation—by force, if necessary. A number of problems facing both the Central Asian states and the Transcaucusus make them vulnerable to Russian efforts to reassert control. On the other hand, as will be shown, there are also a number of Russian weaknesses that hamper Moscow's efforts to extend its influence into these regions.

Russian Interests in Central Asia and the Transcaucasus

The first Russian interest is the Russian-speaking populations in Central Asia. (The Russian minorities in the Transcaucasian states of Georgia, Armenia, and Azerbaizhan are smaller numerically and less of a problem politically than those in Central Asia.) While not all ethnically Russian, the Russian-speaking population belongs to the Russian-language cultural sphere (primarily Russians, Ukrainians, and Jews), which stands apart from the rapidly reviving native-language cultural groups in the Central Asian states. This is particularly true in Kazakhstan, where the Russian cultural sphere still accounts for more than 40 percent of the population, and in Kyrgyzstan, where the share is about 20 percent. The other three Central Asian states have smaller shares: Turkmenistan, 9 percent; Uzbekistan, 8 percent; and Tajikistan, 3 percent.[10] Since 1993 Yeltsin has expressed an increasing proprietary interest in the Russians in the Central Asian states, even demanding dual citizenship arrangements for them in the fall of 1993. While Russian emigration from Central Asia has dropped off over the past few years and the Russian populations do not appear endangered there, many in Moscow see the need to reassert control over Central Asia to prevent a massive refugee problem, which the economically pressed Russian government does not have the resources to house and employ.

A second major Russian interest in Central Asia and the Transcaucasus is economic. A number of Russian factories during the Soviet era were dependent on Central Asian commodities such as Uzbek cotton. When newly independent Uzbekistan sought to sell its cotton on the world market, Russian textile workers were thrown out of work. Thus there are those in Moscow, witnessing the rapid decline of the Russian economy, who want to reincorporate Central Asia and the rest of the "near abroad" to help restore the Russian economy. In the case of the Transcaucasus, the critical issue is one of transportation routes. Russian leaders are increasingly demonstrating the desire to control the railroad and oil pipeline from Azerbaizhan to Grozny in Chechnya. They also express concern about a possible oil pipeline from Azerbaizhan through Georgia to the Black Sea, which would lessen the two countries' economic dependence on Moscow.

A third major Russian interest is national security, as manifested in the desire to rebuild the old Russian defense perimeter and the desire to deny the region to Moscow's rivals. During the Soviet era, the defense perimeter installations were not built around the edge of the Russian Federation (except in the Far East) but on the borders of Central Asia and the Transcaucusus (as well as Moldavia, Belarus, Ukraine, and the Baltic states). To rebuild similar installations around Russia would be exceedingly expensive, and at a time of economic weakness in Russia, virtually impossible. Consequently, Russia has been pressing hard for control of military bases on the periphery of the old USSR. Tajikistan, Georgia, Armenia, and Belarus have acceded to Russian demands, but Azerbaizhan and the Baltic states have rejected them.

A second national security interest is geopolitical. Russia sees itself challenged in Central Asia and the Transcaucasus by Turkey, Iran, and to a lesser extent by the United States, through its oil companies. To preclude major foreign influence in Central Asia and the Transcaucasus, many in Moscow now demand Russian hegemony over the two regions.

A fourth concern for Russia is the threat of radical Islam. In 1992 Moscow appeared to overreact to this problem, thereby getting sucked into Tajikistan's civil war at that time. Since 1993 the Russian leadership has developed a much more realistic evaluation of what is still only a nascent problem in Central Asia, Azerbaizhan, and the Moslem communities of the Northern Caucuses. Nevertheless, given the memories of Afghanistan and the fact that 19 percent of the Russian Federation's population is Muslim (albeit highly secularized), the threat of radical Islam is one that Russian leaders remain mindful of. Their concern is reinforced by the Islamic fighters in Chechnya, which lies just across the border from the Transcaucasus. Consequently, maintaining a forward position in Central Asia, including the Afghan-Tajik border, and bringing the Transcaucasus under control are seen by a number of Russians as ways to prevent the spread of radical Islam into Russia proper.

A fifth Russian interest is preventing the two regions from becoming conduits of narcotics and arms smuggling into the Russian Federation. Crime and narcotics use in Russia have skyrocketed since the collapse of the USSR, and Russians increasingly see Central Asia and the Transcaucasus as the causes of these problems. If Russia were to regain control of these areas, the argument goes, it would go a long way toward stamping out these societal problems.

Taken together, these five interests have motivated many Russians to call for the reestablishment of the old Soviet Union—either rapidly, as the communists want, or step-by-step, as Yeltsin and his advisers are now asserting. Indeed, the communist-dominated Duma openly called for the restoration of the USSR in a mid-March 1996 resolution. In the same month, Sergei Karaganov, chairman of the Collegium of the Council for Foreign and Defense Policy and a member of the Presidential Council, stated, "As far as rapprochement [in the Commonwealth of Independent States] is concerned, we must proceed cautiously when necessary and swiftly whenever we can. In particular, let us move as fast as we can where Belarus and Kazakhstan are concerned."[11]

Similarly, when asked about Russia's interests in Tajikistan, Yeltsin's National Security adviser, Yuri Baturin, summed up Russia's interests not only in Tajikistan, but in Central Asia as a whole: "[First] Tajikistan is a kind of gate to the Commonwealth of Independent States. At this point Russia is not in a position to move the border to the north. It is too costly. In the second place there are military facilities in Tajikistan which we cannot afford to lose."[12] Baturin also listed, as central interests to Russia, Tajikistan's uranium and aluminum and the need to combat the illegal trade in weapons and, especially, narcotics.[13]

Central Asian and Transcaucasian Vulnerabilities

A number of problems in Central Asia and the Transcaucasus make them particularly vulnerable to Russian efforts to regain control. Foremost are the economic problems. The 1995 GNP of Kyrgyzstan was only 50 percent of the 1990 figure. In the same comparison, Kazakhstan registered 45 percent; Uzbekistan, 82 percent; Georgia, 20 percent; Azerbaizhan 38 percent; and Russia itself, only 62 percent.[14] As production dropped, populations have been growing, exacerbating existing problems of unemployment and underemployment. A sharp rise in inflation has wiped out savings and put necessities out of reach for the poorer strata of the population.

The Central Asian states face two additional problems, one being ecological and the other, ethnic. The drying up of the Aral Sea, due to overuse of water from the Syr Darya and Amu Darya rivers, has led not only to water shortages but also to the blowing of poisonous salts over sections of Kazakhstan, Uzbekistan, and Turkmenistan. The overuse of pesticides and fertilizer has poisoned the soil and water and significant numbers of the population. The residue of Soviet nuclear testing in Kazakhstan has also left large tracts of land poisoned.

The Central Asians have their own ethnic problems as well. Tajikistan's population is 25 percent Uzbek, while estimates of the Tajik proportion of Uzbekistan's population range from 5 percent to 15 percent.[15] The intermingling of the Tajik and Uzbek populations has given rise to fears of a "Greater Uzbekistan," or a "Greater Tajikistan," depending on who is concerned. Compounding this problem, some Uzbeks and Tajiks live across the border in Afghanistan, where there are well-established Uzbek and Tajik warlords, and 13 percent of the Kyrgyz population is Uzbek.

As well as sharing the economic problems of their fellow states in Central Asia, Transcaucasian leaders face serious military problems that increase their dependence on Moscow. Armenia has needed Russian military support in its ongoing confrontation with Azerbaizhan over Nagorno-Karabach and has been willing to grant military bases to Russia as a quid pro quo. In the case of Azerbaizhan, one of the primary causes for the ouster of the anti-Russian Popular Front leader Abdulfaz Elchibey was a successful Armenian military offensive that was aided, if not manipulated, by Moscow. In the case of Georgia, separatist movements in Abhazia and Southern Ossetia have been manipulated by Moscow. The purpose was both to oust the anti-Russian Georgian leader Sapumarad Ghamsakourdia and to force his successor, the former Russian foreign minister, Eduard Schevardnadze, to agree to Russian military bases on Georgian soil. The Georgian parliament has yet to ratify the agreement.

Given their economic, ecological, and nationality problems and the absence of strong indigenous armies, the nations of Central Asia and the Transcaucasus appear highly vulnerable to a Russian takeover. Fortunately for those states, however, Russia has encountered a number of serious problems of its own that keep it from extending its influence to the point of hegemony in the two regions.

Russia's Problems

In conducting foreign policy, Russia is hampered by its very weak economy. Currently Moscow simply does not have the capability to provide the capital so desperately needed by the Central Asian and the Transcaucasian states to solve their economic problems.

Russia also faces competition in the region from Turkey and Iran. Turkey has offered credits and technical assistance to both Azerbaizhan and the Turkic-speaking states of Central Asia. Its own economic problems, however, have prevented Turkey from offering large amounts of assistance. Nevertheless, its encouragement of Kazakhstan to use the future Azerbaizhan-Georgia-Turkey oil pipeline may have given the Kazakh government the leverage needed to obtain a favorable agreement from Moscow for the Tenghiz-Novorossisk line previously mentioned.

While in power, Iranian President Rafsanjani deliberately kept a low Islamic profile in Central Asia, in part so as not to alienate Russia, Iran's primary source of arms and nuclear reactors, and in part because it was evident that the region was not ready for an Iranian-style Islamic revolution. Iran has not been hesitant, however, to offer the Central Asian states alternative transportation routes for their raw materials, which would partially free them from dependence on transit routes through Russia.

Yet another problem for Moscow in seeking to control the Transcaucasus and Central Asia was the war in Chechnya. The war exposed the incompetence and weakness of the Russian armed forces, which would make any direct military action against a Central Asian state (except perhaps Tajikistan) or Transcaucasia very problematic. It has also probably slowed the exodus of Russians from most of these states for fear that their sons would have to serve in Chechnya. If their loyalty to their home countries is thereby reinforced, it will be more difficult for nationalists in Moscow to play the "Russian" card.

Despite these problems, regaining control over Central Asia and the Transcaucasus remains a high priority for many in Moscow, and for this reason Russian policy toward both Iran and Turkey is heavily influenced by the "near abroad" factor.

The Gorbachev Legacy

When Mikhail Gorbachev took power in the Soviet Union in March 1985, the Middle East was clearly an area of superpower competition. Moscow backed the Arab rejectionists such as Syria, the PLO, Iraq, Algeria, and Libya in their confrontation with Israel. Moscow viewed Egypt, an ally of the United States, as an enemy. The USSR had no diplomatic relations with Israel, had reduced Jewish emigration from the USSR to less than 1,000 per year (as opposed to a high of 51,000 in 1979), and continued to champion the anti-Israeli "Zionism is Racism" resolution of the United Nations General Assembly. In the Iran-Iraq conflict, the USSR tilted first to Iran, then to Iraq, in an attempt to keep maximum influence in both countries while at the same time trying to prevent the United States from becoming the sole outside guarantor for the Arabs against Iran.[16]

At the time Gorbachev was ousted from power in the collapse of the Soviet Union, there had been a massive transformation in most Soviet policies toward the Middle East. The transformation was accelerated by the failure of the August 1991 abortive coup, which enabled Gorbachev to eliminate many of his most hard-line opponents. The most significant area of change was in Moscow's relations with Israel. Gorbachev restored full diplomatic relations with Israel in October 1991 and joined the United States in cosponsoring a UN resolution reversing the "Zionism is Racism" resolution. Russia also allowed hundreds of thousands of Soviet Jews to emigrate to Israel—much to the discomfiture of the Arab rejectionists like Syria and Iraq. They saw the immigrants, many of whom had advanced degrees, as adding to the military and scientific power of Israel. Despite extensive Arab criticism, Gorbachev allowed the flow of emigrants to continue, primarily to win the favor of the United States, although he justified his action on human rights grounds. Moscow also joined the United States in cosponsoring the Madrid Arab-Israeli peace conference, one more sign of the growing superpower cooperation between the United States and the Soviet Union, although the United States clearly played the dominant role at the conference. Gorbachev also cultivated Egypt, making it the centerpiece of Soviet policy in the Arab world. At the same time, Syrian-Russian relations deteriorated when Gorbachev refused to give Syria the weapons it needed for military parity with Israel.[17]

In the Gulf the degree of change was considerably smaller. Although he initially continued the Brezhnev policy of tilting between Iraq and Iran, by July 1987 Gorbachev had clearly tilted to Iran. After the Iran-Iraq war ended in 1988, Moscow again sought to improve relations with Iraq. The major challenge to Moscow's Gulf policy, however, came with the Iraqi invasion of Kuwait in August 1990. Gorbachev sought to retain influence in Iraq without alienating either the United States or the oil-rich Arab states of the Gulf Cooperation Council, which held out the promise of economic assistance for the USSR's increasingly hard-pressed economy. In doing so, Gorbachev adopted what might be termed a "minimax" strategy—that is, he sought to maintain the maximum amount of influence in Iraq while doing just enough to maintain cooperation with the United States and the Arab members of the anti-Iraqi coalition. In the end, the policy proved to be of limited success, as the U.S.-led coalition decisively defeated Iraq, while Moscow remained on the sidelines. It supported the coalition in the United Nations but did not even supply a hospital ship to the coalition war effort, and it was unsuccessful in seeking to save Iraq from a ground invasion in February 1991. When the war ended, the United States emerged as the dominant foreign power in the Middle East and the military guarantor of the wealthy Arab oil states of the GCC. The USSR was marginalized in the region except for its continuing ties to Iran and some residual influence in Iraq.[18]

As the Soviet Union's collapse accelerated following the August 1991 abortive coup d'état, Soviet policy toward the Middle East appeared to split into two separate lines, Gorbachev's and that of his Middle East adviser, Yevgeny Primakov. To bolster his weakening position at home, Gorbachev sought maximum cooperation with the United States, even if this meant playing "second fiddle," as was very apparent at the Madrid Middle East peace conference. Primakov, who set out on a major Middle East trip in September 1991 to seek economic assistance for the USSR's faltering economy, had another agenda. After visiting Egypt, Saudi Arabia, the United Arab Emirates, Kuwait, Iran, and Turkey, Primakov stated that all these countries "clearly did not want the disintegration of the USSR" and saw the need to preserve its united economic and strategic area. He said that "the leaders I have met want a USSR presence in the Near and Middle East because this would preserve the balance of power. Nobody wants some power to maintain a monopoly position there."[19] Yeltsin at the start of his period of rule in late 1991 would closely adhere to the Gorbachev line but four years later, under heavy pressure from conservative forces in Russia, Yeltsin would sound more like Primakov. Indeed he appointed Primakov to the post of foreign minister in January 1996.

Russia and Iran: A Tactical Alliance

Of all the states in the Middle East, perhaps none is more important to Russia than Iran, as an important actor in the Transcaucasus and Central Asia, as trading partner, and for its strategic position on the Persian Gulf.

Despite misgivings about the call in some Iranian circles for the spread of Islamic radicalism, and about Iran's offer of alternative transportation routes for the states of Central Asia and the Transcaucasus, the Yeltsin regime has found Iran to be an important market for Russian arms. It is a country in which Russia can demonstrate its independence of the United States. Iran is also an ally both in curbing Azerbaizhan's drive to escape Moscow's control and in checking Turkish influence in Central Asia and the Transcaucasus. For its part, the Rafsanjani regime found in Russia a secure source of arms at a time when it was threatened on many sides. Russia is also an important diplomatic link at the time when the United States is trying to isolate it, and an ally in containing the Azerbaizhani irredentist threat against Iran's Azeri population.

The rapprochement between Russia and Iran began in the latter part of the Gorbachev era. After alternately supporting Iran and Iraq, by July 1987 Gorbachev had clearly tilted toward Iran. The relationship between the two countries was solidified in June 1989 when Rafsanjani visited Moscow, where a number of major agreements, including one on military cooperation, were signed. The military agreement permitted Iran to purchase highly sophisticated military aircraft from Moscow, including MIG-29s and SU-24s. At a time when Iran's air force had been badly eroded by the eight-year Iran-Iraq war and by the refusal of the United States to supply spare parts, let alone new planes, the Soviet military equipment was badly needed.

Iran's military dependence on Moscow grew as a result of the 1990–91 Gulf War. The United States, Iran's primary enemy, became the primary military power in the Gulf through defensive agreements with a number of GCC states—which included pre-positioning arrangements for U.S. military equipment. Saudi Arabia, Iran's most important Islamic challenger, also acquired massive amounts of U.S. weaponry. Iraq, a major enemy, though badly damaged by the war, had oil wealth that would support a major military recovery if sanctions were lifted. To Iran's northeast, the war in Afghanistan continued despite the Soviet military withdrawal, with the Shi'a forces backed by Iran often getting the worst of the fighting. Finally, to the north, the collapse of the Soviet Union held out both opportunity and danger for Iran. The opportunity came in the form of the six new Muslim states that emerged (Azerbaizhan, Uzbekistan, Kyrgzystan, Tajikistan, Turkmenistan, and Kazakhstan), in which Iran might exercise influence. The possibility of danger came from one of the most important political forces in Azerbaizhan, the Popular Front, which ruled the country from June 1992 to June 1993. The Popular Front was calling for the unification of newly independent ex-Soviet Azerbaizhan with Iranian Azerbaizhan, a development which, if consummated, could lead to the dismemberment of Iran. (Iran faces a similar, if far less serious problem, with Turkmenistan. If it were to become a wealthy and powerful state as a result of the development of its natural gas resources, it could present an irredentist attraction to the Turkmens living in northeastern Iran.)

Given Iran's need for sophisticated arms, the pragmatic Iranian leader, Hashemi Rafsanjani, was careful not to alienate either the Soviet Union or Russia. Thus, when Azerbaizhan declared its independence from the Soviet Union in November 1991, Iran, unlike Turkey, did not recognize its independence until the USSR had collapsed. Similarly, despite occasional rhetoric from Iranian officials, Rafsanjani ensured that Iran kept a relatively low profile in Azerbaizhan and Central Asia, emphasizing cultural and economic ties rather than Islam as the centerpiece of their relations. The reason was partly that, after more than seventy years of Soviet rule, Islam was in a weak state in the countries of the former Soviet Union. The leaders of the Muslim successor states were all secular Muslims, and the chances for an Iranian-style Islamic revolution were very low. Indeed, some skeptics argued that Iran was simply waiting for mosques to be built and Islam to mature before trying to bring about Islamic revolutions.[20] Nonetheless, the Russian leadership basically saw Iran as acting very responsibly in Central Asia and Transcaucasia, and this view encouraged Russia to continue supplying Iran with modern weaponry—including submarines—despite strong protests from the United States.

Interestingly enough, during 1992, Yeltsin's honeymoon year with the United States, when he was in agreement with Washington on virtually all other Middle Eastern foreign policy issues, the two countries clashed over Russian arms shipments to Iran. There are several possible reasons why, even in 1992, Yeltsin proved willing to risk U.S. displeasure over the sale of arms to Iran. First, there is the hard currency question. Unlike Iraq and Libya, which were under UN sanctions, or Syria, which lacked hard currency to pay for weapons and which already owed Russia $10 billion, Iran could supply Russia with hard currency—badly needed because the Russian economy was going into a tailspin. Second, despite Yeltsin's cultivation of the United States, a number of influential people in the Yeltsin regime, such as Yevgeny Primakov, then chief of one of Russia's intelligence branches, advocated a more independent policy for Russia in the Middle East. Given the fact that the United States had relations with neither Iran nor Iraq, Russia had the opportunity to play a diplomatic role in both countries where the United States was incapable of exercising diplomatic influence. Third, America's NATO allies maintained extensive economic ties with Iran—unlike Iraq or Libya, which were pariah states—although the Salman Rushdie affair and the assassination of Iranian exiles in Western Europe did tend to damage political relations.

Thus, Russia had a certain amount of diplomatic cover for its dealings with Iran. The United States had quarreled with its NATO allies and Japan over their ties with Iran, a process that became even more pronounced when Bill Clinton became president in 1993. Fourth, when Yeltsin came under fire from vocal members of parliament on the center and right of the Russian political spectrum in 1993 and 1994 for being too subservient to the United States, he could point to American criticism of his policy toward Iran—which by 1993 included the promise to sell nuclear reactors—to demonstrate his independence. Indeed, one of the central issues of contention in the May 1995 Moscow summit between Clinton and Yeltsin was the Russian decision, in January 1995, to sell the nuclear reactors, which the United States claimed would speed Iran's acquisition of nuclear weapons. Yeltsin refused to back down on the reactor issue as he had done—under U.S. pressure—with a missile technology sale to India in 1993. Indeed, Yeltsin's submission of the issue to the Gore-Chernomyrdin committee seemed more a face-saving gesture to Clinton than a real concession. But Yeltsin did agree to cancel a proposed gas centrifuge sale to Iran, initially agreed to by Russia's Ministry of Atomic Energy. The sale might have contributed to Iran's more rapid acquisition of nuclear weapons—something very few Russians wanted.

Nonetheless, the Russians regularly asserted that U.S. opposition to the sale of nuclear reactors was due to commercial jealously, not to any genuine fear of Iran acquiring nuclear weapons. By the summer of 1995 Russian-Iranian relations had reached the stage of what the Russian ambassador had begun to call a strategic relationship. With the United States calling for the expansion of NATO, Russian nationalists looked to a closer relationship with Iran as a counterbalance. An article in the newspaper *Sevodnia* noted:

> Cooperation with Iran is more than just a question of money and orders for the Russian atomic industry. Today a hostile Tehran could cause a great deal of unpleasantness for Russia in the North Caucasus and in Tajikistan if it were to really set its mind to supporting the Muslim insurgents with weapons, money and volunteers. On the other hand, a friendly Iran could become an important strategic ally in the future.

> NATO's expansion eastward is making Russia look around hurriedly for at least some kind of strategic allies. In this situation, the anti-

Western and anti-American regime in Iran would be a natural and very important partner. Armed with Russian weapons, including the latest types of sea mines, torpedoes and anti-ship missiles, Iran could, if necessary, completely halt the passage of tankers through the Strait of Hormuz, thereby dealing a serious blow to the haughty West in a very sensitive spot. If, in such a crisis, Russian fighter planes and anti-aircraft missile complexes were to shield Iran from retaliatory strikes by American carrier-based aircraft and cruise missiles, it would be extremely difficult to "open" the Gulf without getting into a large-scale and very costly ground war.[21]

The Russian-Iranian relationship was to hit another high point in 1996 when the Iranian foreign minister, Ali Akbar Velayati, visited Moscow in early March and stated that Iranian-Russian relations were "at their highest level in contemporary history."[22] While in Moscow he joined Primakov in opposing the eastward expansion of NATO, while also emphasizing that Iran was interested in prolonging the truce in Tajikistan and developing cooperation in the Caspian oil shelf zone. One month later, in a radio broadcast to Iran, Russian Deputy Foreign Minister Albert Chernyshev reaffirmed Russia's willingness to stand with Iran against the United States: "Our country opposes the isolation of Iran in the system of international relations that America demands. We believe we can cooperate with Iran. We are doing that now and will continue to do so."[23]

While in the period 1992–96 there was a great deal of Russian-Iranian cooperation, the relationship was not without its problems. As the Iranian economy deteriorated, partly because of U.S. pressure to curb foreign investment in the country and partly because of the Islamic leaders' economic mismanagement, Iran had increasing problems in repaying its debt to Moscow. This led to a drop in Russian military and civilian exports to Iran in 1995. Nonetheless, at the end of 1995, as Russian-Iranian political relations continued to improve, Moscow agreed to reschedule the Iranian debt.[24] It remains to be seen, however, whether Iran can ever develop into the type of economic partner Russia might want in the region. Under these circumstances, the statement of Oleg Davydov, Russia's minister for foreign economic relations, following a visit to Tehran in late 1995 when the Iranian debt was rescheduled, may be seen as somewhat overly optimistic: "Russia considers Iran a strategic partner, a friend, and a neighbor, and the outlook in the field of bilateral economic and technical cooperation including the implementation of joint projects, is excellent."[25]

Other problems primarily reflect the ongoing civil war in Tajikistan and Iran's offer of alternate access routes for Central Asian and Azerbaizhani oil and natural gas. Rafsanjani could not have been very happy either with the Kuwaiti-Russian defense agreement of November 1993 and subsequent joint naval maneuvers, or with Yeltsin's efforts to diplomatically resuscitate Saddam Hussein in 1994 and lift the sanctions against Iraq. A Radio Moscow broadcast to Iran in December 1993 warned Tehran that the favorable prospects for development of Russian-Iranian relations could be greatly harmed "if Iran proposes political conditions, for example, concerning Tajikistan or Russia's military-technical cooperation with the Arab countries of the Persian Gulf."[26]

Tajikistan exemplified for Moscow the threat of Islamic radicalism, which some people in Moscow saw as a formidable problem, particularly in the immediate aftermath of the collapse of the USSR. Ironically, the civil war in Tajikistan did not begin with a radical attempt to seize power but with the ousting of an old-line communist leader by a loose alignment of Western-style democrats and moderate Islamists, primarily from the Eastern provinces of Garm and Pamir. When the communists came back into power, with the help of Uzbek and Russian military forces, many of the Islamists fled across the border into Afghanistan, where they were radicalized and then mounted attacks back across the border into Tajikistan. In the process they killed a number of Russian soldiers guarding the Tajik border and drew Moscow into the heart of the fighting. This posed a serious problem for the Russian leaders. They had no desire to get deeply involved in another Afghanistan-type war, as Deputy Defense Minister Boris Gromov noted.[27] Under these circumstances, an important objective for Yeltsin was a diplomatic settlement of the war in Tajikistan—a country that, unlike the rest of Central Asia, has a Persian rather than Turkic language and culture. Some elements in the Russian Defense Ministry appeared to have their own objectives in Tajikistan, including getting revenge for Russia's defeat at the hands of Islamists in Afghanistan, which differed from Yeltsin's.[28]

In any case, given the fact that many of the leaders of the Islamic opposition, including Akbar Turajanzode, had taken refuge in Iran, it became necessary for Russia to bring Iran into the diplomatic process. By the spring of 1994, with the aid of Iran, Russia managed to get talks started between the opposing Tajik sides, although Russian troops continued to suffer casualties in the fighting along the Tajik-Afghan border. By mid-1996 Russia had partially defused the situation, although there was no agreement between the Tajik government and the rebels, and Russian soldiers continued to suffer casualties (a preliminary agreement was reached in 1997). Throughout the conflict the Rafsanjani regime maintained a low profile and helped Moscow diplomatically. Thus for the time being, at least, the

Russian-Iranian relationship was reinforced. Iran has taken a similar low-profile position toward Russia's invasion of Muslim Chechnya. However, should more ideological and less pragmatic leaders take over in Iran from Rafsanjani, then Iranian aid to the Tajik rebels or to Chechens or other Muslims in the Caucases might well be forthcoming. If this should occur, Russian-Iranian relations would suffer a serious blow.

A second problem in Russian-Iranian relations lies in the area of Iranian offers to provide the Central Asian states and Azerbaizhan with transportation links for the export of their raw materials, particularly oil and natural gas. In its efforts to regain political control over the Central Asian states and Azerbaizhan, Russia has been exploiting its control over oil pipelines and railroad systems, so Iran's offer of alternatives to these states has not been welcome in Moscow. So far, however, only one rail link has been created, the recently opened Mashad-Tedzhen railroad between Iran and Turkmenistan,[29] although there has been an increase in truck traffic through Iran into Central Asia. Nonetheless, for the time being at least, it appears that Iran's offer of alternate transportation links for the oil and natural gas of Central Asia and the Transcaucasus is not a major problem. It is a moot point because of the weakness of the Iranian economy, which is suffering from a high inflation rate (58.8 percent in June 1995 by the Iranian government's own figures) and is heavily burdened by foreign debt. It is unlikely that Iran can provide the funds for pipeline construction out of its own resources, unless there is an unexpectedly sharp rise in oil prices. Given the opposition of the United States, Iran is unlikely to be able to raise the funds for pipeline construction in international capital markets.

The United States has given de facto aid to Yeltsin in his efforts to regain control over Central Asia by publicly discouraging Kazakh leader Nursultan Nazarbayev from exporting its oil via Iran, although a minor oil swap agreement was agreed to in May 1996. The United States has also pressured the Azeri regime of Gaidar Aliev to eliminate a promised offer of 5 percent participation for Iran in Azerbaizhan's Caspian Sea oil consortium. The United States has encouraged alternate transportation routes, through Turkey, for Central Asian and Azeri oil. However, of the two possible routes to Turkey, there is continued conflict between Azerbaizhan and Armenia over Nagorno-Karabakh, and the unsettled conditions in Georgia continue. This makes the Russian routes somewhat more attractive for the oil consortium, assuming an agreement is reached between the Russians and Chechens. Perhaps concerned about the fighting then going on in Chechnya (a cease-fire was signed in late 1996), the Azerbaizhani international operating company decided in October 1995 to authorize two alternate pipelines for Baku's "early oil," one from Baku through Georgia to the Black Sea and the other from Baku to Grozny in Chechnya and then to Novorossisk.

U.S. pressure on Azerbaizhan to drop Iran from the oil consortium led Iran initially to join Russia in claiming that no oil could be developed and shipped without the agreement of all the Caspian littoral states, thus further strengthening Russian influence in both the Transcaucasus and Central Asia. Clearly a rich and powerful Azerbaizhan is not in the Iranian interest, whether under Popular Front leader Abulfaz Elchibey or ex-communist Gaidar Aliev. Nonetheless, in a deft diplomatic move Aliev subsequently got Iran to agree to develop another sector of the Azerbaizhani oil holdings, an action that weakened Russian efforts to limit development of the Caspian Sea.[30]

In sum, since the collapse of the Soviet Union, despite some areas of friction, the Russian-Iranian relationship has basically been beneficial to both sides. For Russia, Iran is an excellent arms market, an area where a newly assertive Russia can demonstrate its role in world affairs, and a tactical ally in curbing Azerbaizhan. For Iran, Russia is a secure source of arms, a diplomatic ally at a time when the United States is seeking to isolate Iran, and a tactical ally in curbing Azerbaizhani irredentism. If Russia continues on its course of increasingly strident nationalism, an even closer Russian-Iranian relationship could develop. Yet there are limits to the relationship. First, the weakness of the Iranian economy may well limit its ability to purchase both military and civilian goods from Russia. Second, should Iran ever acquire the capability of providing oil and natural gas pipelines to Central Asia and the Transcaucasus, Russia's hold over the two regions would be weakened.

Russia, Iraq, and the GCC: Can Moscow Simultaneously Sit on Two Stools?

In the immediate aftermath of the Soviet Union's collapse, Yeltsin adopted an anti-Iraq policy, not only voicing support for the sanctions against Iraq but also dispatching two warships to help enforce the anti-Iraqi embargo in the Persian Gulf. Foreign Minister Andrei Kozyrev made a visit to the GCC states at the end of April 1992 in an effort to get financial support from the oil-rich kingdoms. He succeeded in getting a promise from Oman of $500 million for the development of Russia's oil and gas industry and $100 million for the modernization of its oil fields.[31] While fending off criticism of Russian arms sales to Iran, Kozyrev sought to promote Russian arms sales to the GCC states. (This was also the goal of Defense Minister

Pavel Grachev, who visited the United Arab Emirates in January 1993 and headed a Russian delegation to the International Weapons Fair in Abu Dhabi in February.)

Although this pro-GCC, anti-Iraqi policy was followed by Yeltsin throughout 1992, the Russian leader soon ran into strong criticism. On the far right of the Russian political spectrum was Vladimir Zhirinovsky, who attacked Yeltsin for selling out Iraq, a Russian ally, and called for the unilateral lifting of sanctions on Iraq. More moderate, centrist Russians also questioned the wisdom of Russia's close cooperation with the United States on the embargo, given Iraq's $6 billion debt to Russia and its potential as a future market. On the other side were those who asserted that a unilateral lifting of the embargo would not only seriously damage U.S.-Russian relations (and jeopardize billions of dollars of aid from NATO states), but would also alienate the oil-rich states of the GCC, which Moscow had cultivated since the days of Gorbachev. In addition, they argued, by aiding the GCC states and avoiding any rapprochement with Iraq, Moscow could offer the GCC states an alternative to the protection of the United States and other NATO states.

By January 1993 political pressure from the center and right of the Russian political spectrum began to have its effect on Yeltsin, a politician who has always tacked with the political wind. At that time, Yeltsin began to attack the renewed U.S. bombing of Iraq (although the Russian Foreign Ministry, under the leadership of the then very pro-U.S. Andrei Kozyrev, initially supported the bombing). In addition, Yeltsin began to authorize visits to Iraq by Russian government ministers, and Iraqi ministers began to visit Moscow. In February 1993 Yeltsin sent Igor Melichov, the deputy director of the Middle East Department of the Russian Foreign Ministry, to Iraq. While Melichov reportedly said the goal of his visit was to "strengthen and promote Russian-Iraqi ties," his superior in the Foreign Ministry, Viktor Posuvaliuk, claimed Melichov's comments were taken out of context and were falsely interpreted by foreign journalists.[32] But Posuvaliuk also stated that Russia could not ignore "the potential for Russian-Iraqi cooperation." The moderate Russian newspaper *Nezavisimaya Gazeta* condemned the Melichov visit as stupid because it worked against Russia's goal of the stabilization of the moderate Arab states in the Gulf.[33] Yeltsin, however, persisted in his policy of maintaining low-level contact with Iraq and in some ways moved to embrace the old minimax policy of Gorbachev. These low-level contacts were, however, insufficient for Yeltsin's opponents. In April 1993, the former deputy defense minister of the USSR, General Achalov, a conservative Supreme Soviet deputy, and Duma speaker Ruslan Khasbulatov's chief of staff journeyed to Iraq with a group of right-wing Parliamentarians. In Iraq, Achalov said the Russian people and the former USSR had never betrayed Iraq, but that the Soviet and Russian leaderships had.[34] *Izvestia* on April 8, 1993, responding to Achalov's visit, stated that Iraq would continue to be a place of pilgrimage for the Russian opposition as long as Saddam Hussein remained in power.[35]

In June 1993, following the abortive Iraqi attempt to assassinate former President George Bush, who was visiting Kuwait, the United States again bombed Iraq. Russian Foreign Minister Kozyrev supported the U.S. attack (which Washington had told Moscow of in advance), noting: "We cannot consider hunting presidents, even former ones, to be normal. Tolerating this would be tantamount to endorsing a policy of state terrorism."[36]

Yeltsin's parliamentary opponents denounced the attack on Iraq, and the Supreme Soviet lodged an official protest. Vice President Alexander Rutskoi, an opponent of Yeltsin, condemned Kozryev for his approval of the U.S. attack, asserting that such support meant "ignoring Russia's own national interests."[37] Meanwhile, Yeltsin upgraded Russia's diplomatic contacts with Iraq, dispatching an economic delegation, headed by Oleg Davydov, the minister of external economic relations, to Baghdad in August.[38]

When the crisis between parliament and Yeltsin escalated into a full-scale confrontation in late September 1993, there were rumors in Moscow that Saddam Hussein was bankrolling Yeltsin's opponents.[39] Nonetheless, Yeltsin's victory meant the temporary defeat of his pro-Iraqi opponents, led by Khasbulatov. This may have accelerated negotiations between Moscow and Kuwait on a defense cooperation agreement, which was signed during a visit by Kuwaiti Defense Minister Ali Sabah al-Salim al Sabah to Moscow in late November 1993. According to *Kommersant,* the treaty called for Russia to aid Kuwait in the "elimination of the threat to sovereignty, security and territorial integrity and repelling aggression."[40]

The treaty was a clear rebuff to Iraq, which still refused to recognize Kuwait's independence or the newly demarcated Iraqi-Kuwait border, and to Iraq's supporters in Moscow, as were the joint naval maneuvers conducted by Kuwait and Russia in the Gulf in late December 1993. Indeed, *Pravda,* the primary voice of the Russian right-wing nationalists, noted angrily on January 11, 1994, that because of the naval maneuvers, "the door to cooperation with Iraq—a rich and influential state with which we used to be linked by very close ties—has thereby essentially been slammed shut."[41] Reinforcing what appeared to be a thrust of building up ties to the GCC states, Vice Premier Aleksander Shokhin visited the United Arab Emirates in late November 1993. In the UAE he stated that his visit was taking place within the context of the Russian foreign policy aimed at creating prerequisites for boosting Russian exports. He also noted that Russian foreign policy was becoming more pragmatic. "While ensuring the country's political goals, its main orientation is the solution of Russia's economic problems. Such a policy is more reliable and serves both economic and political purposes."[42]

Having concluded the treaty with Kuwait (thus satisfying the GCC states) and having emphasized the importance of economic goals in Russian foreign policy, Yeltsin made a gesture toward Iraq, thereby continuing his neo-minimax policy. By the spring of 1994 Russian diplomats began to argue that since Saddam Hussein had begun to comply with UN demands on surveillance of its nuclear weapons capability, some gesture acknowledging his changed behavior should be made. One such Russian gesture was an invitation to Iraqi Deputy Prime Minister Tariq Aziz to visit Moscow in July 1994. Russian Deputy Foreign Minister Boris Kolokov, in an *Izvestia* interview, stated that Aziz had been told by Moscow that Russia opposed lifting sanctions until Baghdad recognized Kuwait's independence, agreed to the demarcation of their mutual border, and tried to ascertain the fate of missing Kuwaiti soldiers and civilians. If Iraq did these things, Kolokov indicated, Moscow would vote to lift the sanctions. If they were lifted, Moscow would even resume arms sales to Iraq, thus edging out Western states that would otherwise gain the economic benefit at Russia's expense.[43] Any such supply of arms to Iraq, of course, would damage Russian-GCC relations because the GCC states would now see Russia arming both their major enemies, Iran *and* Iraq.[44] Needless to say, such action by Russia would also severely harm Russian-American relations, which by the fall of 1994 had become strained over a number of issues, including Bosnia, the expansion of NATO, and Russian arms sales to Iran.

In October 1994, however, Russian policy toward Iraq suffered a major embarrassment. At that time, Saddam Hussein again moved his army toward Kuwait, an action that precipitated a massive U.S. reaction. President Clinton moved U.S. troops to Kuwait and warned Saddam not to invade. Yeltsin sought to exploit the situation by sending Kozyrev to Baghdad, where he claimed to have gotten Saddam Hussein's promise to pull back his troops and recognize Kuwait's border and sovereignty—in return for a gradual lifting of the sanctions. Not only was this deal rebuffed by the United States and Britain, it became a moot point because Iraq's parliament did not meet to recognize Kuwait and the Iraqi-Kuwait border. The end result of the crisis was a further strengthening of relations between the United States and the GCC states and a major embarrassment for Russia.

The situation was not alleviated to any major degree when Kozyrev returned to Iraq in November and belatedly extracted the desired promises from the Iraqi parliament.

Despite this embarrassment, Moscow continued to pursue its policy of improving relations with Iraq. At the end of January 1995, an Iraqi parliamentary delegation visited Russia and was received by Prime Minister Chernomyrdin. Deputy Foreign Minister Posuvaliuk warned in February that unless the UN Security Council responded to Iraq's positive steps, the situation in the region would further deteriorate.[45] In August 1995 the Russian deputy foreign minister, who was also the country's highest ranking Middle East specialist, asserted that Russia was "doing more work than others to normalize Kuwait's relations with Iraq." (Kozyrev visited Kuwait on August 2, the fifth anniversary of the Iraqi invasion, to offer Kuwait reassurance.) He also noted that Iraq's "disarmament file is close to being closed and work on the biological file is preceding in the same direction."[46]

Much to Russia's discomfort, however, the temporary defection of Saddam Hussein's son-in-law, Hussein Kamil, to Jordan led to Iraq's disclosure of hidden weapons information. Perhaps seeking to make the best of the situation, a Russian foreign ministry spokesman said, "It is unimportant what considerations Iraq took into consideration in deciding to lift the previous veil of secrecy on military programs. In the end, not motives but the result plays a more important role." The spokesman went on to say that Moscow hoped that the reaction of Washington and of other Russian partners in the UN Security Council "will be adequate to Baghdad's new demonstration of readiness to fulfill the U.N. resolutions."[47] Neither the United States nor the GCC were persuaded by the Russian logic, however, and the sanctions remained in effect.

While Russia was seeking to get the Security Council to lift the sanctions against Iraq, Saddam Hussein continued to dangle the prospects of major economic deals for Russia's hard-pressed economy. In late April 1995, Yuri Shafranik, Russia's energy minister, visited Iraq and offered to resume work on mothballed oil projects from the Soviet era. At the same time, Vagit Alekperov, the enterprising president of Lukoil, stated that his company wanted to develop Iraqi oil. As a result of the Shafranik visit, an agreement was signed providing Russia with drilling rights at two major oil fields in Southern Iraq, as well as rights elsewhere in the country, although they were not to become operative until sanctions were lifted.[48] Meanwhile the Russian Duma, controlled by right-wing forces, voted overwhelmingly on April 21, 1995, to lift the sanctions against Iraq and set forth three goals for Russian policy: (1) to pressure the UN Security Council to repeal the embargo, (2) to collect Iraq's debt if the embargo were to be partially lifted, and (3) to support Russian business investment in Iraq and large-scale co-operation with that country.[49]

The victory of right-wing and communist forces in the Duma elections of December 1995 was good news for Russian-Iraqi relations. In January 1996 Yevgeny Primakov, an old friend of Saddam Hussein, replaced Andrei Kozyrev as foreign minister. While Primakov stated that Russia would continue to observe the sanctions against Iraq and would not lift them unilaterally, the advent of Primakov may have convinced Saddam Hussein to begin to bargain in earnest with the United Nations for an oil-for-food agreement, an action he took one week after Primakov's appointment.[50] And, in order to help entice Russia into even more strongly backing the Iraqi position during the Security Council debates, Iraq made a multibillion dollar agreement with Moscow in mid-February 1996 for oil development and the training of Iraqi oil specialists.[51]

In sum, since 1992 Russia's relations with Iraq have evolved from limited hostility, with Russia actively helping to enforce the U.N. Security Council sanctions against Iraq, to close cooperation with Iraq offering Russia multibillion dollar economic deals and Russia working actively, if not yet successfully, to fully lift the U.N. sanctions.

The evolution of Russian policy has been due to three major factors. First, as Russian politics have moved sharply to the right over the past few years, Yeltsin has sought to move with the political tide and has adopted a foreign policy position independent of that of the United States on many issues, including Iraq. Second is the support for Saddam Hussein among the right wing of the Russian political spectrum. Yeltsin may have felt he could mollify at least part of the opposition by endorsing closer relations with Iraq. The third major factor is economic. The deeply troubled Russian economy was the primary reason for the victories of Yeltsin's right-wing and communist opponents in the Duma elections of December 1993 and December 1995, and the possibility of getting not only repayment of Iraq's $6 billion in debt but also contracts for Russia's armament and oil industries must have loomed large in Kremlin thinking. Indeed, Saddam Hussein skillfully dangled major industrial and military contracts before Russia in a bid to get Yeltsin's support.

So far, Russia has not unilaterally lifted sanctions. In this Yeltsin has embraced the old minimax policy of Gorbachev, seeking to obtain the maximum influence in Iraq without unduly antagonizing either the United States or the GCC. It remains to be seen, however, whether Yeltsin will be able to pursue such a policy successfully once all sanctions are finally lifted. If Russia becomes a major arms supplier to both Iraq and Iran, the GCC states may be driven even closer to the United States. (The possible exception would be Kuwait, which has always considered close ties with Russia an extra insurance policy against both Iraq and Iran.) In any case, there is the lack of GCC investment in Russia over the past few years (Russia is, to be sure, a poor investment risk) and little GCC desire for Russian weaponry, which did poorly in both the Gulf war and the war in Chechnya. Given these facts, and the GCC states' preference for buying their weapons from NATO countries that backed them during the Gulf war, it seems likely that Russian-GCC relations, damaged by both the Gulf war and Russian efforts to lift the Iraqi sanctions, will deteriorate further.

As a consequence Russia may decide to concentrate its efforts on building a sphere of influence in the Gulf covering Iraq and Iran, against which the United States is pursuing a dual containment strategy. Once full sanctions against Iraq are lifted, Russia would become a major military and industrial goods supplier to both Iraq and Iran and could be expected to forge close economic ties with both countries. For Russia's sphere of influence to be effective, however, Russia would have to create at least a modicum of cooperation between Iraq and Iran, heretofore bitter enemies. Whether even Yevgeny Primakov, a skilled diplomat, has the ability to effect such a rapprochement remains to be seen. Achieving it, however, would have to be a major Russian priority, since without improved Iraqi-Iranian cooperation, Russian hopes for a sphere of influence in the Gulf will remain unrealized. All this depends, of course, on the complete lifting of Iraqi sanctions. Russian foreign policy, under the stewardship of Yevgeny Primakov, may now be expected to play an even more energetic role in seeking to have the sanctions lifted.

Russian-Israeli Relations under Yeltsin

In the development of Russian-Israeli relations between 1991 and 1996, there are areas of mutual strong national interest, regardless of domestic politics in either country. Should the communists again come to power in Russia, however, the relationship may well be threatened. There are four major periods in the evolution of the relationship between 1991 and 1996: 1) the honeymoon period, from December 1991 to December 1992; 2) December 1992 to December 1993, when Yeltsin fostered the relationship despite rising domestic opposition from communists and ultranationalists; 3) December 1993 until December 1995, when Russian-Israeli relations, particularly in the areas of trade and diplomacy, flourished despite Yeltsin's adoption of a much more nationalist foreign policy; and 4) January through June 1996, when the further turn to the right by Yeltsin, and the appointment of Yevgeny Primakov as Russia's foreign minister, began to cast a chill on the relationship.

Russian interests in Israel are basically threefold: economic, diplomatic, and cultural. The primary interest is economic. Trade between the countries rose to approximately $650 million dollars in 1995, making Israel the second largest Russian trading partner in the Middle East, after Turkey.[52] The trade includes Israeli supplies of agricultural and high-tech goods to Russia, joint projects such as a $300 million Negev oil shale plant and a $150 million Dead Sea magnesium extraction plant, and cooperation in military technology. In the area of diplomacy, by maintaining good ties with Israel, Russia apparently hopes to keep a door open to the White House even if Russian-U.S. ties become strained, as they increasingly were in the 1994–96 period. A close tie with Israel also enables Russia to play, or at least appear to play, a major role in the Arab-Israeli peace process. This, in turn, has enabled Yeltsin to demonstrate to his domestic opponents that under his leadership, Russia is still playing a significant role in world affairs. Yeltsin was successful in this endeavor until April 1996, when he unsuccessfully sought to mediate the Israeli-Lebanese conflict. As for cultural ties, Israel has more than 800,000 immigrants from the former Soviet Union, almost all of them Russian-speaking—the largest Russian Diaspora outside the former Soviet Union. Israel hosts a large number of Russian artists, pop singers, newspapers, and even cable TV programs.

From the Israeli point of view, there are four central interests in relations with Russia. The first is to maintain the steady flow of immigration, which has provided Israel with a large number of scientists and engineers. The second interest is to prevent the export of nuclear weapons or nuclear materials to Israel's Middle East enemies, including Libya, Iran, and Iraq. The third goal is to develop trade relations with Russia, which supplies Israel with such products as uncut diamonds, metals, and timber. Russia is also the site of numerous joint enterprises begun by Israelis who had emigrated from the former Soviet Union. Finally, Israel hopes for at least an even-handed Russian diplomatic position in the Middle East and, if possible, Russian influence on its erstwhile ally, Syria, to be more flexible in reaching a peace agreement with Israel.

The Year 1992, the Israeli-Russian Honeymoon

Following his accession to power as leader of an independent Russia, Boris Yeltsin initially showed very little interest in Middle Eastern questions. He devoted his time and energy just to consolidating his power and then to gaining approval in the West—particularly in the United States—for Russia as the primary inheritor of the Soviet Union's international responsibilities, including its veto power in the UN Security Council. When Middle East questions arose, Yeltsin tended to follow the U.S. lead on virtually all issues. The Russian president, who appeared anxious to curry favor in the West, at first based his foreign policy on going along with American foreign policy initiatives. Thus, on questions related to the Arab-Israeli conflict, Iraq, and Libya, Yeltsin fully supported U.S. politics.

The only exception to this pattern of Russian support of U.S. Middle East policy, as noted, was in the area of arms sales to Iran, an enemy of both the United States and Israel with which Moscow was seeking close cooperation. In Russian-Israeli relations, the strong rapprochement that had occurred in the last few years of the Soviet Union continued under Yeltsin, as Moscow sought both economic benefits and political dividends from its growing ties to the Jewish states. Thus, when the multilateral phase of the Arab-Israeli peace talks began in Moscow, Russia backed Israeli demands that the PLO be excluded, much as it had been in Madrid.[53]

Following the Madrid conference, Russian-Israeli relations on a bilateral basis continued to improve. The Russian UN ambassador asked Israel to cosponsor the entry of former Soviet Republics into the UN. Yad Vashem, the Israeli Holocaust Memorial, was permitted to photocopy materials from the communist party archives dealing with Jewish issues. The president of the Russian Academy of Natural Sciences proposed the establishment of a foreign branch of the academy in Israel. Natan (Anatoly) Sharansky, the most famous of the former Refusniks living in Israel, was declared innocent of charges that he had spied for the United States. In late April 1992 Russian Vice President Alexander Rutskoi, then still an ally of Yeltsin, visited Israel. In a statement at Ben Gurion Airport near Tel Aviv, he said, "We consider Israel a very important place because of the many Russians who now live here. They form a bridge between us that can enable us to broaden our relations." In giving a toast to Israel on the first day of his visit, he said, "Israel and Russia have a great opportunity for the development of mutual cooperation and a blossoming relationship."[54] A memorandum of understanding on cooperation in agriculture was signed, which Rutskoi said "opens vast prospects for Russo-Israeli business in [the] agrarian sphere."[55]

Following Rutskoi's visit came the Israeli election of Labor Party leader Yitzhak Rabin, who quickly put together a coalition government that spurred the peace process. The election was followed by a state visit by Foreign Minister Shimon Peres to Russia, the first ever by an Israeli foreign minister. Russian Foreign Minister Kozyrev utilized the Peres visit to emphasize Russia's importance in the Middle East peace process, saying, "We want peace in the Middle East and are playing the role of honest brokers, trying to help the sides bring their positions together."[56] Peres said that he hoped the Russian government would continue to play a stabilizing role in the Middle East. For his part, Peres stressed that, given its close ties to the Arab world, Russia could help to bridge the gaps between Israel and its neighbors, contributing to the peace process by fostering joint economic efforts such as a desalinization project.[57] Less than a month later, Peres and Kozyrev signed a major memorandum in New York that called for greater development of Israeli-Russian relations, including increased cooperation between the two countries in the political, legal, economic, and cultural spheres. Peres and Kozyrev also stated their intention to develop political contacts at all levels between Israel and Russia, including the parliaments of both nations. The agreement also called for the strengthening of commercial, economic, scientific, and technological links between the two states, with an eye to encouraging joint investment projects and cooperation between Israeli and Russian business concerns. Finally, the joint memorandum stated that the two foreign ministers would give priority attention to the ongoing peace talks and that Russia, as a cosponsor of the peace process, would continue to actively promote a rapprochement between all parties engaged in the peace talks.

The Middle East peace process ran into obstacles because of an upsurge of fighting in Israel's security zone in Lebanon in November 1992 and the expulsion by Israel in December of more than 400 Hamas activists, whom it accused of inciting the increasing number of attacks on Israelis in the Gaza Strip and in Israel proper. Even with these setbacks, Russian policy did not turn in an anti-Israeli direction but remained very even-handed. A Russian Foreign Ministry statement after the November fighting in Lebanon noted Russia's "serious concern" and called on all conflicting sides in Southern Lebanon to show "maximum restraint."[58] Similarly, a Russian Foreign Ministry communiqué issued after the expulsion of the Hamas activists (which both Russia and the United States condemned in the UN Security Council) noted that "the Russian side is counting on the sides to show maximum restraint in their actions and hopes that the problem with the deportation of hundreds of Palestinians will be humanely settled very soon, taking into account the genuine interests of both the Israelis and Palestinians."[59]

The 1993 Period: Domestic Politics in Russia Becomes a Factor

Yeltsin began to turn away from the United States in the early months of 1993. In an apparent effort to gain support from his critics in parliament, Yeltsin distanced himself from his pro-American Foreign Minister Kozyrev and announced a "balanced" policy for Russia as a "Eurasian state." He also condemned the renewed U.S. bombing of Iraq and asserted that U.S. pressure would not prevent Russia from signing a rocket technology agreement with India.[60] However, while U.S.-Russian relations chilled, Russian-Israeli relations continued to improve. Ruslan Khasbulatov, an outspoken opponent of Yeltsin, visited Israel in early January 1993 as part of a trip to the Middle East. He met with Rabin and announced his support of "businesslike cooperation" between Russia and Israel in the "economic, scientific, cultural and other spheres."[61] Khasbulatov also downplayed the impact of the deportation of Hamas activists, stating that this incident should not disrupt the peace talks because Israel was "seriously intent on the success of the dialogue with the Arabs."[62] Russia and Israel continued to develop their economic, cultural, and diplomatic relations throughout the rest of the year. In February, the Russian government approved a draft agreement on scientific and technical cooperation with Israel, and in September Russia strongly supported the Oslo I accord. Kozyrev, appearing on the White House lawn, emphasized Russia's continuing importance in the Arab-Israeli peace process.

As Israeli-Russian relations deepened, the conflict between Yeltsin and his opponents in parliament worsened, and Russia's ties with Israel became part of the confrontation. *Pravda,* previously the voice of Soviet conservatives and now a major organ of Russia's right wing, on March 13, 1993, condemned the Russian government for following the U.S. lead on the Arab-Israeli conflict. It stated that "since the breakup of the Soviet Union, the opinion of the Russian delegate at the U.N. concerning the Middle East situation has never diverged from the opinion of the U.S. delegate however absurd it has been at times."[63] Then, as the date for the climactic popular referendum on Yeltsin's future approached, *Pravda* denounced Israel for its "extensive" influence in Russia and for its support of Yeltsin.[64]

Yeltsin's victory and parliament's defeat in the referendum did not slow the parliamentary attacks on Yeltsin. Ominously for Israel, a number of parliamentarians, including Khasbulatov and his ally, Vice President Rutskoi (whom Yeltsin was to fire in early September 1993), began to make common cause with the anti-Semitic and anti-Israeli "Red-Browns" on the right wing of the Russian political spectrum during the spring and summer of 1993. Yeltsin's confrontation with his enemies in parliament escalated, and on September 21, frustrated by the constant sabotaging of his domestic programs, Yeltsin issued a decree dissolving parliament. He announced that elections for a new parliament would take place on December 12, 1993. Parliament responded by deposing Yeltsin and declaring Vice President Alexander Rutskoi president. (Rutskoi, Yeltsin's enemy, had once been an ally.) Yeltsin then sealed off the parliament, whose leader, Ruslan Khasbulatov, called for public support. After a failed effort of mediation by the Russian Patriarch, conflict erupted when supporters of the parliamentary side (prominent among them militants of the fascist Alexander Barkashov's Russian National Union) broke through the police barricades around parliament. They seized the Moscow mayor's office (Rutskoi urging them on), then marched on the Ostankino TV center. Led by General Makashov, who had been denouncing the "imperialist-Zionist conspiracy," and other openly anti-Semitic National Salvation Front leaders, the predominantly right-wing supporters of parliament launched an attack on the TV center.

Fortunately for both Israel and Russia's Jewish community, Yeltsin defeated the fascist-supported forces of parliament. Both Khasbulatov and Rutskoi, as well as a number of their right-wing supporters, were imprisoned, if only temporarily. Yeltsin then introduced his own constitution, under which he was given greatly enhanced presidential powers, and announced parliamentary elections in December 1993. A number of political parties began organizing for the elections, not only those supporting Yeltsin but also those supporting the communists and the fascists. Yeltsin's opponents included the Liberal Democratic party head, Vladimir Zhirinovsky, who had been careful to avoid giving overt support to Yeltsin's parliamentary opponents during the October confrontation. Much to Yeltsin's surprise, and to the discomfort of the reform movement in Russia, both the communists and Zhirinovsky's anti-Semitic and anti-Israel Liberal Democratic Party did quite well in the elections. Zhirinovsky's party actually outpolled the pro-Yeltsin Peoples Choice Party of Yegor Gaidar.

The Period 1994–95: Yeltsin Lurches to the Right

In a shift from his confrontational relations with the old parliament, Yeltsin sought to work out a new modus vivendi with the new parliament. Thus he again removed from his government the controversial Yegor Gaidar, and he began to adopt a foreign policy more independent of the United States, in part to meet the criticism of his parliamentary opponents on the center and right. Yeltsin became far more assertive in protecting Russian interests in the "near abroad," using military and economic pressure to help bring such recalcitrant states as Kazakhstan, Georgia, and Azerbaizhan into line. He openly confronted the United States in Bosnia and temporarily succeeded in checking President Clinton's plans to take punitive military action against the Bosnian Serbs and the Serbian regime of Slobodan Milosevic.

The Middle East was also to see a unilateral intervention by Yeltsin, although, as in the case of Bosnia, it seemed more aimed at satisfying Yeltsin's domestic opposition than at challenging the U.S.-led Arab-Israeli peace process. Yeltsin's intervention followed the February 25, 1994, incident in Hebron, when an Israeli settler, possibly intent on sabotaging the Arab-Israeli peace process, killed twenty-nine Arabs praying in the disputed Cave of the Patriarchs. Yeltsin, without coordinating with the United States, urged a return to Madrid to save the peace talks and the introduction of international observers to protect the Palestinians (a position supported by the PLO but rejected by Israel).[65] Yeltsin also dispatched a series of envoys, including Foreign Minister Kozyrev, to Tunis and Jerusalem for talks with the PLO and Israeli leaderships. Finally, he invited both Arafat and Rabin to Moscow on official visits, thereby seeking to demonstrate Russia's centrality as the cosponsor of the Arab-Israeli peace talks.

The Yeltsin strategy seemed to be as follows. Arafat, who had signed the September 13, 1993, agreement with Rabin, had little choice but to return to the talks to get an implementing agreement. If Russia became very active in the diplomacy surrounding the effort to restart the talks, and if, as expected, Arafat agreed to return to the peace talks (as he was to do), then Russia could reap its share of the diplomatic credit for Arafat's return. Such a demonstration of Russia's centrality in a major world trouble spot would not only bolster Yeltsin's prestige but might also (as in Bosnia) help to satisfy his hard-line critics in parliament. Indeed *Pravda,* long a bitter opponent of Yeltsin, noted approvingly on March 15, 1994, that "Russia's current activity in the Near East has been greeted with approval in the Arab world, if not always in essence then at least in form . . . and not just the Near East, but also other areas on our planet have been waiting for this for a long time."[66]

This flurry of diplomacy may have strengthened Yeltsin domestically, and it did no lasting damage to his ties with either the United States or Israel. Moscow quickly abandoned the "Madrid 2" plan, and the PLO and Israel returned to the peace talks after a token international presence was temporarily positioned in Hebron. They reached an agreement on May 4, 1994. During his trip to Moscow, Rabin was warmly welcomed by Yeltsin and Defense Minister Pavel Grachev, and the Israeli prime minister, a former general and chief of staff, was invited to deliver a lecture at the General Staff Academy in Moscow. Yeltsin also promised Rabin that only defensive arms and spare parts would be sold to Syria.[67] (A Russian-Syrian military agreement was signed on April 27, 1994.) While relations between Russia and Syria remained strained, in part because of Syria's $10 billion debt to the former Soviet Union, the Russian leaders also promised Rabin to use their influence with Syria to help find information about Israeli soldiers missing after the 1982 invasion of Lebanon.

Russian-Israeli relations also improved markedly during the rest of 1994 and into 1995. Russia strongly backed the October 1994 Israeli-Jordanian agreement, as well as the Oslo II agreement between Israel and the PLO in September 1995. Russian-Israeli trade boomed, reaching $650 million dollars in 1995, and in the summer of 1995 Russia and Israel established a diplomatic working committee on the Middle East.[68] In late August, balancing its position, Russia announced it also planned to open a mission to the Palestinian authority. The major problem in the Russian-Israeli relationship was the Russian decision to supply Iran with a nuclear reactor, which Israel feared would speed Iran's acquisition of nuclear weapons. Indeed, Rabin journeyed to Moscow in September 1995 in an effort, unsuccessful, to get Moscow to stop the nuclear reactor sale.

Despite the sale, Russian-Israeli relations continued to improve. Prime Minister Chernomyrdin said after Rabin's assassination in early November 1995 that Russia had "lost a friend, a real one." In early December 1995 Russian Defense Minister Pavel Grachev made a major trip to Israel, meeting Peres and the chief of staff, Amnon Shahak. He also visited the Ramat David air force base, Israel's state military industries, Yad Vashem, and Rabin's grave. During his visit a memorandum on military cooperation was signed.[69] Grachev was, however, attacked by Russia's right-wing press for the agreement with Israel. The press accused him of intervening in Russian foreign policy and asserted that his visit was likely to impair Russia's relations with the Arab states.[70]

Grachev's visit may be considered the high-water mark in Russian-Israeli relations during the entire 1991–96 period. Soon after it came the Duma elections of December 1995, which resulted in a major victory for the communists and nationalists and a major defeat for Yeltsin's own party. This resulted in yet a further turn to the right by Yeltsin. Fearing a loss in the June 1996 presidential elections, Yeltsin fired his pro-Western foreign minister, Andrei Kozyrev, along with a number of liberal advisers. He replaced

Kozyrev with Yevgeny Primakov, an Arabist. Although of Jewish birth, Primakov had long been perceived in Israel as a friend of such Arab dictators as Saddam Hussein.

January–June 1996: Ups and Downs of the Primakov Period
in Russian-Israeli Relations

When Primakov took office, the Israeli ambassador to Russia, Aliza Shenhar, sought to put the best possible interpretation on the change in foreign ministers. She said she hoped that Primakov, an expert on the Middle East, could contribute to a settlement in the region. She also stated her hope that the appointment would not lead to a negative revision of Russian policy toward Israel.[71] Unfortunately for Shenhar, and Israel, such a negative revision was soon to occur.

In February an Israeli diplomat was ousted for spying. It is not yet clear whether this was part of a general pattern of getting tough with foreign states (British and Estonian diplomats were also expelled); whether the action was directed specifically against Israel; or whether this was yet another internal foreign policy conflict between the Russian foreign intelligence service and the Russian Foreign Ministry. In any case, the Russian Foreign Ministry tried to play down the incident; Foreign Ministry spokesman Grigory Yasin said that Primakov wanted to solve the problem "on a gentlemanly basis and without publicity."[72] Russia also sent warm condolences to Israel after the terrorist attacks in Jerusalem and Tel Aviv in February and March 1996, and President Yeltsin attended the Sharm el-Sheikh antiterrorism conference, which was convened by President Clinton to show support for Israeli Prime Minister Shimon Peres.

Relations chilled again, however, in April. A right-wing press campaign led by *Pravda* and *Zavtra* protested against Israelis in Russia for "spreading extreme nationalist rightist Zionist propaganda" and cooperating with the Russian mafia. The Russian government withdrew the accreditation of the Jewish Agency in Russia in early April under the pretext that it had not reregistered according to Russian law. This directly threatened Jewish emigration since the Jewish Agency was the main instrument for arranging the exodus of Jews from Russia and the rest of the former Soviet Union. Alexander Bovin, Russia's highly popular ambassador to Israel, noted that it was necessary to differentiate between the accreditation issue, which he termed a "bureaucratic problem," and the "pychological problem which certain circles in Russia have with the Jewish Agency's activities." Bovin added that "some people in Russia find it hard to accept that the [Jewish]

Agency is very well organized, teaches the Jews about Israel and Hebrew, buys them tickets, and helps them leave."[73] *Nezavisimaya Gazeta* was less diplomatic, asserting that "the Jewish Agency was involved in covert activity by collecting information about potential emigrants and so-called Refusniks who are barred from emigrating for security reasons." The newspaper also condemned the Jewish Agency for taking promising scientists out of the country and sending the most talented Jewish children to study in Israel.[74]

Russian-Israeli relations received another blow in late April during the Israeli military operation in Lebanon, which Israeli Prime Minister Peres called "Operation Grapes of Wrath." After taking an even-handed position in the fighting between Israel and Hizbollah in 1992 and 1993, Yeltsin tilted against Israel, denouncing the Israeli military action as "totally unacceptable" and calling for an immediate halt.[75] Primakov initially took a more balanced view, noting that a settlement should not be "at the expense of the interests of either side." He too denounced the Israeli military action against Lebanon as "an unacceptable and totally inappropriate action."[76]

Yeltsin dispatched Primakov to mediate the Lebanese conflict—and once again to demonstrate Russia's importance in the Arab-Israeli peace process. Prime Minister Peres snubbed the Russian foreign minister, saying, "I prefer efforts in this direction [working out a ceasefire in Lebanon] to be concentrated in single hands"—those of the United States.[77] Ultimately, U.S. Secretary of State Warren Christopher was able to work out a ceasefire without Russian participation. Primakov angrily criticized the United States for its efforts to "act singlehandedly," and he asserted that "Russia has been and will be present in the Middle East. We have our interests and responsibilities there and we shall act in the interests of peace and stability."[78] *Izvestia* took a jaundiced view of Primakov's efforts, noting that not even Syria insisted on granting Russia a role in the international committee monitoring the Lebanese cease-fire and calling the failure of the Primakov visit to the Middle East a "palpable defeat" for Russian foreign policy. The Russian newspaper went on to speculate that the reason why the United States no longer wanted to give Russia even the pretense of playing a role in the Middle East was because of recent Russian cozying up to Iran, Iraq, and Libya.[79]

If the United States was giving Russia the Middle East cold shoulder, it was not in Israel's interest to see a deterioration of its ties with Moscow. For this reason, while Primakov was still in Israel, the Israeli Attorney General made a final legal determination that gave Russia ownership of several properties in downtown Jerusalem previously controlled by the Soviet Union.

In sum, in looking at the period from January to June 1996, it is still not clear whether the chill in Russian-Israeli relations was due to a decision by Yeltsin and Primakov to downgrade the relationship, or whether it was due to election-year politics that forced Yeltsin to take a still more assertive position in foreign policy. In any case, given the interests both states have in a good relationship, a major deterioration in Russian-Israeli relations appears unlikely, at least in the short run, unless the communists take power. Indeed, the Israeli elections of May 1996 produced both a new government headed by Binyamin Netanyahu, who called for improved Russian-Israeli relations, and a powerful new political party made up primarily of Russian immigrants (Yisrael B'Aliyah) that called for improved ties.[80] Indeed, Yeltsin's reelection in July and the reregistration of the Jewish Agency in October signaled a turnaround in Russian-Israeli relations, although Russian arms and nuclear equipment sales to Iran remained a problem.

Russian-Turkish Relations: Do Economic Benefits Outweigh Political Problems?

Russian-Turkish relations since 1991 have been, at best, mixed. On the one hand, Turkey is Russia's most important trade partner in the Middle East, and Turkish construction crews are active throughout Russia. On the other hand, Russia sees Turkey as a major competitor in the Transcaucasus and Central Asia, as the leading edge of NATO activity in the two regions, and as a supporter of the Chechen rebellion. For its part, while profiting from trade with Russia, Turkey is uneasy about Russian support for the terrorist PKK and about the continued Russian military presence in Armenia and Georgia, near Turkey's northeastern border. Underlying the tension in the Russian-Turkish relationship are memories of centuries of confrontation as the expanding Russian empire came into conflict with an Ottoman empire on the decline.

When the Soviet Union collapsed, Turkish President Turgut Ozal and some of the Turkish elite saw the opportunity of expanding Turkish influence into Azerbaizhan and throughout Central Asia. Such a development would also enhance Turkey's relationship with the United States after the Cold War ended, when Turkey could serve as a bulwark against Iranian-inspired Islamic radicalism. Ozal's initial optimism led him to pledge more than $1 billion in credits for the newly independent Central Asian states in such areas as banking, education, and transportation. In addition, Turkey established direct air communications with the region; Turkish television beamed programs to the Turkic-speaking countries of the former Soviet Union; and Turkish businessmen established numerous joint ventures in these new countries.

In February 1992, two months after the collapse of the Soviet Union, James Baker, secretary of state of the United States, Turkey's main ally, paid a visit to Central Asia. *Pravda* complained that Baker was doing more there than the entire Russian Foreign Ministry. It warned that the United States was drawing the Islamic states of the former Soviet Union both into the orbit of U.S. policy and into the U.S. view of the world—away from Russia, "their closest neighbor and natural ally."[81] U.S. actions were linked by the Russian right to America's NATO ally, Turkey. Because of its Turkic cultural and linguistic ties to Azerbaizhan, Uzbekistan, Turkmenistan, Kyrgyzstan, and Kazakhstan, Turkey was seen as seeking to create a Turkic alliance on the southern periphery of Russia. In doing so, it would use such devices as the Black Sea Economic Cooperation Zone, which it created, and the Economic Cooperation Organization, in which it shared leadership with Iran.[82] This Russian concern was not baseless; the late Turkish president, Turgut Ozal, had noted in March 1993: "Whatever the shape of things to come, we will be the real elements and most important pieces of the status quo and new order to be established in the region from the Balkans to Central Asia. In this region, there cannot be a status quo or political order that will exclude us."[83]

Besides those in Moscow who feared Turkish political expansion, others there were initially concerned by the threat of "fundamentalist" Islam emanating from Iran, which could infect not only the Muslim states of the former Soviet Union but also the Muslims who live in Russia. For this reason they saw the secular Islamic model of Turkey as a useful counterweight to Iranian Islamic radicalism.[84]

By 1993 the Russian leadership was taking a calmer view of both the threat of Islamic radicalism in Central Asia and the danger of Turkish competition in the region. While Turkish assistance was welcomed by the leaders of Central Asia and Azerbaizhan, it did not lead to the rapid expansion of Turkish influence. In the first place, having just rid themselves of one "big brother," the Central Asians had no desire for another, and they sought to maximize their ties with a number of states in order to avoid dependence on any one.[85] As noted, the economic problems of these states (with the exception of Turkmenistan) were great: rapid inflation, overpopulation, underemployment, water shortages, severe ecological damage, and more. Turkey simply did not have the economic capacity to meet their needs, especially as its own economy was reeling from a 70 percent annual inflation rate. Another factor was the resurgence of the Kurdish uprising, which diverted Turkish attention from Central Asia to more pressing needs at home. Similar concerns of Turkish policy makers were the fighting in the former Yugoslavia, pitting Bosnian Muslims, supported by Turkey, against Serbs and, initially, Croats; the continuing conflict with Greece over Cyprus; and, above all, the war between Armenia and Azerbaizhan.[86] The death of President Ozal, ironically just after he had completed a tour of Central Asia in March 1993, also seemed to weaken Turkish efforts to gain influence in the region, and Turkish leaders had to be disappointed that the Central Asian Muslim leaders did not back the Turkish position on such issues as Cyprus.

In the Transcaucasus, Turkish influence also declined. When the pro-Turkish Azeri president, Abulfaz Elchibey, was ousted in June 1993, he was replaced by former Soviet Politburo member Gaidar Aliev. While certainly not a pawn of Moscow, as he was subsequently to demonstrate, Aliev was less anti-Russian and less pro-Turkish than Elchibey had been. (Aliev has resisted the placement of Russian troops on Azerbaizhan's border with Iran, although he did agree to Azerbaizhan's reentry into the Commonwealth of Independent States.) The Turks not only proved unable to halt the advance of Armenian forces into Azerbaizhan but also could not protect their protege, Elchibey, there.

Moscow's use of economic warfare to gain political obedience from the states on its southern periphery is also a problem for Turkey. By closing pipelines to Kazakh exports of oil and natural gas, and by seeking to pressure Azerbaizhan to reroute the oil it would get from its Caspian offshore oil fields through Russia, rather than through Turkey, Moscow sought to limit Turkish influence.[87] When Turkey responded to this pressure by threatening to limit Russian oil tanker shipments through the Bosporus and Dardanelles Straits, Russia, in turn, responded by planning a pipeline that would circumvent the straits by going through its traditional ally, Bulgaria, and Turkey's enemy, Greece, to the Mediterranean.

Despite Moscow's appearing to have the upper hand by 1995, Turkey did not give up. At the end of October 1994, Turkey hosted a conference of the leaders of the Turkic states of the former Soviet Union. At the conference Turkish President Suleyman Demriel noted that "instead of one, there are seven Turkish flags since the collapse of the Soviet Union"—a remark that reportedly greatly irritated the Russians.[88] Moscow may have taken comfort from one paragraph of the conference's final declaration—that the heads of state reaffirmed their belief in a social order based on *secularism* (my emphasis). The Russians could not have been happy, however, with another paragraph in which the heads of state welcomed the construction of natural gas and oil pipelines to provide Europe with these fuels via Turkey.[89]

Throughout 1995, despite its economic problems, Turkey continued to compete with Russia in Central Asia and the Transcaucasus. During the summer of 1995, Turkey extended credits to Kazakhstan, Uzbekistan, Azerbaizhan, and Georgia. Speaking at the third Turkic summit in Bishkek, Kyrgyzstan, in late August, President Demriel urged the Turkic-speaking states to rid themselves of their dependency on "other powers."[90] The final communiqué of the summit emphasized the need to develop joint projects in oil and natural gas.[91] With the diplomatic groundwork prepared, Turkey stepped up its lobbying efforts to convince the Azerbaizhani international operating company to send oil from Baku through Georgia to the Mediterranean (and Turkey), as well as from Baku to Russia. Turkey's lobbying proved successful when, on October 9, 1995, the consortium endorsed routes through both Russia and Turkey. Should the pipeline through Turkey be constructed as planned, Turkey's position in both Central Asia and the Transcaucasus would be strengthened, as would the independence of new states of the region vis-à-vis Russia; Russia's position in these critical regions of its "near abroad" would be correspondingly weakened.[92]

On the purely bilateral level, Turkish-Russian relations were mixed in the 1992–1996 period. Both countries now share a desire to lift sanctions against Iraq.[93] In addition, the Russians, long interested in gaining markets for their weaponry, have signed arms sales agreements with Turkey. Russia will provide helicopters and combat vehicles in partial repayment of the debt of the former Soviet Union to Turkey, which Moscow inherited.[94] Ironically, at a time when Turkey is under fire from its NATO allies for its repressive acts against the Kurds, Russia has thus become an important, if only partial, substitute arms supplier. Moscow, however, is not above using the Kurdish issue to pressure Turkey. For instance, in February 1994 Russia hosted "The History of Kurdistan" conference, which was cosponsored by an organization affiliated with the PKK—an action protested by the Turkish Foreign Ministry.[95] For its part Russia was unhappy about what it saw as Turkish aid to the Chechen rebels.[96] Yet another area of conflict between Ankara and Moscow is the Russian effort to increase the number of heavy weapons it can station in the Northern Caucuses under the CFE (Conventional Forces in Europe) treaty—claiming instability in Georgia,

Armenia, and Azerbaizhan—something Turkey strongly opposes.[97] Finally, Russia's decision to sell advanced surface-to-air missiles (SAMs) to the Greek government of southern Cyprus also greatly angered the Turks.

Despite these political problems, Russian-Turkish trade continues to grow. Turkey is now Russia's number one trading partner, and formal and informal trade combined are estimated at $8 billion to $10 billion annually. Turkish merchants in Istanbul contributed $5 million to Yeltsin's reelection campaign, and Turkey has become a favorite vacation spot for Russian tourists.[98] Meanwhile, Turkish construction crews are working throughout Russia and were even given the contract to repair the Russian parliament building, badly damaged during the fighting in October 1993.

In sum, Turkey remains an active competitor for Moscow in both Central Asia and the Transcaucasus, although its ability to compete has been limited by economic weaknesses, by governmental instability (which became increasingly evident after the December 1995 Turkish elections), by the PKK-led Kurdish uprising, and by foreign policy problems in Cyprus, Greece, and the Balkans. On a bilateral basis, Russian-Turkish trade relations are strong, and Turkey gets some of its military equipment from Russia. Nonetheless, political ties remain strained, not only by the competition for influence in Central Asia and the Transcaucasus, but also by Russian military activity in Georgia and Armenia, by Russian arms sales to the Greek Cypriots, and by what Turkish leaders perceive as Russian efforts to manipulate the PKK against Turkey. The rise to power of an Islamist-led coalition government in Turkey in late June 1996, the leader of which, Necmettin Erbakan, had long been a foe of Moscow, further alarmed Moscow, but he was to stay in power only one year.

Conclusions

In its policy toward the Middle East from 1991 to 1996, Russia has moved from active cooperation with the United States on virtually all Middle East issues in 1992, to assertions of its independence of U.S. policy in the region in 1996. By the summer of 1996 Moscow clearly was pursuing an independent policy in the region, as indicated by its call for a lifting of the sanctions against Iraq, its mediation attempts in the conflict in Southern Lebanon, and its sale of increasingly sophisticated arms to Iran. There were, however, limits to Russia's degree of assertiveness: it did not unilaterally abolish Russian participation in the sanctions regime, it ultimately acquiesced in American efforts to solve the 1996 fighting in Southern Lebanon, and it backed off from selling a nuclear centrifuge facility to Iran. Such incidents indicate that neither Yeltsin nor his main advisers wish to directly confront the United States in the Middle East. Whether this will change during Yeltsin's second term remains to be seen, as do the prospects under a more nationalist or even communist leader.

In a significant change from Soviet times, domestic politics have had a major role in the formation of Russian policy toward the Middle East as well as toward the rest of the world. Yeltsin's turn to a more assertive position in the Middle East was due in large part to criticism from successive Russian Dumas—each more nationalistic than its predecessor. This was the case not only with the Duma that he ousted by force in October 1993, but also with the even more nationalistic Dumas elected in December 1993 and December 1995. Following the December 1993 Duma election, Yeltsin broke with the United States on policy toward the Arab-Israeli conflict by proposing a return to the Madrid peace talks, and he also began advocating the conditional lifting of sanctions against Iraq. Following the December 1995 Duma elections, in which many more nationalistic and communist legislators were elected, and with the Russian presidential elections only six months away, Yeltsin fired his pro-Western foreign minister, Andrei Kozyrev. He appointed as successor the nationalist Yevgeny Primakov, and he seized on a series of Middle Eastern events to demonstrate to the Russian electorate that he was a leader of international stature.

With Yeltsin's victory in the July 1996 second round of the presidential elections, some of the domestic pressure on the Russian leader may have been relieved. Nonetheless, he still faces a Duma dominated by communists and nationalists, so it is unlikely that Russia's assertive Middle East policy will change markedly.

A third major conclusion to be drawn from this study is that Russian policy toward the Middle East has a very different focus than Soviet policy did in the period from 1955 to 1987, the primary years of Moscow's active competition with the United States in the region. With the collapse of the Soviet Union and the emergence of the former Soviet republics of Central Asia and the Transcaucasus as independent states, the leadership in Moscow perceived that Russia was vulnerable to a series of threats from these areas—from radical Islamism to narcotics and gun-running. Consequently, Russian policy toward Turkey and Iran was heavily influenced by the policies of these two countries toward Central Asia and the Transcaucasus. In the case of Iran, which despite its Islamic revolutionary regime maintained a relatively low profile in the two regions, relations with Russia were very good. By contrast Russian-Turkish relations were badly strained, in large part because of what Moscow saw as Turkish efforts to extend its influence into Central Asia, the Transcaucasus, and even the Caucasus with Turkish aid to the Chechen rebels. Relations were strained despite Turkey's status as by far Russia's leading trade partner among the countries of the Middle East, and despite contributions by Turkish merchants to Yeltsin's reelection campaign.

In the Persian Gulf, Yeltsin pursued the old minimax policy of Gorbachev—trying to maintain the maximum degree of influence in Iraq and Iran without unduly alienating either the oil-rich Gulf Cooperation Council states or the United States (the GCC's primary military ally). With the exception of Kuwait, which sees good relations with Russia as extra insurance against Iraq and Iran, Russia apparently had little success in obtaining loans from, or selling arms to, the Gulf Cooperation Council states. Indeed, the reliance of the regimes of these states on the United States and its NATO allies for defense, as well as the poor showing of Soviet/Russian weaponry in the Gulf War of 1990–91 and the fighting in Chechnya appeared to doom the Russian arms sales and loan efforts. With the advent of Yevgeny Primakov as Russia's foreign minister in January 1996, Moscow seemed to try to carve out a sphere of influence in the Gulf in Iran and Iraq, against which the United States was pursuing a "dual containment" policy and with which the United States had no diplomatic and minimal economic relations. The success of Primakov's policy, however, depends on Russia being able to secure an end to the bitter conflict between Iran and Iraq, and even such a seasoned diplomat as Primakov may have a difficult task in achieving this goal.

The other zone of Russian interest in the Middle East (apart from North Africa, which ranks lowest on Russia's priority list) is Israel and its immediate Arab neighbors: Egypt, Jordan, Syria, Lebanon, and the Palestinians. Here a major reversal has taken place since Soviet times. Israel, which until 1987 had been a pariah to Moscow, was, by 1996, Russia's second largest trade partner in the Middle East. The 800,000 Jews from the former Soviet Union now living in Israel form a strong cultural bond between the two countries as well as making up a large proportion of the joint Russian-Israeli economic ventures. Until the advent of Primakov as Russia's foreign minister, political relations between the two countries were warm. There were numerous high-level visits of Israeli diplomats and political leaders to Moscow and of Russian leaders to Israel. The late Israeli prime minister Yitzhak Rabin even delivered a lecture at the Russian General Staff Academy.

Russian-Israeli political relations cooled somewhat in 1996, in part because of the appointment of Primakov, an Arabist, as Russian foreign minister. Another reason for cooling relations was the Israeli "Grapes of Wrath" operation in Lebanon, when Rabin's successor, Shimon Peres, came into conflict with Primakov. Still another problem was a dispute over Jewish Agency activities in Moscow. However, the new Israeli government formed under Benjamin Netanyahu includes a party of Russian immigrants calling for better relations with Moscow. Their influence may lead to a warming in Israeli-Russian political and diplomatic relations.

Russian foreign policy in the Middle East—as indeed elsewhere in the world—suffers from a lack of coordination. It often appears that independent or quasi-independent fiefdoms are making Russian policy or else deliberately undermining it. Lukoil, one of Russia's leading oil companies, is an excellent example. By joining the Azerbaizhan international operating company, it sabotaged the Russian Foreign Ministry's efforts to prevent Azerbaizhan from independently exploiting the oil from its region of the Caspian Sea. Lukoil also joined the Iranian national oil company in another major deal with Azerbaizhan, thus undercutting Russian efforts to maintain a joint Russian-Iranian policy on the exploitation of the Caspian Sea.

Another major operator pursuing an independent foreign policy is Russia's atomic energy minister, Viktor Mikhailov. In an export-driven strategy reminiscent in some ways of that of President Clinton, Mikhailov, in addition to selling Iran nuclear reactors, also sought to sell it a weapons-capable gas centrifuge plant. A preliminary agreement for its sale was reached, only to be overruled by Yeltsin after heavy pressure from the United States. A third major independent actor in Russian foreign policy is the Defense Ministry. Its operations in Tajikistan, as well as in Chechnya, seemed at times independent of direction from either the Foreign Ministry or from Yeltsin himself. The appointment of Primakov in January 1996 was meant, in part, to ensure greater coordination in Russian foreign policy, although Primakov will not have an easy job in this mission. Similarly the ouster of Grachev as defense minister in June 1996 may lead to a better coordination of military and diplomatic policy, but this too remains to be seen. In any case, the lack of coordination in Russian foreign policy is a major problem for Moscow—a problem that needs to be remedied if Russia is to play a more effective role in the Middle East as well as elsewhere in the world.

Russia has far less influence in the Middle East than the Soviet Union did. Given the weakness of its economy, Moscow no longer has the credits to lavish on its one-time allies like Syria, Iraq, and Libya, and Russia now demands repayment of past loans. The decline in Moscow's influence is a result also of the breakup of the Soviet Union, which physically cut Russia off from the Middle East and the newly independent states of Central Asia and the Transcaucasus. Even its Black Sea fleet, long an instrument of Soviet influence in the Middle East, has been under dispute with Ukraine, while Russia's own Black Sea coast has shrunk to a small fraction of what the Soviet Union's was.

In sum, with a weakened economy and with the newly independent states to its south, Russia is far less a power in the Middle East than the Soviet Union was. Whether a revived economy and more adept diplomacy will enable Moscow to play a more significant role in the region is a question for the future.

Notes

1. Cited in Oles M. Smolansky, "Russia and the Transcaucasus: The Case of Nagorno-Karabach," in *Regional Power Rivalries in the New Eurasia* (Armonk, N.Y.: M.E. Sharpe, 1995), 205.

2. *Rossiskaya Gazeta*, September 23, 1995 (*Foreign Broadcast Information Service Daily Report Central Eurasia* [hereafter *FBIS:FSU*], September 28, 1995, 19–20).

3. For a good survey of the role of the energy companies, see Igor Khripunov and Mary M. Mathews, "Russia's Oil and Gas Interest Group and Its Foreign Policy Agenda." See also Robert V. Barylski, "Russia, the West, and the Caspian Energy Hub."

4. See *Nezavisimaya Gazeta*, March 13, 1996 (*FBIS:FSU*, March 14, 1996, 6).

5. *Kommersant Daily*, August 23, 1995 (*Current Digest of the Soviet Press* [hereafter *CDSP*], vol. 47, no. 34 [1995]: 25).

6. *Novaya Yezhednevnaya Gazeta*, March 14–20, 1996 (*FBIS:FSU*, March 27, 1996, 18).

7. *Finansovaia Ivestia*, February 13, 1996 (*FBIS:FSU*, April 14, 1996, 18).

8. Yeltsin, at the May 1995 summit with President Bill Clinton, was to back away from this offer.

9. See the interview with Primakov in the Italian journal *Limes*, June-September 1996, 53–56 (*FBIS:FSU*, June 13, 1996, 25).

10. The last official census was in 1989. These estimates are based on CIA estimates published in *Current History*, April 1994 (issue devoted to Central Asia), 165, 170, 174, 179, and 184.

11. Moscow TV, March 2, 1995 (*FBIS:FSU*, March 4, 1996, 17).

12. *Novaya Yezhednevnaya Gazeta*, March 14–20, 1996 (*FBIS:FSU*, March 27, 1996, 17).

13. Ibid. See also the interview with General Andrei Nikolaev, director of the Federal Border Service, *Moscow News*, no. 8 (1996): 5.

14. *Delovoy Mir*, March 1, 1996 (*FBIS:FSU*, April 8, 1996 [Supplement], 1).

15. See note 10.

16. For an analysis of the pre-Gorbachev period, see Robert O. Freedman, *Moscow and the Middle East: Soviet Policy since the Invasion of Afghanistan.*

17. The Gorbachev period in the Middle East is discussed in Robert O. Freedman, "Moscow and the Middle East after Iraq's Invasion of Kuwait."

18. Gorbachev's policy during this period is discussed in Robert O. Freedman, "The Soviet Union, the Gulf War and Its Aftermath: A Case Study in Limited Superpower Cooperation."

19. *Tass,* September 20, 1991 (*FBIS:USSR,* September 23, 1991, 10).

20. *Islamic Affairs Analyst,* November 1992, 3.

21. Pavel Felgengauer, *Sevodnya,* May 26, 1995 (*CDSP* 47, no. 21 [1995]: 3).

22. Tehran *IRNA,* March 7, 1996 (*FBIS:FSU,* March 8, 1996, 7).

23. Moscow Voice of Russia World Service, in Persian, April 6, 1996 (*FBIS:FSU,* April 9, 1996, 19).

24. *Interfax,* December 26, 1995 (*FBIS:FSU,* December 27, 1995, 10).

25. Moscow Radio, December 29, 1995 (*FBIS:FSU,* January 2, 1996, 11).

26. Cited in *Izvestia,* December 2, 1993 (*FBIS:FSU,* December 16, 1993, 48).

27. *Interfax,* November 19, 1993 (*FBIS:FSU,* November 22, 1993, 8).

28. Ibid., 6.

29. *Washington Times,* May 18, 1996.

30. See the article by Peter Graff, *Financial Times,* June 5, 1996. Iran invested in the Shakh-Deniz oil and gas field, the second largest in Azerbaizhan. Other investers in the Shakh-Deniz field were Lukoil, British Petroleum, and Norway's Statoil.

31. *Izvestia,* May 5, 1992 (*CDSP* 44, no. 18 [1992]: 15).

32. *Izvestia,* February 10, 1993, as cited in *Commonwealth of Independent States and the Middle East,* Hebrew University of Jerusalem (hereafter *CIS/ME*), vol. 18, no. 2 (February 1993): 17–19.

33. *Ibid.,* 19.

34. *CIS/ME* 18, no. 4 (April 1993): 39.

35. See aso the commentary in *Nezavisimaya Gazeta,* April 16, 1993 (*CDSP* 45, no. 15 [1993]: 22).

36. *Izvestia,* June 29, 1993 (*CDSP* 45, no. 26 [1993]: 13).

37. Interfax, June 28, 1993, cited in *CIS/ME* 18, no. 6 (1993): 28.

38. *Sevodnya,* August 13, 1993 (*CIS/ME* 18, no. 8 [1993]: 3).

39. *Komsomalskaya Pravda,* October 26, 1993 (*CIS/ME* 18, no. 10 [1993]: 31).

40. *Kommersant,* December 1, 1993 (*FBIS;FSU,* December 2, 1993, 11).

41. *Pravda,* January 11, 1994 (*FBIS:FSU,* January 12, 1994, 25).

42. Itar/Tass, November 29, 1993 (*FBIS:FSU,* November 29, 1993, 18).

43. *Izvestia,* August 9, 1994 (*CDSP* 46, no. 32 [1994]: 18).

44. See "Uneasy Eyes on Iraq and Iran," *The Middle East* (London), January 1994, 17. In the late summer of 1994, Kuwait and Russia were to sign another arms deal in which Kuwait reportedly purchased 27 Smerch rockets, rocket launchers, and 60 BMP-3 infantry combat vehicles (*Jane's Defense Weekly,* reprinted in *Washington Times,* September 21, 1994).

45. Interfax, February 2, 1995, cited in *CIS/ME* 20, nos. 2–3 [1995]: 37.

46. *Krasnaya Zvezda*, August 3, 1995 (*FBIS:FSU*, August 4, 1995, 9).

47. Interfax, August 24, 1995 (*FBIS:FSU*, August 25, 1995, 13).

48. *CIS/ME* 20, nos. 4–5 [1995]: 45.

49. Ibid., 46.

50. See the report by Robert Corzine, "Saddam Casts Shadow over Oil Market," *Financial Times*, January 26, 1996.

51. See the report by David Hearst, "Russia signs 'giant' oil deal with Iraq," *Manchester Guardian Weekly*, February 18, 1996.

52. As in the case of trade between Russia and Turkey, the exact amount of Russian-Israeli trade is difficult to determine due to the large amount of "suitcase trade" carried on by Russian tourists visiting Israel. (Author's interview with Israeli Foreign Ministry, July 2, 1996.) The $650 million estimate is taken from *Izvestia*, February 2, 1996 (*CIS/ME*, February 3, 1996, 40).

53. Moscow Radio, January 29, 1992 (*FBIS:FSU*, January 30, 1992, 30).

54. Cited in report by Dan Izenburg, *Jerusalem Post*, April 30, 1992.

55. Itar/Tass, May 1, 1992 (*FBIS:FSU*, May 4, 1992, 16).

56. *Jerusalem Post*, August 21, 1992.

57. *Jerusalem Post*, August 23, 1992.

58. Itar/Tass, October 28, 1992 (*FBIS:FSU*, October 29, 1992, 11).

59. Itar/Tass, December 18, 1992 (*FBIS:FSU*, December 21, 1992, 22).

60. Cited in report by Serge Schmermann, *New York Times*, January 26, 1993.

61. Itar/Tass, January 5, 1993 (*FBIS:FSU*, January 7, 1993, 28). The term "other" spheres of cooperation in Soviet parlance had meant military cooperation, and beginning in 1990 there had been rumors of possible Soviet-Israeli cooperation in the development of military aircraft. The close U.S.-Israeli tie, however, is likely to preclude any Russian-Israeli military cooperation. (Interview by author at Israeli Foreign Ministry, July 2, 1996.)

62. *Ibid.*

63. *Pravda*, March 17, 1993 (*CIS/ME* 18, no. 3, March 1993, 32).

64. *Pravda*, April 24, 1993 (*FBIS:FSU*, April 27, 1993, 12). The referendum basically offered the Russian people a choice between Yeltsin and his reform program, on the one side, and Parliament on the other. It followed a major confrontation between Parliament and Yeltsin. Yeltsin won the referendum.

65. For the official Russian reaction to the Hebron massacre, which was balanced in tone and noted that the Israeli leadership had condemned the incident, see Itar/Tass, February 25, 1994 (*FBIS:FSU*, February 28, 1994, 19).

66. *Pravda*, March 15, 1993 (*FBIS:FSU*, March 16, 1994, 8).

67. Kol Israel (Voice of Israel), April 26, 1994 (*FBIS:FSU*, April 26, 1994, 12).

68. The diplomatic working committee, however, has so far not proven to be very successful (Interviews by the author at Russian Embassy, Tel Aviv, July 1, 1996, and Israeli Foreign Ministry, July 2, 1996).

69. *CIS/ME*, December 1995, 32–33.

70. *Ibid.*, 34.

71. *Sevodnya,* January 23, 1996 (cited in *CIS/ME* nos. 1–2 [1996]: 39).

72. *Izvestia,* February 22, 1996, cited in *CIS/ME,* nos. 1–2 [1996]: 36.

73. Cited in article by Batsheva Tsur, *Jerusalem Post,* May 17, 1996. It should be noted that Brezhnev also described the exit tax on Jewish emigrants from the USSR in 1992 as a "bureaucratic problem." See Robert O. Freedman, "Soviet-American Relations," in Robert O. Freedman, ed., *Soviet Jewry in the Decisive Decade, 1971– 1980* (Durham, N.C.: Duke University Press, 1984), 44.

74. Cited in article by Marily Henry and Batsheva Tsur, *Jerusalem Post,* May 16, 1996. Interviews by the author in Israel in July 1996 with Israeli Absorption Ministry officials revealed that the Jewish Agency was, in fact, doing precisely what *Nezavisimaya Gazeta* was accusing it of doing.

75. Itar/Tass, April 19, 1996 (*FBIS:FSU,* April 19, 1996, 25).

76. Itar/Tass, April 21, 1996 (*FBIS:FSU,* April 23, 1996, 26).

77. Itar/Tass, April 22, 1996 (*FBIS:FSU,* April 23, 1996, 27).

78. Interfax, April 23, 1996 (*FBIS:FSU,* April 24, 1996, 22–23).

79. *Izvestia,* April 30, 1996 (*FBIS:FSU,* April 30, 1996, 21–22).

80. In an interview with the author at the Israeli parliament (Knesset) in Jerusalem on July 3, 1996, a Knesset member of the Yisrael B'Aliyah Party noted that one of the party's priorities would be to improve relations with Russia. In addition, a "senior government official" told the Knesset Immigration and Absorption Committee on July 10, 1996, that the Israeli government, under Peres, had neglected relations with Russia since Rabin's assasination ("Government Neglecting Russia, Knesset Panel Told," by Liat Collins, *Jerusalem Post,* July 11, 1996). See also the article by Yossi Melman "Lo Kdai Lhargiz et Rossia" (It doesn't pay to anger Russia) in *Ha'aretz,* July 8, 1996, and the article by Dov Kontorer, "Novii Charakter Dialoga S Rossii" (New character of the dialogue with Russia), *Vesti* (Jerusalem), July 8, 1996.

81. *Pravda,* February 19, 1992 (*FBIS:FSU,* February 20, 1992, 42).

82. Vladimir Kulistikov, "Turks from the Adriatic to the Great Chinese Wall Are a Threat to Russia," *New Times* (Moscow), no. 20 (1992): 3.

83. Cited in Stephen J. Blank, "Turkey's Strategic Engagement in the Former USSR and U.S. Interests," 56.

84. See Maksim Yusin, "Tehran Declares 'Great Battle' for Influence in Central Asia," *Izvestia,* February 7, 1992 (*CDSP* 44, no. 6 [1992]: 18).

85. Interview by the author, Uzbek Foreign Ministry, Tashkent, Uzbekistan, September 30, 1993. See also Islam Karimov, *Building the Future: Uzbekistan Its Own Model for Transition to a Market Economy.*

86. Turkish correspondent Semih Idiz called 1993 a year that forced Turkish diplomats into a "crisis management mode" (*Turkish Times,* February 1, 1994, 1).

87. For a Russian view of the threat that the Turkish pipeline system would pose to Russia, see Vladimir Iuratev and Anatoly Sheshtakov of the Russian Ministry of Foreign Economic Relations, "Asian Gas Will Flow East: New Alliance Infringes on

Russian Interests," *Nezavisimaya Gazeta,* May 13, 1993 (*CDSP* 45, no. 14 [1993]: 16–18). For a Western view arguing that Moscow is practicing economic warfare over the pipeline issue, see Stephen Blank, *Energy and Security in Transcaucasia,* U.S. Army War College, Carlisle, Pa., September 7, 1994.

88. Cited in report by Baha Gugnor, "Russian Fear of Pan-Turkism Grows," Deutsche Press Agentur, *Washington Times,* November 5, 1994.

89. Istanbul Declaration, *Turkish Times,* November 3, 1994.

90. Cited in *Turkish Times,* September 1, 1995.

91. Ibid.

92. For analyses of the oil pipeline issue, see Marshall Ingwerson, "At Your Local Gas Pump Soon: Caspian Sea Oil," *Christian Science Monitor,* October 11, 1995, and Robert V. Barylski, "Russia, the West and the Caspian Energy Hub."

93. During her visit to Moscow in early September 1993, Turkey's new prime minister, Tansu Ciller, was quoted as saying, "President Yeltsin has agreed to cooperation between Turkey and Russia to lift the anti-Iraqi embargo," *Washington Times,* September 10, 1993.

94. *Izvestia,* July 21, 1994.

95. See Elizabeth Fuller, "Turkish-Russian Relations 1992–1994," *Radio Free Europe/Radio Liberty Research Report* 3, no. 18 (May 6, 1994): 9.

96. Interviews by the author in Turkey in June 1996 indicated that while the Tukish government was apparently not directly aiding the Chechen rebels, private groups in Turkey, especially Islamic groups, were assisting the Chechens.

97. Moscow scored a partial success on the CFE issue in late May 1996, when it was given an additional three years to reduce its heavy equipment (AP report, *Boston Globe,* June 2, 1996).

98. The Laleli district in Istanbul is a center of Russian-Turkish "suitcase trade," and it was primarily merchants from this district who sent the money to aid Yeltsin's campaign. See the report by Dogu Ergil, "Russian Elections and the Future of Turco-Russian Relations," *Turkish Times,* June 23, 1996. So many Russian tourists now come to the Turkish resort of Antalya that there is now a special Russian newspaper for them there, *Antalya Dlya Vas* (Anatolia for you).

Bibliography

Books

Abbas, Mahmud. *Through Secret Channels*. Reading, England: Gamet, 1995.

Abu Amr, Ziad. *Islamic Fundamentalism in the West Bank and Gaza*. Bloomington: Indiana University Press, 1994.

Aburish, Said K. *The Rise, Corruption and Coming Fall of the House of Saud*. New York: St. Martin's Press, 1995.

Aftandilian, Gregory. *Egypt's Bid for Arab Leadership*. New York: Council on Foreign Relations, 1993.

Amnesty International. *Iraq: Human Rights Abuses in Iraqi Kurdistan since 1991*. New York: Amnesty International, February 1995.

Arens, Moshe. *Broken Covenant: American Foreign Policy and the Crisis between the U.S. and Israel*. New York: Simon & Schuster, 1995.

Aronoff, Myron. *Israeli Visions and Divisions*. New Brunswick, N.J.: Transaction, 1987.

———. *Power and Ritual in the Israel Labor Party*. Rev. ed. Armonk, N.Y.: M. E. Sharpe, 1993.

Beblawi, Hazem, and Giacomo Luciani, eds. *The Rentier State*. London: Croom Helm, 1987.

Bidwell, Robin. *The Two Yemens*. Boulder: Westview Press, 1983.

Cantori, Louis, and Drew Ziegler, eds. *Comparative Politics in the Post-Behavioral Era*. Boulder, Col.: Lynn Rienner, 1988.

Caplan, Neil. *The Lausanne Conference, 1949: A Case Study in Middle East Peacemaking*. Tel Aviv: Tel Aviv University, 1993.

Chubin, Shahram. *Iran's National Security Policy: Capabilities, Intentions and Impact*. Washington, D.C.: Carnegie Endowment for International Peace, 1994.

Clawson, Patrick. *Iran's Challenge to the West: How, When, and Why*. Washington, D.C.: Washington Institute for Near East Policy, 1993.

Corbin, Jane. *Gaza First: The Secret Norway Channel to Peace between Israel and the PLO*. London: Bloomsbury, 1994.

Crystal, Jill. *Oil and Politics in the Gulf: Rulers and Merchants in Kuwait and Qatar*. New York: Cambridge University Press, 1990.

Deng, Francis M. *War of Visions: Conflict of Identities in the Sudan*. Washington, D.C.: The Brookings Institution, 1995.

Eliav, Arie Lova. *Land of the Hart: Israelis, Arabs, the Territories, and a Vision of the Future*. Trans. Judith Yalon. Philadelphia: The Jewish Publication Society of America, 1974.

Faour, Muhammad. *The Arab World after Desert Storm*. Washington, D.C.: United States Institute of Peace Press, 1993.

Freedman, Robert O. *Moscow and the Middle East: Soviet Policy since the Invasion of Afghanistan*. Cambridge: Cambridge University Press, 1991.

———, ed. *The Intifada: Its Impact on Israel, the Arab World, and the Superpowers*. Gainesville: University Press of Florida, 1991.

———. *The Middle East after Iraq's Invasion of Kuwait*. Gainesville, University Press of Florida, 1993.

———. *Israel under Rabin*. Boulder: Westview Press, 1995.

Garfinkle, Adam. *Israel and Jordan in the Shadow of War: Functional Ties and Futile Diplomacy in a Small Place*. New York: St. Martin's, 1992.

Gause, F. Gregory III. *Saudi-Yemeni Relations: Domestic Structures and Foreign Influence*. New York: Columbia University Press, 1990.

———. *Oil Monarchies: Domestic and Security Challenges in the Arab Gulf States*. New York: Council on Foreign Relations Press, 1994.

Gruen, George. *The Other Refugees: Impact of Nationalism, Anti-Zionism and the Arab-Israel Conflict on the Jews of the Arab World*. New York: American Jewish Committee, 1987.

Harik, Iliya, and Denis Sullivan, eds. *Privatization and Liberalization in the Middle East*. Bloomington: Indiana University Press, 1992.

Inbar, Efraim. *War and Peace in Israeli Politics*. Boulder, Col.: Lynn Rienner, 1991.

Karimov, Islam. *Building the Future: Uzbekistan Its Own Model for Transition to a Market Economy*. Tashkent: Uzbekistan Publishers, 1993.

Lackner, Helen. *PDR Yemen*. London: Ithaca Press, 1987.

Makovsky, David. *Making Peace with the PLO: The Rabin Government's Road to the Oslo Accord*. Boulder, Col.: Westview Press, 1996.

Metz, Helen Chapin, ed. *Algeria: A Country Study*. Washington, D.C.: Federal Research Division, Library of Congress, 1994.

Middle East Watch. *Genocide in Iraq: The Anfar Campaign against the Kurds*. New York: Human Rights Watch, 1993.

Mylroie, Laurie. *The Future of Iraq*. Washington, D.C.: The Washington Institute for Near East Policy, 1991.

Nachmani, Amikam. *Israel, Turkey and Greece*. London: Frank Cass, 1987.

Nonneman, Gerd. *Iraq, the Gulf States and the War*. London: Ithaca Press, 1986.

Peres, Shimon. *The New Middle East*. New York: Henry Holt, 1993.

———. *Battling for Peace: A Memoir*. New York: Random House, 1995.

Peretz, Don. *Intifada: The Palestinian Uprising*. Boulder, Col.: Westview Press, 1990.

Pipes, Daniel. *Greater Syria: The History of an Ambition*. London and New York: Oxford University Press, 1992.

———. *Syria beyond the Peace Process*. Washington, D.C.: The Washington Institute Policy Papers, no. 40, 1996.

Rielly, John E., ed. *American Public Opinion and U.S. Foreign Policy, 1995*. Chicago: The Chicago Council on Foreign Relations, 1995.

Sadowski, Yahya. *Scuds or Butter? The Political Economy of Arms Control in the Middle East*. Washington, D.C.: The Brookings Institution, 1993.

Seale, Patrick. *Asad: The Struggle for the Middle East*. Berkeley: University of California Press, 1988.

Sullivan, Denis J., *Private Voluntary Organizations in Egypt: Islamic Development, Private Initiative and State Control*. Gainesville: University Press of Florida, 1994.

Tessler, Mark. *A History of the Israeli-Palestinian Conflict*. Bloomington: Indiana University Press, 1994.

Trainer, Bernard. *The Generals' War: The Inside Story of the Conflict in the Gulf*. Boston: Little Brown, 1995.

Tucker, Robert W., and David C. Hendrickson. *The Imperial Temptation: The New World Order and America's Purpose*. New York: Council on Foreign Relations, 1992.

Articles and Chapters

Ajami, Fuad. "The Sorrows of Egypt." *Foreign Affairs* 74, no. 5 (1995): 72–88.

Album, Andrew. "Jordan: Privatisation, Key to Growth." *The Middle East*, February 1996.

Alpher, Yossi. "Settlement and Borders." *Final Status Issues: Israel-Palestinians*, no. 3. Tel Aviv: Jaffee Center for Strategic Studies, 1994.

Arian, Asher. "Israeli Public Opinion and the Intifada." In Robert O. Freedman, ed., *The Intifada*, q.v.

Aronoff, Myron J. "The Labor Party and the Intifada." In Robert O. Freedman, ed., *The Intifada*, q.v.

Aronoff, Myron J., and Pierre M. Atlas. "The Peace Process and Competing Challenges to the Dominant Zionist Discourse." In Ilan Peleg, ed., *The Israel-Palestine Peace Process: Interdisciplinary Perspectives*. Albany: SUNY Press, 1996.

Aruri, Naseer. "Recolonizing the Arabs." *Middle East International*, no. 385 (October 12, 1990).

Bakhash, Shaul. "Iran: The Crisis of Legitimacy." In Martin Kramer, ed., *Middle Eastern Lectures: Number One*. Tel-Aviv: Moshe Dayan Center for Middle Eastern and African Studies; New York: Syracuse University Press, 1995.

———. "Alternative Futures for Iran: Implications for Regional Security." In Geoffrey Kemp and Janice Gross Stein, eds., *Powder Keg in the Middle East*. Washington, D.C.: American Association for the Advancement of Science, 1995.

Barkey, Henri. "Reluctant Neighbors: Reflections on Turkish-Arab Relations." *The Beirut Review* (Spring 1994), 3–22.

————. "Turkey, Islamic Politics, and the Kurdish Question." *World Policy Journal* (Spring 1996), 43–52.

Bar-On, Mordecai. "Israeli Reactions to the Palestinian Uprising." *Journal of Palestine Studies* 17, no. 4 (Summer 1988).

Barylski, Robert V. "Russia, the West, and the Caspian Energy Hub." *Middle East Journal* 49, no. 2 (Spring 1995): 217–32.

Blank, Stephen J. "Turkey's Strategic Engagement in the Former USSR and U.S. Interests." In Stephen Blank et al., eds., *Turkey's Strategic Position at the Crossroads of World Affairs*. Carlisle, Pa.: U.S. Army War College, 1993.

Cantori, Louis J. "Islamic Revivalism: Conservatism and Progress in Contemporary Egypt." In E. Sahliyya, ed., *Religious Resurgence and Politics Worldwide*, 183–94. Albany: SUNY Press, 1990.

————. "Egypt Reenters the Arab State System." In Robert O. Freedman, ed., *The Middle East from the Iran-Contra Affair to the Intifada*, 341–66. Syracuse: Syracuse University Press, 1991.

————. "Unipolarity and Egyptian Hegemony in the Middle East." In Robert O. Freedman, ed., *The Middle East after Iraq's Invasion of Kuwait*, q.v., 335–57.

————. "The Middle East in the New World Order." In Tareq and J. Ismael, eds., *The Gulf War and the New World Order: International Relations of the Middle East*, 451–72. Gainesville: University Press of Florida, 1994.

Carapico, Sheila. "Elections and Mass Politics in Yemen." *Middle East Report*, no. 185 (November/December 1993): 2–6.

————. "From Ballot Box to Battlefield: The War of the Two 'Alis." *Middle East Report*, no. 190 (September/October 1994): 24–27.

Chaudhry, Kiren Aziz. "The Price of Wealth: Business and State in Labor Remittance and Oil Economies." *International Organization* 43, no. 1 (Winter 1989).

————. "The Myths of the Market and the Common History of Late Developers." *Politics and Society* 21, no. 3 (September 1993): 245–74.

Cobban, Helena. "Israel and the Palestinians." In Robert O. Freedman, ed., *Israel under Rabin*, q.v., 91–110.

Dabrowska, Karen. "King Hussein and the Iraqi Opposition." *Middle East International*, January 19, 1996.

al-Dajani, Hisham. *al-idarat al-amrikiyya wa-Israel* (The American administrations and Israel). Damascus: Manshurat Wizarat al-Thaqafa, 1994.

Davis, Eric. "Theorizing Statecraft and Social Change in Arab Oil-Producing Countries." In Eric Davis and Nicolas Gavrielides, eds., *Statecraft in the Middle East*. Miami: Florida International University Press, 1991.

Dekmejian, R. Hrair. "The Rise of Political Islam in Saudi Arabia." *Middle East Journal* 48, no. 4 (Autumn 1994): 627–43.

Denoueux, Guillain. "Tunisie: les elections presidentielles et legislatives, 20 Mars 1994." *Monde Arabe-Maghreb-Machrek*, no. 145 (July/September 1994).

Dessouki, Ali Hilal. "The Primacy of Economics: The Foreign Policy of Egypt." In Bahgat Korany and Ali Hilal Dessouki, eds., *The Foreign Policies of the Arab States*. 2d ed. Boulder, Col.: Westview Press, 1991.

Detalle, Renaud. "The Yemeni Elections Up Close." *Middle East Report*, no. 185 (November/December, 1993): 8–12.

Drake, Laura. "Implosion of Iraq." *Middle East Insight* 12, no. 3 (March/April 1996).

Dunbar, Charles. "The Unification of Yemen: Process, Politics and Prospects." *Middle East Journal* 46, no. 3 (Summer 1992).

Ebeid, Mona Makram. "Egypt's 1995 Elections: One Step Forward, Two Steps Back." *Middle East Policy*, no. 3 (March 1996): 119–36.

Eisenstadt, Michael. "Déjà Vu All Over Again: An Assessment of Iran's Miliatry Build-Up." In Patrick Clawson, ed., *Iran's Strategic Intentions and Capabilities*. Washington, D.C.: National Defense University, Institute for National and Strategic Studies, 1994.

Feuilherade, Peter. "Jordan: Facing the Challenges of Change." *The Middle East*, October 1995.

Flamhaft, Zeva. "Israel and the Arab-Israeli Peace Process." In Fred Lazin and Gregory Mahler, eds., *Israel in the Nineties*. Gainesville: University Press of Florida, 1996.

Francke, Rend Rahim. "Iraq: Race to the Finish Line." *Middle East Insight* 10, no. 4 (July 1994).

Freedman, Robert O. "Moscow and the Middle East after Iraq's Invasion of Kuwait." In Robert O. Freedman, ed., *The Middle East after Iraq's Invasion of Kuwait*, q.v., 74–136.

———. "Courting Baghdad." *Middle East Insight* 12, no. 3 (March/April 1996).

———. "The Soviet Union, the Gulf War and Its Aftermath: A Case Study in Limited Superpower Cooperation." In David W. Lesch, ed., *The Middle East and the United States*, 379–401. Boulder, Col.: Westview Press, 1996.

Friedgut, Theodore. "Israel's Turn toward Peace." In Robert O. Freedman, ed., *Israel under Rabin*, q.v.

Frisch, Hillel. "The PLO and the 1992 Elections—A Skillful Participant?" In Asher Arian and Michael Shamir, eds., *The Elections in Israel, 1992*. Albany: SUNY Press, 1995.

Garfinkle, Adam. "U.S. Decision-Making in the Jordan Crisis of 1970: Correcting the Record." *Political Science Quarterly* (Spring 1985).

———. "The Importance of Being Hussein: Jordanian Foreign Policy and Peace in the Middle East." In Robert O. Freedman, ed., *The Middle East from the Iran-Contra Affair to the Intifada*. Syracuse: Syracuse University Press, 1991.

———. "Allies of Diminishing Returns: The Hashemite Question." *The National Interest*, no. 25 (Fall 1991).

Gerges, Fawaz. "Egyptian-Israeli Relations Turn Sour." *Foreign Affairs* 74, no. 3 (1995): 69–78.

Grissa, Abdelsatar. "The Tunisian State Enterprises and Privatization Policy." In I. William Zartman, ed., *Tunisia: The Political Economy of Reform*. Boulder, Col.: Lynne Rienner Publishers, 1991.

Gruen, George E. "Turkey's Relations with Israel and Its Arab Neighbors." *Middle East Review* 17, no. 3 (Spring 1985): 33–43.

———. "Turkey between the Middle East and the West." In Robert O. Freedman, ed., *The Middle East from the Iran-Contra Affair to the Intifada*, 390–422. Syracuse: Syracuse University Press, 1991).

———. "Turkey's Potential Contribution to Arab-Israel Peace." In *Turkish Review of Middle East Studies*, vol. 7. Istanbul: Foundation for Middle East and Balkan Studies, 1993.

———. "Turkey's Emerging Regional Role." *American Foreign Policy Interests* 17, no. 2 (April 1995): 13–24.

Gunter, Michael. "A De Facto Kurdish State in Northern Iraq." *Third World Quarterly* 14, no. 2 (1993).

———. "The KDP-PUK Conflict in Northern Iraq." *Middle East Journal* 50, no. 2 (Spring 1996).

Habeeb, William Mark. "The Maghribi States and the European Community." In I. William Zartman and William Mark Habeeb, eds., *Polity and Society in Contemporary North Africa*. Boulder, Col.: Westview Press, 1993.

Haddad, Yvonne Yazbeck. "Islamist Perceptions of U.S. Policy in the Middle East." In David Lesch, ed., *The Middle East and the United States: A Historical and Political Assessment*. Boulder, Col.: Westview Press, 1996.

Heidenrich, John G. "The Gulf War: How Many Iraqis Died?" *Foreign Policy*, no. 90 (Spring 1993).

Hirschberg, Peter. "The Trouble with Hebron." *The Jerusalem Report*, July 25, 1996.

Howe, Marvin. "Morocco Is Not Algeria, but Is It Heading in the Same Direction?" *The Washington Report on Middle East Affairs* (January 1996), 16.

Hudson, Michael. "Bipolarity, Rational Calculation and War in Yemen." *Arab Studies Journal* 3, no. 1 (Spring 1995): 9–19.

al-Jabbar, Faleh Abd. "Why the Uprisings Failed." *Middle East Report* (May / June, 1992).

Jarbawi, Ali, "The Triangle of Conflict." *Foreign Policy*, no. 100 (Fall 1995).

Katzmann, Kenneth. "Iraqi Compliance with Cease Fire Agreements." Congressional Research Service report, April 17, 1995.

Kavoossi, Masoud. "Iran's Open Door to Foreign Investors." *U.S.-Iran Review*, July 1993.

———. "Iran's Economy: An Assessment." *U.S.-Iran Review*, January 1994.

———. "Iran's Economy in Transition." *Middle East Insight* (Special Edition: Iran), July / August 1995.

Keren, Michael. "Israeli Professionals and the Peace Process." *Israel Affairs* 1, no. 1 (Autumn 1994): 149–63.

Khalidi, Ahmad. "Current Dilemmas, Future Challenges." *Journal of Palestine Studies* 24, no. 94 (Winter 1995).

Khripunov, Igor, and Mary M. Mathews. "Russia's Oil and Gas Interest Group and Its Foreign Policy Agenda." *Problems of Post-Communism* 43, no. 3 (May / June 1996): 38–48.

Kleiman, Aharon. "New Directions in Israel's Foreign Policy." *Israel Affairs* 1, no. 1 (Autumn 1994): 96–117.

Kohen, Sami. "Contacts with Central Asian States as a Foundation for 'Pan-Turkism'." *The Washington Report on Middle East Affairs*, August–September 1992.

Komali-Zadeh, Bahman. "Officials Discuss Inflation, Ways to Curb Money Supply." *Iran Business Monitor*, April 1994.

———. "Bigger Deficit Feared as Government Ups Spending 40 Percent." *Iran Business Monitor*, July 1995.

Lake, Anthony, "Confronting Backlash States." *Foreign Affairs* 73 (March/April 1994).

Lesch, Ann Mosely. "Confrontation in the Southern Sudan." *The Middle East Journal* 40, no. 3 (Summer 1986).

———. "Sudan's Foreign Policy: In Search of Arms, Aid and Allies." In John O. Voll, ed., *Sudan: State and Society in Crisis*. Bloomington: Indiana University Press, 1991.

———. "Negotiations in the Sudan." In David R. Smock, ed., *Foreign Intervention in Sub-Saharan Africa: Making War and Waging Peace*. Washington, D.C.: U.S. Institute of Peace, 1993.

———. "Israeli Negotiations with Syria, Lebanon and Jordan: The Security Dimension." In Robert O. Freedman, ed., *Israel under Rabin*, q.v.

Lifton, Robert K. "Talking with Asad: A Visit to the Middle East in Transition." *Middle East Insight*, September/October 1994.

Mandelbaum, Michael. "Foreign Policy as Social Work." *Foreign Affairs* 75 (January/February 1996).

Marr, Phebe. "Iraq's Future, Plus ça Change . . . or Something Better?" In Ibrahim Ibrahim, ed., *The Gulf Crisis: Background and Consequences*. Washington, D.C.: Georgetown University Press, 1992.

Mortimer, Robert. "Islam and Multiparty Politics in Algeria." *The Middle East Journal* 45, no. 4 (Autumn 1991): 583–86.

———. "Islamists, Soldiers and Democrats: The Second Algerian War." *The Middle East Journal* 50, no. 1 (Winter 1996): 24–27.

Muslih, Muhammad. "The Shift in Palestinian Thinking." *Current History* 91 (January 1992).

———. "Palestinian Civil Society." *The Middle East Journal* 47, no. 2 (Spring 1993).

Peleg, Ilan. "The Likud under Rabin II: Between Ideological Purity and Pragmatic Readjustment." In Robert O. Freedman, ed., *Israel under Rabin*, q.v., 143–67.

Perthes, Volker. "Syria's Parliamentary Elections: Remodeling Asad's Political Base." *Middle East Report*, January/February 1992.

Poelling, Sylvia. "Investment Law No. 10: Which Future for the Private Sector." In Eberhard Kienle, ed., *Contemporary Syria: Liberalization between Cold War and Cold Peace*. London: British Academic Press and the University of London, 1994.

Qasimiyya, Khayriyya. *al-watan al-Arabi wal-nidham al-'alami, awda ile al-madi wa-waqfa 'inda al-hadir* (The Arab homeland and the world order, a retrospective review and a look at the present). Damascus: al-Dawudi Press, 1994.

Rubin, Barry. "U.S.-Israel Relations and Israel's 1992 Election." In Asher Arian and Michael Shamir, eds., *The Elections in Israel, 1992*. Albany: SUNY Press, 1995.

al-Rumayhi, Muhammad. "Halat al-laharb wal-lasilim . . . thaqafiyyan" (The cultural dimension of the state of war and no peace). *al-Arabi*, no. 449 (April 1996).

Shlaim, Avi. "Prelude to the Accord: Likud, Labor, and the Palestinians." *Journal of Palestine Studies*, no. 23 (Winter 1994).

Stork, Joe. "The Middle East Arms Bazaar after the Gulf War." *Middle East Report*, November/December 1995.

Tal, Lawrence. "Dealing with Radical Islam: The Case of Jordan." *Survival* 37, no. 3 (Autumn 1995).

Trevan, Tim. "UNSCOM Faces Entirely New Verification Challenges in Iraq." *Arms Control Today* 23, no. 3 (April 1993).

Viorst, Milton. "The Limits of Revolution." *Foreign Affairs* 75 (November/December 1995).

Warburton, David. "The Conventional War in Yemen." *Arab Studies Journal* 3, no. 1 (Spring 1995): 20–44.

Wright, Robin. "Dateline Tehran: A Revolution Implodes." *Foreign Policy* no. 102 (Summer 1996).

Yuchtman-Yaar, Ephraim. "The Israeli Public and the Intifada: Attitude Change or Entrenchment?" In Ehud Sprinzak and Larry Diamond, eds., *Israeli Democracy under Stress*. Boulder, Col.: Lynne Rienner, 1993.

About the Authors

Myron Aronoff is professor of anthropology and political science at Rutgers University. He is the author of *Frontiertown: The Politics of Community Building in Israel*; *Israeli Visions and Divisions*; and *Power and Ritual in the Israel Labor Party*. He has written extensively about various aspects of Israeli society, culture, and politics, with a particular focus on political culture.

Yael Aronoff is a Ph.D. candidate in the Department of Political Science at Columbia University. Her research interests include the Middle East peace process as well as peacekeeping and collective security. She has previously been a Javits Fellow in the Senate Foreign Relations Committee and a political appointee in the Pentagon's Office of Humanitarian and Refugee Affairs.

Shaul Bakhash is Clarence Robinson Professor of History at George Mason University. He has written extensively on Iranian politics and served on a mission of American Middle East specialists to the Soviet Union. He is the author of *Iran: Monarchy, Bureaucracy and Reform under the Qajars, 1848–1896*, and *The Politics of Oil and Revolution in Iran*.

Louis J. Cantori is professor of political science at the University of Maryland, Baltimore County, and is also a consultant to numerous agencies of the U.S. government, including the AID project in Egypt and the Directorate of Planning of the Middle East headquarters of the U.S. Air Force. Among his publications are *Local Politics and Development in the Middle East* and *Comparative Politics in the Post-Behavioral Era*.

Mary-Jane Deeb is editor of the *Middle East Journal* and a professor of international relations in the School of International Service at American University in Washington, D.C. She is a specialist in North African affairs who has written extensively about the region and has worked for the U.S. Agency for International Development, the U.N. Economic Commission for Western Asia, UNICEF, and AMIDEAST in Beirut during the civil war.

Robert O. Freedman is Peggy Meyerhoff Pearlstone Professor of Political Science and president of Baltimore Hebrew University. He has written and edited numerous books on the Middle East, among them *Soviet Policy toward the Middle East since 1970* and *Moscow and the Middle East: Soviet Policy since the Invasion of Afghanistan*. He is also the editor of *Israel under Rabin* and *The Middle East after Iraq's Invasion of Kuwait*.

Adam Garfinkle is executive editor of *The National Interest*, adjunct professor of American foreign policy at the School for Advanced International Studies of Johns Hopkins University, and an associate scholar at the Foreign Policy Research Institute in Philadelphia. Among his many publications are *War, Water, and Negotiation in the Middle East*; *The Case of the Palestine-Syria Border, 1916–23*, and *Israel and Jordan in the Shadow of War*.

F. Gregory Gause III is an associate professor of political science at the University of Vermont. He has written extensively about politics in the Arabian Peninsula and is the author of *Saudi-Yemen Relations: Domestic Structure and Foreign Influence* and *Oil Monarchies: Domestic and Security Challenges in the Arab Gulf States*.

George E. Gruen is an adjunct professor of international relations at Columbia University and a visiting scholar at Columbia's Middle East Institute. He is a specialist on Turkey, and in his latest book, *The Water Crisis: The Next Middle East Conflict?* he discusses the impact of regional water issues on the prospects for achieving Arab-Israeli and Palestinian-Israeli peace.

Raymond Hinnebusch is a professor in the Department of Political Science at the University of St. Andrews, Scotland. He has written extensively on Syrian politics, and among his publications are *Syria and the Middle East Peace Process* and *Authoritarian Power and State Formation in Ba'athist Syria*.

Ann Mosely Lesch is professor of political science at Villanova University and associate director of its Center for Arab and Islamic Studies. Her most recent books are *Transition to Palestinian Self-Government: Practical Steps toward Israeli-Palestinian Peace* and *Egypt and the Palestinians from Camp David to the Intifada*.

Phebe Marr is a professor at the National Defense University in Washington, D.C. She was previously associate professor of Middle East history at the University of Tennessee and at California State University, and she was chair of the Near East and North Africa program at the Foreign Service Institute. Her numerous books and articles on the Middle East include *Riding the Tiger: The Middle East Challenge after the Cold War*.

Muhammad Muslih is professor of political science at the C.W. Post Campus of Long Island University. He has written extensively on Syrian, Palestinian, and Arab politics. Among his publications are *The Origin of Palestinian Nationalism* and *Political Ties in the Arab World*. He also has a book forthcoming on Syria.

Don Peretz is professor emeritus at Binghamton University (SUNY). He is the author of *The Arab-Israeli Dispute; Palestinian Refugees; The Middle East Peace Process; The Intifada: The Palestinian Uprising;* and *Government and Politics of Israel* (with Gideon Doron), now in its third edition.

Mark Rosenblum is professor of history at Queens College of the City University of New York, where he is the director of the Michael Harrington Center and chair of its Middle East Project. Among his publications on the Middle East are a series of studies on the Oslo peace process published in the Michael Harrington Center's Working Papers: *Israel and the PLO: From Negotiating a "Piece of Paper" to Implementing "Peace on the Ground"* and *Euphoria with the King, Angst with Arafat, Anticipation with Assad: Hope without Delusion*.

Index